CENGAGE
Learning®

BSTAT, Second Edition
Gerald Keller

Senior Vice President, Global Product Manager,
 Higher Education:
 Jack W. Calhoun

Product Director:
 Joe Sabatino

VP, 4LTR & Learning Solutions Strategy,
 Institutional: Neil Marquardt

Product Development Manager, 4LTR Press:
 Steven Joos

Content Developer: Kendra Brown

Project Manager, 4LTR Press: Pierce Denny

Product Assistant: Anne Merrill

Marketing Director: Kristen Hurd

Senior Marketing Communications Manager:
 Libby Shipp

Marketing Coordinator:
 Christopher Walz

Sr. Content Project Manager:
 Holly Henjum

Media Developer:
 Chris Valentine

Manufacturing Planner:
 Ron Montgomery

Production Service:
 MPS Limited

Rights Acquisition Specialist:
 Deanna Ettinger

Senior Art Director:
 Stacy Jenkins Shirley

Interior and Cover Design:
 Craig Ramsdell

Cover Image:
 © Glowimages/Getty Images

For product information and technology assistance, contact us at
Cengage Learning Customer & Sales Support, 1-800-354-9706

For permission to use material from this text or product,
submit all requests online at **www.cengage.com/permissions**
Further permissions questions can be emailed to
permissionrequest@cengage.com

Windows is a registered trademark of the Microsoft Corporation used herein under license. Macintosh and Power Macintosh are registered trademarks of Apple Computer, Inc. used herein under license.

Library of Congress Control Number: 2013945443

Student Edition ISBN 13: 978-1-285-44771-1

Student Edition ISBN 10: 1-285-44771-9

Student Edition PKG ISBN 13: 978-1-285-44768-1

Student Edition PKG ISBN 10: 1-285-44768-9

Cengage Learning
200 First Stamford Place, 4th Floor
Stamford, CT 06902
USA

Cengage Learning is a leading provider of customized learning solutions with office locations around the globe, including Singapore, the United Kingdom, Australia, Mexico, Brazil, and Japan. Locate your local office at: **www.cengage .com/global**

Cengage Learning products are represented in Canada by Nelson Education, Ltd.

To learn more about Cengage Learning Solutions, visit **www.cengage.com**

Purchase any of our products at your local college store or at our preferred online store **www.cengagebrain.com**

Printed in the United States of America
1 2 3 4 5 6 7 17 16 15 14 13

Brief Contents

1 What Is Statistics? 2

2 Graphical and Tabular Descriptive Techniques 10

3 Numerical Descriptive Techniques 34

4 Data Collection and Sampling 54

5 Probability 64

6 Random Variables and Discrete Probability Distributions 80

7 Continuous Probability Distributions 96

8 Sampling Distributions 120

9 Introduction to Estimation 134

10 Introduction to Hypothesis Testing 148

11 Inference about a Population 168

12 Inference about Comparing Two Populations, Part 1 184

13 Inference about Comparing Two Populations, Part 2 206

14 Analysis of Variance 220

15 Chi-Squared Tests 240

16 Simple Linear Regression and Correlation 254

17 Multiple Regression 276

18 Review of Statistical Inference 294

Appendix A Data File Sample Statistics 300

Appendix B Tables 303

Appendix C Answers to Selected Even-Numbered Exercises 323

Appendix D A Guide to Statistical Techniques 329

Appendix E Index of Computer Output and Instructions 331

Index 332

USE THE TOOLS.

- Rip out the Review Cards in the back of your book to study.

Or Visit CourseMate to:

- Read, search, highlight, and take notes in the Interactive eBook
- Review Flashcards (Print or Online) to master key terms
- Test yourself with Auto-Graded Quizzes
- Bring concepts to life with Games, Videos, and Animations!

Go to CourseMate for **BSTAT2** to begin using these tools.
Access at **www.cengagebrain.com**

Complete the Speak Up
survey in CourseMate at
www.cengagebrain.com

 Follow us at
www.facebook.com/4ltrpress

Contents

1 What Is Statistics? 2

1-1 Key Statistical Concepts 6

1-2 Large Real Data Sets 7

1-3 Statistics and the Computer 8

2 Graphical and Tabular Descriptive Techniques 10

2-1 Types of Data and Information 12

2-2 Pie and Bar Charts 14

2-3 Histograms and Stem-and-Leaf Displays 18

2-4 Line Charts 24

2-5 Scatter Diagrams 27

3 Numerical Descriptive Techniques 34

3-1 Measures of Central Location 36

3-2 Measures of Variability 39

3-3 Measures of Relative Standing and Box Plots 42

3-4 Measures of Linear Relationship 47

4 Data Collection and Sampling 54

4-1 Methods of Collecting Data 55

4-2 Sampling 57

4-3 Sampling Plans 58

4-4 Sampling and Nonsampling Errors 61

5 Probability 64

5-1 Assigning Probability to Events 65

5-2 Joint, Marginal, and Conditional Probability 68

5-3 Probability Rules and Trees 72

5-4 Identifying the Correct Method 75

6 Random Variables and Discrete Probability Distributions 80

6-1 Random Variables and Probability Distributions 82

6-2 Binomial Distribution 86

6-3 Poisson Distribution 90

7 Continuous Probability Distributions 96

7-1 Probability Density Functions 98

7-2 Normal Distribution 100

7-3 Other Continuous Distributions 108

8 Sampling Distributions 120

8-1 Sampling Distribution of the Mean 121

8-2 Sampling Distribution of a Proportion 127

9 Introduction to Estimation 134

9-1 Concepts of Estimation 135

9-2 Estimating the Population Proportion 138

9-3 Selecting the Sample Size to Estimate the Proportion 143

10 Introduction to Hypothesis Testing 148

10-1 Concepts of Hypothesis Testing 149

10-2 Testing the Population Proportion 152

10-3 Calculating the Probability of a Type II Error 160

10-4 The Road Ahead 164

11 Inference about a Population 168

11-1 Inference about a Population Mean 170

11-2 Inference about a Population Variance 175

11-3 Review of Inference about a Population Proportion 179

12 Inference about Comparing Two Populations, Part 1 184

12-1 Inference about the Difference between Two Means: Independent Samples 185

12-2 Inference about the Difference between Two Means: Matched Pairs Experiment 196

13 Inference about Comparing Two Populations, Part 2 206

13-1 Inference about the Ratio of Two Population Variances 207

13-2 Inference about the Difference between Two Population Proportions 210

14 Analysis of Variance 220

14-1 One-Way Analysis of Variance 221

14-2 Multiple Comparisons 227

14-3 Randomized Block (Two-Way) Analysis of Variance 232

15 Chi-Squared Tests 240

15-1 Chi-Squared Goodness-of-Fit Test 241

15-2 Chi-Squared Test of a Contingency Table 244

16 Simple Linear Regression and Correlation 254

16-1 Model 256

16-2 Estimating the Coefficients 256

16-3 Error Variable: Required Conditions 260

16-4 Assessing the Model 261

16-5 Using the Regression Equation 269

17 Multiple Regression 276

17-1 Model and Required Conditions 277

17-2 Estimating the Coefficients and Assessing the Model 278

17-3 Regression Diagnostics 284

18 Review of Statistical Inference 294

Appendix A Data File Sample Statistics 300

Appendix B Tables 303

1 Binomial Probabilities 303

2 Poisson Probabilities 307

3 Cumulative Standardized Normal Probabilities 309

4 Critical Values of the Student t Distribution 311

5 Critical Values of the χ^2 Distribution 312

6(a) Critical Values of the F-Distribution: $A = .05$ 313

6(b) Values of the F-Distribution: $A = .025$ 315

6(c) Values of the F-Distribution: $A = .01$ 317

6(d) Values of the F-Distribution: $A = .005$ 319

7(a) Critical Values of the Studentized Range, $\alpha = .05$ 321

7(b) Critical Values of the Studentized Range, $\alpha = .01$ 322

Appendix C Answers to Selected Even-Numbered Exercises 323

Appendix D A Guide to Statistical Techniques 329

Appendix E Index of Computer Output and Instructions 331

Index 332

Tear-Out Cards

4LTR Press solutions are designed for today's learners through the continuous feedback of students like you. Tell us what you think about **BSTAT2** and help us improve the learning experience for future students.

YOUR FEEDBACK MATTERS.

Complete the Speak Up
survey in CourseMate at
www.cengagebrain.com

 Follow us at
www.facebook.com/4ltrpress

CHAPTER 1

What Is Statistics?

objectives

1-1 **Key Statistical Concepts**

1-2 **Large Real Data Sets**

1-3 **Statistics and the Computer**

INTRODUCTION

Statistics is a way to get information from data. That's it! Most of this textbook is devoted to describing how, when, and why managers and statistics practitioners[1] conduct statistical procedures. You may ask, "If that's all there is to statistics, then why is this book (and most other statistics books) so large?" The answer is that there are different kinds of information and data to which students of applied statistics should be exposed. We demonstrate some of these with three examples here, one of which is featured later in this book.

---

[1] The term *statistician* is used to describe so many different kinds of occupations that it no longer has any meaning. It is used, for example, to describe both a person who calculates baseball statistics and an individual educated in statistical principles. We will describe the former as a *statistics practitioner* and the latter as a *statistician*. A statistics practitioner is a person who uses statistical techniques properly. Examples of statistics practitioners include the following:

1. a financial analyst who develops stock portfolios based on historical rates of return;
2. an economist who uses statistical models to help explain and predict variables such as inflation rate, unemployment rate, and changes in the gross domestic product; and
3. a market researcher who surveys consumers and converts the responses into useful information.

Our goal in this book is to convert you into one such capable individual.

The term *statistician* refers to an individual who works with the mathematics of statistics. His or her work involves research that develops techniques and concepts that in the future may help the statistics practitioner. Statisticians are also statistics practitioners, frequently conducting empirical research and consulting. If you're taking a statistics course, your instructor is probably a statistician.

EXAMPLE 1.1

Business Statistics Marks

A student who is enrolled in a business program is attending his first class of the required statistics course. The student is somewhat apprehensive because he believes the myth that the course is difficult. To alleviate his anxiety, the student asks the professor about last year's marks. Because, like all other statistics professors, this one is friendly and helpful, he obliges the student and provides a list of the final marks, which are composed of term work plus the final exam. What information can the student obtain from the list?

This is a typical statistics problem. The student has the data (marks) and needs to apply statistical techniques to get the information he requires. This is a function of **descriptive statistics**.

Peter Dazeley/Photographer's Choice/Getty Images

Descriptive Statistics

Descriptive statistics deals with methods of organizing, summarizing, and presenting data in a convenient and informative way. One form of descriptive statistics uses graphical techniques that allow statistics practitioners to present data in ways that make it easy for the reader to extract useful information. In Chapter 2, we will present a variety of graphical methods.

Another form of descriptive statistics uses numerical techniques to summarize data. One such method that you have already used frequently calculates the average or mean. We can compute the mean mark of last year's statistics course by summing the marks and dividing by the number of marks. Chapter 3 introduces several numerical statistical measures that describe different features of the data.

The actual technique we use depends on what specific information we would like to extract. In Example 1.1, we can see at least three important pieces of information. The first is the "typical" mark. We call this a *measure of central location*. The average is this type of measure. Another measure of central location is the median which is the mark that divides the top half from the bottom half. Suppose the student was told that the average mark last year was 67. Is this enough information to reduce his anxiety? The student would likely respond "no" because he would like to know whether most of the marks were close to 67 or were scattered far below and above the average. He needs a *measure of variability*. The simplest such measure is the *range*, which is calculated by subtracting the smallest number from the largest. Suppose the largest mark is 96 and the smallest is 24. Unfortunately, this provides little information. We need other measures, and these will be introduced in Chapter 3. Moreover, the student must determine more about the marks. In particular, he needs to know how the marks are distributed between 24 and 96. The best way to do this is to use a graphical technique, the histogram, which will be introduced in Chapter 2.

EXAMPLE 1.2

Pepsi's Exclusivity Agreement with a University

In the last few years, colleges and universities have signed exclusivity agreements with a variety of private companies. These agreements bind the university to sell that company's products exclusively on the campus. Many of the agreements involve food and beverage firms.

A large university with a total enrollment of about 50,000 students has offered Pepsi-Cola an exclusivity agreement that would give Pepsi exclusive rights to sell its products at all university facilities for the next year with an option for future years. In return, the university would receive 35% of the on-campus revenues and an additional lump sum of $200,000 per year. Pepsi has been given 2 weeks to respond.

The management at Pepsi quickly reviews what it knows. The market for soft drinks is measured in terms of 12-ounce cans. Pepsi currently sells an average of 22,000 cans per week (over the 40 weeks of the year that the university operates). The cans sell for an average of one dollar each. The costs including labor amount to 30 cents per can. Pepsi is unsure of its market share but suspects it is considerably less than 50%. A quick analysis reveals that if its current market share were 25%, then, with an exclusivity agreement, Pepsi would sell 88,000 (22,000 is 25% of 88,000) cans per week or 3,520,000 cans per year. The gross revenue would be computed as follows:[2]

---

[2] We have created an Excel spreadsheet that does the calculations for this case. To access it, click **Excel Workbooks** and **Example 1.2**. The only cell you may alter is cell C3, which contains the average number of soft drinks sold per week per student, assuming a total of 88,000 drinks sold per year.

Gross revenue = 3,520,000 × $1.00/can
= $3,520,000

This figure must be multiplied by 65% because the university would rake in 35% of the gross. Thus,

Gross revenue after deducting 35% university take = 65% × $3,520,000 = $2,288,000

The total cost of 30 cents per can (or $1,056,000) and the annual payment to the university of $200,000 are subtracted to obtain the net profit:

Net profit = $2,288,000 − $1,056,000
− $200,000 = $1,032,000

Pepsi's current annual profit is

40 weeks × 22,000 cans/week × $.70
= $616,000

If the current market share is 25%, the potential gain from the agreement is

$1,032,000 − $616,000 = $416,000

The only problem with this analysis is that Pepsi does not know how many soft drinks are sold weekly at the university. Coke is not likely to supply Pepsi with information about its sales, which together with Pepsi's line of products constitute virtually the entire market.

Pepsi assigned a recent university graduate to survey the university's students to supply the missing information. Accordingly, she organizes a survey that asks 500 students to keep track of the number of soft drinks they purchase in the next 7 days. The responses are stored in a file named Xm01-02 available from our Web site.

Inferential Statistics

The information we would like to acquire in Example 1.2 is an estimate of annual profits from the exclusivity agreement. The data are the numbers of cans of soft drinks consumed in 7 days by the 500 students in the sample. We can use descriptive techniques to learn more about the data. In this case, however, we are not so much interested in what the 500 students are reporting as we are in knowing the mean number of soft drinks consumed by all 50,000 students on campus. To accomplish this goal, we need another branch of statistics—**inferential statistics**.

Inferential statistics is a body of methods used to draw conclusions or inferences about characteristics of populations based on sample data. The population in question in this example is the soft drink consumption

© Mark Richards/PhotoEdit

of the university's 50,000 students. The cost of interviewing each student would be prohibitive and extremely time consuming. Statistical techniques make such endeavors unnecessary. Instead, we can sample a much smaller number of students (the sample size is 500) and infer from the data the number of soft drinks consumed by all 50,000 students. We can then estimate annual profits for Pepsi.

EXAMPLE 10.1
Exit Polls
(see Chapter 10)

When an election for political office takes place, the television networks cancel regular programming and provide election coverage instead. When the ballots are counted, the results are reported. However, for important offices such as president or senator in large states, the networks actively compete to see which will be the first to predict a winner. This is done through *exit polls* in which a random sample of voters who exit polling booths are asked who they voted for. From the data, the sample proportion of voters supporting the candidates is computed. A statistical technique is applied to determine whether there is enough evidence to infer that the leading candidate will garner enough votes to win. Suppose that the exit poll results from the state of Florida during the 2000 year elections were recorded. Although there were a number of candidates running for president, the exit pollsters recorded only the votes of the two candidates who had any chance of winning: Republican candidate George W. Bush and Democrat Albert Gore. The results (900 people who voted for either Bush or Gore) were stored on a file (Xm10-01), which can be downloaded from our Web site. The network analysts would like to know whether they can conclude that George W. Bush will win the state of Florida.

Example 10.1 describes a very common application of statistical inference. The population the television networks wanted to make inferences about is the approximately 5 million Floridians who voted for Bush or Gore for president. The sample consisted of the 900 people randomly selected by the polling company who voted for either of the two main candidates. The characteristic of the population that we would like to know is the proportion of the Florida total electorate that voted for Bush. Specifically, we would like to know whether more than 50% of the electorate voted for Bush (counting only those who voted for either the Republican or Democratic candidate). Because we will not ask every one of the 5 million actual voters who they voted for, it must be made clear that we cannot predict the outcome with 100% certainty. This is a fact that statistics practitioners and even students of statistics must understand. A sample that is only a small fraction of the size of the population can lead to correct inferences only a certain percentage of the time. You will find that statistics practitioners can control that fraction and usually set it between 90% and 99%.

Incidentally, on the night of the United States election in November 2000, the networks goofed badly. Using exit polls as well as the results of previous elections, all four networks concluded at about 8 P.M. that Al Gore would win the state of Florida. Shortly after 10 P.M., with a large percentage of the actual vote having been counted, the networks reversed course and declared that George W. Bush would win Florida. By 2 A.M., another verdict was declared: the result was too close to call. This experience is often used by statistics instructors when they teach how *not* to use statistics.

Contrary to what you probably believed, notice that data are not necessarily numbers. The marks in Example 1.1 and the number of soft drinks consumed in a week in Example 1.2, of course, are numbers, but the votes in Example 10.1 are not. In Chapter 2, we will discuss the different types of data you will encounter in statistical applications and how to deal with them.

1-1 Key Statistical Concepts

Statistical inference problems involve three key concepts: the population, the sample, and the statistical inference. We now discuss each concept in more detail.

1-1a Population

A **population** is the group of all items of interest to a statistics practitioner. It is frequently very large and may, in fact, be infinitely large. In the language of statistics, *population* does not necessarily refer to a group of people. It may, for example, refer to the population of diameters of ball bearings produced at a large plant. In Example 1.2, the population of interest consists of the 50,000 students on campus. In Example 10.1 the population consists of the Floridians who voted for Bush or Gore.

A descriptive measure of a population is called a **parameter**. The parameter of interest in Example 1.2 is the mean number of soft drinks consumed by all the students at the university. The parameter in Example 10.1 is the proportion of the 5 million Florida voters who voted for Bush. In most applications of inferential statistics, the parameter represents the information we need.

1-1b Sample

A **sample** is a set of data drawn from the population. A descriptive measure of a sample is called a **statistic**. We use statistics to make inferences about parameters. In Example 1.2, the statistic we would compute is the mean number of soft drinks consumed in the last week by the 500 students in the sample. We would then use the sample mean to infer the value of the population mean, from which we can estimate the profit. In Example 10.1,

© Anatoliy Samara/Shutterstock.com

we compute the proportion of the sample of 900 Floridians who voted for Bush. The sample statistic is then used to make inferences about the population of all 5 million votes. In other words, we predict the election results even before the actual count.

1-1c Statistical Inference

Statistical inference is the process of making an estimate, prediction, or decision about a population based on sample data. Because populations are almost always very large, investigating each member of the population would be impractical and expensive. It is far easier and cheaper to take a sample from the population of interest and draw conclusions or make estimates about the population on the basis of information provided by the sample. However, such conclusions and estimates will not always be correct. For this reason, we build into the statistical inference a measure of reliability. There are two such measures: the **confidence level** and the **significance level**. The *confidence level* is the proportion of times that an estimating procedure will be correct. In Example 1.2, we could produce an estimate of the average number of soft drinks to be consumed by all 50,000 students that has a confidence level of 95%. In other words, in the long run, estimates based on this form of statistical inference will be correct 95% of the time. When the purpose of the statistical inference is to draw a conclusion about a population, the *significance level* measures how frequently the conclusion will be wrong in the long run. For example, suppose that as a

result of the analysis in Example 10.1, we conclude that more than 50% of the electorate will vote for George W. Bush and thus he will win the state of Florida. A 5% significance level means that, in the long run, this type of conclusion will be wrong 5% of the time.

1-2 Large Real Data Sets

© Glowimages

The author believes that you learn statistics by doing statistics. In life after college and university, we expect that our students will have access to large amounts of real data that must be summarized to acquire the information needed to make decisions. To provide practice in this vital skill. We have included on our Web site two sets of large real data sets. Their sources are the General Social Survey (GSS) and the American National Election Survey (ANES).

1-2a General Social Survey

Since 1972, the General Social Survey has been tracking American attitudes on a wide variety of topics. Except for the United States census, the GSS is the most frequently used source of information about American society. The surveys now conducted every second year measure hundreds of variables and thousands of observations. We have included the results of the last six surveys (years 2002, 2004, 2006, 2008, 2010, and 2012) stored as GSS2002, GSS2004, GSS2006, GSS2008, GSS2010, and GSS2012, respectively. The survey sizes are 2,765, 2,812, 4,510, 2,023, 2,044, and 1974, respectively. We have reduced the number of variables to about 60 and have deleted the responses that are known as *missing* data ("Don't know," "Refused," etc.).

We have included some demographic variables such as, age, gender, race, income, and education. Others measure political views, support for various government activities, and work. The full lists of variables for each year are stored on our Web site in Appendixes GSS2002, GSS2004, GSS2006, GSS2008, GSS2010, and GSS2012.

We have scattered throughout this book examples and exercises drawn from these data sets.

1-2b American National Election Survey

The goal of the American National Election Survey is to provide data about why Americans vote as they do. The surveys are conducted in the years of presidential elections. We have included data from the 2004 and 2008 surveys. Like the General Social Survey, the ANES includes demographic variables. It also deals with interest in the presidential election as well as variables that describe political beliefs and affiliations. Web site Appendixes ANES2004 and ANES2008 contain the names and definitions of the variables.

The 2008 surveys overly sampled black and Hispanic voters. We have "adjusted" these data by randomly deleting responses from these two racial groups.

As is the case with the General Social Surveys, we have removed the missing data.

1-3 Statistics and the Computer

In virtually all applications of statistics, the statistics practitioner must deal with large amounts of data. For instance, Example 1.2 involves 500 observations. To estimate annual profits, the statistics practitioner would have to perform computations on the data; although the calculations do not require any great mathematical skill, the sheer amount of arithmetic makes this aspect of the statistical method time consuming and tedious.

Fortunately, numerous commercially prepared computer programs are available to perform the arithmetic. We have chosen to use Microsoft Excel, which is a spreadsheet program, and Minitab, a statistical software package. We chose Excel because we believe that it is and will continue to be the most popular spreadsheet package. One drawback, however, is that it does not offer a complete set of the statistical techniques that we introduce in this book. Consequently, we have created add-ins that can be loaded onto your computer to enable you to use Excel for all statistical procedures introduced in this book. The add-ins can be downloaded from our Web site. When installed, they will appear as Data Analysis Plus© on Excel's menu. Also available on the Web site are introductions to Excel and Minitab and detailed instructions for both software packages.

A large proportion of the examples and exercises feature large data sets that are also stored on the Web site. These are denoted with the file name. We demonstrate the solution to the statistical examples in three ways: manually, by employing Excel, and by using Minitab. Moreover, we will provide detailed instructions for all techniques.

The files contain the data needed to produce the solution. However, in many real applications of statistics, additional data are collected. For example, the interviewer at exit polls often records the gender and asks the voter for other information, including race, religion, education, and income. Many other data sets are similarly constructed. In later chapters, we will return to these files and require other statistical techniques to extract the needed information. (Files that contain additional data are denoted by an asterisk on the file name.)

The approach we prefer to take is to minimize the time spent on manual computations and to focus instead on selecting the appropriate method for dealing with a problem and on interpreting the output after the computer has performed the necessary computations. In this way, we hope to demonstrate that statistics can be as interesting and as practical as any other subject in your curriculum.

EXERCISES

1.1 In your own words, define and give an example of each of the following statistical terms:

a. population
b. sample
c. parameter
d. statistic
e. statistical inference

1.2 Briefly describe the difference between descriptive statistics and inferential statistics.

1.3 A politician running for the office of mayor of a city with 25,000 registered voters commissions a survey. In the survey, 48% of the 200 registered voters interviewed say they plan to vote for her.

a. What is the population of interest?
b. What is the sample?
c. Is the value 48% a parameter or a statistic? Explain.

1.4 A manufacturer of computer chips claims that less than 10% of his products are defective. When 1,000 chips were drawn from a large production, 7.5% were found to be defective.

a. What is the population of interest?
b. What is the sample?
c. What is the parameter?
d. What is the statistic?
e. Does the value 10% refer to the parameter or to the statistic?
f. Is the value 7.5% a parameter or a statistic?
g. Explain briefly how the statistic can be used to make inferences about the parameter to test the claim.

1.5 Suppose you believe that graduates who have majored in *your* subject are generally offered higher salaries on graduating than graduates of other programs. Describe a statistical experiment that could help test your belief.

1.6 You are shown a coin that its owner says is fair in the sense that it will produce the same number of heads and tails when flipped a very large number of times.

a. Describe an experiment to test this claim.
b. What is the population in your experiment?
c. What is the sample?
d. What is the parameter?
e. What is the statistic?
f. Describe briefly how statistical inference can be used to test the claim.

1.7 Suppose that in Exercise 1.6 you decide to flip the coin 100 times.

a. What conclusion would you be likely to draw if you observed 95 heads?
b. What conclusion would you be likely to draw if you observed 55 heads?
c. Do you believe that if you flip a perfectly fair coin 100 times you will always observe exactly 50 heads? If you answered "No," what numbers do you think are possible? If you answered "Yes," how many heads would you observe if you flipped the coin twice? Try it several times and report the results.

1.8 [Xr01-08] The owner of a large fleet of taxis is trying to estimate his costs for next year's operations. Fuel is one major cost. To estimate fuel purchases, the owner needs to know the total distance his taxis will travel next year, the cost of a gallon of fuel, and the fuel mileage of his taxis. The owner has been provided with the first two figures (distance estimate and cost of a gallon of fuel). However, because of the high cost of gasoline, the owner has recently converted his taxis to operate on natural gas. He has measured and recorded the natural gas mileage (in miles per gallon) for 50 taxis.

a. What is the population of interest?
b. What is the parameter the owner needs?
c. What is the sample?
d. What is the statistic?
e. Describe briefly how the statistic will produce the kind of information the owner wants.

CHAPTER 2

Graphical and Tabular Descriptive Techniques

objectives

2-1 Types of Data and Information

2-2 Pie and Bar Charts

2-3 Histograms and Stem-and-Leaf Displays

2-4 Line Charts

2-5 Scatter Diagrams

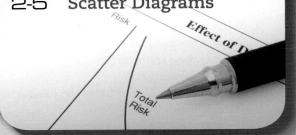

GENERAL SOCIAL SURVEY: HOW EDUCATED ARE AMERICAN ADULTS?

[GSS2012*] In Chapter 1, we described two real large-scale surveys. One was the General Social Survey (GSS), which deals with a wide variety of topics. One question asked in the 2012 survey addressed the question of how educated American adults were. The question was,

Indicate your highest degree completed.

The variable was stored as (DEGREE)

0   Left high school

1   Completed high school

2   Completed junior college

3   Completed bachelor's degree

4   Completed graduate degree

Summarize these data and describe what you have learned.

On pages 17–18 you will find our answer.

In Chapter 1, we pointed out that statistics is divided into two basic areas: descriptive statistics and inferential statistics. The purpose of this chapter, together with the next one, is to present the principal methods that fall under the heading of descriptive statistics. In this chapter, we introduce graphical and tabular methods that allow managers to summarize data visually to produce useful information that is often used in decision making. Another class of descriptive techniques, numerical methods, is introduced in Chapter 3.

Descriptive statistics involves arranging, summarizing, and presenting a set of data in such a way that useful information is produced. Its methods use graphical techniques and numerical descriptive measures (such as averages) to summarize and present the data, allowing managers to make decisions based on the information generated.

In both the preface and Chapter 1, we pointed out that a critical part of your education as statistics practitioners includes an understanding not only of *how* to draw graphs and calculate statistics but also *when* to use each technique that we cover. The two most important factors that determine the appropriate method to use are the type of data and the information that is needed. Both are discussed next.

2-1 Types of Data and Information

The objective of statistics is to extract information from data. There are different types of data and information. To help explain this important principle, we need to define some terms.

A **variable** is some characteristic of a population or sample. For example, the mark on a statistics exam is a characteristic of statistics exams that is certainly of interest to readers of this book. We usually represent the name of the variable using uppercase letters such as X, Y, and Z.

The **values** of the variable are the possible observations of the variable. The values of statistics exam marks are the integers between 0 and 100 (assuming the exam is marked out of 100).

Data are the observed values of a variable. For example, suppose that we observe the midterm test marks of 10 students, which are

| 67 | 74 | 71 | 83 | 93 | 55 | 48 | 82 | 68 | 62 |

These are the data from which we will extract the information we seek. Incidentally, data is plural for **datum**. The mark of one student is a datum.

When most people think of data they think of sets of numbers. However, there are three types of data. They are interval, nominal, and ordinal data.[1]

Interval data are real numbers, such as heights, weights, incomes, and distances. We also refer to this type of data as **quantitative** or **numerical**.

The values of **nominal** data are categories. For example, responses to questions about marital status produce nominal data. The values of this variable are single, married, divorced, and widowed. Notice that the values are not numbers but words that describe the categories. We often record nominal data by arbitrarily assigning a different number to each category. Nominal data are also called **qualitative** or **categorical**.

The third type of data is ordinal. **Ordinal** data appear to be nominal, but their values are in order. For example, at the completion of most college and university courses, students are asked to evaluate the course. The variables are the ratings of various aspects of the course, including the professor. Suppose that in a particular college the values are

poor, fair, good, very good, and excellent

The difference between nominal and ordinal types of data is that the values of the latter are in order. Consequently, when assigning codes to the values, we should maintain the order of the values. For example, we can record the students' evaluations as

1 = Poor, 2 = Fair, 3 = Good, 4 = Very good, 5 = Excellent

Because the only constraint that we impose on our choice of codes is that the order must be maintained, we can use any set of codes that are in order. For example, we can also assign the following codes:

6 = Poor, 18 = Fair, 23 = Good, 45 = Very good, 88 = Excellent

The use of any code that preserves the order of the data will produce exactly the same result.

2-1a Calculations for Types of Data

Interval Data

All calculations are permitted on interval data. We often describe a set of interval data by calculating the average. For example, the average of the 10 marks listed above is 70.3.

---

[1] There are actually four types of data, the fourth being ratio data. However, for statistical purposes there is no difference between ratio and interval data, so we combine the two types.

Nominal Data

Because the codes of nominal data are completely arbitrary, we cannot perform any calculations on these codes. To understand why, consider a survey that asks people to report their marital status. Suppose that the first 10 people surveyed gave the following responses:

single, married, married, married, widowed, single, married, married, single, divorced

Using the codes

1 = Single, 2 = Married, 3 = Divorced, 4 = Widowed

we would record these responses as

1 2 2 2 4 1 2 2 1 3

The average of these numerical codes is 2.0. Does this mean that the average person is married? Now suppose four more persons were interviewed, three of them widowed and one divorced. The data are given here:

1 2 2 2 4 1 2 2 1 3 4 4 4 3

The average of these 14 codes is 2.5. Does this mean that the average person is married, but halfway to getting divorced? The answer to both questions is obviously "No." This example illustrates a fundamental truth about nominal data: calculations based on the codes used to store this type of data are meaningless. All that we are permitted to do with nominal data is count the occurrences of each category. Thus, we would describe the 14 observations by counting the number of each marital status category and reporting the frequency as shown in the following table.

Category	Code	Frequency
Single	1	3
Married	2	5
Divorced	3	2
Widowed	4	4

© Cengage Learning

2-1b Ordinal Data

The most important aspect of ordinal data is the order of the values. As a result, the only permissible calculations are those that involve a ranking process. For example, we can place all the data in order and select the code that lies in the middle. As we discuss in Chapter 3, this descriptive measurement is called the *median*.

2-1c Hierarchy of Data

The data types can be placed in order of the permissible calculations. At the top of the list we place the interval data type because virtually *all* computations are allowed. The nominal data type is at the bottom because *no* calculations other than determining frequencies are permitted. (We are permitted to perform calculations using the frequencies of codes. However, this differs from performing calculations on the codes themselves.) In between interval and nominal data lies the ordinal data type. Permissible calculations are ones that rank the data.

Higher-level data types may be treated as lower-level ones. For example, in universities and colleges we convert the marks in a course, which are interval, to letter grades, which are ordinal. Some graduate courses feature only a pass or fail designation. In this case, the interval data are converted to nominal. It is important to point out that when we convert higher-level data to lower-level data we lose information. For example, a mark of 89 on an accounting course exam gives far more information about the performance of that student than does a letter grade of B, which is the letter grade for marks between 80 and 90. As a result we do not convert data unless it is necessary to do so.

It is also important to note that we cannot treat lower-level data types as higher-level types.

2-1d Interval, Ordinal, and Nominal Variables

The variables whose observations constitute our data will be given the same name as the type of data. Thus, for example, interval data are the observations of an interval variable.

2-1e Problem Objectives and Information

In presenting the different types of data, we introduced a critical factor in deciding which statistical procedure to use. A second factor is the type of information we need to produce from our data. We discuss the different types of information in greater detail in Section 10-3 when we introduce *problem objectives*. However, in Chapters 2 and 3 we will use statistical techniques to describe a set of data and the relationship between two variables. In Section 2-2, we introduce graphical and tabular techniques employed to describe a set of nominal data. Section 2-3 introduces graphical methods to describe a set of interval data. In Section 2-4, we present a graphical technique to describe a time series. Section 2-5 presents methods to describe the relationship between two interval variables.

2-2 Pie and Bar Charts

As we discussed in Section 2-1, the only allowable calculation on nominal data is to count the frequency of each value of the variable. We can summarize the data in a table that presents the categories and their counts called a **frequency distribution**. A **relative frequency distribution** lists the categories and the proportion with which each occurs. We can use graphical techniques to present a picture of the data. There are two graphical methods we can use: the **bar chart** and the **pie chart**.

EXAMPLE 2.1

Light Beer Preference Survey

[Xm02-01*] In 2012, total light beer sales was approximately $50 billion (*Source:* Bloomberg.com). With this large a market, breweries often need to know more about who is buying their products. The marketing manager of a major brewery wanted to analyze the light beer sales among college and university students who drink light beer. A random sample of 285 graduating students was asked to report which of the following is their favorite light beer:

1 = Bud Light, 2 = Busch Light, 3 = Coors Light, 4 = Michelob Light, 5 = Miller Lite, 6 = Natural Light, 7 = Other brands

The responses were recorded using the codes 1, 2, 3, 4, 5, 6, and 7, respectively. The data are listed here, and the entire data set is stored on our Web site. The name of the file is listed in the margin. The file also contains each graduate's identification number and gender. The additional data are not needed in this example but will be used later in this book to produce other information for the manager. (Examples and exercises with additional data are indicated with an asterisk next to the file name.)

Construct a frequency and relative frequency distribution for these data and graphically summarize the data by producing a bar chart and a pie chart.

SOLUTION

To extract useful information requires the application of a statistical or graphical technique. To choose the appropriate technique, we must first identify the type of data. In this example, the data are nominal because the numbers represent categories. The only calculation permitted on nominal data is to count the number of occurrences of each category. Hence, we count the number of 1s, 2s, 3s, 4s, 5s, 6s, and 7s. The list of the categories and their counts constitute the frequency distribution. The relative frequency

Light Beer Preferences

1	1	1	1	2	4	3	5	1	3	1	3	7	5	1
1	5	2	1	5	1	3	3	3	1	1	5	3	1	5
5	1	1	3	3	5	5	6	3	5	3	5	5	5	1
1	2	1	1	5	5	3	2	1	6	1	1	4	5	1
3	3	5	4	7	6	6	4	4	6	5	2	1	1	5
3	3	1	3	5	3	3	7	3	7	2	1	5	7	
3	6	2	6	3	6	6	6	5	6	1	1	6	3	
7	1	1	1	5	1	3	1	3	7	7	2	1	1	
2	5	3	1	1	3	1	1	7	5	3	2	1	1	
6	5	7	1	3	2	1	3	1	1	7	5	5	6	
1	4	6	1	3	1	1	5	5	5	1	1	5	5	
6	1	3	3	1	3	7	1	1	1	2	4	1	1	
3	3	7	5	5	1	1	3	5	1	5	4	5	3	
4	1	4	5	3	1	5	3	3	3	1	1	5	3	
5	6	4	3	5	6	4	6	5	5	5	5	3	1	
2	3	2	7	5	1	6	6	2	3	3	3	1	1	
5	1	4	6	3	5	1	1	2	1	5	6	1	1	
5	1	3	5	1	1	1	3	7	3	1	6	3	1	
2	2	5	1	3	5	5	2	3	1	1	3	6	1	
1	1	1	7	3	1	5	3	3	3	5	3	1	7	

Table 2.1 Frequency and Relative Frequency Distributions for Example 2.1

Light Beer Brand	Frequency	Relative Frequency (%)
Bud Light	90	31.6
Busch Light	19	6.7
Coors Light	62	21.8
Michelob Light	13	4.6
Miller Lite	59	20.7
Natural Light	25	8.8
Other brands	17	6.0
Total	285	100

© Cengage Learning

distribution is produced by converting the frequencies into proportions. The frequency and relative frequency distributions are combined in Table 2.1.

As we promised in Chapter 1 (and the preface) we demonstrate the solution of all examples in this book using three approaches (where feasible): manually, using Excel, and using Minitab.

Excel

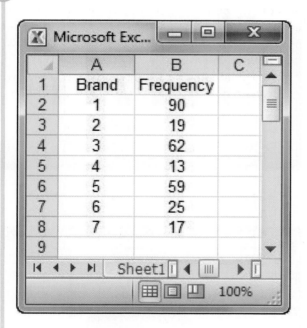

INSTRUCTIONS

1. Type or import the data into one or more columns. (Open Xm02-01.)

2. Activate any empty cell and type

```
=COUNTIF ([Input range], [Criteria])
```

Input range are the cells that contain the data. In this example, the range is B1:B286. The criteria are the

codes you want to count: (1) (2) (3) (4) (5) (6) (7). To count the number of 1s (Bud Light), type

```
=COUNTIF (B1:B286, 1)
```

and the frequency will appear in the dialog box. Change the criteria to produce the frequency of the other categories.

Minitab

Tally for Discrete Variables: Brand

Brand	Count	Percent
1	90	31.58
2	19	6.67
3	62	21.75
4	13	4.56
5	59	20.70
6	25	8.77
7	17	5.96

$N = 285$

© Cengage Learning

INSTRUCTIONS

(Specific commands for this example are highlighted.)

1. Type or import the data into one column. (Open Xm02-01.)

2. Click **Stat**, **Tables**, and **Tally Individual Variables**.

3. Type or use the **Select** button to specify the name of the variable or the column where the data are stored in the **Variables** box (Brand). Under **Display**, click **Counts** and **Percents**.

INTERPRET

Budweiser, Coors, and Miller are by far the most popular light beers among college and university seniors.

2-2a Bar and Pie Charts

The information contained in the data is summarized well in the table. However, graphical techniques generally catch a reader's eye more quickly than a table of numbers. Two graphical techniques can be used to display the results shown in the table. A **bar chart** is used to display frequencies; a **pie chart** graphically shows relative frequencies.

The bar chart is created by drawing a rectangle representing each category. The height of the rectangle represents the frequency. The base is arbitrary. Figure 2.1 depicts the manually drawn bar chart for Example 2.1.

If we wish to emphasize the relative frequencies instead of drawing the bar chart, we draw the pie chart. A pie chart is simply a circle subdivided into slices that represent the categories. It is drawn so that the size of each

Figure 2.1 Bar Chart for Example 2.1

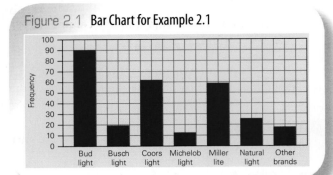

© Cengage Learning

slice is proportional to the percentage corresponding to that category. For example, because the entire circle is composed of 360 degrees, a category that contains 25% of the observations is represented by a slice of the pie that contains 25% of 360 degrees, or 90 degrees. The number of degrees for each category in Example 2.1 is shown in Table 2.2.

Table 2.2 Proportion in Each Category in Example 2.1

Light Beer Brand	Relative Frequency (%)	Slice of the Pie (Degrees)
Bud Light	31.6	113.7
Busch Light	6.7	24.0
Coors Light	21.8	78.3
Michelob Light	4.6	16.4
Miller Lite	20.7	74.5
Natural Light	8.8	31.6
Other brands	6.0	21.5
Total	100.00	360

© Cengage Learning

Figure 2.2 was drawn from these results.

Figure 2.2 Pie Chart for Example 2.1

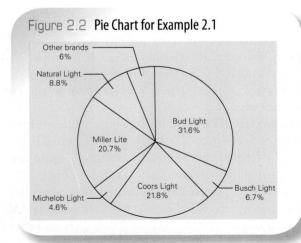

© Cengage Learning

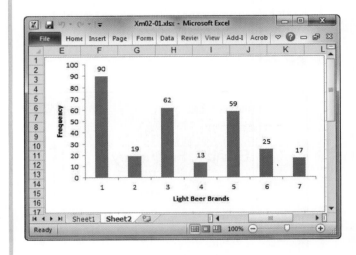

© Aleksandr Bryliaev/Shutterstock.com

Excel

Here are Excel's bar and pie charts.

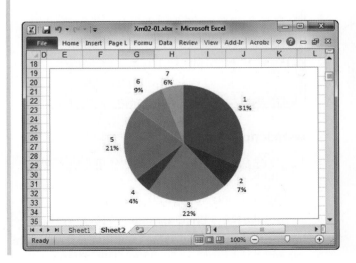

1. After creating the frequency distribution, highlight the column of frequencies.

2. For a bar chart, click **Insert**, **Column**, and the first **2-D Column**.

3. Click **Chart Tools**. (If it does not appear, click inside the box containing the bar chart.) Next, click **Layout**. This will allow you to make changes to the chart. We removed the **Gridlines**, the **Legend**, and clicked the **Data Labels** to create the titles.

4. For a pie chart, click **Pie** and **Chart Tools** to edit the graph.

Minitab

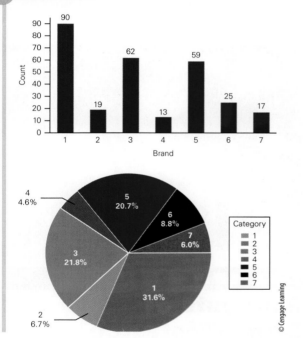

© Cengage Learning

1. Type or import the data into one column. (Open Xm02-01.)

For a bar chart:

2. Click **Graph** and **Bar Chart**.

3. In the **Bars represent** box, click **Counts of unique values** and select **Simple**.

4. Type or use the **Select** button to specify the variable in the **Variables** box (Brand).

We clicked **Labels** and added the title and clicked **Data Labels** and **use y-value labels** to display the frequencies at the top of the columns.

For a pie chart:

2. Click **Graph** and **Pie Chart**.

3. Click **Chart** and **Counts of unique values**. Then in the **Categorical variables** box, type or use the **Select** button to specify the variable (Brand).

We clicked **Labels** and added the title. We clicked **Slice Labels** and clicked **Category name** and **Percent**.

INTERPRET

The bar chart focuses on the frequencies. As you can see, Bud Light is the most popular light beer, with 90 college and university seniors selecting it as their favorite. Coors Light and Miller Lite are the second and third most popular light beers.

The pie chart focuses on the proportions. Bud Light is the choice of almost one-third of college seniors.

GENERAL SOCIAL SURVEY

HOW EDUCATED ARE AMERICAN ADULTS: SOLUTION

In this problem, the data are ordinal because the responses are in order from least amount of education to most. However, we will treat the data as nominal. To summarize a set of nominal data, we can use a frequency distribution, a bar chart, or a pie chart. We'll use all three to answer the question.

Frequency and Relative Frequency Distribution

Education	Frequency	Relative Frequency (%)
Left high school	288	14.6
Completed high school	976	49.4
Completed junior college	151	7.7
Completed bachelor's degree	354	17.9
Completed graduate degree	205	10.4
TOTAL	1,974	100

© Cengage Learning

Bar Chart

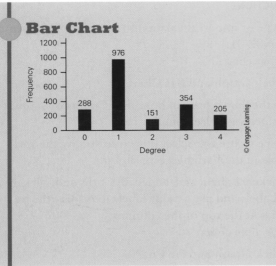

Pie Chart

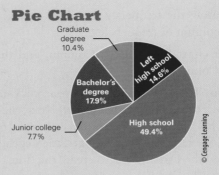

The relative frequencies and the pie chart provide the most information. About 50% of American adults finished high school only, and more than a quarter have a bachelor's degree or more.

We complete this section by describing when bar and pie charts are used to summarize and present data.

Factors That Identify When to Use Frequency and Relative Frequency Tables, Bar Charts, and Pie Charts

1. Objective: Describe a single set of data.
2. Data type: Nominal (or ordinal)

2-3 Histograms and Stem-and-Leaf Displays

In this section, we introduce two graphical methods that are used when the data are interval. The more important of these graphical methods is the histogram. As you will see, the histogram not only is a powerful graphical technique used to summarize interval data but also is used to help explain an important aspect of probability (see Chapter 7).

EXAMPLE 2.2
Analysis of Long-Distance Telephone Bills

[Xm02-02] After the telephone industry was deregulated, several new companies were created to compete in the business of providing long-distance telephone service. In almost all cases, these companies competed on price because the service each offered was similar. Pricing a service or product in the face of stiff competition is difficult. Factors to be considered include supply, demand, price elasticity, and the actions of competitors. Long-distance packages may employ per-minute charges, a flat monthly rate, or some combination of the two. Determining the appropriate rate structure is facilitated by acquiring information about the behaviors of customers, especially the size of monthly long-distance bills.

Long-Distance Telephone Bills

42.19	39.21	75.71	8.37	1.62	28.77	35.32	13.9	114.67	15.3
38.45	48.54	88.62	7.18	91.1	9.12	117.69	9.22	27.57	75.49
29.23	93.31	99.5	11.07	10.88	118.75	106.84	109.94	64.78	68.69
89.35	104.88	85	1.47	30.62	0	8.4	10.7	45.81	35
118.04	30.61	0	26.4	100.05	13.95	90.04	0	56.04	9.12
110.46	22.57	8.41	13.26	26.97	14.34	3.85	11.27	20.39	18.49
0	63.7	70.48	21.13	15.43	79.52	91.56	72.02	31.77	84.12
72.88	104.84	92.88	95.03	29.25	2.72	10.13	7.74	94.67	13.68
83.05	6.45	3.2	29.04	1.88	9.63	5.72	5.04	44.32	20.84
95.73	16.47	115.5	5.42	16.44	21.34	33.69	33.4	3.69	100.04
103.15	89.5	2.42	77.21	109.08	104.4	115.78	6.95	19.34	112.94
94.52	13.36	1.08	72.47	2.45	2.88	0.98	6.48	13.54	20.12
26.84	44.16	76.69	0	21.97	65.9	19.45	11.64	18.89	53.21
93.93	92.97	13.62	5.64	17.12	20.55	0	83.26	1.57	15.3
90.26	99.56	88.51	6.48	19.7	3.43	27.21	15.42	0	49.24
72.78	92.62	55.99	6.95	6.93	10.44	89.27	24.49	5.2	9.44
101.36	78.89	12.24	19.6	10.05	21.36	14.49	89.13	2.8	2.67
104.8	87.71	119.63	8.11	99.03	24.42	92.17	111.14	5.1	4.69
74.01	93.57	23.31	9.01	29.24	95.52	21	92.64	3.03	41.38
56.01	0	11.05	84.77	15.21	6.72	106.59	53.9	9.16	45.77

As part of a larger study, a long-distance company wanted to acquire information about the monthly bills of new subscribers in the first month after signing with the company. The company's marketing manager conducted a survey of 200 new residential subscribers and recorded the first month's bills. The general manager planned to present his findings to senior executives. What information can be extracted from these data?

SOLUTION

There is little information developed by casually reading through the 200 observations. The manager can probably see that most of the bills are under $100, but that is likely to be the extent of the information garnered from browsing through the data. If he examines the data more carefully, he may discover that the smallest bill is $0 and the largest is $119.63. He has now developed some information. However, his presentation to senior executives will be most unimpressive if no other information is produced. For example, someone is likely to ask how the numbers are distributed between 0 and 119.63. Are there many small bills and few large bills? What is the "typical" bill? Are the bills somewhat similar or do they vary considerably?

To help answer these questions and others like them, the marketing manager can construct a frequency distribution from which a histogram can be drawn. In the previous section, a frequency distribution was created by counting the number of times each category of the nominal variable occurred. We create a frequency distribution for interval data by counting the number of observations that fall into each of a series of intervals, called **classes**, that cover the complete range of observations. We discuss how to decide the number of classes and the upper and lower limits of the intervals later. We have chosen eight classes defined in such a way that each observation falls into one and only one class. These classes are defined as follows:

CLASSES

Amounts that are . . .
Less than or equal to 15

Amounts that are . . .
More than 15 but less than or equal to 30

Amounts that are . . .
More than 30 but less than or equal to 45

Amounts that are . . .
More than 45 but less than or equal to 60

Amounts that are . . .
More than 60 but less than or equal to 75

Amounts that are . . .
More than 75 but less than or equal to 90

Amounts that are . . .
More than 90 but less than or equal to 105

Amounts that are . . .

More than 105 but less than or equal to 120

Notice that the intervals do not overlap, so there is no uncertainty about which interval to assign to any observation. Moreover, because the smallest number is 0 and the largest is 119.63, every observation will be assigned to a class. Finally, the intervals are equally wide. Although this is not essential, it makes the task of reading and interpreting the graph easier.

To create the frequency distribution manually, we count the number of observations that fall into each interval. Table 2.3 presents the frequency distribution.

Table 2.3 Frequency Distribution of the Long-Distance Bills in Example 2.2

Class Limits	Frequency
0 to 15*	71
15 to 30	37
30 to 45	13
45 to 60	9
60 to 75	10
75 to 90	18
90 to 105	28
105 to 120	14
Total	200

*Classes contain observations greater than their lower limits (except for the first class) and less than or equal to their upper limits.

© Cengage Learning

Although the frequency distribution provides information about how the numbers are distributed, the information is more easily understood and imparted by drawing a picture or graph. The graph is called a **histogram**. A histogram is created by drawing rectangles whose bases are the intervals and whose heights are the **frequencies**. Figure 2.3 exhibits the histogram that was drawn by hand.

Figure 2.3 Histogram for Example 2.2

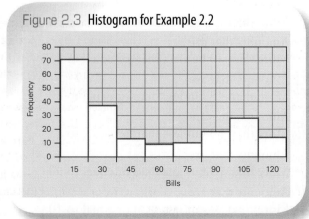

© Cengage Learning

Excel

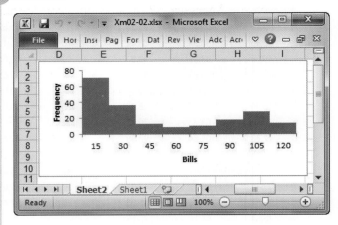

INSTRUCTIONS

1. Type or import the data into one column. (Open Xm02-02.) In another column, type the upper limits of the class intervals. Excel calls them *bins*. (You can put any name in the first row; we typed "Bills.")

2. Click **Data**, **Data Analysis**, and **Histogram**. If Data Analysis does not appear in the menu box, see Web site Appendix A1.

3. Specify the **Input Range** (A1:A201) and the **Bin Range** (B1:B9). Click **Chart Output**. Click **Labels** if the first row contains names.

4. To remove the gaps, place the cursor over one of the rectangles and click the right button of the mouse. With the left button, click **Format Data Series . . . .** Move the pointer to **Gap Width** and use the slider to change the number from 150 to 0.

Except for the first class, Excel counts the number of observations in each class that are greater than the lower limit and less than or equal to the upper limit.

Note that the numbers along the horizontal axis represent the upper limits of each class, although they appear to be placed in the centers. If you wish, you can replace these numbers with the actual midpoints by making changes to the frequency distribution in cells A1:B14 (change 15 to 7.5, 30 to 22.5, . . ., and 120 to 112.5).

You can also convert the histogram to list relative frequencies instead of frequencies. To do so, change the frequencies to relative frequencies by dividing each frequency by 200—that is, replace 71 by .355, 37 by .185, . . ., and 14 by .07.

If you have difficulty with this technique, turn to Web site Appendix A2 or A3; both provide step-by-step instructions for Excel as well as troubleshooting tips.

Minitab

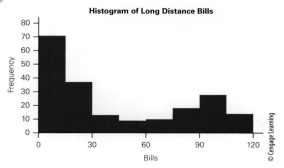

Histogram of Long Distance Bills

Note that Minitab counts the number of observations in each class that are strictly less than their upper limits.

INSTRUCTIONS

1. Type or import the data into one column. (Open Xm02-02.)

2. Click **Graph**, **Histogram . . .**, and **Simple**.

3. Type or use the **Select** button to specify the name of the variable in the **Graph variables** box (Bills). Click **Data View**.

4. Click **Data Display** and **Bars**. Minitab will create a histogram using its own choices of class intervals.

5. To choose your own classes, double-click the horizontal axis. Click **Binning**.

6. Under **Interval Type** choose **Cutpoint**. Under **Interval Definition**, choose **Midpoint/Cutpoint positions** and type in your choices (0 15 30 45 60 75 90 105 120).

INTERPRET

The histogram gives us a clear view of the way the bills are distributed. About half the monthly bills are small ($0 to $30), a few bills are in the middle range ($30 to $75), and a relatively large number of long-distance bills are at the high end of the range. It would appear from this sample of first-month long-distance bills that the company's customers are split unevenly between light and heavy users of long-distance telephone service. If the company assumes that this pattern will continue, it must address a number of pricing issues. For example, customers who incurred large monthly bills may be targets of

competitors who offer flat rates for 15-minute or 30-minute calls. The company needs to know more about these customers. With the additional information, the marketing manager may suggest an alteration of the company's pricing.

2-3a Determining the Number of Class Intervals

The number of class intervals we select depends entirely on the number of observations in the data set. The more observations we have, the larger the number of class intervals we need to use to draw a useful histogram. Table 2.4 provides guidelines on choosing the number of classes. In Example 2.2 we had 200 observations. The table tells us to use 7, 8, 9, or 10 classes.

Table 2.4 **Approximate Number of Classes in Frequency Distributions**

Number of Observations	Number of Classes
Less than 50	5–7
50–200	7–9
200–500	9–10
500–1,000	10–11
1,000–5,000	11–13
5,000–50,000	13–17
More than 50,000	17–20

2-3b Class Interval Widths

We determine the approximate width of the classes by subtracting the smallest observation from the largest and dividing the difference by the number of classes. Thus,

$$\text{Class width} = \frac{\text{Largest} - \text{Smallest Observation}}{\text{Number of Classes}}$$

In Example 2.2, we calculated

$$\text{Class width} = \frac{119.63 - 0}{8} = 14.95$$

We often round the result to some convenient value. We then define our class limits by selecting a lower limit for the first class from which all other limits are determined. The only condition we apply is that the first class interval must contain the smallest observation. In Example 2.2, we rounded the class width to 15 and set the lower limit of the first class to 0. Thus, the first class is defined as "Amounts that are greater than or equal to 0 but less than or equal to 15." (Minitab users should remember that the classes are defined as the number of observations that are *strictly less* than their upper limits.)

Table 2.4 provides guidelines only. It is more important to choose classes that are easy to interpret. For example, suppose that we have recorded the marks on an exam of the 100 students registered in the course where the highest mark is 94 and the lowest is 48. Table 2.4 suggests that we use 7, 8, or 9 classes. Suppose we choose 8. Thus,

$$\text{Class width} = \frac{94 - 48}{8} = 5.75$$

which we would round to 6. We could then produce a histogram whose upper limits of the class intervals are 50, 56, 62, . . ., 98. Because of the rounding and the way in which we defined the class limits, the number of classes is 9. However, a histogram that is easier to interpret would be produced using classes whose widths are 5. In other words, the upper limits would be 50, 55, 60, . . ., 95. The number of classes in this case would be 10.

2-3c Shapes of Histograms

The purpose of drawing histograms, like that of all other statistical techniques, is to acquire information. Once we have the information, we frequently need to describe what we've learned to others. We describe the shape of histograms on the basis of the following characteristics.

2-3d Symmetry

A histogram is said to be **symmetric** if, when we draw a vertical line down the center of the histogram, the two sides are identical in shape and size. Figure 2.4 depicts three symmetric histograms.

2-3e Skewness

A skewed histogram is one with a long tail extending to either the right or the left. The former is called **positively skewed**, and the latter is called **negatively skewed**. Figure 2.5 shows examples of both. Incomes of employees in large firms tend to be positively skewed because there is a large number of relatively low-paid workers and a small number of well-paid executives. The time taken by students to write exams is frequently negatively skewed because only a few students hand in their exams early; most prefer to reread their papers and hand them in near the end of the scheduled test period.

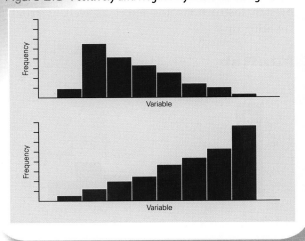

Figure 2.5 **Positively and Negatively Skewed Histograms**

© Cengage Learning

2-3f Number of Modal Classes

As we discuss in Chapter 3, a *mode* is the observation that occurs with the greatest frequency. A **modal class** is the class with the largest number of observations. A **unimodal histogram** is one with a single peak. The histogram in Figure 2.6 is unimodal. A **bimodal histogram** is one with two peaks that are not necessarily equal in height. Bimodal histograms often indicate that two different distributions are present. Figure 2.7 depicts bimodal histograms.

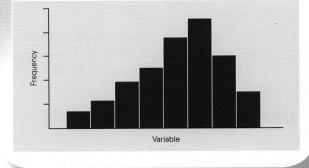

Figure 2.6 **A Unimodal Histogram**

© Cengage Learning

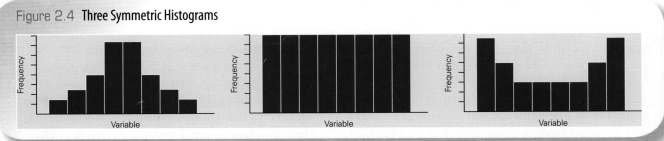

Figure 2.4 **Three Symmetric Histograms**

© Cengage Learning

Figure 2.7 Bimodal Histograms

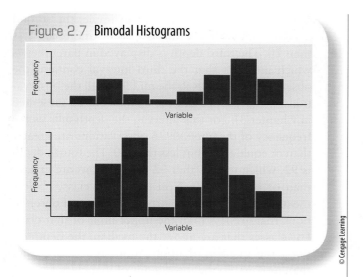

2-3g Bell Shape

A special type of symmetric unimodal histogram is one that is bell shaped. In Chapter 7, we will explain why this type of histogram is important. Figure 2.8 exhibits a bell-shaped histogram.

Figure 2.8 Bell-Shaped Histogram

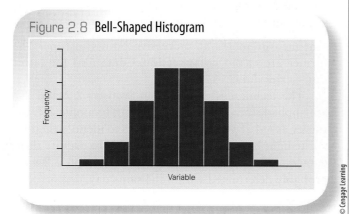

2-3h Stem-and-Leaf Display

One drawback of the histogram is that we lose potentially useful information by classifying the observations. In Example 2.2, we learned that 71 observations fall between 0 and 15. By classifying the observations, we did acquire useful information. However, the histogram focuses our attention on the frequency of each class and by doing so sacrifices whatever information was contained in the actual observations. A statistician named John Tukey introduced the **stem-and-leaf display**, which is a method that to some extent overcomes this loss.

The first step in developing a stem-and-leaf display is to split each observation into two parts: a stem and a leaf. There are several different ways to do this. For example, the number 12.3 can be split so that the

stem is 12 and the leaf is 3. In this definition, the stem consists of the digits to the left of the decimal, and the leaf is the digit to the right of the decimal. Another method can define the stem as 1 and the leaf as 2 (ignoring the 3). In this definition, the stem is the number of tens and the leaf is the number of ones. We'll use this definition to create a stem-and-leaf display for Example 2.2.

The first observation is 42.19. Thus, the stem is 4 and the leaf is 2. The second observation is 38.45, which has a stem of 3 and a leaf of 8. We continue converting each number in this way. The stem-and-leaf display consists of listing the stems 0, 1, 2, . . ., 11. After each stem, we list that stem's leaves, usually in ascending order. Figure 2.9 depicts the manually created stem-and-leaf display.

Figure 2.9 Stem-and-Leaf Display for Example 2.2

Stem	Leaf
0	0000000001111122222233333455555566666667788889999
1	0000011112333333344555555667889999
2	0000111112344666778999
3	001335589
4	124445589
5	33566
6	3458
7	022224556789
8	334457889999
9	00112222233344555999
10	001344446699
11	0124557889

As you can see, the stem-and-leaf display is similar to a histogram turned on its side. The length of each line represents the frequency in the class interval defined by the stems. The advantage of the stem-and-leaf display over the histogram is that we can see the actual observations.

Excel

Stem-and-Leaf Display

Stems	Leaves
0	->00000000011111222222333333455555566666667788889999999
1	->00000111123333333445555556678899999
2	->0000111112344666677899999
3	->001335589
4	->12445589
5	->33566
6	->3458
7	->022224556789
8	->334457889999
9	->00112222233344555999
10	->001344446699
11	->0124557889

INSTRUCTIONS

1. Type or import the data into one column. (Open Xm02-02.)

2. Click **Add-ins**, **Data Analysis Plus**, and **Stem-and-Leaf Display**.

3. Specify the **Input Range** (A1:A201). Click one of the values of **Increment** (the increment is the difference between stems) (10).

Minitab

Stem-and-Leaf Display: Bills

```
Stem-and-leaf of Bills  N = 200
Leaf Unit = 1.0
  52   0  00000000011111222222333333455555566666667788889999999
  85   1  00000111123333333445555556678899999
 (23)  2  0000111112344666677899999
  92   3  001335589
  83   4  12445589
  75   5  33566
  70   6  3458
  66   7  022224556789
  54   8  334457889999
  42   9  00112222233344555999
  22  10  001344446699
  10  11  0124557889
```

INSTRUCTIONS

1. Type or import the data into one column. (Open Xm02-02.)

2. Click **Graph** and **Stem-and-Leaf . . . .**

3. Type or use the **Select** button to specify the variable in the **Variables** box (Bills). Type the increment in the **Increment** box (10).

The numbers in the left column are called **depths**. Each depth counts the number of observations that are on its line or beyond. For example, the second depth is 85, which means 85 observations are less than 20. The third depth is displayed in parentheses, which indicates that the third interval contains the observation that falls in the middle of all the observations, a statistic we call the *median* (to be presented in Chapter 3). For this interval, the depth tells us the frequency of the interval: 23 observations are greater than or equal to 20 but less than 30. The fourth depth is 92, which tells us that 92 observations are greater than or equal to 30. Notice that for classes below the median, the depth reports the number of observations that are less than the upper limit of that class. For classes that are above the median, the depth reports the number of observations that are greater than or equal to the lower limit of that class.

2-4 Line Charts

Besides classifying data by type, we can also classify them according to whether the observations are measured at the same time or whether they represent measurements at successive points in time. The former are called **cross-sectional data** and the latter **time-series data**.

The techniques described in Sections 2-2 and 2-3 are applied to cross-sectional data. In Example 2.1, the survey asked 285 graduating seniors to identify their favorite light beer. The likely time period to acquire these data was 2 or 3 days. All the data for Example 2.2 were probably determined within the same day.

2-4a Line Chart

Time-series data are often graphically depicted on a **line chart**, which is a plot of the variable over time. It is created by plotting the value of the variable on the vertical axis and the time periods on the horizontal axis.

In the last few years, the price of gasoline has been increasing, which raises the question: is the recent price of gasoline high compared to the past prices?

EXAMPLE 2.3

Price of Gasoline

[Xm02-03] We recorded the monthly average retail price of gasoline since January 1976. Some of these data are displayed below. Draw a line chart to describe these data and briefly describe the results.

Year	Month	Price per Gallon ($)
1976	1	60.5
1976	2	60.0
1976	3	59.4
1976	4	59.2
1976	5	60.0
1976	6	61.6
1976	7	62.3
1976	8	62.8
1976	9	63.0
1976	10	62.9
1976	11	62.9
1976	12	62.6

2012	1	339.9
2012	2	357.2
2012	3	386.8
2012	4	392.7
2012	5	379.2
2012	6	355.2
2012	7	345.1
2012	8	370.7
2012	9	385.6
2012	10	378.6
2012	11	348.8
2012	12	350.0

© Cengage Learning

SOLUTION

Figure 2.10 is the line chart for the average monthly gasoline prices.

Figure 2.10 Line Chart for Example 2.3

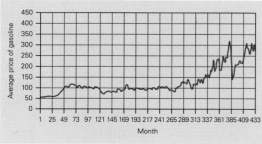

© Cengage Learning

Excel

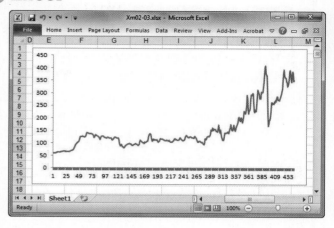

INSTRUCTIONS

1. Type or import the data into one column. (Open Xm02-03.)

2. Highlight the column of data. Click **Insert, Line,** and the first **2-D Line.** Click **Chart Tools** and **Layout** to make whatever changes you wish.

   You can draw two or more line charts (for two or more variables) by highlighting all columns of data you wish to graph.

Minitab

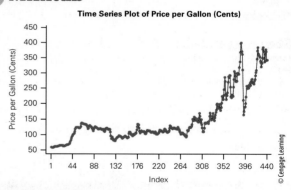

© Cengage Learning

INSTRUCTIONS

1. Type or import the data into one column. (Open Xm02-03.)

2. Click **Graph** and **Time Series Plot . . . .** Click **Simple.**

3. In the **Series** box, type or use the **Select** button to specify the variable (Price). Click **Time/Scale.**

4. Click the **Time** tab; under **Time Scale,** click **Index.**

INTERPRET

The price of gasoline rose from about $.60 to over a dollar in the late 1970s (months 1 to 49), fluctuated between $.90 and $1.50 until 2000 (months

APPLICATIONS IN ECONOMICS

MEASURING INFLATION: CONSUMER PRICE INDEX

Inflation is the increase in the prices for goods and services. In most countries, inflation is measured using the Consumer Price Index (CPI). The Consumer Price Index works with a basket of some 300 goods and services in the United States (and a similar number in other countries), including such diverse items as food, housing, clothing, transportation, health, and recreation. The basket is defined for the "typical" or "average" middle-income family, and the set of items and their weights are revised periodically (every 10 years in the United States and every 7 years in Canada).

Prices for each item in this basket are computed on a monthly basis, and the CPI is computed from these prices. Here's how it works. We start by setting a period of time as the base. In the United States, the base is the years 1982–1984. Suppose that the basket of goods and services cost $1,000 during this period. Thus, the base is $1,000, and the CPI is set at 100. Suppose that in the next month (January 1985) the price increases to $1,010. The CPI for January 1985 is calculated in the following way.

$$\text{CPI(January 1985)} = \frac{1,010}{1,000} \times 100 = 101$$

If the price increases to 1,050 in the next month, the CPI is

$$\text{CPI(February 1985)} = \frac{1,050}{1,000} \times 100 = 105$$

Even though it was never really intended to serve as the official measure of inflation, the CPI has come to be interpreted in this way by the general public. Pension-plan payments, Social Security, and some labor contracts are automatically linked to the CPI and automatically indexed (so it is claimed) to the level of inflation. Despite its flaws, the Consumer Price Index is used in numerous applications. One application involves adjusting prices by removing the effect of inflation, making it possible to track the "real" changes in a time series of prices.

In Example 2.3, the figures shown are the actual prices measured in what are called *current* dollars. To remove the effect of inflation, we divide the monthly prices by the CPI for that month and multiply by 100. These prices are then measured in *constant* 1982–1984 dollars. This makes it easier to see what has happened to the prices of the goods and services of interest.

We created two data sets to help you calculate prices in constant 1982–1984 dollars. File Ch02:\\CPI-Annual and Ch02:\\CPI-Monthly list the values of the CPI in which 1982–1984 is set at 100 for annual values and monthly values, respectively.

49 to 313), then rose rapidly to month 396 before dropping sharply. It started to rise again until the last month listed.

EXAMPLE 2.4

Price of Gasoline in 1982–1984 Constant Dollars

[Xm02-04] Remove the effect of inflation in Example 2.3 to determine whether gasoline prices are higher than they have been in the past.

SOLUTION

Here are the 1976 to 2012 average monthly prices of gasoline, the CPI, and the adjusted prices.

The adjusted figures for all months were used in the line chart produced by Excel (see Figure 2.11). Minitab charts are similar.

Year	Month	Price per Gallon	CPI	Adjusted Price
1976	1	60.5	55.8	108.4
1976	2	60.0	55.9	107.3
1976	3	59.4	56	106.1
1976	4	59.2	56.1	105.5
1976	5	60.0	56.4	106.4
1976	6	61.6	56.7	108.6
1976	7	62.3	57	109.3
1976	8	62.8	57.3	109.6
1976	9	63.0	57.6	109.4
1976	10	62.9	57.9	108.6
1976	11	62.9	58.1	108.3
1976	12	62.6	58.4	107.2

© Cengage Learning

2012	1	339.9	227.6	149.3
2012	2	357.2	228.3	156.5
2012	3	386.8	229.0	168.9
2012	4	392.7	229.0	171.5
2012	5	379.2	228.7	165.8
2012	6	355.2	228.9	155.2
2012	7	345.1	228.8	150.8
2012	8	370.7	230.0	161.2
2012	9	385.6	231.2	166.8
2012	10	378.6	231.6	163.5
2012	11	348.8	231.1	150.9
2012	12	350.0	231.1	151.4

INTERPRET

Using constant 1982–1984 dollars, we can see that the average price of a gallon of gasoline hit its peak in the middle of 2008 (month 390). From there it dropped rapidly and then rose more or less steadily until the end of 2012. At that point the adjusted price was about the same as the adjusted price in 1978 (month 49).

2-5 Scatter Diagrams

Statistics practitioners frequently need to know how two interval variables are related. For example, financial analysts need to understand how the returns of individual stocks and the returns of the entire market are related. Marketing managers need to understand the relationship between sales and advertising. Economists develop statistical techniques to describe the relationship between such variables as unemployment rates and inflation. The technique is called a **scatter diagram**.

To draw a scatter diagram, we need data for two variables. In applications in which one variable depends to some degree on the other variable, we label the dependent variable Y and the other variable, called the *independent variable*, X. For example, an individual's income depends somewhat on the number of years of education. Accordingly, we identify income as the dependent variable and label it Y, and we identify years of education as the independent variable and label it X. In other cases in which no dependency is evident, we label the variables arbitrarily.

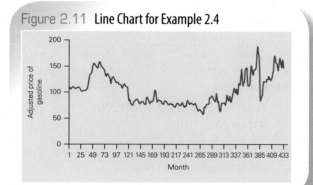

Figure 2.11 **Line Chart for Example 2.4**

Excel

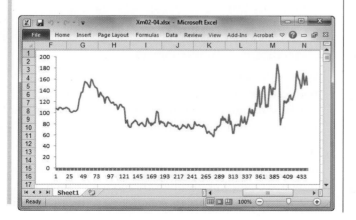

EXAMPLE 2.5

Analyzing the Relationship between Price and Size of Houses

[Xm02-05] A real estate agent wanted to know to what extent the selling price of a home is related to its size. To acquire this information, he took a sample of 12 homes that had recently sold, recording the price in thousands of dollars and the size in square feet. These data are listed in the following table. Use a graphical technique to describe the relationship between size and price.

Size	Price
2,354	315
1,807	229
2,637	355
2,024	261
2,241	234
1,489	216
3,377	308
2,825	306
2,302	289
2,068	204
2,715	265
1,833	195

SOLUTION

Using the guideline just stated, we label the price of the house Y (dependent variable) and the size X (independent variable). Figure 2.12 depicts the scatter diagram.

Excel

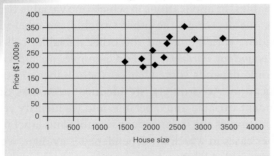

Figure 2.12 Scatter Diagram for Example 2.5

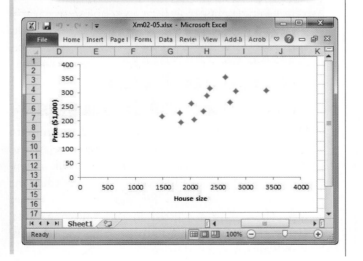

INSTRUCTIONS

1. Type or import the data into two adjacent columns. Store variable X in the first column and variable Y in the next column. (Open Xm02-05.)

2. Click **Insert** and **Scatter**.

3. To make cosmetic changes, click **Chart Tools** and **Layout**. (We chose to add titles and remove the gridlines.) If you wish to change the scale, click **Axes, Primary Horizontal Axis** or **Primary Vertical Axes, More Primary Horizontal** or **Vertical Axis Options . . .**, and make the changes you want.

Minitab

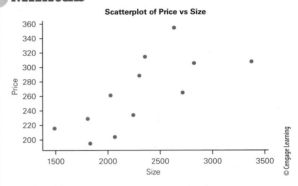

INSTRUCTIONS

1. Type or import the data into two columns. (Open Xm02-05.)

2. Click **Graph** and **Scatterplot . . . .**

3. Click **Simple.**

4. Type or use the **Select** button to specify the variable to appear on the Y-axis (Price) and the X-axis (Size).

INTERPRET

The scatter diagram reveals that, in general, the greater the size of the house, the greater the price. However, other variables also determine price. Further analysis may reveal what these other variables are.

2-5a Patterns of Scatter Diagrams

As was the case with histograms, we frequently need to describe verbally how two variables are related. The two most important characteristics are the strength and direction of the linear relationship.

Linearity

To determine the strength of the linear relationship, we draw a straight line through the points in such a way that the line represents the relationship. If most of the points fall close to the line, we say that there is a **linear relationship**. If most of the points appear to be scattered randomly with only a semblance of a straight line, then there is either no or, at best, a weak linear relationship. Figure 2.13 depicts several scatter diagrams that exhibit various levels of linearity.

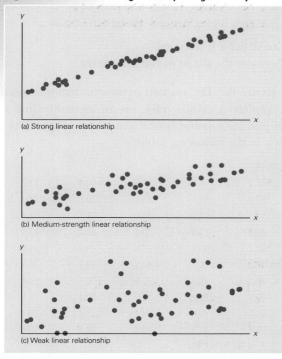

Figure 2.13 **Scatter Diagrams Depicting Linearity**

(a) Strong linear relationship

(b) Medium-strength linear relationship

(c) Weak linear relationship

© Cengage Learning

In drawing the line freehand, we would attempt to draw it so that it passes through the middle of the data. Unfortunately, different people drawing a straight line through the same set of data will produce somewhat different lines. Fortunately, statisticians have produced an objective way to draw the straight line. The method is called the *least squares method*, and it will be presented in Chapters 16 and 17.

Note that there may well be some other type of relationship, such as a quadratic or exponential one.

Direction

If, in general, when one variable increases and the other also does, we say that there is a **positive linear relationship**. When the two variables tend to move in opposite directions, we describe the nature of their association as a **negative linear relationship**. See Figure 2.14 for examples of scatter diagrams depicting a positive linear relationship, a negative linear relationship, no relationship, and a nonlinear relationship.

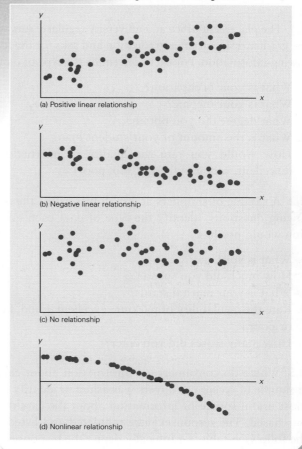

Figure 2.14 **Scatter Diagrams Describing Direction**

(a) Positive linear relationship

(b) Negative linear relationship

(c) No relationship

(d) Nonlinear relationship

© Cengage Learning

2-5b Interpreting a Strong Linear Relationship

In interpreting the results of a scatter diagram, it is important to understand that if two variables are linearly related it does not mean that one is causing the other. In fact, we can never conclude that one variable causes another variable. We can express this more eloquently as

Correlation is not Causation.

We close this section by reviewing the factors that identify the use of the scatter diagram.

Factors That Identify When to Use a Scatter Diagram

1. Objective: Describe the relationship between two variables
2. Data type: Interval

2.1 The placement office at a university regularly surveys the graduates 1 year after graduation and asks for the following information. For each, determine the type of data.

a. What is your occupation?
b. What is your income?
c. What degree did you obtain?
d. What is the amount of your student loan?
e. How would you rate the quality of instruction? (excellent, very good, good, fair, poor)

2.2 A sample of shoppers at a mall was asked the following questions. Identify the type of data each question would produce.

a. What is your age?
b. How much did you spend?
c. What is your marital status?
d. Rate the availability of parking: excellent, good, fair, or poor.
e. How many stores did you enter?

2.3 Where do consumers get information about cars? A sample of recent car buyers was asked to identify the most useful source of information about the cars they purchased. The responses were tabulated and listed in the following table. Graphically depict the responses.

Source	Frequencies
Consumer guide	172
Dealership	93
Word of mouth	40
Internet	26

2.4 An increasing number of statistics courses use a computer and software rather than manual calculations. A survey of statistics instructors asked each to report the software his or her course uses. The responses and frequencies are listed next.

Software	Frequencies
Excel	34
Minitab	17
SAS	3
SPSS	4
Other	12

a. Produce a relative frequency distribution.
b. Graphically summarize the data so that the proportions are depicted.
c. What do the charts tell you about the software choices?

2.5 [Xr02-05] The number of items rejected daily by a manufacturer because of defects was recorded for the past 30 days. The results are as follows.

4 9 13 7 5 8 12 15 5 7 3 8 15 17 19
6 4 10 8 22 16 9 5 3 9 19 14 13 18 7

a. Construct a histogram.
b. Describe the shape of the histogram.

2.6 [Xr02-06] The amount of time (in seconds) needed to complete a critical task on an assembly line was measured for a sample of 50 assemblies. These data are shown in the following table.

30.3	34.5	31.1	30.9	33.7
31.9	33.1	31.1	30.0	32.7
34.4	30.1	34.6	31.6	32.4
32.8	31.0	30.2	30.2	32.8
31.1	30.7	33.1	34.4	31.0
32.2	30.9	32.1	34.2	30.7
30.7	30.7	30.6	30.2	33.4
36.8	30.2	31.5	30.1	35.7
30.5	30.6	30.2	31.4	30.7
30.6	37.9	30.3	34.1	30.4

a. Draw a stem-and-leaf display.
b. Draw a histogram.
c. Describe the histogram.

2.7 [Xr02-07] A survey of individuals in a mall asked 60 people how many stores they will enter during this visit to the mall. The responses are shown in the following table. Draw a histogram and describe your findings.

3	2	4	3	3	9
2	4	3	6	2	2
8	7	6	4	5	1
5	2	3	1	1	7
3	4	1	1	4	8
0	2	5	4	4	4
6	2	2	5	3	8
4	3	1	6	9	1
4	4	1	0	4	6
5	5	5	1	4	3

2.8 [Xr02-08] The United States spends more money on health care than any other country. To gauge how fast costs are increasing, the following table was produced that lists the total health care expenditures in the United States annually for 1981 to 2009 (expenditures are in $billions).

a. Graphically present these data.
b. Use the data in CPI-Annual to remove the effect of inflation. Graph the results and describe your findings.

Year	Health Expenditure
1981	294
1982	331
1983	365
1984	402
1985	440
1986	472
1987	513
1988	574
1989	639
1990	714
1991	782
1992	849
1993	913
1994	962
1995	1017
1996	1069
1997	1125
1998	1191
1999	1265
2000	1353
2001	1470
2002	1603
2003	1732
2004	1895
2005	2021
2006	2152
2007	2284
2008	2391
2009	2486

Source: *Statistical Abstract of the United States*, 2012, Table 135.

2.9 [Xr02-09] The gross national product (GNP) is the sum total of the economic output of the citizens (nationals) of a country. It is an important measure of the wealth of a country. The following table lists the year and the GNP in billions of current dollars for the United States.

Year	GNP
1980	2822
1981	3160
1982	3290
1983	3572

Year	GNP
1984	3967
1985	4244
1986	4478
1987	4754
1988	5124
1989	5508
1990	5835
1991	6022
1992	6371
1993	6699
1994	7109
1995	7444
1996	7870
1997	8356
1998	8811
1999	9381
2000	9989
2001	10338
2002	10691
2003	11211
2004	11959
2005	12736
2006	13471
2007	14193
2008	14583
2009	14117
2010	14708
2011	15328

Source: U.S. Bureau of Economic Activity.

a. Graph the GNP. What have you learned?
b. Use the data in CPI-Annual to compute the per capita GNP in constant 1982–1984 dollars. Graph the results and describe your findings.

2.10 [Xr02-10] The average daily U.S. oil consumption and production (thousands of barrels) is shown for the years 1973 to 2011. Use a graphical technique to describe these figures. What does the graph tell you?

Year	Con-sumption	Prod-uction	Year	Con-sumption	Prod-uction
1973	17,318	9,209	1993	17,328	6,847
1974	16,655	8,776	1994	17,721	6,662
1975	16,323	8,376	1995	17,730	6,561
1976	17,460	8,132	1996	18,308	6,465
1977	18,443	8,245	1997	18,618	6,452
1978	18,857	8,706	1998	18,913	6,253
1979	18,527	8,551	1999	19,515	5,882
1980	17,060	8,597	2000	19,699	5,822
1981	16,061	8,572	2001	19,647	5,801
1982	15,301	8,649	2002	19,758	5,746

(continued)

Year	Con-sumption	Prod-uction	Year	Con-sumption	Prod-uction
1983	15,228	8,689	2003	20,034	5,645
1984	15,722	8,879	2004	20,731	5,435
1985	15,726	8,972	2005	20,799	5,147
1986	16,277	8,683	2006	20,686	5,088
1987	16,666	8,349	2007	20,684	5,077
1988	17,284	8,140	2008	19,496	4,999
1989	17,327	7,615	2009	18,771	5,352
1990	16,988	7,356	2010	19,178	5,479
1991	16,710	7,418	2011	18,949	5,656
1992	17,031	7,172			

Source: U.S. Department of Energy: Monthly Energy Review

2.11 [Xr02-11] How has the size of government changed? To help answer this question, we recorded the U.S. federal budget receipts and outlays (billions of current dollars) for the years 1980 to 2011.

Year	Receipts	Outlays	Year	Receipts	Outlays
1980	517.1	590.9	1996	1,453.1	1,560.5
1981	599.3	678.2	1997	1,579.3	1,601.3
1982	617.8	745.7	1998	1,721.8	1,652.6
1983	600.6	808.4	1999	1,827.5	1,701.9
1984	666.5	851.9	2000	2,025.2	1,789.1
1985	734.1	946.4	2001	1,991.2	1,863.9
1986	769.2	990.4	2002	1,853.2	2,011.0
1987	854.4	1,004.1	2003	1,782.3	2,159.9
1988	909.3	1,064.5	2004	1,880.1	2,292.8
1989	991.2	1,143.6	2005	2,153.6	2,472.0
1990	1,032.0	1,253.2	2006	2,406.9	2,655.0
1991	1,055.0	1,324.4	2007	2,568.0	2,728.7
1992	1091.3	1381.7	2008	2,524.0	2,982.5
1993	1,154.4	1,409.5	2009	2,105.0	3,517.7
1994	1,258.6	1,461.9	2010	2,162.7	3,456.2
1995	1,351.8	1,515.8	2011	2,173.7	3,818.8

Source: Statistical Abstract of the United States, 2012, Table 469.

a. Use a graphical technique to describe the receipts and outlays of the annual U.S. federal government budgets since 1980.
b. Calculate the difference between receipts and outlays. If the difference is positive, then the result is a surplus. If the difference is negative, then the results show a deficit. Graph the surplus or deficit variable and describe the results.

2.12 [Xr02-12] In a university where calculus is a prerequisite for the statistics course, a sample of

15 students was drawn. The marks for calculus and statistics were recorded for each student. The data are shown in the following table.

Calculus	Statistics
65	74
58	72
93	84
68	71
74	68
81	85
58	63
85	73
88	79
75	65
63	62
79	71
80	74
54	68
72	73

a. Draw a scatter diagram of the data.
b. What does the graph tell you about the relationship between the marks in calculus and statistics?

2.13 [Xr02-13] The growing interest in and use of the Internet is forcing many companies into considering ways to sell their products on the Web, so it is of interest to these companies to determine who is using the Web. A statistics practitioner undertook a study to determine how education and Internet use are connected. She took a random sample of 15 adults (20 years of age and older) and asked them to report the years of education they had completed and the number of hours of Internet use in the previous week. These data are shown in the following table.

Education	Internet Use
11	10
11	5
8	0
13	14
17	24
11	0
11	15
11	12
19	20
13	10
15	5
9	8
15	12
15	15
11	0

a. Employ a suitable graph to depict the data.

b. Does it appear that there is a linear relationship between the two variables? If so, describe it.

The following exercises require a computer and software.

2.14 [Xr02-14] What are the most important characteristics of colleges and universities? This question was asked of a sample of college-bound high school seniors. The responses are

1 = Location, 2 = Majors, 3 = Reputation, 4 = Career focus, 5 = Community, 6 = Number of students.

The results are stored using the codes. Use a graphical technique to summarize and present the data.

2.15 [Xr02-15] Who applies to MBA programs? To help determine the background of the applicants, a sample of 230 applicants to a university's business school was asked to report their undergraduate degree. The degrees were recorded using these codes.

1 = BA, 2 = BBA, 3 = B.Eng, 4 = BSc, 5 = Other

a. Determine the frequency distribution.

b. Draw a bar chart.

c. Draw a pie chart.

d. What do the charts tell you about the sample of MBA applicants?

2.16 [Xr02-16] The annual income for a sample of 200 first-year accountants were recorded. Summarize these data using a graphical method. Describe your results.

2.17 [Xr02-17] The number of customers entering a bank in the first hour of operation for each of the last 200 days was recorded. Use a graphical technique to extract information. Describe your findings.

2.18 [Xr02-18] The lengths of time (in minutes) to serve 420 customers at a local restaurant were recorded.

a. How many bins should a histogram of these data contain?

b. Draw a histogram using the number of bins specified in part a.

c. Is the histogram symmetric or skewed?

d. Is the histogram bell shaped?

2.19 [Xr02-19] The marks of 320 students on an economics midterm test were recorded. Use a graphical technique to summarize these data. What does the graph tell you?

2.20 [Xr02-20] The monthly value of U.S. exports to Canada (in $millions) and imports from Canada from 1985 to 2012 were recorded. (*Source:* Federal Reserve Economic Data)

a. Draw a line chart of U.S. exports to Canada.

b. Draw a line chart of U.S. imports from Canada.

c. Calculate the trade balance and draw a line chart.

d. What do all the charts reveal?

2.21 [Xr02-21] The Dow Jones Industrial Average was recorded monthly for the years 1950 to 2012. Use a graph to describe these numbers. (*Source: The Wall Street Journal*)

2.22 Refer to Exercise 2.21. Use the CPI-Monthly file to measure the Dow Jones Industrial Average in 1982–1984 constant dollars. What have you learned?

2.23 [Xr02-23] In an attempt to determine the factors that affect the amount of energy used, 200 households were analyzed. In each, the number of occupants and the amount of electricity used were measured.

a. Draw a graph of the data.

b. What have you learned from the graph?

2.24 [Xr02-24] One general belief held by observers of the business world is that taller men earn more money than shorter men. In a University of Pittsburgh study, 250 MBA graduates, all about 30 years old, were polled and asked to report their height (in inches) and their annual income (to the nearest $1,000).

a. Draw a scatter diagram of the data.

b. What have you learned from the scatter diagram?

2.25 [Xr02-25] An analyst employed at a commodities trading firm wanted to explore the relationship between prices of grains and livestock. Theoretically, the prices should move in the same direction because as the price of livestock increases, more livestock are bred, resulting in a greater demand for grains to feed them. The analyst recorded the monthly grains and livestock subindexes for 1971 to 2008. (Subindexes are based on the prices of several similar commodities. For example, the livestock subindex represents the prices of cattle and hogs.) Using a graphical technique, describe the relationship between the two subindexes and report your findings. (*Source:* Bridge Commodity Research Bureau.)

2.26 [Xr02-26] It is generally believed that higher interest rates result in less employment because companies are more reluctant to borrow to expand their business. To determine whether there is a relationship between bank prime rate and unemployment, an economist collected the monthly prime bank rate and the monthly unemployment rate for the years 1950 to 2012. Use a graphical technique to supply your answer. (*Source:* Federal Reserve Economic Data, St. Louis Fed.)

CHAPTER 3

Numerical Descriptive Techniques

objectives

3-1 Measures of Central Location

3-2 Measures of Variability

3-3 Measures of Relative Standing and Box Plots

3-4 Measures of Linear Relationship

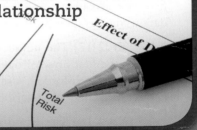

DO MORE EDUCATED PEOPLE WATCH LESS TELEVISION?

[GSS2012*] In 2012, the General Social Survey asked American adults the following questions.

> What is the highest year of school completed of respondent?
>
> On average days how many hours do you spend watching television?

The variables were stored as TVHOURS (Responses: 0 to 24) and EDUC (Responses: 0 to 20).

> We would like to know whether more educated people watch less television.
>
> After the statistical technique is presented, we return to this problem and solve it.

© thumb/iStockPhoto

In Chapter 2, we presented several graphical techniques that describe data. In this chapter, we introduce numerical descriptive techniques that allow the statistics practitioner to be more precise in describing various characteristics of a sample or population. These techniques are critical to the development of statistical inference.

As we pointed out in Chapter 2, arithmetic calculations can be applied to interval data only. Consequently, most of the techniques introduced here may be used only to numerically describe interval data. However, some of the techniques can be used for ordinal data, and one of the techniques can be employed for nominal data.

When we introduced the histogram, we commented that there are several bits of information that we look for. The first is the location of the center of the data. In Section 3-1, we will present measures of central location. Another important characteristic that we seek from a histogram is the spread of the data. The spread will be measured more precisely by measures of variability, which we present in Section 3-2. Section 3-3 introduces measures of relative standing and another graphical technique: the box plot.

In Section 2-5, we introduced the scatter diagram, which is a graphical method that we use to analyze the relationship between two interval variables. The numerical counterparts to the scatter diagram are called *measures of linear relationship*, and they are presented in Section 3-4.

Recall the terms introduced in Chapter 1: population, sample, parameter, and statistic. A parameter is a descriptive measurement about a population, and a statistic is a descriptive measurement about a sample. In this chapter, we introduce a dozen descriptive measurements. We describe how to calculate both the population parameter and the sample statistic for each measurement. However, in most realistic applications,

populations are very large—in fact, virtually infinite. The formulas describing the calculation of parameters are not practical, and they are seldom used. They are provided here primarily to teach the concept and the notation. In Chapter 6, we introduce probability distributions, which describe populations. At that time, we show how parameters are calculated from probability distributions. In general, small data sets of the type we feature in this book are samples.

3-1 Measures of Central Location

We use three different measures to describe the center of a set of data. The first is the best known, the **arithmetic mean**, which we'll refer to simply as the *mean*. Students may be more familiar with its other name: the *average*. The mean is computed by summing the observations and dividing by the number of observations. We label the observations in a sample $x_1, x_2, \ldots, x_n$, where x_1 is the first observation, x_2 is the second, and so on until x_n, where n is the sample size. As a result, the sample mean is denoted $\bar{x}$. In a population, the number of observations is labeled N, and the population mean is denoted by μ (Greek letter *mu*).

Mean

$$\text{Population mean: } \mu = \frac{\sum_{i=1}^{N} x_i}{N}$$

$$\text{Sample mean: } \bar{x} = \frac{\sum_{i=1}^{n} x_i}{n}$$

The second most popular measure of central location is the *median*.

Median

The **median** is calculated by placing all the observations in order (ascending or descending). The observation that falls in the middle is the median. The sample and population medians are computed in the same way.

When there is an even number of observations, the median is determined by averaging the two observations in the middle.

The third and last measure of central location that we present here is the *mode*.

Mode

The **mode** is defined as the observation (or observations) that occurs with the greatest frequency. Both the statistic and parameter are computed in the same way.

For populations and large samples, it is preferable to report the modal class, which we defined in Chapter 2.

There are several problems with using the mode as a measure of central location. First, in a small sample it may not be a very good measure. Second, it may not be unique.

EXAMPLE 3.1

Measures of Central Location for Time Spent on the Internet

A sample of 10 adults was asked to report the number of hours they spent on the Internet the previous month. The results are listed here. Manually calculate the sample mean, median, and mode.

0   7   12   5   33   14   8   0   9   22

SOLUTION

MEAN

Using our notation, we have $x_1 = 0, x_2 = 7, \ldots, x_{10} = 22$, and $n = 10$. The sample mean is

$$\bar{x} = \frac{\sum_{i=1}^{n} x_i}{n} = \frac{0 + 7 + 12 + 5 + 33 + 14 + 8 + 0 + 9 + 22}{10}$$

$$= \frac{110}{10} = 11.0$$

MEDIAN

When placed in ascending order, the data appear as follows:

0   0   5   7   8   9   12   14   22   33

The median is the average of the fifth and sixth observations (the middle two), which are 8 and 9, respectively. Thus, the median is 8.5.

MODE

All observations except 0 occur once. There are two 0s. Thus, the mode is 0. As you can see, this is a poor measure of central location. It is nowhere near the center of the data. Compare this with the mean 11.0 and median 8.5 and you can appreciate that in this example the mean and median are superior measures.

EXAMPLE 3.2

Measures of Central Location for Long-Distance Telephone Bills

[Xm02-02] Refer to Example 2.2. Find the mean, median, and mode of the long-distance telephone bills.

SOLUTION

MEAN

To calculate the mean, we add the observations and divide the sum by the size of the sample. Thus,

$$\bar{x} = \frac{\sum_{i=1}^{n} x_i}{n} = \frac{42.19 + 38.45 + \ldots + 45.77}{200}$$

$$= \frac{8717.52}{200} = 43.59$$

USING THE COMPUTER

Excel
INSTRUCTIONS

Type or import the data into one or more columns. (Open Xm02-02.) Type into any empty cell

```
=AVERAGE([Input range])
```

For Example 3.2, we would type into any cell

```
=AVERAGE(A1:A201)
```

The active cell would store the mean as 43.5876.

Minitab
INSTRUCTIONS

1. Type or import the data into one column. (Open Xm02-02.)

2. Click **Calc** and **Column Statistics . . . .** Specify **Mean** in the **Statistic** box. Type or use the **Select** button to specify the **Input variable** and click **OK.** The sample mean is outputted in the session window as 43.5876.

MEDIAN

All the observations were placed in order. We observed that the 100th and 101st observations are 26.84 and 26.97, respectively. Thus, the median is the average of these two numbers:

$$\text{Median} = \frac{26.84 + 26.97}{2} = 26.905$$

Excel
INSTRUCTIONS

To calculate the median, substitute **MEDIAN** in place of **AVERAGE** in the instructions for the mean. The median is reported as 26.905.

Minitab
INSTRUCTIONS

Follow the instructions for the mean to compute the mean except click **Median** instead of **Mean.** The median is outputted as 26.905 in the session window.

INTERPRET

Half the observations are below 26.905, and half the observations are above 26.905.

MODE

An examination of the 200 observations reveals that, except for 0, it appears that each number is unique. However, there are 8 zeros, which indicate that the mode is 0.

Excel

Excel reports that the mode is 0.

Minitab

Minitab does not compute the mode directly. However, it will provide a count of the frequency of each number. The number associated with the largest frequency is the mode, 0.

3-1a Mean, Median, Mode: Which Is Best?

With three measures from which to choose, which one should we use? There are several factors to consider when making our choice of measure of central location. The mean is generally our first selection. However, there are several circumstances when the median is better. The mode is seldom the best measure of central location. One advantage the median holds is that it is not as sensitive to extreme values as is the mean. To illustrate, consider the data in Example 3.1. The mean was 11.0, and the median was 8.5. Now suppose that the respondent who reported 33 hours actually reported 133 hours (obviously an Internet addict). The mean becomes

$$\bar{x} = \frac{\sum_{i=1}^{n} x_i}{n} = \frac{0 + 7 + 12 + 5 + 133 + 14 + 8 + 0 + 22}{10}$$

$$= \frac{210}{10} = 21.0$$

This value is exceeded by only 2 of the 10 observations in the sample, making this statistic a poor measure of *central* location. The median stays the same. When there is a relatively small number of extreme observations (either very small or very large, but not both), the median usually produces a better measure of the center of the data.

To see another advantage of the median over the mean, suppose you and your classmates have taken a statistics test, and the instructor is returning the graded tests. What piece of information is most important to you? The answer, of course, is *your* mark. What is the next important bit of information? The answer is how well you performed relative to the class. Most students ask their instructor for the class mean. This is the wrong statistic to request. You want the *median* because it divides the class into two halves. This information allows

you to identify which half of the class your mark falls into. The median provides this information; the mean does not. Nevertheless, the mean can also be useful in this scenario. If there are several sections of the course, then the section means can be compared to determine whose class performed best (or worst).

3-1b Excel and Minitab: Printing All the Measures of Central Location plus Other Statistics

Both Excel and Minitab can produce the measures of central location plus a variety of others that we will introduce in later sections.

Excel

Excel Output for Example 3.2

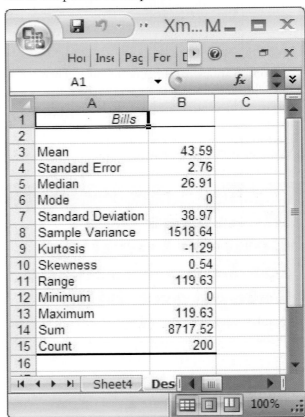

	Bills
Mean	43.59
Standard Error	2.76
Median	26.91
Mode	0
Standard Deviation	38.97
Sample Variance	1518.64
Kurtosis	-1.29
Skewness	0.54
Range	119.63
Minimum	0
Maximum	119.63
Sum	8717.52
Count	200

Excel reports the mean, median, and mode as the same values we obtained previously. Most of the other statistics will be discussed later.

INSTRUCTIONS

1. Type or import the data into one column. (Open Xm02-02.)

2. Click **Data, Data Analysis,** and **Descriptive Statistics.**

3. Specify the **Input Range** (A1:A201) and click **Summary statistics.**

Minitab

Minitab Output for Example 3.2

Descriptive Statistics: Bills

```
Variable N N* Mean StDev Variance Sum Minimum Median Maximum
Bills 200 0 43.59 38.97 1518.64 8717.52 0.00 26.91 119.63
N for
Variable Range Mode Mode
Bills 119.63  0  8
```

INSTRUCTIONS

1. Type or import the data into one column. (Open Xm02-02.)

2. Click **Stat, Basic Statistics,** and **Display Descriptive Statistics . . . .**

3. Type or use **Select** to identify the name of the variable or column (Bills). Click **Statistics . . .** to add or delete particular statistics.

3-1c Measures of Central Location for Ordinal and Nominal Data

When the data are interval, we can use any of the three measures of central location. However, for ordinal and nominal data, the calculation of the mean is not valid. Because the calculation of the median begins by placing the data in order, this statistic is appropriate for ordinal data. The mode, which is determined by counting the frequency of each observation, is appropriate for nominal data. However, nominal data do not have a "center," so we cannot interpret the mode of nominal data in that way. It is generally pointless to compute the mode of nominal data.

Here is a summary of the numerical techniques introduced in this section and when to use them.

Factors That Identify When to Compute the Mean

1. **Objective:** Describe a single set of data

2. **Type of data:** Interval

3. **Descriptive measurement:** Central location

Factors That Identify When to Compute the Median

1. **Objective:** Describe a single set of data

2. **Type of data:** Ordinal or interval

3. **Descriptive measurement:** Central location

Factors That Identify When to Compute the Mode

1. **Objective:** Describe a single set of data

2. **Type of data:** Nominal, ordinal, interval

3-2 Measures of Variability

The statistics introduced in Section 3-1 serve to provide information about the central location of the data. However, as we have already discussed in Chapter 2, other characteristics of data also are of interest to practitioners of statistics. One such characteristic is the spread or variability of the data. In this section, we introduce three **measures of variability**. We begin with the simplest: the range.

Range

Range = Largest observation – Smallest observation

The advantage of the range is its simplicity. The disadvantage is also its simplicity. Because the range is calculated from only two observations, it tells us nothing about the other observations. Consider the following two sets of data.

| Set 1: | 4 | 4 | 4 | 4 | 4 | 50 |
| Set 2: | 4 | 8 | 15 | 24 | 39 | 50 |

The range of both sets is 46. The two sets of data are completely different and yet their ranges are the same. To measure variability, we need other statistics that incorporate all the data and not just two observations.

3-2a Variance

The **variance** and its related measure, the **standard deviation**, are arguably the most important statistics. They are used to measure variability, but, as you will discover, they play a vital role in almost all statistical inference procedures.

Variance

$$\text{Population variance: } \sigma^2 = \frac{\sum_{i=1}^{N}(x_i - \mu)^2}{N}$$

$$\text{Sample variance}[1]: s^2 = \frac{\sum_{i=1}^{n}(x_i - \overline{x})^2}{n-1}$$

The population variance is represented by σ^2 (the Greek letter sigma squared).

Examine the formula for the sample variance s^2. It may appear to be illogical that in calculating s^2 we divide the sum of squared deviations by $n-1$ rather than by n. However, we do so for the following reason. Population parameters in practical settings are seldom known. One of the objectives of statistical inference is to estimate the parameter from the statistic. For example, we estimate the population mean μ from the sample mean $\overline{x}$. Although it is not obviously logical, the statistic created by dividing $\Sigma(x_i - \overline{x})^2$ by $n-1$ is a better estimator than the one created by dividing by n. We will discuss this issue in greater detail in Section 9-1.

To compute the sample variance s^2, we begin by calculating the sample mean $\overline{x}$. Next, we compute the difference (also called the **deviation**) between each observation and the mean. We square the deviations and sum. Finally, we divide the sum of squared deviations by $n-1$.

We'll illustrate with a simple example. Suppose that we have the following observations of the numbers of hours five students spent studying statistics last week:

8   4   9   11   3

The mean is

$$\overline{x} = \frac{8 + 4 + 9 + 11 + 3}{5} = \frac{35}{5} = 7$$

For each observation, we determine its deviation from the mean. The deviation is squared and the sum of squares determined as shown in Table 3.1.

Table 3.1 Calculation of Sample Variance

x_i	$(x_i - \overline{x})$	$(x_i - \overline{x})^2$
8	$(8 - 7) = 1$	$(1)^2 = 1$
4	$(4 - 7) = -3$	$(-3)^2 = 9$
9	$(9 - 7) = 2$	$(2)^2 = 4$
11	$(11 - 7) = 4$	$(4)^2 = 16$
3	$(3 - 7) = -4$	$(-4)^2 = 16$
	$\sum_{i=1}^{5}(x_i - \overline{x}) = 0$	$\sum_{i=1}^{5}(x_i - \overline{x})^2 = 46$

The sample variance is

$$s^2 = \frac{\sum_{i=1}^{n}(x_i - \overline{x})^2}{n-1} = \frac{46}{5-1} = 11.5$$

The calculation of this statistic raises several questions. Why do we square the deviations before averaging? If you examine the deviations, you will see that some of the deviations are positive and some are negative. When you add them together, the sum is 0. This will always be the case because the sum of the positive deviations will always equal the sum of the negative deviations. Consequently, we square the deviations to avoid the "canceling effect."

What is the unit of measurement of the variance? Because we squared the deviations, we also squared the units. In this illustration, the units were hours (of study). Thus, the sample variance is 11.5 hours^2.

[1]Technically, the variance of the sample is calculated by dividing the sum of squared deviations by n. The statistic computed by dividing the sum of squared deviations by $n-1$ is called the *sample variance corrected for the mean*. Because this statistic is used extensively, we will shorten its name to *sample variance*.

EXAMPLE 3.3

Summer Jobs

The following are the number of summer jobs a sample of six students applied for. Find the mean and variance of these data.

17   15   23   7   9   13

SOLUTION

The mean of the six observations is

$$\bar{x} = \frac{17 + 15 + 23 + 7 + 9 + 13}{6} = \frac{84}{6} = 14 \text{ jobs}$$

The sample variance is

$$s^2 = \frac{\sum\limits_{i=1}^{n} (x_i - \bar{x})^2}{n - 1}$$

$$= \frac{(17 - 14)^2 + (15 - 14)^2 + (23 - 14)^2 + (7 - 14)^2 + (9 - 14)^2 + (13 - 14)^2}{6 - 1}$$

$$= \frac{9 + 1 + 81 + 49 + 25 + 1}{5} = \frac{166}{5}$$

$$= 33.2 \text{ jobs}^2$$

(OPTIONAL) SHORTCUT METHOD FOR VARIANCE

The calculations for larger data sets are quite time consuming. The following shortcut for the sample variance may help lighten the load.

Shortcut for Sample Variance

$$s^2 = \frac{1}{n-1} \left[\sum_{i=1}^{n} x_i^2 - \frac{\left(\sum_{i=1}^{n} x_i\right)^2}{n} \right]$$

To illustrate we'll do Example 3.3 again.

$$\sum_{i=1}^{n} x_i^2 = 17^2 + 15^2 + 23^2 + 7^2 + 9^2 + 13^2 = 1{,}342$$

$$\sum_{i=1}^{n} x_i = 17 + 15 + 23 + 7 + 9 + 13 = 84$$

$$\left(\sum_{i=1}^{n} x_i\right)^2 = 84^2 = 7056$$

$$s^2 = \frac{1}{n-1} \left[\sum_{i=1}^{n} x_i^2 - \frac{\left(\sum_{i=1}^{n} x_i\right)^2}{n} \right]$$

$$= \frac{1}{6-1} \left[1342 - \frac{7056}{6} \right]$$

$$= 33.2 \text{ jobs}^2$$

Notice that we produced the same exact answer.

Excel
INSTRUCTIONS
Follow the instructions to compute the mean (page 37) except type VAR instead of AVERAGE.

Minitab
INSTRUCTIONS
Click **Stat**, **Basic Statistics**, and **Display Descriptive Statistics . . .**, and then select the variable. Click **Statistics** and **Variance**.

3-2b Interpreting the Variance

We calculated the variance in Example 3.3 to be 33.2 jobs^2. What does this statistic tell us? Unfortunately, the variance provides us with only a rough idea about the amount of variation in the data. However, this statistic is useful when comparing two or more sets of data of the same type of variable. If the variance of one data set is larger than that of a second data set, we interpret that to mean that the observations in the first set display more variation than the observations in the second set.

The problem of interpretation is caused by the way the variance is computed. Because we squared the deviations from the mean, the unit attached to the variance is the square of the unit attached to the original observations. In other words, in Example 3.3, the unit of the data is jobs; the unit of the variance is jobs squared. This contributes to the problem of interpretation. We resolve this difficulty by calculating another related measure of variability.

3-2c Standard Deviation

Standard Deviation

Population standard deviation: $\sigma = \sqrt{\sigma^2}$

Sample standard deviation: $s = \sqrt{s^2}$

The standard deviation is simply the positive square root of the variance. Thus, in Example 3.3, the sample standard deviation is

$$s = \sqrt{s^2} = \sqrt{33.2} = 5.76 \text{ jobs}$$

Notice that the unit associated with the standard deviation is the unit of the original data set.

Interpreting the Standard Deviation

Knowing the mean and standard deviation allows the statistics practitioner to extract useful bits of information. The information depends on the shape of the histogram. If the histogram is bell shaped, we can use the **Empirical Rule**.

Empirical Rule

1. Approximately 68% of all observations fall within one standard deviation of the mean.

2. Approximately 95% of all observations fall within two standard deviations of the mean.

3. Approximately 99.7% of all observations fall within three standard deviations of the mean.

EXAMPLE 3.4

Using the Empirical Rule to Interpret Standard Deviation

After an analysis of the returns on an investment, a statistics practitioner discovered that the histogram is bell shaped and that the mean and standard deviation are 10% and 8%, respectively. What can you say about the way the returns are distributed?

SOLUTION

Because the histogram is bell shaped, we can apply the Empirical Rule. Thus, the following apply.

1. Approximately 68% of the returns lie between 2% (the mean minus one standard deviation = $10 - 8$) and 18% (the mean plus one standard deviation = $10 + 8$).

2. Approximately 95% of the returns lie between −6% [the mean minus two standard deviations = $10 - 2(8)$] and 26% [the mean plus two standard deviations = $10 + 2(8)$].

3. Approximately 99.7% of the returns lie between −14% [the mean minus three standard deviations = $10 - 3(8)$] and 34% [the mean plus three standard deviations = $10 + 3(8)$].

3-2d Measures of Variability for Ordinal and Nominal Data

The measures of variability introduced in this section can be used only for interval data. The next section will feature a measure that can be used to describe the variability of ordinal data. There are no measures of variability for nominal data.

We complete this section by reviewing the factors that identify the use of measures of variability.

Factors That Identify When to Compute the Range, Variance, and Standard Deviation

1. **Objective:** Describe a single set of data

2. **Type of Data:** Interval

3. **Descriptive measurement:** Variability

3-3 Measures of Relative Standing and Box Plots

Measures of relative standing are designed to provide information about the position of particular values relative to the entire data set. We've already presented one measure of relative standing, the median, which is also a measure of central location. Recall that the median divides the data set into halves, allowing the statistics practitioner to determine which half of the data set each observation lies in. The statistics we're about to introduce will give you much more detailed information.

Percentile

The *P*th **percentile** is the value for which *P* percent are less than that value and $(100 - P)\%$ are greater than that value.

The scores and the percentiles of the SAT (Scholastic Achievement Test) and the GMAT (Graduate Management Admission Test), as well as various other admissions tests, are reported to students taking them. Suppose, for example, that your SAT score is reported to be at the 60th percentile. This means that 60% of all the other marks are below yours and 40% are above it. You now know exactly where you stand relative to the population of SAT scores.

We have special names for the 25th, 50th, and 75th percentiles. Because these three statistics divide the set of data into quarters, these measures of relative standing are also called **quartiles**. The *first* or *lower quartile* is labeled Q_1. It is equal to the 25th percentile. The *second quartile*, Q_2 is equal to the 50th percentile, which is also the median. The *third* or *upper quartile*, Q_3 is equal to the 75th percentile. Incidentally, many people confuse the terms *quartile* and *quarter*. A common error is to state that someone is in the lower *quartile* of a group when they actually mean that someone is in the lower *quarter* of a group.

Besides quartiles, we can also convert percentiles into quintiles and deciles. **Quintiles** divide the data into fifths, and **deciles** divide the data into tenths.

Locating Percentiles

The following formula allows us to approximate the location of any percentile.

Location of a Percentile

$$L_p = (n + 1)\frac{p}{100}$$

where L_p is the location of the Pth percentile.

EXAMPLE 3.5

Percentiles of Time Spent on the Internet

Calculate the 25th, 50th, and 75th percentiles (first, second, and third quartiles) of the data in Example 3.1.

SOLUTION

Placing the 10 observations in ascending order, we get

0 0 5 7 8 9 12 14 22 33

The location of the 25th percentile is

$$L_{25} = (10 + 1)\frac{25}{100} = (11)(.25) = 2.75$$

The 25th percentile is three-quarters of the distance between the second (which is 0) and the third (which is 5) observations. Three-quarters of the distance is

$$(.75)(5 - 0) = 3.75$$

Because the second observation is 0, the 25th percentile is $0 + 3.75 = 3.75$.

To locate the 50th percentile, we substitute $P = 50$ into the formula and produce

$$L_{50} = (10 + 1)\frac{50}{100} = (11)(.5) = 5.5$$

which means that the 50th percentile is halfway between the fifth and sixth observations. The fifth and sixth observations are 8 and 9, respectively. The 50th percentile is 8.5. This is the median calculated in Example 4.3.

The 75th percentile's location is

$$L_{75} = (10 + 1)\frac{75}{100} = (11)(.75) = 8.25$$

Thus, it is located one-quarter of the distance between the eighth and the ninth observations, which are 14 and 22, respectively. One-quarter of the distance is

$$(.25)(22 - 14) = 2$$

which means that the 75th percentile is

$$14 + 2 = 16$$

EXAMPLE 3.6

Quartiles of Long-Distance Telephone Bills

[Xm02-02] Determine the quartiles for Example 2.2.

SOLUTION

Excel

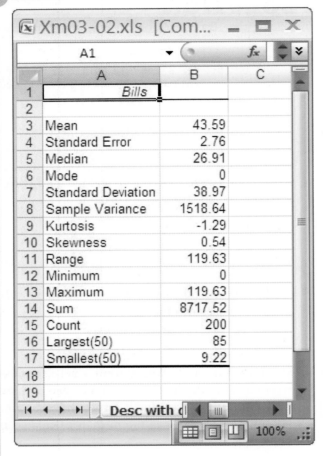

INSTRUCTIONS

Follow the instructions for **Descriptive Statistics** (page 38). In the dialog box, click **Kth Largest** and type in the integer closest to $n/4$. Repeat for **Kth Smallest**, typing in the integer closest to $n/4$.

Excel approximates the third and first quartiles in the following way. The **Largest(50)** is 85, which is the number such that 150 numbers are below it and 49 numbers are above it. The **Smallest(50)** is 9.22, which is the number such that 49 numbers are below it and 150 numbers are above it. The median is 26.91, a statistic we discussed in Example 3.4.

Minitab

Minitab outputs the first and third quartiles as Q1 (9.28) and Q3 (84.94), respectively. (See page 39.)

We can often get an idea of the shape of the histogram from the quartiles. For example, if the first and second quartiles are closer to each other than the second and third quartiles are, then the histogram is positively skewed. If the first and second quartiles are farther apart than the second and third quartiles, then the histogram is negatively skewed. If the difference between the first and second quartiles is approximately equal to the difference between the second and third quartiles, the histogram is approximately symmetric. The box plot described subsequently is particularly useful in this regard.

3-3a Interquartile Range

The quartiles can be used to create another measure of variability, the interquartile range, which is defined as follows.

Interquartile Range

$$\text{Interquartile range} = Q_3 - Q_1$$

The **interquartile range** measures the spread of the middle 50% of the observations. Large values of this statistic mean that the first and third quartiles are far apart, indicating a high level of variability.

EXAMPLE 3.7

Interquartile Range of Long-Distance Telephone Bills

[Xm02-02] Determine the interquartile range for Example 2.2.

SOLUTION

Using Excel's approximations of the first and third quartiles, we find

$$\text{Interquartile range} = Q_3 - Q_1 = 85 - 9.22$$
$$= 75.78$$

3-3b Box Plots

Now that we have introduced quartiles we can present one more graphical technique: the **box plot**. This technique graphs five statistics, the minimum and maximum observations, and the first, second, and third quartiles. It also depicts other features of a set of data. Figure 3.1 exhibits the box plot of the data in Example 3.1.

Figure 3.1 Box Plot for Example 3.1

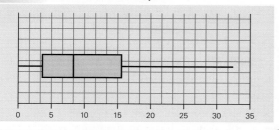

© Cengage Learning

The three vertical lines of the box are the first, second, and third quartiles. The lines extending to the left and right are called *whiskers*. Any points that lie outside the whiskers are called *outliers*. The whiskers extend outward to the smaller of 1.5 times the interquartile range or to the most extreme point that is not an outlier.

Outliers

Outliers are unusually large or small observations. Because an outlier is considerably removed from the main body of the data set, its validity is suspect. Consequently, outliers should be checked to determine that they are not the result of an error in recording their values. Outliers can also represent unusual observations that should be investigated. For example, if a salesperson's performance is an outlier on the high end of the distribution, then the company could profit by determining what sets that salesperson apart from the others.

EXAMPLE 3.8

Box Plot of Long-Distance Telephone Bills

[Xm02-02] Draw the box plot for Example 2.2.

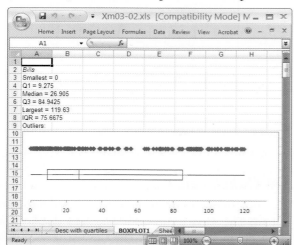

SOLUTION

Excel

INSTRUCTIONS

1. Type or import the data into one column or two or more adjacent columns. (Open Xm02-02.)

2. Click **Add-Ins, Data Analysis Plus,** and **Box Plot.**

3. Specify the **Input Range** (A1:A201).

A box plot will be created for each column of data that you have specified or highlighted.

Notice that the quartiles produced in the **Box Plot** are not exactly the same as those produced by **Descriptive Statistics.** The **Box Plot** command uses a slightly different method than the **Descriptive Methods** command.

Minitab

Box Plot of Bills

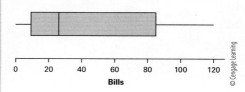

© Cengage Learning

INSTRUCTIONS

1. Type or import the data into one column or more columns. (Open Xm02-02.)

2. Click **Graph** and **Box Plot** . . . .

3. Click **Simple** if there is only one column of data or **Multiple Y's** if there are two or more columns.

4. Type or **Select** the variable or variables in the **Graph variables** box. (Bills).

5. The box plot will be drawn so that the values (Bills) will appear on the vertical axis. To turn the box plot on its side click **Scale** . . . , **Axes and Ticks,** and **Transpose value and category scales.**

INTERPRET

The smallest value is 0 and the largest is 119.63. The first, second, and third quartiles are 9.275, 26.905, and 84.9425, respectively. The interquartile range is 75.6675. One and one-half times the interquartile range is $1.5 \times 75.6675 = 113.5013$. Outliers are defined as any observations that are less than $9.275 - 113.5013 = -104.226$ and any observations that are larger than $84.9425 + 113.5013 = 198.4438$. The whisker to the left extends only to 0, which is the smallest observation that is not an outlier. The whisker to the right extends to 119.63, which is the largest observation that is not an outlier. There are no outliers.

The box plot is particularly useful when comparing two or more data sets.

© Photodisc/Getty Images

EXAMPLE 3.9

Comparing Service Times of Fast-Food Restaurants' Drive-Throughs

[Xm03-09] A large number of fast-food restaurants with drive-through windows offer drivers and their passengers the advantages of quick service. To measure how good the service is, an organization called QSR planned a study in which the amount of time taken by a sample of drive-through customers at each of five restaurants was recorded. Compare the five sets of data using a box plot and interpret the results.

SOLUTION

We use the computer and our software to produce the box plots.

Excel

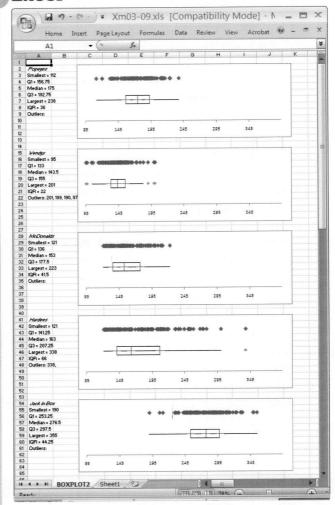

Minitab

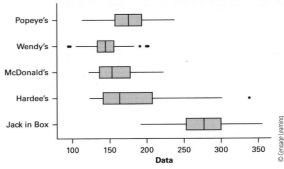

© Cengage Learning

INTERPRET

Wendy's times appear to be the lowest and most consistent. The service times for Hardee's display considerably more variability. The slowest service times are provided by Jack in the Box. The service times for Popeye's, Wendy's, and Jack in the Box seem to be symmetric. However, the times for McDonald's and Hardee's are positively skewed.

3-3c Measures of Relative Standing and Variability for Ordinal Data

Because the measures of relative standing are computed by ordering the data, these statistics are appropriate for ordinal as well as for interval data. Furthermore, because the interquartile range is calculated by taking the difference between the upper and lower quartiles, it too can be employed to measure the variability of ordinal data.

Here are the factors that tell us when to use the techniques presented in this section.

Factors That Identify When to Compute Percentiles and Quartiles

1. **Objective:** Describe a single set of data
2. **Type of data:** Interval or ordinal
3. **Descriptive measurement:** Relative standing

Factors That Identify When to Compute the Interquartile Range

1. **Objective:** Describe a single set of data
2. **Type of data:** Interval or ordinal
3. **Descriptive measurement:** Variability

3-4 Measures of Linear Relationship

In Chapter 2, we introduced the scatter diagram, a graphical technique that describes the relationship between two interval variables. At that time, we pointed out that we were particularly interested in the direction and strength of the linear relationship. We now present two numerical measures of linear relationship that provide this information. They are the **covariance** and the **coefficient of correlation**.

3-4a Covariance

As we did in Chapter 2, we label one variable X and the other Y.

Covariance

Population covariance: $\sigma_{xy} = \dfrac{\sum\limits_{i=1}^{N}(x_i - \mu_x)(y_i - \mu_y)}{N}$

Sample covariance: $s_{xy} = \dfrac{\sum\limits_{i=1}^{n}(x_i - \overline{x})(y_i - \overline{y})}{n-1}$

The denominator in the calculation of the sample covariance is $n - 1$, not the more logical n for the same reason that we divide by $n - 1$ to calculate the sample variance (see page 40). If you plan to compute the sample covariance manually, here is a shortcut calculation.

Shortcut for Sample Covariance

$$s_{xy} = \frac{1}{n-1}\left[\sum_{i=1}^{n}x_i y_i - \frac{\sum\limits_{i=1}^{n}x_i \sum\limits_{i=1}^{n}y_i}{n}\right]$$

We would like to extract two pieces of information. The first is the sign of the covariance, which tells us the nature of the relationship. The second is the magnitude, which describes the strength of the association. Unfortunately, the magnitude may be difficult to judge. For example, if you're told that the covariance between two variables is 500 does this mean that there is a strong linear relationship? The answer is that it is impossible to judge without additional statistics. Fortunately, we can improve on the information provided by this statistic by creating another one.

3-4b Coefficient of Correlation

The coefficient of correlation is defined as the covariance divided by the standard deviations of the variables.

Coefficient of Correlation

Population coefficient of correlation: $\rho = \dfrac{\sigma_{xy}}{\sigma_x \sigma_y}$

Sample coefficient of correlation: $r = \dfrac{s_{xy}}{s_x s_y}$

The population parameter is denoted by the Greek letter rho.

The advantage that the coefficient of correlation has over the covariance is that the former has a set lower and upper limit. The limits are -1 and $+1$, respectively; that is,

$$-1 \le r \le +1 \quad \text{and} \quad -1 \le \rho \le +1$$

When the coefficient of correlation equals -1, there is a negative linear relationship and the scatter diagram exhibits a straight line. When the coefficient of correlation equals $+1$, there is a perfect positive relationship. When the coefficient of correlation equals 0, there is no linear relationship. All other values of correlation are judged in relation to these three values.

3-4c Comparing the Scatter Diagram, Covariance, and Coefficient of Correlation

The scatter diagram depicts relationships graphically; the covariance and the coefficient of correlation describe the linear relationship numerically. Figures 3.2, 3.3, and 3.4 depict three scatter diagrams. To show how the graphical and numerical techniques compare, we calculated the covariance and the coefficient of correlation for each. (The data are stored in files Fig 03-02, Fig 03-03, and Fig 03-04.) As you can see, Figure 3.2 depicts a strong positive relationship between the two variables. The covariance is 36.87, and the coefficient of correlation is .9641. The variables in Figure 3.3 produced a relatively strong negative linear relationship; the covariance and coefficient of correlation are -34.18 and $-.8791$, respectively. The covariance and coefficient of correlation for the data in Figure 3.4 are 2.07 and .1206, respectively. There is no apparent linear relationship in this figure.

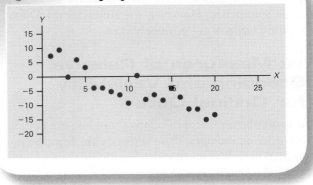

Figure 3.3 **Strong Negative Linear Relationship**

© Cengage Learning

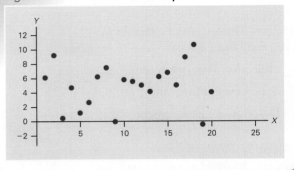

Figure 3.4 **No Linear Relationship**

© Cengage Learning

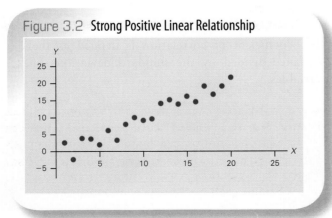

Figure 3.2 **Strong Positive Linear Relationship**

© Cengage Learning

EXAMPLE 3.10

Analyzing the Relationship Between Price and Size of Houses, II

[Xm02-05] Refer to Example 2.5. Calculate the covariance and the coefficient of correlation. Interpret the statistics.

SOLUTION

The dependent variable is the price of the house and the independent variable is the size. To calculate the covariance and the coefficient of correlation we need the sum of X, Y, XY, X^2, and Y^2.

House	X	Y	XY	X²	Y²
1	2,354	315	741,510	5,541,316	99,225
2	1,807	229	413,803	3,265,249	52,441
3	2,637	355	936,135	6,953,769	126,025
4	2,024	261	528,264	4,096,576	68,121
5	2,241	234	524,394	5,022,081	54,756
6	1,489	216	321,624	2,217,121	46,656
7	3,377	308	1,040,116	11,404,129	94,864
8	2,825	306	864,450	7,980,625	93,636
9	2,302	289	665,278	5,299,204	83,521
10	2,068	204	421,872	4,276,624	41,616
11	2,715	265	719,475	7,371,225	70,225
12	1,833	195	357,435	3,359,889	38,025
Total	27,672	3,177	7,534,356	66,787,808	869,111

© Cengage Learning

Covariance:

$$s_{xy} = \frac{1}{n-1}\left[\sum_{i=1}^{n}x_iy_i - \frac{\sum_{i=1}^{n}x_i\sum_{i=1}^{n}y_i}{n}\right]$$

$$= \frac{1}{12-1}\left[7,534,356 - \frac{(27,672)(3,177)}{12}\right]$$

$$= 18,927$$

Variance of X:

$$s_x^2 = \frac{1}{n-1}\left[\sum_{i=1}^{n}x_i^2 - \frac{\left(\sum_{i=1}^{n}x_i\right)^2}{n}\right]$$

$$= \frac{1}{12-1}\left[66,787,808 - \frac{(27,672)^2}{12}\right]$$

$$= 270,561$$

Standard deviation of X is

$$s_x = \sqrt{s_x^2} = \sqrt{270,561} = 520$$

Variance of Y:

$$s_y^2 = \frac{1}{n-1}\left[\sum_{i=1}^{n}y_i^2 - \frac{\left(\sum_{i=1}^{n}y_i\right)^2}{n}\right]$$

$$= \frac{1}{12-1}\left[869,111 - \frac{(3,177)^2}{12}\right]$$

$$= 2,545$$

Standard deviation of Y:

$$s_y = \sqrt{s_y^2} = \sqrt{2,545} = 50.5$$

The coefficient of correlation is

$$r = \frac{s_{xy}}{s_xs_y} = \frac{18,927}{(520)(50.5)} = .7208$$

Excel
INSTRUCTIONS

Type or import the data into two columns. (Open Xm02-05.) Type the following into any empty cell.

```
=CORREL[Input range of one variable],
    [Input range of second variable])
```

In this example, we would enter

```
=CORREL (A1:A13, B1:B13)
```

To calculate the covariance, replace **CORREL** with **COVAR**.

Unfortunately, Excel computes the population covariance. You can convert the parameter to the statistic by multiplying Excel's covariance by $n/(n-1)$, in this example 12/11.

Minitab

Correlations: Size, Price
Pearson correlation of Size and Price = 0.721

INSTRUCTIONS

1. Type or import the data into two columns. (Open Xm02-05.)
2. Click **Stat, Basic Statistics** and **Correlation . . . .**
3. In the **Variables** box, type **Select** the variables (**Size, Price**).

Covariances: Size, Price

	Size	Price
Size	270561.45	
Price	18926.73	2545.48

INSTRUCTIONS

Click **Covariance . . .** instead of **Correlation . . .** in step 2 above.

INTERPRET

The coefficient of correlation is .7208, which tells us that there is a positive linear relationship between the size and price of the houses. Because the coefficient of correlation is closer to 1 than to 0, we say that the linear relationship is quite strong.

DO MORE EDUCATED PEOPLE WATCH LESS TELEVISION? SOLUTION

Excel calculated the coefficient of correlation as $-.1966$, indicating that there is a weak negative relationship between EDUC and TVHOURS. The answer to the question is yes, more educated people watch less television.

3-4d Interpreting Correlation

Because of its importance we remind you about the correct interpretation of the analysis of the relationship between two interval variables that we discussed in Chapter 2. In other words, if two variables are linearly related, it does not mean that X causes Y. It may mean that another variable causes both X and Y or that Y causes X. Remember

Correlation is not Causation

We complete this section with a review of when to use the techniques introduced in this section.

Factors That Identify When to Compute Covariance and Coefficient of Correlation

1. **Objective:** Describe the relationship between two variables
2. **Type of data:** Interval

EXERCISES

3.1 A sample of 12 people was asked how much change they had in their pockets and wallets. The responses (in cents) are

52 25 15 0 104 44 60 30 33 81 40 5

Determine the mean, median, and mode for these data.

3.2 The number of sick days due to colds and flu last year was recorded by a sample of 15 adults. The data are

5 7 0 3 15 6 5 9 3 8 10 5 2 0 12

Compute the mean, median, and mode.

Exercises 3.3 to 3.5 require the use of a computer and software.

3.3 [Xr03-03] The starting salaries of a sample of 125 recent MBA graduates are recorded.

a. Determine the mean and median of these data.
b. What do these two statistics tell you about the starting salaries of MBA graduates?

3.4 [Xr03-04] To determine whether changing the color of their invoices would improve the speed of payment, a company selected 200 customers at random and sent their invoices on blue paper. The number of days until the bills were paid was recorded. Calculate the mean and median of these data. Report what you have discovered.

3.5 [Xr03-05] In an effort to slow drivers, traffic engineers painted a solid line 3 feet from the curb over the entire length of a road and filled the space with diagonal lines. The lines made the road look narrower. A sample of car speeds was taken after the lines were drawn.

a. Compute the mean, median, and mode of these data.
b. Briefly describe the information you acquired from each statistic calculated in part a.

3.6 Calculate the variance of the following data.

9 3 7 4 1 7 5 4

3.7 Determine the variance and standard deviation of the following sample.

12 6 22 31 23 13 15 17 21

3.8 Examine the three samples listed here. Without performing any calculations, indicate which sample has the largest amount of variation and which sample has the smallest amount of variation. Explain how you produced your answer.

a. 17 29 12 16 11
b. 22 18 23 20 17
c. 24 37 6 39 29

3.9 Refer to Exercise 3.8. Calculate the variance for each part. Was your answer in Exercise 3.8 correct?

3.10 A friend calculates a variance and reports that it is −25.0. How do you know that he has made a serious calculation error?

3.11 Create a sample of five numbers whose mean is 6 and whose standard deviation is 0.

3.12 A set of data whose histogram is bell shaped yields a mean and standard deviation of 50 and 4, respectively. Approximately what proportion of observations

a. are between 46 and 54?
b. are between 42 and 58?
c. are between 38 and 62?

3.13 A set of data whose histogram is bell shaped yields a mean and standard deviation of 70 and 12, respectively. What is the approximate proportion of observations that

a. are between 46 and 94?
b. are between 34 and 106?

Exercises 3.14 to 3.16 require a computer and software.

3.14 [Xr03-14] There has been much media coverage of the high cost of medicinal drugs in the United States. One concern is the large variation from pharmacy to pharmacy. To investigate a consumer advocacy group took a random sample of 100 pharmacies around the country and recorded the price (in dollars per 100 pills) of Prozac. Compute the range, variance, and standard deviation of the prices. Discuss what these statistics tell you.

3.15 [Xr03-15] Many traffic experts argue that the most important factor in accidents is not the average speed of cars but the amount of variation. Suppose that the speeds of a sample of 200 cars were taken over a stretch of highway that has seen numerous accidents. Compute the variance and standard deviation of the speeds, and interpret the results.

3.16 [Xr03-16] Variance is often used to measure quality in production-line products. Suppose that a sample of steel rods that are supposed to be exactly 100 cm long is taken. The length of each is determined, and the results are recorded. Calculate the variance and the standard deviation. Briefly describe what these statistics tell you.

3.17 Calculate the first, second, and third quartiles of the following sample.

5 8 2 9 5 3 7 4 2 7 4 10 4 3 5

3.18 Find the third and eighth deciles (30th and 80th percentiles) of the following data set.

26 23 29 31 24 22 15 31 30 20

3.19 Find the first and second quintiles (20th and 40th percentiles) of the data shown here.

52 61 88 43 64 71 39 73 51 60

3.20 Determine the first, second, and third quartiles of the following data.

10.5 14.7 15.3 17.7 15.9 12.2 10.0 14.1 13.9 18.5 13.9 15.1 14.7

3.21 Draw the box plot of the following set of data.

9 28 15 21 12 22 29 20 23 31 11 19 24 16 13

Exercises 3.22 to 3.24 require a computer and software.

3.22 [Xr03-22] Accountemps, a company that supplies temporary workers, sponsored a survey of 100 executives. All were asked to report the number of minutes they spend screening each job resume they receive.

a. Compute the quartiles.
b. What information did you derive from the quartiles? What does this suggest about writing your resume?

3.23 [Xr03-23] The career counseling center at a university wanted to learn more about the starting salaries of the university's graduates. All were asked to report the highest salary offer received. The survey also asked each graduate to report the degree and starting salary (column 1 = BA, column 2 = BSc, column 3 = BBA, column 4 = other). Draw box plots to compare the four groups of starting salaries. Report your findings.

3.24 [Xr03-24] For many restaurants, the amount of time customers linger over coffee and dessert negatively affect profits. To learn more about this variable, a sample of 200 restaurant groups was observed, and the amount of time customers spent in the restaurant was recorded.

a. Calculate the quartiles of these data.
b. What do these statistics tell you about the amount of time spent in this restaurant?

3.25 The covariance of two variables has been calculated to be −150. What does the statistic tell you about the relationship between the two variables?

3.26 Refer to Exercise 3.25. You've now learned that the two sample standard deviations are 16 and 12. Calculate the coefficient of correlation. What does this statistic tell you about the relationship between the two variables?

3.27 [Xr03-27] Are the marks one receives in a course related to the amount of time spent studying the subject? To analyze this mysterious possibility, a student took a random sample of 10 students who had enrolled in an accounting class last semester. He asked each to report his or her mark in the course and the total number of hours spent studying accounting. These data are listed here.

Marks	Time Spent Studying
77	40
63	42
79	37
86	47
51	25
78	44
83	41
90	48
65	35
47	28

a. Calculate the covariance.
b. Calculate the coefficient of correlation.
c. What do the statistics calculated above tell you about the relationship between marks and study time?

The following exercises require a computer and software.

3.28 [Xr03-28] When the price of crude oil increases, do oil companies drill more oil wells? To determine the strength and nature of the relationship, an economist recorded the price of a barrel of domestic crude oil (West Texas crude) and the number of exploratory oil wells drilled for each month from 1973 to 2010. Analyze the data and explain what you have discovered. (*Source:* U.S. Department of Energy.)

3.29 [Xr03-29] One way to measure the extent of unemployment is through the help wanted index, which measures the number of want ads in the nation's newspapers. The higher the index, the greater the demand for workers. Another measure is the unemployment rate among insured workers. An economist wanted to know whether these two variables are related and, if so, how. He acquired the help wanted index and unemployment rates for each month between 1951 and 2006 (last year available). Determine the strength and direction of the relationship. (*Source:* U.S. Department of Labor Statistics.)

4LTR Press solutions are designed for today's learners through the continuous feedback of students like you. Tell us what you think about **BSTAT2** and help us improve the learning experience for future students.

YOUR FEEDBACK MATTERS.

Complete the Speak Up survey in CourseMate at www.cengagebrain.com

 Follow us at www.facebook.com/4ltrpress

CHAPTER 4

Data Collection and Sampling

objectives

4-1 Methods of Collecting Data

4-2 Sampling

4-3 Sampling Plans

4-4 Sampling and Nonsampling Errors

SAMPLING AND THE CENSUS

The census, which is conducted every 10 years in the United States, serves an important function. It is the basis for deciding how many congressional representatives and how many votes in the electoral college each state will have. Businesses often use the information derived from the census to help make decisions about products, advertising, and plant locations.

One problem with the census is the issue of undercounting, which occurs when some people are not included. For example, the 1990 census reported that 12.05% of adults were African American; the true value was 12.41%. To address undercounting, the Census Bureau adjusts the numbers it gets from the census. The adjustment is based on another survey. The mechanism is called the Accuracy and Coverage Evaluation. Using sampling methods described in this chapter, the Census Bureau is able to adjust the numbers in American subgroups. For example, the bureau may discover that the number of Hispanics has been undercounted or that the number of people living in California has not been accurately counted.

Later in this chapter we'll discuss how the sampling is conducted and how the adjustments are made.

In Chapter 1, we briefly introduced the concept of statistical inference—the process of inferring information about a population from a sample. Because information about populations can usually be described by parameters, the statistical technique used generally deals with drawing inferences about population parameters from sample statistics. (Recall that a parameter is a measurement about a population, and a statistic is a measurement about a sample.)

In this chapter, we will discuss the basic concepts and techniques of sampling itself. But first we take a look at various sources for collecting data.

4-1 Methods of Collecting Data

Most of this book addresses the problem of converting data into information. The question arises, "Where do data come from?" The answer is that there are a large number of methods that produce data. Before we proceed, however, we'll remind you of the definition of data introduced in Section 2-1. Data are the observed values of a variable—that is, we define a variable or variables that are of interest to us and then proceed to collect observations of those variables.

4-1a Direct Observation

The simplest method of obtaining data is by direct observation. When data are gathered in this way, they are said to be **observational**. For example, suppose that a researcher for a pharmaceutical company wants to determine whether aspirin actually reduces the incidence of heart attacks. Observational data may be gathered by selecting a sample of men and women and asking each whether he or she has taken aspirin regularly over the past 2 years. Each person also would be asked whether he or she had suffered a heart attack over the same period. The proportions reporting heart attacks would be compared, and a statistical technique that is

introduced in Chapter 13 would be used to determine whether aspirin is effective in reducing the likelihood of heart attacks. There are many drawbacks to this method. One of the most critical is that it is difficult to produce useful information in this way. For example, if the statistics practitioner concludes that people who take aspirin suffer fewer heart attacks, can we conclude that aspirin is effective? It may be that people who take aspirin tend to be more heath conscious, and health-conscious people tend to have fewer heart attacks. The one advantage to direct observation is that it is relatively inexpensive.

4-1b Experiments

A more expensive but better way to produce data is through experiments. Data produced in this manner are called **experimental**. In the aspirin illustration, a statistics practitioner can randomly select men and women. The sample would be divided into two groups. One group would take aspirin regularly, and the other would not. After 2 years, the statistics practitioner would determine the proportion of people in each group who had suffered a heart attack, and again statistical methods would be used to determine whether aspirin works. If we find that the aspirin group suffered fewer heart attacks, then we may more confidently conclude that taking aspirin regularly is a healthy decision.

4-1c Surveys

One of the most familiar methods of collecting data is the **survey**, which solicits information from people concerning such things as their income, family size, and opinions on various issues. We're all familiar, for example, with

opinion polls that accompany each political election. The Gallup Poll and the Harris Survey are two well-known surveys of public opinion whose results are often reported by the media. But the majority of surveys are conducted for private use. Private surveys are used extensively by market researchers to determine the preferences and attitudes of consumers and voters. The results can be used for a variety of purposes: from helping to determine the target market for an advertising campaign to modifying a candidate's platform in an election campaign. As an illustration, consider a television network that has hired a market-research firm to provide the network with a profile of owners of luxury automobiles, including what they watch on television and at what times. The network could then use this information to develop a package of recommended time slots for Cadillac commercials, including costs, that it would present to General Motors. It is quite likely that many students reading this book will one day be marketing executives who will "live and die" by such market-research data.

An important aspect of surveys is the **response rate**. This rate is the proportion of all people who were selected who complete the survey. As we discuss in the next section, a low response rate can destroy the validity of any conclusion resulting from the statistical analysis. Statistics practitioners need to ensure that data are reliable.

4-1d Personal Interview

Many researchers feel that the best way to survey people is by means of a personal interview, which involves an interviewer soliciting information from a respondent by asking prepared questions. A personal interview has the advantage of having a higher expected response rate than other methods of data collection. In addition, there will probably be fewer incorrect responses resulting from respondents misunderstanding some questions, because the interviewer can clarify misunderstandings when asked to. But the interviewer must also be careful not to say too much for fear of biasing the response. To avoid introducing such biases, as well as to reap the potential benefits of a personal interview, the interviewer must be well trained in proper interviewing techniques and be well informed on the purpose of the study. The main disadvantage of personal interviews is that they are expensive, especially when travel is involved.

4-1e Telephone Interview

A telephone interview is usually less expensive, but it is also less personal and has a lower expected response rate. Unless the issue is of interest, many people will refuse to respond to telephone surveys. This problem is exacerbated by telemarketers trying to sell something.

4-1f Self-Administered Survey

A third popular method of data collection is the self-administered questionnaire, which is usually mailed to a sample of people. This is an inexpensive method of conducting a survey and is therefore attractive when the number of people to be surveyed is large. But self-administered questionnaires usually have a low response rate and may have a relatively high number of incorrect responses from respondents who misunderstand some questions.

Whatever method is used to collect primary data, we need to know something about sampling, the subject of the next section.

4-2 Sampling

The chief motive for examining a sample rather than a population is cost. Statistical inference permits us to draw conclusions about a population parameter based on a sample that is quite small in comparison to the size of the population. For example, television executives want to know the proportion of television viewers who watch a network's programs. Because 100 million people may be watching television in the United States on a given evening, determining the actual proportion of the population that is watching certain programs is impractical and prohibitively expensive. The Nielsen ratings provide approximations of the desired information by observing what is watched by a sample of 5,000 television households. The proportion of households watching a particular program can be calculated in the Nielsen sample. This sample proportion is then used as an **estimate** of the proportion of all households (the population proportion) that watched the program.

We know that the sample proportion of television households is probably not exactly equal to the population proportion we want to estimate. Nonetheless, the sample statistic can come quite close to the parameter it is designed to estimate if the **target population** (the population about which we want to draw inferences) and the **sampled population** (the actual population from which the sample has been taken) are the same. In practice, these may not be the same. One of statistics' most famous failures illustrates this phenomenon.

The *Literary Digest* was a popular magazine of the 1920s and 1930s that had correctly predicted the outcomes of several presidential elections. In 1936, the *Digest* predicted that the Republican candidate, Alfred Landon, would defeat the Democratic incumbent, Franklin D. Roosevelt, by a 3 to 2 margin. But in that election, Roosevelt defeated Landon in a landslide victory, garnering the support of 62% of the electorate. The source of this blunder was the sampling procedure, and there were two distinct mistakes.[1] First, the *Digest* sent out 10 million sample ballots to prospective voters. However, most of the names of these people were taken from the *Digest*'s subscription list and from telephone directories. Subscribers to the magazine and people who owned telephones tended to be wealthier than average and such people then, as today, tended to vote Republican. Second, only 2.3 million ballots were returned resulting in a self-selected sample.

Self-selected samples are almost always biased, because the individuals who participate in them are more keenly interested in the issue than are other members of the population. You often find similar surveys conducted today when radio and television stations ask people to call and give their opinion on an issue of interest. Again, only listeners who are concerned about the topic and have enough patience to get through to the station will be included in the sample. Hence, the sampled population is composed entirely of people who

---

[1] Many statisticians ascribe the *Literary Digest*'s statistical debacle to the wrong causes. For an understanding of what really happened, read Maurice C. Bryson, "The Literary Digest Poll: Making of a Statistical Myth" *American Statistician* 30(4) (November 1976): 184–185.

are interested in the issue, whereas the target population is made up of all the people within the listening radius of the radio station. As a result, the conclusions drawn from such surveys are frequently wrong.

4-3 Sampling Plans

Our objective in this section is to introduce three different sampling plans: simple random sampling, stratified random sampling, and cluster sampling. We begin our presentation with the most basic design.

4-3a Simple Random Sampling

Simple Random Sample
A **simple random sample** is a sample selected in such a way that every possible sample with the same number of observations is equally likely to be chosen.

One way to conduct a simple random sample is to assign a number to each element in the population, write these numbers on individual slips of paper, toss them into a hat, and draw the required number of slips (the sample size, n) from the hat. This is the kind of procedure that occurs in raffles, when all the ticket stubs go into a large rotating drum from which the winners are selected.

Sometimes the elements of the population are already numbered. For example, virtually all adults have Social Security numbers (in the United States) or Social Insurance numbers (in Canada); all employees of large corporations have employee numbers; many people have driver's license numbers, medical plan numbers, student numbers, and so on. In such cases, choosing which sampling procedure to use is simply a matter of deciding how to select from among these numbers.

After each element of the chosen population has been assigned a unique number, sample numbers can be selected at random. A computer can be used to perform this function.

EXAMPLE 4.1
Random Sample of Income Tax Returns

A government income tax auditor has been given responsibility for 1,000 tax returns. A computer is used to check the arithmetic of each return. However, to determine whether the returns have been completed honestly, the auditor must check each entry and confirm its veracity. Because it takes, on average, 1 hour to completely audit a return and she has only 1 week to complete the task, the auditor has decided to randomly select 40 returns. The returns are numbered from 1 to 1,000. Use a computer random number generator to select the sample for the auditor.

SOLUTION

We generated 50 numbers between 1 and 1,000 even though we needed only 40 numbers. We did so because it is likely that there will be some duplicates. We will use the first 40 unique random numbers to select our sample. The following numbers were generated by Excel. The instructions for both Excel and Minitab are provided here. [Notice that the 24th and 36th (counting down the columns) numbers generated were the same: 467.]

Computer-Generated Random Numbers

383	246	372	952	75
101	46	356	54	199
597	33	911	706	65
900	165	467	817	359
885	220	427	973	488
959	18	304	467	512
15	286	976	301	374
408	344	807	751	986
864	554	992	352	41
139	358	257	776	231

Excel
INSTRUCTIONS

1. Click **Data, Data Analysis,** and **Random Number Generation.**

2. Specify the **Number of Variables (1)** and the **Number of Random Numbers (50).**

3. Select **Uniform Distribution.**

4. Specify the range of the uniform distribution (**Parameters**): 0 and **1.**

5. Click **OK.** Column A will fill with 50 numbers that range between 0 and 1.

6. Multiply column A by 1,000 and store the products in column B.

7. Make cell C1 active, and click f_x, **Math & Trig, ROUNDUP,** and **OK.**

8. Specify the first number to be rounded. (**B1**)

9. Type the **number of digits** (decimal places) (**0**). Click **OK**.

10. Complete column C.

The first five steps command Excel to generate 50 uniformly distributed random numbers between 0 and 1 to be stored in column A. Steps 6 through 10 convert these random numbers to integers between 1 and 1,000. Each tax return has the same probability $(1/1,000 = .001)$ of being selected. Thus, each member of the population is equally likely to be included in the sample.

Minitab

INSTRUCTIONS

1. Click **Calc, Random Data,** and **Integer....**

2. Type the number of random numbers you wish (**50**).

3. Specify where the numbers are to be stored (**C1**).

4. Specify the **Minimum value** (**1**).

5. Specify the **Maximum value** (**1000**). Click **OK**.

INTERPRET

The auditor would examine the tax returns selected by the computer. She would pick returns numbered 383, 101, 597, . . . , 352, 776, and 75 (the first 40 unique numbers). Each return would be audited to determine whether they are fraudulent. If the objective is to audit these 40 returns, then no statistical procedure would be employed. However, if the objective is to estimate the proportion of all 1,000 returns that are dishonest, then she would use one of the inferential techniques presented later in this book.

4-3b Stratified Random Sampling

In making inferences about a population, we attempt to extract as much information as possible from a sample. The basic sampling plan, simple random sampling, often accomplishes this goal at low cost. Other methods, however, can be used to increase the amount of information about the population. One such procedure is *stratified random sampling.*

Stratified Random Sample
A **stratified random sample** is obtained by separating the population into mutually exclusive sets, or strata, and then drawing simple random samples from each stratum.

Examples of criteria for separating a population into strata (and of the strata themselves) follow.

1 Gender
Male
Female

2 Age
Less than 20
20–30
31–40
41–50
51–60
More than 60

3 Occupation
Professional
Clerical
Blue collar
Other

4 Household income
Less than $25,000
$25,000–$39,999
$40,000–$60,000
More than $60,000

To illustrate, suppose a public opinion survey is to be conducted to determine how many people favor a tax increase. A stratified random sample could be obtained by selecting a random sample of people from each of the four income groups we just described. We usually stratify in a way that enables us to obtain particular kinds of information. In this example, we would like to know whether people in the different income categories differ in their opinions about the proposed tax increase, because the tax increase will affect the strata differently. We avoid stratifying when there is no connection between the survey and the strata. For example, little purpose is served in trying to determine whether people within religious strata have divergent opinions about the tax increase.

One advantage of stratification is that, besides acquiring information about the entire population, we can also make inferences within each stratum or compare strata. For instance, we can estimate what proportion of the lowest income group favors the tax increase, or we can compare the highest and lowest income groups to determine whether they differ in their support of the tax increase.

Any stratification must be done in such a way that the strata are mutually exclusive: each member of the population must be assigned to exactly one stratum. After the population has been stratified in this way, we can use simple random sampling to generate the complete sample. There are several ways to do this. For example, we can draw random samples from each of the four income groups according to their proportions in the population. Thus, if in the population the relative frequencies of the four groups are as listed here, our sample will be stratified in the same proportions. If a total sample of 1,000 is to be drawn, then we will randomly select 250 from stratum 1, 400 from stratum 2, 300 from stratum 3, and 50 from stratum 4.

Stratum	Income Categories ($)	Population Proportions (%)
1	Less than 25,000	25
2	25,000–39,999	40
3	40,000–60,000	30
4	More than 60,000	5

The problem with this approach, however, is that if we want to make inferences about the last stratum, a sample of 50 may be too small to produce useful information. In such cases, we usually increase the sample size of the smallest stratum to ensure that the sample data provide enough information for our purposes. An adjustment must then be made before we attempt to draw inferences about the entire population. The required procedure is beyond the level of this book. We recommend that anyone planning such a survey consult an expert statistician or a reference book on the subject. Better still, become an expert statistician yourself by taking additional statistics courses.

4-3c Cluster Sampling

Cluster Sample
A **cluster sample** is a simple random sample of groups or clusters of elements.

Cluster sampling is particularly useful when it is difficult or costly to develop a complete list of the population members (making it difficult and costly to generate a simple random sample). It is also useful whenever the population elements are widely dispersed geographically. For example, suppose we wanted to estimate the average annual household income in a large city. To use simple random sampling, we would need a complete list of households in the city from which to sample. To use stratified random sampling, we would need the list of households, and we would also need to have each household categorized by some other variable (such as age of household head) in order to develop the strata. A less expensive alternative would be to let each block

within the city represent a cluster. A sample of clusters could then be randomly selected, and every household within these clusters could be questioned to determine income. By reducing the distances the surveyor must cover to gather data, cluster sampling reduces the cost.

But cluster sampling also increases sampling error (see Section 4-4), because households belonging to the same cluster are likely to be similar in many respects, including household income. This can be partially offset by using some of the cost savings to choose a larger sample than would be used for a simple random sample.

4-3d Sample Size

Whichever type of sampling plan you select, you still have to decide what size sample to use. Determining the appropriate sample size will be addressed in Chapter 9. Until then, we can rely on our intuition, which tells us that the larger the sample size is, the more accurate we can expect the sample estimates to be.

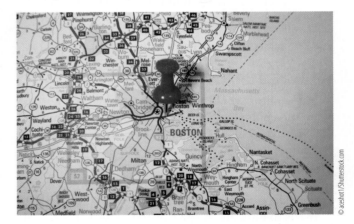

SAMPLING AND THE CENSUS

To adjust for undercounting, the Census Bureau conducts cluster sampling. The clusters are geographic blocks. For the year 2000 census, the Bureau randomly sampled 11,800 blocks, which contained 314,000 housing units. Each unit was intensively revisited to ensure that all residents were counted. From the results of this survey, the Census Bureau estimated the number of people missed by the first census in various subgroups, defined by several variables including gender, race, and age. Because of the importance of determining state populations, adjustments were made to state totals. For example, by comparing the results of the census and of the sampling, the bureau determined that the undercount in the state of Texas was 1.7087%. The official census produced a state population of 20,851,820. Taking 1.7087% of this total produced an adjustment of 356,295. Using this method changed the population of the state of Texas to 21,208,115.

Note that this process is politically contentious. The controversy centers on the way in which subgroups are defined. Changing the definition alters the undercounts, making this statistical technique subject to politicking.

4-4 Sampling and Nonsampling Errors

Two major types of error can arise when a sample of observations is taken from a population: *sampling error* and *nonsampling error*. Anyone reviewing the results of sample surveys and studies, as well as statistics practitioners conducting surveys and applying statistical techniques, should understand the sources of these errors.

4-4a Sampling Error

Sampling error refers to differences between the sample and the population that exist only because of the observations that happened to be selected for the sample. Sampling error is an error that we expect to occur when we make a statement about a population that is based only on the observations contained in a sample taken from the population. To illustrate, suppose that we wish to determine the mean annual income of North American blue-collar workers. To determine this parameter, we would have to ask each North American blue-collar worker what his or her income is and then calculate the mean of all the responses. Because the size of this population is several million, the task is both expensive and impractical. We can use statistical inference to estimate the mean income μ of the population if we are willing to accept less than 100% accuracy. We record the incomes of a sample of the workers and find the mean $\bar{x}$ of this sample of incomes. This *sample mean* is an estimate of the desired population mean. But the value of the sample mean will deviate from the population mean simply by chance, because the value of the sample mean depends on which incomes just happened to be selected for the sample. The difference between

the true (unknown) value of the population mean and its estimate the sample mean is the sampling error. The size of this deviation may be large simply because of bad luck—bad luck that a particularly unrepresentative sample happened to be selected. The only way we can reduce the expected size of this error is to take a larger sample.

Given a fixed sample size, the best we can do is state the probability that the sampling error is less than a certain amount (as we will discuss in Chapter 9). It is common today for such a statement to accompany the results of an opinion poll. If an opinion poll states that, based on sample results, the incumbent candidate for mayor has the support of 54% of eligible voters in an upcoming election, the statement may be accompanied by the following explanatory note: "This percentage is correct to within three percentage points, 19 times out of 20." This statement means that we estimate that the actual level of support for the candidate is between 51% and 57%, and that in the long run this type of procedure is correct 95% of the time.

4-4b Nonsampling Error

Nonsampling error is more serious than sampling error, because taking a larger sample won't diminish the size, or the possibility of occurrence, of this error. Even a census can (and probably will) contain nonsampling errors. **Nonsampling errors** result from mistakes made in the acquisition of data or from the sample observations being selected improperly.

1. *Errors in data acquisition.* This type of error arises from the recording of incorrect responses. Incorrect responses may be the result of incorrect measurements being taken because of faulty equipment, mistakes made during transcription from primary sources, inaccurate recording of data because of the misinterpretation of terms, or inaccurate responses to questions concerning sensitive issues such as sexual activity or possible tax evasion.

2. *Nonresponse error* **Nonresponse error** refers to error (or **bias**) introduced when responses are not obtained from some members of the sample. When this happens, the sample observations that are collected may not be representative of the target population, resulting in biased results (as was discussed in Section 4-2). Nonresponse can occur for a number of reasons. An interviewer may be unable to contact a person listed in the sample, or the sampled person may refuse to respond for some reason. In either case, responses are not obtained from a sampled person, and bias is introduced. The problem of nonresponse is even greater when self-administered questionnaires are used rather than

an interviewer, who can attempt to reduce the nonresponse rate by means of callbacks. As noted previously, the *Literary Digest* fiasco resulted largely from a high nonresponse rate, which led to a biased, self-selected sample.

3. *Selection bias.* **Selection bias** occurs when the sampling plan is such that some members of the target population cannot possibly be selected for inclusion in the sample. Together with nonresponse error, selection bias played a role in the *Literary Digest* poll being so wrong, because voters without telephones or subscriptions to *Literary Digest* were excluded from possible inclusion in the sample taken.

EXERCISES

4.1 Briefly describe the difference between observational and experimental data.

4.2 A soft drink manufacturer has been supplying its cola drink in bottles to grocery stores and in cans to small convenience stores. The company is analyzing sales of this cola drink to determine which type of packaging is preferred by consumers.

a. Is this study observational or experimental? Explain your answer.
b. Outline a better method for determining whether a store will be supplied with cola in bottles or in cans so that future sales data will be more helpful in assessing the preferred type of packaging.

4.3 a. Briefly describe how you might design a study to investigate the relationship between smoking and lung cancer.
b. Is your study in part (a) observational or experimental? Explain why.

4.4 a. List three methods of conducting a survey of people.
b. Give an important advantage and disadvantage of each of the methods listed in part (a).

4.5 Discuss how the data from the Nielsen ratings can be used by television executives and potential advertisers.

4.6 For each of the following sampling plans, indicate why the target population and the sampled population are not the same.

a. To determine the opinions and attitudes of customers who regularly shop at a particular mall, a surveyor stands outside a large department store in the mall and randomly selects people to participate in the survey.
b. A library wants to estimate the proportion of its books that have been damaged. The librarians decide to select one book per shelf as a sample by measuring 12 inches from the left edge of each shelf and selecting the book in that location.
c. Political surveyors visit 200 residences during one afternoon to ask eligible voters present in the house at the time whom they intend to vote for.

4.7 a. Describe why the *Literary Digest* poll of 1936 has become infamous.
b. What caused this poll to be so wrong?

4.8 a. What is meant by a self-selected sample?
b. Give an example of a recent poll that involved a self-selected sample.
c. Why are self-selected samples not desirable?

4.9 A regular feature in a newspaper asks readers to respond via e-mail to a survey that requires a yes or no response. In the following day's newspaper, the percentage of yes and no responses are reported. Discuss why we should ignore these statistics.

4.10 Suppose your statistics professor distributes a questionnaire about the course. One of the questions asks, "Would you recommend this course to a friend?" Can the professor use the results to infer something about all statistics courses? Explain.

4.11 A statistics practitioner would like to conduct a survey to ask people their views on a proposed new shopping mall in their community. According to the latest census, there are 500 households in the community. The statistician has numbered each household (from 1 to 500), and she would like to randomly select 25 of these households to participate in the study. Use Excel or Minitab to generate the sample.

4.12 A safety expert wants to determine the proportion of cars in his state with worn tire treads. The state license plate contains six digits. Use Excel or Minitab to generate a sample of 20 cars to be examined.

4.13 A large university campus has 60,000 students. The president of the students' association wants to conduct a survey of the students to determine their views on an increase in the student activity fee. She would like to acquire information about all the students but would also like to compare the school of business, the faculty of arts and sciences, and the graduate school. Describe a sampling plan that accomplishes these goals.

4.14 A telemarketing firm has recorded the households that have purchased one or more of the company's products. These number in the millions. The company would like to conduct a survey of purchasers to acquire information about their attitude concerning the timing of the telephone calls. The president of the company would like to know the views of all purchasers but would also like to compare the attitudes of people in the West, South, North, and East. Describe a suitable sampling plan.

4.15 The operations manager of a large plant with four departments wants to estimate the person-hours lost per month from accidents. Describe a sampling plan that would be suitable for estimating the plant-wide loss and for comparing departments.

4.16 A statistics practitioner wants to estimate the mean age of children in his city. Unfortunately, he does not have a complete list of households. Describe a sampling plan that would be suitable for his purposes.

4.17 a. Explain the difference between sampling error and nonsampling error.
b. Which type of error in part (a) is more serious? Why?

4.18 Briefly describe three types of nonsampling error.

4.19 Is it possible for a sample to yield better results than a census? Explain.

CHAPTER 5

Probability

objectives

5-1 Assigning Probability to Events

5-2 Joint, Marginal, and Conditional Probability

5-3 Probability Rules and Trees

5-4 Identifying the Correct Method

DIVERSITY INDEX

Every ten years the United States government conducts a census. Among many other pieces of information, the Census Bureau records the race or ethnicity of the residents of every county in every state. From these results, the bureau calculated a "diversity index" that measured the probability that two people chosen at random were of different races or ethnicities. Suppose that the census determined that in one Wisconsin county 80% of residents are white, 15% are black, and 5% are Asian. Calculate the diversity index for this county. (See page 75 for the answer.)

In Chapters 2 and 3, we introduced graphical and numerical descriptive methods. Although the methods are useful on their own, we are particularly interested in developing statistical inference. As we pointed out in Chapter 1, statistical inference is the process by which we acquire information about populations from samples. A critical component of inference is *probability* because it provides the link between the population and the sample.

5-1 Assigning Probability to Events

To introduce probability, we must first define a *random experiment*.

Random Experiment

A **random experiment** is an action or process that leads to one of several possible outcomes.

Here are six illustrations of random experiments and their outcomes.

Illustration 1. Experiment: Flip a coin.
Outcomes: Heads and tails

Illustration 2. Experiment: Record marks on a statistics test (out of 100).
Outcomes: Numbers between 0 and 100

Illustration 3. Experiment: Record grade on a statistics test.
Outcomes: A, B, C, D, and F

Illustration 4. Experiment: Record student evaluations of a course.
Outcomes: Poor, fair, good, very good, and excellent

Illustration 5. Experiment: Measure the time to assemble a computer.
Outcomes: Number whose smallest possible value is 0 seconds with no predefined upper limit

Illustration 6. Experiment: Record the party that a voter will vote for in an upcoming election.
Outcomes: Party A, Party B, . . .

The first step in assigning probabilities is to produce a list of the outcomes. The listed outcomes must be **exhaustive**, which means that all possible outcomes must be included. In addition, the outcomes must be **mutually exclusive**—that is, no two outcomes can occur at the same time.

To understand the concept of exhaustive outcomes, consider this list of the outcomes of the toss of a die:

1 2 3 4 5

This list is not exhaustive, because we have omitted 6.

The concept of mutual exclusiveness can be seen by listing the following outcomes in illustration 2:

0–50, 50–60, 60–70, 70–80, 80–100

If these intervals include both the lower and upper limits, then these outcomes are not mutually exclusive because two outcomes can occur for any student. For example, if a student receives a mark of 70, both the third and fourth outcomes occur.

Note that we could produce more than one list of exhaustive and mutually exclusive outcomes. For example, here is another list of outcomes for illustration 3:

Pass and fail

A list of exhaustive and mutually exclusive outcomes is called a *sample space* and is denoted by *S*. The outcomes are denoted by $O_1, O_2, \ldots, O_k$.

Sample Space
A **sample space** of a random experiment is a list of all possible outcomes of the experiment. The outcomes must be exhaustive and mutually exclusive.

Using set notation, we represent the sample space and its outcomes as

$$S = \{O_1, O_2, \ldots, O_k\}$$

Once a sample space has been prepared, we begin the task of assigning probabilities to the outcomes. There are three ways to assign probability to outcomes. However it is done, two rules govern probabilities, as we show in the next box.

Requirements of Probabilities
Given a sample space $S = \{O_1, O_2, \ldots, O_k\}$, the probabilities assigned to the outcomes must satisfy two requirements.

1. The probability of any outcome must lie between 0 and 1; that is,

    $$0 \leq P(O_i) \leq 1 \qquad \text{for each } i$$

    [Note: $P(O_i)$ is the notation we use to represent the probability of outcome *i*.]

2. The sum of the probabilities of all the outcomes in a sample space must be 1; that is,

    $$\sum_{i=1}^{k} P(O_i) = 1$$

5-1a Three Approaches to Assigning Probabilities

The **classical approach** is used by mathematicians to help determine probability associated with games of chance. For example, the classical approach specifies that the probabilities of heads and tails in the flip of a balanced coin are equal to each other. Because the sum of the probabilities must be 1, the probability of heads and the probability of tails are both 50%. Similarly, the six possible outcomes of the toss of a balanced die have the same probability; each is assigned a probability of 1/6. In some experiments, it is necessary to develop mathematical ways to count the number of outcomes.

For example, to determine the probability of winning a lottery, we need to determine the number of possible combinations.

The **relative frequency approach** defines probability as the long-run relative frequency with which an outcome occurs. For example, suppose that we know that of the last 1,000 students who took the statistics course you're now taking, 200 received a grade of A. The relative frequency of A's is then 200/1000, or 20%. This figure represents an estimate of the probability of obtaining a grade of A in the course. It is only an estimate because the relative frequency approach defines probability as the "long-run" relative frequency. One thousand students do not constitute the long run. The larger the number of students whose grades we have observed, the better the estimate becomes. In theory, we would have to observe an infinite number of grades to determine the exact probability.

When it is not reasonable to use the classical approach and there is no history of the outcomes, we have no alternative but to employ the **subjective approach**. In the subjective approach, we define probability as the degree of belief that we hold in the occurrence of an event. An excellent example is derived from the field of investment. An investor would like to know the probability that a particular stock will increase in value. Using the subjective approach, the investor would analyze a number of factors associated with the stock and the stock market in general and, using his or her judgment, assign a probability to the outcomes of interest.

5-1b Defining Events

An individual outcome of a sample space is called a **simple event**. All other events are composed of the simple events in a sample space.

Event

An **event** is a collection or set of one or more simple events in a sample space.

In illustration 2, we can define the event, achieve a grade of A, as the set of numbers that lie between 80 and 100, inclusive. Using set notation, we have

$$A = \{80, 81, 82, \ldots, 99, 100\}$$

Similarly,

$$F = \{0, 1, 2 \ldots, 48, 49\}$$

5-1c Probability of Events

We can now define the probability of any event.

Probability of an Event

The **probability of an event** is the sum of the probabilities of the simple events that constitute the event.

For example, suppose that in illustration 3 we employed the relative frequency approach to assign probabilities to the simple events as follows:

$$P(A) = .20$$
$$P(B) = .30$$
$$P(C) = .25$$
$$P(D) = .15$$
$$P(F) = .10$$

The probability of the event, pass the course, is

$$P(\text{Pass the course}) = P(A) + P(B) + P(C) + P(D)$$
$$= .20 + .30 + .25 + .15 = .90$$

5-1d Interpreting Probability

No matter what method was used to assign probability, we interpret it using the relative frequency approach for an infinite number of experiments. For example, an investor may have used the subjective approach to determine that there is a 65% probability that a particular stock's price will increase over the next month. However, we interpret the 65% figure to mean that if we had an infinite number of stocks with exactly the same economic and market characteristics as the one the investor will buy, 65% of them would increase in price over the next month. Similarly, we can determine that the probability of throwing a 5 with a balanced die is 1/6. We may have used the classical approach to determine this probability. However, we interpret the number as the proportion of times that a 5 is observed on a balanced die thrown an infinite number of times.

This relative frequency approach is useful to interpret probability statements such as those heard from weather forecasters or scientists. You will also discover that this is the way we link the population and the sample in statistical inference.

© Arno van Ulmen/Shutterstock.com

© Glowimages

5-2 Joint, Marginal, and Conditional Probability

In the previous section, we described how to produce a sample space and assign probabilities to the simple events in the sample space. Although this method of determining probability is useful, we need to develop more sophisticated methods. In this section, we discuss how to calculate the probability of more complicated events from the probability of related events. Here is an illustration of the process.

The sample space for the toss of a die is

$S = \{1, 2, 3, 4, 5, 6\}$

If the die is balanced, then the probability of each simple event is 1/6. In most parlor games and casinos, players toss two dice. To determine playing and wagering strategies, players need to compute the probabilities of various totals of the two dice. For example, the probability of tossing a total of 3 with two dice is 2/36. This probability was derived by creating combinations of the simple events. There are several different types of combinations. One of the most important types is the **intersection** of two events.

5-2a Intersection

Intersection of Events *A* and *B*

The intersection of events *A* and *B* is the event that occurs when both *A* and *B* occur. It is denoted as

A and *B*

The probability of the intersection is called the **joint probability**.

For example, one way to toss a 3 with two dice is to toss a 1 on the first die *and* a 2 on the second die, which is the intersection of two simple events. Incidentally, to compute the probability of a total of 3, we need to combine this intersection with another intersection, namely, a 2 on the first die and a 1 on the second die. This type of combination is called a *union* of two events, and it will be described later in this section. Here is another illustration.

Applications in Finance
Mutual Funds

A mutual fund is a pool of investments made on behalf of people who share similar objectives. In most cases, a professional manager who has been educated in finance and statistics manages the fund. He or she makes decisions to buy and sell individual stocks and bonds in accordance with a specified investment philosophy. For example, there are funds that concentrate on other publicly traded mutual fund companies. Other mutual funds specialize in Internet (so-called dot-coms) stocks whereas others buy stocks of biotech firms. Surprisingly, most mutual funds do not outperform the market. In other words, the increase in the net asset value (NAV) of the mutual fund is often less than the increase in the value of stock indexes that represent their stock markets. One reason for this is the management expense ratio (MER), which is a measure of the costs charged to the fund by the manager to cover expenses, including the salary and bonus of the managers. The MERs for most funds range from .5% to more than 4%. The ultimate success of the fund depends on the skill and knowledge of the fund manager. This raises the question: Which managers do best?

EXAMPLE 5.1

Determinants of Success among Mutual Fund Managers, Part 1[1]

Why are some mutual fund managers more successful than others? One possible factor is where a manager earned his or her MBA. Suppose that a potential investor examined the relationship between how well

---

[1] This example is adapted from "Are Some Mutual Fund Managers Better than Others? Cross-Sectional Patterns in Behavior and Performance" by Judith Chevalier and Glenn Ellison, Working paper 5852, National Bureau of Economic Research.

the mutual fund performs and where the fund manager earned the MBA. After the analysis, Table 5.1, a table of joint probabilities, was developed. Analyze these probabilities and interpret the results.

Table 5.1 **Determinants of Success among Mutual Fund Managers, Part 1**

	Mutual Fund Outperforms Market	Mutual Fund Does Not Outperform Market
Top 20 MBA Program	.11	.29
Not Top 20 MBA Program	.06	.54

© Cengage Learning

Table 5.1 tells us that the joint probability that a mutual fund outperforms the market *and* that its manager graduated from a top-20 MBA program is .11; that is, 11% of all mutual funds outperform the market and their managers graduated from a top-20 MBA program. The other three joint probabilities are defined similarly:

The probability that a mutual fund outperforms the market and its manager did not graduate from a top-20 MBA program is .06.

The probability that a mutual fund does not outperform the market and its manager graduated from a top-20 MBA program is .29.

The probability that a mutual fund does not outperform the market and its manager did not graduate from a top-20 MBA program is .54.

To help make our task easier, we'll use notation to represent the events. Let

A_1 = Fund manager graduated from a top-20 MBA program

A_2 = Fund manager did not graduate from a top-20 MBA program

B_1 = Fund outperforms the market

B_2 = Fund does not outperform the market

Thus,

$P(A_1 \text{ and } B_1) = .11$
$P(A_2 \text{ and } B_1) = .06$
$P(A_1 \text{ and } B_2) = .29$
$P(A_2 \text{ and } B_2) = .54$

5-2b Marginal Probability

The joint probabilities in Table 5.1 allow us to compute various probabilities. **Marginal probabilities,** computed by adding across rows or down columns, are

so named because they are calculated in the margins of the table.

Adding across the first row produces

$$P(A_1 \text{ and } B_1) + P(A_1 \text{ and } B_2) = .11 + .29 = .40$$

Notice that both intersections state that the manager graduated from a top-20 MBA program (represented by A_1). Thus, when randomly selecting mutual funds, the probability that its manager graduated from a top-20 MBA program is .40. Expressed as relative frequency, 40% of all mutual fund managers graduated from a top-20 MBA program.

Adding across the second row:

$$P(A_2 \text{ and } B_1) + P(A_2 \text{ and } B_2) = .06 + .54 = .60$$

This probability tells us that 60% of all mutual fund managers did not graduate from a top-20 MBA program (represented by A_2). Notice that the probability that a mutual fund manager graduated from a top-20 MBA program and the probability that the manager did not graduate from a top-20 MBA program add to 1.

Adding down the columns produces the following marginal probabilities.

Column 1: $P(A_1 \text{ and } B_1) + P(A_2 \text{ and } B_1)$
$= .11 + .06 = .17$
Column 2: $P(A_1 \text{ and } B_2) + P(A_2 \text{ and } B_2)$
$= .29 + .54 = .83$

These marginal probabilities tell us that 17% of all mutual funds outperform the market and that 83% of mutual funds do not outperform the market.

Table 5.2 lists all the joint and marginal probabilities.

Table 5.2 **Joint and Marginal Probabilities**

	Mutual Fund Outperforms Market	Mutual Fund Does Not Outperform Market	Totals
Top-20 MBA Program	$P(A_1 \text{ and } B_1) = .11$	$P(A_1 \text{ and } B_2) = .29$	$P(A_1) = .40$
Not Top-20 MBA Program	$P(A_2 \text{ and } B_1) = .06$	$P(A_2 \text{ and } B_2) = .54$	$P(A_2) = .60$
Totals	$P(B_1) = .17$	$P(B_2) = .83$	1.00

© Cengage Learning

5-2c Conditional Probability

We frequently need to know how two events are related. In particular, we would like to know the probability of one event given the occurrence of another related event. For example, we would certainly like to know the probability that a fund managed by a graduate of a top-20

MBA program will outperform the market. Such a probability will allow us to make an informed decision about where to invest our money. This probability is called a **conditional probability** because we want to know the probability that a fund will outperform the market *given* the condition that the manager graduated from a top-20 MBA program. The conditional probability that we seek is represented by

$$P(B_1|A_1)$$

where the "|" represents the word *given*. Here is how we compute this conditional probability.

The marginal probability that a manager graduated from a top-20 MBA program is .40, which is made up of two joint probabilities. They are the probability that the mutual fund outperforms the market and the manager graduated from a top-20 MBA program [$P(A_1$ and $B_1)$] and the probability that the fund does not outperform the market and the manager graduated from a top-20 MBA program [$P(A_1$ and $B_2)$]. Their joint probabilities are .11 and .29, respectively. We can interpret these numbers in the following way. On average for every 100 mutual funds, 40 will be managed by a graduate of a top-20 MBA program. Of these 40 managers, on average 11 of them will manage a mutual fund that will outperform the market. Thus, the conditional probability is 11/40 = .275. Notice that this ratio is the same as the ratio of the joint probability to the marginal probability .11/.40. All conditional probabilities can be computed this way.

Conditional Probability

The probability of event A given event B is

$$P(A|B) = \frac{P(A \text{ and } B)}{P(B)}$$

The probability of event B given event A is

$$P(B|A) = \frac{P(A \text{ and } B)}{P(A)}$$

EXAMPLE 5.2

Determinants of Success among Mutual Fund Managers, Part 2

Suppose that in Example 5.1 we select one mutual fund at random and discover that it did not outperform the market. What is the probability that a graduate of a top-20 MBA program manages it?

SOLUTION

We wish to find a conditional probability. The condition is that the fund did not outperform the market (event B_2), and the event whose probability we seek is that the fund is managed by a graduate of a top-20 MBA program (event A_1). Thus, we want to compute the following probability:

$$P(A_1|B_2)$$

Using the conditional probability formula, we find

$$P(A_1|B_2) = \frac{P(A_1 \text{ and } B_2)}{P(B_2)} = \frac{.29}{.83} = .349$$

Thus, 34.9% of all mutual funds that do not outperform the market are managed by top-20 MBA program graduates.

The calculation of conditional probabilities raises the question of whether the two events, the fund outperformed the market and the manager graduated from a top-20 MBA program, are related, a subject we tackle next.

5-2d Independence

One of the objectives of calculating conditional probability is to determine whether two events are related. In particular, we would like to know whether they are **independent events**.

Independent Events

Two events A and B are said to be independent if

$$P(A|B) = P(A)$$

or

$$P(B|A) = P(B)$$

Put another way, two events are independent if the probability of one event is not affected by the occurrence of the other event.

EXAMPLE 5.3

Determinants of Success among Mutual Fund Managers, Part 3

Determine whether the event that the manager graduated from a top-20 MBA program and the event the fund outperforms the market are independent events.

SOLUTION

We wish to determine whether A_1 and B_1 are independent. To do so we must calculate the probability of A_1 given B_1; that is,

$$P(A_1 | B_1) = \frac{P(A_1 \text{ and } B_1)}{P(B_1)} = \frac{.11}{.17} = .647$$

The marginal probability that a manager graduated from a top-20 MBA program is

$$P(A_1) = .40$$

Because the two probabilities are not equal, we conclude that the two events are dependent.

Incidentally, we could have made the decision by calculating $P(B_1 | A_1) = .275$ and observing that it is not equal to $P(B_1) = .17$.

Note that there are three other combinations of events in this problem. They are $(A_1 \text{ and } B_2)$, $(A_2 \text{ and } B_1)$, $(A_2 \text{ and } B_2)$ [ignoring mutually exclusive combinations $(A_1 \text{ and } A_2)$ and $(B_1 \text{ and } B_2)$, which are dependent]. In each combination, the two events are dependent. In this type of problem, in which there are only four combinations, if one combination is dependent, all four will be dependent. Similarly, if one combination is independent, all four will be independent. This rule does not apply to any other situation.

5-2e Union

Another event that is the combination of other events is the *union*.

Union of Events *A* and *B*

The **union** of events A and B is the event that occurs when either A or B or both occur. It is denoted as

A or B

EXAMPLE 5.4

Determinants of Success among Mutual Fund Managers, Part 4

Determine the probability that a randomly selected fund outperforms the market or the manager graduated from a top-20 MBA program.

SOLUTION

We want to compute the probability of the union of two events

$$P(A_1 \text{ or } B_1)$$

The union A_1 or B_1 consists of three events. In other words, the union occurs whenever any of the following joint events occurs:

1. fund outperforms the market and the manager graduated from a top-20 MBA program;

2. fund outperforms the market and the manager did not graduate from a top-20 MBA program; and

3. fund does not outperform the market and the manager graduated from a top-20 MBA program.

Their probabilities are

$$P(A_1 \text{ and } B_1) = .11$$
$$P(A_2 \text{ and } B_1) = .06$$
$$P(A_1 \text{ and } B_2) = .29$$

Thus, the probability of the union, the fund outperforms the market or the manager graduated from a top-20 MBA program, is the sum of the three probabilities; that is,

$$\begin{aligned} P(A_1 \text{ or } B_1) &= P(A_1 \text{ and } B_1) + P(A_2 \text{ and } B_1) \\ &\quad + P(A_1 \text{ and } B_2) \\ &= .11 + .06 + .29 = .46 \end{aligned}$$

Notice that there is another way to produce this probability. Of the four probabilities in Table 5.1, the only one representing an event that is not part of the union is the probability of the event the fund does not outperform the market and the manager did not graduate from a top-20 MBA program. That probability is

$$P(A_2 \text{ and } B_2) = .54$$

which is the probability that the union *does not* occur. Thus, the probability of the union is

$$P(A_1 \text{ or } B_1) = 1 - P(A_2 \text{ and } B_2) = 1 - .54 = .46.$$

Thus, we determined that 46% of mutual funds either outperform the market or are managed by a top-20 MBA program graduate or have both characteristics.

5-3 Probability Rules and Trees

In Section 5-2, we introduced intersection and union and described how to determine the probability of the intersection and the union of two events. In this section, we present other methods of determining these probabilities. We introduce three rules that enable us to calculate the probability of more complex events from the probability of simpler events.

5-3a Complement Rule

The **complement** of event A is the event that occurs when event A does not occur. The complement of event A is denoted by A^C. The complement rule defined here derives from the fact that the probability of an event and the probability of the event's complement must sum to 1.

Complement Rule

$$P(A^C) = 1 - P(A)$$

for any event A.

We will demonstrate the use of this rule after we introduce the next rule.

5-3b Multiplication Rule

The **multiplication rule** is used to calculate the joint probability of two events. It is based on the formula for conditional probability supplied in the previous section; that is, from the following formula

$$P(A|B) = \frac{P(A \text{ and } B)}{P(B)}$$

we derive the multiplication rule simply by multiplying both sides by $P(B)$.

Multiplication Rule

The joint probability of any two events A and B is

$$P(A \text{ and } B) = P(B)P(A|B)$$

or altering the notation

$$P(A \text{ and } B) = P(A)P(B|A)$$

If A and B are independent events, $P(A|B) = P(A)$ and $P(B|A) = P(B)$. It follows that the joint probability of two independent events is simply the product of the probabilities of the two events. We can express this as a special form of the multiplication rule.

Multiplication Rule for Independent Events

The joint probability of any two independent events A and B is

$$P(A \text{ and } B) = P(A)P(B)$$

EXAMPLE 5.5

Selecting Two Students without Replacement

A graduate statistics course has seven male and three female students. The professor wants to select two students at random to help her conduct a research project. What is the probability that the two students chosen are female?

SOLUTION

Let A represent the event that the first student chosen is female and B represent the event that the second student chosen is also female. We want the joint probability $P(A \text{ and } B)$. Consequently, we apply the multiplication rule:

$$P(A \text{ and } B) = P(A)P(B|A)$$

Because there are 3 female students in a class of 10, the probability that the first student chosen is female is

$$P(A) = 3/10$$

After the first student is chosen, only nine students are left. Given that the first student chosen was female, only two female students are left. It follows that

$$P(B|A) = 2/9$$

Thus, the joint probability is

$$P(A \text{ and } B) = P(A)P(B|A) = \left(\frac{3}{10}\right)\left(\frac{2}{9}\right) = \frac{6}{90} = .067$$

EXAMPLE 5.6

Selecting Two Students with Replacement

Refer to Example 5.5. The professor who teaches the course is suffering from the flu and will be unavailable for two classes. The professor's replacement will teach the next two classes. His style is to select one student at random and pick on him or her to answer questions during that class. What is the probability that the two students chosen are female?

SOLUTION

The form of the question is the same as in Example 5.5. We wish to compute the probability of choosing two female students. However, the experiment is slightly different. It is now possible to choose the *same* student in each of the two classes the replacement teaches. Thus, A and B are independent events, and we apply the multiplication rule for independent events:

$$P(A \text{ and } B) = P(A)P(B)$$

The probability of choosing a female student in each of the two classes is the same; that is,

$$P(A) = 3/10 \text{ and } P(B) = 3/10$$

Hence,

$$P(A \text{ and } B) = P(A)P(B) = \left(\frac{3}{10}\right)\left(\frac{3}{10}\right) = \frac{9}{100} = .09$$

5-3c Addition Rule

The **addition rule** enables us to calculate the probability of the union of two events.

Addition Rule

The probability that event A, or event B, or both occur is

$$P(A \text{ or } B) = P(A) + P(B) - P(A \text{ and } B)$$

If you're like most students, you're wondering why we subtract the joint probability from the sum of the probabilities of A and B. To understand why this is necessary, examine Table 5.2 (page 69), which we have reproduced here as Table 5.3.

Table 5.3 Joint and Marginal Probabilities

	B_1	B_2	Totals
A_1	$P(A_1 \text{ and } B_1) = .11$	$P(A_1 \text{ and } B_2) = .29$	$P(A_1) = .40$
A_2	$P(A_2 \text{ and } B_1) = .06$	$P(A_2 \text{ and } B_2) = .54$	$P(A_2) = .60$
Totals	$P(B_1) = .17$	$P(B_2) = .83$	1.00

© Cengage Learning

This table summarizes how the marginal probabilities were computed. For example, the marginal probability of A_1 and the marginal probability of B_1 were calculated as

$$P(A_1) = P(A_1 \text{ and } B_1) + P(A_1 \text{ and } B_2) = .11 + .29$$
$$= .40$$
$$P(B_1) = P(A_1 \text{ and } B_1) + P(A_2 \text{ and } B_1) = .11 + .06$$
$$= .17$$

If we now attempt to calculate the probability of the union of A_1 and B_1 by summing their probabilities, we find

$$P(A_1) + P(B_1) = .11 + .29 + .11 + .06$$

Notice that we added the joint probability of A_1 and B_1 (which is .11) twice. To correct the double counting, we subtract the joint probability from the sum of the probabilities of A_1 and B_1. Thus,

$$P(A_1 \text{ or } B_1) = P(A_1) + P(B_1) - P(A_1 \text{ and } B_1)$$
$$= [.11 + .29] + [.11 + .06] - .11$$
$$= .40 + .17 - .11 = .46$$

This is the probability of the union of A_1 and B_1, which we calculated in Example 5.4 (page 71).

As was the case with the multiplication rule, there is a special form of the addition rule. When two events are mutually exclusive (which means that the two events cannot occur together), their joint probability is 0.

Addition Rule for Mutually Exclusive Events

The probability of the union of two mutually exclusive events A and B is

$$P(A \text{ or } B) = P(A) + P(B)$$

EXAMPLE 5.7

Applying the Addition Rule

In a large city, two newspapers are published, the *Sun* and the *Post*. The circulation departments report that 22% of the city's households have a subscription to the *Sun* and 35% subscribe to the *Post*. A survey reveals that 6% of all households subscribe to both newspapers. What proportion of the city's households subscribe to either newspaper?

SOLUTION

We can express this question as, What is the probability of selecting a household at random that subscribes to the *Sun*, the *Post*, or both? Another way of asking the question is, What is the probability that a randomly selected household subscribes to *at least one* of the newspapers? It is now clear that we seek the probability of the union, and we must apply the addition rule. Let A = the household subscribes to the *Sun* and B = the household subscribes to the *Post*. We perform the following calculation:

$$P(A \text{ or } B) = P(A) + P(B) - P(A \text{ and } B)$$
$$= .22 + .35 - .06 = .51$$

The probability that a randomly selected household subscribes to either newspaper is .51. Expressed as relative frequency, 51% of the city's households subscribe to either newspaper.

5-3d Probability Trees

An effective and simpler method of applying the probability rules is the probability tree, wherein the events in an experiment are represented by lines. The resulting figure resembles a tree, hence the name. We will illustrate the probability tree with several examples, including two that we addressed using the probability rules alone.

In Example 5.5, we wanted to find the probability of choosing two female students, where the two choices had to be different. The tree diagram in Figure 5.1 describes this experiment. Notice that the first two branches represent the two possibilities, female and male students, on the first choice. The second set of branches represents the two possibilities on the second choice. The probabilities of female and male student chosen first are 3/10 and 7/10, respectively. The probabilities for the second set of branches are conditional probabilities based on the choice of the first student selected.

We calculate the joint probabilities by multiplying the probabilities on the linked branches. Thus, the probability of choosing two female students is $P(F \text{ and } F) = (3/10)(2/9) = 6/90$. The remaining joint probabilities are computed similarly.

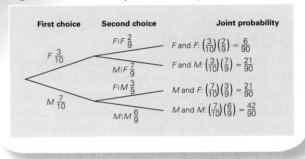

Figure 5.1 Probability Tree for Example 5.5

In Example 5.6, the experiment was similar to that of Example 5.5. However, the student selected on the first choice was returned to the pool of students and was eligible to be chosen again. Thus, the probabilities on the second set of branches remain the same as the probabilities on the first set, and the probability tree is drawn with these changes, as shown in Figure 5.2.

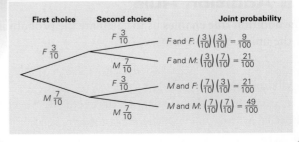

Figure 5.2 Probability Tree for Example 5.6

The advantage of a probability tree on this type of problem is that it restrains its users from making the wrong calculation. Once the tree is drawn and the probabilities of the branches inserted, virtually the only allowable calculation is the multiplication of the probabilities of linked branches. An easy check on those calculations is available. The joint probabilities at the ends of the branches must sum to 1 because all possible events are listed. In both figures notice that the joint probabilities do indeed sum to 1.

The special form of the addition rule for mutually exclusive events can be applied to the joint probabilities. In both probability trees, we can compute the probability that one student chosen is female and one is male simply by adding the joint probabilities. For the tree in Example 5.5, we have

$$P(F \text{ and } M) + P(M \text{ and } F) = 21/90 + 21/90$$
$$= 42/90$$

In the probability tree in Example 5.6, we find

$$P(F \text{ and } M) + P(M \text{ and } F) = 21/100 + 21/100$$
$$= 42/100$$

DIVERSITY INDEX: SOLUTION

Figure 5.3 **Probability Tree Diversity Index**

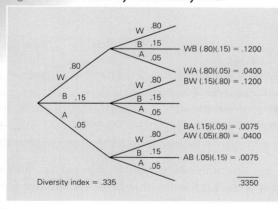

Diversity index = .335

© Cengage Learning

© Glowimages

As we've previously pointed out, the emphasis in this book will be on identifying the correct statistical technique to use. Although it is difficult to offer strict rules on which probability method to use, nevertheless we can provide some general guidelines.

In the examples and exercises in this text (and most other introductory statistics books), the key issue is whether joint probabilities are provided or are required.

5-4a Joint Probabilities Are Given

In Section 5-2, we addressed problems where the joint probabilities were given. In these problems, we can compute marginal probabilities by adding across rows and down columns. We can use the joint and marginal probabilities to compute conditional probabilities, for which a formula is available. This allows us to determine whether the events described by the table are independent or dependent.

We can also apply the addition rule to compute the probability that either of two events occur.

5-4b Joint Probabilities Are Required

The previous section introduced three probability rules and probability trees. We need to apply some or all of these rules in circumstances where one or more joint probabilities are required. We apply the multiplication rule (either by formula or through a probability tree) to calculate the probability of intersections. In some problems we're interested in adding these joint probabilities. We're actually applying the addition rule for mutually exclusive events here. We also frequently use the complement rule.

EXERCISES

5.1 The sample space of the toss of a fair die is

$$S = \{1, 2, 3, 4, 5, 6\}$$

If the die is balanced each simple event has the same probability. Find the probability of the following events.

a. An even number
b. A number less than or equal to 4
c. A number greater than or equal to 5

5.2 Four candidates are running for mayor. The four candidates are Adams, Brown, Collins, and Dalton. Determine the sample space of the results of the election.

5.3 Refer to Exercise 5.2. Employing the subjective approach a political scientist has assigned the following probabilities:

P(Adams wins) = .42
P(Brown wins) = .09
P(Collins wins) = .27
P(Dalton wins) = .22

Determine the probabilities of the following events.

a. Adams loses.
b. Either Brown or Dalton wins.
c. Either Adams, Brown, or Collins wins.

5.4 The manager of a computer store has kept track of the number of computers sold per day. On the basis of this information, the manager produced the following list of the number of daily sales.

Number of Computers Sold	Probability
0	.08
1	.17
2	.26
3	.21
4	.18
5	.10

a. If we define the experiment as observing the number of computers sold tomorrow, determine the sample space.
b. Use set notation to define the event, sell more than 3 computers.
c. What is the probability of selling 5 computers?
d. What is the probability of selling 2, 3, or 4 computers?
e. What is the probability of selling 6 computers?

5.5 Discrimination in the workplace is illegal and companies that do so are often sued. The female instructors at a large university recently lodged a complaint about the most recent round of promotions from assistant professor to associate professor. An analysis of the relationship between gender and promotion produced the following joint probabilities.

	Promoted	Not Promoted
Female	.03	.12
Male	.17	.68

a. What is the rate of promotion among female assistant professors?
b. What is the rate of promotion among male assistant professors?
c. Is it reasonable to accuse the university of gender bias?

5.6 A department store analyzed its most recent sales and determined the relationship between the way the customer paid for the item and the price category of the item. The joint probabilities in the following table were calculated.

	Cash	Credit Card	Debit Card
Under $20	.09	.03	.04
$20–$100	.05	.21	.18
Over $100	.03	.23	.14

a. What proportion of purchases was paid by debit card?
b. Find the probability that a credit card purchase was over $100.
c. Determine the proportion of purchases made by credit card or by debit card.

5.7 The following table lists the probabilities of unemployed females and males and their educational attainment.

	Female	Male
Less than high school	.077	.110
High school graduate	.154	.201
Some college/university-no degree	.141	.129
College/university graduate	.092	.096

Source: *Statistical Abstract of the United States*, 2009, Table 607.

a. If one unemployed person is selected at random, what is the probability that he or she did not finish high school?
b. If an unemployed female is selected at random, what is the probability that she has a college or university degree?
c. If an unemployed high school graduate is selected at random, what is the probability that he is a male?

5.8 A restaurant chain routinely surveys customers and among other questions asks each customer whether he or she would return and to rate the quality of food. Summarizing hundreds of thousands of questionnaires produced this table of joint probabilities.

Rating	Customer Will Return	Customer Will Not Return
Poor	.02	.10
Fair	.08	.09
Good	.35	.14
Excellent	.20	.02

a. What proportion of customers say that they will return and rate the restaurant's food as good?
b. What proportion of customers who say that they will return rate the restaurant's food as good?
c. What proportion of customers who rate the restaurant's food as good say that they will return?
d. Discuss the differences in your answers to parts (a), (b), and (c).

5.9 The issue of health-care coverage in the United States is becoming a critical issue in American politics. A large-scale study was undertaken to determine who is and is not covered. From this study the following table of joint probabilities was produced.

Age Category	Has Health Insurance	Does Not Have Health Insurance
25–34	.167	.085
35–44	.209	.061
45–54	.225	.049
55–64	.177	.026

Source: U.S. Department of Health and Human Services.

If one person is selected at random, find the following probabilities.

a. P(Person has health insurance)
b. P(Person 55–64 has no health insurance)
c. P(Person without health insurance is between 25 and 34 years old)

5.10 A firm has classified its customers in two ways: (1) according to whether the account is overdue and (2) whether the account is new (less than 12 months) or old. An analysis of the firm's records provided the input for the following table of joint probabilities.

	Overdue	Not Overdue
New	.06	.13
Old	.52	.29

One account is randomly selected.

a. If the account is overdue, what is the probability that it is new?
b. If the account is new, what is the probability that it is overdue?
c. Is the age of the account related to whether it is overdue? Explain.

5.11 An aerospace company has submitted bids on two separate federal government defense contracts. The company president believes that there is a 40% probability of winning the first contract. If they win the first contract, the probability of winning the second is 70%. However, if they lose the first contract, the president thinks that the probability of winning the second contract decreases to 50%.

a. What is the probability that they win both contracts?
b. What is the probability that they lose both contracts?
c. What is the probability that they win only one contract?

5.12 A foreman for an injection-molding firm admits that on 10% of his shifts, he forgets to shut off the injection machine on his line. This causes the machine to overheat, increasing the probability from 2% to 20% that a defective molding will be produced during the early morning run. What proportion of moldings from the early morning run is defective?

5.13 A study undertaken by the Miami–Dade Supervisor of Elections revealed that 44% of registered voters are Democrats, 37% are Republicans, and 19% are others. If two registered voters are selected at random, what is the probability that both of them have the same party affiliation?

5.14 The chartered financial analyst (CFA) is a designation earned after taking three annual exams (CFA I, II, and III). The exams are taken in early June. Candidates who pass an exam are eligible to take the exam for the next level in the following year. The pass rates for levels I, II, and III are .57, .73, and .85, respectively. Suppose that 3,000 candidates take the level I exam, 2,500 take the level II exam, and 2,000 take the level III exam. Suppose that one student is selected at random. What is the probability that he or she has passed the exam? (Source: Institute of Financial Analysts)

5.15 The Nickels restaurant chain regularly conducts surveys of its customers. Respondents are asked to assess food quality, service, and price. The responses are

    Excellent   Good   Fair

They are also asked whether they would come back. After analyzing the responses, an expert in probability determined that 87% of customers say that they will return. Of those who so indicate, 57% rate the restaurant as excellent, 36% rate it as good, and the remainder rate it as fair. Of those who say that they won't return, the probabilities are 14%, 32%, and 54%, respectively. What proportion of customers rate the restaurant as good?

5.16 A financial analyst estimates that the probability that the economy will experience a recession in the next 12 months is 25%. She also believes that if the economy encounters a recession, the probability that her mutual fund will increase in value is 20%. If there is no recession, the probability that the mutual fund will increase in value is 75%. Find the probability that the mutual fund's value will increase.

5.17 The effect of an antidepressant drug varies from person to person. Suppose that the drug is effective on 80% of women and 65% of men. It is known that 66% of the people who take the drug are women. What is the probability that the drug is effective?

5.18 A telemarketer sells magazine subscriptions over the telephone. The probability of a busy signal or no answer is 65%. If the telemarketer does make contact, the probability of 0, 1, 2, or 3 magazine subscriptions sold is .5, .25, .20, and .05, respectively. Find the probability that in one call she sells no magazines.

5.19 A statistics professor believes that there is a relationship between the number of missed classes and the grade on his midterm test. After examining his records, he produced the following table of joint probabilities.

	Student Fails Test	Student Passes Test
Student Misses Fewer than 5 Classes	.02	.86
Student Misses 5 or More Classes	.09	.03

a. What is the pass rate on the midterm test?
b. What proportion of students who miss 5 or more classes passes the midterm test?
c. What proportion of students who miss fewer than 5 classes passes the midterm test?
d. Are the events independent?

5.20 Casino Windsor conducts surveys to determine the opinions of its customers. Among other questions respondents are asked to give their opinion about "Your overall impression of Casino Windsor." The responses are

    Excellent   Good   Average   Poor

In addition, the gender of the respondent is noted. After analyzing the results the following table of joint probabilities was produced.

Rating	Women	Men
Excellent	.27	.22
Good	.14	.10
Average	.06	.12
Poor	.03	.06

a. What proportion of customers rate Casino Windsor as excellent?
b. Determine the probability that a male customer rates Casino Windsor as excellent.
c. Find the probability that a customer who rates Casino Windsor as excellent is a man.
d. Are gender and rating independent? Explain your answer.

5.21 How does level of affluence affect health care? To address one dimension of the problem a group of heart attack victims was selected. Each was categorized as a low-, medium-, or high-income earner. Each was also categorized as having survived or died. A demographer notes that in our society 21% fall into the low-income group, 49% are in the medium-income group, and 30% are in the high-income group. Furthermore, an analysis of heart attack victims reveals that 12% of low-income people, 9% of medium-income people, and 7% of high-income people die of heart attacks. Find the probability that a heart attack victim survives.

5.22 A statistics professor and his wife are planning to take a 2-week vacation in Hawaii, but they can't decide whether to spend 1 week on each of the islands of Maui and Oahu, 2 weeks on Maui, or 2 weeks on Oahu. Placing their faith in random chance, they insert two Maui brochures in one envelope, two Oahu brochures in a second envelope, and one brochure from each island in a third envelope. The professor's wife will select one envelope at random and their vacation schedule will be based on the brochures of the islands so selected. After his wife randomly selects an envelope, the professor removes one brochure from the envelope (without looking at the second brochure) and observes that it is a Maui brochure. What is the probability that the other brochure in the envelope is a Maui brochure? (Proceed with caution; the problem is more difficult than it appears.)

5.23 A union's executive conducted a survey of its members to determine what the membership felt were the important issues to be resolved during upcoming negotiations with management. The results indicate that 74% felt that job security was an important issue, whereas 65% identified pension benefits as an important issue. Of those who felt that pension benefits were important, 60% also felt that job security was an important issue. One member is selected at random.

a. What is the probability that he or she felt that both job security and pension benefits were important?

b. What is the probability that the member felt that at least one of these two issues was important?

CHAPTER 6

Random Variables and Discrete Probability Distributions

objectives

6-1 Random Variables and Probability Distributions

6-2 Binomial Distribution

6-3 Poisson Distribution

HOW MUCH DO YOU EXPECT TO WIN BUYING LOTTERY TICKETS?

It costs one dollar to buy a lottery ticket, which has five prizes. The prizes and the probability that a player wins the prize are listed here. Calculate the expected value of the payoff.

Prize ($)	Probability
1 million	1/10 million
200,000	1/1 million
50,000	1/500,000
10,000	1/50,000
1,000	1/10,000

© Cengage Learning

© thumb/iStockPhoto

In this chapter, we extend the concepts and techniques of probability introduced in Chapter 5. We present random variables and probability distributions, which are essential in the development of statistical inference.

Here is a brief glimpse into the wonderful world of statistical inference. Suppose you flip a coin 100 times and count the number of heads. The objective is to determine whether we can infer from the count that the coin is not balanced. It is reasonable to believe that observing a large number of heads (say, 90) or a small number (say, 15) would be a statistical indication of an unbalanced coin. However, where do we draw the line? At 75 or 65 or 55? Without knowing the probability of the frequency of the number of heads from a balanced coin, we cannot draw any conclusions from the sample of 100 coin flips.

The concepts and techniques of probability introduced in this chapter will allow us to calculate the probability we seek. As a first step, we introduce random variables and probability distributions.

6-1 Random Variables and Probability Distributions

Consider an experiment in which we flip two balanced coins and observe the results. We can represent the events as

> heads on the first coin and heads on the second coin,
>
> heads on the first coin and tails on the second coin,
>
> tails on the first coin and heads on the second coin, and
>
> tails on the first coin and tails on the second coin.

However, we can list the events in a different way. Instead of defining the events by describing the outcome of each coin, we can count the number of heads (or, if we wish, the number of tails). Thus, the events are now

2 heads

1 heads

1 heads

0 heads

The number of heads is called the **random variable**. We often label the random variable X, and we're interested in the probability of each value of X. Thus, in this illustration the values of X are 0, 1, and 2.

Here is another example. In many parlor games as well as in the game of craps played in casinos, the player tosses two dice. One way of listing the events is to describe the number on the first die and the number on the second die as follows.

1, 1	1, 2	1, 3	1, 4	1, 5	1, 6
2, 1	2, 2	2, 3	2, 4	2, 5	2, 6
3, 1	3, 2	3, 3	3, 4	3, 5	3, 6
4, 1	4, 2	4, 3	4, 4	4, 5	4, 6
5, 1	5, 2	5, 3	5, 4	5, 5	5, 6
6, 1	6, 2	6, 3	6, 4	6, 5	6, 6

However, in almost all games the player is primarily interested in the total. Accordingly, we can list the totals of the two dice instead of the individual numbers.

2	3	4	5	6	7
3	4	5	6	7	8
4	5	6	7	8	9
5	6	7	8	9	10
6	7	8	9	10	11
7	8	9	10	11	12

If we define the random variable X as the total of the two dice, then X can equal 2, 3, 4, 5, 6, 7, 8, 9, 10, 11, and 12.

Random Variable

A random variable is a function or rule that assigns a number to each outcome of an experiment.

In some experiments, the outcomes are numbers. For example, when we observe the return on an investment or measure the amount of time to assemble a computer, the experiment produces events that are numbers. Simply stated, the value of a random variable is a numerical event.

There are two types of random variables: discrete and continuous. A **discrete random variable** is one that can take on a countable number of values. For example, if we define X as the number of heads observed in an experiment that flips a coin 10 times, the values of X are 0, 1, 2, . . . 10. The variable X can assume a total of 11 values. Obviously, we counted the number of values; hence X is discrete.

A **continuous random variable** is one whose values are uncountable. An excellent example of a continuous random variable is the amount of time to complete a task. For example, let $X =$ time to write a statistics exam in a university where the time limit is 3 hours and students cannot leave before 30 minutes. The smallest value of X is 30 minutes. If we attempt to count the number of values that X can take on, we need to identify the next value. Is it 30.1 minutes? 30.01 minutes? 30.001 minutes? None of these is the second possible value of X because there exist numbers larger than 30 and smaller than 30.001. It becomes clear that we cannot identify the second, or third, or any other values of X (except for the largest value 180 minutes). Thus, we cannot count the number of values, and X is continuous.

A **probability distribution** is a table, formula, or graph that describes the values of a random variable and the probability associated with these values. We will address discrete probability distributions in the rest of this chapter and cover continuous distributions in Chapter 7.

As we noted above, an uppercase letter will represent the *name* of the random variable, usually X. Its lowercase counterpart will represent the value of the random variable. Thus, we represent the probability that the random variable X will equal x as

$$P(X = x)$$

or more simply

$$P(x)$$

6-1a Discrete Probability Distributions

The probabilities of the values of a discrete random variable may be derived by means of probability tools such as tree diagrams or by applying one of the definitions of probability. However, two fundamental requirements apply as stated in the box.

Requirements for a Distribution of a Discrete Random Variable

1. $0 \leq P(x) \leq 1$ for all x
2. $\displaystyle\sum_{\text{all } x} P(x) = 1$

where the random variable can assume values x and $P(x)$ is the probability that the random variable is equal to x.

These requirements are equivalent to the rules of probability provided in Chapter 5. To illustrate, consider the following example.

EXAMPLE 6.1

Probability Distribution of Persons per Household

The *Statistical Abstract of the United States* is published annually. It contains a wide variety of information based on the census as well as other sources. The objective is to provide information about a variety of different aspects of the lives of the country's residents. One of the questions asks households to report the number of persons living in the household. The following table summarizes the data. Develop the probability distribution of the random variable defined as the number of persons per household.

Number of Persons	Number of Households (Millions)
1	31.1
2	38.6
3	18.8
4	16.2
5	7.2
6	2.7
7 or more	1.4
Total	116.0

Source: *Statistical Abstract of the United States*, 2009, Table 61.

SOLUTION

The probability of each value of X, the number of persons per household, is computed as the relative frequency. We divide the frequency for each value of X by the total number of households, producing the following probability distribution.

x	$P(x)$
1	31.1/116.0 = .268
2	38.6/116.0 = .333
3	18.8/116.0 = .162
4	16.2/116.0 = .140
5	7.2/116.0 = .062
6	2.7/116.0 = .023
7 or more	1.4/116.0 = .012
Total	1.000

© Cengage Learning

As you can see, the requirements are satisfied. Each probability lies between 0 and 1, and the total is 1.

We interpret the probabilities in the same way we did in Chapter 5. For example, if we select one household at random, the probability that it has three persons is

$$P(3) = .162$$

We can also apply the addition rule for mutually exclusive events. (The values of X are mutually exclusive; a household can have 1, 2, 3, 4, 5, 6, or

7 or more persons.) The probability that a randomly selected household has four or more persons is

$$P(X \geq 4) = P(4) + P(5) + P(6) + P(7 \text{ or more})$$
$$= .140 + .062 + .023 + .012 = .237$$

In Example 6.1, we calculated the probabilities using census information about the entire population. The next example illustrates the use of the techniques introduced in Chapter 5 to develop a probability distribution.

EXAMPLE 6.2

Probability Distribution of the Number of Sales

A mutual fund salesperson has arranged to call on three people tomorrow. Based on past experience, the salesperson knows that there is a 20% chance of closing a sale on each call. Determine the probability distribution of the number of sales the salesperson will make.

SOLUTION

We can use the probability rules and trees introduced in Section 5-3. Figure 6.1 displays the probability tree for this example. Let $X =$ the number of sales.

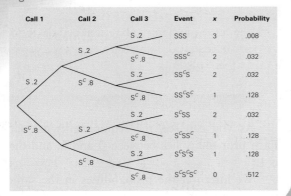

Figure 6.1

The tree exhibits each of the eight possible outcomes and their probabilities. We see that there is one outcome that represents no sales, and its probability is $P(0) = .512$. There are three outcomes

representing one sale, each with probability .128, so we add these probabilities. Thus,

$$P(1) = .128 + .128 + .128 = 3(.128) = .384$$

The probability of two sales is computed similarly:

$$P(X) = 3(.032) = .096$$

There is one outcome where there are three sales:

$$P(3) = .008$$

The probability distribution of X is listed in Table 6.1.

Table 6.1 Probability Distribution of the Number of Sales in Example 6.2

x	P(x)
0	.512
1	.384
2	.096
3	.008

6-1b Probability Distributions and Populations

The importance of probability distributions derives from their use as representatives of populations. In Example 6.1, the distribution provided us with information about the population of numbers of persons per household.

Describing the Population/ Probability Distribution

In Chapter 3, we showed how to calculate the mean, variance, and standard deviation of a population. The formulas we provided were based on knowing the value of the random variable for each member of the population. For example, if we want to know the mean and variance of annual income of all North American blue-collar workers, we would record each of their incomes and use the formulas introduced in Chapter 3:

$$\mu = \frac{\sum_{i=1}^{N} X_i}{N}$$

$$\sigma^2 = \frac{\sum_{i=1}^{N} (X_i - \mu)^2}{N}$$

where X_1 is the income of the first blue-collar worker, X_2 is the second worker's income, and so on. It is likely

that N equals several million. As you can appreciate, these formulas are seldom used in practical applications because populations are so large. It is unlikely that we would be able to record all the incomes in the population of North American blue-collar workers. However, probability distributions often represent populations. Rather than record each of the many observations in a population, we list the values and their associated probabilities as we did in deriving the probability distribution of the number of persons per household in Example 6.1 and the number of successes in three calls by the salesperson in Example 6.2. These can be used to compute the mean and variance of the population.

The population mean is the weighted average of all of its values. The weights are the probabilities. This parameter is also called the **expected value** of X and is represented by $E(X)$.

Population Mean

$$E(X) = \mu = \sum_{\text{all } x} xP(x)$$

The population variance is calculated similarly. It is the weighted average of the squared deviations from the mean.

6-1c **Population Variance**

$$V(X) = \sigma^2 = \sum_{\text{all } x} (x - \mu)^2 P(x)$$

There is a shortcut calculation that simplifies the calculations for the population variance. This formula is not an approximation; it will yield the same value as the formula above.

Shortcut Calculation for Population Variance

$$V(X) = \sigma^2 = \sum_{\text{all } x} x^2 P(x) - \mu^2$$

The standard deviation is defined as in Chapter 3.

6-1d **Population Standard Deviation**

$$\sigma = \sqrt{\sigma^2}$$

EXAMPLE 6.3

Describing the Population of the Number of Persons per Household

Find the mean, variance, and standard deviation for the population of the number of persons per household in Example 6.1.

SOLUTION

For this example we will assume that the last category is exactly 7 persons. The mean of X is

$$
\begin{aligned}
E(X) = \mu = \sum_{\text{all } x} xP(x) &= 1P(1) + 2P(2) + 3P(3) \\
&\quad + 4P(4) + 5P(5) + 6P(6) + 7P(7) \\
&= 1(.268) + 2(.333) + 3(.162) + 4(.140) \\
&\quad + 5(.062) + 6(.023) + 7(.012) \\
&= 2.513
\end{aligned}
$$

Notice that the random variable can assume integer values only, yet the mean is 2.513.

The variance of X is

$$V(X) = \sigma^2 = \sum_{\text{all } x} (x - \mu)^2 P(x)$$
$$= (1 - 2.513)^2 (.268) + (2 - 2.513)^2 (.333)$$
$$+ (3 - 2.513)^2 (.162) + (4 - 2.513)^2 (.140)$$
$$+ (5 - 2.513)^2 (.062) + (6 - 2.513)^2 (.023)$$
$$+ (7 - 2.513)^2 (.012) = 1.958$$

To demonstrate the shortcut method, we'll use it to recompute the variance:

$$\sum_{\text{all } x} x^2 P(x) = 1^2(.268) + 2^2(.333) + 3^2(.162)$$
$$+ 4^2(.140) + 5^2(.062) + 6^2(.023)$$
$$+ 7^2(.012) = 8.273$$

and

$$\mu = 2.513$$

Thus,

$$\sigma^2 = \sum_{\text{all } x} x^2 P(x) - \mu^2 = 8.273 - (2.513)^2 = 1.958$$

The standard deviation is

$$\sigma = \sqrt{\sigma^2} = \sqrt{1.958} = 1.399$$

These parameters tell us that the mean and standard deviation of the number of persons per household are 2.513 and 1.399, respectively.

HOW MUCH DO YOU EXPECT TO WIN BUYING LOTTERY TICKETS: SOLUTION

The expected value is

$$E(X) = 1 \text{ million}(1/10 \text{ million}) + 200{,}000(1/1 \text{ million})$$
$$+ 50{,}000(1/500{,}000) + 10{,}000(1/50{,}000)$$
$$+ 1000(1/10{,}000)$$
$$= .1 + .2 + .1 + .2 + .1 = .7$$

The expected value of a lottery ticket that costs $1.00 is 70 cents. In the long run, the player loses 30 cents for each lottery ticket purchased.

6-2 Binomial Distribution

Now that we've introduced probability distributions in general, we need to introduce several specific probability distributions. In this section, we present the *binomial distribution*.

The binomial distribution is the result of a *binomial experiment*, which has the following properties.

Binomial Experiment

1. The **binomial experiment** consists of a fixed number of trials. We represent the number of trials by n.

2. Each trial has two possible outcomes. We label one outcome a *success,* and the other a *failure*.

3. The probability of success is p. The probability of failure is $1 - p$.

4. The trials are independent, which means that the outcome of one trial does not affect the outcomes of any other trials.

If properties 2, 3, and 4 are satisfied, then we say that each trial is a **Bernoulli process**. Adding property 1 yields the binomial experiment. The random variable of a binomial experiment is defined as the number of successes in the n trials. It is called the **binomial random variable**. Here are three examples of binomial experiments.

1. Flip a coin 10 times. The two outcomes per trial are heads and tails. The terms *success* and *failure* are arbitrary. We can label either outcome success. However, we generally call success anything we're looking for. For example, if we were betting on heads, we would label heads a success. If the coin is fair, the probability of heads is 50%. Thus, $p = .5$. Finally, we can see that the trials are independent, because the outcome of one coin flip cannot possibly affect the outcomes of other flips.

2. Draw five cards out of a shuffled deck. We can label as success whatever card we seek. For example, if we wish to know the probability of receiving five

clubs, a club is labeled a success. On the first draw, the probability of a club is $13/52 = .25$. However, if we draw a second card without replacing the first card and shuffling, the trials are not independent. To see why, suppose that the first draw is a club. If we draw again without replacement, the probability of drawing a second club is $12/51$, which is not .25. In this experiment, the trials are *not* independent. Hence, this is not a binomial experiment. However, if we replace the card and shuffle before drawing again, the experiment is binomial. Note that in most card games, we do not replace the card, and as a result the experiment is not binomial.

3. A political survey asks 1,500 voters who they intend to vote for in an approaching election. In most elections in the United States, there are only two candidates: the Republican and Democratic nominees. Thus, we have two outcomes per trial. The trials are independent, because the choice of one voter does not affect the choice of other voters. In Canada, and in other countries with a parliamentary system of government, there are usually several candidates in the race. However, we can label a vote for our favored candidate (or the party that is paying us to do the survey) a success and all the others are failures.

As you will discover, the third example is a very common application of statistical inference. The actual value of p is unknown, and the job of the statistics practitioner is to estimate its value. By understanding the probability distribution that uses p, we will be able to develop the statistical tools to estimate p.

6-2a **Binomial Random Variable**

The binomial random variable is the number of successes in the experiment's n trials. It can take on values $0, 1, 2, \ldots n$. Thus, the random variable is discrete. To proceed, we must be capable of calculating the probability associated with each value.

Using a probability tree, we draw a series of branches as depicted in Figure 6.2. The stages represent the outcomes for each of the n trials. At each stage, there are two branches representing success and failure. To calculate the probability that there are X successes in n trials, we note that for each success in the sequence we must multiply by p. And if there are X successes, there must be $n - X$ failures. For each failure in the sequence, we multiply by $1 - p$. Thus, the probability

for each sequence of branches that represent x successes and $n - x$ failures has probability

$$p^x(1 - p)^{n-x}$$

There are a number of branches that yield x successes and $n - x$ failures. For example, there are two ways to produce exactly one success and one failure in two trials: SF and FS. To count the number of branch sequences that produce x successes and $n - x$ failures, we use the combinatorial formula

$$C_x^n = \frac{n!}{x!(n - x)!}$$

where $n! = n(n - 1)(n - 2)\ldots(2)(1)$. For example, $3! = 3(2)(1) = 6$. Incidentally, although it may not appear to be logical, $0! = 1$.

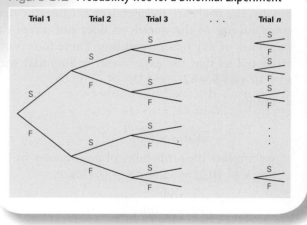

Figure 6.2 **Probability Tree for a Binomial Experiment**

© Cengage Learning

Pulling together the two components of the probability distribution yields the following.

Binomial Probability Distribution

The probability of x successes in a binomial experiment with n trials and probability of success $= p$ is

$$P(x) = \frac{n!}{x!(n - x)!} p^x(1 - p)^{n-x} \text{ for } x = 0, 1, 2, \ldots, n$$

EXAMPLE 6.4

Pat Statsdud and the Statistics Quiz

Pat Statsdud is a student taking a statistics course. Unfortunately, Pat is not a good student. Pat does not read the textbook before class, does not do homework, and regularly misses class. Pat intends to rely on luck to pass the next quiz. The quiz consists of 10 multiple-choice questions. Each question has five possible answers, only one of which is correct. Pat plans to guess the answer to each question.

a. What is the probability that Pat gets no answers correct?

b. What is the probability that Pat gets two answers correct?

SOLUTION

The experiment consists of 10 identical trials, each with two possible outcomes and where success is defined as a correct answer. Because Pat intends to guess, the probability of success is 1/5 or .2. Finally, the trials are independent because the outcome of any of the questions does not affect the outcomes of any other questions. These four properties tell us that the experiment is binomial with $n = 10$ and $p = .2$.

a. From

$$P(x) = \frac{n!}{x!(n - x)!} p^x(1 - p)^{n-x}$$

we produce the probability of no successes by letting $n = 10$, $p = .2$, and $x = 0$. Hence,

$$P(0) = \frac{10!}{0!(10 - 0)!} (.2)^0(1 - .2)^{10-0}$$

The combinatorial part of the formula is $\frac{10!}{0!10!}$, which is 1. This is the number of ways to get 0 correct and 10 incorrect. Obviously, there is only one way to produce $X = 0$. And because $(.2)^0 = 1$,

$$P(X = 0) = 1(1)(.8)^{10} = .1074$$

b. The probability of two correct answers is computed similarly by substituting $n = 10$, $p = .2$, and $x = 2$:

$$P(x) = \frac{n!}{x!(n - x)!} p^x(1 - p)^{n-x}$$

$$P(0) = \frac{10!}{2!(10 - 2)!} (.2)^2(1 - .2)^{10-2}$$

$$= \frac{(10)(9)(8)(7)(6)(5)(4)(3)(2)(1)}{(2)(1)(8)(7)(6)(5)(4)(3)(2)(1)} (.04)(.1678)$$

$$= 45(.006712)$$

$$= .3020$$

In this calculation, we discovered that there are 45 ways to get exactly two correct and eight incorrect answers, and that each such outcome has probability .006712. Multiplying the two numbers produces a probability of .3020.

6-2b Cumulative Probability

The formula of the binomial distribution allows us to determine the probability that X equals individual values. In Example 6.4, the values of interest were 0 and 2. There are many circumstances in which we wish to find the probability that a random variable is less than or equal to a value. In other words, we want to determine $P(X \leq x)$, where x is that value. Such a probability is called a **cumulative probability**.

EXAMPLE 6.5
Will Pat Fail the Quiz?

Find the probability that Pat fails the quiz. A mark is considered a failure if it is less than 50%.

SOLUTION

In this quiz, a mark of less than 5 is a failure. Because the marks must be integers, a mark of 4 or less is a failure. We wish to determine $P(X \leq 4)$. So,

$$P(X \leq 4) = P(0) + P(1) + P(2) + P(3) + P(4)$$

From Example 6.4, we know $P(0) = .1074$ and $P(2) = .3020$. Using the binomial formula, we find $P(1) = .2684$, $P(3) = .2013$, and $P(4) = .0881$. Thus,

$$P(X \leq 4) = .1074 + .2684 + .3020 + .2013$$
$$+ .0881$$
$$= .9672$$

There is a 96.72% probability that Pat will fail the quiz by guessing the answer for each question.

6-2c Binomial Table

There is another way to determine binomial probabilities. Table 1 in Appendix B provides cumulative binomial probabilities for selected values of n and p. We can use this table to answer the question in Example 6.5 where we need $P(X \leq 4)$. Refer to Table 1, find $n = 10$, and then find $p = .20$ in that table. The values in that column are $P(X \leq x)$ for $x = 0, 1, 2, \ldots, 10$, which are shown in Table 6.2.

Table 6.2 Cumulative Binomial Probabilities with $n = 10$ and $p = .2$

x	P(X ≤ x)
0	.1074
1	.3758
2	.6778
3	.8791
4	.9672
5	.9936
6	.9991
7	.9999
8	1.000
9	1.000
10	1.000

© Cengage Learning

The first cumulative probability is $P(X \leq 0)$, which is $P(0) = .1074$. The probability we need for Example 6.5 is $P(X \leq 4) = .9672$, which is the same value we obtained manually.

We can use the table and the complement rule to determine probabilities of the type $P(X \geq x)$. For example, to find the probability that Pat will pass the quiz, we note that

$$P(X \leq 4) + P(X \geq 5) = 1$$

Thus,

$$P(X \geq 5) = 1 - P(X \leq 4) = 1 - .9672 = .0328$$

Using Table 1 to Find the Binomial Probability $P(X \geq x)$

$$P(X \geq x) = 1 - P(X \leq [x - 1])$$

The table is also useful in determining the probability of an individual value of X. For example, to find the probability that Pat will get exactly two right answers we note that

$$P(X \leq 2) = P(0) + P(1) + P(2)$$

and

$$P(X \leq 1) = P(0) + P(1)$$

The difference between these two cumulative probabilities is $p(2)$. Thus,

$$P(2) = P(X \leq 2) - P(X \leq 1) = .6778 - .3758$$
$$= .3020$$

Using Table 1 to Find the Binomial Probability $P(X = x)$

$$P(x) = P(X \leq x) - P(X \leq [x - 1])$$

6-2d Using the Computer

● Excel

INSTRUCTIONS

Type the following into any empty cell.

`=BINOMDIST([x], [n], [p], [True] or [False])`

Typing "True" calculates a cumulative probability, and typing "False" computes the probability of an individual value of X. For Example 6.4a type

`=BINOMDIST(0, 10, .2, False)`

For Example 6.5, enter

`=BINOMDIST(4, 10, .2, True)`

● Minitab

INSTRUCTIONS

This is the first of six probability distributions for which we provide instructions. All work in the same way. Click **Calc**, **Probability Distributions**, and the specific distribution whose probability you wish to compute. In this case, select **Binomial. . . .** Check either **Probability** or **Cumulative probability**. If you wish to make a probability statement about one value of x, specify **Input constant** and type the value of x.

If you wish to make probability statements about several values of x from the same binomial distribution, type the values of x into a column before checking **Calc**. Choose **Input column** and type the name of the column. Finally, enter the components of the distribution. For the binomial, enter the **Number of trials** n and the **Event Probability** p.

6-2e Mean and Variance of a Binomial Distribution

Statisticians have developed general formulas for the mean, variance, and standard deviation of a binomial random variable. They are

$$\mu = np$$
$$\sigma^2 = np(1 - p)$$
$$\sigma = \sqrt{np(1 - p)}$$

EXAMPLE 6.6

Pat Statsdud Has Been Cloned!

Suppose that a professor has a class full of students like Pat (a nightmare!). What is the mean mark? What is the standard deviation?

SOLUTION

The mean mark for a class of Pat Statsduds is

$$\mu = np = 10(.2) = 2$$

The standard deviation is

$$\sigma = \sqrt{np(1 - p)} = \sqrt{10(.2)(1 - .2)} = 1.26$$

6-3 Poisson Distribution

Another useful discrete probability distribution is the **Poisson distribution**, named after its French creator. Like the binomial random variable, the **Poisson random variable** is the number of occurrences of events, which we'll continue to call *successes*. The difference between the two random variables is that a binomial random variable is the number of successes in a set number of trials, whereas a Poisson random variable is the number of successes in an interval of time or specific region of space. Here are several examples of Poisson random variables.

1. The number of cars arriving at a service station in 1 hour. (The interval of time is 1 hour.)

2. The number of flaws in a bolt of cloth. (The specific region is a bolt of cloth.)

3. The number of accidents in 1 day on a particular stretch of highway. (The interval is defined by both time, 1 day, and space, the particular stretch of highway.)

The Poisson experiment is described in the box.

Poisson Experiment

A **Poisson experiment** is characterized by the following properties:

1. The number of successes that occur in any interval is independent of the number of successes that occur in any other interval.

2. The probability of a success in an interval is the same for all equal-size intervals.

3. The probability of a success in an interval is proportional to the size of the interval.

4. The probability of more than one success in an interval approaches 0 as the interval becomes smaller.

Poisson Random Variable

The Poisson random variable is the number of successes that occur in a period of time or an interval of space in a Poisson experiment.

There are several ways to derive the probability distribution of a Poisson random variable. However, all are beyond the mathematical level of this book. We simply provide the formula and illustrate how it is used.

Poisson Probability Distribution

The probability that a Poisson random variable assumes a value of x in a specific interval is

$$P(x) = \frac{e^{-\mu}\mu^x}{x!} \qquad \text{for } x = 0, 1, 2, \ldots$$

where μ is the mean number of successes in the interval or region and e is the base of the natural logarithm (approximately 2.71828). Incidentally, the variance of a Poisson random variable is equal to its mean; that is, $\sigma^2 = \mu$.

EXAMPLE 6.7

Probability of the Number of Typographical Errors in Textbooks

A statistics instructor has observed that the number of typographical errors in new editions of textbooks varies considerably from book to book. After some analysis, he concludes that the number of errors is Poisson distributed with a mean of 1.5 per 100 pages. The instructor randomly selects 100 pages of a new book. What is the probability that there are no typographical errors?

SOLUTION

We want to determine the probability that a Poisson random variable with a mean of 1.5 is equal to 0. Using the formula

$$P(x) = \frac{e^{-\mu}\mu^x}{x!}$$

and substituting $x = 0$ and $\mu = 1.5$, we get

$$P(0) = \frac{e^{-1.5}1.5^0}{0!} = \frac{(2.71828)^{-1.5}(1)}{1} = .2231$$

The probability that in the 100 pages selected there are no errors is .2231.

Notice that in Example 6.7 we wanted to find the probability of 0 typographical errors in 100 pages given a mean of 1.5 typos in 100 pages. The next example illustrates how we calculate the probability of events where the intervals or regions do not match.

EXAMPLE 6.8

Probability of the Number of Typographical Errors in 400 Pages

Refer to Example 6.7. Suppose that the instructor has just received a copy of a new statistics book. He notices that there are 400 pages.

a. What is the probability that there are no typos?

b. What is the probability that there are five or fewer typos?

SOLUTION

The specific region that we're interested in is 400 pages. To calculate Poisson probabilities associated with this region, we must determine the mean number of typos per 400 pages. Because the mean is specified as 1.5 per 100 pages, we multiply this figure by 4 to convert to 400 pages. Thus, $\mu = 6$ typos per 400 pages.

a. The probability of no typos is

$$P(0) = \frac{e^{-6}6^0}{0!} = \frac{(2.71828)^{-6}(1)}{1} = .002479$$

b. We want to determine the probability that a Poisson random variable with a mean of 6 is 5 or less—that is, we want to calculate

$$P(X \le 5) = P(0) + P(1) + P(2) + P(3) + P(4) + P(5)$$

To produce this probability we need to compute the six probabilities in the summation.

$$P(0) = .002479$$

$$P(1) = \frac{e^{-\mu}\mu^x}{x!} = \frac{e^{-6}6^1}{1!} = \frac{(2.71828)^{-6}(6)}{1} = .01487$$

$$P(2) = \frac{e^{-\mu}\mu^x}{x!} = \frac{e^{-6}6^2}{2!} = \frac{(2.71828)^{-6}(36)}{2} = .04462$$

$$P(3) = \frac{e^{-\mu}\mu^x}{x!} = \frac{e^{-6}6^3}{3!} = \frac{(2.71828)^{-6}(216)}{6} = .08924$$

$$P(4) = \frac{e^{-\mu}\mu^x}{x!} = \frac{e^{-6}6^4}{4!} = \frac{(2.71828)^{-6}(1296)}{24} = .1339$$

$$P(5) = \frac{e^{-\mu}\mu^x}{x!} = \frac{e^{-6}6^5}{5!} = \frac{(2.71828)^{-6}(7776)}{120} = .1606$$

Thus,

$$\begin{aligned} P(X \le 5) &= .002479 + .01487 + .04462 \\ &\quad + .08924 + .1339 + .1606 \\ &= .4457 \end{aligned}$$

The probability of observing 5 or fewer typos in this book is .4457.

6-3a Poisson Table

As was the case with the binomial distribution, a table is available that makes it easier to compute Poisson probabilities of individual values of x as well as cumulative and related probabilities.

Table 2 in Appendix B provides cumulative Poisson probabilities for selected values of μ. This table makes it easy to find cumulative probabilities like those in Example 6.8, part (b), where we found $P(X \le 5)$.

To do so, find $\mu = 6$ in Table 2. The values in that column are $P(X \le x)$ for $x = 0, 1, 2, \ldots$, which are shown in Table 6.3.

Table 6.3 **Cumulative Poisson Probabilities for $\mu = 6$**

x	P(X ≤ x)
0	.0025
1	.0174
2	.0620
3	.1512
4	.2851
5	.4457
6	.6063
7	.7440
8	.8472
9	.9161
10	.9574
11	.9799
12	.9912
13	.9964
14	.9986
15	.9995
16	.9998
17	.9999
18	1.0000

© Cengage Learning

Theoretically, a Poisson random variable has no upper limit. The table provides cumulative probabilities until the sum is 1.0000 (using four decimal places).

The first cumulative probability is $P(X \leq 0)$, which is $P(0) = .0025$. The probability we need for Example 6.8, part (b), is $P(X \leq 5) = .4457$, which is the same value we obtained manually.

Like Table 1 for binomial probabilities, Table 2 can be used to determine probabilities of the type $P(X \geq x)$. For example, to find the probability that in Example 6.8 there are six or more typos, we note that $P(X \leq 5) + P(X \geq 6) = 1$. Thus,

$$P(X \geq 6) = 1 - P(X \leq 5) = 1 - .4457 = .5543$$

Using Table 2 to Find the Poisson Probability $P(X \geq x)$

$$P(X \geq x) = 1 - P(X \leq [x - 1])$$

We can also use the table to determine the probability of one individual value of X. For example, to find the probability that the book contains exactly 10 typos, we note that

$$P(X \leq 10) = P(0) + P(1) + \cdots + P(9) + P(10)$$

and

$$P(X \leq 9) = P(0) + P(1) + \cdots + P(9)$$

EXERCISES

6.1 The amount of money students earn on their summer jobs is a random variable.

a. What are the possible values of this random variable?
b. Are the values countable? Explain.
c. Is there a finite number of values? Explain.
d. Is the random variable discrete or continuous? Explain.

6.2 The mark on a statistics exam that consists of 100 multiple-choice questions is a random variable.

a. What are the possible values of this random variable?
b. Are the values countable? Explain.
c. Is there a finite number of values? Explain.
d. Is the random variable discrete or continuous? Explain.

The difference between these two cumulative probabilities is $P(10)$. Thus,

$$P(10) = P(X \leq 10) - P(X \leq 9) = .9574 - .9161$$
$$= .0413$$

Using Table 2 to Find the Poisson Probability $P(X = x)$

$$P(x) = P(X \leq x) - P(X \leq [x - 1])$$

6-3b Using the Computer

Excel

INSTRUCTIONS

Type the following into any empty cell:

    =POISSON([x], [µ], [True] or [False])

We calculate the probability in Example 6.7 by typing

    =POISSON(0, 1.5, False)

For Example 6.8, we type

    =POISSON(5, 6, True)

Minitab

INSTRUCTIONS

Click **Calc**, **Probability Distributions**, and **Poisson . . .**, and type the mean.

6.3 An Internet pharmacy advertises that it will deliver the over-the-counter products that customers purchase in 3 to 6 days. The manager of the company wanted to be more precise in its advertising. Accordingly, she recorded the number of days it took to deliver to customers. From the data, the following probability distribution was developed.

Number of Days	Probability
0	0
1	0
2	.01
3	.04
4	.28
5	.42
6	.21
7	.02
8	.02

a. What is the probability that a delivery will be made within the advertised 3- to 6-day period?
b. What is the probability that a delivery will be late?
c. What is the probability that a delivery will be early?

6.4 The probability that a university graduate will be offered no jobs within a month of graduation is estimated to be 5%. The probability of receiving one, two, and three job offers has similarly been estimated to be 43%, 31%, and 21%, respectively. Determine the following probabilities.

a. A graduate is offered fewer than two jobs.
b. A graduate is offered more than one job.

6.5 The number of pizzas delivered to university students each month is a random variable with the following probability distribution.

X	P(X)
0	.1
1	.3
2	.4
3	.2

a. Find the probability that a student has received delivery of two or more pizzas this month.
b. Determine the mean and variance of the number of pizzas delivered to students each month.

6.6 The manager of a bookstore recorded the number of customers who arrive at a checkout counter every 5 minutes and calculated the following distribution. Calculate the mean and standard deviation of the random variable.

x	P(x)
0	.10
1	.20
2	.25
3	.25
4	.20

6.7 A shopping mall estimates the probability distribution of the number of stores mall customers actually enter, as shown in the table.

x	P(x)
0	.04
1	.19
2	.22
3	.28
4	.12
5	.09
6	.06

Find the mean and standard deviation of the number of stores entered.

6.8 You have been given the choice of receiving $500 in cash or receiving a gold coin that has a face value of $100. However, the actual value of the gold coin depends on its gold content. You are told that the coin has a 40% probability of being worth $400, a 30% probability of being worth $900, and a 30% probability of being worth its face value. Basing your decision on expected value, should you choose the coin?

6.9 The owner of a small firm has just purchased a personal computer, which she expects will serve her for the next 2 years. The owner has been told that she "must" buy a surge suppressor to provide protection for her new hardware against possible surges or variations in the electrical current, which have the capacity to damage the computer. The amount of damage to the computer depends on the strength of the surge. It has been estimated that there is a 1% chance of incurring $400 damage, a 2% chance of incurring $200 damage, and a 10% chance of $100 damage. An inexpensive suppressor, which would provide protection for only one surge can be purchased. How much should the owner be willing to pay if she makes decisions on the basis of expected value?

6.10 A sign on the gas pumps of a chain of gasoline stations encourages customers to have their oil checked, claiming that one out of four cars needs to have oil added. If this is true, what is the probability of the following events?

a. One out of the next four cars needs oil.
b. Two out of the next eight cars need oil.
c. Three out of the next 12 cars need oil.

6.11 The leading brand of dishwasher detergent has a 30% market share. A sample of 25 dishwasher detergent customers was taken. What is the probability that 10 or fewer customers chose the leading brand?

6.12 A student majoring in accounting is trying to decide on the number of firms to which he should apply. Given his work experience and grades, he can expect to receive a job offer from 70% of the firms to which he applies. The student decides to apply to only four firms. What is the probability that he receives no job offers?

6.13 In the United States, voters who are neither Democrat nor Republican are called independent. It is believed that 10% of all voters are independent. A survey asked 25 people to identify themselves as Democrat, Republican, or independent.

a. What is the probability that none of the people are independent?
b. What is the probability that fewer than five people are independent?
c. What is the probability that more than two people are independent?

6.14 Major software manufacturers offer a help line that allows customers to call and receive assistance in solving their problems. However, because of the volume of calls, customers frequently are put on hold. One software manufacturer claims that only 20% of callers are put on hold. Suppose that 100 customers call. What is the probability that more than 25 of them are put on hold?

6.15 A statistics practitioner working for Major League Baseball determined the probability that the hitter will be out on ground balls is .75. In a game where there are 20 ground balls, find the probability that all of them were outs.

6.16 In the game of roulette, a steel ball is rolled onto a wheel that contains 18 red, 18 black, and two green slots. If the ball is rolled 25 times, find the probabilities of the following events.

a. The ball falls into the green slots two or more times.
b. The ball does not fall into any green slots.
c. The ball falls into black slots 15 or more times.
d. The ball falls into red slots 10 or fewer times.

6.17 According to a Gallup Poll conducted March 5–7, 2001, 52% of American adults think that protecting

the environment should be given priority over developing U.S. energy supplies. Thirty-six percent think that developing energy supplies is more important, and 6% believe the two are equally important. The rest had no opinion. Suppose that a sample of 100 American adults is quizzed on the subject. What is the probability of the following events?

a. Fifty or more think that protecting the environment should be given priority.
b. Thirty or fewer think that developing energy supplies is more important.
c. Five or fewer have no opinion.

6.18 According to the U.S. census, one-third of all businesses are owned by women. If we select 25 businesses at random, what is the probability that 10 or more of them are owned by women?

6.19 The final exam in a one-term statistics course is taken in the December exam period. Students who are sick or have other legitimate reasons for missing the exam are allowed to write a deferred exam scheduled for the first week in January. A statistics professor has observed that only 2% of all students legitimately miss the December final exam. Suppose that the professor has 40 students registered this term.

a. How many students can the professor expect to miss the December exam?
b. What is the probability that the professor will not have to create a deferred exam?

6.20 The number of accidents that occur at a busy intersection is Poisson distributed, with a mean of 3.5 per week. Find the probability of the following events.

a. No accidents in one week
b. Five or more accidents in one week
c. One accident today

6.21 Snowfalls occur randomly and independently over the course of winter in a Minnesota city. The average is one snowfall every 3 days.

a. What is the probability of five snowfalls in 2 weeks?
b. Find the probability of a snowfall today.

6.22 In older cities across North America, infrastructure is deteriorating, including water lines that supply homes and businesses. A report to the Toronto city council recorded an average of 30 water-line breaks per 100 kilometers per year in the city of Toronto. Outside of Toronto, the average number of breaks is 15 per 100 kilometers per year.

a. Find the probability that in a stretch of 100 kilometers in Toronto there are 35 or more breaks next year.
b. Find the probability that there are 12 or fewer breaks in a stretch of 100 kilometers outside of Toronto next year.

6.23 The number of bank robberies that occur in a large North American city is Poisson distributed with a mean of 1.8 per day. Find the probabilities of the following events.

a. Three or more bank robberies in a day
b. Between 10 and 15 (inclusive) robberies during a 5-day period

6.24 According to climatologists, the long-term average for Atlantic storms is 9.6 per season (June 1 to November 30), with 6.0 becoming hurricanes and 2.3 becoming intense hurricanes. Find the probability of the following events. (Source: *Globe and Mail*, December 3, 2004.)

a. Ten or more Atlantic storms
b. Five or fewer hurricanes
c. Three or more intense hurricanes

Continuous Probability Distributions

objectives

7-1   Probability Density Functions

7-2   Normal Distribution

7-3   Other Continuous Distributions

MINIMUM GMAT SCORE TO ENTER EXECUTIVE MBA PROGRAM

A university has just approved a new executive MBA Program. The new director believes that the new program must be seen as having high standards to maintain the business school's prestigious image. Accordingly, the faculty council decides that one of the entrance requirements will be that applicants must score in the top 1% of GMAT (Graduate Management Admission Test) scores. The director knows that GMAT scores are normally distributed with a mean of 490 and a standard deviation of 61. The only thing she doesn't know is what the minimum GMAT score for admission should be.

After introducing the normal distribution, we will return to this question and answer it. (See page 107.)

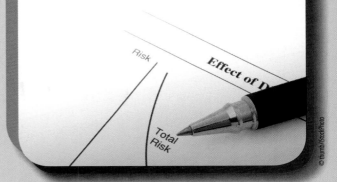

This chapter completes our presentation of probability by introducing continuous random variables and their distributions. In Chapter 6, we introduced discrete probability distributions that are employed to calculate the probability associated with discrete random variables. In Section 6-2, we introduced the binomial distribution, which allows us to determine the probability that the random variable equals a particular value (the number of successes). In this way we connected the population represented by the probability distribution with a sample of nominal data. This chapter introduces continuous probability distributions, which are used to calculate the probability associated with an interval variable. By doing so, we develop the link between a population and a sample of interval data.

Andris Torms/Shutterstock.com

Commercial Eye/Iconica/Getty Images

BSTAT

7-1 Probability Density Functions

A continuous random variable is one that can assume an uncountable number of values. Because this type of random variable is so different from a discrete variable, we need to treat it completely differently. First, we cannot list the possible values because there is an infinite number of them. Second, because there is an infinite number of values, the probability of each individual value is virtually 0. Consequently, we can determine the probability of only a range of values. To illustrate how this is done, consider the histogram we created for the long-distance telephone bills (Example 2.2), which is depicted in Figure 7.1.

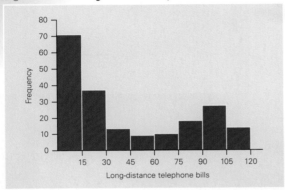

Figure 7.1 **Histogram for Example 2.2**

We found, for example that the relative frequency of the interval 15 to 30 was 37/200. Using the relative frequency approach, we estimate that the probability that a randomly selected long-distance bill will fall between $15 and $30 is 37/200 = .185. We can similarly estimate the probabilities of the other intervals in the histogram.

Interval	Relative Frequency
$0 \leq X \leq 15$	71/200
$15 < X \leq 30$	37/200
$30 < X \leq 45$	13/200
$45 < X \leq 60$	9/200
$60 < X \leq 75$	10/200
$75 < X \leq 90$	18/200
$90 < X \leq 105$	28/200
$105 < X \leq 120$	14/200

Notice that the sum of the probabilities equals 1. To proceed, we set the values along the vertical axis so that the *area* in all the rectangles together adds to 1. We accomplish this by dividing each relative frequency by the width of the interval, which is 15. The result is a rectangle over each interval whose *area* equals the probability that the random variable will fall into that interval.

To determine probabilities of ranges other than the ones created when we drew the histogram, we apply the same approach. For example, the probability that a long-distance bill will fall between $50 and $80 is equal to the area between 50 and 80 as shown in Figure 7.2.

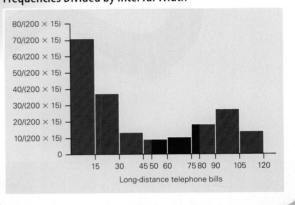

Figure 7.2 **Histogram for Example 2.2: Relative Frequencies Divided by Interval Width**

The areas in each shaded rectangle are calculated and added together as shown in the following table.

Interval	Height of Rectangle	Base Multiplied by Height
$50 < X \leq 60$	$9/(200 \times 15) = .00300$	$(60 - 50) \times .00300 = .030$
$60 < X \leq 75$	$10/(200 \times 15) = .00333$	$(75 - 60) \times .00333 = .050$
$75 < X \leq 80$	$18/(200 \times 15) = .00600$	$(80 - 75) \times .00600 = .030$
		Total = .110

We estimate that the probability that a randomly selected long-distance bill falls between $50 and $80 is .11.

If the histogram is drawn with a large number of small intervals, we can smooth the edges of the rectangles to produce a smooth curve as shown in Figure 7.3. In many cases, it is possible to determine a function $f(x)$ that approximates the curve. The function is called a **probability density function**. Its requirements are stated in the box.

Figure 7.3 **Density Function for Example 2.2**

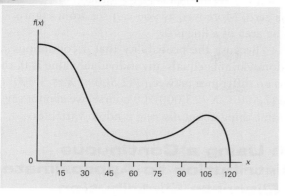

Figure 7.4 **Uniform Distribution**

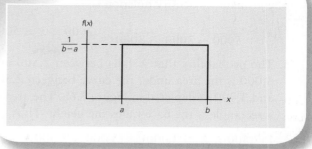

To calculate the probability of any interval, simply find the area under the curve. For example, to find the probability that X falls between x_1 and x_2 determine the area in the rectangle whose base is $x_2 - x_1$ and whose height is $1/(b - a)$. Figure 7.5 depicts the area we wish to find. As you can see, it is a rectangle and the area of a rectangle is found by multiplying the base times the height.

Requirements for a Probability Density Function

The following requirements apply to a probability density function $f(x)$ whose range is $a \le x \le b$.

1. $f(x) \ge 0$ for all x between a and b.

2. The total area under the curve between a and b is 1.0.

Integral calculus can often be used to calculate the area under a curve. Fortunately, the probabilities corresponding to continuous probability distributions that we deal with do not require this mathematical tool. The distributions will be either simple or too complex for calculus. Let's start with the simplest continuous distribution.

7-1a Uniform Distribution

To illustrate how we find the area under the curve that describes a probability density function, consider the **uniform probability distribution**, which is also called the **rectangular probability distribution**.

Uniform Probability Density Function

The uniform distribution is described by the function

$$f(x) = \frac{1}{b - a} \text{ where } a \le x \le b$$

The function is graphed in Figure 7.4. You can see why the distribution is called *rectangular*.

Figure 7.5 $P(x_1 < X < x_2)$

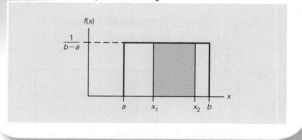

Thus,

$$P(x_1 < X < x_2) = \text{base} \times \text{height} = (x_2 - x_1) \times \frac{1}{b - a}$$

EXAMPLE 7.1

Uniformly Distributed Gasoline Sales

The amount of gasoline sold daily at a service station is uniformly distributed with a minimum of 2,000 gallons and a maximum of 5,000 gallons.

a. Find the probability that daily sales will fall between 2,500 and 3,000 gallons.

b. What is the probability that the service station will sell at least 4,000 gallons?

c. What is the probability that the station will sell exactly 2,500 gallons?

SOLUTION

The probability density function is

$$f(x) = \frac{1}{5000 - 2000} = \frac{1}{3000} \qquad 2000 \le x \le 5000$$

a. The probability that X falls between 2,500 and 3,000 is the area under the curve between 2,500 and 3,000 as depicted in Figure 7.6a. The area of a rectangle is the base times the height. Thus,

$$P(2{,}500 \le X \le 3{,}000) = (3{,}000 - 2{,}500)$$
$$\times \left(\frac{1}{3{,}000}\right)$$
$$= .1667$$

b. $P(X \ge 4{,}000) = (5{,}000 - 4{,}000)$
$$\times \left(\frac{1}{3{,}000}\right)$$
$$= .3333$$

[See Figure 7.6(b).]

c. $P(X = 2{,}500) = 0$

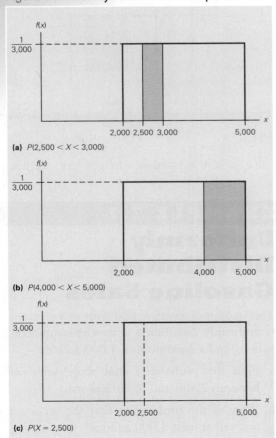

Figure 7.6 **Density Functions for Example 7.1**

(a) $P(2{,}500 < X < 3{,}000)$

(b) $P(4{,}000 < X < 5{,}000)$

(c) $P(X = 2{,}500)$

Because there is an uncountable infinite number of values of X, the probability of each individual value is zero. Moreover, as you can see from Figure 7.6c, the area of a line is 0.

Because the probability that a continuous random variable equals any individual value is 0, there is no difference between $P(2{,}500 \le X \le 3{,}000)$ and $P(2{,}500 < X < 3{,}000)$. Of course, we cannot say the same thing about discrete random variables.

7-1b Using a Continuous Distribution to Approximate a Discrete Distribution

In our definition of discrete and continuous random variables, we distinguish between them by noting whether the number of possible values is countable or uncountable. However, in practice, we frequently use a continuous distribution to approximate a discrete one when the number of values the variable can assume is countable but large. For example, the number of possible values of weekly income is countable. The values of weekly income expressed in dollars are 0, .01, .02, ... Although there is no set upper limit we can easily identify (and thus, count) all the possible values. Consequently, weekly income is a discrete random variable. However, because it can assume such a large number of values, we prefer to employ a continuous probability distribution to determine the probability associated with such variables. In the next section, we introduce the normal distribution, which is often used to describe discrete random variables that can assume a large number of values.

7-2 Normal Distribution

The **normal distribution** is the most important of all probability distributions because of its crucial role in statistical inference.

Normal Density Function

The probability density function of a **normal random variable** is

$$f(x) = \frac{1}{\sigma\sqrt{2\pi}} e^{-\frac{1}{2}\left(\frac{x-\mu}{\sigma}\right)^2} \qquad -\infty < x < \infty$$

where $e = 2.71828\ldots$ and $\pi = 3.14159\ldots.$

Figure 7.7 depicts a normal distribution. Notice that the curve is symmetric about its mean, and the random variable ranges between $-\infty$ and $+\infty$.

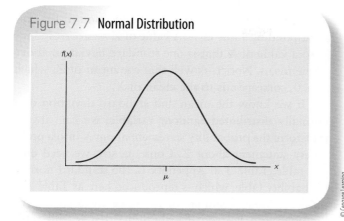

Figure 7.7 **Normal Distribution**

The normal distribution is described by two parameters, the mean μ and the standard deviation σ. In Figure 7.8, we demonstrate the effect of changing the value of μ. Obviously, increasing μ shifts the curve to the right and decreasing μ shifts it to the left.

Figure 7.8 **Normal Distributions with the Same Variance but Different Means**

Figure 7.9 describes the effect of σ. Larger values of σ widen the curve and smaller ones narrow it.

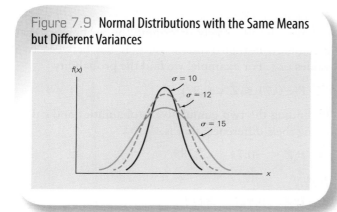

Figure 7.9 **Normal Distributions with the Same Means but Different Variances**

7-2a Calculating Normal Probabilities

To calculate the probability that a normal random variable falls into any interval, we must compute the area in the interval under the curve. Unfortunately, the function is not as simple as the uniform precluding the use of simple mathematics or even integral calculus. Instead we will resort to using a probability table similar to Tables 1 and 2 in Appendix B, which are used to calculate binomial and Poisson probabilities, respectively. Recall that to determine binomial probabilities from Table 1 we needed probabilities for selected values of n and p. Similarly, to find Poisson probabilities we needed probabilities for each value of μ that we chose to include in Table 2. It would appear then that we will need a separate table for normal probabilities for a selected set of values of μ and σ. Fortunately, this won't be necessary. Instead, we reduce the number of tables needed to one by standardizing the random variable. We standardize a random variable by subtracting its mean and dividing by its standard deviation. When the variable is normal, the transformed variable is called a **standard normal random variable** and is denoted by Z—that is,

$$Z = \frac{X - \mu}{\sigma}$$

The probability statement about X is transformed by this formula into a statement about Z. To understand how we proceed, consider the following example.

EXAMPLE 7.2

Normally Distributed Gasoline Sales

At another gas station, suppose the daily demand for regular gasoline is normally distributed with a mean of 1,000 gallons and a standard deviation of 100 gallons. The station manager has just opened the station for business and notes that there is exactly 1,100 gallons of regular gasoline in storage. The next delivery is scheduled later today at the close of business. The manager would like to know the probability that he will have enough regular gasoline to satisfy today's demands.

SOLUTION

The amount of gasoline on hand will be sufficient to satisfy demand if the demand is less than the supply. We label the demand for regular gasoline as X, and we want to find the probability $P(X \leq 1,100)$.

Note that because X is a continuous random variable, we can also express the probability as $P(X < 1,100)$ because the area for $X = 1,100$ is 0.

Figure 7.10 describes a normal curve with mean of 1,000, standard deviation of 100, and the area we want to find.

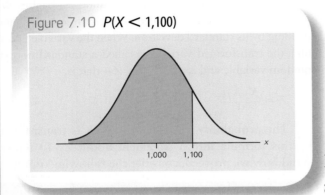

Figure 7.10 $P(X < 1,100)$

The first step is to standardize X. However, if we perform any operations on X, we must perform the same operations on 1,100. Thus,

$$P(X < 1,100) = P\left(\frac{X - \mu}{\sigma} < \frac{1,100 - 1,000}{100}\right)$$
$$= P(Z < 1.00)$$

Figure 7.11 describes the transformation that has taken place. Notice that the variable X was

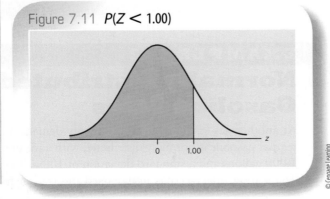

Figure 7.11 $P(Z < 1.00)$

transformed into Z, and 1,100 was transformed into 1.00. However, the area has not changed. In other words, the probability that we wish to compute $P(X < 1,100)$ is identical to $P(Z < 1.00)$.

The values of Z specify the location of the corresponding value of X. A value of $Z = 1$ corresponds to a value of X that is one standard deviation above the mean. Notice as well that the mean of Z, which is 0, corresponds to the mean of X.

If we know the mean and standard deviation of a normally distributed random variable, we can always transform the probability statement about X into a probability statement about Z. Consequently, we need only one table, Table 3 in Appendix B, the standard normal probability table, which is reproduced here as Table 7.1.

This table is similar to the ones we used for the binomial and Poisson distributions; that is, this table lists cumulative probabilities $P(Z < z)$ for values of z ranging from -3.09 to $+3.09$.

To use the table, we simply find the value of z and read the probability. For example, the probability $P(Z < 2.00)$ is found by finding 2.0 in the left margin and under the heading .00 finding .9772. The probability $P(Z < 2.01)$ is found in the same row but under the heading .01. It is .9778.

Returning to Example 7.2, the probability we seek is found in Table 7.1 by finding 1.0 in the left margin. The number to its right under the heading .00 is .8413. See Figure 7.12.

As was the case with Tables 1 and 2, we can also determine the probability that the standard normal random variable is greater than some value of z. For example, we find the probability that Z is greater than 1.80 by determining the probability that Z is less than 1.80 and subtracting that value from 1. Applying the complement rule, we get

$$P(Z > 1.80) = 1 - P(Z < 1.80) = 1 - .9641$$
$$= .0359$$

See Figure 7.13.

We can also easily determine the probability that a standard normal random variable lies between two values of z. For example, we find the probability

$$P(-0.71 < Z < 0.92)$$

By finding the two cumulative probabilities and calculating their difference; that is,

$$P(Z < -0.71) = .2389$$

and

$$P(Z < 0.92) = .8212$$

Table 7.1 Normal Probabilities (Table 3 in Appendix B)

z	0.00	0.01	0.02	0.03	0.04	0.05	0.06	0.07	0.08	0.09
−3.0	0.0013	0.0013	0.0013	0.0012	0.0012	0.0011	0.0011	0.0011	0.0010	0.0010
−2.9	0.0019	0.0018	0.0018	0.0017	0.0016	0.0016	0.0015	0.0015	0.0014	0.0014
−2.8	0.0026	0.0025	0.0024	0.0023	0.0023	0.0022	0.0021	0.0021	0.0020	0.0019
−2.7	0.0035	0.0034	0.0033	0.0032	0.0031	0.0030	0.0029	0.0028	0.0027	0.0026
−2.6	0.0047	0.0045	0.0044	0.0043	0.0041	0.0040	0.0039	0.0038	0.0037	0.0036
−2.5	0.0062	0.0060	0.0059	0.0057	0.0055	0.0054	0.0052	0.0051	0.0049	0.0048
−2.4	0.0082	0.0080	0.0078	0.0075	0.0073	0.0071	0.0069	0.0068	0.0066	0.0064
−2.3	0.0107	0.0104	0.0102	0.0099	0.0096	0.0094	0.0091	0.0089	0.0087	0.0084
−2.2	0.0139	0.0136	0.0132	0.0129	0.0125	0.0122	0.0119	0.0116	0.0113	0.0110
−2.1	0.0179	0.0174	0.0170	0.0166	0.0162	0.0158	0.0154	0.0150	0.0146	0.0143
−2.0	0.0228	0.0222	0.0217	0.0212	0.0207	0.0202	0.0197	0.0192	0.0188	0.0183
−1.9	0.0287	0.0281	0.0274	0.0268	0.0262	0.0256	0.0250	0.0244	0.0239	0.0233
−1.8	0.0359	0.0351	0.0344	0.0336	0.0329	0.0322	0.0314	0.0307	0.0301	0.0294
−1.7	0.0446	0.0436	0.0427	0.0418	0.0409	0.0401	0.0392	0.0384	0.0375	0.0367
−1.6	0.0548	0.0537	0.0526	0.0516	0.0505	0.0495	0.0485	0.0475	0.0465	0.0455
−1.5	0.0668	0.0655	0.0643	0.0630	0.0618	0.0606	0.0594	0.0582	0.0571	0.0559
−1.4	0.0808	0.0793	0.0778	0.0764	0.0749	0.0735	0.0721	0.0708	0.0694	0.0681
−1.3	0.0968	0.0951	0.0934	0.0918	0.0901	0.0885	0.0869	0.0853	0.0838	0.0823
−1.2	0.1151	0.1131	0.1112	0.1093	0.1075	0.1056	0.1038	0.1020	0.1003	0.0985
−1.1	0.1357	0.1335	0.1314	0.1292	0.1271	0.1251	0.1230	0.1210	0.1190	0.1170
−1.0	0.1587	0.1562	0.1539	0.1515	0.1492	0.1469	0.1446	0.1423	0.1401	0.1379
−0.9	0.1841	0.1814	0.1788	0.1762	0.1736	0.1711	0.1685	0.1660	0.1635	0.1611
−0.8	0.2119	0.2090	0.2061	0.2033	0.2005	0.1977	0.1949	0.1922	0.1894	0.1867
−0.7	0.2420	0.2389	0.2358	0.2327	0.2296	0.2266	0.2236	0.2206	0.2177	0.2148
−0.6	0.2743	0.2709	0.2676	0.2643	0.2611	0.2578	0.2546	0.2514	0.2483	0.2451
−0.5	0.3085	0.3050	0.3015	0.2981	0.2946	0.2912	0.2877	0.2843	0.2810	0.2776
−0.4	0.3446	0.3409	0.3372	0.3336	0.3300	0.3264	0.3228	0.3192	0.3156	0.3121
−0.3	0.3821	0.3783	0.3745	0.3707	0.3669	0.3632	0.3594	0.3557	0.3520	0.3483
−0.2	0.4207	0.4168	0.4129	0.4090	0.4052	0.4013	0.3974	0.3936	0.3897	0.3859
−0.1	0.4602	0.4562	0.4522	0.4483	0.4443	0.4404	0.4364	0.4325	0.4286	0.4247
−0.0	0.5000	0.4960	0.4920	0.4880	0.4840	0.4801	0.4761	0.4721	0.4681	0.4641
0.0	0.5000	0.5040	0.5080	0.5120	0.5160	0.5199	0.5239	0.5279	0.5319	0.5359
0.1	0.5398	0.5438	0.5478	0.5517	0.5557	0.5596	0.5636	0.5675	0.5714	0.5753
0.2	0.5793	0.5832	0.5871	0.5910	0.5948	0.5987	0.6026	0.6064	0.6103	0.6141
0.3	0.6179	0.6217	0.6255	0.6293	0.6331	0.6368	0.6406	0.6443	0.6480	0.6517
0.4	0.6554	0.6591	0.6628	0.6664	0.6700	0.6736	0.6772	0.6808	0.6844	0.6879
0.5	0.6915	0.6950	0.6985	0.7019	0.7054	0.7088	0.7123	0.7157	0.7190	0.7224
0.6	0.7257	0.7291	0.7324	0.7357	0.7389	0.7422	0.7454	0.7486	0.7517	0.7549
0.7	0.7580	0.7611	0.7642	0.7673	0.7704	0.7734	0.7764	0.7794	0.7823	0.7852
0.8	0.7881	0.7910	0.7939	0.7967	0.7995	0.8023	0.8051	0.8078	0.8106	0.8133
0.9	0.8159	0.8186	0.8212	0.8238	0.8264	0.8289	0.8315	0.8340	0.8365	0.8389
1.0	0.8413	0.8438	0.8461	0.8485	0.8508	0.8531	0.8554	0.8577	0.8599	0.8621
1.1	0.8643	0.8665	0.8686	0.8708	0.8729	0.8749	0.8770	0.8790	0.8810	0.8830
1.2	0.8849	0.8869	0.8888	0.8907	0.8925	0.8944	0.8962	0.8980	0.8997	0.9015
1.3	0.9032	0.9049	0.9066	0.9082	0.9099	0.9115	0.9131	0.9147	0.9162	0.9177
1.4	0.9192	0.9207	0.9222	0.9236	0.9251	0.9265	0.9279	0.9292	0.9306	0.9319
1.5	0.9332	0.9345	0.9357	0.9370	0.9382	0.9394	0.9406	0.9418	0.9429	0.9441
1.6	0.9452	0.9463	0.9474	0.9484	0.9495	0.9505	0.9515	0.9525	0.9535	0.9545
1.7	0.9554	0.9564	0.9573	0.9582	0.9591	0.9599	0.9608	0.9616	0.9625	0.9633
1.8	0.9641	0.9649	0.9656	0.9664	0.9671	0.9678	0.9686	0.9693	0.9699	0.9706

(continued)

Table 7.1 Normal Probabilities (Table 3 in Appendix B) *(continued)*

z	0.00	0.01	0.02	0.03	0.04	0.05	0.06	0.07	0.08	0.09
1.9	0.9713	0.9719	0.9726	0.9732	0.9738	0.9744	0.9750	0.9756	0.9761	0.9767
2.0	0.9772	0.9778	0.9783	0.9788	0.9793	0.9798	0.9803	0.9808	0.9812	0.9817
2.1	0.9821	0.9826	0.9830	0.9834	0.9838	0.9842	0.9846	0.9850	0.9854	0.9857
2.2	0.9861	0.9864	0.9868	0.9871	0.9875	0.9878	0.9881	0.9884	0.9887	0.9890
2.3	0.9893	0.9896	0.9898	0.9901	0.9904	0.9906	0.9909	0.9911	0.9913	0.9916
2.4	0.9918	0.9920	0.9922	0.9925	0.9927	0.9929	0.9931	0.9932	0.9934	0.9936
2.5	0.9938	0.9940	0.9941	0.9943	0.9945	0.9946	0.9948	0.9949	0.9951	0.9952
2.6	0.9953	0.9955	0.9956	0.9957	0.9959	0.9960	0.9961	0.9962	0.9963	0.9964
2.7	0.9965	0.9966	0.9967	0.9968	0.9969	0.9970	0.9971	0.9972	0.9973	0.9974
2.8	0.9974	0.9975	0.9976	0.9977	0.9977	0.9978	0.9979	0.9979	0.9980	0.9981
2.9	0.9981	0.9982	0.9982	0.9983	0.9984	0.9984	0.9985	0.9985	0.9986	0.9986
3.0	0.9987	0.9987	0.9987	0.9988	0.9988	0.9989	0.9989	0.9989	0.9990	0.9990

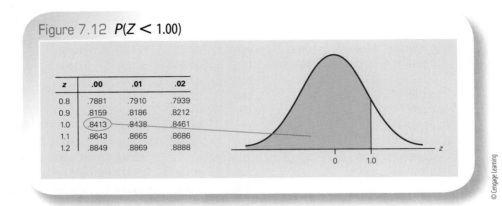

Figure 7.12 $P(Z < 1.00)$

z	.00	.01	.02
0.8	.7881	.7910	.7939
0.9	.8159	.8186	.8212
1.0	.8413	.8438	.8461
1.1	.8643	.8665	.8686
1.2	.8849	.8869	.8888

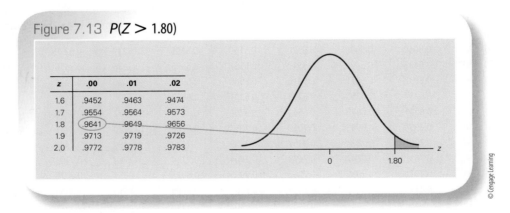

Figure 7.13 $P(Z > 1.80)$

z	.00	.01	.02
1.6	.9452	.9463	.9474
1.7	.9554	.9564	.9573
1.8	.9641	.9649	.9656
1.9	.9713	.9719	.9726
2.0	.9772	.9778	.9783

Hence,

$$P(-0.71 < Z < 0.92) = P(Z < 92) - P(Z < -0.71)$$
$$= .8212 - .2389 = .5823$$

Figure 7.14 depicts this calculation.

Notice that the largest value of z in the table is 3.09, and that $P(Z < 3.09) = .9990$. This means that

$$P(Z > 3.09) = 1 - .9990 = .0010$$

However, because the table lists no values beyond 3.09, we approximate any area beyond 3.10 as 0; that is,

$$P(Z > 3.10) = P(Z < -3.10) \approx 0$$

Recall that in Tables 1 and 2 we were able to use the table to find the probability that X is *equal* to some value of x, but we won't do the same with the normal table. Remember that the normal random variable is

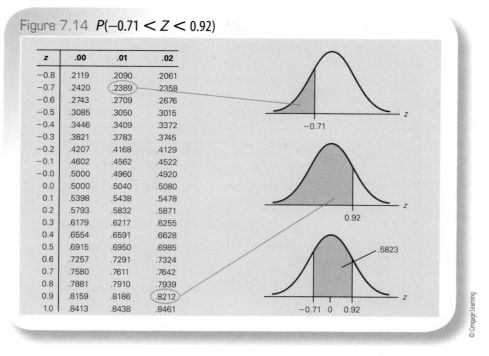

Figure 7.14 $P(-0.71 < Z < 0.92)$

z	.00	.01	.02
−0.8	.2119	.2090	.2061
−0.7	.2420	.2389	.2358
−0.6	.2743	.2709	.2676
−0.5	.3085	.3050	.3015
−0.4	.3446	.3409	.3372
−0.3	.3821	.3783	.3745
−0.2	.4207	.4168	.4129
−0.1	.4602	.4562	.4522
−0.0	.5000	.4960	.4920
0.0	.5000	.5040	.5080
0.1	.5398	.5438	.5478
0.2	.5793	.5832	.5871
0.3	.6179	.6217	.6255
0.4	.6554	.6591	.6628
0.5	.6915	.6950	.6985
0.6	.7257	.7291	.7324
0.7	.7580	.7611	.7642
0.8	.7881	.7910	.7939
0.9	.8159	.8186	.8212
1.0	.8413	.8438	.8461

continuous and the probability that a continuous random variable is equal to any single value is 0.

7-2b Finding Values of Z

There is a family of problems that require us to determine the value of Z given a probability. We use the notation Z_A to represent the value of z such that the area to its right under the standard normal curve is A. In other words, Z_A is a value of a standard normal random variable such that

$$P(Z > Z_A) = A$$

Figure 7.15 depicts this notation.

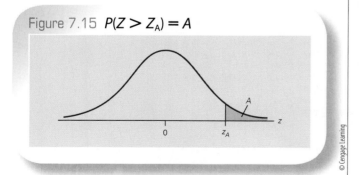

Figure 7.15 $P(Z > Z_A) = A$

To find Z_A for any value of A requires us to use the standard normal table backward. As you saw in Example 7.2, to find a probability about Z, we must find the value of z in the table and determine the probability associated with it. To use the table backward, we need to specify a probability and then determine the z-value associated with it. We'll demonstrate by finding $z_{.025}$. Figure 7.16 depicts the standard normal curve and $z_{.025}$. Because of the format of the standard normal table, we begin by determining the area *less than* $z_{.025}$, which is $1 - .025 = .9750$. (Notice that we expressed this probability with four decimal places to make it easier for you to see what you need to do.) We now search through the probability part of the table looking for .9750. When we locate it, we see that the z-value associated with it is 1.96.

Thus, $z_{.025} = 1.96$, which means that $P(Z > 1.96) = .025$.

EXAMPLE 7.3

Finding $z_{.05}$

Find the value of a standard normal random variable such that the probability that the random variable is greater than it is 5%.

SOLUTION

We wish to determine $z_{.05}$. Figure 7.17 depicts the normal curve and $z_{.05}$. If .05 is the area in the tail, then the probability less than $z_{.05}$ must be $1 - .05 = .9500$. To find $z_{.05}$, we search the table looking for the probability .9500. We don't find this probability, but we find two values that are equally close: .9495 and .9505. The Z-values associated with these probabilities are 1.64 and 1.65, respectively. The average is taken as $z_{.05}$. Thus, $z_{.05} = 1.645$.

Figure 7.16 $Z_{.025}$

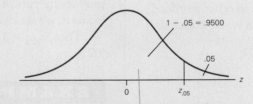

z	.00	.01	.02	.03	.04	.05	.06	.07	.08	.09
1.0	.8413	.8438	.8461	.8485	.8508	.8531	.8554	.8577	.8599	.8621
1.1	.8643	.8665	.8686	.8708	.8729	.8749	.8770	.8790	.8810	.8830
1.2	.8849	.8869	.8888	.8907	.8925	.8944	.8962	.8980	.8997	.9015
1.3	.9032	.9049	.9066	.9082	.9099	.9115	.9131	.9147	.9162	.9177
1.4	.9192	.9207	.9222	.9236	.9251	.9265	.9279	.9292	.9306	.9319
1.5	.9332	.9345	.9357	.9370	.9382	.9394	.9406	.9418	.9429	.9441
1.6	.9452	.9463	.9474	.9484	.9495	.9505	.9515	.9525	.9535	.9545
1.7	.9554	.9564	.9573	.9582	.9591	.9599	.9608	.9616	.9625	.9633
1.8	.9641	.9649	.9656	.9664	.9671	.9678	.9686	.9693	.9699	.9706
1.9	.9713	.9719	.9726	.9732	.9738	.9744	.9750	.9756	.9761	.9767
2.0	.9772	.9778	.9783	.9788	.9793	.9798	.9803	.9808	.9812	.9817
2.1	.9821	.9826	.9830	.9834	.9838	.9842	.9846	.9850	.9854	.9857
2.2	.9861	.9864	.9868	.9871	.9875	.9878	.9881	.9884	.9887	.9890
2.3	.9893	.9896	.9898	.9901	.9904	.9906	.9909	.9911	.9913	.9916
2.4	.9918	.9920	.9922	.9925	.9927	.9929	.9931	.9932	.9934	.9936
2.5	.9938	.9940	.9941	.9943	.9945	.9946	.9948	.9949	.9951	.9952
2.6	.9953	.9955	.9956	.9957	.9959	.9960	.9961	.9962	.9963	.9964
2.7	.9965	.9966	.9967	.9968	.9969	.9970	.9971	.9972	.9973	.9974
2.8	.9974	.9975	.9976	.9977	.9977	.9978	.9979	.9979	.9980	.9981
2.9	.9981	.9982	.9982	.9983	.9984	.9984	.9985	.9985	.9986	.9986
3.0	.9987	.9987	.9987	.9988	.9988	.9989	.9989	.9989	.9990	.9990

Figure 7.17 $Z_{.05}$

z	.00	.01	.02	.03	.04	.05	.06	.07	.08	.09
1.0	.8413	.8438	.8461	.8485	.8508	.8531	.8554	.8577	.8599	.8621
1.1	.8643	.8665	.8686	.8708	.8729	.8749	.8770	.8790	.8810	.8830
1.2	.8849	.8869	.8888	.8907	.8925	.8944	.8962	.8980	.8997	.9015
1.3	.9032	.9049	.9066	.9082	.9099	.9115	.9131	.9147	.9162	.9177
1.4	.9192	.9207	.9222	.9236	.9251	.9265	.9279	.9292	.9306	.9319
1.5	.9332	.9345	.9357	.9370	.9382	.9394	.9406	.9418	.9429	.9441
1.6	.9452	.9463	.9474	.9484	.9495	.9505	.9515	.9525	.9535	.9545
1.7	.9554	.9564	.9573	.9582	.9591	.9599	.9608	.9616	.9625	.9633
1.8	.9641	.9649	.9656	.9664	.9671	.9678	.9686	.9693	.9699	.9706
1.9	.9713	.9719	.9726	.9732	.9738	.9744	.9750	.9756	.9761	.9767
2.0	.9772	.9778	.9783	.9788	.9793	.9798	.9803	.9808	.9812	.9817
2.1	.9821	.9826	.9830	.9834	.9838	.9842	.9846	.9850	.9854	.9857
2.2	.9861	.9864	.9868	.9871	.9875	.9878	.9881	.9884	.9887	.9890
2.3	.9893	.9896	.9898	.9901	.9904	.9906	.9909	.9911	.9913	.9916
2.4	.9918	.9920	.9922	.9925	.9927	.9929	.9931	.9932	.9934	.9936
2.5	.9938	.9940	.9941	.9943	.9945	.9946	.9948	.9949	.9951	.9952
2.6	.9953	.9955	.9956	.9957	.9959	.9960	.9961	.9962	.9963	.9964
2.7	.9965	.9966	.9967	.9968	.9969	.9970	.9971	.9972	.9973	.9974
2.8	.9974	.9975	.9976	.9977	.9977	.9978	.9979	.9979	.9980	.9981
2.9	.9981	.9982	.9982	.9983	.9984	.9984	.9985	.9985	.9986	.9986
3.0	.9987	.9987	.9987	.9988	.9988	.9989	.9989	.9989	.9990	.9990

EXAMPLE 7.4

Finding $-z_{.05}$

Find the value of a standard normal random variable such that the probability that the random variable is less than that value is 5%.

SOLUTION

Because the standard normal curve is symmetric about 0, we wish to find $-z_{.05}$. In Example 7.4, we found $z_{.05} = 1.645$. Thus, $-z_{.05} = -1.645$. See Figure 7.18.

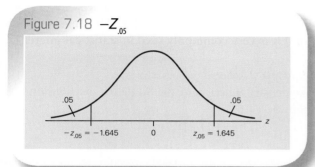

Figure 7.18 $-Z_{.05}$

MINIMUM GMAT SCORE TO ENTER EXECUTIVE MBA PROGRAM: SOLUTION

Figure 7.19 depicts the distribution of GMAT scores. We've labeled the minimum score needed to enter the new MBA Program $X_{.01}$ such that

$$P(X > X_{.01}) = .01$$

Below the normal curve, we depict the standard normal curve and $z_{.01}$. We can determine the value of $z_{.01}$ as we did Example 7.4. In the standard normal table, we find $1 - .01 = .9900$ (its closest value in the table is .9901) and the Z-value 2.33. Thus, the standardized value of $x_{.01}$ is $z_{.01} = 2.33$. To find $x_{.01}$, we must *unstandardize* $z_{.01}$. We do so by solving for $x_{.01}$ in the equation

$$z_{.01} = \frac{X_{.01} - \mu}{\sigma}$$

Substituting $z_{.01} = 2.33$, $\mu = 490$, and $\sigma = 61$, we find

$$2.33 = \frac{X_{.01} - 490}{61}$$

Solving we get

$$x_{.01} = 2.33(61) + 490 = 632.13$$

Rounding up (GMAT scores are integers), we find that the minimum GMAT score to enter the Executive MBA Program is 633.

© Cengage Learning

Figure 7.19 **Minimum GMAT Score**

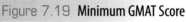

z	.00	.01	.02	.03	.04
1.0	.8413	.8438	.8461	.8485	.8508
1.1	.8643	.8665	.8686	.8708	.8729
1.2	.8849	.8869	.8888	.8907	.8925
1.3	.9032	.9049	.9066	.9082	.9099
1.4	.9192	.9207	.9222	.9236	.9251
1.5	.9332	.9345	.9357	.9370	.9382
1.6	.9452	.9463	.9474	.9484	.9495
1.7	.9554	.9564	.9573	.9582	.9591
1.8	.9641	.9649	.9656	.9664	.9671
1.9	.9713	.9719	.9726	.9732	.9738
2.0	.9772	.9778	.9783	.9788	.9793
2.1	.9821	.9826	.9830	.9834	.9838
2.2	.9861	.9864	.9868	.9871	.9875
2.3	.9893	.9896	.9898	.9901	.9904
2.4	.9918	.9920	.9922	.9925	.9927
2.5	.9938	.9940	.9941	.9943	.9945
2.6	.9953	.9955	.9956	.9957	.9959
2.7	.9965	.9966	.9967	.9968	.9969
2.8	.9974	.9975	.9976	.9977	.9977
2.9	.9981	.9982	.9982	.9983	.9984
3.0	.9987	.9987	.9987	.9988	.9988

© Cengage Learning

7-2c Using the Computer

Excel Instructions

We can use Excel to compute probabilities as well as values of X and Z. To compute cumulative normal probabilities $P(X < x)$, type (in any cell)

$$= \texttt{NORMDIST([X],[\mu],[\sigma],True)}$$

(Typing "True" yields a cumulative probability. Typing "False" will produce the value of the normal density function, a number with little meaning.)

If you type 0 for μ and 1 for σ, you will obtain standard normal probabilities. Alternatively, type **NORMSDIST** instead of **NORMDIST** and enter the value of z.

In Example 7.2, we found $P(X < 1,100) = P(Z < 1.00) = .8413$. To instruct Excel to calculate this probability, we enter

$$\texttt{=NORMDIST(1100, 1000, 100, True)}$$

or

$$\texttt{=NORMSDIST(1.00)}$$

To calculate a value for Z_A, type

$$\texttt{=NORMSINV([1 - A])}$$

In Example 7.4, we would type

$$\texttt{=NORMSINV(.95)}$$

and produce 1.6449. We calculated $Z_{.05} = 1.645$.

To calculate a value of x given the probability $P(X > x) = A$, enter

$$= \texttt{NORMINV([1 - A], } \mu, \sigma\texttt{)}$$

The chapter-opening example would be solved by typing

$$\texttt{=NORMINV(.99, 490, 61)}$$

which yields 632.

Minitab Instructions

We can use Minitab to compute probabilities as well as values of X and Z.

Check **Calc**, **Probability Distributions**, and **Normal . . .** and either **Cumulative probability** [to determine $P(X < x)$] or **Inverse cumulative probability** to find the value of x. Specify the **Mean** and **Standard deviation**.

7-3 Other Continuous Distributions

In this section, we introduce three more continuous distributions which are used extensively in statistical inference.

7-3a Student t Distribution

The Student t distribution was first derived by William S. Gosset in 1908. (Gosset published his findings under the pseudonym "Student" and used the letter t to represent the random variable, hence the **Student t distribution**, which is also called the Student's t distribution.) It is very commonly used in statistical inference.

Student t Density Function

The density function of the Student t distribution is as follows:

$$f(t) = \frac{\Gamma[(\nu + 1)/2]}{\sqrt{\nu\pi}\Gamma(\nu/2)} \left[1 + \frac{t^2}{\nu}\right]^{-(\nu+1)/2}$$

where ν (Greek letter nu) is the parameter of the Student t distribution called the **degrees of freedom**, $\pi = 3.14159$ (approximately), and Γ is the gamma function whose definition is not needed here.

The mean and variance of a Student t random variable are

$$E(t) = 0$$

and

$$V(t) = \frac{\nu}{\nu - 2} \text{ for } \nu > 2$$

Figure 7.20 depicts the Student t distribution. As you can see, this distribution is similar to the standard normal distribution. Both are symmetrical about 0. (Both random variables have a mean of 0.) We describe the Student t distribution as mound shaped, whereas the normal distribution is bell shaped.

Figure 7.20 **Student t Distribution**

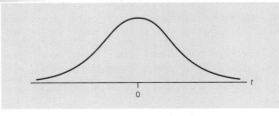

Figure 7.21 shows both a Student t and the standard normal distributions. The former is more widely spread out than the latter. [The variance of a standard normal random variable is 1, whereas the variance of a Student t random variable is $\nu/(\nu - 2)$, which is greater than 1 for all ν.]

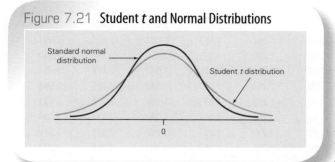

Figure 7.21 **Student t and Normal Distributions**

Figure 7.22 depicts Student t distributions with several different degrees of freedom. Notice that for larger degrees of freedom the Student t distribution's dispersion is smaller. For example, when $\nu = 10$, $V(t) = 1.25$; when $\nu = 50$, $V(t) = 1.042$; and when $\nu = 200$, $V(t) = 1.010$. As ν grows larger, the Student t distribution approaches the standard normal distribution.

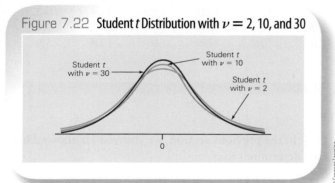

Figure 7.22 **Student t Distribution with $\nu = 2, 10,$ and 30**

Student t Probabilities

For each value of ν (the number of degrees of freedom), there is a different Student t distribution. If we wanted to calculate probabilities of the Student t random variable manually as we did for the normal random variable, then we would need a different table for each ν, which is not practical. Alternatively, we can use Microsoft Excel or Minitab. The instructions are given later in this section.

Determining Student t Values

As you will discover later in this book, the Student t distribution is used extensively in statistical inference. And for inferential methods we often need to find values of the random variable. To determine values of a normal random variable, we used Table 3 backward. Finding values of a Student t random variable is considerably easier. Table 4 in Appendix B (reproduced here as Table 7.2) lists values of $t_{A,\nu}$, which are the values of a Student t random variable with ν degrees of freedom such that

$$P(t > t_{A,\nu}) = A$$

Figure 7.23 depicts this notation.

Observe that $t_{A,\nu}$ is provided for degrees of freedom ranging from 1 to 200 and ∞. To read this table, simply identify the degrees of freedom and find that value or the closest number to it if it is not listed. Then locate the column representing the t_A value you wish. For example, if we want the value of t with 10 degrees of freedom such that the area under the Student t curve is .05, we locate 10 in the first column and move across this row until we locate the number under the heading $t_{.05}$. From Table 7.3, we find

$$t_{.05,10} = 1.812$$

If the number of degrees of freedom is not shown, find its closest value. For example, suppose we wanted to find $t_{.025,32}$. Because 32 degrees of freedom is not listed, we find the closest number of degrees of freedom, which is 30, and use $t_{.025,30} = 2.042$ as an approximation.

Because the Student t distribution is symmetric about 0, the value of t such that the area to its *left* is A, is $-t_{A,\nu}$. For example, the value of t with 10 degrees of freedom such that the area to its left is .05 is

$$-t_{.050,10} = -1.812$$

Notice the last row in the Student t table. The number of degrees of freedom is infinite and the t values are identical (except for the number of decimal places) to the values of z. For example,

$$t_{.10,\infty} = 1.282$$
$$t_{.05,\infty} = 1.645$$
$$t_{.025,\infty} = 1.960$$
$$t_{.01,\infty} = 2.326$$
$$t_{.005,\infty} = 2.576$$

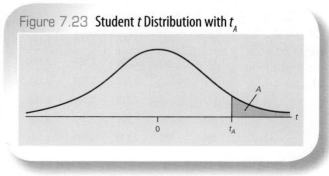

Figure 7.23 **Student t Distribution with t_A**

Table 7.2 Critical Values of t

v	$t_{.100}$	$t_{.050}$	$t_{.025}$	$t_{.010}$	$t_{.005}$	v	$t_{.100}$	$t_{.050}$	$t_{.025}$	$t_{.010}$	$t_{.005}$
1	3.078	6.314	12.71	31.82	63.66	29	1.311	1.699	2.045	2.462	2.756
2	1.886	2.920	4.303	6.965	9.925	30	1.310	1.697	2.042	2.457	2.750
3	1.638	2.353	3.182	4.541	5.841	35	1.306	1.690	2.030	2.438	2.724
4	1.533	2.132	2.776	3.747	4.604	40	1.303	1.684	2.021	2.423	2.704
5	1.476	2.015	2.571	3.365	4.032	45	1.301	1.679	2.014	2.412	2.690
6	1.440	1.943	2.447	3.143	3.707	50	1.299	1.676	2.009	2.403	2.678
7	1.415	1.895	2.365	2.998	3.499	55	1.297	1.673	2.004	2.396	2.668
8	1.397	1.860	2.306	2.896	3.355	60	1.296	1.671	2.000	2.390	2.660
9	1.383	1.833	2.262	2.821	3.250	65	1.295	1.669	1.997	2.385	2.654
10	1.372	1.812	2.228	2.764	3.169	70	1.294	1.667	1.994	2.381	2.648
11	1.363	1.796	2.201	2.718	3.106	75	1.293	1.665	1.992	2.377	2.643
12	1.356	1.782	2.179	2.681	3.055	80	1.292	1.664	1.990	2.374	2.639
13	1.350	1.771	2.160	2.650	3.012	85	1.292	1.663	1.988	2.371	2.635
14	1.345	1.761	2.145	2.624	2.977	90	1.291	1.662	1.987	2.368	2.632
15	1.341	1.753	2.131	2.602	2.947	95	1.291	1.661	1.985	2.366	2.629
16	1.337	1.746	2.120	2.583	2.921	100	1.290	1.660	1.984	2.364	2.626
17	1.333	1.740	2.110	2.567	2.898	110	1.289	1.659	1.982	2.361	2.621
18	1.330	1.734	2.101	2.552	2.878	120	1.289	1.658	1.980	2.358	2.617
19	1.328	1.729	2.093	2.539	2.861	130	1.288	1.657	1.978	2.355	2.614
20	1.325	1.725	2.086	2.528	2.845	140	1.288	1.656	1.977	2.353	2.611
21	1.323	1.721	2.080	2.518	2.831	150	1.287	1.655	1.976	2.351	2.609
22	1.321	1.717	2.074	2.508	2.819	160	1.287	1.654	1.975	2.350	2.607
23	1.319	1.714	2.069	2.500	2.807	170	1.287	1.654	1.974	2.348	2.605
24	1.318	1.711	2.064	2.492	2.797	180	1.286	1.653	1.973	2.347	2.603
25	1.316	1.708	2.060	2.485	2.787	190	1.286	1.653	1.973	2.346	2.602
26	1.315	1.706	2.056	2.479	2.779	200	1.286	1.653	1.972	2.345	2.601
27	1.314	1.703	2.052	2.473	2.771	∞	1.282	1.645	1.960	2.326	2.576
28	1.313	1.701	2.048	2.467	2.763						

© Cengage Learning

Table 7.3 Finding $t_{.05,10}$

Degrees of Freedom	$t_{.10}$	$t_{.05}$	$t_{.025}$	$t_{.01}$	$t_{.005}$
1	3.078	6.314	12.706	31.821	63.657
2	1.886	2.920	4.303	6.965	9.925
3	1.638	2.353	3.182	4.541	5.841
4	1.533	2.132	2.776	3.747	4.604
5	1.476	2.015	2.571	3.365	4.032
6	1.440	1.943	2.447	3.143	3.707
7	1.415	1.895	2.365	2.998	3.499
8	1.397	1.860	2.306	2.896	3.355
9	1.383	1.833	2.262	2.821	3.250
10	1.372	1.812	2.228	2.764	3.169
11	1.363	1.796	2.201	2.718	3.106
12	1.356	1.782	2.179	2.681	3.055

© Cengage Learning

In the previous section, we showed (or showed how we determine) that

$$z_{.10} = 1.28$$
$$z_{.05} = 1.645$$
$$z_{.025} = 1.96$$
$$z_{.01} = 2.33$$
$$z_{.005} = 2.575$$

7-3b Using the Computer

Excel Instructions

To compute Student t probabilities, type

```
=TDIST([x], [v], [Tails])
```

where x must be positive, v is the number of degrees of freedom, and Tails is 1 or 2. Typing 1 for Tails produces the area to the right of x. Typing 2 for Tails produces the area to the right of x plus the area to the left of $-x$. For example,

$$=\texttt{TDIST(2,50,1)} = .02547$$

and

$$=\texttt{TDIST(2,50,2)} = .05095$$

To determine t_A, type

$$=\texttt{TINV([2A], [}v\texttt{])}$$

For example, to find $t_{.05,200}$ enter

$$=\texttt{TINV(.10,200)}$$

yielding 1.6525.

Minitab Instructions

Click **Calc, Probability Distributions**, and **t...** and type the **Degrees of freedom**.

7-3c Chi-Squared Distribution

The density function of another very useful random variable is exhibited next.

Chi-Squared Density Function

The chi-squared density function is

$$f(\chi^2) = \frac{1}{\Gamma(v/2)} \frac{1}{2^{v/2}} (\chi^2)^{(v/2)-1} e^{-\chi^2/2} \qquad \chi^2 > 0$$

The parameter v is the number of degrees of freedom, which like the degrees of freedom of the Student t distribution, affects the shape.

Figure 7.24 depicts a **chi-squared distribution**. As you can see, it is positively skewed, ranging between 0 and ∞. Like that of the Student t distribution, its shape depends on its number of degrees of freedom. The effect of increasing the degrees of freedom is seen in Figure 7.25.

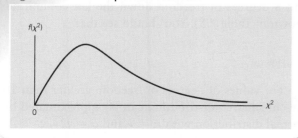

Figure 7.24 **Chi-Squared Distribution**

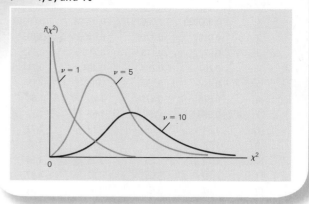

Figure 7.25 **Chi-Squared Distribution with** $v = 1, 5,$ **and 10**

The mean and variance of a chi-squared random variable are

$$E(\chi^2) = v$$

and

$$V(\chi^2) = 2v$$

Determining Chi-Squared Values

The value of χ^2 with v degrees of freedom such that the area to its right under the chi-squared curve is equal to A is denoted $\chi^2_{A,v}$. We cannot use $-\chi^2_{A,v}$ to represent the point such that the area to its *left* is A (as we did with the standard normal and Student t values) because χ^2 is always greater than 0. To represent left-tail critical values, we note that if the area to the left of a point is A, then the area to its right must be $1 - A$ because the entire area under the chi-squared curve (as well as all continuous distributions) must equal 1. Thus, $\chi^2_{1-A,v}$ denotes the point such that the area to its left is A. See Figure 7.26.

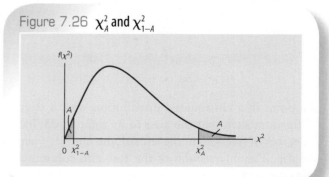

Figure 7.26 χ^2_A **and** χ^2_{1-A}

Table 5 in Appendix B (reproduced here as Table 7.4) lists critical values of the chi-squared distribution for degrees of freedom equal to 1 to 30, 40, 50, 60, 70, 80, 90, and 100. For example, to find

Table 7.4 Critical Values of χ^2

ν	$\chi^2_{.995}$	$\chi^2_{.990}$	$\chi^2_{.975}$	$\chi^2_{.950}$	$\chi^2_{.900}$	$\chi^2_{.100}$	$\chi^2_{.050}$	$\chi^2_{.025}$	$\chi^2_{.010}$	$\chi^2_{.005}$
1	0.000039	0.000157	0.000982	0.00393	0.0158	2.71	3.84	5.02	6.63	7.88
2	0.0100	0.0201	0.0506	0.103	0.211	4.61	5.99	7.38	9.21	10.6
3	0.072	0.115	0.216	0.352	0.584	6.25	7.81	9.35	11.3	12.8
4	0.207	0.297	0.484	0.711	1.06	7.78	9.49	11.1	13.3	14.9
5	0.412	0.554	0.831	1.15	1.61	9.24	11.1	12.8	15.1	16.7
6	0.676	0.872	1.24	1.64	2.20	10.6	12.6	14.4	16.8	18.5
7	0.989	1.24	1.69	2.17	2.83	12.0	14.1	16.0	18.5	20.3
8	1.34	1.65	2.18	2.73	3.49	13.4	15.5	17.5	20.1	22.0
9	1.73	2.09	2.70	3.33	4.17	14.7	16.9	19.0	21.7	23.6
10	2.16	2.56	3.25	3.94	4.87	16.0	18.3	20.5	23.2	25.2
11	2.60	3.05	3.82	4.57	5.58	17.3	19.7	21.9	24.7	26.8
12	3.07	3.57	4.40	5.23	6.30	18.5	21.0	23.3	26.2	28.3
13	3.57	4.11	5.01	5.89	7.04	19.8	22.4	24.7	27.7	29.8
14	4.07	4.66	5.63	6.57	7.79	21.1	23.7	26.1	29.1	31.3
15	4.60	5.23	6.26	7.26	8.55	22.3	25.0	27.5	30.6	32.8
16	5.14	5.81	6.91	7.96	9.31	23.5	26.3	28.8	32.0	34.3
17	5.70	6.41	7.56	8.67	10.09	24.8	27.6	30.2	33.4	35.7
18	6.26	7.01	8.23	9.39	10.86	26.0	28.9	31.5	34.8	37.2
19	6.84	7.63	8.91	10.12	11.65	27.2	30.1	32.9	36.2	38.6
20	7.43	8.26	9.59	10.85	12.44	28.4	31.4	34.2	37.6	40.0
21	8.03	8.90	10.28	11.59	13.24	29.6	32.7	35.5	38.9	41.4
22	8.64	9.54	10.98	12.34	14.04	30.8	33.9	36.8	40.3	42.8
23	9.26	10.20	11.69	13.09	14.85	32.0	35.2	38.1	41.6	44.2
24	9.89	10.86	12.40	13.85	15.66	33.2	36.4	39.4	43.0	45.6
25	10.52	11.52	13.12	14.61	16.47	34.4	37.7	40.6	44.3	46.9
26	11.16	12.20	13.84	15.38	17.29	35.6	38.9	41.9	45.6	48.3
27	11.81	12.88	14.57	16.15	18.11	36.7	40.1	43.2	47.0	49.6
28	12.46	13.56	15.31	16.93	18.94	37.9	41.3	44.5	48.3	51.0
29	13.12	14.26	16.05	17.71	19.77	39.1	42.6	45.7	49.6	52.3
30	13.79	14.95	16.79	18.49	20.60	40.3	43.8	47.0	50.9	53.7
40	20.71	22.16	24.43	26.51	29.05	51.8	55.8	59.3	63.7	66.8
50	27.99	29.71	32.36	34.76	37.69	63.2	67.5	71.4	76.2	79.5
60	35.53	37.48	40.48	43.19	46.46	74.4	79.1	83.3	88.4	92.0
70	43.28	45.44	48.76	51.74	55.33	85.5	90.5	95.0	100	104
80	51.17	53.54	57.15	60.39	64.28	96.6	102	107	112	116
90	59.20	61.75	65.65	69.13	73.29	108	113	118	124	128
100	67.33	70.06	74.22	77.93	82.36	118	124	130	136	140

the point in a chi-squared distribution with 8 degrees of freedom such that the area to its right is .05, locate 8 degrees of freedom in the left column and $\chi^2_{.050}$ across the top. The intersection of the row and column contains the number we seek, as shown in Table 7.5; that is,

$$\chi^2_{.050,8} = 15.5$$

To find the point in the same distribution such that the area to its *left* is .05, find the point such that the

area to its *right* is .95. Locate $\chi^2_{.950}$ across the top row and 8 degrees of freedom down the left column (also shown in Table 7.5). You should see that

$$\chi^2_{.950,8} = 2.73$$

For values of degrees of freedom greater than 100, the chi-squared distribution can be approximated by a normal distribution with $\mu = \nu$ and $\sigma = \sqrt{2\nu}$.

Table 7.5 Critical Values of $\chi^2_{.05,8}$ and $\chi^2_{.950,8}$

Degrees of Freedom	$\chi^2_{.995}$	$\chi^2_{.990}$	$\chi^2_{.975}$	$\chi^2_{.950}$	$\chi^2_{.900}$	$\chi^2_{.100}$	$\chi^2_{.050}$	$\chi^2_{.025}$	$\chi^2_{.010}$	$\chi^2_{.005}$
1	0.000039	0.000157	0.000982	0.00393	0.0158	2.71	3.84	5.02	6.63	7.88
2	0.0100	0.0201	0.0506	0.103	0.211	4.61	5.99	7.38	9.21	10.6
3	0.072	0.115	0.216	0.352	0.584	6.25	7.81	9.35	11.3	12.8
4	0.207	0.297	0.484	0.711	1.06	7.78	9.49	11.1	13.3	14.9
5	0.412	0.554	0.831	1.15	1.61	9.24	11.1	12.8	15.1	16.7
6	0.676	0.872	1.24	1.64	2.20	10.6	12.6	14.4	16.8	18.5
7	0.989	1.24	1.69	2.17	2.83	12.0	14.1	16.0	18.5	20.3
8	1.34	1.65	2.18	2.73	3.49	13.4	15.5	17.5	20.1	22.0
9	1.73	2.09	2.70	3.33	4.17	14.7	16.9	19.0	21.7	23.6
10	2.16	2.56	3.25	3.94	4.87	16.0	18.3	20.5	23.2	25.2
11	2.60	3.05	3.82	4.57	5.58	17.3	19.7	21.9	24.7	26.8

© Cengage Learning

7-3d Using the Computer

Excel Instructions
To calculate $P(\chi^2 > x)$ type into any cell

$$=\textbf{CHIDIST([x], [v])}$$

For example, **CHIDIST**(6.25139,3) = .1000.

To determine $\chi_{A,v}$ type

$$=\textbf{CHIINV([A], [v])}$$

For example, **CHIINV**(.10,3) = 6.25139.

Minitab Instructions
Click **Calc, Probability Distributions,** and **Chi-square....** Specify the **Degrees of freedom.**

7-3e F Distribution

The density function of the **F distribution** is given in the box.

F Density Function

$$f(F) = \frac{\Gamma\left(\dfrac{v_1 + v_2}{2}\right)}{\Gamma\left(\dfrac{v_1}{2}\right)\Gamma\left(\dfrac{v_2}{2}\right)}\left(\dfrac{v_1}{v_2}\right)^{\frac{v_1}{2}}\dfrac{F^{\frac{v_1-2}{2}}}{\left(1+\dfrac{v_1 F}{v_2}\right)^{\frac{v_1+v_2}{2}}} \qquad F > 0$$

where F ranges from 0 to ∞ and v_1 and v_2 are the parameters of the distribution called *degrees of freedom*. For reasons that are clearer in Chapter 12, we call v_1 the *numerator degrees of freedom* and v_2 the *denominator degrees of freedom*.

The mean and variance of an F random variable are

$$E(F) = \frac{v_2}{v_2 - 2} \qquad v_2 > 2$$

and

$$V(F) = \frac{2v_2^2(v_1 + v_2 - 2)}{v_1(v_2 - 2)^2(v_2 - 4)} \qquad v_2 > 4$$

Notice that the mean depends only on the denominator degrees of freedom and that for large v_2 the mean of the F distribution is approximately 1. Figure 7.27 describes the density function when it is graphed. As you can see, the F distribution is positively skewed. Its actual shape depends on the two numbers of degrees of freedom.

Figure 7.27 F Distribution

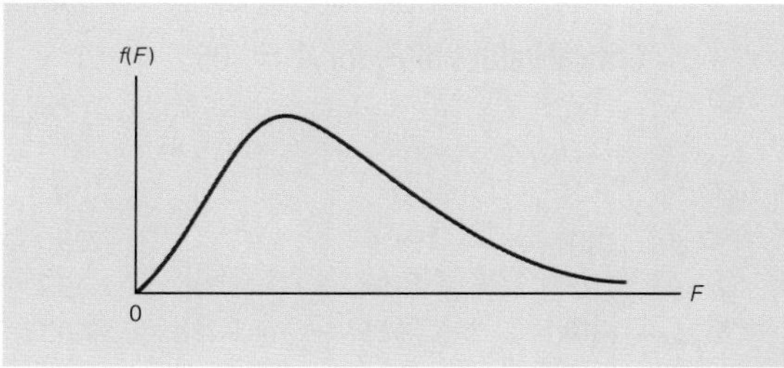

© Cengage Learning

Determining Values of F
We define F_{A,v_1,v_2} as the value of F with v_1 and v_2 degrees of freedom such that the area to its right under the curve is A; that is,

$$P(F > F_{A,v_1,v_2}) = A$$

Because the F random variable, like the chi-squared, can equal only positive values, we define F_{1-A,v_1,v_2} as the value such that the area to its left is A. Figure 7.28 depicts this notation. Table 6 in Appendix B provides values of F_{A,v_1,v_2} for $A = .05, .025, .01$, and $.005$. Part of Table 6 is reproduced here as Table 7.6.

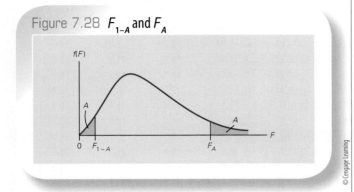

Figure 7.28 F_{1-A} and F_A

Values of F_{1-A,v_1,v_2} are unavailable. However, we do not need them because we can determine F_{1-A,v_1,v_2} from F_{A,v_1,v_2}. In other words, statisticians can show that

$$F_{1-A,v_1,v_2} = \frac{1}{F_{A,v_2,v_1}}$$

To determine any critical value, find the numerator degrees of freedom v_1 across the top of Table 6 and the denominator degrees of freedom v_2 down the left column. The intersection of the row and column contains the number we seek. To illustrate, suppose that we want to find $F_{.05,5,7}$. Table 7.7 shows how this point is found. Locate the numerator degrees of freedom, 5, across the top and the denominator degrees of freedom, 7, down the left column. The intersection is 3.97. Thus, $F_{.05,5,7} = 3.97$.

Note that the order in which the degrees of freedom appear is important. To find $F_{.05,7,5}$ (numerator degrees of freedom = 7, and denominator degrees of freedom = 5), we locate 7 across the top and 5 down the side. The intersection is $F_{.05,7,5} = 4.88$.

Suppose that we want to determine the point in an F distribution with $v_1 = 4$ and $v_2 = 8$ such that the area to its right is .95. Thus,

$$F_{.95,4,8} = \frac{1}{F_{.05,8,4}} = \frac{1}{6.04} = .166$$

7-3f Using the Computer

Excel Instructions

For probabilities, type

$$\texttt{=FDIST([X], [v_1], [v_2])}$$

For example, **FDIST**(3.97,5,7) = .05.

To determine F_{A,v_1,v_2} type

$$\texttt{=FINV([A], [v_1], [v_2])}$$

For example, **FINV**(.05,5,7) = 3.97.

Minitab Instructions

Click **Calc, Probability Distributions**, and **F. . .** Specify the **Numerator degrees of freedom** and the **Denominator degrees of freedom**.

Table 7.6 **Critical Values of F_A for $A = .05$**

					v_1					
v_2	1	2	3	4	5	6	7	8	9	10
1	161	199	216	225	230	234	237	239	241	242
2	18.5	19.0	19.2	19.2	19.3	19.3	19.4	19.4	19.4	19.4
3	10.1	9.55	9.28	9.12	9.01	8.94	8.89	8.85	8.81	8.79
4	7.71	6.94	6.59	6.39	6.26	6.16	6.09	6.04	6.00	5.96
5	6.61	5.79	5.41	5.19	5.05	4.95	4.88	4.82	4.77	4.74
6	5.99	5.14	4.76	4.53	4.39	4.28	4.21	4.15	4.10	4.06
7	5.59	4.74	4.35	4.12	3.97	3.87	3.79	3.73	3.68	3.64
8	5.32	4.46	4.07	3.84	3.69	3.58	3.50	3.44	3.39	3.35
9	5.12	4.26	3.86	3.63	3.48	3.37	3.29	3.23	3.18	3.14
10	4.96	4.10	3.71	3.48	3.33	3.22	3.14	3.07	3.02	2.98
11	4.84	3.98	3.59	3.36	3.20	3.09	3.01	2.95	2.90	2.85
12	4.75	3.89	3.49	3.26	3.11	3.00	2.91	2.85	2.80	2.75
13	4.67	3.81	3.41	3.18	3.03	2.92	2.83	2.77	2.71	2.67
14	4.60	3.74	3.34	3.11	2.96	2.85	2.76	2.70	2.65	2.60
15	4.54	3.68	3.29	3.06	2.90	2.79	2.71	2.64	2.59	2.54
16	4.49	3.63	3.24	3.01	2.85	2.74	2.66	2.59	2.54	2.49
17	4.45	3.59	3.20	2.96	2.81	2.70	2.61	2.55	2.49	2.45

(continued)

Table 7.6 Critical Values of F_A for $A = .05$ (continued)

v_2	v_1 1	2	3	4	5	6	7	8	9	10
18	4.41	3.55	3.16	2.93	2.77	2.66	2.58	2.51	2.46	2.41
19	4.38	3.52	3.13	2.90	2.74	2.63	2.54	2.48	2.42	2.38
20	4.35	3.49	3.10	2.87	2.71	2.60	2.51	2.45	2.39	2.35
22	4.30	3.44	3.05	2.82	2.66	2.55	2.46	2.40	2.34	2.30
24	4.26	3.40	3.01	2.78	2.62	2.51	2.42	2.36	2.30	2.25
26	4.23	3.37	2.98	2.74	2.59	2.47	2.39	2.32	2.27	2.22
28	4.20	3.34	2.95	2.71	2.56	2.45	2.36	2.29	2.24	2.19
30	4.17	3.32	2.92	2.69	2.53	2.42	2.33	2.27	2.21	2.16
35	4.12	3.27	2.87	2.64	2.49	2.37	2.29	2.22	2.16	2.11
40	4.08	3.23	2.84	2.61	2.45	2.34	2.25	2.18	2.12	2.08
45	4.06	3.20	2.81	2.58	2.42	2.31	2.22	2.15	2.10	2.05
50	4.03	3.18	2.79	2.56	2.40	2.29	2.20	2.13	2.07	2.03
60	4.00	3.15	2.76	2.53	2.37	2.25	2.17	2.10	2.04	1.99
70	3.98	3.13	2.74	2.50	2.35	2.23	2.14	2.07	2.02	1.97
80	3.96	3.11	2.72	2.49	2.33	2.21	2.13	2.06	2.00	1.95
90	3.95	3.10	2.71	2.47	2.32	2.20	2.11	2.04	1.99	1.94
100	3.94	3.09	2.70	2.46	2.31	2.19	2.10	2.03	1.97	1.93
120	3.92	3.07	2.68	2.45	2.29	2.18	2.09	2.02	1.96	1.91
140	3.91	3.06	2.67	2.44	2.28	2.16	2.08	2.01	1.95	1.90
160	3.90	3.05	2.66	2.43	2.27	2.16	2.07	2.00	1.94	1.89
180	3.89	3.05	2.65	2.42	2.26	2.15	2.06	1.99	1.93	1.88
200	3.89	3.04	2.65	2.42	2.26	2.14	2.06	1.98	1.93	1.88
∞	3.84	3.00	2.61	2.37	2.21	2.10	2.01	1.94	1.88	1.83

Table 7.7 $F_{.05,5,7}$

v_2 \ v_1	Numerator Degrees of Freedom								
	1	2	3	4	5	6	7	8	9
1	161	199	216	225	230	234	237	239	241
2	18.5	19.0	19.2	19.2	19.3	19.3	19.4	19.4	19.4
3	10.1	9.55	9.28	9.12	9.01	8.94	8.89	8.85	8.81
4	7.71	6.94	6.59	6.39	6.26	6.16	6.09	6.04	6.00
5	6.61	5.79	5.41	5.19	5.05	4.95	4.88	4.82	4.77
6	5.99	5.14	4.76	4.53	4.39	4.28	4.21	4.15	4.1
7	5.59	4.74	4.35	4.12	3.97	3.87	3.79	3.73	3.68
8	5.32	4.46	4.07	3.84	3.69	3.58	3.5	3.44	3.39
9	5.12	4.26	3.86	3.63	3.48	3.37	3.29	3.23	3.18
10	4.96	4.10	3.71	3.48	3.33	3.22	3.14	3.07	3.02

Chapter 7: Continuous Probability Distributions   115

7.1 The weekly output of a steel mill is a uniformly distributed random variable that lies between 110 and 175 metric tons.

a. Compute the probability that the steel mill will produce more than 150 metric tons next week.
b. Determine the probability that the steel mill will produce between 120 and 160 metric tons next week.

7.2 The amount of time it takes for a student to complete a statistics quiz is uniformly distributed between 30 and 60 minutes. One student is selected at random. Find the probability of the following events.

a. The student requires more than 55 minutes to complete the quiz.
b. The student completes the quiz in a time between 30 and 40 minutes.
c. The student completes the quiz in exactly 37.23 minutes.

7.3 Refer to Exercise 7.2. The professor wants to reward (with bonus marks) students who are in the lowest quarter of completion times. What completion time should he use for the cutoff for awarding bonus marks?

7.4 Battery manufacturers compete on the basis of the amount of time their products last in cameras and toys. A manufacturer of alkaline batteries has observed that its batteries last for an average of 26 hours when used in a toy racing car. The amount of time is normally distributed with a standard deviation of 2.5 hours.

a. What is the probability that the battery lasts between 24 and 28 hours?
b. What is the probability that the battery lasts longer than 28 hours?
c. What is the probability that the battery lasts less than 24 hours?

7.5 It is said that sufferers of a cold virus experience symptoms for 7 days. However, the amount of time is actually a normally distributed random variable whose mean is 7.5 days and whose standard deviation is 1.2 days.

a. What proportion of cold sufferers experiences less than 4 days of symptoms?
b. What proportion of cold sufferers experiences symptoms for between 7 and 10 days?

7.6 The long-distance calls made by the employees of a company are normally distributed with a mean of 6.3 minutes and a standard deviation of 2.2 minutes. Find the probability that a call

a. lasts between 5 and 10 minutes.
b. lasts more than 7 minutes.
c. lasts less than 4 minutes.

7.7 Travelbyus is an Internet-based travel agency that allows customers to see videos of the cities they plan to visit. The number of hits daily is a normally distributed random variable with a mean of 10,000 and a standard deviation of 2,400.

a. What is the probability of getting more than 12,000 hits?
b. What is the probability of getting fewer than 9,000 hits?

7.8 A new gas- and electric-powered hybrid car has recently hit the market. The distance traveled on 1 gallon of fuel is normally distributed with a mean of 65 miles and a standard deviation of 4 miles. Find the probability of the following events.

a. The car travels more than 70 miles per gallon.
b. The car travels less than 60 miles per gallon.
c. The car travels between 55 and 70 miles per gallon.

7.9 The top-selling Red and Voss tire is rated 70,000 miles, which means nothing. In fact, the distance the tires can run until they wear out is a normally distributed random variable with a mean of 82,000 miles and a standard deviation of 6,400 miles.

a. What is the probability that a tire wears out before 70,000 miles?
b. What is the probability that a tire lasts more than 100,000 miles?

7.10 Because of relatively high interest rates, most consumers attempt to pay off their credit card bills promptly. However, this is not always possible. An analysis of the amount of interest paid monthly by a bank's Visa cardholders reveals that the amount is normally distributed with a mean of $27 and a standard deviation of $7.

a. What proportion of the bank's Visa cardholders pay more than $30 in interest?
b. What proportion of the bank's Visa cardholders pay more than $40 in interest?
c. What proportion of the bank's Visa cardholders pay less than $15 in interest?
d. What interest payment is exceeded by only 20% of the bank's Visa cardholders?

7.11 How much money does a typical family of four spend at McDonald's restaurants per visit? The amount is a normally distributed random variable whose mean is $16.40 and whose standard deviation is $2.75.

a. Find the probability that a family of four spends less than $10.
b. What is the amount below which only 10% of families of four spend at McDonald's?

7.12 The lifetimes of lightbulbs that are advertised to last for 5,000 hours are normally distributed with a mean of 5,100 hours and a standard deviation of 200 hours. What is the probability that a bulb lasts longer than the advertised figure?

7.13 Refer to Exercise 7.12. If we wanted to be sure that 98% of all bulbs last longer than the advertised figure, what figure should be advertised?

7.14 The number of pages printed before replacing the cartridge in a laser printer is normally distributed with a mean of 11,500 pages and a standard deviation of 800 pages. A new cartridge has just been installed.

a. What is the probability that the printer produces more than 12,000 pages before this cartridge must be replaced?
b. What is the probability that the printer produces fewer than 10,000 pages?

7.15 Refer to Exercise 7.14. The manufacturer wants to provide guidelines to potential customers advising

them of the minimum number of pages they can expect from each cartridge. How many pages should it advertise if the company wants to be correct 99% of the time?

7.16 The final marks in a statistics course are normally distributed with a mean of 70 and a standard deviation of 10. The professor must convert all marks to letter grades. She decides that she wants 10% A's, 30% B's, 40% C's, 15% D's, and 5% F's. Determine the cutoffs for each letter grade.

7.17 Mensa is an organization whose members possess IQs that are in the top 2% of the population. It is known that IQs are normally distributed with a mean of 100 and a standard deviation of 16. Find the minimum IQ needed to be a Mensa member.

Some of the following exercises require the use of a computer and software.

7.18 Use the t table (Table 4) to find the following values of t.

a. $t_{.10,15}$ b. $t_{.10,23}$ c. $t_{.025,83}$ d. $t_{.05,195}$

7.19 Use the t table (Table 4) to find the following values of t.

a. $t_{.005,33}$ b. $t_{.10,600}$ c. $t_{.05,4}$ d. $t_{.01,20}$

7.20 Use a computer to find the following values of t.

a. $t_{.10,15}$ b. $t_{.10,23}$ c. $t_{.025,83}$ d. $t_{.05,195}$

7.21 Use a computer to find the following values of t.

a. $t_{.05,143}$ b. $t_{.01,12}$ c. $t_{.025,\infty}$ d. $t_{.05,100}$

7.22 Use a computer to find the following probabilities.

a. $P(t_{64} > 2.12)$ b. $P(t_{27} > 1.90)$ c. $P(t_{159} > 1.33)$
d. $P(t_{550} > 1.85)$

7.23 Use a computer to find the following probabilities.

a. $P(t_{141} > .94)$ b. $P(t_{421} > 2.00)$ c. $P(t_{1000} > 1.96)$
d. $P(t_{82} > 1.96)$

7.24 Use the χ^2 table (Table 5) to find the following values of χ^2.

a. $\chi^2_{.10,5}$ b. $\chi^2_{.01,100}$ c. $\chi^2_{.95,18}$ d. $\chi^2_{.99,60}$

7.25 Use the χ^2 table (Table 5) to find the following values of χ^2.

a. $\chi^2_{.90,26}$ b. $\chi^2_{.01,30}$ c. $\chi^2_{.10,1}$ d. $\chi^2_{.99,80}$

7.26 Use a computer to find the following values of χ^2.

a. $\chi^2_{.25,66}$ b. $\chi^2_{.40,100}$ c. $\chi^2_{.50,17}$ d. $\chi^2_{.10,17}$

7.27 Use a computer to find the following values of χ^2.

a. $\chi^2_{.99,55}$ b. $\chi^2_{.05,800}$ c. $\chi^2_{.99,43}$ d. $\chi^2_{.10,233}$

7.28 Use a computer to find the following probabilities.

a. $P(\chi^2_{73} > 80)$ b. $P(\chi^2_{200} > 125)$ c. $P(\chi^2_{88} > 60)$
d. $P(\chi^2_{1000} > 450)$

7.29 Use a computer to find the following probabilities.

a. $P(\chi^2_{250} > 250)$ b. $P(\chi^2_{36} > 25)$ c. $P(\chi^2_{600} > 500)$
d. $P(\chi^2_{120} > 100)$

7.30 Use the F table (Table 6) to find the following values of F.

a. $F_{.05,3,7}$ b. $F_{.05,7,3}$ c. $F_{.025,5,20}$ d. $F_{.01,12,60}$

7.31 Use the F table (Table 6) to find the following values of F.

a. $F_{.025,8,22}$ b. $F_{.05,20,30}$ c. $F_{.01,9,18}$ d. $F_{.025,24,10}$

7.32 Use a computer to find the following values of F.

a. $F_{.05,70,70}$ b. $F_{.01,45,100}$ c. $F_{.025,36,50}$ d. $F_{.05,500,500}$

7.33 Use a computer to find the following values of F.

a. $F_{.01,100,150}$ b. $F_{.05,25,125}$ c. $F_{.01,11,33}$ d. $F_{.05,300,800}$

7.34 Use a computer to find the following probabilities.

a. $P(F_{7,20} > 2.5)$ b. $P(F_{18,63} > 1.4)$ c. $P(F_{34,62} > 1.8)$
d. $P(F_{200,400} > 1.1)$

7.35 Use a computer to find the following probabilities.

a. $P(F_{600,800} > 1.1)$ b. $P(F_{35,100} > 1.3)$ c. $P(F_{66,148} > 2.1)$
d. $P(F_{17,37} > 2.8)$

THE IN-CROWD

Share your 4LTR Press story on Facebook at
www.facebook.com/4ltrpress for a chance to win.

 To learn more about the In-Crowd opportunity 'like' us on Facebook.

CHAPTER 8

Sampling Distributions

objectives

8-1 Sampling Distribution of the Mean

8-2 Sampling Distribution of a Proportion

SALARIES OF A BUSINESS SCHOOL'S GRADUATES

Deans and other faculty members in professional schools often monitor how well the graduates of their programs fare in the job market. Information about the types of jobs and their salaries may provide useful information about the success of the program.

In the advertisements for a large university, the dean of the School of Business claims that the average salary of the school's graduates one year after graduation is $800 per week with a standard deviation of $100. A second-year student in the business school who has just completed his statistics course would like to check whether the claim about the mean is correct. He does a survey of 25 people who graduated 1 year ago and determines their weekly salary. He discovers the sample mean to be $750. To interpret his finding, he needs to calculate the probability that a sample of 25 graduates would have a mean of $750 or less when the population mean is $800 and the standard deviation is $100. After calculating the probability, he needs to draw some conclusion. (See page 126 for the answer.)

This chapter introduces the *sampling distribution*, a fundamental element in statistical inference. We remind you that statistical inference is the process of converting data into information. Here are the parts of the process we have thus far discussed:

1. Parameters describe populations.

2. Parameters are almost always unknown.

3. We take a random sample of a population to obtain the necessary data.

4. We calculate one or more statistics from the data.

For example, to estimate a population mean, we compute the sample mean. Although there is very little chance that the sample mean and the population mean are identical, we would expect them to be quite close. However, for the purposes of statistical inference, we need to be able to measure how close. The sampling distribution provides this service. It plays a crucial role in the process, because the measure of proximity it provides is the key to statistical inference.

8-1 Sampling Distribution of the Mean

As the name suggests, a **sampling distribution** is created by sampling. There are two ways to create a sampling distribution. The first is to actually draw samples of the same size from a population, calculate the statistic of interest, and then use descriptive techniques

to learn more about the sampling distribution. The second method relies on the rules of probability and the laws of expected value and variance to derive the sampling distribution. We'll demonstrate the latter approach by developing the sampling distribution of the mean of two dice.

8-1a **Sampling Distribution of the Mean of Two Dice**

The population is created by throwing a fair die infinitely many times, with the random variable X indicating the number of spots showing on any one throw. The probability distribution of the random variable X is shown in the following table.

x	p(x)
1	1/6
2	1/6
3	1/6
4	1/6
5	1/6
6	1/6

The population is infinitely large, because we can throw the die infinitely many times (or at least imagine doing so). From the definitions of expected value and variance presented in Section 6-1, we calculate the population mean, variance, and standard deviation.

Population mean:

$$\mu = \sum x P(x)$$
$$= 1(1/6) + 2(1/6) + 3(1/6) + 4(1/6) + 5(1/6) + 6(1/6)$$
$$= 3.5$$

Population variance:

$$\sigma^2 = \sum (x - \mu)^2 P(x)$$
$$= (1 - 3.5)^2(1/6) + (2 - 3.5)^2(1/6)$$
$$\quad + (3 - 3.5)^2(1/6) + (4 - 3.5)^2(1/6)$$
$$\quad + (5 - 3.5)^2(1/6) + (6 - 3.5)^2(1/6)$$
$$= 2.92$$

Population standard deviation:

$$\sigma = \sqrt{\sigma^2} = \sqrt{2.92} = 1.71$$

The sampling distribution of the mean of two dice is created by drawing samples of size 2 from the population. In other words, we toss two dice. Figure 8.1 depicts this process in which we compute the mean for each sample. Because the value of the sample mean varies randomly from sample to sample, we can regard $\overline{X}$ as a new random variable created by sampling. Table 8.1 lists all the possible samples and their corresponding values of $\overline{x}$.

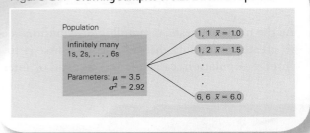

Figure 8.1 Drawing Samples of Size 2 from a Population

Table 8.1 All Samples of Size 2 and Their Means

Sample	$\overline{x}$	Sample	$\overline{x}$	Sample	$\overline{x}$
1, 1	1.0	3, 1	2.0	5, 1	3.0
1, 2	1.5	3, 2	2.5	5, 2	3.5
1, 3	2.0	3, 3	3.0	5, 3	4.0
1, 4	2.5	3, 4	3.5	5, 4	4.5
1, 5	3.0	3, 5	4.0	5, 5	5.0
1, 6	3.5	3, 6	4.5	5, 6	5.5
2, 1	1.5	4, 1	2.5	6, 1	3.5
2, 2	2.0	4, 2	3.0	6, 2	4.0
2, 3	2.5	4, 3	3.5	6, 3	4.5
2, 4	3.0	4, 4	4.0	5, 4	5.0
2, 5	3.5	4, 5	4.5	5, 5	5.5
2, 6	4.0	4, 6	5.0	6, 6	6.0

There are 36 different possible samples of size 2; because each sample is equally likely, the probability of any one sample being selected is 1/36. However, $\overline{x}$ can assume only 11 different possible values: 1.0, 1.5, 2.0, . . . , 6.0, with certain values of $\overline{x}$ occurring more frequently than others. The value $\bar{x} = 1.0$ occurs only once, so its probability is 1/36. The value $\bar{x} = 1.5$ can occur in two ways: (1,2) and (2,1), each having the same probability 1/36. Thus, $P(\bar{x} = 1.5) = 2/36$. The probabilities of the other values of $\bar{x}$ are determined in similar fashion, and the resulting **sampling distribution of $\bar{X}$** is shown in Table 8.2.

Table 8.2	Sampling Distribution of $\bar{x}$
$\bar{x}$	$P(\bar{x})$
1.0	1/36
1.5	2/36
2.0	3/36
2.5	4/36
3.0	5/36
3.5	6/36
4.0	5/36
4.5	4/36
5.0	3/36
5.5	2/36
6.0	1/36

© Cengage Learning

The most interesting aspect of the sampling distribution of $\bar{X}$ is how different it is from the distribution of X, as can be seen in Figure 8.2.

Figure 8.2 **Distributions of X and $\bar{X}$**

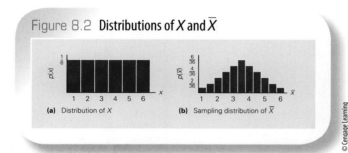

(a) Distribution of X **(b)** Sampling distribution of $\bar{X}$

© Cengage Learning

We can also compute the mean, variance, and standard deviation of the sampling distribution. Once again, using the definitions of expected value and variance, we determine the following parameters of the sampling distribution.

Mean of the sampling distribution of $\bar{X}$:

$$\mu_{\bar{x}} = \sum \bar{x}\,P(\bar{x})$$
$$= 1.0(1/36) + 1.5(2/36) + \cdots + 6.0(1/36)$$
$$= 3.5$$

Notice that the mean of the sampling distribution of $\bar{X}$ is equal to the mean of the population of the toss of a die computed previously.

Variance of the sampling distribution of $\bar{X}$:

$$\sigma_{\bar{x}}^2 = \sum (\bar{x} - \mu_{\bar{x}})^2\,P(\bar{x})$$
$$= (1.0 - 3.5)^2(1/36) + (1.5 - 3.5)^2(2/36) + \cdots$$
$$+ (6.0 - 3.5)^2(1/36)$$
$$= 1.46$$

It is no coincidence that the variance of the sampling distribution of $\bar{X}$ is exactly half of the variance of the population of the toss of a die (computed previously as $\sigma^2 = 2.92$).

Standard deviation of the sampling distribution of $\bar{X}$:

$$\sigma_{\bar{x}} = \sqrt{\sigma_{\bar{x}}^2} = \sqrt{1.46} = 1.21$$

It is important to recognize that the distribution of $\bar{X}$ is different from the distribution of X as depicted in Figure 8.2. However, the two random variables are related. Their means are the same ($\mu_{\bar{x}} = \mu = 3.5$), and their variances are related ($\sigma_{\bar{x}}^2 = \sigma^2/2$).

Don't get lost in the terminology and notation. Remember that μ and σ^2 are the parameters of the population of X. To create the sampling distribution of $\bar{X}$, we repeatedly drew samples of size $n = 2$ from the population and calculated $\bar{x}$ for each sample. Thus, we treat $\bar{X}$ as a brand-new random variable with its own distribution, mean, and variance. The mean is denoted $\mu_{\bar{x}}$, and the variance is denoted $\sigma_{\bar{x}}^2$.

If we now repeat the sampling process with the same population but with other values of n, we produce somewhat different sampling distributions of $\bar{X}$. Figure 8.3 shows the sampling distributions of $\bar{X}$ when $n = 5, 10$, and 25.

For each value of n, the mean of the sampling distribution of $\bar{X}$ is the mean of the population from which we're sampling; that is,

$$\mu_{\bar{x}} = \mu = 3.5$$

The variance of the sampling distribution of the sample mean is the variance of the population divided by the sample size; that is,

$$\sigma_{\bar{x}}^2 = \frac{\sigma^2}{n}$$

The standard deviation of the sampling distribution is called the **standard error of the mean**; that is,

$$\sigma_{\bar{x}} = \frac{\sigma}{\sqrt{n}}$$

As you can see, the variance of the sampling distribution of $\bar{X}$ is less than the variance of the population we're sampling from all sample sizes. Thus, a randomly selected value of $\bar{X}$ (the mean of the number of spots observed in, say, five throws of the die) is likely to be

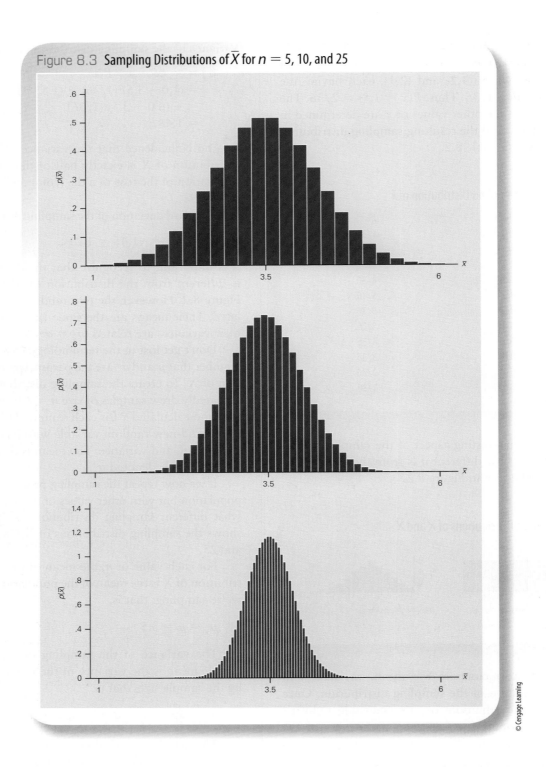

© Cengage Learning

closer to the mean value of 3.5 than is a randomly se-lected value of X (the number of spots observed in one throw). Indeed, this is what you would expect, because in five throws of the die you are likely to get some 5s and 6s and some 1s and 2s, which will tend to offset one another in the averaging process and produce a

sample mean reasonably close to 3.5. As the number of throws of the die increases, the probability that the sample mean will be close to 3.5 also increases. Thus, we observe in Figure 8.3 that the sampling distribution of $\overline{X}$ becomes narrower (or more concentrated about the mean) as n increases.

Another thing that happens as n gets larger is that the sampling distribution of $\overline{X}$ becomes increasingly bell shaped. This phenomenon is summarized in the **central limit theorem**.

Central Limit Theorem

The sampling distribution of the mean of a random sample drawn from any population is approximately normal for a sufficiently large sample size. The larger the sample size, the more closely the sampling distribution of $\overline{X}$ will resemble a normal distribution.

The accuracy of the approximation alluded to in the central limit theorem depends on the probability distribution of the population and on the sample size. If the population is normal, then $\overline{X}$ is normally distributed for all values of n. If the population is nonnormal, then $\overline{X}$ is approximately normal only for larger values of n. In many practical situations, a sample size of 30 may be sufficiently large to allow us to use the normal distribution as an approximation for the sampling distribution of $\overline{X}$. However, if the population is extremely nonnormal (for example, bimodal and highly skewed distributions), the sampling distribution will also be nonnormal even for moderately large values of n.

We can now summarize what we know about the sampling distribution of the sample mean for large populations.

Sampling Distribution of the Sample Mean

1. $\mu_{\bar{x}} = \mu$
2. $\sigma_{\bar{x}}^2 = \sigma^2/n$ and $\sigma_{\bar{x}} = \sigma/\sqrt{n}$
3. If X is normal, $\overline{X}$ is normal. If X is nonnormal, $\overline{X}$ is approximately normal for sufficiently large sample sizes. The definition of "sufficiently large" depends on the extent of nonnormality of X.

EXAMPLE 8.1
Contents of a 32-Ounce Bottle

The foreman of a bottling plant has observed that the amount of soda in each 32-ounce bottle is actually a normally distributed random variable, with a mean of 32.2 ounces and a standard deviation of .3 ounce.

a. If a customer buys one bottle, what is the probability that the bottle will contain more than 32 ounces?

b. If a customer buys a carton of four bottles, what is the probability that the mean amount of the four bottles will be greater than 32 ounces?

SOLUTION

a. Because the random variable is the amount of soda in one bottle, we want to find $P(X > 32)$, where X is normally distributed, $\mu = 32.2$, and $\sigma = .3$. Hence,

$$P(X > 32) = P\left(\frac{X - \mu}{\sigma} > \frac{32 - 32.2}{.3}\right)$$
$$= P(Z > -.67)$$
$$= 1 - P(Z < -.67)$$
$$= 1 - .2514 = .7486$$

b. Now we want to find the probability that the mean amount of four filled bottles exceeds 32 ounces. In other words, we want $P(\overline{X} > 32)$. From our previous analysis and from the central limit theorem, we know the following:

1. $\overline{X}$ is normally distributed.

2. $\mu_{\bar{x}} = \mu = 32.2$

3. $\sigma_{\bar{x}} = \sigma/\sqrt{n} = .3/\sqrt{4} = .15$

Hence,

$$P(\overline{X} > 32) = P\left(\frac{\overline{X} - \mu_{\bar{x}}}{\sigma_{\bar{x}}} > \frac{32 - 32.2}{.15}\right)$$
$$= P(Z > -1.33) = 1 - P(Z < -1.33)$$
$$= 1 - .0918 = .9082$$

Figure 8.4 illustrates the distributions used in this example.

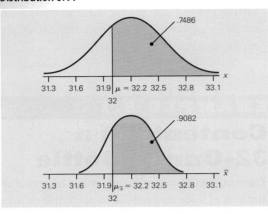

Figure 8.4 **Distribution of X and Sampling Distribution of $\overline{X}$**

In Example 8.1(b), we began with the assumption that both μ and σ were known. Then, using the sampling distribution, we made a probability statement about $\overline{X}$. Unfortunately, the values of μ and σ are not usually known, so an analysis such as that in Example 8.1 cannot usually be conducted. However, we can use the sampling distribution to infer something about an unknown value of μ on the basis of a sample mean.

SALARIES OF A BUSINESS SCHOOL'S GRADUATES: SOLUTION

We want to find the probability that the sample mean is less than \$750. Thus, we seek

$$P(\overline{X} < 750)$$

The distribution of X, the weekly income, is likely to be positively skewed but not sufficiently so to make the distribution of $\overline{X}$ nonnormal. As a result, we may assume that $\overline{X}$ is normal with mean $\mu_{\bar{x}} = \mu = 800$ and standard deviation $\sigma_{\bar{x}} = \sigma/\sqrt{n} = 100/\sqrt{25} = 20$. Thus,

$$P(\overline{X} < 750) = P\left(\frac{\overline{X} - \mu_{\bar{x}}}{\sigma_{\bar{x}}} < \frac{750 - 800}{20}\right)$$
$$= P(Z < -2.5) = .0062$$

Figure 8.5 illustrates the distribution.

The probability of observing a sample mean as low as \$750 when the population mean is \$800 is extremely small. Because this event is quite unlikely, we would have to conclude that the dean's claim is not justified.

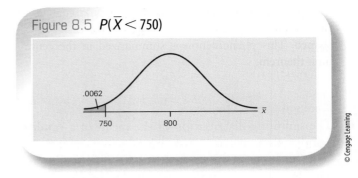

Figure 8.5 $P(\overline{X} < 750)$

8-1b Using the Sampling Distribution for Inference

Our conclusion in the chapter-opening example illustrates how the sampling distribution can be used to make inferences about population parameters. The first form of inference is estimation, which we introduce in the next chapter. In preparation for this momentous occasion, we'll present another way of expressing the probability associated with the sampling distribution.

Recall the notation introduced in Section 7-2 (see page 105). We defined Z_A to be the value of z such that the area to the right of Z_A under the standard normal curve is equal to A. We also showed that $z_{.025} = 1.96$. Because the standard normal distribution is symmetric about 0, the area to the left of -1.96 is also .025. The area between -1.96 and 1.96 is .95. Figure 8.6 depicts this notation. We can express the notation algebraically as

$$P(-1.96 < Z < 1.96) = .95$$

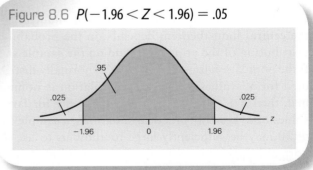

Figure 8.6 $P(-1.96 < Z < 1.96) = .05$

In this section, we established that

$$Z = \frac{\overline{X} - \mu}{\sigma/\sqrt{n}}$$

is standard normally distributed. Substituting this form of Z into the previous probability statement, we produce

$$P\left(-1.96 < \frac{\overline{X} - \mu}{\sigma/\sqrt{n}} < 1.96\right) = .95$$

With a little algebraic manipulation (multiply all three terms by $\sigma/\sqrt{n}$ and add μ to all three terms), we determine

$$P\left(\mu - 1.96\frac{\sigma}{\sqrt{n}} < \overline{X} < \mu + 1.96\frac{\sigma}{\sqrt{n}}\right) = .95$$

Returning to the chapter-opening example where $\mu = 800$, $\sigma = 100$, and $n = 25$, we compute

$$P\left(800 - 1.96\frac{100}{\sqrt{25}} < \overline{X} < 800 + 1.96\frac{100}{\sqrt{25}}\right) = .95$$

Thus, we can say that

$$P(760.8 < \overline{X} < 839.2) = .95$$

This tells us that there is a 95% probability that a sample mean drawn from a population whose mean is 800 (the dean's claim) will fall between 760.8 and 839.2. Because the sample mean was computed to be \$750, we would have to conclude that the dean's claim is not supported by the statistic.

Changing the probability from .95 to .90 changes the probability statement to

$$P\left(\mu - 1.645\frac{\sigma}{\sqrt{n}} < \overline{X} < \mu + 1.645\frac{\sigma}{\sqrt{n}}\right) = .90$$

We can also produce a general form of this statement:

$$P\left(\mu - z_{\alpha/2}\frac{\sigma}{\sqrt{n}} < \overline{X} < \mu + z_{\alpha/2}\frac{\sigma}{\sqrt{n}}\right) = 1 - \alpha$$

In this formula α (Greek letter *alpha*) is the probability that $\overline{X}$ does not fall into the interval. To apply this formula, all we need do is substitute the values for μ, σ, n, and α. For example, with $\mu = 800$, $\sigma = 100$, $n = 25$ and $\alpha = .01$, we produce

$$P\left(\mu - z_{.005}\frac{\sigma}{\sqrt{n}} < \overline{X} < \mu + z_{.005}\frac{\sigma}{\sqrt{n}}\right) = 1 - .01$$

$$P\left(800 - 2.575\frac{100}{\sqrt{25}} < \overline{X} < 800 + 2.575\frac{100}{\sqrt{25}}\right) = .99$$

$$P(748.5 < \overline{X} < 851.5) = .99$$

which is another probability statement about $\overline{X}$. In Section 9-2, we will use a similar type of probability statement to derive the first statistical inference technique.

8-2 Sampling Distribution of a Proportion

In Section 6-2, we introduced the binomial distribution whose parameter is p, the probability of success in any trial. To compute binomial probabilities, we assumed that p was known. However, in the real world, p is unknown,

requiring the statistics practitioner to estimate its value from a sample. The estimator of a population proportion of successes is the sample proportion. In other words, we count the number of successes in a sample and compute

$$\hat{P} = \frac{X}{n}$$

($\hat{P}$ is read as *p-hat*) where X is the number of successes and n is the sample size. When we take a sample of size n, we're actually conducting a binomial experiment; as a result X is binomially distributed. Thus, the probability of any value of $\hat{P}$ can be calculated from its value of X. For example, suppose that we have a binomial experiment with $n = 10$ and $p = .4$. To find the probability that the sample proportion $\hat{P}$ is less than or equal to .50, we find the probability that X is less than or equal to 5 (because $5/10 = .50$). From Table 1 in Appendix B, we find with $n = 10$ and $p = .4$

$$P(\hat{P} \le .50) = P(X \le 5) = .8338$$

We can calculate the probability associated with other values of $\hat{P}$ similarly.

Discrete distributions such as the binomial do not lend themselves easily to the kinds of calculation needed for inference. And inference is the reason we need sampling distributions. Fortunately, we can approximate the binomial distribution by a normal distribution.

What follows is an explanation of how and why the normal distribution can be used to approximate a binomial distribution. Disinterested readers can skip to page 129 where we present the **approximate sampling distribution of a sample proportion**.

8-2a (Optional) Normal Approximation to the Binomial Distribution

Recall how we introduced continuous probability distributions in Chapter 7. We developed the density function by converting a histogram so that the total area in the rectangles equaled 1. We can do the same for a binomial distribution. To illustrate, let X be a binomial random variable with $n = 20$ and $p = .5$. We can easily determine the probability of each value of X, where $X = 0, 1, 2, \ldots,$ 19, 20. A rectangle representing a value of x is drawn so that its area equals the probability. We accomplish this by letting the height of the rectangle equal the probability and the base of the rectangle equal 1. Thus, the base of each rectangle for x is the interval $x - .5$ to $x + .5$. Figure 8.7 depicts this graph. As you can see, the rectangle representing $x = 10$ is the rectangle whose base is the interval 9.5 to 10.5 and whose height is $P(X = 10) = .1762$.

© Glowimages

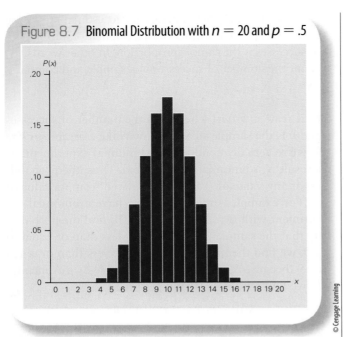

Figure 8.7 **Binomial Distribution with** $n = 20$ **and** $p = .5$

© Cengage Learning

If we now smooth the ends of the rectangles, we produce a bell-shaped curve as seen in Figure 8.8. Thus, to use the normal approximation, all we need to do is find the area under the *normal* curve between 9.5 and 10.5.

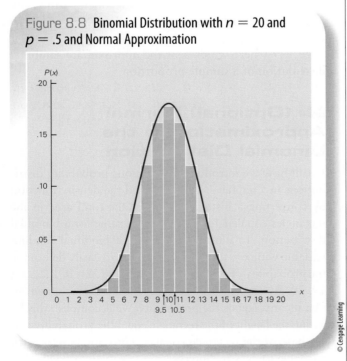

Figure 8.8 **Binomial Distribution with** $n = 20$ **and** $p = .5$ **and Normal Approximation**

© Cengage Learning

To find normal probabilities requires us to first standardize X by subtracting the mean and dividing by the standard deviation. The values for μ and σ are

derived from the binomial distribution being approximated. In Section 6-2 we pointed out that

$$\mu = np$$

and

$$\sigma = \sqrt{np(1 - p)}$$

For $n = 20$ and $p = .5$, we have

$$\mu = np = 20(.5) = 10$$

and

$$\sigma = \sqrt{np(1 - p)} = \sqrt{20(.5)(1 - .5)} = 2.24$$

To calculate the probability that $X = 10$ using the normal distribution requires that we find the area under the normal curve between 9.5 and 10.5; that is,

$$P(X = 10) \approx P(9.5 < Y < 10.5)$$

where Y is a normal random variable approximating the binomial random variable X. We standardize Y and use Table 3 of Appendix B to find

$$P(9.5 < Y < 10.5)$$
$$= P\left(\frac{9.5 - 10}{2.24} < \frac{Y - \mu}{\sigma} < \frac{10.5 - 10}{2.24}\right)$$
$$= P(-.22 < Z < .22) = (Z < .22)$$
$$- P(Z < -.22) = .5871 - .4129 = .1742$$

The actual probability that X equals 10 is

$$P(X = 10) = .1762$$

As you can see, the approximation is quite good.

Notice that to draw a binomial distribution, which is discrete, it was necessary to draw rectangles whose bases were constructed by adding and subtracting .5 to the values of X. The .5 is called the **continuity correction factor**.

The approximation for any other value of X would proceed in the same manner. In general, the binomial probability $P(X = x)$ is approximated by the area under a normal curve between $x - .5$ and $x + .5$. To find the binomial probability $P(X \leq x)$, we calculate the area under the normal curve to the left of $x + .5$. For the same binomial random variable, the probability that its value is less than or equal to 8 is $P(X \leq 8) = .2517$. The normal approximation is

$$P(X \leq 8) \approx P(Y < 8.5) = P\left(\frac{Y - \mu}{\sigma} < \frac{8.5 - 10}{2.24}\right)$$
$$= P(Z < -.67) = .2514$$

We find the area under the normal curve to the right of $x - .5$ to determine the binomial probability $P(X \geq x)$. To illustrate, the probability that the binomial random variable (with $n = 20$ and $p = .5$) is greater than or equal to 14 is $P(X \geq 14) = .0577$. The normal approximation is

$$P(X \geq 14) \approx P(Y > 13.5)$$

$$= P\left(\frac{Y - \mu}{\sigma} > \frac{13.5 - 10}{2.24}\right) = P(Z > 1.56) = .0594$$

8-2b Omitting the Correction Factor for Continuity

When calculating the probability of *individual* values of X as we did when we computed the probability that X equals 10 above, the correction factor *must* be used. If we don't, we are left with finding the area in a line, which is 0. When computing the probability of a *range* of values of X, we can omit the correction factor. However, the omission of the correction factor will decrease the accuracy of the approximation. For example, if we approximate $P(X \leq 8)$ as we did previously except without the correction factor, we find

$$P(X \leq 8) \approx P(Y < 8) = P\left(\frac{Y - \mu}{\sigma} < \frac{8 - 10}{2.24}\right)$$

$$= P(Z < -.89) = .1867$$

The absolute size of the error between the actual cumulative binomial probability and its normal approximation is quite small when the values of x are in the tail regions of the distribution. For example, the probability that a binomial random variable with $n = 20$ and $p = .5$ is less than or equal to 3 is

$$P(X \leq 3) = .0013$$

The normal approximation with the correction factor is

$$P(X \leq 3) \approx P(Y < 3.5) = P\left(\frac{Y - \mu}{\sigma} < \frac{3.5 - 10}{2.24}\right)$$

$$= P(Z < -2.90) = .0019$$

The normal approximation without the correction factor is (using Excel)

$$P(X \leq 3) \approx P(Y < 3) = P\left(\frac{Y - \mu}{\sigma} < \frac{3 - 10}{2.24}\right)$$

$$= P(Z < -3.13) = .0009$$

For larger values of n, the differences between the normal approximation with and without the correction factor are small even for values of X near the center of the distribution. For example, the probability that a binomial random variable with $n = 1000$ and $p = .3$ is less than or equal to 260 is

$$P(X \leq 260) = .0029 \text{ (using Excel)}$$

The normal approximation with the correction factor is

$$P(X \leq 260) \approx P(Y < 260.5)$$

$$= P\left(\frac{Y - \mu}{\sigma} < \frac{260.5 - 300}{14.49}\right) = P(Z < -2.73)$$

$$= .0032$$

The normal approximation without the correction factor is

$$P(X \leq 260) \approx P(Y < 260)$$

$$= P\left(\frac{Y - \mu}{\sigma} < \frac{260 - 300}{14.49}\right) = P(Z < -2.76)$$

$$= .0029$$

As we pointed out, the normal approximation of the binomial distribution is made necessary by the needs of statistical inference. As you will discover, statistical inference generally involves the use of large values of n, and the part of the sampling distribution that is of greatest interest lies in the tail regions. The correction factor was a temporary tool that allowed us to convince you that a binomial distribution can be approximated by a normal distribution. Now that we have done so, we will use the normal approximation of the binomial distribution to approximate the sampling distribution of a sample proportion, and in such applications the correction factor will be omitted.

8-2c Approximate Sampling Distribution of a Sample Proportion

Using the laws of expected value and variance, we can determine the mean, variance, and standard deviation of $\hat{P}$. We will summarize what we have learned.

Sampling Distribution of a Sample Proportion

1. $\hat{P}$ is approximately normally distributed provided that np and $n(1 - p)$ are greater than or equal to 5.

2. The expected value: $E(\hat{P}) = p$

3. The variance: $V(\hat{P}) = \sigma_{\hat{p}}^2 = \dfrac{p(1 - p)}{n}$

4. The standard deviation: $\sigma_{\hat{p}} = \sqrt{p(1 - p)/n}$

(The standard deviation of $\hat{P}$ is called the **standard error of the proportion**.)

The sample size requirement is theoretical because in practice much larger sample sizes are needed for the normal approximation to be useful.

his popularity has not changed, what is the probability that more than half of the sample would vote for him?

SOLUTION

The number of respondents who would vote for the representative is a binomial random variable with $n = 300$ and $p = .52$. We want to determine the probability that the sample proportion is greater than 50%; that is, we want to find $P(\hat{P} > .50)$.

We now know that the sample proportion $\hat{P}$ is approximately normally distributed with mean $p = .52$ and standard deviation $= \sqrt{p(1-p)/n} = \sqrt{(.52)(.48)/300} = .0288$.

Thus, we calculate

$$P(\hat{P} > .50) = P\left(\frac{\hat{P} - p}{\sqrt{p(1-p)/n}} > \frac{.50 - .52}{.0288}\right)$$
$$= P(Z > -.69) = 1 - P(Z < -.69)$$
$$= 1 - .2451 = .7549$$

If we assume that the level of support remains at 52%, the probability that more than half the sample of 300 people would vote for the representative is .7549.

© AP Photo/Alice Keeney

EXAMPLE 8.2
Political Survey

In the last election, a state representative received 52% of the votes cast. One year after the election, the representative organized a survey that asked a random sample of 300 people whether they would vote for him in the next election. If we assume that

EXERCISES

8.1 Let X represent the result of the toss of a fair die. Find the following probabilities.

a. $P(X = 1)$
b. $P(X = 6)$

8.2 Let $\overline{X}$ represent the mean of the toss of two fair dice. Use the probabilities listed in Table 8.2 to determine the following probabilities.

a. $P(\overline{X} = 1)$
b. $P(\overline{X} = 6)$

8.3 An experiment consists of tossing five balanced dice. Find the following probabilities. (Determine the exact probabilities as we did in Tables 8.1 and 8.2 for two dice.)

a. $P(\overline{X} = 1)$
b. $P(\overline{X} = 6)$

8.4 Refer to Exercises 8.1 to 8.3. What do the probabilities tell you about the variances of X and $\overline{X}$?

8.5 A normally distributed population has a mean of 40 and a standard deviation of 12. What does the central limit theorem say about the sampling distribution of the mean if samples of size 100 are drawn from this population?

8.6 Refer to Exercise 8.5. Suppose that the population is not normally distributed. Does this change your answer? Explain.

8.7 The heights of North American women are normally distributed with a mean of 64 inches and a standard deviation of 2 inches.

a. What is the probability that a randomly selected woman is taller than 66 inches?
b. A random sample of four women is selected. What is the probability that the sample mean height is greater than 66 inches?
c. What is the probability that the mean height of a random sample of 100 women is greater than 66 inches?

8.8 Refer to Exercise 8.7. If the population of women's heights is not normally distributed, which if any of the questions can you answer? Explain.

8.9 The amount of time the university professors devote to their jobs per week is normally distributed with a mean of 52 hours and a standard deviation of 6 hours.

a. What is the probability that a professor works for more than 60 hours per week?
b. Find the probability that the mean amount of work per week for three randomly selected professors is more than 60 hours.
c. Find the probability that if three professors are randomly selected all three work for more than 60 hours per week.

8.10 The number of pizzas consumed per month by university students is normally distributed with a mean of 10 and a standard deviation of 3.

a. What proportion of students consume more than 12 pizzas per month?
b. What is the probability that in a random sample of 25 students more than 275 pizzas are consumed? (*Hint:* What is the mean number of pizzas consumed by the sample of 25 students?)

8.11 The manufacturer of cans of salmon that are supposed to have a net weight of 6 ounces tells you that the net weight is actually a normal random variable with a mean of 6.05 ounces and a standard deviation of .18 ounces. Suppose that you draw a random sample of 36 cans.

a. Find the probability that the mean weight of the sample is less than 5.97 ounces.
b. Suppose your random sample of 36 cans of salmon produced a mean weight that is less than 5.97 ounces. Comment on the statement made by the manufacturer.

8.12 The number of customers who enter a supermarket each hour is normally distributed with a mean of 600 and a standard deviation of 200. The supermarket is open 16 hours per day. What is the probability that the total number of customers who enter the supermarket in one day is greater than 10,000? (*Hint:* Calculate the average hourly number of customers necessary to exceed 10,000 in one 16-hour day.)

8.13 The sign on the elevator in the Peters Building, which houses the School of Business and Economics at Wilfrid Laurier University, states, "Maximum Capacity 1,140 Kilograms (2500 Pounds) or 16 Persons." A professor of statistics wonders what the probability is that 16 persons would weigh more than 1,140 kilograms. Discuss what the professor needs (besides the ability to perform the calculations) in order to satisfy his curiosity.

8.14 Refer to Exercise 8.13. Suppose that the professor discovers that the weights of people who use the elevator are normally distributed with an average of 75 kilograms and a standard deviation of 10 kilograms. Calculate the probability that the professor seeks.

8.15 The time it takes for a statistics professor to mark his midterm test is normally distributed with a mean of 4.8 minutes and a standard deviation of 1.3 minutes. There are 60 students in the professor's class. What is the probability that he needs more than 5 hours to mark all the midterm tests? (The 60 midterm tests of the students in this year's class can be considered a random sample of the many thousands of midterm tests the professor has marked and will mark.)

8.16 Refer to Exercise 8.15. Does your answer change if you discover that the times needed to mark a midterm test are not normally distributed?

8.17 The proportion of eligible voters in the next election who will vote for the incumbent is assumed to be 55%. What is the probability that in a random sample of 500 voters less than 49% say they will vote for the incumbent?

8.18 The assembly line that produces an electronic component of a missile system has historically resulted in a 2% defective rate. A random sample of 800 components is drawn. What is the probability that the defective rate is greater than 4%? Suppose that in the random sample the defective rate is 4%. What does that suggest about the defective rate on the assembly line?

8.19 a. The manufacturer of aspirin claims that the proportion of headache sufferers who get relief with just two aspirins is 53%. What is the probability that in a random sample of 400 headache sufferers, less than 50% obtain relief? If 50% of the sample actually obtained relief, what does this suggest about the manufacturer's claim?

b. Repeat part (a) using a sample of 1,000.

8.20 The manager of a restaurant in a commercial building has determined that the proportion of customers who drink tea is 14%. What is the probability that in the next 100 customers at least 10% will be tea drinkers?

8.21 A commercial for a manufacturer of household appliances claims that 3% of all its products require a service call in the first year. A consumer protection association wants to check the claim by surveying 400 households that recently purchased one of the company's appliances. What is the probability that more than 5% require a service call within the first year? What would you say about the commercial's honesty if in a random sample of 400 households 5% report at least one service call?

8.22 The Laurier Company's brand has a market share of 30%. Suppose a survey asks 1,000 consumers of the product which brand they prefer. What is the probability that more than 32% of the respondents say they prefer the Laurier brand?

8.23 A university bookstore claims that 50% of its customers are satisfied with the service and prices.

a. If this claim is true, what is the probability that in a random sample of 600 customers less than 45% are satisfied?

b. Suppose that in a random sample of 600 customers, 270 express satisfaction with the bookstore. What does this tell you about the bookstore's claim?

8.24 A psychologist believes that 80% of male drivers continue to drive when lost, hoping to find the location they seek rather than ask directions. To examine this belief, he took a random sample of 350 male drivers and asked each what they did when lost. If the belief is true, determine the probability that less than 75% said they continue driving.

8.25 The Red Lobster restaurant chain regularly surveys its customers. On the basis of these surveys, the management of the chain claims that 75% of its customers rate the food as excellent. A consumer testing service wants to examine the claim by asking 460 customers to rate the food. What is the probability that less than 70% rate the food as excellent?

USE THE TOOLS.

- Rip out the Review Cards in the back of your book to study.

Or Visit CourseMate to:

- Read, search, highlight, and take notes in the Interactive eBook
- Review Flashcards (Print or Online) to master key terms
- Test yourself with Auto-Graded Quizzes
- Bring concepts to life with Games, Videos, and Animations!

Go to CourseMate for **BSTAT2** to begin using these tools.
Access at **www.cengagebrain.com**

Complete the Speak Up
survey in CourseMate at
www.cengagebrain.com

Follow us at
www.facebook.com/4ltrpress

©iStockphoto.com/A-Digit | © Cengage Learning 2011

CHAPTER 9

Introduction to Estimation

objectives

9-1   Concepts of Estimation

9-2   Estimating the Population Proportion

9-3   Selecting the Sample Size to Estimate the Proportion

GENERAL SOCIAL SURVEY: NUMBER OF AMERICANS WORKING FOR GOVERNMENTS

[GSS2008*] In the United States as well as other countries, governments have been expanding their programs requiring the hiring of new employees. To help assess this trend, we would like to know the number of Americans who work for government. Fortunately, the General Social Survey asked the following question.

Are you employed by the federal, state, or local government, or by a private employer?

WRKGOVT: 1 = Government, 2 = Private.

Estimate with 95% confidence the number of Americans who work for government.

In 2008, there were 230,151,000 American adults (18 years of age and older). (*Source: Statistical Abstract of the United States,* 2009, Table 7.) (See page 141 for the solution.)

Having discussed descriptive statistics (Chapter 3), probability distributions (Chapters 6 and 7), and sampling distributions (Chapter 8), we are ready to tackle statistical inference. As we explained in Chapter 1, *statistical inference* is the process by which we acquire information and draw conclusions about populations from samples. There are two general procedures for making inferences about populations: *estimation* and *hypothesis testing*. In this chapter, we introduce the concepts and foundations of estimation. In Chapter 10, we describe the fundamentals of hypothesis testing. Because most of what we do in the remainder of this book applies the concepts of estimation and hypothesis testing, understanding Chapters 9 and 10 is vital to your development as a statistics practitioner.

9-1) Concepts of Estimation

As its name suggests, the objective of estimation is to determine the approximate value of a population parameter on the basis of a sample statistic. For example, the sample proportion is employed to estimate the population proportion. We refer to the sample proportion (denoted $\hat{P}$) as the *estimator* of the population proportion. Once the sample proportion has been computed, its value is called the *estimate*. In this chapter, we will introduce the statistical process in which we estimate a population proportion using sample data. In the rest of the book, we use the concepts and techniques introduced here for other parameters.

9-1a Point and Interval Estimators

We can use sample data to estimate a population parameter in two ways. First, we can compute the value of the estimator and consider that value as the estimate of the parameter. Such an estimator is called a *point estimator*.

Point Estimator

A **point estimator** draws inferences about a population by estimating the value of an unknown parameter using a single value or point.

There are three drawbacks to using point estimators. First, it is virtually certain that the estimate will be wrong. (The probability that a continuous random variable will equal a specific value is 0. In other words, the probability that $\hat{p}$ will exactly equal p is 0.) Second, we often need to know how close the estimator is to the parameter. Third, in drawing inferences about a population, it is intuitively reasonable to expect that a large sample will produce more accurate results, because it contains more information than a smaller sample does. But point estimators don't have the capacity to reflect the effects of larger sample sizes. As a consequence, we use the second method of estimating a population parameter: the *interval estimator*.

Interval Estimator

An **interval estimator** draws inferences about a population by estimating the value of an unknown parameter using an interval.

As you will see, the interval estimator is affected by the sample size; because it possesses this feature, we will deal mostly with interval estimators in this text.

To illustrate the difference between point and interval estimators, suppose a pollster wants to estimate the proportion of voters who will support a particular proposition in an upcoming election. From a sample of 500 people selected at random, she calculates the sample proportion to be 40%. The point estimate is the sample proportion. In other words, she estimates the proportion of all voters who support the proposition in the entire population to be 40%. Using the technique described subsequently, she may instead use an interval estimate; she estimates that the population proportion lies between 35% and 45%.

Numerous applications of estimation occur in the real world. For example, television network executives want to know the proportion of television viewers who are tuned in to their networks, an economist wants to know the mean income of university graduates, and a medical researcher wishes to estimate the recovery rate of heart attack victims treated with a new drug. In each case, to accomplish the objective exactly, the statistics practitioner would have to examine each member of the population and then calculate the parameter of interest. For instance, network executives would have to ask each person in the country what he or she is watching to determine the proportion of people who are watching their shows. Because there are millions of television viewers, the task is both impractical and prohibitively expensive. An alternative is to take a random sample from this population, calculate the sample proportion, and use that as an estimator of the population proportion. The use of the sample proportion to estimate the population proportion seems logical. The selection of the sample statistic to be used as an estimator, however, depends on the characteristics of that statistic. Naturally, we want to use the statistic with the most desirable qualities for our purposes.

One desirable quality of an estimator is *unbiasedness*.

Unbiased Estimator

An **unbiased estimator** of a population parameter is an estimator whose expected value is equal to that parameter.

This means that if you were to take an infinite number of samples and calculate the value of the estimator in each sample, the average value of the estimators would equal the parameter. This amounts to saying that, on average, the sample statistic is equal to the parameter.

We know that the sample mean $\overline{X}$ is an unbiased estimator of the population mean μ. In presenting the sampling distribution of $\overline{X}$ in Section 8-1, we stated that

$E(\overline{X}) = \mu$. We also know that the sample proportion is an unbiased estimator of the population proportion because $E(\hat{P}) = p$.

Recall that in Chapter 3 we defined the sample variance as

$$s^2 = \sum \frac{(x_i - \overline{x})^2}{n - 1}$$

At the time, it seemed odd that we divided by $n - 1$ rather than by n. The reason for choosing $n - 1$ was to make $E(s^2) = \sigma^2$ so that this definition makes the sample variance an unbiased estimator of the population variance. Had we defined the sample variance using n in the denominator, then the resulting statistic would be a biased estimator of the population variance, one whose expected value is less than the parameter.

Knowing that an estimator is unbiased only assures us that its expected value equals the parameter; it does not tell us how close the estimator is to the parameter. Another desirable quality is that as the sample size grows larger, the sample statistic should come closer to the population parameter. This quality is called *consistency*.

Consistency

An unbiased estimator is said to be **consistent** if the difference between the estimator and the parameter grows smaller as the sample size grows larger.

The measure we use to gauge closeness is the variance (or the standard deviation). Thus, $\overline{X}$ is a consistent estimator of μ, because the variance of $\overline{X}$ is σ^2/n. This implies that as n grows larger, the variance of $\overline{X}$ grows smaller. As a consequence, an increasing proportion of sample means falls close to μ. Similarly, $\hat{P}$ is a consistent estimator of p because it is unbiased and the variance of $\hat{P}$ is $p(1 - p)/n$, which grows smaller as n grows larger.

Figure 9.1 depicts two sampling distributions of $\overline{X}$ when samples are drawn from the same population.

One sampling distribution is based on samples of size 25, and the other is based on samples of size 100. The former is more spread out than the latter.

A third desirable quality is *relative efficiency*, which compares two unbiased estimators of a parameter.

Relative Efficiency

If there are two unbiased estimators of a parameter, the one whose variance is smaller is said to be **relatively more efficient**.

We have already seen that the sample mean is an unbiased estimator of the population mean and that its variance is σ^2/n. Statisticians have established that the sample median is an unbiased estimator but that its variance is greater than that of the sample mean (when the population is normal). As a consequence, the sample mean is relatively more efficient than the sample median when estimating the population mean.

In the remaining chapters of this book, we will present the statistical inference of a number of different population parameters. In each case, we will select a sample statistic that is unbiased and consistent. When there is more than one such statistic, we will choose the one that is relatively efficient to serve as the estimator.

9-1b Developing an Understanding of Statistical Concepts

In this section, we described three desirable characteristics of estimators: unbiasedness, consistency, and relative efficiency. An understanding of statistics requires that you know that there are several potential estimators for each parameter but that we choose the estimators used in this book because they possess these characteristics.

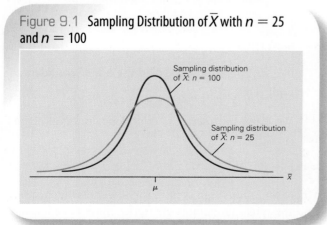

Figure 9.1 **Sampling Distribution of $\overline{X}$ with $n = 25$ and $n = 100$**

Sampling distribution of $\overline{X}$: $n = 100$

Sampling distribution of $\overline{X}$: $n = 25$

© Cengage Learning

Jupiterimages/Workbook Stock/Getty Images

9-2 Estimating the Population Proportion

One of the most common uses of this technique is in political polling. The objective is to estimate the proportion of voters who support each candidate. The best estimator of a population proportion is the sample proportion $\hat{p}$ that we introduced in Section 8-2. We defined $\hat{p}$ as the number of successes divided by the sample size; that is, $\hat{p} = \frac{x}{n}$. We showed that $\hat{p}$ is approximately normally distributed with a mean of p and a standard deviation of $\sqrt{p(1-p)/n}$. Recall that in Chapter 8 we referred to the standard deviation of $\hat{p}$ as the standard error.[1]

We can express this in the following way.

$$Z = \frac{\hat{p} - p}{\sqrt{p(1-p)/n}}$$

In Chapter 7, we introduced the notation Z_A which is the value of Z such that the area (probability) to its right is A. We also showed that $Z_{.025} = 1.96$. Because the standard normal distribution is symmetric about 0, the value of Z such that the area to its *left* is A is $-Z_A$. Thus, for example $-Z_{.025}$ is equal to -1.96. Figure 9.2 displays these notations.

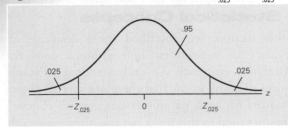

Figure 9.2 **Normal Distribution with $-Z_{.025}$ and $Z_{.025}$**

We can express this as

$$P(-Z_{.025} < Z < Z_{.025}) = .95$$

And because $Z = \dfrac{\hat{p} - p}{\sqrt{p(1-p)/n}}$, we can substitute this

value into the probability statement

$$P\left(-Z_{.025} < \frac{\hat{p} - p}{\sqrt{p(1-p)/n}} < Z_{.025}\right) = .95$$

[1] Since Chapter 6 we've been using the convention in which an uppercase letter (usually X) represents a random variable and a lowercase letter (usually x) represents one of its values. However, in the formulas used in statistical inference, the distinction between the variable and its value becomes blurred.

With a little mathematical work, we can rewrite:

$$P\left(\hat{p} - 1.96\sqrt{\frac{p(1-p)}{n}} < p < \hat{p} + 1.96\sqrt{\frac{p(1-p)}{n}}\right) = .95$$

We can do the same thing with different probabilities. For example, for a 90% probability, we would have

$$P\left(\hat{p} - 1.645\sqrt{\frac{p(1-p)}{n}} < p < \hat{p} + 1.645\sqrt{\frac{p(1-p)}{n}}\right) = .90$$

Or we can generalize

$$P\left(\hat{p} - Z_{\alpha/2}\sqrt{\frac{p(1-p)}{n}} < p < \hat{p} + Z_{\alpha/2}\sqrt{\frac{p(1-p)}{n}}\right) = 1 - \alpha$$

where α (Greek letter *alpha*) can be any number between 0 and 1. In this form, notice that the population proportion is in the center of the interval created by adding and subtracting $Z_{\alpha/2}$ standard errors to and from the sample proportion. It is important for you to understand that this is merely another form of probability statement about the sample proportion. This equation says that, with repeated sampling from this population, the proportion of values of $\hat{p}$ for which the interval

$$\hat{p} - Z_{\alpha/2}\sqrt{\frac{p(1-p)}{n}}, \hat{p} + Z_{\alpha/2}\sqrt{\frac{p(1-p)}{n}}$$

includes the population proportion p is equal to $1 - \alpha$. This form of probability statement is very useful to us because we can use it to estimate a population proportion. However, there is a problem with the standard error: if p is unknown, how do we calculate it? We get around this problem by estimating p in the standard error using the sample proportion $\hat{p}$. By doing so, we produce the **confidence interval estimator of p**.

Confidence Interval Estimator of p

$$\hat{p} - Z_{\alpha/2}\sqrt{\frac{\hat{p}(1-\hat{p})}{n}}, \hat{p} + Z_{\alpha/2}\sqrt{\frac{\hat{p}(1-\hat{p})}{n}}$$

The probability $1 - \alpha$ is called the **confidence level**.

$\hat{p} - Z_{\alpha/2}\sqrt{\dfrac{\hat{p}(1-\hat{p})}{n}}$ is called the **lower confidence limit (LCL)**.

$\hat{p} + Z_{\alpha/2}\sqrt{\dfrac{\hat{p}(1-\hat{p})}{n}}$ is called the **upper confidence limit (UCL)**.

We often represent the confidence interval estimator as

$$\hat{p} \pm Z_{\alpha/2}\sqrt{\frac{\hat{p}(1-\hat{p})}{n}}$$

where the minus sign defines the lower confidence limit and the plus sign defines the upper confidence limit.

To apply this formula, we specify the confidence level $1 - \alpha$, from which we determine α, $\alpha/2$, and $Z_{\alpha/2}$ (from Table 3 in Appendix B). Because the confidence level is the probability that the interval includes the actual value of p, we generally set $1 - \alpha$ close to 1 (usually between .90 and .99).

In Table 9.1, we list four commonly used confidence levels and their associated values of $Z_{\alpha/2}$. For example, if the confidence level is $1 - \alpha = .95$, $\alpha = .05$, $\alpha/2 = .025$, and $Z_{\alpha/2} = Z_{.025} = 1.96$. The resulting confidence interval estimator is then called the **95% confidence interval estimator of** p.

Table 9.1 **Four Commonly Used Confidence Levels and** $z_{\alpha/2}$

$1 - \alpha$	α	$\alpha/2$	$z_{\alpha/2}$
.90	.10	.05	$z_{.05} = 1.645$
.95	.05	.025	$z_{.025} = 1.96$
.98	.02	.01	$z_{.01} = 2.33$
.99	.01	.005	$z_{.005} = 2.575$

© Cengage Learning

The following example illustrates how statistical techniques are applied. It also illustrates how we intend to solve problems in the rest of this book. The solution process that we advocate and use throughout this book is by and large the same one that statistics practitioners use to apply their skills in the real world. The process is divided into three stages. Simply stated, the stages are (1) the activities we perform before the calculations, (2) the calculations, and (3) the activities we perform after the calculations.

In stage 1, we determine the appropriate statistical technique to employ. Of course, for this example you will have no difficulty identifying the technique, because at this point you know only one. (In practice, stage 1 also addresses the problem of *how* to gather the data. The methods used in the examples and exercises are described in the problem.)

In the second stage, we calculate the statistics. We will do this in three ways.[2] To illustrate how the computations are completed, we will do the arithmetic manually with the assistance of a calculator. Solving problems by hand often provides insights into the statistical inference technique. In addition, we will use the computer in two ways. First, in Excel we will use the Analysis ToolPak (**Data** menu item **Data Analysis**) or the add-ins we created for this book (**Add-Ins** menu

___

[2] We anticipate that students in most statistics classes will use only one of the three methods of computing statistics: the choice made by the instructor. If such is the case, readers are directed to ignore the other two.

item **Data Analysis Plus**). Finally, we will use Minitab, one of the easiest software packages to use.

In the third and last stage of the solution, we intend to interpret the results and deal with the question presented in the problem. To be capable of properly interpreting statistical results, one needs to have an understanding of the fundamental principles underlying statistical inference.

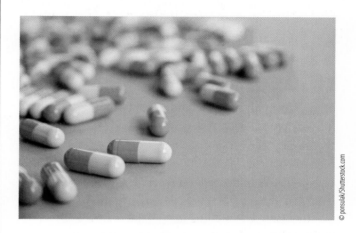

© ponsulak/Shutterstock.com

EXAMPLE 9.1
Prescription Drugs

[Xm09-01] Because television newscast audiences tend to be older (and because older people suffer from a variety of medical ailments) pharmaceutical companies' advertising often appears on national news in the three networks (ABC, CBS, and NBC). The ads concern prescription drugs such as those to treat heartburn. To determine how effective the ads are, a survey was undertaken. Adults 50 and older who regularly watch network newscasts were asked whether they had contacted their physician to ask about one of the prescription drugs advertised during the newscast. The responses (1 = No and 2 = Yes) were recorded. Estimate with 95% confidence the fraction of adults 50 and older who have contacted their physician to inquire about a prescription drug.

SOLUTION
IDENTIFY

The population of interest is Americans 50 and older who regularly watch network news. Our task is to estimate the proportion who contact their physician to ask about the advertised pharmaceutical. The parameter is p and its estimator is

$$\hat{p} \pm Z_{\alpha/2}\sqrt{\frac{\hat{p}(1 - \hat{p})}{n}}$$

The next step is to perform the calculations. As we discussed previously, we will perform the calculations in three ways: manually, using Excel, and using Minitab.

COMPUTE
Manually

We need three values to construct the confidence interval estimate of p. They are:

Sample size n

Number of successes X (Code = 2)

$Z_{\alpha/2}$

By analyzing the data, we find that $n = 693$ and $x = 104$. Thus,

$$\hat{p} = \frac{x}{n} = \frac{104}{693} = .150$$

The confidence level is set at 95%; thus, $1 - \alpha = .95$, $\alpha = 1 - .95 = .05$, and $\alpha/2 = .025$.

From Table 3 in Appendix B or from Table 9.1, we find

$$Z_{\alpha/2} = Z_{.025} = 1.96$$

Substituting $\hat{p}$, n, and $Z_{\alpha/2}$ into the confidence interval estimator, we find

$$\hat{p} \pm Z_{\alpha/2}\sqrt{\frac{\hat{p}(1-\hat{p})}{n}} = .150 \pm 1.96\sqrt{\frac{(.150)(1-.150)}{693}}$$
$$= .150 \pm .026$$

The lower and upper confidence limits are LCL = .124 and UCL = .176.

Excel

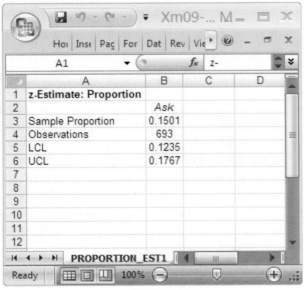

INSTRUCTIONS

1. Type or import the data into one column. (Open Xm09-01.)

2. Click **Add-Ins**, **Data Analysis Plus**, and **Z Estimate: Proportion**.

3. Fill in the dialog box: **Input Range** (A1:A694), click **Labels** if the first row contains the name of the variable, and specify the confidence level by typing the value of $\alpha(.05)$.

Minitab

Test and CI for One Proportion: Ask

```
Event = 2

Variable    X    N    Sample p         95% CI

Ask        104  693   0.150072   (0.123482, 0.176662)

Using the normal approximation.
```

INSTRUCTIONS

The data must represent successes and failures. The codes can be numbers or text. There can be only two kinds of entries, one representing success and the other representing failure. If numbers are used, then Minitab will interpret the larger one as a success.

1. Type or import that data into one column. (Open Xm09-01.)

2. Click **Stat**, **Basic Statistics**, and **1 Proportion** . . . .

3. Type or use the **Select** button to specify the name of the variable or the column in which it is stored in the **Samples in columns** box (Ask) and click **Options** . . . .

4. Type the value for the confidence level (.95), and in the **Alternative** box select **not equal**. Click **Use test and interval based on normal distribution**.

INTERPRET

We estimate that the proportion lies between .124 and .176.

9-2a Estimating the Total Number of Successes in a Large Finite Population

The technique in this section assumes infinitely large populations. When the population is large and finite, we can estimate the total number of successes in the population.

To produce the confidence interval estimator of the total, we multiply the lower and upper confidence limits of the interval estimator of the proportion of successes by

GENERAL SOCIAL SURVEY: NUMBER OF AMERICANS WORKING FOR GOVERNMENTS: SOLUTION

IDENTIFY

The problem objective is to describe a population when data are nominal. The parameter to be estimated is p, the proportion of American adults working for the government.

COMPUTE

The following is the Excel printout for the estimate of the proportion of American adults who work for the government. The Minitab output is similar. (Minitab users will have to recode the data so that working for the government is the higher of the two codes.)

To estimate the total number we multiply the total number of American adults by the lower and upper limits.

> Number: LCL = 230,151,000(.1619)
>   = 37,270,284
> UCL = 230,151,000(.1963) = 45,175,453

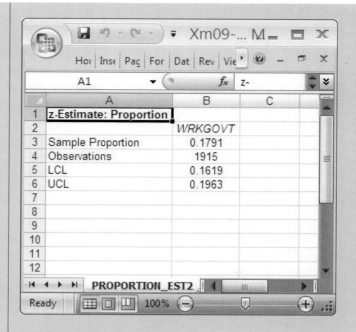

INTERPRET

We estimate that the number of American adults working for government lies between 37,270,284 and 45,175,453.

the population size. The confidence interval estimator of the total number of successes in a large finite population is

$$N\left(\hat{p} \pm z_{\alpha/2}\sqrt{\frac{\hat{p}(1-\hat{p})}{n}}\right)$$

We will use this estimator in the chapter-opening example and several exercises.

9-2b Interpreting the Confidence Interval Estimate

Some people erroneously interpret the confidence interval estimate in Example 9.1 to mean that there is a 95% probability that the population proportion lies between .124 and .176. This interpretation is wrong because it implies that the population proportion is a variable about which we can make probability statements. In fact, the population proportion is a fixed but unknown quantity. Consequently, we cannot interpret the confidence interval estimate of p as a probability statement about p. To translate the confidence interval estimate properly, we must remember that the confidence interval estimator was derived from the sampling distribution of the sample proportion. In Section 8-2, we used the sampling distribution to make probability statements about

the sample proportion. Although the form has changed, the confidence interval estimator is also a probability statement about the sample proportion. It states that there is $1 - \alpha$ probability that the sample proportion will be equal to a value such that the interval

$$\hat{p} - Z_{\alpha/2}\sqrt{\frac{\hat{p}(1-\hat{p})}{n}} \text{ to } \hat{p} + Z_{\alpha/2}\sqrt{\frac{\hat{p}(1-\hat{p})}{n}}$$

will include the population proportion. Once the sample proportion is computed, the interval acts as the lower and upper limits of the interval estimate of the population proportion.

As an illustration, suppose we want to estimate the proportion of heads when flipping a fair coin. Because the coin is fair, we know that the proportion of heads is $p = .5$. Pretend now that we don't know that $p = .5$ and that we want to estimate its value. To estimate p, we draw a sample of size $n = 400$ (we flip the coin 400 times) and calculate $\hat{p}$. The confidence interval estimator of p is shown next. (We'll use the actual value of the standard error instead of its estimator.)

$$\hat{p} \pm Z_{\alpha/2}\sqrt{\frac{p(1-p)}{n}}$$

The 90% confidence interval estimator is

$$\hat{p} \pm Z_{\alpha/2}\sqrt{\frac{p(1-p)}{n}} = \hat{p} \pm 1.645\sqrt{\frac{(.5)(1-.5)}{400}}$$
$$= \hat{p} \pm .0411$$

This notation means that, if we repeatedly draw samples of size 400 from this population, 90% of the values of $\hat{p}$ will be such that p would lie somewhere between the lower limit $\hat{p} - .0411$ and the upper limit $\hat{p} + .0411$, and 10% of the values of $\hat{p}$ will produce intervals that would not include p. Now, imagine that we draw 40 samples of 400 observations each. The values of $\hat{p}$ and the resulting confidence interval estimates of p are shown in Table 9.2. Notice that not all the intervals include the true value of the parameter. Samples 3, 5, 13, and 28 produce values of $\hat{p}$ that in turn produce intervals that exclude $p = .5$.

Table 9.2 **90% Confidence Interval Estimates of p**

Sample	$\hat{p}$	LCL	UCL	Does Interval Include $p = .5$?
1	0.505	0.464	0.546	Yes
2	0.473	0.431	0.514	Yes
3	0.558	0.516	0.599	No
4	0.530	0.489	0.571	Yes
5	0.440	0.399	0.481	No
6	0.540	0.499	0.581	Yes
7	0.483	0.441	0.524	Yes
8	0.463	0.422	0.504	Yes
9	0.478	0.436	0.519	Yes
10	0.525	0.484	0.566	Yes
11	0.528	0.486	0.569	Yes
12	0.483	0.441	0.524	Yes
13	0.555	0.514	0.596	No
14	0.480	0.439	0.521	Yes
15	0.495	0.454	0.536	Yes
16	0.490	0.449	0.531	Yes
17	0.535	0.494	0.576	Yes
18	0.500	0.459	0.541	Yes
19	0.478	0.436	0.519	Yes
20	0.505	0.464	0.546	Yes
21	0.523	0.481	0.564	Yes
22	0.503	0.461	0.544	Yes
23	0.470	0.429	0.511	Yes
24	0.533	0.491	0.574	Yes
25	0.480	0.439	0.521	Yes
26	0.495	0.454	0.536	Yes
27	0.485	0.444	0.526	Yes
28	0.455	0.414	0.496	No
29	0.480	0.439	0.521	Yes
30	0.493	0.451	0.534	Yes
31	0.495	0.454	0.536	Yes
32	0.508	0.466	0.549	Yes

(continued)

Table 9.2 *(continued)*

Sample	$\hat{p}$	LCL	UCL	Does Interval Include $p = .5$?
33	0.525	0.484	0.566	Yes
34	0.525	0.484	0.566	Yes
35	0.515	0.474	0.556	Yes
36	0.533	0.491	0.574	Yes
37	0.510	0.469	0.551	Yes
38	0.495	0.454	0.536	Yes
39	0.500	0.459	0.541	Yes
40	0.505	0.464	0.546	Yes

Students often react to this situation by asking, What went wrong with samples 3, 5, 13, and 28? The answer is, nothing. Statistics does not promise 100% certainty. In fact, in this illustration, we expected 90% of the intervals to include $p = .5$ and 10% to exclude $p = .5$. Because we produced 40 intervals, we expected that 4.0 (10% of 40) intervals would not contain $p = .5$.[3] It is important to understand that, even when the statistics practitioner performs experiments properly, a certain proportion (in this example, 10%) of the experiments will produce incorrect estimates by random chance.

We can improve the confidence associated with the interval estimate. If we let the confidence level $1 - \alpha$ equal .95, the 95% confidence interval estimator is

$$\hat{p} \pm Z_{\alpha/2}\sqrt{\frac{p(1-p)}{n}} = \hat{p} \pm 1.96\sqrt{\frac{(.5)(1-.5)}{400}}$$
$$= \hat{p} \pm .0490$$

Because this interval is wider, it is more likely to include the value of p. If you redo Table 9.2, this time using a 95% confidence interval estimator, only samples 3, 5, and 13 will produce intervals that do not include $p = .5$ (Notice that we expected 5% of the intervals to exclude p and that we actually observed $3/40 = 7.5\%$.) The 99% confidence interval estimator is

$$\hat{p} \pm Z_{\alpha/2}\sqrt{\frac{p(1-p)}{n}} = \hat{p} \pm 2.575\sqrt{\frac{(.5)(1-.5)}{400}}$$
$$= \hat{p} \pm .0644$$

Applying this interval estimate to the sample proportions listed in Table 9.2 would result in having all 40 interval estimates include the population proportion $p = .5$. (We expected 1% of the intervals to exclude p; we observed $0/40 = 0\%$.)

---

[3] In this illustration, exactly 10% of the sample proportions produced interval estimates that excluded the value of p, but this will not always be the case. Remember, we expect 10% of the sample proportions in the long run to result in intervals excluding p. This group of 40 sample proportions does not constitute "the long run."

In actual practice, only one sample will be drawn, and thus only one value of $\hat{p}$ will be calculated. The resulting interval estimate will either correctly include the parameter or incorrectly exclude it. Unfortunately, statistics practitioners do not know whether they are correct in each case; they know only that, in the long run, they will incorrectly estimate the parameter some of the time. Statistics practitioners accept that as a fact of life.

We summarize our calculations in Example 9.1 as follows. We estimate that the proportion of American adults in the population of interest who contact their physicians to inquire about the advertised pharmaceutical falls between .124 and .176, and this type of estimator is correct 95% of the time. Thus, the confidence level applies to our estimation procedure and not to any one interval. Incidentally, news media often refer to the 95% figure as "19 times out of 20," which emphasizes the long-run aspect of the confidence level.

9-2c Information and the Width of the Interval

Interval estimation, like all other statistical techniques, is designed to convert data into information. However, a wide interval provides little information. For example, suppose that as a result of a statistical study we estimate with 95% confidence that the proportion of voters who intend to vote for the incumbent lies between .09 and .88. This interval is so wide that very little information was derived from the data. Suppose, however, that the interval estimate was .43 to .48. This interval is much narrower, providing us with much more precise information about the proportion.

The width of the confidence interval estimate of p is a function of the sample proportion $\hat{p}$, the sample size n, and the confidence level $1 - \alpha$. Consider Example 9.1, where the interval estimate was $.150 \pm .026$.

Although we have no control over the value of $\hat{p}$, we do have the power to select values for the other two elements. In Example 9.1 we chose a 95% confidence level. If we had chosen 90% instead, the interval estimate would have been

$$\hat{p} \pm Z_{\alpha/2}\sqrt{\frac{\hat{p}(1-\hat{p})}{n}} = .150 \pm 1.645\sqrt{\frac{(.150)(1-.150)}{693}} = .150 \pm .022$$

A 99% confidence level results in this interval estimate:

$$\hat{p} \pm Z_{\alpha/2}\sqrt{\frac{\hat{p}(1-\hat{p})}{n}} = .150 \pm 2.575\sqrt{\frac{(.150)(1-.150)}{693}} = .150 \pm .035$$

As you can see, increasing the confidence level widens the interval; decreasing it narrows the interval. However, a large confidence level is generally desirable because that means a larger proportion of confidence interval estimates will be correct in the long run. There is a direct relationship between the width of the interval and the confidence level. This is because we need to widen the interval in order to be more confident in the estimate. (The analogy is that to be more likely to capture a butterfly, we need a larger butterfly net.) The trade-off between increased confidence and the resulting wider confidence interval estimates must be resolved by the statistics practitioner. As a general rule, however, 95% confidence is considered "standard."

The third element is the sample size. Had the sample size been 2,772 (four times the original sample size of 693), the confidence interval estimate would become

$$\hat{p} \pm Z_{\alpha/2}\sqrt{\frac{\hat{p}(1-\hat{p})}{n}} = .150 \pm 1.96\sqrt{\frac{(.150)(1-.150)}{2772}} = .150 \pm .013$$

Increasing the sample size fourfold decreases the width of the interval by half. A larger sample size provides more potential information. The increased amount of information is reflected in a narrower interval. However, there is another trade-off: increasing the sample size increases the sampling cost.

In the next section, we discuss how to determine the sample size to estimate a population proportion.

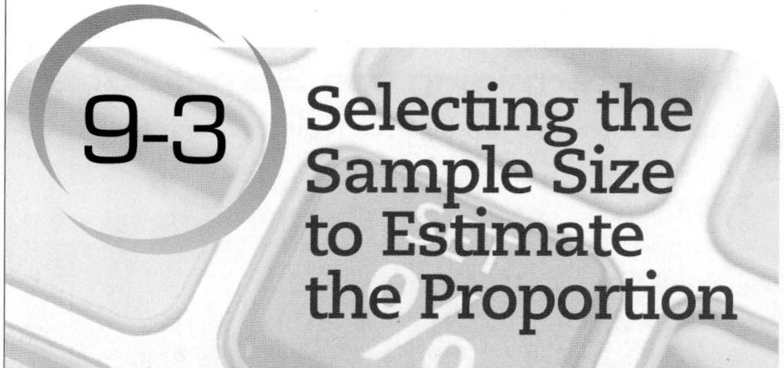

9-3 Selecting the Sample Size to Estimate the Proportion

© Glowimages

As we discussed in the previous section, if the interval estimate is too wide, it provides little information. In Example 9.1, the interval estimate was .124 to .176. This interval may be too wide to be effective. Fortunately, statistics practitioners can control the width of the interval by determining the sample size necessary to produce narrow intervals.

To understand how and why we can determine the sample size, we discuss the error of estimation.

9-3a Error of Estimation

In Chapter 4, we pointed out that sampling error is the difference between the sample and the population that exists only because of the observations that happened to be selected for the sample. Now that we have discussed estimation we can define the sampling error as the difference between an estimator and a parameter. We can also define this difference as the **error of estimation**. In this chapter, this can be expressed as the difference between $\hat{p}$ and p. In our derivation of the confidence interval estimator of p (see page 138), we expressed the following probability:

$$P\left(-Z_{\alpha/2} < \frac{\hat{p} - p}{\sqrt{p(1-p)/n}} < Z_{\alpha/2}\right) = 1 - \alpha$$

This can also be expressed as

$$P\left(-Z_{\alpha/2}\sqrt{\frac{p(1-p)}{n}} < \hat{p} - p < +Z_{\alpha/2}\sqrt{\frac{p(1-p)}{n}}\right)$$
$$= 1 - \alpha$$

This tells us that the difference between $\hat{p}$ and p lies between $-Z_{\alpha/2}\sqrt{p(1-p)/n}$ and $+Z_{\alpha/2}\sqrt{p(1-p)/n}$ with probability $1 - \alpha$. Expressed another way, we have with probability $1 - \alpha$:

$$|\hat{p} - p| < Z_{\alpha/2}\sqrt{\frac{p(1-p)}{n}}$$

In other words, the error of estimation is less than $Z_{\alpha/2}\sqrt{p(1-p)/n}$. We interpret this to mean that $Z_{\alpha/2}\sqrt{p(1-p)/n}$ is the maximum error of estimation that we are willing to tolerate. We label this value B, which stands for the **bound on the error of estimation**; that is,

$$B = Z_{\alpha/2}\sqrt{\frac{p(1-p)}{n}}$$

9-3b Determining the Sample Size

Solving for n, we produce the required sample size as indicated in the following box.

Sample Size to Estimate a Proportion

$$n = \left(\frac{Z_{\alpha/2}\sqrt{p(1-p)}}{B}\right)^2$$

To illustrate the use of this formula, suppose that in a brand preference survey we want to estimate the proportion of consumers who prefer our company's brand to within .03 with 95% confidence. This means that the bound on the error of estimation is $B = .03$. Because $1 - \alpha = .95, \alpha = .05, \alpha/2 = .025$, and $Z_{\alpha/2} = Z_{.025} = 1.96$, therefore

$$n = \left(\frac{1.96\sqrt{p(1-p)}}{.03}\right)^2$$

To solve for n, we need to know p. Unfortunately, this value is unknown, and because the sample has not yet been taken we cannot estimate it with $\hat{p}$. At this point, we can use either of two methods to solve for n.

Method 1

If we have no knowledge of even the approximate value of p, then we let $p = .5$. We choose $p = .5$ because the product $p(1 - p)$ equals its maximum value at $p = .5$. (Figure 9.3 illustrates this point.) This, in turn, results in a conservative value of n; as a result, the confidence interval will be no wider than the interval $\hat{p} \pm .03$. If $\hat{p}$ does not equal .5 when the sample is drawn, then the confidence interval estimate will be better (that is, narrower) than planned. Thus,

$$n = \left(\frac{1.96\sqrt{(.5)(.5)}}{.03}\right)^2 = (32.67)^2 = 1,068$$

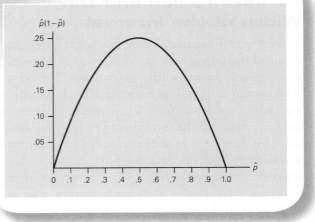

Figure 9.3 **Plot of p versus $(1 - p)$**

If it turns out that $\hat{p} = .5$, then the interval estimate is $\hat{p} \pm .03$. If not, the interval estimate will be narrower. For instance, if it turns out that $\hat{p} = .2$, then the estimate is $\hat{p} \pm .024$, which is better than we had planned.

Method 2

If we have some idea about the value of p, we can use that quantity to determine n. For example, if we believe that p will turn out to be approximately .2, we can solve for n as follows:

$$n = \left(\frac{1.96\sqrt{(.2)(.8)}}{.03}\right)^2 = (26.13)^2 = 683$$

Notice that this produces a smaller value of n (thus reducing sampling costs) than does method 1. If $\hat{p}$ actually lies between .2 and .8, however, the estimate will not be as good as we wanted, because the interval will be wider than desired.

Method 1 is often used to determine the sample size used in public opinion surveys reported by newspapers, magazines, television, and radio. These polls usually estimate proportions to within 3%, with 95% confidence. If you've ever wondered why opinion polls almost always estimate proportions to within 3%, consider the sample size required to estimate a proportion to within 1%:

$$n = \left(\frac{1.96\sqrt{(.5)(.5)}}{.01} \right)^2 = (98)^2 = 9,604$$

The sample size 9,604 is 9 times the sample size needed to estimate a proportion to within 3%. Thus, to divide the width of the interval by 3 requires multiplying the sample size by 9. The cost would also increase considerably. For most applications, the increase in accuracy (created by decreasing the width of the confidence interval estimate) does not overcome the increased cost. Confidence interval estimates with 5% or 10% bounds (sample sizes 385 and 97, respectively) are generally considered too wide to be useful. Thus, the 3% bound provides a reasonable compromise between cost and accuracy.

EXERCISES

9.1 a. In a random sample of 500 observations, we found the proportion of successes to be 48%. Estimate with 95% confidence the population proportion of successes.
b. Repeat part (a) with $n = 200$.
c. Repeat part (a) with $n = 1000$.
d. Describe the effect on the confidence interval estimate of increasing the sample size.

9.2 a. The proportion of successes in a random sample of 400 was calculated as 50%. Estimate the population proportion with 95% confidence.
b. Repeat part (a) with $\hat{p} = 33\%$.
c. Repeat part (a) with $\hat{p} = 10\%$.
d. Discuss the effect on the width of the confidence interval estimate of reducing the sample proportion.

9.3 A statistics practitioner working for Major League Baseball wants to supply radio and television commentators with interesting statistics. He observed several hundred games and counted the number of times a runner on first base attempted to steal second base. He found there were 373 such events, of which 259 were successful. Estimate with 95% confidence the proportion of all attempted thefts of second base that are successful.

9.4 A dean of a business school wanted to know whether the graduates of her school used a statistical inference technique during their first year of employment after graduation. She surveyed 314 graduates and asked about the use of statistical techniques. After tallying the responses, she found that 204 used statistical inference within one year of graduation. Estimate with 90% confidence the proportion of all business school graduates who use their statistical education within a year of graduation.

9.5 What type of educational background do CEOs have? In one survey, 344 CEOs of medium and large companies were asked whether they had an MBA degree. There were 97 MBAs. Estimate with 95% confidence the proportion of all CEOs of medium and large companies who have MBAs.

9.6 The GO transportation system of buses and commuter trains operates on the honor system. Train travelers are expected to buy their tickets before boarding the train. Only a small number of people will be checked on the train to see whether they bought a ticket. Suppose that a random sample of 400 train travelers was sampled, and 68 of them had failed to buy a ticket. Estimate with 95% confidence the proportion of all train travelers who do not buy a ticket.

9.7 Refer to Exercise 9.6. Assuming that there are 1 million travelers per year and the fare is $3, estimate with 95% confidence the amount of revenue lost each year.

Exercises 9.8 to 9.15 require the use of a computer and software. The answers may be calculated manually. See Appendix A for the sample statistics.

9.8 [Xr09-08*] There is a looming crisis in universities and colleges across North America. In most places, enrollments are increasing, which requires more instructors. However, there are not enough PhD's to fill the vacancies now. Moreover, among current professors, a large proportion are nearing retirement age. On top of these problems, some universities allow professors older than 60 to retire early. To help devise a plan to deal with the crisis, a consultant surveyed 521 professors ages 55 to 64 and asked each whether he or she intended to retire before 65. The responses are 1 = No and 2 = Yes. Estimate with 95% confidence the proportion of professors who plan on early retirement.

9.9 Refer to Exercise 9.8. If the number of professors between ages 55 and 64 is 75,000, estimate the total number of such professors who plan to retire early.

9.10 [Xr09-10] According to the Internal Revenue Service, in 2009 the top 5% of American income earners earned more than $153,542, and the top 1% earned more than $388,806. The top 1% pay slightly more than 40% of all federal income taxes. To determine whether Americans are aware of these figures, *Investor's Business Daily* randomly sampled American adults and asked, "What share do you think the rich (earning more than $388,806) pay in income taxes?" The categories are (1) 0–10%, (2) 10–20%, (3) 20–30%, (4) 30–40%, and (5) more than 40%. The data are stored using the codes 1 to 5. Estimate with 95% confidence the proportion of Americans who knew that the rich pay more than 40% of all federal income taxes.

9.11 [Xr09-11] An increasing number of people are giving gift certificates as Christmas presents. To measure the extent of this practice, a random sample of people was asked (survey conducted December 26–29) whether they had received a gift certificate for Christmas. The responses are recorded as 1 = No and 2 = Yes. Estimate with 95% confidence the proportion of people who received a gift certificate for Christmas.

9.12 [Xr09-12] An important decision faces Christmas holiday celebrators: buy a real or an artificial tree? A sample of 1,508 male and female respondents 18 years of age and older was interviewed. Respondents were asked whether they preferred a real (1) or an artificial (2) tree. If 6 million Canadian households buy Christmas trees, estimate with 95% confidence the total number of Canadian households that would prefer artificial Christmas trees. (*Source: Toronto Star*, November 29, 2006.)

9.13 [Xr09-13] Statistical techniques play a vital role in helping advertisers determine how many viewers watch the shows they sponsor. Although several companies sample television viewers to determine what shows they watch, the best known is the A. C. Nielsen firm. The Nielsen ratings are based on a random sample

of approximately 5,000 of the 115 million households in the United States with at least one television (in 2010). A meter attached to the televisions in the selected households keeps track of when the televisions are turned on and what channels they are tuned to. The data are sent to Nielsen's computers every night from which the company computes the ratings and sponsors can determine the number of viewers and the potential value of any commercials. The results from Sunday, February 14, 2010, for the time slot 9:00 to 9:30 P.M. have been recorded using the following codes:

Network	Show	Code
ABC	*Extreme Makeover: Home Edition*	1
CBS	*Undercover Boss*	2
Fox	*Family Guy*	3
NBC	*Vancouver Winter Olympics*	4
Television turned off or watched some other channel		5

Source: tvbythenumbers.com February 15, 2010.

NBC would like to use the data to estimate how many of the households were tuned to its coverage of the Vancouver Winter Olympics.

9.14 [Xr09-14] A new credit card company is investigating various market segments to determine whether it is profitable to direct its advertising specifically at each one. One of the market segments is composed of Hispanic people. The latest census indicates that there are 31,669,000 Hispanic adults (18 and older) in the United States (*Source: Statistical Abstract of the United States*, 2012, Table 10). A survey of 475 Hispanics asked how they usually paid for products they purchase. The responses are

1. Cash
2. Check
3. Visa
4. MasterCard
5. Other credit card

Estimate with 95% confidence the number of Hispanics in the United States who usually pay by credit card.

9.15 [Xr09-15*] A California university is investigating expanding its evening programs. It wants to target people between 25 and 54 years old who have completed high school but did not complete college or university. To help determine the extent and type of offerings, the university needs to know the size of its target market. A survey of 320 California adults was drawn, and each person was asked to identify his or her highest educational attainment. The responses are

1. Did not complete high school
2. Completed high school only
3. Some college or university
4. College or university graduate

The *Statistical Abstract of the United States* (2012, Table 16) indicates that there are 15,753,000 Californians between the ages of 25 and 54. Estimate with 95% confidence the number of Californians between 25 and 54 years of age who are in the market segment the university wishes to target.

9.16 Determine the sample size necessary to estimate a population proportion to within .03 with 90% confidence, assuming you have no knowledge of the approximate value of the sample proportion.

9.17 Suppose that you used the sample size calculated in Exercise 9.16 and found $\hat{p} = .5$.

a. Estimate the population proportion with 90% confidence.
b. Is this the result you expected? Explain.

9.18 Suppose that you used the sample size calculated in Exercise 9.16 and found $\hat{p} = .75$.

a. Estimate the population proportion with 90% confidence.
b. Is this the result you expected? Explain.

c. If you were hired to conduct this analysis, would the person who hired you be satisfied with the interval estimate you produced? Explain.

9.19 Redo Exercise 9.16 assuming that you know that the sample proportion will be no less than .75.

9.20 Suppose that you used the sample size calculated in Exercise 9.19 and found $\hat{p} = .75$.

a. Estimate the population proportion with 90% confidence.
b. Is this the result you expected? Explain.

9.21 Suppose that you used the sample size calculated in Exercise 9.19 and found $\hat{p} = .92$.

a. Estimate the population proportion with 90% confidence.
b. Is this the result you expected? Explain.
c. If you were hired to conduct this analysis, would the person who hired you be satisfied with the interval estimate you produced? Explain.

9.22 Suppose that you used the sample size calculated in Exercise 9.19 and found $\hat{p} = .5$.

a. Estimate the population proportion with 90% confidence.
b. Is this the result you expected? Explain.
c. If you were hired to conduct this analysis, would the person who hired you be satisfied with the interval estimate you produced? Explain.

CHAPTER 10

Introduction to Hypothesis Testing

objectives

10-1   Concepts of Hypothesis Testing

10-2   Testing the Population Proportion

10-3   Calculating the Probability of a Type II Error

10-4   The Road Ahead

AMERICAN NATIONAL ELECTION SURVEY: DO SURVEY RESULTS MATCH THE ELECTION RESULTS?

[ANES2008*] In the 2008 presidential election, Barack Obama received 53% of the vote. The American National Election Survey asked some of those surveyed before the election for whom they voted (WHOVOTE). 1 = Barack Obama, 3 = John McCain, 7 = Other. Can we infer that the survey results differ from the actual vote for Barack Obama? If so, suggest possible reasons.

After we've introduced the required tools, we'll return to this question and answer it (see page 160).

In Chapter 9, we introduced estimation and showed how it is used. Now we're going to present the second general procedure of making inferences about a population: hypothesis testing. The purpose of this type of inference is to determine whether enough statistical evidence exists to enable us to conclude that a belief or hypothesis about a parameter is supported by the data. You will discover that hypothesis testing has a wide variety of applications in business and economics, as well as in many other fields. This chapter will lay the foundation on which the rest of the book is based. As such, it represents a critical contribution to your development as a statistics practitioner.

10-1 Concepts of Hypothesis Testing

The term **hypothesis testing** is likely new to most readers, but the concepts underlying hypothesis testing are quite familiar. There are a variety of nonstatistical applications of hypothesis testing, the best known of which is a criminal trial.

When a person is accused of a crime, he or she faces a trial. The prosecution presents its case, and a jury must make a decision on the basis of the evidence presented. In fact, the jury conducts a test of hypothesis. Actually, two hypotheses are tested. The first is called the

null **hypothesis** and is represented by H_0 (pronounced "*H*-nought": *nought* is a British term for zero). It is

H_0: The defendant is innocent.

The second is called the **alternative** or **research hypothesis** and is denoted H_1. In a criminal trial, it is

H_1: The defendant is guilty.

Of course, jury members do not know which hypothesis is correct. They must make a decision on the basis of the evidence presented by both the prosecution and the defense. There are only two possible decisions: convict or acquit the defendant. In statistical parlance, convicting the defendant is equivalent to *rejecting the null hypothesis in favor of the alternative*. In other words, the jury is saying that there was enough evidence to conclude that the defendant was guilty. Acquitting a defendant is phrased as *not rejecting the null hypothesis in favor of the alternative*, which means that the jury decided that there was not enough evidence to conclude that the defendant was guilty. Notice that we do not say that we accept the null hypothesis. In a criminal trial, that would be interpreted as finding the defendant innocent. Our justice system does not allow this decision.

There are two possible errors. A **Type I error** occurs when we reject a true null hypothesis. A **Type II error** is defined as not rejecting a false null hypothesis. In the criminal trial, a Type I error is made when an innocent person is wrongly convicted. A Type II error occurs when a guilty defendant is acquitted. The probability of a Type I error is denoted by α (Greek letter alpha), which is also called the **significance level**. The probability of a Type II error is denoted by β (Greek letter beta). The error probabilities α and β are inversely related, meaning that any attempt to reduce one will increase the other. Table 10.1 summarizes the terminology and the concepts.

© James Steidl/Shutterstock

up so that the probability of a Type I error is small. This is arranged by placing the burden of proof on the prosecution (the prosecution must prove guilt, and the defense need not prove anything) and by having judges instruct the jury to find the defendant guilty only if there is "evidence beyond a reasonable doubt." In the absence of enough evidence, the jury must acquit even though there may be some evidence of guilt. The consequence of this arrangement is that the probability of acquitting guilty people is relatively large. Oliver Wendell Holmes, a United States Supreme Court justice, once phrased the relationship between the probabilities of Type I and Type II errors in the following way: "Better to acquit 100 guilty men than convict one innocent one." In Justice Holmes's opinion, the probability of a Type I error should be 1/100 of the probability of a Type II error.

The critical concepts in hypothesis testing follow.

1. There are two hypotheses. One is called the *null hypothesis*, and the other the *alternative* or *research hypothesis*.

2. The testing procedure begins with the assumption that the null hypothesis is true.

3. The goal of the process is to determine whether there is enough evidence to infer that the alternative hypothesis is true.

4. There are two possible decisions:

   Conclude that there is enough evidence to support the alternative hypothesis.

   Conclude that there is not enough evidence to support the alternative hypothesis.

Table 10.1 Terminology of Hypothesis Testing

Decision	H_0 Is True (Defendant Is Innocent)	H_0 Is False (Defendant Is Guilty)
REJECT Convict defendant	Type I Error P(Type I Error) $= \alpha$	Correct decision
DO NOT REJECT Acquit defendant	Correct decision	Type II Error P(Type II Error) $= \beta$

© Cengage Learning

In our justice system, Type I errors are regarded as more serious. As a consequence, the system is set

5. Two possible errors can be made in any test. A Type I error occurs when we reject a true null hypothesis, and a Type II error occurs when we don't reject a false null hypothesis. The probabilities of Type I and Type II errors are

$$P(\text{Type I error}) = \alpha$$

$$P(\text{Type II error}) = \beta$$

Let's extend these concepts to statistical hypothesis testing.

In statistics, we frequently test hypotheses about parameters. The hypotheses we test are generated by questions that managers need to answer.

Suppose that in Example 9.1 we are not so much interested in estimating the proportion of viewers of the pharmaceutical ads who contact their physicians but want to know if the proportion is different from 10%, which is the goal of the pharmaceutical companies. Thus, we want to determine whether we can infer that the proportion p is not equal to 10%. We can rephrase the question so that it now reads, Is there enough evidence to conclude that p is not equal to 10%? This wording is analogous to the criminal trial wherein the jury is asked to determine whether there is enough evidence to conclude that the defendant is guilty. Thus, the alternative (research) hypothesis is

$$H_1: p \neq .10$$

In a criminal trial, the process begins with the assumption that the defendant is innocent. In a similar fashion, we start with the assumption that the parameter equals the value we're testing. Consequently, we would assume that $p = .10$ and that the null hypothesis is expressed as

$$H_0: p = .10$$

When we state the hypotheses, we list the null first followed by the alternative hypothesis. To determine whether the proportion is different from .10, we test

$$H_0: p = .10$$
$$H_1: p \neq .10$$

Now suppose that in this illustration the advertisements are based on an analysis that revealed that the actual proportion is .10. After changing the advertising, we suspect that there has been an increase in the proportion. To test whether there is evidence of an increase, we would specify the alternative hypothesis as

$$H_1: p > .10$$

Because we know that the proportion before the new advertisement was (and maybe still is) .10, the null hypothesis would state

$$H_0: p = .10$$

Further suppose that we do not know the actual proportion, but the current advertising approach is based on the assumption that the proportion is *less than or equal to .10*. We would like to know whether the advertising campaign increases the proportion to a quantity larger than .10. In this scenario, the hypotheses become

$$H_0: p \leq .10$$
$$H_1: p > .10$$

Notice that in both illustrations the alternative hypothesis is designed to determine whether there is enough evidence to conclude that the proportion is greater than .10. Although the two null hypotheses are different (one states that the proportion is equal to .10, and the other states that the proportion is less than or equal to .10), when the test is conducted the process begins by assuming that the proportion is *equal to* .10. In other words, no matter the form of the null hypothesis, we use the equal sign in the null hypothesis. Here is the reason. If there is enough evidence to conclude that the alternative hypothesis (the proportion is greater than .10) is true when we assume that the proportion is *equal to* .10, we would certainly draw the same conclusion when we assume that the proportion is a value that is *less than* .10. As a result, the null hypothesis will always state that the parameter equals the value specified in the alternative hypothesis.

To emphasize this point, suppose we now want to determine whether there has been a decrease in the proportion. We express the null and alternative hypotheses as

$$H_0: p = .10$$
$$H_1: p < .10$$

The hypotheses are often set up to reflect a manager's decision problem in which the null hypothesis represents the *status quo*. Often this takes the form of some course of action such as maintaining a particular advertising approach. If there is evidence of an increase or decrease in the value of the parameter, then a new course of action will be taken. Examples include deciding to produce a new product, switching to a better drug to treat an illness, and sentencing a defendant to prison.

The next element in the procedure is to randomly sample the population and calculate the sample proportion. This is called the **test statistic**. The test statistic is the criterion on which we base our decision about the hypotheses. (In the criminal trial analogy, this is equivalent to the evidence presented in the case.) The test statistic is based on the best estimator of the parameter. In Chapter 9, we stated that the best estimator of a population proportion p is the sample proportion $\hat{p}$.

If the test statistic's value is inconsistent with the null hypothesis, we reject the null hypothesis and infer that the alternative hypothesis is true. For example, if we're trying to decide whether the proportion is greater than .10, a large value of $\hat{p}$ (say, .25) would provide enough evidence. If $\hat{p}$ is close to .10 (say, .11), we would say that this does not provide much evidence to infer that the proportion is greater than .10. In the absence of sufficient evidence, we do not reject the null hypothesis in favor of the alternative. (In the absence of sufficient evidence of guilt, a jury finds the defendant not guilty.)

In a criminal trial, "sufficient evidence" is defined as "evidence beyond a reasonable doubt." In statistics, we need to use the test statistic's sampling distribution to define *sufficient evidence*. We will do so in the next section.

10-2 Testing the Population Proportion

To illustrate the process, consider the following example.

EXAMPLE 10.1

Election Day Exit Poll

[Xm10-01] When an election for political office takes place, the television networks cancel regular programming and instead provide election coverage. When the ballots are counted, the results are reported. However, for important offices such as president or senator in large states, the networks actively compete to see which will be the first to predict a winner. This is done through exit polls,[1] in which a random sample of voters who exit the polling booth is asked for whom they voted. From the data, the sample proportion of voters supporting the candidates is computed. A statistical technique is applied to determine whether there is enough evidence to infer that the leading candidate will garner enough votes to win. Suppose that in the exit poll from the state of Florida during the 2000 year elections, the pollsters recorded only the votes of the two candidates who had any chance of winning: Democrat Albert Gore (code = 1) and Republican George W. Bush (code = 2). The polls close at 8 P.M. Can the networks conclude from these data that the Republican candidate will win the state? Should the network announce at 8:01 P.M. that the Republican candidate will win?

SOLUTION
IDENTIFY

The parameter to be tested is the proportion of all voters in Florida who voted for George Bush. The network wants to determine whether it can declare the Republican to be the winner at 8:01 P.M. The winner is the one who gets more than 50% of the votes. Hence, the alternative hypothesis is

$$H_1: p > .50$$

---

[1] Warren Mitofsky is generally credited for creating the election day exit poll in 1967 when he worked for CBS News. Mitofsky claimed to have correctly predicted 2,500 elections and was wrong only six times. Exit polls are considered so accurate that when the exit poll and the actual election result differ, some newspaper and television reporters claim that the election result is wrong! In the 2004 presidential election, the exit poll showed John Kerry leading in Ohio. However, when the ballots were counted, George Bush won the state of Ohio. Conspiracy theorists now believe that the Ohio election was stolen by the Republicans using the exit poll as their "proof." However, Mitofsky's own analysis found that the exit poll was improperly conducted, resulting in many Republican voters refusing to participate in the poll. Blame was placed on poorly trained interviewers. (Source: *Amstat News*, December 2006.)

which makes the null hypothesis

$$H_0: p = .50$$

As we pointed out in Chapter 9, the best estimator of a population proportion is the sample proportion $\hat{p}$ defined as

$$\hat{p} = \frac{x}{n}$$

where x is the number of successes (in this example, the number of votes for George Bush) and n is the sample size. An analysis of the data yielded the following: $x = 477$ and $n = 900$. Thus,

$$\hat{p} = \frac{x}{n} = \frac{477}{900} = .530$$

To conduct this test, we need to ask and answer the question, Is a sample proportion of .530 sufficiently larger than .50 to conclude that the population proportion is greater than .50?

There are two approaches to answering this question. The first is called the *rejection region method*. It can be used in conjunction with the computer, but it is mandatory for those computing statistics manually. The second is the *p-value approach*, which in general can be employed only in conjunction with a computer and statistical software. We recommend, however, that users of statistical software be familiar with both approaches.

10-2a Rejection Region

It seems reasonable to reject the null hypothesis in favor of the alternative if the value of the sample proportion is large relative to .50. If we had calculated the sample proportion to be, say, .75, it would be quite apparent that the null hypothesis is false, and we would reject it. On the other hand, values of $\hat{p}$ close to .50, such as .51, do not allow us to reject the null hypothesis because it is entirely possible to observe a sample proportion of .51 from a population whose proportion is .50. Unfortunately, the decision is not always so obvious. In this example, the sample proportion was calculated to be .530, a value apparently neither very far away from nor very close to .50. To make a decision about this sample proportion, we set up the *rejection region*.

Rejection Region
The **rejection region** is a range of values such that if the test statistic falls into that range, we decide to reject the null hypothesis in favor of the alternative hypothesis.

Suppose we define the value of the sample proportion that is just large enough to reject the null hypothesis as $\hat{p}_L$. The rejection region is

$$\hat{p} > \hat{p}_L$$

Because a Type I error is defined as rejecting a true null hypothesis, and the probability of committing a Type I error is α, it follows that

$$\alpha = P \text{ (rejecting } H_0 \text{ given that } H_0 \text{ is true)}$$
$$= P \text{ (} \hat{p} > \hat{p}_L \text{ given that } H_0 \text{ is true)}$$

Figure 10.1 depicts the sampling distribution and the rejection region.

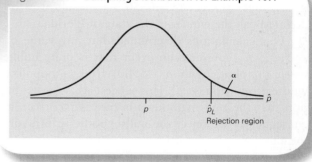

Figure 10.1 Sampling Distribution for Example 10.1

From Section 8-2, we know that the sampling distribution of $\hat{p}$ is approximately normal, with mean p and standard deviation $\sigma = \sqrt{p(1-p)/n}$. As a result, we can standardize $\hat{p}$ and obtain the following probability:

$$P\left(\frac{\hat{p} - p}{\sqrt{p(1-p)/n}} > \frac{\hat{p}_L - p}{\sqrt{p(1-p)/n}} \right)$$
$$= P\left(Z > \frac{\hat{p}_L - p}{\sqrt{p(1-p)/n}} \right) = \alpha$$

From Section 7-2, we defined z_α to be the value of a standard normal random variable such that

$$P(Z > z_\alpha) = \alpha$$

Because both probability statements involve the same distribution (standard normal) and the same probability (α), it follows that the limits are identical. Thus,

$$\frac{\hat{p}_L - p}{\sqrt{p(1-p)/n}} = z_\alpha$$

Because the probabilities defined above are conditional on the null hypothesis being true, we have $p = .5$. To calculate the rejection region, we need a value of α, the significance level. We'll let α be 5%. It follows that $z_\alpha = z_{.05} = 1.645$. We can now calculate the value of $\hat{p}_L$:

$$\frac{\hat{p}_L - p}{\sqrt{p(1-p)/n}} = z_\alpha$$

$$\frac{\hat{p}_L - .50}{\sqrt{.50(1-.50)/900}} = 1.645$$

$$\hat{p}_L = .527$$

Therefore, the rejection region is

$$\hat{p} > .527$$

The sample proportion was computed to be .530. Because the test statistic (sample proportion) is in the rejection region (it is greater than .527), we reject the null hypothesis. Thus, there is sufficient evidence to infer that the proportion of all Florida voters who voted for George Bush is greater than .50. As a result, we would declare Bush the winner in the state of Florida.

Our calculations determined that any value of $\hat{p}$ above .527 represents an event that is quite unlikely when sampling (with $n = 900$) from a population whose proportion is .50. This suggests that the assumption that the null hypothesis is true is incorrect, and consequently we reject the null hypothesis in favor of the alternative hypothesis.

10-2b Standardized Test Statistic

The preceding test used the test statistic $\hat{p}$. As a result, the rejection region had to be set up in terms of $\hat{p}$. An easier method specifies that the test statistic be the standardized value of $\hat{p}$. In other words, we use the **standardized test statistic**

$$z = \frac{\hat{p} - p}{\sqrt{p(1-p)/n}}$$

and the rejection region consists of all values of z that are greater than z_α. Algebraically, the rejection region is

$$z > z_\alpha$$

We can redo Example 10.1 using the standardized test statistic.

The rejection region is

$$z > z_\alpha = z_{.05} = 1.645$$

The value of the test statistic is calculated next:

$$z = \frac{\hat{p} - p}{\sqrt{p(1-p)/n}} = \frac{.530 - .50}{\sqrt{.5(1-.5)/900}} = 1.80$$

Because 1.80 is greater than 1.645, reject the null hypothesis and conclude that there is enough evidence to infer that the proportion is greater than .50.

As you can see, the conclusions we draw from using the test statistic $\hat{p}$ and the standardized test statistic z are identical. Figures 10.2 and 10.3 depict the two sampling distributions, highlighting the equivalence of the two tests.

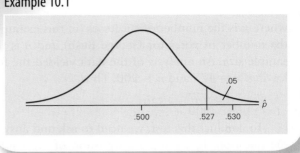

Figure 10.2 Sampling Distribution of $\hat{p}$ for Example 10.1

© Cengage Learning

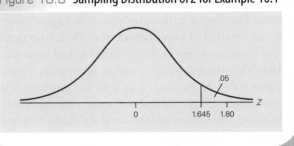

Figure 10.3 Sampling Distribution of Z for Example 10.1

© Cengage Learning

Because it is convenient and because statistical software packages employ it, the standardized test statistic will be used throughout this book. For simplicity, we will refer to the *standardized test statistic* simply as the *test statistic*.

Incidentally, when a null hypothesis is rejected, the test is said to be **statistically significant** at whatever significance level the test was conducted. Summarizing Example 10.1, we would say that the test was significant at the 5% significance level.

10-2c *p*-Value

There are several drawbacks to the rejection region method. Foremost among them is the type of information provided by the result of the test. The rejection region method produces a yes or no response to the question, Is there sufficient statistical evidence to infer that the alternative hypothesis is true? The implication is that the result of the test of hypothesis will be converted automatically into one of two possible courses of action: one action as a result of rejecting the null hypothesis in favor of the alternative and another as a result of not rejecting the null hypothesis in favor of the alternative. In Example 10.1, the rejection of the null hypothesis seems to imply that the network would declare Bush the winner in the state of Florida at 8:01.

In fact, this is not the way in which the result of a statistical analysis is utilized. The statistical procedure is only one of several factors considered by a manager when making a decision. In Example 10.1, the network executive discovered that there was enough statistical evidence to conclude that the proportion of Florida voters who voted for George is greater than .50. However, before taking any action, the executive would like to consider a number of factors, including the cost and probability of making an error—in this case, a Type I error.

What is needed to take full advantage of the information available from the test result and make a better decision is a measure of the amount of statistical evidence supporting the alternative hypothesis so that it can be weighed in relation to the other factors, especially the financial ones. The *p-value* of a test provides this measure.

p-Value

The ***p*-value** of a test is the probability of observing a test statistic at least as extreme as the one computed given that the null hypothesis is true.

In Example 10.1, the *p*-value is the probability of observing a sample proportion at least as large as .530 when the population proportion is .50. Thus,

$$p\text{-value} = P(\hat{p} > .530)$$
$$= P\left(\frac{\hat{p} - p}{\sqrt{p(1-p)/n}} > \frac{.530 - .50}{\sqrt{.50(1-.50)/900}} \right)$$
$$= P(Z > 1.80) = 1 - P(Z < 1.80)$$
$$= 1 - .9641 = .0359$$

Figure 10.4 describes this calculation.

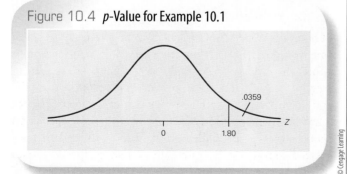

Figure 10.4 *p*-Value for Example 10.1

© Cengage Learning

10-2d Interpreting the *p*-Value

To properly interpret the results of an inferential procedure, you must remember that the technique is based on the sampling distribution. The sampling distribution allows us to make probability statements about a sample statistic, assuming knowledge of the population parameter. Thus, the probability of observing a sample proportion at least as large as .530 from a population whose proportion is .50 is .0359, which is quite small. In other words, we have just observed an unlikely event, an event so unlikely that we seriously doubt the assumption that began the process: the null hypothesis is true. Consequently, we have reason to reject the null hypothesis and support the alternative.

Students may be tempted to simplify the interpretation by stating that the *p*-value is the probability that the null hypothesis is true. Don't! As was the case with interpreting the confidence interval estimator, you cannot make a probability statement about a parameter. It is not a random variable.

The *p*-value of a test provides valuable information because it is a measure of the amount of statistical evidence that supports the alternative hypothesis. To understand this interpretation fully, refer to Table 10.2, which lists several values of $\hat{p}$, their *z*-statistics, and *p*-values for Example 10.1. Notice that the closer $\hat{p}$ is to the hypothesized proportion .50, the larger the *p*-value. The farther $\hat{p}$ is above .50, the smaller the *p*-value is. Values of $\hat{p}$ far above .50 tend to indicate that the alternative hypothesis is true. Thus, the smaller the *p*-value, the more the statistical evidence supports the alternative hypothesis. Figure 10.5 graphically depicts the information in Table 10.2.

This raises the question, How small does the *p*-value have to be to infer that the alternative hypothesis is true? In general, the answer depends on a number of factors, including the costs of making Type I and Type II errors. In Example 10.1, a Type I error would occur if the network concludes that Bush won when, in fact, he did not. A Type II error means that the network did not conclude from the exit polls that Bush had won when, in fact, he did. A Type I error is far more expensive because the network would have to admit sometime later in the evening that they were wrong, which would hurt their credibility and perhaps decrease the number of viewers in the next election. The consequence of a Type II error is simply to delay the announcement that Bush had won.

If the cost of a Type I error is high, then we attempt to minimize its probability. In the rejection region method, we do so by setting the significance level quite low, say, 1%. Using the *p*-value method, we would insist that the *p*-value be quite small, providing sufficient

Figure 10.5 *p*-Values for Example 10.1

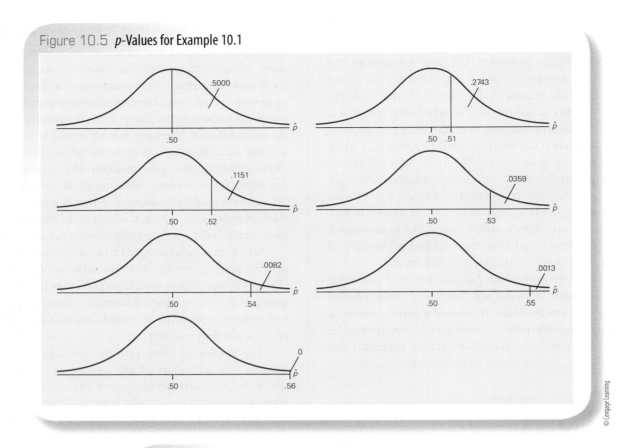

© Cengage Learning

Table 10.2 Test Statistics and *p*-Values for Example 10.1

Sample Proportion $\hat{p}$	Test Statistic $z = \dfrac{\hat{p} - p}{\sqrt{p(1-p)/n}} = \dfrac{\hat{p} - .50}{\sqrt{.50(1-.50)/900}}$	*p*-Value
.50	0	.5000
.51	0.60	.2743
.52	1.20	.1151
.53	1.80	.0359
.54	2.40	.0082
.55	3.00	.0013
.56	3.60	0

© Cengage Learning

evidence to infer that the population proportion is greater than .50 before declaring on air that Bush won.

This is exactly what happened on the evening of the U.S. presidential elections in November 2000. Shortly after the polls closed at 8 P.M., all the networks declared that the Democratic candidate Albert Gore would win the state of Florida. A couple of hours later, the networks admitted that a mistake had been made and the Republican candidate George W. Bush had won. Several hours later, they again admitted a mistake and finally declared the race too close to call. Fortunately for each network, all the networks made the same mistake.

© AP Photo/Ed Reinke

However, if one network had not done this, it would have developed a better track record, which could have been used in future advertisements for news shows and likely drawn more viewers.

10-2e Describing the *p*-Value

Statistics practitioners can translate *p*-values using the following descriptive terms:

> If the *p*-value is less than .01, then we say that there is *overwhelming* evidence to infer that the alternative hypothesis is true. We also say that the test is **highly significant**.

> If the *p*-value lies between .01 and .05, then there is *strong* evidence to infer that the alternative hypothesis is true. The result is deemed to be **significant**.

> If the *p*-value is between .05 and .10, then we say that there is *weak* evidence to indicate that the alternative hypothesis is true. When the *p*-value is greater than 5%, we say that the result is **not statistically significant**.

> When the *p*-value exceeds .10, we say that there is little or no evidence to infer that the alternative hypothesis is true.

Figure 10.6 summarizes these terms.

10-2f The *p*-Value and Rejection Region Methods

If we so choose, we can use the *p*-value to make the same type of decisions we make in the rejection region method. The rejection region method requires the decision maker to select a significance level from which the rejection region is constructed. We then decide to reject or not reject the null hypothesis. Another way of making that type of decision is to compare the *p*-value with the selected value of the significance level. If the *p*-value is less than α, then we judge the *p*-value to be small enough to reject the null hypothesis. If the *p*-value is greater than α, then we do not reject the null hypothesis.

10-2g Solving Manually, Using Excel, and Using Minitab

As you have already seen, we offer three ways to solve statistical problems. When we perform the calculations manually, we will use the rejection region approach. We will set up the rejection region using the test statistic's sampling distribution and associated table (in Appendix B). The calculations will be performed manually and a reject–do not reject decision will be made. In this chapter, it is possible to compute the *p*-value of the test manually. However, in later chapters we will be using test statistics that are not normally distributed, making it impossible to calculate the *p*-values manually. In these instances, manual calculations require the decision to be made via the rejection region method only.

Most software packages that compute statistics, including Excel and Minitab, print the *p*-value of the test. When we employ the computer, we will not set up the rejection region. Instead we will focus on the interpretation of the *p*-value.

Excel

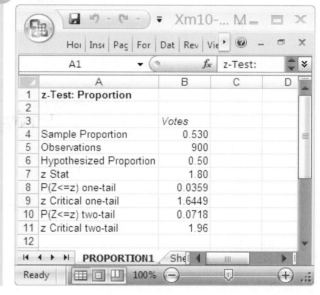

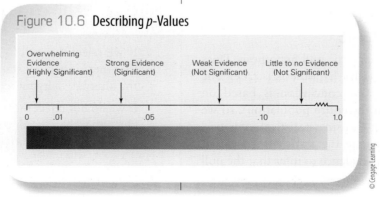

Figure 10.6 **Describing *p*-Values**

1. Type or import the data into one column. (Open Xm10-01.)

2. Click **Add-Ins, Data Analysis Plus,** and **Z-Test: Proportion.**

3. Specify the **Input Range** (A1:A901), type the **Code for Success** (2), the **Hypothesized Proportion** (.5), and a value of α(.05).

Minitab

Test and CI for One Proportion: Votes

Test of p = 0.5 vs p > 0.5

Event = 2

Variable	X	N	Sample p	95% Lower Bound	Z-Value	P-Value
Votes	477	900	0.530000	0.502635	1.80	0.036

Using the normal approximation.

INSTRUCTIONS

See page 140 for how the data must be stored.

1. Type or import the data into one column. (Open Xm10-01.)

2. Click **Stat, Basic Statistics,** and **1 Proportion. . . .**

3. Use the **Select** button or type the name of the variable or its column in the **Samples in columns** box (Votes) and check **Perform hypothesis test** and type the **Hypothesized proportion** (.5).

4. Click **Options . . .** and specify the **Alternative hypothesis (greater than).** To use the normal approximation of the binomial, click **Use test and interval based on normal approximation.**

Minitab calculates a one-sided confidence interval estimate when we're conducting a one-tail test.

10-2h Interpreting the Results of a Test

In Example 10.1, we rejected the null hypothesis. Does this prove that the alternative hypothesis is true? The answer is, No, because our conclusion is based on sample data (and not on the entire population), so we can never *prove* anything by using statistical inference. Consequently, we summarize the test by stating that there is enough statistical evidence to infer that the null hypothesis is false and that the alternative hypothesis is true.

Now suppose that $\hat{p}$ had equaled .520 instead of .530. We would then have calculated $z = 1.20$ (*p*-value = .1151), which is not in the rejection region. Could we conclude on this basis that there is enough statistical evidence to infer that the null hypothesis is true and hence that $p = .50$? Again, the answer is No, because it is absurd to suggest that a sample proportion of .520 provides enough evidence to infer that the population proportion is .50. (If it proved anything, it would prove that the population proportion is .520.) Because we're testing a single value of the parameter under the null hypothesis, we can never have enough statistical evidence to establish that the null hypothesis is true (unless we sample the entire population). (The same argument is valid if you set up the null hypothesis as $p \leq .50$. It would be illogical to conclude that a sample proportion of .52 provides enough evidence to conclude that the population proportion is *less than or equal to .50*.)

Consequently, if the value of the test statistic does not fall into the rejection region (or the *p*-value is large), rather than, say, we accept the null hypothesis (which implies that we're stating that the null hypothesis is true), then we state that we do not reject the null hypothesis, and we conclude that not enough evidence exists to show that the alternative hypothesis is true. Although it may appear to be the case, we are not being overly technical. Your ability to set up tests of hypotheses properly and to interpret their results correctly very much depends on your understanding of this point. The point is that the conclusion is based on the alternative hypothesis. In the final analysis, there are only two possible conclusions of a test of hypothesis.

Conclusions of a Test of Hypothesis

If we reject the null hypothesis, then we conclude that there is enough statistical evidence to infer that the alternative hypothesis is true.

If we do not reject the null hypothesis, then we conclude that there is not enough statistical evidence to infer that the alternative hypothesis is true.

Observe that the alternative hypothesis is the focus of the conclusion. It represents what we are investigating. That is why it is also called the *research hypothesis*. Whatever you're trying to show statistically must be represented by the alternative hypothesis (bearing in mind that you have only three choices for the alternative hypothesis: the parameter is greater than, less than, or not equal to the value specified in the null hypothesis).

When we introduced statistical inference in Chapter 9, we pointed out that the first step in the solution is to identify the technique. When the problem involves hypothesis testing, part of this process is the specification of the hypotheses. Because the alternative hypothesis represents the condition we're researching, we will identify it first. The null hypothesis automatically follows because the null hypothesis must specify equality. However, by tradition, when we list the two hypotheses, the null hypothesis comes first, followed by the alternative hypothesis. All examples in this book will follow that format.

10-2i One-Tail Tests

The test we performed in Example 10.1 is called a **one-tail test** because the entire rejection region is in one tail of the bell curve. In this example, it was the right tail because we wanted to determine whether there was enough evidence to infer that p is greater than .50. Another one-tail test would be conducted if the hypotheses were

$$H_0: p = .50$$

$$H_1: p < .50$$

If the significance level is set at, say, 1%, then the rejection region would be $z < -z_\alpha = -z_{.01} = -2.33$. Notice that the critical value is negative and that the rejection region is in the *left* tail of the normal distribution. This is so because the alternative hypothesis specifies that p is *less than* .50. Suppose that now $\hat{p} = .49$. We calculate the p-value as

$$P(\hat{p} < .49) = P\left(\frac{\hat{p} - p}{\sqrt{p(1-p)/n}} < \frac{.49 - .50}{\sqrt{.50(1 - .50)/900}}\right)$$
$$= P(Z < -.60) = .2743$$

Figure 10.7 depicts the sampling distribution.

Figure 10.7 **Sampling Distribution for Test** $H_1: p < .5$

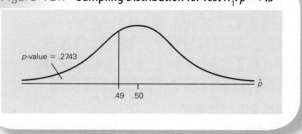

10-2j Two-Tail Tests

A **two-tail test** is performed when the alternative hypothesis specifies that the proportion is *not equal* to the value specified in the null hypothesis; that is,

$$H_0: p = .50$$

$$H_1: p \neq .50$$

The rejection region would be two tailed because there are two circumstances where the null hypothesis would be rejected in favor of the alternative hypothesis. In other words, when $\hat{p}$ is large relative to .50 or small relative to .50, the rejection region is two sided:

$$z < -z_{\alpha/2} \quad \text{or} \quad z > z_{\alpha/2}$$

We often list the rejection as

$$|z| > z_{\alpha/2}$$

Notice that the critical values are defined by dividing the significance level by 2. Figure 10.8 shows this situation.

Figure 10.8 **Two-Tail Test**

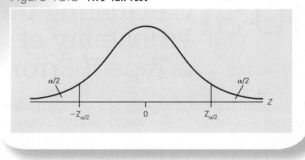

To calculate the p-value of a two-tail test, we calculate the tail area and double it. To illustrate, suppose that in Example 10.1 we wanted to test to determine whether we can infer that the proportion was not equal to .50. The p-value is calculated in the following way:

$$p\text{-value} = 2 \times P(\hat{p} > .530) = 2(.0359) = .0718$$

In other words, we determine the area in one tail of the sampling distribution and then double it.

AMERICAN NATIONAL ELECTION SURVEY: DO SURVEY RESULTS MATCH THE ELECTION RESULTS? SOLUTION

IDENTIFY

The problem objective is to describe the population of votes when the data are nominal. The parameter is p the proportion of American adults who now say that they voted for Barack Obama in the 2008 election. In that election, Obama garnered 53% of the votes. We want to know whether voters' recollection of whom they voted for in the 2008 presidential election is accurate. Thus, we test

$$H_0: p = .53$$
$$H_1: p \neq .53$$

COMPUTE

Here is the Excel printout. Minitab's is similar. (Minitab users will have to recode the data so that a vote for Obama is the higher code, and votes for the other two are combined with a lower code.)

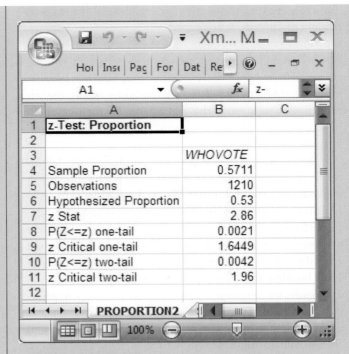

	A	B	C
1	z-Test: Proportion		
2			
3		WHOVOTE	
4	Sample Proportion	0.5711	
5	Observations	1210	
6	Hypothesized Proportion	0.53	
7	z Stat	2.86	
8	P(Z<=z) one-tail	0.0021	
9	z Critical one-tail	1.6449	
10	P(Z<=z) two-tail	0.0042	
11	z Critical two-tail	1.96	
12			

PROPORTION2

INTERPRET

The p-value of the two-tail test is .0042, providing more than enough evidence to conclude that voters' memory of the subject is poor. It is possible that the result represents the bandwagon effect in which people want to join the winning side.

10-3 Calculating the Probability of a Type II Error

To properly interpret the results of a test of hypothesis requires that you be able to specify an appropriate significance level or to judge the p-value of a test. However, it also requires that you have an understanding of the relationship between Type I and Type II errors. In this section, we describe how the probability of a Type II error is computed and interpreted.

Recall Example 10.1, in which we conducted the test using the sample proportion as the test statistic. We computed the rejection region (with $\alpha = .05$) as

$$\hat{p} > .527$$

A Type II error occurs when a false null hypothesis is not rejected. In Example 10.1, if $\hat{p}$ is less than .527,

we will not reject the null hypothesis. If we do not reject the null hypothesis, then the network will not announce that Bush has won when, in fact, he did win. The probability of this occurring is the probability of a Type II error. It is defined as

$$\beta = P(\hat{p} < .527, \text{ given that the null hypothesis is false})$$

The condition that the null hypothesis is false tells us only that the proportion is not equal to .50. If we want to compute β, then we need to specify a value for p. Suppose that when the population proportion (the exact proportion of Florida voters who voted for Bush) is 56%, the Bush victory is so clear-cut that the network would hate to postpone announcing the result. As a result, the network would like to determine the probability of not announcing the victory of Bush at 8:01 P.M. Because calculating probability from an approximately normal sampling distribution requires a value of p (as well as n), we will calculate the probability of not announcing that Bush has won when p is *equal* to .56:

$$\beta = P\,(\hat{p} < .527, \text{given that } p = .56)$$

We know that $\hat{p}$ is approximately normally distributed with mean p and standard deviation $\sqrt{p(1-p)/n}$. To proceed, we standardize $\hat{p}$ and use the standard normal table (Table 3 in Appendix B):

$$\beta = P\left|\frac{\hat{p} - p}{\sqrt{p(1-p)/n}} < \frac{.527 - .56}{\sqrt{(.56)(1-.56)/900}}\right|$$
$$= P(Z < -1.99) = .0233$$

This tells us that when the population proportion is actually .56, the probability of incorrectly not rejecting the null hypothesis is .0233. Figure 10.9 graphically depicts how the calculation was performed. Notice that to calculate the probability of a Type II error, we had to express the rejection region in terms of the unstandardized test statistic $\hat{p}$, and we had to specify a value for p other than the one shown in the null hypothesis.

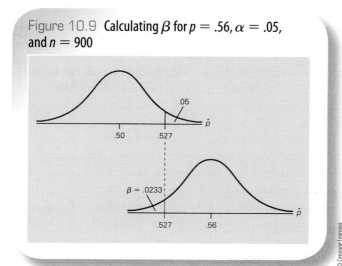

Figure 10.9 **Calculating β for $p = .56$, $\alpha = .05$, and $n = 900$**

10-3a **Effect on β of Changing α**

Suppose that in the previous illustration we had used a significance level of 1% instead of 5%. The rejection region expressed in terms of the standardized test statistic would be

$$z > z_{.01} = 2.33$$

or

$$\frac{\hat{p}_L - p}{\sqrt{p(1-p)/n}} = \frac{\hat{p}_L - .50}{\sqrt{(.50)(1-.50)/900}} > 2.33$$

Solving for $\hat{p}$, we find the rejection region in terms of the unstandardized test statistic:

$$\hat{p} > .539$$

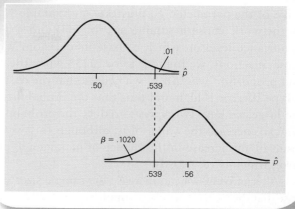

Figure 10.10 **Calculating β for $p = .56$, $\alpha = .01$, and $n = 900$**

The probability of a Type II error when $p = .56$ is

$$\beta = P\left|\frac{\hat{p} - p}{\sqrt{p(1-p)/n}} < \frac{.539 - .56}{\sqrt{(.56)(1-.56)/900}}\right|$$
$$= P(Z < -1.27) = .1020$$

Figure 10.10 depicts this calculation. Compare this figure with Figure 10.9. As you can see, by decreasing the significance level from 5% to 1%, we have shifted the critical value of the rejection region to the right and thus enlarged the area where the null hypothesis is not rejected. The probability of a Type II error increases from .0233 to .1020.

This calculation illustrates the inverse relationship between the probabilities of Type I and Type II errors alluded to in Section 10-1. It is important to understand this relationship. From a practical point of view, it tells us that if you want to decrease the probability of a Type I error (by specifying a small value of α), you increase the probability of a Type II error. In applications where the cost of a Type I error is considerably larger than the cost of a Type II error, this is appropriate. In fact, a significance level of 1% or less is probably justified. However, when the cost of a Type II error is relatively large, a significance level of 5% or more may be appropriate.

Unfortunately, there is no simple formula to determine what the significance level should be. It is necessary for the manager to consider the costs of both mistakes in deciding what to do. Judgment and knowledge of the factors in the decision are crucial.

10-3b **Judging the Test**

There is another important concept to be derived from this section. A statistical test of hypothesis is effectively defined by the significance level and the sample size, both of which are selected by the statistics practitioner. We can judge how well the test functions by calculating the probability of a Type II error at some value of the parameter. To illustrate, in Example 10.1 the network chose a sample size of 900 and a 5% significance level on which to base its decision. With those selections, we found β to be .0233 when the actual proportion was .56. If we believe that the cost of a Type II error is high and thus that the probability is too large, we have two ways to reduce the probability. We can increase the value of α, although this would result in an increase in the chance of making a Type I error, which is very costly.

Alternatively, we can increase the sample size. Suppose that the manager chose a sample size of 1,800 (twice the original sample size of 900). We'll now recalculate β with $n = 1,800$ (and $\alpha = .05$). The rejection region is

$$z > z_{.05} = 1.645$$

or

$$\frac{\hat{p} - .50}{\sqrt{(.50)(1 - .50)/1800}} > 1.645$$

which yields

$$\hat{p} > .519$$

The probability of a Type II error is

$$\beta = P\left(\frac{\hat{p} - p}{\sqrt{p(1 - p)/n}} < \frac{.519 - .56}{\sqrt{(.56)(1 - .56)/1800}} \right)$$
$$= P(Z < -3.50) = 0 \text{ (approximately)}$$

See Figure 10.11.

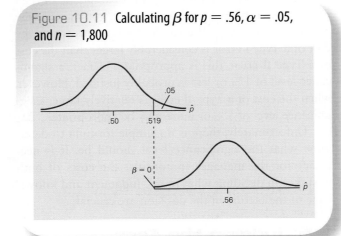

Figure 10.11 Calculating β for $p = .56$, $\alpha = .05$, and $n = 1,800$

© Cengage Learning

In this case, we maintained the same value of α (.05), but we reduced the probability of not announcing the

Bush victory at 8:01 P.M. when the actual proportion is .56 to virtually 0.

10-3c Developing an Understanding of Statistical Concepts: Larger Sample Size Equals More Information Equals Better Decisions

Figure 10.11 displays the previous calculation. When compared with Figure 10.9, we can see that the sampling distribution of the proportion is narrower because the standard error of the proportion $\sqrt{p(1 - p)/n}$ becomes smaller as n increases. Narrower distributions represent more information. The increased information is reflected in a smaller probability of a Type II error.

The calculation of the probability of a Type II error for $n = 900$ and for $n = 1,800$ illustrates a concept whose importance cannot be overstated. By increasing the sample size, we reduce the probability of a Type II error. By reducing the probability of a Type II error, we make this type of error less frequently. Hence, larger sample sizes allow us to make better decisions in the long run. This finding lies at the heart of applied statistical analysis and reinforces the book's first sentence, "Statistics is a way to get information from data."

Throughout this book we introduce a variety of applications in accounting, finance, marketing, operations management, human resources management, and economics. In all such applications, the statistics practitioner must make a decision that involves converting data into information. The more information, the better the decision. Without such information, decisions must be based on guesswork, instinct, and luck. W. Edwards Deming, a famous statistician, said it best: "Without data you're just another person with an opinion."

10-3d Power of a Test

Another way to express how well a test performs is to report its *power*: the probability of its leading us to reject the null hypothesis when it is false. Thus, the power of a test is $1 - \beta$.

When more than one test can be performed in a given situation, we would naturally prefer to use the test that is correct more frequently. Given the same alternative hypothesis, sample size, and significance level, if one test has a higher power than a second test, then the first test is said to be more powerful.

Left-Tail Test

Here is an example of computing the probability of a Type II error when conducting a left-tail test. The hypotheses are

$H_0: p = .30$
$H_1: p < .30$

With $\alpha = .10$ and $n = 100$, we want to calculate β when $p = .25$.

Step 1 is to find the rejection region in terms of the sample proportion. Because the alternative hypothesis specifies *less than*, the rejection region is $z < -z_\alpha$. Thus,

$$\frac{\hat{p} - p}{\sqrt{p(1-p)/n}} < -z_\alpha$$

$$\frac{\hat{p} - .30}{\sqrt{(.30)(1-.30)/100}} < -1.28$$

$$\hat{p} < .2413$$

Step 2 is to find the probability that $\hat{p}$ does not fall into the rejection region when $p = .25$; that is, $P(\hat{p} > .2413 \text{ when } p = .25)$. We proceed by standardizing:

$$\beta = P\left(\frac{\hat{p} - p}{\sqrt{p(1-p)/n}} > \frac{.2413 - .25}{\sqrt{(.25)(1-.25)/100}}\right)$$
$$= P(Z > -.20) = 1 - .4207 = .5793$$

Two-Tail Test

A two-tail test is conducted when the alternative hypothesis specifies that the parameter is *not equal* to the value indicated in the null hypothesis. For example.

$H_0: p = .60$
$H_1: p \ne .60$

With $\alpha = .05$ and $n = 1,600$, we want to calculate β when $p = .61$.

The rejection region is $z < -z_{\alpha/2}$ or $z > z_{\alpha/2}$. We need to find the left-tail and right-tail critical values.

Left-tail critical value:

$$\frac{\hat{p} - p}{\sqrt{p(1-p)/n}} < -z_{\alpha/2}$$

$$\frac{\hat{p} - .60}{\sqrt{(.60)(1-.60)/1600}} < -1.96$$

$$\hat{p} < .5760$$

Right-tail critical value:

$$\frac{\hat{p} - p}{\sqrt{p(1-p)/n}} > z_{\alpha/2}$$

$$\frac{\hat{p} - .60}{\sqrt{(.60)(1-.60)/1600}} > 1.96$$

$$\hat{p} > .6240$$

$$\beta = P(.5760 < \hat{p} < .6240 \text{ given that } p = .61)$$

$$\beta = P\left(\frac{.5760 - .61}{\sqrt{(.61)(1-.61)/1600}}\right.$$
$$\left. < \frac{\hat{p} - p}{\sqrt{p(1-p)/n}} < \frac{.6240 - .61}{\sqrt{(.61)(1-.61)/1600}}\right)$$
$$= P(-2.79 < Z < 1.15) = .8749 - .0026 = .8723$$

10-3e Using the Computer

Excel

We have made it possible to utilize Excel to calculate β for any test of hypothesis about a population proportion.

Open the **Beta-proportion** workbook. There are three worksheets: **Right-tail test**, **Left-tail test**, and **Two-tail test**. Find the appropriate worksheet for the test of hypothesis you are analyzing and type values for p (under the null hypothesis), n, α, and p (actual value under the alternative hypothesis).

The accompanying printout was produced by selecting the **Right-tail Test** worksheet and substituting $p = .50$ (under the null hypothesis), $n = 900$, $\alpha = .05$, and $p = .56$ (under the alternative hypothesis).

You can use the **Left-tail Test** worksheet to compute the probability of Type II errors when the alternative hypothesis states that the proportion is less than a specified value. The **Two-tail Test** worksheet is used to compute β for two-tail tests.

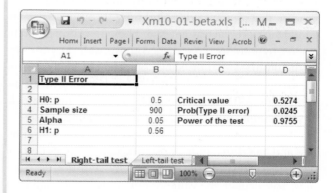

Minitab

Minitab computes the power of the test.

Power and Sample Size

Test for one Proportion

Testing p = 0.5 (versus > 0.5)
Alpha = 0.05

Comparison p	Sample Size	Power
0.56	900	0.975545

INSTRUCTIONS

1. Click **Stat**, **Power** and **Sample Size**, and **1 Proportion** . . . .

2. Specify the sample size in the **Sample Sizes** box (900). (You can specify more than one value of *n*. Minitab will compute the power for each value.) Type the **Comparison proportions** (.56). (You can specify more than one value.)

3. Type the **Hypothesized proportion** (.50)

4. Click **Options** . . . and specify the **Alternative Hypothesis** (greater than) and the **Significance level** (.05).

10-4 The Road Ahead

We had two principal goals to accomplish in Chapters 9 and 10. First, we wanted to present the concepts of estimation and hypothesis testing. Second, we wanted to show how to produce confidence interval estimates and conduct tests of hypotheses. The importance of both of these goals should not be underestimated. Almost everything that follows this chapter will involve either estimating a parameter or testing a set of hypotheses. Consequently, Sections 9-2 and 10-2 set the pattern for the way in which statistical techniques are applied. It is no exaggeration to state that if you understand how to produce and use confidence interval estimates and how to conduct and interpret hypothesis tests, then you are well on your way to the ultimate goal of being competent at analyzing, interpreting, and presenting data. It is fair for you to ask what more you must accomplish to achieve this goal. The answer, simply put, is much more of the same.

In the chapters that follow, we plan to present about two and half dozen different statistical techniques that can be (and frequently are) employed by statistics practitioners. To calculate the value of test statistics or confidence interval estimates requires nothing more than the ability to add, subtract, multiply, divide, and compute square roots. If you intend to use the computer, all you need to know are the commands. The key, then, to applying statistics is knowing which formula to calculate or which set of commands to issue. Thus, the real challenge of the subject lies in being able to define the problem and identify which statistical method is the most appropriate one to use.

A number of factors determine which statistical method should be used, but two are especially important:

the type of data and the purpose of the statistical inference. In Chapter 2, we pointed out that there are effectively three types of data: interval, ordinal, and nominal.

The second key factor in determining the statistical technique is the purpose of doing the work. Every statistical method has some specific objective. We address five such objectives in this book.

10-4a Problem Objectives

1. **Describe a population.** Our objective here is to describe some property of a population of interest. The decision about which property to describe is generally dictated by the type of data. For example, suppose the population of interest consists of all purchasers of home computers. If we are interested in the purchasers' incomes (for which the data are interval), we may calculate the mean or the variance to describe that aspect of the population. But if we are interested in the brand of computer that has been bought (for which the data are nominal), all we can do is compute the proportion of the population that purchases each brand.

2. **Compare two populations.** In this case, our goal is to compare a property of one population with a corresponding property of a second population. For example, suppose the populations of interest are male and female purchasers of computers. We could compare the means of their incomes, or we could compare the proportion of each population that purchases a certain brand. Once again, the data type generally determines what kinds of properties we compare.

3. **Compare two or more populations.** We might want to compare the average income in each of several locations in order, for example, to decide where to build a new shopping center. Or we might want to compare the proportions of defective items in a number of production lines in order to determine which line is the best. In each case, the problem objective involves comparing two or more populations.

4. **Analyze the relationship between two variables.** There are numerous situations in which we want to know how one variable is related to another. Governments need to know what effect rising interest rates have on the unemployment rate. Companies want to investigate how the sizes of their advertising budgets influence sales volume. In most of the problems in this introductory text, the two variables to be analyzed will be of the same type,

Table 10.3 Guide to Statistical Inference Showing Where Each Technique Is Introduced

Problem Objective	Data Type		
	Nominal	Ordinal	Interval
Describe a population	Sections 11-3, 15-1	Not covered	Sections 11-1, 11.2
Compare two populations	Sections 13-2, 15-2	Web-site appendix	Sections 12-1, 12-2, 13.1, Web-site appendix
Compare two or more populations	Section 15-2	Web-site appendix Web-site appendix	Chapter 14
Analyze the relationship between two variables	Section 15-2	Web-site appendix	Chapter 16 Web-site appendix
Analyze the relationship among two or more variables	Not covered	Not covered	Chapter 17

© Cengage Learning

either both interval or both nominal; we will not attempt to cover the fairly large body of statistical techniques that has been developed to deal with two variables of different types.

5. **Analyze the relationship among two or more variables.** Our objective here is usually to forecast one variable (called the *dependent variable*) on the basis of several other variables (called *independent variables*). We will deal with this problem only in situations in which all the variables are interval.

Table 10.3 lists the types of data and the five problem objectives. For each combination, the table specifies the chapter or section where the appropriate statistical technique is presented. For your convenience, a more detailed version of this table is reproduced inside the front cover of this book. (Note that we have stored the inferential techniques for ordinal data in a Web-site appendix.)

10-4b Derivations

Because this book is about statistical applications, we assume that our readers have little interest in the mathematical derivations of the techniques described. However, it might be helpful for you to have some understanding about the process that produces the formulas.

As described previously, factors such as the problem objective and the type of data determine the parameter to be estimated and tested. For each parameter, statisticians have determined which statistic to use. That statistic has a sampling distribution that can usually be expressed as a formula. For example, in this chapter, the parameter of interest was the population proportion p whose best estimator is the sample proportion $\hat{p}$. The sampling distribution of $\hat{p}$ is approximately normal with mean p and standard deviation $\sqrt{p(1-p)/n}$. The sampling distribution can be described by the formula

$$z = \frac{\hat{p} - p}{\sqrt{p(1-p)/n}}$$

This formula also describes the test statistic for p. With a little algebra, we were able to derive (in Section 9-2) the confidence interval estimator of p.

In future chapters, we will repeat this process, which in several cases involves the introduction of a new sampling distribution. Although its shape and formula will differ from the sampling distribution used in this chapter, the pattern will be the same. In general, the formula that expresses the sampling distribution will describe the test statistic. Then some algebraic manipulation (which we will not show) produces the interval estimator. Consequently, we will reverse the order of presentation of the two techniques. In other words, we will present the test of hypothesis first, followed by the confidence interval estimator.

EXERCISES

Exercises 10.1–10.3 feature nonstatistical applications of hypothesis testing. For each, identify the hypotheses, define Type I and Type II errors, and discuss the consequences of each error. In setting up the hypotheses, you will have to consider where to place the "burden of proof."

10.1 It is the responsibility of the federal government to judge the safety and effectiveness of new drugs. There are two possible decisions: approve the drug or disapprove the drug.

10.2 You are faced with two investments. One is very risky, but the potential returns are high. The other is safe, but the potential is quite limited. Pick one.

10.3 You are the pilot of a jumbo jet. You smell smoke in the cockpit. The nearest airport is less than 5 minutes away. Should you land the plane immediately?

10.4 Several years ago in a high-profile case, a defendant was acquitted in a double-murder trial but was subsequently found responsible for the deaths in a civil trial. (Guess the name of the defendant—the answer is in Appendix C.) In a civil trial, the plaintiff (the victims' relatives) are required only to show that the preponderance of evidence points to the guilt of the defendant. Aside from the other issues in the cases, discuss why these results are logical.

Exercises 10.5 and 10.6 are what-if analyses designed to determine what happens to the test statistics and p-values when elements of the statistical inference change.

10.5 a. Calculate the p-value of the test of the following hypotheses given that $\hat{p} = .63$ and $n = 100$:

$H_0: p = .60$
$H_1: p > .60$

b. Repeat part (a) with $n = 200$.
c. Repeat part (a) with $n = 400$.
d. Describe the effect on the p-value of increasing the sample size.

10.6 a. A statistics practitioner wants to test the following hypotheses:

$H_0: p = .70$
$H_1: p < .70$

A random sample of 100 produced $\hat{p} = .67$. Calculate the p-value of the test.

b. Repeat part (a) with $\hat{p} = .68$.
c. Repeat part (a) with $\hat{p} = .69$.
d. Describe the effect on the z-statistic and its p-value of increasing the sample proportion.

10.7 In some states, the law requires drivers to turn on their headlights when driving in the rain. A highway patrol officer believes that less than one-quarter of all drivers follow this rule. As a test, he randomly samples 200 cars driving in the rain and counts the number whose headlights are turned on. He finds this number to be 41. Does the officer have enough evidence at the 10% significance level to support his belief?

10.8 Has the recent drop in airplane passengers resulted in better on-time performance? Before the recent downturn, one airline bragged that 92% of its flights were on time. A random sample of 165 flights completed this year reveals that 153 were on time. Can we conclude at the 5% significance level that the airline's on-time performance has improved?

10.9 The Miami Beach tourist agency claims that the percentage of days in the winter (December 21 to March 21) when the highest daily temperature exceeds 75 degrees is more than 80%. A random sample of 250 days reveals that in 212 days the highest daily temperature exceeded 75 degrees. Can we infer at the 10% significance level that the tourist agency is correct?

Exercises 10.10 to 10.14 require the use of a computer and software. The answers may be calculated manually. See Appendix A for the sample statistics. Use a 5% significance level unless specified otherwise.

10.10 [Xr10-10] The results of an annual Claimant Satisfaction Survey of policyholders who have had a claim with State Farm Insurance Company revealed a 90% satisfaction rate for claim service. To check the accuracy of this claim, a random sample of State Farm claimants was asked to rate whether they were satisfied with the quality of the service (1 = Satisfied and 2 = Unsatisfied). Can we infer that the satisfaction rate is less than 90%?

10.11 [Xr10-11] A professor of business statistics recently adopted a new textbook. At the completion of the course, 100 randomly selected students were asked to assess the book. The responses are as follows:

Excellent (1), Good (2), Adequate (3), Poor (4)

The results are stored using the codes in parentheses. Do the data allow us to conclude at the 10% significance level that more than 50% of all business students would rate the book as excellent?

10.12 Refer to Exercise 10.11. Do the data allow us to conclude at the 10% significance level that more than 90% of all business students would rate it as at least adequate?

10.13 [Xr10-13] According to the American Contract Bridge League, bridge hands that contain two four-card suits, one three-card suit, and one two-card suit (4-4-3-2) occur with 21.55% probability. Suppose that a bridge-playing statistics professor with much too much time on his hands tracked the number of hands over a one-year period and recorded the following hands with 4-4-3-2 distribution (code 2) and some other distribution (code 1). All hands were shuffled and dealt by the players at a bridge club. Determine whether the proportion of 4-4-3-2 hands differ from the theoretical probability. If the answer is yes, propose a reason to explain the result.

10.14 [Xr10-14] According to the latest census, the number of households in a large metropolitan area is 425,000. The home-delivery department of the local newspaper reports that 104,320 households receive daily home delivery. To increase home-delivery sales, the marketing department launches an expensive advertising campaign. A financial analyst tells the publisher that for the campaign to be successful, home-delivery sales must increase to more than 110,000 households. Anxious to see whether the campaign is working, the publisher authorizes a telephone survey of 400 households within 1 week of the beginning of the campaign and asks each household head whether he or she has the newspaper delivered. The responses were recorded, with 2 = yes and 1 = no.
a. Do these data indicate that the campaign will increase home-delivery sales?
b. Do these data allow the publisher to conclude that the campaign will be successful?

10.15 Calculate the probability of a Type II error for the following test of hypothesis, given that $p = .37$.

$$H_0: p = .4$$
$$H_1: p < .4$$
$$\alpha = .05, n = 400$$

10.16 Find the probability of a Type II error for the following test of hypothesis, given that $p = .15$.

$$H_0: p = .2$$
$$H_1: p \neq .2$$
$$\alpha = .10, n = 750$$

10.17 Determine β for the following test of hypothesis, given that $p = .74$.

$$H_0: p = .75$$
$$H_1: p > .75$$
$$\alpha = .01, n = 2,500$$

10.18 A statistics practitioner wants to test the following hypotheses:

$$H_0: p = .5$$
$$H_1: p > .5$$
$$\alpha = .05, n = 1,000$$

a. Find the probability of a Type II error when $p = .52$.
b. Repeat part (a) with $\alpha = .02$.
c. Describe the effect on β of decreasing α.

10.19 a. Calculate the probability of a Type II error for the following hypotheses when $p = .23$:

$$H_0: p = .25$$
$$H_1: p < .25$$
$$\alpha = .05, n = 350$$

b. Repeat part (a) with $\alpha = .15$.
c. Describe the effect on β of increasing α.

10.20 a. Find the probability of a Type II error for the following test of hypothesis, given that $p = .82$.

$$H_0: p = .8$$
$$H_1: p > .8$$
$$\alpha = .10, n = 400$$

b. Repeat part (a) with $n = 1,600$.
c. Describe the effect on β of increasing n.

10.21 Refer to Exercise 10.7. Calculate the probability of a Type II error when the actual proportion is .20.

10.22 Refer to Exercise 10.8. Calculate the probably of a Type II error when the on-time proportion is 95%.

10.23 Refer to Exercise 10.9. Find β when the proportion of days when the high is above 75 degrees is actually 83%.

10.24 Refer to Exercise 10.10. If the actual satisfaction rate is 85% determine the probability of a Type II error.

10.25 Refer to Exercise 10.11. Find the probability of a Type II error when 55% of students rate the book as excellent.

CHAPTER 11

Inference about a Population

objectives

11-1 Inference about a Population Mean

11-2 Inference about a Population Variance

11-3 Review of Inference about a Population Proportion

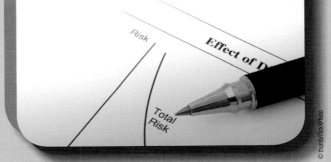

GENERAL SOCIAL SURVEY: HOW MUCH TIME DO AMERICAN ADULTS SPEND WATCHING TELEVISION?

[GSS2012*] Television networks' revenue depends on advertising, the price of which is based on the number of viewers. It is useful to know how much time is spent by Americans watching television. The General Social Survey in 2012 asked the following question:

On average days how many hours do you spend watching television?

TVHOURS (Range 1–24)

Estimate with 95% confidence the mean number of hours American adults spend watching television per day.

After presenting the appropriate technique we will show our answer. See page 175.

In the previous two chapters, we introduced the concepts of statistical inference and showed how to estimate and test a population proportion. The purpose, then, of Chapters 9 and 10 was to set the pattern for the way in which we plan to present other statistical techniques. In other words, we will begin by identifying the parameter to be estimated or tested. We will then specify the parameter's estimator (each parameter has an estimator chosen because of the characteristics we discussed at the beginning of Chapter 9) and its sampling distribution. The sampling distribution is usually the formula for the test statistic. Using simple mathematics, statisticians have derived the interval estimator. This pattern will be used repeatedly as we introduce new techniques.

In Section 10-4, we described the five problem objectives addressed in this book, and we laid out the order of presentation of the statistical methods. In this chapter, we will present techniques employed when the problem objective is to describe a population. When the data are interval, the parameters of interest are the population mean μ and the population variance σ^2. In Section 11-1, we describe how to make inferences about the population mean. In Section 11-2, we continue to deal with interval data, but our parameter of interest becomes the population variance.

Chapters 9 and 10 introduced estimation and hypothesis testing, respectively using the population proportion to illustrate. We'll briefly review the details in Section 11-3.

11-1 Inference about a Population Mean

In Chapter 8, we introduced the sampling distribution of the sample mean $\bar{x}$. The sampling distribution of $\bar{x}$ is normal or approximately normal with mean μ (population mean) and standard deviation $\sigma/\sqrt{n}$ (called the *standard error of the mean*). This can be summarized by the formula

$$z = \frac{\bar{x} - \mu}{\sigma/\sqrt{n}}$$

We would like to use that formula as the test statistic for μ and then use the formula to develop the confidence interval estimator of μ. Unfortunately, there is a major flaw that inhibits us from these goals. The problem is that in virtually all realistic scenarios if the population mean, μ, is unknown, then so is the population standard deviation σ. We will overcome this hurdle in the same way we dealt with the unknown standard error in developing the interval estimator of the population proportion in Chapter 9. We substitute the sample standard deviation s in place of the unknown population standard deviation σ. The result is called a t-statistic because that is what mathematician William S. Gosset called it. In 1908, Gosset showed that the t-statistic defined as

$$t = \frac{\bar{x} - \mu}{s/\sqrt{n}}$$

is Student t distributed when the sampled population is normal. (Gosset published his findings under the pseudonym "Student," hence the **Student t distribution**.) Recall that we introduced the Student t distribution in Section 7-3.

Test Statistic for μ

The test statistic for testing hypotheses about μ is

$$t = \frac{\bar{x} - \mu}{s/\sqrt{n}}$$

which is Student t distributed with $\nu = n - 1$ degrees of freedom, provided that the population is normal.

With exactly the same logic used to develop the confidence interval estimator in Section 9-2, we derive the confidence interval estimator of μ when the population is normal.

Confidence Interval Estimator of μ

$$\bar{x} \pm t_{\alpha/2}\frac{s}{\sqrt{n}} \quad \nu = n - 1$$

EXAMPLE 11.1

Newspaper Recycling Plant

[Xm11-01*] It is likely that in the near future nations will have to do more to save the environment. Possible actions include reducing energy use and recycling. Currently, most products manufactured from recycled material are considerably more expensive than those manufactured from material found in the earth. For example, it is approximately three times as expensive to produce glass bottles from recycled glass as from silica sand, soda ash, and limestone, all plentiful materials mined in numerous countries. It is more expensive to manufacture aluminum cans from recycled cans than from bauxite. Newspapers are an exception. It can be profitable to recycle newspaper. A major expense is the collection from homes. In recent years, a number of companies have gone into the business of collecting used newspapers from households and recycling them. A financial analyst for one such company has recently computed that the firm would make a profit if the mean weekly newspaper collection from each household exceeded 2.0 pounds. In a study to determine the feasibility of a recycling plant, a random sample of 148 households was drawn from a large community, and the weekly weight of newspapers discarded for recycling for each household was recorded and listed next. Do these data provide sufficient evidence to allow the analyst to conclude that a recycling plant would be profitable?

Weights of Discarded Newspapers

2.5	0.7	3.4	1.8	1.9	2.0	1.3	1.2	2.2	0.9	2.7	2.9	1.5	1.5	2.2
3.2	0.7	2.3	3.1	1.3	4.2	3.4	1.5	2.1	1.0	2.4	1.8	0.9	1.3	2.6
3.6	0.8	3.0	2.8	3.6	3.1	2.4	3.2	4.4	4.1	1.5	1.9	3.2	1.9	1.6
3.0	3.7	1.7	3.1	2.4	3.0	1.5	3.1	2.4	2.1	2.1	2.3	0.7	0.9	2.7
1.2	2.2	1.3	3.0	3.0	2.2	1.5	2.7	0.9	2.5	3.2	3.7	1.9	2.0	3.7
2.3	0.6	0.0	1.0	1.4	0.9	2.6	2.1	3.4	0.5	4.1	2.2	3.4	3.3	0.0
2.2	4.2	1.1	2.3	3.1	1.7	2.8	2.5	1.8	1.7	0.6	3.6	1.4	2.2	2.2
1.3	1.7	3.0	0.8	1.6	1.8	1.4	3.0	1.9	2.7	0.8	3.3	2.5	1.5	2.2
2.6	3.2	1.0	3.2	1.6	3.4	1.7	2.3	2.6	1.4	3.3	1.3	2.4	2.0	
1.3	1.8	3.3	2.2	1.4	3.2	4.3	0.0	2.0	1.8	0.0	1.7	2.6	3.1	

SOLUTION
IDENTIFY

The problem objective is to describe the population of the amounts of newspaper discarded by each household in the population. The data are interval, indicating that the parameter to be tested is the population mean. Because the financial analyst needs to determine whether the mean is greater than 2.0 pounds, the alternative hypothesis is

$H_1: \mu > 2.0$

As usual, the null hypothesis states that the mean is equal to the value listed in the alternative hypothesis:

$H_0: \mu = 2.0$

The test statistic is

$t = \dfrac{\bar{x} - \mu}{s/\sqrt{n}} \quad \nu = n - 1$

COMPUTE
Manually

The manager believes that the cost of a Type I error (concluding that the mean is greater than 2 when it isn't) is quite high. Consequently, he sets the significance level at 1%. The rejection region is

$t > t_{\alpha, n-1} = t_{.01, 147} \approx t_{.01, 150} = 2.351$

To calculate the value of the test statistic, we need to calculate the sample mean $\bar{x}$ and the sample standard deviation s. From the data, we determine

$\sum x_i = 322.7 \quad \text{and} \quad \sum x_i^2 = 845.1$

Thus,

$\bar{x} = \dfrac{\sum x_i}{n} = \dfrac{322.7}{148} = 2.18$

$s^2 = \dfrac{\sum x_i^2 - \dfrac{\left(\sum x_i\right)^2}{n}}{n - 1} = \dfrac{845.1 - \dfrac{(322.7)^2}{148}}{148 - 1} = .962$

and

$s = \sqrt{s^2} = \sqrt{.962} = .981$

The value of μ is to be found in the null hypothesis. It is 2.0. The value of the test statistic is

$t = \dfrac{\bar{x} - \mu}{s/\sqrt{n}} = \dfrac{2.18 - 2.0}{.981/\sqrt{148}} = 2.23$

Because 2.23 is not greater than 2.351, we cannot reject the null hypothesis in favor of the alternative.

Excel

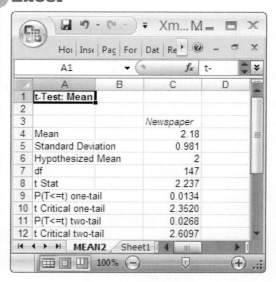

INSTRUCTIONS

1. Type or import the data into one column. (Open Xm11-01.)

2. Click **Add-Ins, Data Analysis Plus,** and *t*-**Test: Mean.**

3. Specify the **Input Range** (A1:A149), the **Hypothesized Mean** (2), and α(.01).

Minitab

One-Sample *T*: Newspaper

Test of mu = 2 vs > 2

Variable	N	Mean	StDev	SE Mean	95% Lower Bound	T	P
Newspaper	148	2.1804	0.9811	0.0807	2.0469	2.24	0.013

INSTRUCTIONS

1. Type or import the data into one column. (Open Xm11-01.)

2. Click **Stat, Basic Statistics,** and **1-Sample *t* . . . .**

3. Type or use the **Select** button to specify the name of the variable or the column in the **Samples in columns** box (Newspaper), choose **Perform hypothesis test** and type the value of μ in the **Hypothesized mean** box (2), and click **Options . . . .**

4. Select one of **less than, not equal,** or **greater than** in the **Alternative** box (greater than).

INTERPRET

The value of the test statistic is $t = 2.24$, and its *p*-value is .0134. There is not enough evidence to infer that the mean weight of discarded newspapers is greater than 2.0. Note that there is some evidence; the *p*-value is .0134. However, because we wanted the probability of a Type I error to be small, we insisted on a 1% significance level. Thus, we cannot conclude that the recycling plant would be profitable.

© Franck Boston/Shutterstock.com

EXAMPLE 11.2

Tax Collected from Audited Returns

[Xm11-02] In a recent year, 134,543,000 tax returns were filed in the United States. The Internal Revenue Service (IRS) examined 1.03% or 1,385,000 of them to determine if they were correctly done. To determine how well the auditors are performing, a random sample of these returns was drawn and the additional tax was reported, which is listed next. Estimate with 95% confidence the mean additional income tax collected from the 1,385,000 files audited. (Adapted from U.S. Internal Revenue Service, *IRS Data Book*, annual, Publication 55B.)

SOLUTION
IDENTIFY

The problem objective is to describe the population of additional income tax. The data are interval, hence the parameter is the population mean μ. The question asks us to estimate this parameter. The confidence interval estimator is

$$\bar{x} \pm t_{\alpha/2}\frac{s}{\sqrt{n}}$$

COMPUTE
Manually

From the data, we determine

$$\sum x_i = 2,087,080 \text{ and } \sum x_i^2 = 27,216,444,599$$

Thus,

$$\bar{x} = \frac{\sum x_i}{n} = \frac{2,087,080}{184} = 11,343$$

and

$$s^2 = \frac{\sum x_i^2 - \frac{\left(\sum x_i\right)^2}{n}}{n-1}$$

$$= \frac{27,216,444,599 - \frac{(2,087,080)^2}{184}}{184-1}$$

$$= 19,360,979$$

Additional Income Tax

15731.15	15594.25	8724.17	11374.34	13197.31	10312.43
6364.09	18662.69	8214.82	9316.70	12132.27	15602.60
7116.91	10463.63	12155.59	3977.52	12672.99	10253.46
12890.47	10070.18	4453.51	14034.78	16409.30	20352.98
11853.56	11603.00	10363.78	11830.85	13676.91	9153.78
10665.40	11255.04	8220.39	15968.90	4278.77	16178.15
6635.94	14491.35	13851.38	7313.00	11985.47	17387.08
12254.47	5128.84	9748.55	15078.81	8658.68	13689.50
7619.82	10102.60	15482.87	9904.92	5172.77	7932.38
9524.40	11010.64	10174.46	15923.39	14994.48	10576.01
17041.16	3694.86	10451.61	18292.65	13789.65	16494.25
7648.54	9761.73	16359.09	5318.50	10429.75	1554.77
7678.23	15018.60	14362.03	15467.99	12984.66	14461.00
9198.38	7589.68	13716.94	14588.00	8672.97	12708.45
7951.54	2732.71	12834.86	7977.11	4023.16	16068.56
6660.60	4740.91	11541.49	9952.42	16493.69	15052.86
11493.30	9326.62	11558.31	10007.03	15651.35	12563.35
7792.70	7308.05	7224.16	16132.63	13991.80	4247.18
10147.98	13760.60	9714.45	0.00	18070.00	6996.54
17712.81	7220.72	15002.06	12870.00	13188.00	7863.68
19276.94	22132.00	12613.92	6645.67	12770.00	12971.50
9320.49	14258.93	17276.46	11801.96	4614.75	18461.05
7821.41	2994.88	8126.62	8941.16	9521.19	21480.96
6774.85	11271.67	13054.84	13739.98	10813.72	15999.38
9389.68	2690.57	4978.82	18259.38	14666.33	
10730.14	17390.36	10481.09	15677.43	1974.11	
4798.18	8402.68	6959.23	16069.51	10831.23	
17192.61	0.00	13224.15	11819.80	12071.03	
7730.51	12744.79	12865.30	17389.63	19326.79	
12387.27	16284.14	14898.40	5927.63	11507.15	
17110.60	7100.00	13617.28	15855.37	10443.33	
17415.28	16386.49	11235.86	7666.54	5972.11	

Thus

$$s = \sqrt{s^2} = \sqrt{19{,}360{,}979} = 4{,}400$$

Because we want a 95% confidence interval estimate, $1 - \alpha = .95$, $\alpha = .05$, $\alpha/2 = .025$, and $t_{\alpha/2,\nu} = t_{.025,183} \approx t_{.025,180} = 1.973$. Thus, the 95% confidence interval estimate of μ is

$$\bar{x} \pm t_{\alpha/2}\frac{s}{\sqrt{n}} = 11{,}343 \pm 1.973\frac{4{,}400}{\sqrt{184}}$$
$$= 11{,}343 \pm 640$$

or

$$LCL = \$10{,}703 \quad UCL = \$11{,}983$$

● Excel

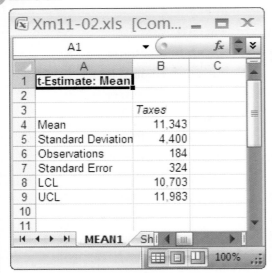

	A	B	C
1	t-Estimate: Mean		
2			
3		*Taxes*	
4	Mean	11,343	
5	Standard Deviation	4,400	
6	Observations	184	
7	Standard Error	324	
8	LCL	10,703	
9	UCL	11,983	
10			
11			

INSTRUCTIONS

1. Type or import the data into one column. (Open Xm11-02.)

2. Click **Add-Ins, Data Analysis Plus**, and *t*-**Estimate: Mean.**

3. Specify the **Input Range** (A1:A185) and (.05).

● Minitab

One-Sample *T*: Taxes

Variable	N	Mean	StDev	SE Mean	95% CI
Taxes	184	11343	4400	324	(10703, 11983)

INSTRUCTIONS

Follow the instructions for the *t*-test of μ except select not equal in the **Alternative** box.

INTERPRET

We estimate that the mean additional tax collected lies between $10,703 and $11,983. We can use this estimate to help decide whether the IRS is auditing the individuals who should be audited.

11-1a Checking the Required Conditions

When we introduced the Student *t* distribution, we pointed out that the *t*-statistic is Student *t* distributed if the population from which we've sampled is normal. However, statisticians have shown that the mathematical process that derived the Student *t* distribution is **robust**, which means that if the population is nonnormal, the results of the *t*-test and confidence interval

estimate are still valid provided that the population is not *extremely* nonnormal.[1] To check this requirement, we draw the histogram and determine whether it is far from bell shaped. Figures 11.1 and 11.2 depict the Excel histograms for Examples 11.1 and 11.2, respectively. (The Minitab histograms are similar.) Both histograms suggest that the variables are not extremely nonnormal.

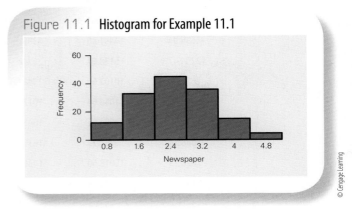

Figure 11.1 **Histogram for Example 11.1**

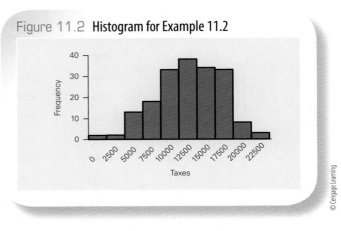

Figure 11.2 **Histogram for Example 11.2**

11-1b Estimating the Totals of Finite Populations

The inferential techniques introduced thus far were derived by assuming infinitely large populations. In practice, however, most populations are finite. (Infinite populations are usually the result of some endlessly repeatable process, such as flipping a coin or selecting items with replacement.)

Finite populations allow us to use the confidence interval estimator of a mean to produce a confidence interval estimator of the population total. To estimate the total, we multiply the lower and upper confidence limits

---

[1] Statisticians have shown that when the sample size is large, the results of a *t*-test and estimator of a mean are valid even when the population is extremely nonnormal. The sample size required depends on the extent of nonnormality.

IDENTIFY

The objective is to describe a population, the amount of television watched by American adults, and the data are interval. Thus the parameter to be estimated is μ.

COMPUTE

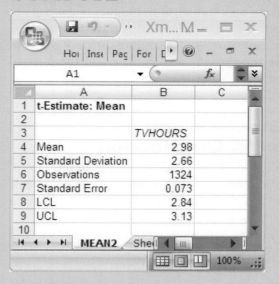

INTERPRET

American adults spend an average of between 2.84 and 3.13 hours per day watching television.

---

of the estimate of the mean by the population size. Thus, the confidence interval estimator of the total is

$$N\left[\bar{x} \pm t_{\alpha/2}\frac{s}{\sqrt{n}}\right]$$

For example, suppose that we wish to estimate the total amount of additional income tax collected from the 1,385,000 returns that were examined. The 95% confidence interval estimate of the total is

$$N\left[\bar{x} \pm t_{\alpha/2}\frac{s}{\sqrt{n}}\right] = 1,385,000\ (11,343 \pm 640)$$

which is

$$LCL = 14,823,655,000 \quad \text{and}$$
$$UCL = 16,596,455,000$$

We complete this section with a review of how we identify the techniques introduced in this section.

Factors That Identify the t-Test and Estimator of μ

1. **Problem objective:** Describe a population
2. **Data type:** Interval
3. **Type of descriptive measurement:** Central location

11-2 Inference about a Population Variance

In Section 11-1, where we presented the inferential methods about a population mean, we were interested in acquiring information about the central location of the population. As a result, we tested and estimated the population mean. If we are interested instead in drawing inferences about a population's variability, then the parameter we need to investigate is the population variance σ^2.

One application of the use of variance comes from operations management. Quality technicians attempt to ensure that their company's products consistently meet specifications. One way of judging the consistency of a production process is to compute the variance of the size, weight, or volume of the product; that is, if the variation in product size, weight, or volume is large, then it is likely that an unsatisfactorily large number of products will lie outside the specifications for that product.

The task of deriving the test statistic and the interval estimator provides us with another opportunity to show how statistical techniques in general are developed. We begin by identifying the best estimator. That estimator has a sampling distribution from which we produce the test statistic and the interval estimator.

11-2a Statistic and Sampling Distribution

The estimator of σ^2 is the sample variance introduced in Section 3-2. The statistic s^2 has the desirable characteristics presented in Section 9-1; that is, s^2 is an unbiased, consistent estimator of σ^2.

Statisticians have shown that the sum of squared deviations from the mean $\sum(x_i - \bar{x})^2$ [which is equal to $(n-1)s^2$] divided by the population variance is chi-squared distributed with $\nu = n - 1$ degrees of freedom provided that the sampled population is normal. The statistic

$$\chi^2 = \frac{(n-1)s^2}{\sigma^2}$$

is called the **chi-squared statistic** (χ^2-statistic). The chi-squared distribution was introduced in Section 7-3.

11-2b Testing and Estimating a Population Variance

As we discussed in Section 10-4, the formula that describes the sampling distribution is the formula of the test statistic.

Test Statistic for σ^2

The test statistic used to test hypotheses about σ^2 is

$$\chi^2 = \frac{(n-1)s^2}{\sigma^2}$$

which is chi-squared distributed with $\nu = n - 1$ degrees of freedom when the population random variable is normally distributed with variance equal to σ^2.

Using the notation introduced in Section 7-3, we can make the following probability statement:

$$P\left(\chi^2_{1-\alpha/2} < \chi^2 < \chi^2_{\alpha/2}\right) = 1 - \alpha$$

Substituting

$$\chi^2 = \frac{(n-1)s^2}{\sigma^2}$$

and with some algebraic manipulation, we derive the confidence interval estimator of a population variance.

Confidence Interval Estimator of σ^2

$$\text{Lower confidence limit (LCL)} = \frac{(n-1)s^2}{\chi^2_{\alpha/2}}$$

$$\text{Upper confidence limit (UCL)} = \frac{(n-1)s^2}{\chi^2_{1-\alpha/2}}$$

© Alexey Stiop/Shutterstock.com

EXAMPLE 11.3

Consistency of a Container-Filling Machine, Part 1

[Xm11-03] Container-filling machines are used to package a variety of liquids, including milk, soft drinks, and paint. Ideally, the amount of liquid should vary only slightly, because large variations will cause some containers to be underfilled (cheating the customer) and some to be overfilled (resulting in costly waste). The president of a company that developed a new type of machine boasts that this machine can fill 1-liter (1,000 cubic centimeters) containers so consistently that the variance of the fills will be less than 1 cubic centimeter^2. To examine the veracity of the claim, a random sample of 25-liter fills was taken, and the results (cubic centimeters) recorded. These data are listed here. Do these data allow the president to make this claim at the 5% significance level?

Fills

999.6	1,000.7	999.3	1,000.1	999.5
1,000.5	999.7	999.6	999.1	997.8
1,001.3	1,000.7	999.4	1000.0	998.3
999.5	1,000.1	998.3	999.2	999.2
1,000.4	1,000.1	1,000.1	999.6	999.9

SOLUTION
IDENTIFY

The problem objective is to describe the population of l-liter fills from this machine. The data are interval, and we're interested in the variability of the fills. It follows that the parameter of interest is the population variance. Because we want to determine whether there is enough evidence to support the claim, the alternative hypothesis is

$$H_1: \sigma^2 < 1$$

The null hypothesis is

$$H_0: \sigma^2 = 1$$

and the test statistic we will use is

$$\chi^2 = \frac{(n-1)s^2}{\sigma^2}$$

COMPUTE
Manually

Using a calculator, we find

$$\sum x_i = 24{,}992.0 \quad \text{and} \quad \sum x_i^2 = 24{,}984{,}017.76$$

Thus,

$$s^2 = \frac{\sum x_i^2 - \frac{\left(\sum x_i\right)^2}{n}}{n-1} = \frac{24{,}984{,}017.76 - \frac{(24{,}992.0)^2}{25}}{25-1}$$

$$= .6333$$

The value of the test statistic is

$$\chi^2 = \frac{(n-1)s^2}{\sigma^2} = \frac{(25-1)(.6333)}{1} = 15.20$$

The rejection region is

$$\chi^2 < \chi^2_{1-\alpha,n-1} = \chi^2_{1-.05,25-1} = \chi^2_{.95,24} = 13.85$$

Because 15.20 is not less than 13.85, we cannot reject the null hypothesis in favor of the alternative.

Excel

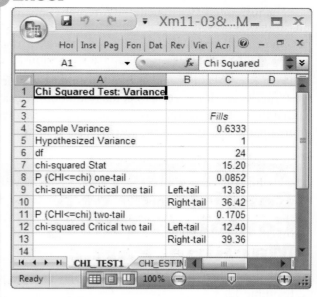

	A	B	C	D
1	Chi Squared Test: Variance			
2				
3			Fills	
4	Sample Variance		0.6333	
5	Hypothesized Variance		1	
6	df		24	
7	chi-squared Stat		15.20	
8	P (CHI<=chi) one-tail		0.0852	
9	chi-squared Critical one tail	Left-tail	13.85	
10		Right-tail	36.42	
11	P (CHI<=chi) two-tail		0.1705	
12	chi-squared Critical two tail	Left-tail	12.40	
13		Right-tail	39.36	
14				

INSTRUCTIONS

1. Type or import the data into one column. (Open Xm11-03.)

2. Click **Add-Ins, Data Analysis Plus,** and **Chi-squared Test: Variance.**

3. Specify the **Input Range** (A1:A26), type the **Hypothesized Variance** (1) and the value of (.05).

The value of the test statistic is 15.20. $P(\text{CHI}<=\text{chi})$ one-tail is the probability $P(\chi^2 < 15.20)$, which is equal to .0852. Because this is a one-tail test, the p-value is .0852.

Minitab

Test and CI for One Variance: Fills

```
Null hypothesis          Sigma-squared = 1
Alternative hypothesis   Sigma-squared < 1

Test
Variable   Method       Statistic   DF   P-Value
Fills      Chi-Square   15.20       24   0.085
```

INSTRUCTIONS

Some of the output has been deleted.

1. Type or import the data into one column. (Open Xm11-03.)

2. Click **Stat, Basic Statistics,** and **1 Variance . . .**

3. Select **Samples in columns** in the **Data** box. Type or use the **Select** button to specify the name of the variable or the column in the **Columns** box (Fills).

4. Click **Perform hypothesis test,** select **Hypothesized variance,** and type the value of σ^2 (1) in the **Value** box.

5. Click **Options** . . . and select one of **less than, not equal,** or **greater than** in the **Alternative** box (less than).

INTERPRET

There is not enough evidence to infer that the claim is true. As we discussed before, the result does not say that the variance is equal to 1; it merely states that we are unable to show that the variance is less than 1.

EXAMPLE 11.4

Consistency of a Container-Filling Machine, Part 2

Estimate with 99% confidence the variance of fills in Example 11.3.

SOLUTION
IDENTIFY

In the solution to Example 11.3, we found $(n - 1)s^2$ to be 15.20. From Table 5 in Appendix B, we find

$$\chi^2_{\alpha/2, n-1} = \chi^2_{.005, 24} = 45.6$$

$$\chi^2_{1-\alpha/2, n-1} = \chi^2_{.995, 24} = 9.89$$

Thus,

$$\text{LCL} = \frac{(n - 1)s^2}{\chi^2_{\alpha/2}} = \frac{15.20}{45.6} = .3333$$

$$\text{UCL} = \frac{(n - 1)s^2}{\chi^2_{1-\alpha/2}} = \frac{15.20}{9.89} = 1.537$$

We estimate that the variance of fills is a number that lies between .3333 and 1.537.

Excel

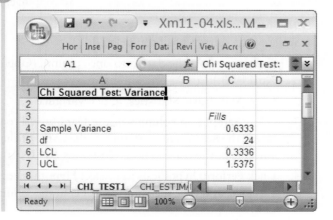

INSTRUCTIONS

1. Type or import the data into one column. (Open Xm11-03.)

2. Click **Add-Ins, Data Analysis Plus,** and **Chi-squared Estimate: Variance.**

3. Specify the **Input Range** (A1:A26) and (.01).

Minitab

Test and CI for One Variance: Fills

99% Confidence Intervals

Variable	Method	CI for StDev	CI for Variance
Fills	Chi-Square	(0.578, 1.240)	(0.334, 1.537)

INSTRUCTIONS

Some of the output has been deleted.

1. Follow the first three steps in the chi-squared test of σ^2. Do not click **Perform hypothesis test.**

2. Click **Options** . . . **Type the confidence level** (.99) and select **not equal** in the **Alternative** box.

INTERPRET

In Example 11.3, we saw that there was not sufficient evidence to infer that the population variance is less than 1. Here we see that σ^2 is estimated to lie between .3333 and 1.537. Part of this interval is above 1, which tells us that the variance may be larger than 1, confirming the conclusion we reached in Example 11.3. We may be able to use the estimate to predict the percentage of overfilled and underfilled bottles. This may allow us to choose among competing machines.

11-2c Checking the Required Condition

Like the *t*-test and estimator of μ introduced in Section 11-1, the chi-squared test and estimator of σ^2 theoretically require that the sample population be normal. In practice, however, the technique is valid so long as the population is not extremely nonnormal. We can gauge the extent of nonnormality by drawing the histogram. Figure 11.3 depicts Excel's version of this histogram. As you can see, the fills appear to be somewhat asymmetric. However, the variable does not appear to be very nonnormal. We conclude that the normality requirement is not seriously violated.

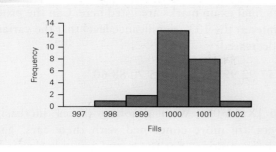

Figure 11.3 **Histogram for Examples 11.3 and 11.4**

Here is how we recognize when to use the techniques introduced in this section.

Factors That Identify the Chi-Squared Test and Estimator of σ^2

1. **Problem objective:** Describe a population

2. **Data type:** Interval

3. **Type of descriptive measurement:** Variability

11-3 Review of Inference about a Population Proportion

We have already introduced inference about a population proportion in Chapters 9 and 10. We include this review because we need to put these techniques into the technique-identification framework.

When the problem objective is to draw inferences about a single population and the data are nominal, the parameter to be estimated or tested is the population proportion p. In Example 9.1, the population was Americans 50 and older who regularly watch network news on television. The data were nominal; the values are "No" (code = 1) and "Yes" (code = 2). Consequently, we wanted to estimate p, the proportion of the population who had contacted their physicians to ask about the advertised pharmaceutical.

In Example 10.1, the problem objective is to describe the population of votes in the state. The data are nominal because the values are "Democrat" (code = 1) and "Republican" (code = 2). Thus, the parameter to be tested is the proportion of votes in the entire state who are for the Republican candidate. Because we want to determine whether the network can declare the Republican to be the winner at 8:01 P.M., the alternative hypothesis is

$$H_1: p > .5$$

which makes the null hypothesis

$$H_0: p = .5$$

Test Statistic for p

$$z = \frac{\hat{p} - p}{\sqrt{p(1 - p)/n}}$$

which is approximately normal for np and $n(1 - p)$ greater than 5.

Confidence Interval Estimator of p

$$\hat{p} \pm z_{\alpha/2} \sqrt{\hat{p}(1 - \hat{p})/n}$$

which is valid provided that $n\hat{p}$ and $n(1 - \hat{p})$ are greater than 5.

Factors that Identify the z-Test and Interval Estimator of p

1. **Problem objective:** Describe a population

2. **Data type:** Nominal

11.1 [Xr11-01] A diet doctor claims that the average North American is more than 20 pounds overweight. To test this claim, a random sample of 20 North Americans was weighed, and the difference between their actual weight and their ideal weight was calculated. The data are listed here. Do these data allow us to infer at the 5% significance level that the doctor's claim is true?

16 23 18 41 22 18 23 19 22 15 18 35 16 15 17 19 23 15 16 26

11.2 [Xr11-02] A parking-control officer is conducting an analysis of the amount of time left on parking meters. A quick survey of 15 cars that have just left their metered parking spaces produced the following times (in minutes). Estimate with 95% confidence the mean amount of time left for all the city's meters.

22 15 1 14 0 9 17 31 18 26 23 15 33 28 20

11.3 [Xr11-03] University bookstores order books that instructors adopt for their courses. The number of copies ordered matches the projected demand. However, at the end of the semester, the bookstore has too many copies on hand and must return them to the publisher. A bookstore has a policy that the proportion of books returned should be kept as small as possible. The average is supposed to be less than 10%. To see whether the policy is working, a random sample of book titles was drawn, and the fraction of the total originally ordered that are returned is recorded and listed here. Can we infer at the 10% significance level that the mean proportion of returns is less than 10%?

4 15 11 7 5 9 4 3 5 8

11.4 [Xr11-04] The weights of a random sample of cereal boxes that are supposed to weigh 1 pound are listed here. Estimate the variance of the entire population of cereal box weights with 90% confidence.

1.05 1.03 .98 1.00 .99 .97 1.01 .96

11.5 [Xr11-05] After many years of teaching, a statistics professor computed the variance of the marks on her final exam and found it to be $\sigma^2 = 250$. She recently made changes to the way in which the final exam is marked and wondered whether this would result in a reduction in the variance. A random sample of this year's final exam marks are listed here. Can the professor infer at the 10% significance level that the variance has decreased?

57 92 99 73 62 64 75 70 88 60

11.6 [Xr11-06] With gasoline prices increasing, drivers are more concerned with their cars' gasoline consumption. For the past 5 years, a driver has tracked the gas mileage of his car and found that the variance from fill-up to fill-up was $\sigma^2 = 23$ mpg^2. Now that his car is 5 years old, he would like to know whether the variability of gas mileage has changed. He recorded the gas mileage from his last eight fill-ups; these are listed here. Conduct a test at a 10% significance level to infer whether the variability has changed.

28 25 29 25 32 36 27 24

11.7 [Xr11-07] During annual checkups physicians routinely send their patients to medical laboratories to have various tests performed. One such test determines the cholesterol level in patients' blood. However, not all tests are conducted in the same way. To acquire more information, a man was sent to 10 laboratories and had his cholesterol level measured in each. The results are listed here. Estimate with 95% confidence the variance of these measurements.

188 193 186 184 190 195 187 190 192 196

The following exercises require the use of a computer and software. The answers may be calculated manually. See Appendix A for the sample statistics. Use a 5% significance level unless specified otherwise.

11.8 [Xr11-08*] A growing concern for educators in the United States is the number of teenagers who have part-time jobs while they attend high school. It is generally believed that the amount of time teenagers spend working is deducted from the amount of time devoted to schoolwork. To investigate this problem, a school guidance counselor took a random sample of 200 15-year-old high school students and asked how many hours per week each worked at a part-time job. Estimate with 95% confidence the mean amount of time all 15-year-old high school students devote per week to part-time jobs.

11.9 [Xr11-09] Bankers and economists watch for signs that the economy is slowing. One statistic they monitor is consumer debt, particularly credit card debt. The Federal Reserve conducts surveys of consumer finances every 3 years. The last survey determined that 23.8% of American households have no credit cards and another 31.2% of the households paid off their most recent credit card bills. The remainder, approximately 50 million households, did not pay their credit card bills in the previous month. A random sample of these households was drawn. Each household in the sample reported how much credit card debt it currently carries. The Federal Reserve would like an estimate (with 95% confidence) of the total credit card debt in the United States.

11.10 [Xr11-10] OfficeMax, a chain that sells a wide variety of office equipment, often features sales of products whose prices are reduced because of rebates. Some rebates are so large that the effective price becomes $0. The goal is to lure customers into the store to buy other nonsale items. A secondary objective is to acquire addresses and telephone numbers to sell to telemarketers and other mass marketers. During one week in January, OfficeMax offered a 100-pack of CD-ROMs (regular price $29.99 minus $10 instant rebate, $12 manufacturer's rebate, and $8 OfficeMax mail-in rebate). The number of packages was limited, and no rain checks were issued. In all the OfficeMax stores, there were 2,800 packages in stock. All were sold. A random sample of 122 buyers was undertaken. Each was asked to report the total value of the other purchases made that day. Estimate with 95% the total spent on other products purchased by those who bought the CD-ROMs.

11.11 [Xr11-11] To help estimate the size of the disposable razor market, a random sample of men was asked to count the number of shaves they used each razor for. Assume that each razor is used once per day. Estimate with 95% confidence the number of days a pack of 10 razors will last.

11.12 [Xr11-12] Because of the enormity of the viewing audience, firms that advertise during the Super Bowl create special commercials that tend to be quite entertaining. Thirty-second commercials cost $2.3 million during the 2001 Super Bowl game. A random sample of people who watched the game was asked how many commercials they watched in their entirety. Do these data allow us to infer that the mean number of commercials watched is greater than 15?

11.13 [Xr11-13] On a per capita basis, the United States spends far more on health than any other country. To help assess the costs, annual surveys are undertaken. One such survey asks a sample of Americans to report the number of times they visited a health care professional in the year. The data for 2006 were recorded. In 2006, the United States population was 299,157,000. Estimate with 95% confidence the total number of visits to a health-care professional. (Adapted from the *Statistical Abstract of the United States*, 2009, Table 158.)

11.14 [Xr11-14] Companies that sell groceries over the Internet are called *e-grocers*. Customers enter their orders, pay by credit card, and receive deliveries by truck. A potential e-grocer analyzed the market and determined that to be profitable the average order would have to exceed $85. To determine whether an e-grocery would be profitable in one large city, she offered the service and recorded the size of the order for a random sample of customers. Can we infer from these data that an e-grocery will be profitable in this city?

11.15 [Xr11-15] One important factor in inventory control is the variance of the daily demand for the product. A management scientist has developed the optimal order quantity and reorder point, assuming that the variance is equal to 250. Recently, the company has experienced some inventory problems, which induced the operations manager to doubt the assumption. To examine the problem, the manager took a sample of 25 days and recorded the demand.

a. Do these data provide sufficient evidence at the 5% significance level to infer that the management scientist's assumption about the variance is wrong?
b. What is the required condition for the statistical procedure in part (a)?
c. Does it appear that the required condition is not satisfied?

11.16 [Xr11-16] Some traffic experts believe that the major cause of highway collisions is the differing speeds of cars. In other words, when some cars are driven slowly while others are driven at speeds well in excess of the speed limit, cars tend to congregate in bunches, increasing the probability of accidents. Thus, the greater the variation in speeds, the greater will be the number of collisions that occur. Suppose that one expert believes that when the variance exceeds 18 mph², the number of accidents will be unacceptably high. A random sample of the speeds of 245 cars on a highway with one of the highest accident rates in the country is taken. Can we conclude at the 10% significance level that the variance in speeds exceeds 18 mph²?

11.17 [Xr11-17] The job-placement service at a university observed the not unexpected result of the variance in marks and work experience of the university's graduates: some graduates received numerous offers, whereas others received far fewer. To learn more about the problem, a survey of 90 recent graduates was conducted in which they were asked how many job offers they received. Estimate with 90% confidence the variance in the number of job offers made to the university's graduates.

11.18 [Xr11-18] One problem facing the manager of maintenance departments is when to change the bulbs in streetlamps. If bulbs are changed only when they burn out, it is quite costly to send crews out to change only one bulb at a time. This method also requires someone to report the problem; in the meantime, the light is off. If each bulb lasts approximately the same amount of time, they can all be replaced periodically, producing significant cost savings in maintenance. Suppose that a financial analysis of the lights at Yankee Stadium has concluded that it will pay to replace all of the light-bulbs at the same time if the variance of the lives of the bulbs is less than 200 hours². The lengths of life of the last 100 bulbs were recorded. What conclusion can be drawn from these data? Use a 5% significance level.

11.19 [Xr11-19] Home blood-pressure monitors have been on the market for several years. This device allows people with high blood pressure to measure their own and determine whether additional medication is necessary. Concern has been expressed about inaccurate readings. To judge the severity of the problem, a laboratory technician measured his own blood pressure 25 times using the leading brand of monitors. Estimate the population variance with 95% confidence.

11.20 [Xr11-20*] The JC Penney department store chain segments the market for women's apparel by its identification of values. The three segments are

1. Conservative
2. Traditional
3. Contemporary

Questionnaires about personal and family values are used to identify which segment a woman falls into. Suppose that the questionnaire was sent to a random sample of 1,836 women. Each woman was classified using the codes 1, 2, and 3. The latest census reveals that there are 120,728,000 adult women in the United States (*Statistical Abstract of the United States*, 2012, Table 7). Use a 95% confidence level.

a. Estimate the proportion of adult American women who are classified as traditional.
b. Estimate the size of the traditional market segment.

11.21 [Xr11-21] Most life insurance companies are leery about offering policies to people older than 64. When they do, the premiums must be high enough to overcome the predicted length of life. The president of one life insurance company was thinking about offering special discounts to Americans older than 64 who held full-time jobs. The plan was based on the belief that full-time workers older than 64 are likely to be in good health and would likely live well into their 80s. To help decide what to do, he organized a survey of a random sample of the 40,268,000 American adults older than 64 (*Statistical Abstract of the United States*, 2012, Table 7). He asked a random sample of 325 Americans older than 64 whether they currently hold a full-time job (1 = No, 2 = Yes). Estimate with 95% confidence the size of this market segment.

11.22 [Xr11-22] An advertising company was awarded the contract to design advertising for Rolls Royce automobiles. An executive in the firm decided to pitch the product not only to the affluent in the United States but also to those who think they are in the top 1% of income earners in the country. A survey was undertaken that asked, among other questions, respondents 25 and older where their annual income ranked. The following responses were given:

1 = Top 1%
2 = Top 5% but not top 1%
3 = Top 10% but not top 5%
4 = Top 25% but not top 10%
5 = Bottom 75%

Estimate with 90% confidence the number of Americans 25 and older who believe they are in the top 1% of income earners. The number of Americans older than

25 is 203,892,000 (*Statistical Abstract of the United States*, 2012, Table 7).

11.23 [Xr11-23] Suppose the survey in the previous exercise also asked those who were not in the top 1% whether they believed that within 5 years they would be in the top 1% (1 = will not be in top 1% within 5 years, 2 = will be in top 1% within 5 years). Estimate with 95% confidence the number of Americans who believe that they will be in the top 1% of income earners within 5 years.

11.24 [Xr11-24] Opinion Research International surveyed people whose household incomes exceed $50,000 and asked each for their top money-related New Year's resolutions. The responses are:

1. Get out of credit card debt.
2. Retire before age 65.
3. Die broke.
4. Make do with current finances.
5. Look for higher-paying job.

Estimate with 90% confidence the proportion of people whose household incomes exceed $50,000 and whose top money-related resolution is to get out of credit card debt.

11.25 [Xr11-25] In 2010, there were 117,538,000 households in the United States. There were 78,833,000 family households made up of married couples, single-male households, and single-female households. To determine how many of each type a survey was undertaken. The results were stored using the codes 1 = married couple, 2 = single male, and 3 = single female. Estimate with 95% confidence the total number of American households with married couples. (Adapted from *Statistical Abstract of the United States*, 2012, Table 59)

Inference about Comparing Two Populations, Part 1

objectives

12-1 Inference about the Difference between Two Means: Independent Samples

12-2 Inference about the Difference between Two Means: Matched Pairs Experiment

AMERICAN NATIONAL ELECTION SURVEY: ARE REPUBLICANS MORE EDUCATED THAN DEMOCRATS?

[ANES2008*] The American National Election Survey asked the following questions.

1. What is the highest grade of school or year of college completed? (EDUC: Range 0, 1, . . . , 16, 17 = 17+)

2. Do you think of yourself as Democrat, Republican, Independent, or what? PARTY: 1 = Democrat, 2 = Republican, 3 = Independent, 4 = Other party, 5 = No preference.

Conduct a test to determine whether Republicans have more years of education than do Democrats. We will provide our answer on pages 193–194.

In this chapter and the next one, we present a variety of techniques whose objective is to compare two populations. In this chapter, we deal with interval variables; the parameter of interest is the difference between two means. The difference between Sections 12-1 and 12-2 introduces yet another factor that determines the correct statistical method—the design of the experiment used to gather the data.

12-1 Inference about the Difference between Two Means: Independent Samples

In order to test and estimate the difference between two population means, the statistics practitioner draws random samples from each of two populations. In this section, we discuss independent samples. In Section 12-2, where we present the matched pairs experiment, the distinction between independent samples and matched pairs will be made clear. For now, we define independent samples as samples completely unrelated to one another.

Figure 12.1 depicts the sampling process. Observe that we draw a sample of size n_1 from population 1 and a sample of size n_2 from population 2. For each sample, we compute the sample means and sample variances.

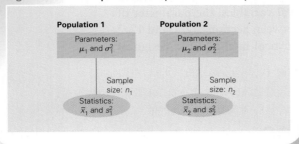

Figure 12.1 **Independent Samples from Two Populations**

The best estimator of the difference between two population means $\mu_1 - \mu_2$ is the difference between two sample means, $\bar{x}_1 - \bar{x}_2$. The sampling distribution of $\bar{x}_1 - \bar{x}_2$ is derived in a way similar to the way the sampling distribution of $\bar{x}$ was derived in Chapter 8.

Sampling Distribution of $\bar{x}_1 - \bar{x}_2$

1. $\bar{x}_1 - \bar{x}_2$ is normally distributed if the populations are normal and approximately normal if the populations are nonnormal and the sample sizes are large.

2. The expected value of $\bar{x}_1 - \bar{x}_2$ is

$$E(\bar{x}_1 - \bar{x}_2) = \mu_1 - \mu_2$$

3. The variance of $\bar{x}_1 - \bar{x}_2$ is

$$V(\bar{x}_1 - \bar{x}_2) = \frac{\sigma_1^2}{n_1} + \frac{\sigma_2^2}{n_2}$$

The standard error of $\bar{x}_1 - \bar{x}_2$ is

$$\sqrt{\frac{\sigma_1^2}{n_1} + \frac{\sigma_2^2}{n_2}}$$

Thus,

$$z = \frac{(\bar{x}_1 - \bar{x}_2) - (\mu_1 - \mu_2)}{\sqrt{\dfrac{\sigma_1^2}{n_1} + \dfrac{\sigma_2^2}{n_2}}}$$

is a standard normal (or approximately normal) random variable. It follows that the test statistic is

$$z = \frac{(\bar{x}_1 - \bar{x}_2) - (\mu_1 - \mu_2)}{\sqrt{\dfrac{\sigma_1^2}{n_1} + \dfrac{\sigma_2^2}{n_2}}}$$

The interval estimator is

$$(\bar{x}_1 - \bar{x}_2) \pm z_{\alpha/2} \sqrt{\frac{\sigma_1^2}{n_1} + \frac{\sigma_2^2}{n_2}}$$

However, these formulas are rarely used because the population variances σ_1^2 and σ_2^2 are virtually always unknown. Consequently, it is necessary to estimate the standard error of the sampling distribution as we did in Chapter 11. The way to do this depends on whether the two unknown population variances are equal. When they are equal, the test statistic is defined in the following way.

Test Statistic for $\mu_1 - \mu_2$ When $\sigma_1^2 = \sigma_2^2$

$$t = \frac{(\bar{x}_1 - \bar{x}_2) - (\mu_1 - \mu_2)}{\sqrt{s_p^2\left(\dfrac{1}{n_1} + \dfrac{1}{n_2}\right)}} \qquad v = n_1 + n_2 - 2$$

where

$$s_p^2 = \frac{(n_1 - 1)s_1^2 + (n_2 - 1)s_2^2}{n_1 + n_2 - 2}$$

The quantity s_p^2 is called the **pooled variance estimator**. The requirement that the population variances be equal makes this calculation feasible, because we need only one estimate of the common value of σ_1^2 and σ_2^2. It makes sense for us to use the pooled variance estimator because, in combining both samples, we produce a better estimate.

The test statistic is Student t distributed with $n_1 + n_2 - 2$ degrees of freedom, provided that the two populations are normal. The confidence interval estimator is derived by mathematics that by now has become routine.

Confidence Interval Estimator of $\mu_1 - \mu_2$ When $\sigma_1^2 = \sigma_2^2$

$$(\bar{x}_1 - \bar{x}_2) \pm t_{\alpha/2} \sqrt{s_p^2\left(\frac{1}{n_1} + \frac{1}{n_2}\right)} \qquad v = n_1 + n_2 - 2$$

We will refer to these formulas as the **equal-variances test statistic** and **equal-variances confidence interval estimator**, respectively.

When the population variances are unequal, we cannot use the pooled variance estimate. Instead, we estimate each population variance with its sample variance. Unfortunately, the sampling distribution of the resulting statistic

$$\frac{(\bar{x}_1 - \bar{x}_2) - (\mu_1 - \mu_2)}{\sqrt{\dfrac{s_1^2}{n_1} + \dfrac{s_2^2}{n_2}}}$$

is neither normally nor Student t distributed. However, it can be approximated by a Student t distribution with degrees of freedom equal to

$$v = \frac{(s_1^2/n_1 + s_2^2/n_2)^2}{\dfrac{(s_1^2/n_1)^2}{n_1 - 1} + \dfrac{(s_2^2/n_2)^2}{n_2 - 1}}$$

(It is usually necessary to round this number to the nearest integer.) The test statistic and confidence interval estimator are easily derived from the sampling distribution.

Test Statistic for $\mu_1 - \mu_2$ When $\sigma_1^2 \neq \sigma_2^2$

$$t = \frac{(\bar{x}_1 - \bar{x}_2) - (\mu_1 - \mu_2)}{\sqrt{\dfrac{s_1^2}{n_1} + \dfrac{s_2^2}{n_2}}} \qquad \nu = \frac{(s_1^2/n_1 + s_2^2/n_2)^2}{\dfrac{(s_1^2/n_1)^2}{n_1 - 1} + \dfrac{(s_2^2/n_2)^2}{n_2 - 1}}$$

Confidence Interval Estimator of $\mu_1 - \mu_2$ When $\sigma_1^2 \neq \sigma_2^2$

$$(\bar{x}_1 - \bar{x}_2) \pm t_{\alpha/2} \sqrt{\frac{s_1^2}{n_1} + \frac{s_2^2}{n_2}} \qquad \nu = \frac{(s_1^2/n_1 + s_2^2/n_2)^2}{\dfrac{(s_1^2/n_1)^2}{n_1 - 1} + \dfrac{(s_2^2/n_2)^2}{n_2 - 1}}$$

We will refer to these formulas as the **unequal-variances test statistic** and **unequal-variances confidence interval estimator**, respectively.

The question naturally arises, How do we know when the population variances are equal? The answer is that because σ_1^2 and σ_2^2 are unknown, we can't know for certain whether they're equal. However, we can perform a statistical test to determine whether there is evidence to infer that the population variances differ. We conduct the F-test of the ratio of two variances, which we briefly present here and save the details for Section 13-1.

Testing the Population Variances

The hypotheses to be tested are

$$H_0: \sigma_1^2/\sigma_2^2 = 1$$

$$H_1: \sigma_1^2/\sigma_2^2 \neq 1$$

The test statistic is the ratio of the sample variances s_1^2/s_2^2, which is F distributed with degrees of freedom $\nu_1 = n_1 - 1$ and $\nu_2 = n_2 - 1$. Recall that we introduced the F distribution in Section 7-3. The required condition is the same as that for the t-test of $\mu_1 - \mu_2$, which is that both populations are normally distributed.

This is a two-tail test so that the rejection region is

$$F > F_{\alpha/2, \nu_1, \nu_2} \qquad \text{or} \qquad F < F_{1-\alpha/2, \nu_1, \nu_2}$$

Put simply, we will reject the null hypothesis that states that the population variances are equal when the ratio of the sample variances is large or if it is small.

Table 6 in Appendix B, which lists the critical values of the F distribution, defines "large" and "small."

12-1a Decision Rule: Equal-Variances or Unequal-Variances t-Tests and Estimators

Recall that we can never have enough statistical evidence to conclude that the null hypothesis is true. This means that we can only determine whether there is enough evidence to infer that the population variances *differ*. Accordingly, we adopt the following rule: we will use the equal-variances test statistic and confidence interval estimator unless there is evidence (based on the F-test of the population variances) to indicate that the population variances are unequal, in which case we will apply the unequal-variances test statistic and confidence interval estimator.

Jay Brousseau/Stone/Getty Images

EXAMPLE 12.1

Direct and Broker-Purchased Mutual Funds[1]

[Xm12-01] Millions of investors buy mutual funds, choosing from thousands of possibilities. Some funds can be purchased directly from banks or other financial institutions, whereas others must be purchased through brokers, who charge a fee for this service. This raises the question, Can investors do better by buying mutual funds directly than by purchasing mutual funds through brokers?

[1] Source: D. Bergstresser, J. Chalmers, and P. Tufano, "Assessing the Costs and Benefits of Brokers in the Mutual Fund Industry." Working paper.

To help answer this question, a group of researchers randomly sampled the annual returns from mutual funds that can be acquired directly and mutual funds that are bought through brokers and recorded the net annual returns, which are the returns on investment after deducting all relevant fees. These are listed next.

Can we conclude at the 5% significance level that directly purchased mutual funds outperform mutual funds bought through brokers?

Direct					Broker				
9.33	4.68	4.23	14.69	10.29	3.24	3.71	16.4	4.36	9.43
6.94	3.09	10.28	−2.97	4.39	−6.76	13.15	6.39	−11.07	8.31
16.17	7.26	7.1	10.37	−2.06	12.8	11.05	−1.9	9.24	−3.99
16.97	2.05	−3.09	−0.63	7.66	11.1	−3.12	9.49	−2.67	−4.44
5.94	13.07	5.6	−0.15	10.83	2.73	8.94	6.7	8.97	8.63
12.61	0.59	5.27	0.27	14.48	−0.13	2.74	0.19	1.87	7.06
3.33	13.57	8.09	4.59	4.8	18.22	4.07	12.39	−1.53	1.57
16.13	0.35	15.05	6.38	13.12	−0.8	5.6	6.54	5.23	−8.44
11.2	2.69	13.21	−0.24	−6.54	−5.75	−0.85	10.92	6.87	−5.72
1.14	18.45	1.72	10.32	−1.06	2.59	−0.28	−2.15	−1.69	6.95

SOLUTION
IDENTIFY

To answer the question, we need to compare the population of returns from direct and the returns from broker-bought mutual funds. The data are obviously interval (we've recorded real numbers). This problem objective–data type combination tells us that the parameter to be tested is the difference between two means $\mu_1 - \mu_2$. The hypothesis to be tested is that the mean net annual return from directly purchased mutual funds (μ_1) is larger than the mean of broker-purchased funds (μ_2). Hence, the alternative hypothesis is

$$H_1: (\mu_1 - \mu_2) > 0$$

As usual, the null hypothesis automatically follows:

$$H_0: (\mu_1 - \mu_2) = 0$$

To decide which of the t-tests of $\mu_1 - \mu_2$ to apply, we conduct the F-test of σ_1^2/σ_2^2.

$$H_0: \sigma_1^2/\sigma_2^2 = 1$$
$$H_1: \sigma_1^2/\sigma_2^2 \neq 1$$

COMPUTE
Manually

From the data we calculated the following statistics:

$$s_1^2 = 37.49 \quad \text{and} \quad s_2^2 = 43.34$$

Test statistic: $F = s_1^2/s_2^2 = 37.49/43.34 = 0.86$

Rejection region: $F > F_{\alpha/2,\nu_1,\nu_2} = F_{.025,49,49} \approx F_{.025,50,50} = 1.75$

or

$$F < F_{1-\alpha/2,\nu_1,\nu_2} = F_{.975,49,49} = 1/F_{.025,49,49} \approx 1/F_{.025,50,50}$$
$$= 1/1.75 = .57$$

Because $F = .86$ is not greater than 1.75 or smaller than .57, we cannot reject the null hypothesis.

Excel

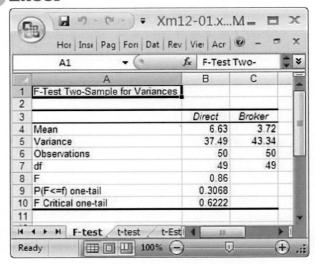

The value of the test statistic is $F = .86$. Excel outputs the one-tail p-value. Because we're conducting a two-tail test, we double that value. Thus, the p-value of the test we're conducting is $2 \times .3068 = .6136$.

INSTRUCTIONS

1. Type or import the data into two columns. (Open Xm12-01.)

2. Click **Data, Data Analysis,** and **F-Test Two-Sample for Variances.**

3. Specify the **Variable 1 Range** (A1:A51) and the **Variable 2 Range** (B1:B51). Type a value for α(.05)

Minitab

Test and CI for Two Variances: Direct, Broker

Null hypothesis	Variance(Direct)/Variance (Broker) = 1
Alternative hypothesis	Variance(Direct)/Variance (Broker) not = 1
Significance level	Alpha = 0.05

	DF1	DF2	Statistic	P-Value
F TEST (NORMAL)	49	49	0.86	0.614

INSTRUCTIONS

(Note: Some of the printout has been omitted.)

1. Type or import the data into two columns. (Open Xm12-01.)
2. Click **Stat**, **Basic Statistics**, and **2 Variances** . . . .
3. Specify Samples in different columns in the **Data** box. Specify the names of the **First** and **Second** samples.
4. Click **Options** . . . Select Variance 1/Variance 2 in the **Hypothesized ratio** box. Type 1 in the **Value** box.
5. Choose one of **less than**, **not equal**, or **greater than** in the **Alternative** box (not equal).

INTERPRET

There is not enough evidence to infer that the population variances differ. It follows that we must apply the equal-variances t-test of $\mu_1 - \mu_2$.

The hypotheses are

$H_0: (\mu_1 - \mu_2) = 0$
$H_1: (\mu_1 - \mu_2) > 0$

COMPUTE
Manually

From the data we calculated the following statistics:

$$\bar{x}_1 = 6.63, \bar{x}_2 = 3.72, s_1^2 = 37.49, s_2^2 = 43.34$$

The pooled variance estimator is

$$s_p^2 = \frac{(n_1 - 1)s_1^2 + (n_2 - 1)s_2^2}{n_1 + n_2 - 2}$$

$$= \frac{(50 - 1)37.49 + (50 - 1)43.34}{50 + 50 - 2} = 40.42$$

The number of degrees of freedom of the test statistic is

$$\nu = n_1 + n_2 - 2 = 50 + 50 - 2 = 98$$

The rejection region is

$$t > t_{\alpha, \nu} = t_{.05, 98} \approx t_{.05, 100} = 1.660$$

We determine that the value of the test statistic is

$$t = \frac{(\bar{x}_1 - \bar{x}_2) - (\mu_1 - \mu_2)}{\sqrt{s_p^2\left(\frac{1}{n_1} + \frac{1}{n_2}\right)}}$$

$$= \frac{(6.63 - 3.72) - 0}{\sqrt{40.42\left(\frac{1}{50} + \frac{1}{50}\right)}} = 2.29$$

Excel

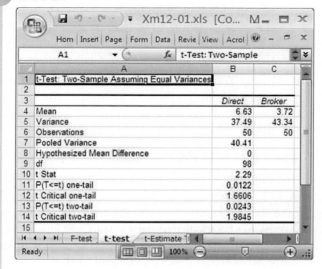

INSTRUCTIONS

1. Type or import the data into two columns. (Open Xm12-01.)
2. Click **Data**, **Data Analysis**, and **t-Test: Two-Sample Assuming Equal Variances**.
3. Specify the **Variable 1 Range** (A1:A51) and the **Variable 2 Range** (B1:B51). Type the value of the **Hypothesized Mean Difference**[2] (0) and type a value for α(.05).

Minitab

Two-Sample *T*-Test and CI: Direct, Broker

```
Two-sample T for Direct vs Broker
          N    Mean    StDev    SE Mean
Direct   50    6.63    6.12     0.87
Broker   50    3.72    6.58     0.93

Difference = mu (Direct) - mu (Broker)
Estimate for difference: 2.91
95% lower bound for difference: 0.80
T-Test of difference = 0 (vs >): T-value = 2.29
P-Value = 0.012  DF = 98
Both use Pooled StDev = 6.3572
```

---

[2] This term is technically incorrect. Because we're testing $\mu_1 - \mu_2$, Excel should ask for and output the "Hypothesized Difference between Means."

INSTRUCTIONS

1. Type or import the data into two columns. (Open Xm12-01.)

2. Click **Stat**, **Basic Statistics**, and **2-Sample t . . . .**

3. If the data are stacked, use the **Samples in one column** box to specify the names of the variables. If the data are unstacked (as in Example 12.1) specify the **First** and **Second** variables in the **Samples in different columns** box (Direct, Broker). (See the discussion on Data Formats on page 195 for a discussion of stacked and unstacked data.) Click **Assume equal variances**. Click **Options . . . .**

4. In the **Test difference** box, type the value of the parameter under the null hypothesis (0) and select one of **less than**, **not equal**, or **greater than** for the **Alternative** hypothesis (greater than).

INTERPRET

The value of the test statistic is 2.29. The one-tail p-value is .0122. We observe that the p-value of the test is small (and the test statistic falls into the rejection region). As a result, we conclude that there is sufficient evidence to infer that on average directly purchased mutual funds outperform broker-purchased mutual funds.

12-1b Estimating $\mu_1 - \mu_2$: Equal Variances

In addition to testing a value of the difference between two population means, we can also estimate the difference between means. Next, we compute the 95% confidence interval estimate of the difference between the mean return for direct and broker mutual funds.

COMPUTE

Manually

The confidence interval estimator of the difference between two means with equal population variances is

$$(\bar{x}_1 - \bar{x}_2) \pm t_{\alpha/2} \sqrt{s_p^2 \left(\frac{1}{n_1} + \frac{1}{n_2} \right)}$$

The 95% confidence interval estimate of the difference between the return for directly purchased mutual funds and the mean return for broker-purchased mutual funds is

$$(\bar{x}_1 - \bar{x}_2) \pm t_{\alpha/2} \sqrt{s_p^2 \left(\frac{1}{n_1} + \frac{1}{n_2} \right)}$$

$$= (6.63 - 3.72) \pm 1.984 \sqrt{40.42 \left(\frac{1}{50} + \frac{1}{50} \right)}$$

$$= 2.91 \pm 2.52$$

The lower and upper limits are .39 and 5.43.

Excel

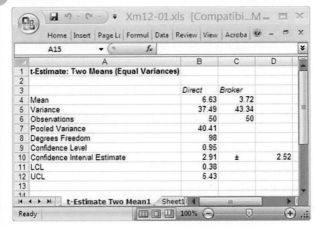

INSTRUCTIONS

1. Type or import the data into two columns. (Open Xm12-01.)

2. Click **Add-Ins**, **Data Analysis Plus**, and **t-Estimate: Two Means**.

3. Specify the **Variable 1 Range** (A1:A51) and the **Variable 2 Range** (B1:B51). Click **Independent Samples with Equal Variances** and the value for α (.05).

Minitab

Two-Sample T-Test and CI: Direct, Broker

```
Difference = mu(Direct) − mu(Broker)
Estimate for difference: 2.91
95% CI for difference: (0.38, 5.43)
```

INSTRUCTIONS

Some of the printout has been deleted. To produce a confidence interval estimate, follow the instructions for the test but specify **not equal** for the **Alternative**. Minitab will conduct a two-tail test and produce the confidence interval estimate.

INTERPRET

We estimate that the return on directly purchased mutual funds is on average between .38 and 5.43 percentage points larger than broker-purchased mutual funds.

EXAMPLE 12.2

Effect of New CEO in Family-Run Businesses[3]

[Xm12-02] What happens to the family-run business when the boss' son or daughter takes over? Does the business do better after the change if the new boss is the offspring of the owner or does the business do better when an outsider is made chief executive officer (CEO)? In pursuit of an answer, researchers randomly selected 140 firms between 1994 and 2002, 30% of which passed ownership to an offspring and 70% appointed an outsider as CEO. For each company, the researchers calculated the operating income as a proportion of assets in the year before and the year after the new CEO took over. The change (operating income after − operating income before) in this variable was recorded and is listed next. Do these data allow us to infer that the effect of making an offspring CEO is different from the effect of hiring an outsider as CEO?

Offspring			Outsider						
−1.95	0.91	−3.15	0.69	−1.05	1.58	−2.46	3.33	−1.32	−0.51
0	−2.16	3.27	−0.95	−4.23	−1.98	1.59	3.2	5.93	8.68
0.56	1.22	−0.67	−2.2	−0.16	4.41	−2.03	0.55	−0.45	1.43
1.44	0.67	2.61	2.65	2.77	4.62	−1.69	−1.4	−3.2	−0.37
1.5	−0.39	1.55	5.39	−0.96	4.5	0.55	2.79	5.08	−0.49
1.41	−1.43	−2.67	4.15	1.01	2.37	0.95	5.62	0.23	−0.08
−0.32	−0.48	−1.91	4.28	0.09	2.44	3.06	−2.69	−2.69	−1.16
−1.7	0.24	1.01	2.97	6.79	1.07	4.83	−2.59	3.76	1.04
−1.66	0.79	−1.62	4.11	1.72	−1.11	5.67	2.45	1.05	1.28
−1.87	−1.19	−5.25	2.66	6.64	0.44	−0.8	3.39	0.53	1.74
−1.38	1.89	0.14	6.31	4.75	1.36	1.37	5.89	3.2	−0.14
0.57	−3.7	2.12	−3.04	2.84	0.88	0.72	−0.71	−3.07	−0.82
3.05	−0.31	2.75	−0.42	−2.1	0.33	4.14	4.22	−4.34	0
2.98	−1.37	0.3	−0.89	2.07	−5.96	3.04	0.46	−1.16	2.68

© Cengage Learning

SOLUTION
IDENTIFY

The objective is to compare two populations, and the data are interval. It follows that the parameter of interest is the difference between two population means $\mu_1 - \mu_2$ where μ_1 is the mean difference for companies where the owner's son or daughter became CEO and μ_2 is the mean difference for companies who appointed an outsider as CEO.

To determine whether to apply the equal or unequal variances t-test we use the F-test of two variances.

$$H_0: \sigma_1^2/\sigma_2^2 = 1$$
$$H_1: \sigma_1^2/\sigma_2^2 \neq 1$$

COMPUTE
Manually

From the data, we calculated the following statistics:

$$s_1^2 = 3.79 \quad \text{and} \quad s_2^2 = 8.03$$

Test statistic: $F = s_1^2/s_2^2 = 3.79/8.03 = 0.47$

The degrees of freedom are $v_1 = n_1 - 1 = 42 - 1 = 41$ and $v_2 = n_2 - 1 = 98 - 1 = 97$

Rejection region: $F > F_{\alpha/2,v_1,v_2} = F_{.025,41,97} \approx F_{.025,40,100} = 1.64$

or

$$F < F_{1-\alpha/2,v_1,v_2} = F_{.975,41,97} \approx 1/F_{.025,97,41} \approx 1/F_{.025,100,40}$$

$$= 1/1.74 = .57$$

Because $F = .47$ is less than .57, we reject the null hypothesis.

---

[3] Source: M. Bennedsen and K. Nielsen, Copenhagen Business School, and D. Wolfenzon, New York University Working Paper.

Excel

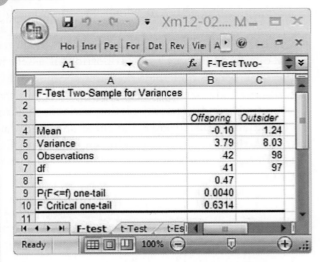

The value of the test statistic is $F = .47$, and the p-value = $2 \times .0040 = .0080$.

Minitab

Test and CI for Two Variances: Offspring, Outsider

Null hypothesis	Variance (Offspring)/Variance (Outsider) = 1
Alternative hypothesis	Variance (Offspring)/Variance (Outsider) not = 1
Significance level	Alpha = 0.05

	DF1	DF2	Statistic	P-Value
F Test (normal)	41	97	0.47	0.008

INTERPRET

There is enough evidence to infer that the population variances differ. The appropriate technique is the unequal-variances t-test of $\mu_1 - \mu_2$.

Because we want to determine whether there is a *difference* between means, the alternative hypothesis is

$$H_1: (\mu_1 - \mu_2) \neq 0$$

and the null hypothesis is

$$H_0: (\mu_1 - \mu_2) = 0$$

COMPUTE
Manually

From the data we calculated the following statistics:

$$\bar{x}_1 = -.10, \bar{x}_2 = 1.24, s_1^2 = 3.79, s_2^2 = 8.03$$

The number of degrees of freedom of the test statistic is

$$\nu = \frac{(s_1^2/n_1 + s_2^2/n_2)^2}{\dfrac{(s_1^2/n_1)^2}{n_1 - 1} + \dfrac{(s_2^2/n_2)^2}{n_2 - 1}} = \frac{(3.79/42 + 8.03/98)^2}{\dfrac{(3.79/42)^2}{42 - 1} + \dfrac{(8.03/98)^2}{98 - 1}}$$

$$= 110.75 \text{ rounded to } 111$$

The rejection region is

$$t < -t_{\alpha/2,\nu} = -t_{.025,111} \approx -t_{.025,110} = -1.982$$

or $\quad t > t_{\alpha/2,\nu} = t_{.025,111} \approx 1.982$

The value of the test statistic is computed next:

$$t = \frac{(\bar{x}_1 - \bar{x}_2) - (\mu_1 - \mu_2)}{\sqrt{\left(\dfrac{s_1^2}{n_1} + \dfrac{s_2^2}{n_2}\right)}} = \frac{(-.10 - 1.24) - (0)}{\sqrt{\left(\dfrac{3.79}{42} + \dfrac{8.03}{98}\right)}}$$

$$= -3.22$$

Excel

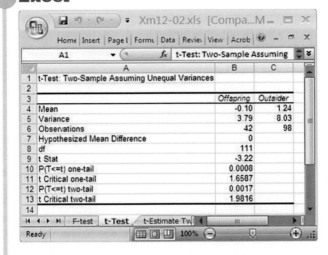

INSTRUCTIONS

Follow the instructions for Example 12.1 except at step 2 click **Data, Data Analysis,** and **t-Test: Two-Sample Assuming Unequal Variances.**

Minitab
Two-Sample T-Test and CI: Offspring, Outsider

Two-sample T for Offspring vs Outsider

	N	Mean	StDev	SE Mean
Offspring	42	-0.10	1.95	0.30
Outsider	98	1.24	2.83	0.29

Difference = mu (Offspring) - mu (Outsider)
Estimate for difference: -1.336
95% CI for difference: (-2.158, -0.514)
T-Test of difference = 0 (vs not =): T-Value = -3.22 P-Value = 0.002 DF = 110

INSTRUCTIONS

Follow the instructions for Example 12.1 except at step 3 do not click **Assume equal variances.**

INTERPRET

The t-statistic is -3.22, and its p-value is .0017. Accordingly, we conclude that there is sufficient evidence to infer that the mean changes in operating income between offspring and outsider CEOs differ.

12-1c Estimating $\mu_1 - \mu_2$: Unequal Variances

We can also draw inferences about the difference between the two population means by calculating the confidence interval estimator. We use the unequal-variances confidence interval estimator of $\mu_1 - \mu_2$ and a 95% confidence level.

COMPUTE

Manually

$$(\bar{x}_1 - \bar{x}_2) \pm t_{\alpha/2} \sqrt{\left(\frac{s_1^2}{n_1} + \frac{s_2^2}{n_2}\right)}$$

$$= (-.10 - 1.24) \pm 1.982 \sqrt{\left(\frac{3.79}{42} + \frac{8.03}{98}\right)}$$

$$= -1.34 \pm .82$$

$$\text{LCL} = -2.16 \quad \text{and} \quad \text{UCL} = -.52$$

Excel

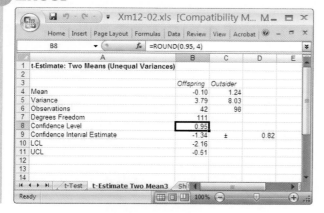

INSTRUCTIONS

1. Type or import the data into two columns. (Open Xm12-02.)

2. Click **Add-Ins, Data Analysis Plus,** and **t-Estimate: Two Means**.

3. Specify the **Variable 1 Range** (A1:A43) and the **Variable 2 Range** (B1:B99). Click **Independent Samples with Unequal Variances** and the value for α (.05).

Minitab

Minitab prints the confidence interval estimate as part of the output of the test statistic. However, you must specify the **Alternative** hypothesis as **not equal** to produce a two-sided interval.

INTERPRET

We estimate that the mean change in operating incomes for outsiders exceeds the mean change in the operating income for offspring lies between .51 and 2.16 percentage points.

12-1d Checking the Required Condition

Both the equal-variances and unequal-variances techniques require that the populations be normally

AMERICAN NATIONAL ELECTION SURVEY: ARE REPUBLICANS MORE EDUCATED THAN DEMOCRATS? SOLUTION

IDENTIFY

The data are interval (years of education), and the problem objective is to compare two populations (Democrats and Republicans). The samples are independent. The parameter to be tested is $\mu_1 - \mu_2$, where the Democrats are population 1 and the Republicans are population 2. To determine whether to use the equal-variances or unequal-variances *t*-test of $\mu_1 - \mu_2$, we conducted the *F*-test of two variances. The Excel results are shown next.

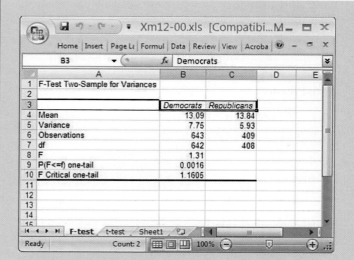

The two-tail p-value is .0032. Thus, the appropriate technique is the unequal-variances t-test. Because we want to know whether there is enough evidence to infer that Republicans are more educated than Democrats, we test

$$H_0: (\mu_1 - \mu_2) = 0$$

$$H_1: (\mu_1 - \mu_2) < 0$$

Here is the Excel printout:

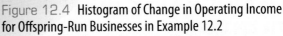

	A	B	C
1	t-Test: Two-Sample Assuming Unequal Variances		
2			
3		Democrats	Republicans
4	Mean	13.09	13.84
5	Variance	7.75	5.93
6	Observations	643	409
7	Hypothesized Mean Difference	0	
8	df	951	
9	t Stat	-4.65	
10	P(T<=t) one-tail	1.88E-06	
11	t Critical one-tail	1.6465	
12	P(T<=t) two-tail	3.77E-06	
13	t Critical two-tail	1.9625	

INTERPRET

The Excel printout reveals that there is sufficient evidence to infer that Republicans are more educated than Democrats.

distributed.[4] As before, we can check to see whether the requirement is satisfied by drawing the histograms of the data.

To illustrate, we used Excel (Minitab histograms are almost identical) to create the histograms for Example 12.1 (Figures 12.2 and 12.3) and Example 12.2 (Figures 12.4 and 12.5). Although the histograms are not perfectly bell shaped, it appears that in both examples the data are at least approximately normal. Because this technique is robust, we can be confident in the validity of the results.

Figure 12.2 **Histogram of Rates of Return for Directly Purchased Mutual Funds in Example 12.1**

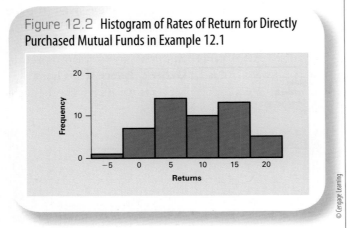

Figure 12.3 **Histogram of Rates of Return for Broker-Purchased Mutual Funds in Example 12.1**

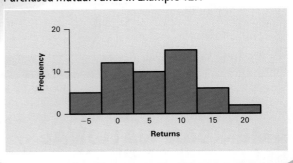

Figure 12.4 **Histogram of Change in Operating Income for Offspring-Run Businesses in Example 12.2**

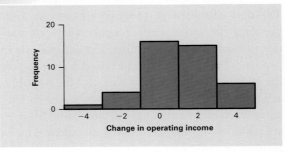

---

[4] As we pointed out in Chapter 11, large sample sizes can overcome the effects of extreme nonnormality.

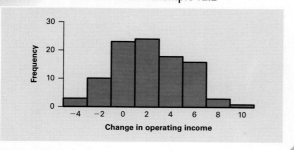

Figure 12.5 **Histogram of Change in Operating Income for Outsider-Run Businesses in Example 12.2**

12-1e Violation of the Required Condition

When the normality requirement is unsatisfied, we can use a nonparametric technique—the Wilcoxon rank sum test—to replace the equal-variances test of $\mu_1 - \mu_2$. We have no alternative to the unequal-variances test of $\mu_1 - \mu_2$ when the populations are very nonnormal. Nonparametric techniques are available from our Web site.

12-1f Data Formats

There are two formats for storing the data when drawing inferences about the difference between two means. The first, which you have seen demonstrated in both Examples 12.1 and 12.2, is called *unstacked*, wherein the observations from sample 1 are stored in one column and the observations from sample 2 are stored in a second column. We may also store the data in *stacked* format. In this format, all the observations are stored in one column. A second column contains the codes, usually 1 and 2, that indicate from which sample the corresponding observation was drawn. Here is an example of unstacked data.

Column 1 (Sample 1)	Column 2 (Sample 2)
12	18
19	23
13	25

Here are the same data in stacked form.

Column 1	Column 2
12	1
19	1
13	1
18	2
23	2
25	2

Understand that the data need not be in order. Hence, they could have been stored in this way:

Column 1	Column 2
18	2
25	2
13	1
12	1
23	2
19	1

If there are two populations to compare and only one variable, then it is probably better to record the data in unstacked form. However, it is frequently the case that we want to observe several variables and compare them. For example, suppose that we survey male and female MBAs and ask each to report his or her age, income, and number of years of experience. These data are usually stored in stacked form using the following format.

Column 1: Code identifying female (1) and male (2)

Column 2: Age

Column 3: Income

Column 4: Years of experience

To compare ages, we would use columns 1 and 2. Columns 1 and 3 are used to compare incomes, and columns 1 and 4 are used to compare experience levels.

Most statistical software requires one format or the other. Some but not all of Excel's techniques require unstacked data. Some of Minitab's procedures allow either format, whereas others specify only one. Fortunately, both of our software packages allow the statistics practitioner to alter the format. (See the Web-site appendix's Excel and Minitab Instructions for Stacking and Unstacking Data.) We say "fortunately" because this allowed us to store the data in either form. In fact, we've used both forms to allow you to practice your ability to manipulate the data as necessary. You will need this ability to perform statistical techniques in this and other chapters in this book.

Here is a summary of how we recognize the techniques presented in this section.

Factors That Identify the Equal-Variances *t*-Test and Estimator of $\mu_1 - \mu_2$

1. **Problem objective:** Compare two populations

2. **Data type:** Interval

3. **Descriptive measurement:** Central location

4. **Experimental design:** Independent samples

5. **Population variances:** Equal

Factors That Identify the Unequal-Variances *t*-Test and Estimator of $\mu_1 - \mu_2$

1. **Problem objective:** Compare two populations

2. **Data type:** Interval

3. **Descriptive measurement:** Central location

4. **Experimental design:** Independent samples

5. **Population variances:** Unequal

12-2 Inference about the Difference between Two Means: Matched Pairs Experiment

We continue our presentation of statistical techniques that address the problem of comparing two populations of interval data. In Section 12-1, the parameter of interest was the difference between two population means, where the data were generated from independent samples. In this section, the data are gathered from a matched pairs experiment. To understand why matched pairs experiments are needed and how we deal with data produced in this way, consider the following example.

EXAMPLE 12.3

Comparing Salary Offers for Finance and Marketing MBA Majors, Part 1

[Xm12-03] In the last few years, a number of Web-based companies that offer job-placement services have been created. The manager of one such company wanted to investigate the job offers recent MBAs were obtaining. In particular, she wanted to know whether finance majors were being offered higher salaries than marketing majors. In a preliminary study, she randomly sampled 50 recently graduated MBAs, half of whom majored in finance and half in marketing. From each graduate she obtained the highest salary offer (including benefits). These data are listed here. Can we infer that finance majors obtain higher salary offers than do marketing majors among MBAs?

Highest Salary Offer Made to Finance Majors								
61,228	51,836	20,620	73,356	84,186	79,782	29,523	80,645	76,125
62,531	77,073	86,705	70,286	63,196	64,358	47,915	86,792	75,155
65,948	29,392	96,382	80,644	51,389	61,955	63,573		

Highest Salary Offer Made to Marketing Majors								
73,361	36,956	63,627	71,069	40,203	97,097	49,442	75,188	59,854
79,816	51,943	35,272	60,631	63,567	69,423	68,421	56,276	47,510
58,925	78,704	62,553	81,931	30,867	49,091	48,843		

SOLUTION
IDENTIFY

The objective is to compare two populations of interval data. The parameter is the difference between two means $\mu_1 - \mu_2$ (where μ_1 = mean highest salary offer to finance majors and μ_2 = mean highest salary offer to marketing majors). Because we want to determine whether finance majors are offered higher salaries, the alternative hypothesis will specify that μ_1 is greater than μ_2. The F-test for variances was conducted, and the results indicate that there is not enough evidence to infer that the population variances differ. Hence, we use the equal-variances test statistic. The hypotheses are

$$H_0: (\mu_1 - \mu_2) = 0$$
$$H_1: (\mu_1 - \mu_2) > 0$$

Test statistic: $t = \dfrac{(\bar{x}_1 - \bar{x}_2) - (\mu_1 - \mu_2)}{\sqrt{s_p^2\left(\dfrac{1}{n_1} + \dfrac{1}{n_2}\right)}}$

COMPUTE
Manually

From the data, we calculated the following statistics:

$$\bar{x}_1 = 65,624, \bar{x}_2 = 60,423, s_1^2 = 360,433,294,$$

$$s_2^2 = 262,228,559$$

$$s_p^2 = \frac{(n_1 - 1)s_1^2 + (n_2 - 1)s_2^2}{n_1 + n_2 - 2}$$

$$= \frac{(25 - 1)(360,433,294) + (25 - 1)(262,228,559)}{25 + 25 - 2}$$

$$= 311,330,926$$

The value of the test statistic is computed next.

$$t = \frac{(\bar{x}_1 - \bar{x}_2) - (\mu_1 - \mu_2)}{\sqrt{s_p^2\left(\dfrac{1}{n_1} + \dfrac{1}{n_2}\right)}}$$

$$= \frac{(65,624 - 60,423) - (0)}{\sqrt{311,330,926\left(\dfrac{1}{25} + \dfrac{1}{25}\right)}} = 1.04$$

The number of degrees of freedom of the test statistic is

$$\nu = n_1 + n_2 - 2 = 25 + 25 - 2 = 48$$

The rejection region is

$$t > t_{\alpha,\nu} = t_{.05,48} \approx 1.676$$

Excel

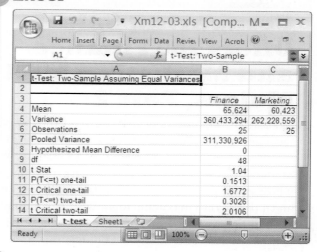

	A	B	C
1	t-Test: Two-Sample Assuming Equal Variances		
2			
3		Finance	Marketing
4	Mean	65,624	60,423
5	Variance	360,433,294	262,228,559
6	Observations	25	25
7	Pooled Variance	311,330,926	
8	Hypothesized Mean Difference	0	
9	df	48	
10	t Stat	1.04	
11	P(T<=t) one-tail	0.1513	
12	t Critical one-tail	1.6772	
13	P(T<=t) two-tail	0.3026	
14	t Critical two-tail	2.0106	

Minitab

Two-Sample T-Test and CI: Finance, Marketing

```
Two-sample T for Finance vs Marketing

            N    Mean   StDev   SE Mean
Finance    25   65624   18985     3797
Marketing  25   60423   16193     3239

Difference = mu (Finance) - mu (Marketing)
Estimate for difference: 5201.00
95% lower bound for difference: -3169.42
T-Test of difference = 0 (vs >): T-Value = 1.04
P-Value = 0.151  DF = 48
Both use Pooled StDev = 17644.5722
```

INTERPRET

The value of the test statistic ($t = 1.04$) and its p-value (.1513) indicate that there is very little evidence to support the hypothesis that finance majors receive higher salary offers than marketing majors.

Notice that we have some evidence to support the alternative hypothesis. The difference in sample means is

$$(\bar{x}_1 - \bar{x}_2) = (65,624 - 60,423) = 5,201$$

However, we judge the difference between sample means in relation to the standard error of $\bar{x}_1 - \bar{x}_2$. As we've already calculated,

$$s_p^2 = 311,330,926 \quad \text{and} \quad \sqrt{s_p^2\left(\frac{1}{n_1} + \frac{1}{n_2}\right)} = 4,991$$

Consequently, the value of the test statistic is $t = 5,201/4,991 = 1.04$, a value that does not allow us to infer that finance majors attract higher salary offers. We can see that although the difference between the sample means was quite large, the variability of the data as measured by s_p^2 was also large, resulting in a small test statistic value.

EXAMPLE 12.4

Comparing Salary Offers for Finance and Marketing MBA Majors, Part 2

[Xm12-04] Suppose now that we redo the experiment in the following way. We examine the transcripts of finance and marketing MBA majors. We randomly select a finance and a marketing major whose grade point average (GPA) falls between 3.92 and 4 (based on a maximum of 4). We then randomly select a finance and a marketing major whose GPA is between 3.84 and 3.92. We continue this process until the 25th pair of finance and marketing majors is selected whose GPA fell between 2.0 and 2.08. (The minimum GPA required for graduation is 2.0.) As we did in Example 12.3, we recorded the highest salary offer. These data, together with the GPA group, are listed here. Can we conclude from these data that finance majors draw larger salary offers than do marketing majors?

Group	Finance	Marketing
1	95,171	89,329
2	88,009	92,705
3	98,089	99,205
4	106,322	99,003
5	74,566	74,825
6	87,089	77,038
7	88,664	78,272
8	71,200	59,462
9	69,367	51,555
10	82,618	81,591
11	69,131	68,110
12	58,187	54,970
13	64,718	68,675
14	67,716	54,110
15	49,296	46,467
16	56,625	53,559
17	63,728	46,793
18	55,425	39,984
19	37,898	30,137
20	56,244	61,965
21	51,071	47,438
22	31,235	29,662
23	32,477	33,710
24	35,274	31,989
25	45,835	38,788

© Cengage Learning

SOLUTION

The experiment described in Example 12.3 is one in which the samples are independent. In other words, there is no relationship between the observations in one sample and the observations in the second sample. However, in this example, the experiment was designed in such a way that each observation in one sample is matched with an observation in the other sample. The matching is conducted by selecting finance and marketing majors with similar GPAs. Thus, it is logical to compare the salary offers for finance and marketing majors in each group. This is called a **matched pairs experiment**. We now describe how we conduct the test.

© Kurhan/Shutterstock.com

For each GPA group, we calculate the matched pair difference between the salary offers for finance and marketing majors.

Group	Finance	Marketing	Difference
1	95,171	89,329	5,842
2	88,009	92,705	−4,696
3	98,089	99,205	−1,116
4	106,322	99,003	7,319
5	74,566	74,825	−259

(*continued*)

Group	Finance	Marketing	Difference
6	87,089	77,038	10,051
7	88,664	78,272	10,392
8	71,200	59,462	11,738
9	69,367	51,555	17,812
10	82,618	81,591	1,027
11	69,131	68,110	1,021
12	58,187	54,970	3,217
13	64,718	68,675	−3,957
14	67,716	54,110	13,606
15	49,296	46,467	2,829
16	56,625	53,559	3,066
17	63,728	46,793	16,935
18	55,425	39,984	15,441
19	37,898	30,137	7,761
20	56,244	61,965	−5,721
21	51,071	47,438	3,633
22	31,235	29,662	1,573
23	32,477	33,710	−1,233
24	35,274	31,989	3,285
25	45,835	38,788	7,047

© Cengage Learning

In this experimental design, the parameter of interest is the **mean of the population of differences**, which we label μ_D. Note that μ_D does, in fact, equal $\mu_1 - \mu_2$, but we test μ_D because of the way the experiment was designed. Hence, the hypotheses to be tested are

$$H_0: \mu_D = 0$$
$$H_1: \mu_D > 0$$

We have already presented inferential techniques about a population mean. Recall that in Chapter 11 we introduced the t-test of μ. Thus, to test hypotheses about μ_D, we use the following test statistic.

Test Statistic for μ_D

$$t = \frac{\overline{x}_D - \mu_D}{s_D/\sqrt{n_D}}$$

which is Student t distributed with $v = n_D - 1$ degrees of freedom, provided that the differences are normally distributed.

Aside from the subscript D, this test statistic is identical to the one presented in Chapter 11. We conduct the test in the usual way.

COMPUTE

Manually

Using the differences computed above, we find the following statistics:

$$\overline{x}_D = 5,065 \quad \text{and} \quad s_D = 6,647$$

from which we calculate the value of the test statistic:

$$t = \frac{\overline{x}_D - \mu_D}{s_D/\sqrt{n_D}} = \frac{5,065 - 0}{6,647/\sqrt{25}} = 3.81$$

The rejection region is

$$t > t_{\alpha,v} = t_{.05,24} = 1.711$$

Excel

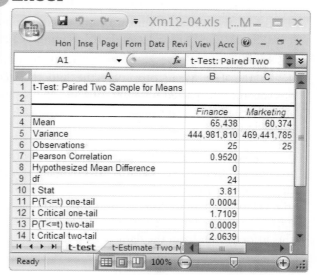

Excel prints the sample means, variances, and sample sizes for each sample, which implies that the procedure uses these statistics. It doesn't. The technique is based on computing the paired differences from which the mean, variance, and sample size are determined. Excel should have printed these statistics.

INSTRUCTIONS

1. Type or import the data into two columns. (Open Xm12-04.)

2. Click **Data, Data Analysis,** and **t-Test: Paired Two-Sample for Means.**

3. Specify the **Variable 1 Range** (B1:B26) and the **Variable 2 Range** (C1:C26). Type the value of **the Hypothesized Mean Difference** (0) and specify a value for α(.05).

Minitab

Paired T-Test and CI: Finance, Marketing

```
Paired T for Finance - Marketing

              N     Mean     StDev    SE Mean
Finance      25   65438.2   21094.6   4218.9
Marketing    25   60373.7   21666.6   4333.3
Difference   25   5064.52   6646.90   1329.38

95% lower bound for mean difference: 2790.11
T-Test of mean difference = 0 (vs > 0): T-Value =
3.81  P-Value = 0.000
```

INSTRUCTIONS

1. Type or import the data into two columns. (Open Xm12-04.)

2. Click **Stat, Basic Statistics,** and **Paired t . . . .**

3. Select the variable names of the **First sample** (Finance) and **Second sample** (Marketing). Click **Options . . . .**

4. In the **Test Mean** box, type the hypothesized mean of the paired difference (0) and specify the **Alternative** (greater than).

INTERPRET

The value of the test statistic is $t = 3.81$ with a p-value of .0004. There is now overwhelming evidence to infer that finance majors obtain higher salary offers than marketing majors. By redoing the experiment as matched pairs, we were able to extract this information from the data.

12-2a Estimating the Mean Difference

We derive the confidence interval estimator of μ_D using the usual form for the confidence interval.

Confidence Interval Estimator of μ_D

$$\bar{x}_D \pm t_{\alpha/2} \frac{s_D}{\sqrt{n_D}}$$

EXAMPLE 12.5

Comparing Salary Offers for Finance and Marketing MBA Majors, Part 3

[Xm12-04] Compute the 95% confidence interval estimate of the mean difference in salary offers between finance and marketing majors in Example 12.4.

SOLUTION
COMPUTE
Manually

The 95% confidence interval estimate of the mean difference is

$$\bar{x}_D \pm t_{\alpha/2} \frac{s_D}{\sqrt{n_D}} = 5{,}065 \pm 2.064 \frac{6{,}647}{\sqrt{25}}$$

$$= 5{,}065 \pm 2{,}744$$

$$\text{LCL} = 2321 \qquad \text{and} \qquad \text{UCL} = 7809$$

Excel

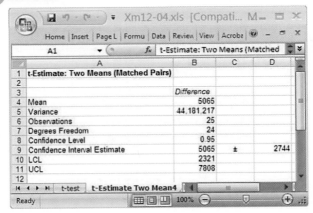

INSTRUCTIONS

1. Type or import the data into two columns. (Open Xm12-04.)

2. Click **Add-Ins, Data Analysis Plus,** and **t-Estimate: Two Means.**

3. Specify the **Variable 1 Range** (A1:A51) and the **Variable 2 Range** (B1:B51). Click **Matched Pairs** and the value for α (.05).

Minitab

Paired *T*-Test and CI: Finance, Marketing

```
Paired T for Finance - Marketing

              N     Mean     StDev    SE Mean
Finance      25   65438.2   21094.6   4218.9
Marketing    25   60373.7   21666.6   4333.3
Difference   25   5064.52   6646.90   1329.38

95% CI for mean difference: (2320.82, 7808.22)
T-Test of mean difference = 0 (vs not = 0):
T-Value = 3.81  P-Value = 0.001
```

INSTRUCTIONS

Follow the instructions to test the paired difference. However, you must specify **not equal** for the **Alternative** hypothesis to produce the two-sided confidence interval estimate of the mean difference.

INTERPRET

We estimate that the mean salary offer to finance majors exceeds the mean salary offer to marketing majors by an amount that lies between $2,321 and $7,808 (using the computer output).

12-2b Independent Samples or Matched Pairs: Which Experimental Design Is Better?

Examples 12.3 and 12.4 demonstrated that the experimental design is an important factor in statistical inference. However, these two examples raise several questions about experimental designs.

1. Why does the matched pairs experiment result in concluding that finance majors receive higher salary offers than do marketing majors, whereas the independent samples experiment could not?

2. Should we always use the matched pairs experiment? In particular, are there disadvantages to its use?

3. How do we recognize when a matched pairs experiment has been performed?

Here are our answers.

1. The matched pairs experiment worked in Example 12.4 by reducing the variation in the data. To understand this point, examine the statistics from both examples. In Example 12.3, we found $\bar{x}_1 - \bar{x}_2 = 5,201$. In Example 12.4, we computed $\bar{x}_D = 5,065$. Thus, the numerators of the two test statistics were quite similar. However, the test statistic in Example 12.3 was much larger than the test statistic in Example 12.4 because of the standard errors. In Example 12.3, we calculated

$$s_p^2 = 311,330,926 \quad \text{and} \quad \sqrt{s_p^2\left(\frac{1}{n_1} + \frac{1}{n_2}\right)} = 4,991$$

Example 12.4 produced

$$s_D = 6,647 \text{ and } \frac{s_D}{\sqrt{n_D}} = 1,329$$

As you can see, the difference in the test statistics was caused not by the numerator, but by the denominator. This raises another question: Why was the variation in the data of Example 12.3 so much greater than the variation in the data of Example 12.4? If you examine the data and statistics from Example 12.3, you will find that there was a great deal of variation *between* the salary offers in each sample. In other words, some MBA graduates received high salary offers and others relatively low ones. This high level

of variation, as expressed by s_p^2, made the difference between the sample means appear to be small. As a result, we could not conclude that finance majors attract higher salary offers.

Looking at the data from Example 12.4, we see that there is very little variation between the observations of the paired differences. The variation caused by different GPAs has been decreased markedly. The smaller variation causes the value of the test statistic to be larger. Consequently, we conclude that finance majors obtain higher salary offers.

2. Will the matched pairs experiment always produce a larger test statistic than the independent samples experiment? The answer is, not necessarily. Suppose that in our example we found that companies did not consider grade point averages when making decisions about how much to offer the MBA graduates. In such circumstances, the matched pairs experiment would result in no significant decrease in variation when compared to independent samples. It is possible that the matched pairs experiment may be less likely to reject the null hypothesis than the independent samples experiment. The reason can be seen by calculating the degrees of freedom. In Example 12.3, the number of degrees of freedom was 48, whereas in Example 12.4, it was 24. Even though we had the same number of observations (25 in each sample), the matched pairs experiment had half the number of degrees of freedom as the equivalent independent samples experiment. For exactly the same value of the test statistic, a smaller number of degrees of freedom in a Student t distributed test statistic yields a larger p-value. What this means is that if there is little reduction in variation to be achieved by the matched pairs experiment, the statistics practitioner should choose instead to conduct the experiment with independent samples.

3. As you've seen, in this book we deal with questions arising from experiments that have already been conducted. Consequently, one of your tasks is to determine the appropriate test statistic. In the case of comparing two populations of interval data, you must decide whether the samples are independent (in which case the parameter is $\mu_1 - \mu_2$) or matched pairs (in which case the parameter is μ_D) to select the correct test statistic. To help you do so, we suggest you ask and answer the following question: Does some natural relationship exist between each pair of observations that provides a logical reason to compare the first observation of sample 1 with the first observation of sample 2, the second observation of sample 1 with

the second observation of sample 2, and so on? If so, then the experiment was conducted by matched pairs. If not, it was conducted using independent samples.

12-2c Checking the Required Condition

The validity of the results of the t-test and estimator of μ_D depends on the normality of the differences (or large enough sample sizes). The histogram of the differences (not shown) is positively skewed but not enough so that the normality requirement is violated.

12-2d Violation of Required Condition

If the differences are very nonnormal, we cannot use the t-test of μ_D. We can, however, employ a nonparametric technique: the Wilcoxon signed rank sum test for matched pairs (Web-site appendix).

Here is a summary of how we determine when to use these techniques.

Factors That Identify the t-Test and Estimator of μ_D

1. **Problem objective:** Compare two populations
2. **Data type:** Interval
3. **Descriptive measurement:** Central location
4. **Experimental design:** Matched pairs

EXERCISES

12.1 [Xr12-01] A number of restaurants feature a device that allows credit card users to swipe their cards at the table. It allows the user to specify a percentage or a dollar amount to leave as a tip. In an experiment to see how the device works, a random sample of credit card users was drawn. Some paid the usual way and some used the new device. The percent left as a tip was recorded and listed below. Can we infer that users of the device leave larger tips?

Usual	Device
10.3	13.6
15.2	15.7
13.0	12.9
9.9	13.2
12.1	12.9
13.4	13.4
12.2	12.1
14.9	13.9
13.2	15.7
12.0	15.4
	17.4

12.2 [Xr12-02] How do drivers react to sudden large increases in the price of gasoline? To help answer the question, a statistician recorded the speeds of cars as they passed a large service station. He recorded the speeds (mph) in the same location after the service station sign showed that the price of gasoline had risen by 15 cents. Can we conclude that the speeds differ?

Speeds Before Price Increase											
43	36	31	30	28	36	27	36	35	30	32	36

Speeds After Price Increase											
32	33	36	31	32	29	28	39	26	30	32	30

12.3 [Xr12-03] How effective are antilock brakes (ABS)? These brakes pump very rapidly rather than lock, and thus they help to prevent skids. As a test, a car buyer organized an experiment. He hit the brakes and, using a stopwatch, recorded the number of seconds it took to stop an ABS-equipped car and another identical car without ABS. The speeds when the brakes were applied and the number of seconds each took to stop on dry pavement are listed here. Can we infer that ABS is better?

Speeds	ABS	Non-ABS
20	3.6	3.4
25	4.1	4.0
30	4.8	5.1
35	5.3	5.5
40	5.9	6.4
45	6.3	6.5
50	6.7	6.9
55	7.0	7.3

12.4 [Xr12-04] In a preliminary study to determine whether the installation of a camera designed to catch cars that go through red lights affects the number of violators, the number of red-light runners was recorded for each day of the week before and after the camera was installed. These data are listed here. Can we infer that the camera reduces the number of red-light runners?

Day	Before	After
Sunday	7	8
Monday	21	18
Tuesday	27	24
Wednesday	18	19
Thursday	20	16
Friday	24	19
Saturday	16	16

The following exercises require the use of a computer and software. The answers may be calculated manually. See Appendix A for the sample statistics. Use a 5% significance level unless specified otherwise.

12.5 [Xr12-05] The president of Tastee Inc., a baby-food producer, claims that her company's product is superior to that of her leading competitor, because babies gain weight faster with her product. (This is a good thing for babies.) To test this claim, a survey was undertaken. Mothers of newborn babies were asked which baby food they intended to feed their babies. Those who responded Tastee or the leading competitor were asked to keep track of their babies' weight gains over the next 2 months. There were 15 mothers who indicated that they would feed their babies Tastee and 25 who responded that they would feed their babies the product of the leading competitor. Each baby's weight gain (in ounces) was recorded.

a. Can we conclude, using weight gain as our criterion, that Tastee baby food is indeed superior?

b. Estimate with 95% confidence the difference between the mean weight gains of the two products.

c. Check to ensure that the required condition(s) is satisfied.

12.6 [Xr12-06] Automobile insurance companies consider many factors when setting rates, including age, marital status, and miles driven per year. To determine the effect of gender, a random sample of young male and female drivers was surveyed (all younger than 25 and with at least 2 years of driving experience). Each was asked how many miles he or she had driven in the past year. The distances (in thousands of miles) are stored in stacked format (column 1 = driving distances, and column 2 identifies the gender where 1 = male and code 2 = female).

a. Can we conclude that male and female drivers differ in the numbers of miles driven per year?

b. Estimate with 95% confidence the difference in mean distance driven by male and female drivers.

c. Check to ensure that the required condition(s) of the techniques used in parts (a) and (b) is satisfied.

12.7 [Xr12-07] One factor in low productivity is the amount of time wasted by workers. Wasted time includes time spent cleaning up mistakes, waiting for more material and equipment, and performing any other activity not related to production. In a project designed to examine the problem, an operations management consultant took a survey of 200 workers in companies that were classified as successful (on the basis of their latest annual profits) and another 200 workers from unsuccessful companies. The amount of time (in hours) wasted during a standard 40-hour workweek was recorded for each worker.

a. Do these data provide enough evidence at the 1% significance level to infer that the amount of time wasted in unsuccessful firms exceeds that of successful ones?

b. Estimate with 95% confidence how much more time is wasted in unsuccessful firms than in successful ones.

12.8 [Xr12-08] It is often useful for companies to know who their customers are and how they became customers. In a study of credit card use, a random sample of cardholders who applied for the credit card and a random sample of credit cardholders who were contacted by telemarketers or by mail were drawn. The total purchases made by each last month were recorded. Can we conclude from these data that differences exist on average between the two types of customers?

12.9 [Xr12-09] Traditionally, wine has been sold in glass bottles with cork stoppers. The stoppers are supposed to keep air out of the bottle because oxygen is the enemy of wine, particularly red wine. Recent research appears to indicate that metal screw caps are more effective in keeping air out of the bottle. However, metal caps are perceived to be inferior and usually associated with cheaper brands of wine. To determine if this perception is wrong, a random sample of 130 people who drink at least one bottle per week on average was asked to participate in an experiment. All were given the same wine in two types of bottles. One group was given a corked bottle, and the other group of people was given a bottle with a metal cap and asked to taste the wine and indicate what they think the retail price of the wine should be. Determine whether there is enough evidence to conclude that bottles of wine with metal caps are perceived to be cheaper.

12.10 [Xr12-10] Studies have shown that tired children have trouble learning because neurons become incapable of forming new synaptic connections that are necessary to encode memory. The problem is that the school day starts too early. Awakened at dawn, teenage brains are still releasing melatonin, which makes them sleepy. Several years ago, Edina, Minnesota, changed its high school start from 7:25 A.M. to 8:30 A.M. The SAT scores for a random sample of students taken before the change and a random sample of SAT scores after the change were recorded. Can we infer from the data that SAT scores increased after the change in the school start time?

12.11 [Xr12-11] Tire manufacturers are constantly researching ways to produce tires that last longer. New innovations are tested by professional drivers on race-tracks. However, any promising inventions are also test-driven by ordinary drivers. The latter tests are closer to what the tire company's customers will actually experience. To determine whether a new steel-belted radial tire lasts longer than the company's current model, suppose two new-design tires were installed on the rear wheels of 20 randomly selected cars and two existing-design tires were installed on the rear wheels of another 20 cars. All drivers were told to drive in their usual way until the tires wore out. The number of miles driven by each driver was recorded. Can the company infer that the new tire will last longer, on average, than the existing tire?

12.12 [Xr12-12] Researchers at the University of Ohio surveyed 219 students and found that 148 had Facebook accounts. All students were asked for their current grade point average. Do the data allow us to infer that Facebook users have lower GPAs?

12.13 [Xr12-13] A restaurant located in an office building decides to adopt a new strategy for attracting customers to the restaurant. Every week it advertises in the city newspaper. To assess how well the advertising is working, the restaurant owner recorded the weekly gross sales for the 15 weeks after the campaign began and the weekly gross sales for the 24 weeks immediately before the campaign. Can the restaurateur conclude that the advertising campaign is successful?

12.14 [Xr12-14] One measure of the state of the economy is the amount of money homeowners pay on their mortgage each month. To determine the extent of change between this year and 5 years ago a random sample of 150 homeowners was drawn. The monthly mortgage payments for each homeowner for this year and for 5 years ago were recorded. (The amounts have been adjusted so that we're comparing constant dollars.) Can we infer that mortgage payments have risen over the past 5 years?

12.15 [Xr12-15] Do waiters or waitresses earn larger tips? To answer this question, a restaurant consultant undertook a preliminary study. The study involved measuring the percentage of the total bill left as a tip for one randomly selected waiter and one randomly selected waitress in each of 50 restaurants during a 1-week period. What conclusions can we draw from these data?

12.16 [Xr12-16] To determine the effect of advertising in the Yellow Pages, Bell Telephone took a sample of 40 retail stores that did not advertise in the Yellow Pages last year but did so this year. The annual sales (in thousands of dollars) for each store in both years were recorded.

a. Estimate with 90% confidence the improvement in sales between the 2 years.
b. Can we infer that advertising in the Yellow Pages improves sales?
c. Check to ensure that the required condition(s) of the techniques used in parts (a) and (b) is satisfied.
d. Would it be advantageous to perform this experiment with independent samples? Explain why or why not.

12.17 [Xr12-17] Because of the high cost of energy, homeowners in northern climates need to find ways to cut their heating costs. A building contractor wanted to investigate the effect on heating costs of increasing the insulation. As an experiment, he located a large sub-development built around 1970 with minimal insulation. His plan was to insulate some of the houses and compare the heating costs in the insulated homes with those that remained uninsulated. However, it was clear to him that the size of the house was a critical factor in determining heating costs. Consequently, he found 16 pairs of houses of identical sizes ranging from about 1,200 to 2,800 square feet. He insulated one house in each pair (levels of R20 in the walls and R32 in the attic) and left the other house unchanged. The heating cost for the following winter season was recorded for each house.

a. Do these data allow the contractor to infer at the 10% significance level that the heating cost for insulated houses is less than that for the uninsulated houses?
b. Estimate with 95% confidence the mean savings due to insulating the house.
c. What is the required condition for the use of the techniques in parts (a) and (b)?

12.18 [Xr12-18] The cost of health care is rising faster than most other items. To learn more about the problem, a survey was undertaken to determine whether differences in health-care expenditures exist between men and women. The survey randomly sampled men and women aged 21, 22, . . . , 65 and determined the total amount spent on health care. Do these data allow us to infer that men and women spend different amounts on health care? (Source: Bureau of Labor Statistics, Consumer Expenditure Survey.)

12.19 [Xr12-19] The fluctuations in the stock market induce some investors to sell and move their money into more stable investments. To determine the degree to which recent fluctuations affected ownership, a random sample of 170 people who confirmed that they owned some stock was surveyed. The values of the holdings were recorded at the end of last year and at the end of the year before. Can we infer that the value of the stock holdings has decreased?

12.20 [Xr12-20] Are Americans more deeply in debt this year compared to last year? To help answer this question, a statistics practitioner randomly sampled Americans this year and last year. The sampling was conducted so that the samples were matched by the age of the head of the household. For each, the ratio of debt payments to household income was recorded. Can we infer that the ratios are higher this year than last?

12.21 [Xr12-21] The growing use of bicycles to commute to work has caused many cities to create exclusive bicycle lanes. These lanes are usually created by disallowing parking on streets that formerly allowed curbside parking. Merchants on such streets complain that the removal of parking will cause their businesses to suffer. To examine this problem, the mayor of a large city decided to launch an experiment on one busy street that had 1-hour parking meters. The meters were removed, and a bicycle lane was created. The mayor asked

the three businesses (a dry cleaner, a doughnut shop, and a convenience store) in one block to record daily sales for 2 complete weeks (Sunday to Saturday) before the change and 2 complete weeks after the change. The data are stored as follows. Column 1 = day of the week, column 2 = sales before change for dry cleaner, column 3 = sales after change for dry cleaner, column 4 = sales before change for doughnut shop, column 5 = sales after change for doughnut shop, column 6 = sales before change for convenience store, and column 7 = sales after change for convenience store. What conclusions can you draw from these data?

12.22 [Xr12-22] Refer to Exercise 12.11. Suppose now we redo the experiment in the following way. On 20 randomly selected cars, one of each type of tire is installed on the rear wheels, and as before the cars are driven until the tires wear out. The number of miles until wear-out occurred was recorded. Can we conclude from these data that the new tire is superior?

12.23 Refer to Exercises 12.11 and 12.22. Explain why the matched pairs experiment produced significant results, whereas the independent samples t-test did not.

12.24 [Xr12-24] Every April, Americans and Canadians fill out their tax return forms. Many turn to tax-preparation companies to do this tedious job. The question arises, Are there differences between companies? In an experiment, two of the largest companies were asked to prepare the tax returns of a sample of 55 taxpayers. The amounts of tax payable were recorded. Can we conclude that company 1's service results in higher tax payable?

12.25 [Xr12-25] Research scientists at a pharmaceutical company have recently developed a new nonprescription sleeping pill. They decide to test its effectiveness by measuring the time it takes for people to fall asleep after taking the pill. Preliminary analysis indicates that the time to fall asleep varies considerably from one person to another. Consequently, they organize the experiment in the following way. A random sample of 100 volunteers who regularly suffer from insomnia is chosen. Each person is given one pill containing the newly developed drug and one placebo. (They do not know whether the pill they are taking is the placebo or the real thing, and the order of use is random.) Each participant is fitted with a device that measures the time until sleep occurs. Can we conclude that the new drug is effective?

Inference about Comparing Two Populations, Part 2

objectives

13-1 Inference about the Ratio of Two Population Variances

13-2 Inference about the Difference between Two Population Proportions

GENERAL SOCIAL SURVEY: GENDER AND THE DECISION TO WORK FOR ONE'S SELF

[GSS2012*] The deep recession of 2008–2010 may have changed patterns of employment. Because of the large number of layoffs, an increasing number of individuals have chosen to work for themselves. The question arises:

> Do men and women (SEX: 1 = Male and
>
> 2 = Female) differ in their decision to work
>
> for themselves? (WRKSLF: 1 = self-employed, 2 = someone else).

Conduct a test to answer the question.

On pages 215–216 we will provide our answer.

Chapter 12 introduced the techniques we use to compare two populations of interval data when we want to draw inferences about the two populations' central location. This chapter continues the work of Chapter 12.

13-1 Inference about the Ratio of Two Population Variances

This section discusses the statistical technique to use when the problem objective is to compare two populations and the data are interval. However, our interest is in comparing variability. Here we will study the ratio of two population variances. We make inferences about the ratio because the sampling distribution is based on ratios rather than differences.

We will proceed in a manner that is probably becoming quite familiar.

13-1a Parameter

As you will see shortly, we compare two population variances by determining the ratio. Consequently, the parameter is σ_1^2/σ_2^2.

13-1b Statistic and Sampling Distribution

The estimator of the parameter σ_1^2/σ_2^2 is the ratio of the two sample variances drawn from their respective populations s_1^2/s_2^2.

The sampling distribution of s_1^2/s_2^2 is said to be F distributed provided that we have independently sampled from two normal populations. (The F distribution was introduced in Section 7-3.)

This statistic is F distributed with $\nu_1 = n_1 - 1$ and $\nu_2 = n_2 - 1$ degrees of freedom. Recall that ν_1 is called the **numerator degrees of freedom** and ν_2 is called the **denominator degrees of freedom**.

13-1c Testing and Estimating a Ratio of Two Variances

In this book, our null hypothesis will always specify that the two variances are equal. As a result, the ratio will equal 1. Thus, the null hypothesis will always be expressed as

$$H_0: \sigma_1^2/\sigma_2^2 = 1$$

The alternative hypothesis can state that the ratio σ_1^2/σ_2^2 is not equal to 1, greater than 1, or less than 1. Technically, the test statistic is

$$F = \frac{s_1^2/\sigma_1^2}{s_2^2/\sigma_2^2}$$

However, under the null hypothesis, which states that $\sigma_1^2/\sigma_2^2 = 1$, the test statistic becomes as follows.

Test Statistic for σ_1^2/σ_2^2

The test statistic employed to test that σ_1^2/σ_2^2 is equal to 1 is

$$F = \frac{s_1^2}{s_2^2}$$

which is F distributed with $\nu_1 = n_1 - 1$ and $\nu_2 = n_2 - 1$ degrees of freedom provided that the populations are normal.

With the usual algebraic manipulation, we can derive the confidence interval estimator of the ratio of two population variances.

Confidence Interval Estimator of σ_1^2/σ_2^2

$$\text{LCL} = \left(\frac{s_1^2}{s_2^2}\right)\frac{1}{F_{\alpha/2,\nu_1,\nu_2}}$$

$$\text{UCL} = \left(\frac{s_1^2}{s_2^2}\right)F_{\alpha/2,\nu_2,\nu_1}$$

where $\nu_1 = n_1 - 1$ and $\nu_2 = n_2 - 1$

© AP Photo/Ival Lawson Jr.

EXAMPLE 13.1

Testing the Quality of Two Bottle-Filling Machines

[Xm13-01] In Example 11.3, we applied the chi-squared test of a variance to determine whether there was sufficient evidence to conclude that the population variance was less than 1.0. Suppose that the statistics practitioner also collected data from another container-filling machine and recorded the fills of a randomly selected sample. Can we infer at the 5% significance level that the second machine is superior in its consistency?

SOLUTION
IDENTIFY

The problem objective is to compare two populations for which the data are interval. Because we want information about the consistency of the two machines, the parameter we wish to test is σ_1^2/σ_2^2, where σ_1^2 is the variance of machine 1 and σ_2^2 is the variance for machine 2. We need to conduct the F-test of σ_1^2/σ_2^2 to determine whether the variance of population 2 is less than that of population 1. Expressed differently, we wish to determine whether there is enough evidence to infer that σ_1^2 is larger than σ_2^2. Hence, the hypotheses we test are

$$H_0: \sigma_1^2/\sigma_2^2 = 1$$

$$H_1: \sigma_1^2/\sigma_2^2 > 1$$

COMPUTE
Manually

The sample variances are $s_1^2 = .6333$ and $s_2^2 = .4528$.
The value of the test statistic is

$$F = \frac{s_1^2}{s_2^2} = \frac{.6333}{.4528} = 1.40$$

The rejection region is

$$F > F_{\alpha,\nu_1,\nu_2} = F_{.05,24,24} = 1.98$$

Because the value of the test statistic is not greater than 1.98, we cannot reject the null hypothesis.

Excel

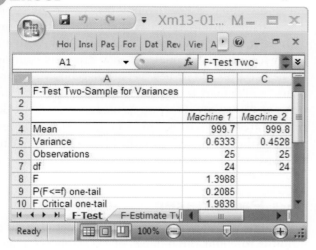

INSTRUCTIONS

1. Type or import the data into two columns. (Open Xm13-01.)

2. Click **Data, Data Analysis**, and **F-Test Two-Sample for Variances**.

3. Specify the **Variable 1 Range** (A1:A26) and the **Variable 2 Range** (B1:B26). Type a value for α(.05)

Minitab

Test and CI for Two Variances: Machine 1, Machine 2

Null hypothesis	Variance(Machine 1)/ Variance(Machine 2) = 1			
Alternative hypothesis	Variance(Machine 1)/ Variance(Machine 2) > 1			
Significance level	Alpha = 0.05			
	DF1	DF2	Statistic	P-Value
F Test (normal)	24	24	1.40	0.208

INSTRUCTIONS

Note: Some of the printout has been omitted. Follow the instructions on page 189.

INTERPRET

There is not enough evidence to infer that the variance of machine 2 is less than the variance of machine 1.

The histograms (not shown) are sufficiently bell shaped to allow us to assume that the normality requirement for this test is satisfied.

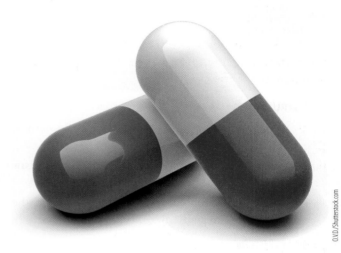

EXAMPLE 13.2

Estimating the Ratio of the Variances in Example 13.1

[Xm13-01] Determine the 95% confidence interval estimate of the ratio of the two population variances in Example 13.1.

SOLUTION
COMPUTE
Manually

We find

$$F_{\alpha/2,\nu_1,\nu_2} = F_{.025,24,24} = 2.27$$

Thus,

$$\text{LCL} = \left(\frac{s_1^2}{s_2^2}\right)\frac{1}{F_{\alpha/2,\nu_1,\nu_2}} = \left(\frac{.6333}{.4528}\right)\frac{1}{2.27} = .616$$

$$\text{UCL} = \left(\frac{s_1^2}{s_2^2}\right)F_{\alpha/2,\nu_2,\nu_1} = \left(\frac{.6333}{.4528}\right)2.27 = 3.17$$

We estimate that σ_1^2/σ_2^2 lies between .616 and 3.17.

Excel

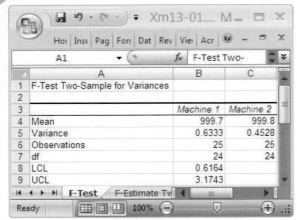

INSTRUCTIONS

1. Type or import the data into two columns. (Open Xm13-01.)

2. Click **Add-ins, Data Analysis Plus,** and **F Estimate 2 Variances.**

3. Specify the **Variable 1 Range** (A1:A26) and the **Variable 2 Range** (B1:B26). Type a value for α(.05).

Minitab

Test and CI for Two Variances: Machine 1, Machine 2

```
Statistics
Variable    N    StDev    Variance
Machine 1   25   0.796    0.633
Machine 2   25   0.673    0.453
Ratio of variances = 1.399
95% Confidence Interval

                             CI for
Distribution   CI for StDev   Variance
of Data          Ratio         Ratio
Normal        (0.785, 1.782)  (0.616, 3.174)
```

INSTRUCTIONS

Note: Some of the printout has been omitted. Follow the instructions to conduct the *F*-test but specify **not equal.**

INTERPRET

As we pointed out in Chapter 11, we can often use a confidence interval estimator to test hypotheses. In this example, the interval estimate excludes the value of 1. Consequently, we can draw the same conclusion as we did in Example 13.1.

Factors that Identify the *F*-Test and Estimator of σ_1^2/σ_2^2

1. **Problem objective:** Compare two populations
2. **Data type:** Interval
3. **Descriptive measurement:** Variability

13-2 Inference about the Difference between Two Population Proportions

In this section, we present the procedures for drawing inferences about the difference between populations whose data are nominal. The number of applications of these techniques is almost limitless. For example, pharmaceutical companies test new drugs by comparing new against old or new versus placebo. Marketing managers compare market shares before and after advertising campaigns. Operations managers compare defective rates between two machines. Political pollsters measure the difference in popularity before and after an election.

13-2a Parameter

When data are nominal, the only meaningful computation is to count the number of occurrences of each type of outcome and calculate proportions. Consequently, the parameter to be tested and estimated in this section is the difference between two population proportions $p_1 - p_2$.

13-2b Statistic and Sampling Distribution

To draw inferences about $p_1 - p_2$, we take a sample of size n_1 from population 1 and a sample of size n_2 from population 2. For each sample, we count the number of successes (recall that we call anything we're looking for a success), which we label x_1 and x_2, respectively. The sample proportions are then computed:

$$\hat{p}_1 = \frac{x_1}{n_1} \quad \text{and} \quad \hat{p}_2 = \frac{x_2}{n_2}$$

Statisticians have proven that the statistic $\hat{p}_1 - \hat{p}_2$ is an unbiased consistent estimator of the parameter $p_1 - p_2$. Using the same mathematics as we did in Chapter 8 to derive the sampling distribution of the sample proportion $\hat{p}$, we determine the sampling distribution of the difference between two sample proportions.

Sampling Distribution of $\hat{p}_1 - \hat{p}_2$

1. The statistic $\hat{p}_1 - \hat{p}_2$ is approximately normally distributed provided that the sample sizes are large enough so that $n_1 p_1$, $n_1(1 - p_1)$, $n_2 p_2$, and $n_2(1 - p_2)$ are all greater than or equal to 5. [Because p_1 and p_2 are unknown, we express the sample size requirement as $n_1\hat{p}_1$, $n_1(1 - \hat{p}_1)$, $n_2\hat{p}_2$, and $n_2(1 - \hat{p}_2)$ are greater than or equal to 5.]

2. The mean of $\hat{p}_1 - \hat{p}_2$ is

$$E(\hat{p}_1 - \hat{p}_2) = p_1 - p_2$$

3. The variance of $\hat{p}_1 - \hat{p}_2$ is

$$V(\hat{p}_1 - \hat{p}_2) = \frac{p_1(1 - p_1)}{n_1} + \frac{p_2(1 - p_2)}{n_2}$$

The standard error is

$$\sigma_{\hat{p}_1 - \hat{p}_2} = \sqrt{\frac{p_1(1 - p_1)}{n_1} + \frac{p_2(1 - p_2)}{n_2}}$$

Thus, the variable

$$z = \frac{(\hat{p}_1 - \hat{p}_2) - (p_1 - p_2)}{\sqrt{\frac{p_1(1 - p_1)}{n_1} + \frac{p_2(1 - p_2)}{n_2}}}$$

is approximately standard normally distributed.

13-2c Testing and Estimating the Difference between Two Proportions

We would like to use the z-statistic just described as our test statistic; however, the standard error of $\hat{p}_1 - \hat{p}_2$, which is

$$\sigma_{\hat{p}_1 - \hat{p}_2} = \sqrt{\frac{p_1(1 - p_1)}{n_1} + \frac{p_2(1 - p_2)}{n_2}}$$

is unknown, because both p_1 and p_2 are unknown. As a result, the standard error of $\hat{p}_1 - \hat{p}_2$ must be estimated from the sample data. There are two different estimators of this quantity, and the determination of which one to use depends on the null hypothesis. If the null hypothesis states that $p_1 - p_2 = 0$, then the hypothesized equality of the two population proportions allows us to pool the data from the two samples to produce an estimate of the common value of the two proportions p_1 and p_2. The **pooled proportion estimate** is defined as

$$\hat{p} = \frac{x_1 + x_2}{n_1 + n_2}$$

Thus, the estimated standard error of $\hat{p}_1 - \hat{p}_2$ is

$$\sqrt{\frac{\hat{p}(1 - \hat{p})}{n_1} + \frac{\hat{p}(1 - \hat{p})}{n_2}} = \sqrt{\hat{p}(1 - \hat{p})\left(\frac{1}{n_1} + \frac{1}{n_2}\right)}$$

The principle used in estimating the standard error of $\hat{p}_1 - \hat{p}_2$ is analogous to that applied in Section 12-1 to produce the pooled variance estimate s_p^2, which is used to test $\mu_1 - \mu_2$ with σ_1^2 and σ_2^2 unknown but equal. The principle roughly states that, where possible, pooling data from two samples produces a better estimate of the standard error. Here, pooling is made possible by hypothesizing (under the null hypothesis) that $p_1 = p_2$. (In Section 12-1, we used the pooled variance estimate because we assumed that $\sigma_1^2 = \sigma_2^2$.) We will call this application Case 1.

Test Statistic for $p_1 - p_2$: Case 1
If the null hypothesis specifies

$$H_0: (p_1 - p_2) = 0$$

the test statistic is

$$z = \frac{(\hat{p}_1 - \hat{p}_2) - (p_1 - p_2)}{\sqrt{\hat{p}(1 - \hat{p})\left(\frac{1}{n_1} + \frac{1}{n_2}\right)}}$$

Because we hypothesize that $p_1 - p_2 = 0$, we simplify the test statistic to

$$z = \frac{(\hat{p}_1 - \hat{p}_2)}{\sqrt{\hat{p}(1 - \hat{p})\left(\frac{1}{n_1} + \frac{1}{n_2}\right)}}$$

The second case applies when, under the null hypothesis, we state that $p_1 - p_2 = D$, where D is some value other than 0. Under such circumstances, we cannot pool the sample data to estimate the standard error of $\hat{p}_1 - \hat{p}_2$. The appropriate test statistic is described next as Case 2.

Test Statistic for $p_1 - p_2$: Case 2
If the null hypothesis specifies

$$H_0: (p_1 - p_2) = D \qquad (D \neq 0)$$

the test statistic is

$$z = \frac{(\hat{p}_1 - \hat{p}_2) - (p_1 - p_2)}{\sqrt{\frac{\hat{p}_1(1 - \hat{p}_1)}{n_1} + \frac{\hat{p}_2(1 - \hat{p}_2)}{n_2}}}$$

which can also be expressed as

$$z = \frac{(\hat{p}_1 - \hat{p}_2) - D}{\sqrt{\frac{\hat{p}_1(1 - \hat{p}_1)}{n_1} + \frac{\hat{p}_2(1 - \hat{p}_2)}{n_2}}}$$

Notice that this test statistic is determined by simply substituting the sample statistics $\hat{p}_1$ and $\hat{p}_2$ in the standard error of $\hat{p}_1 - \hat{p}_2$.

You will find that, in most practical applications (including the exercises in this book), Case 1 applies. In most problems, we want to know whether the two population proportions differ—that is,

$$H_1: (p_1 - p_2) \neq 0$$

or if one proportion exceeds the other—that is,

$$H_1: (p_1 - p_2) > 0 \qquad \text{or} \qquad H_1: (p_1 - p_2) < 0$$

In some other problems, however, the objective is to determine whether one proportion exceeds the other by a specific nonzero quantity. In such situations, Case 2 applies.

We derive the interval estimator of $p_1 - p_2$ in the same manner we have been using since Chapter 9.

Confidence Interval Estimator of $p_1 - p_2$

$$(\hat{p}_1 - \hat{p}_2) \pm z_{\alpha/2} \sqrt{\frac{\hat{p}_1(1 - \hat{p}_1)}{n_1} + \frac{\hat{p}_2(1 - \hat{p}_2)}{n_2}}$$

This formula is valid when $n_1\hat{p}_1$, $n_1(1 - \hat{p}_1)$, $n_2\hat{p}_2$, and $n_2(1 - \hat{p}_2)$ are greater than or equal to 5.

Notice that the standard error is estimated using the individual sample proportions rather than the pooled proportion. In this procedure, we cannot assume that the population proportions are equal as we did in the Case 1 test statistic.

© oksana2010/Shutterstock.com

EXAMPLE 13.3

Test Marketing of Package Designs, Part 1

[Xm13-03] The General Products Company produces and sells a variety of household products. Because of stiff competition, one of its products,

bath soap, is not selling well. Hoping to improve sales, General Products decides to introduce more attractive packaging. The company's advertising agency has developed two new designs. The first design features several bright colors to distinguish it from other brands. The second design is light green in color with just the company's logo on it. As a test to determine which design is better, the marketing manager selected two supermarkets. In one supermarket, the soap was packaged in a box using the first design; the second supermarket used the second design. The product scanner at each supermarket tracked every buyer of soap over a 1-week period. The supermarkets recorded the last four digits of the scanner code for each of the five brands of soap the supermarket sold. The code for the General Products brand of soap is 9077 (the other codes are 4255, 3745, 7118, and 8855). After the trial period, the scanner data were transferred to a computer file. Because the first design is more expensive, management has decided to use this design only if there is sufficient evidence to allow it to conclude that the first design is better. Should management switch to the brightly colored design or the simple green one?

SOLUTION
IDENTIFY

The problem objective is to compare two populations. The first is the population of soap sales in supermarket 1, and the second is the population of soap sales in supermarket 2. The data are nominal because the values are "buy General Products soap" and "buy other companies' soap." These two factors tell us that the parameter to be tested is the difference between two population proportions $p_1 - p_2$ (where p_1 and p_2 are the proportions of soap sales that are a General Products brand in supermarkets 1 and 2, respectively). Because we want to know whether there is enough evidence to adopt the brightly colored design, the alternative hypothesis is

$$H_1: (p_1 - p_2) > 0$$

The null hypothesis must be

$$H_0: (p_1 - p_2) = 0$$

which tells us that this is an application of Case 1. Thus, the test statistic is

$$z = \frac{(\hat{p}_1 - \hat{p}_2)}{\sqrt{\hat{p}(1 - \hat{p})\left(\frac{1}{n_1} + \frac{1}{n_2}\right)}}$$

COMPUTE
Manually

To compute the test statistic manually requires the statistics practitioner to tally the number of successes in each sample, where success is represented by the code 9077. Reviewing all the sales reveals that

$$x_1 = 180 \quad n_1 = 904 \quad x_2 = 155 \quad n_2 = 1,038$$

The sample proportions are

$$\hat{p}_1 = \frac{180}{904} = .1991 \quad \text{and} \quad \hat{p}_2 = \frac{155}{1,038} = .1493$$

The pooled proportion is

$$\hat{p} = \frac{180 + 155}{904 + 1,038} = \frac{335}{1,942} = .1725$$

The value of the test statistic is

$$z = \frac{(\hat{p}_1 - \hat{p}_2)}{\sqrt{\hat{p}(1 - \hat{p})\left(\frac{1}{n_1} + \frac{1}{n_2}\right)}}$$

$$= \frac{(.1991 - .1493)}{\sqrt{(.1725)(1 - .1725)\left(\frac{1}{904} + \frac{1}{1,038}\right)}} = 2.90$$

A 5% significance level seems to be appropriate. Thus, the rejection region is

$$z > z_\alpha = z_{.05} = 1.645$$

Excel

INSTRUCTIONS

1. Type or import the data into two adjacent columns. (Open Xm13-03.)

2. Click **Add-Ins, Data Analysis Plus,** and **Z-Test: 2 Proportions.**

3. Specify the **Variable 1 Range** (A1:A905) and the **Variable 2 Range** (B1:B1039). Type the **Code for Success** (9077), the **Hypothesized Difference** (0), and a value for α(.05).

Minitab

Test and CI for Two Proportions: Supermarket 1, Supermarket 2

```
Event = 9077

Variable          X      N    Sample p
Supermarket  1   180    904   0.199115
Supermarket  2   155   1038   0.149326
```

Difference = p (Supermarket 1) − p (Supermarket 2)

Estimate for difference: 0.0497894

95% lower bound for difference: 0.0213577

Test for difference = 0 (vs > 0): z = 2.90
P-Value = 0.002

INSTRUCTIONS

1. Type or import the data into two adjacent columns. (Open Xm13-03.) Recode the data if necessary. In this example the code representing the General Products soap is 9077. All the other brands were recoded so that they were all some number less than 9077. (We recoded them all as 1.). Remember that Minitab allows only two codes, the higher one being treated as a success.

2. Click **Stat, Basic Statistics,** and **2 Proportions. . . .**

3. In the **Samples in different columns,** specify the **First** (Supermarket 1) and **Second** (Supermarket 2) samples. Click **Options. . . .**

4. Type the value of the **Test difference** (0), specify the **Alternative** hypothesis (greater than), and click **Use pooled estimate of p for test.**

INTERPRET

The value of the test statistic is $z = 2.90$; its p-value is .0019. There is enough evidence to infer that the brightly colored design is more popular than the simple design. As a result, it is recommended that management switch to the first design.

EXAMPLE 13.4

Test Marketing of Package Designs, Part 2

[Xm13-03] Suppose that in Example 13.3 the additional cost of the brightly colored design requires that it outsell the simple design by more than 3%. Should management switch to the brightly colored design?

SOLUTION
IDENTIFY

The alternative hypothesis is

$$H_1: (p_1 - p_2) > .03$$

and the null hypothesis follows as

$$H_0: (p_1 - p_2) = .03$$

Because the null hypothesis specifies a nonzero difference, we would apply the Case 2 test statistic.

COMPUTE
Manually

The value of the test statistic is

$$z = \frac{(\hat{p}_1 - \hat{p}_2) - (p_1 - p_2)}{\sqrt{\dfrac{\hat{p}_1(1 - \hat{p}_1)}{n_1} + \dfrac{\hat{p}_2(1 - \hat{p}_2)}{n_2}}}$$

$$= \frac{(.1991 - .1493) - (.03)}{\sqrt{\dfrac{.1991(1 - .1991)}{904} + \dfrac{.1493(1 - .1493)}{1038}}}$$

$$= 1.14$$

Excel

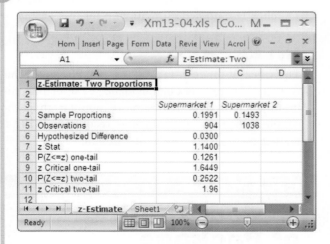

INSTRUCTIONS

Use the same commands we used previously, except specify that the **Hypothesized Difference** is .03. Excel will apply the Case 2 test statistic when a nonzero value is typed.

Minitab

Test and CI for Two Proportions: Supermarket 1, Supermarket 2

```
Event = 9077

Variable            X      N     Sample p
Supermarket  1     180    904    0.199115
Supermarket  2     155   1038    0.149326

Difference = p (Supermarket 1) – p (Supermarket 2)
Estimate for difference: 0.0497894
95% lower bound for difference: 0.0213577
Test for difference = 0.03 (vs > 0.03): Z = 1.14
P-Value = 0.126
```

INSTRUCTIONS

Use the same commands detailed previously, except at step 4 specify that the **Test difference** is .03 and do not click **Use pooled estimate of p for test.**

INTERPRET

There is not enough evidence to infer that the proportion of soap customers who buy the product with the brightly colored design is more than 3% higher than the proportion of soap customers who buy the product with the simple design. In the absence of sufficient evidence, the analysis suggests that the product should be packaged using the simple design.

EXAMPLE 13.5

Test Marketing of Package Designs, Part 3

[Xm13-03] To help estimate the difference in profitability, the marketing manager in Examples 13.3 and 13.4 would like to estimate the difference between the two proportions. A confidence level of 95% is suggested.

SOLUTION
IDENTIFY

The parameter is $p_1 - p_2$, which is estimated by the following confidence interval estimator:

$$(\hat{p}_1 - \hat{p}_2) \pm z_{\alpha/2} \sqrt{\frac{\hat{p}_1(1 - \hat{p}_1)}{n_1} + \frac{\hat{p}_2(1 - \hat{p}_2)}{n_2}}$$

COMPUTE
Manually

The sample proportions have already been computed. They are

$$\hat{p}_1 = \frac{180}{904} = .1991 \qquad \text{and} \qquad \hat{p}_2 = \frac{155}{1038} = .1493$$

The 95% confidence interval estimate of $p_1 - p_2$ is

$$(\hat{p}_1 - \hat{p}_2) \pm z_{\alpha/2}\sqrt{\frac{\hat{p}_1(1 - \hat{p}_1)}{n_1} + \frac{\hat{p}_2(1 - \hat{p}_2)}{n_2}}$$

$$= (.1991 - .1493)$$

$$\pm 1.96\sqrt{\frac{.1991(1 - .1991)}{904} + \frac{.1493(1 - .1493)}{1038}}$$

$$= .0498 \pm .0339$$

$$\text{LCL} = .0159 \qquad \text{and} \qquad \text{UCL} = .0837$$

Excel

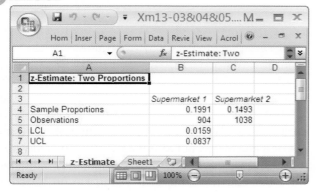

INSTRUCTIONS

1. Type or import the data into two adjacent columns. (Open Xm13-03.)

2. Click **Add-Ins, Data Analysis Plus,** and **Z-Estimate: 2 Proportions.**

3. Specify the **Variable 1 Range** (A1:A905) and the **Variable 2 Range** (B1:B1039). Specify the **Code for Success** (9077) and a value for α(.05).

Minitab

Test and CI for Two Proportions: Supermarket 1, Supermarket 2

```
Event = 9077

Variable          X      N      Sample p
Supermarket   1   180    904    0.199115
Supermarket   2   155    1038   0.149326

Difference = p (Supermarket 1) − p (Supermarket 2)
Estimate for difference: 0.0497894
95% CI for difference:(0.0159109, 0.0836679)
Test for difference = 0 (vs not = 0): Z = 2.88
P-Value = 0.004
```

INSTRUCTIONS

Follow the commands to test hypotheses about two proportions. Specify the alternative hypothesis as **not equal,** and do not click **Use pooled estimate of p for test.**

INTERPRET

We estimate that the market share for the brightly colored design is between 1.59% and 8.37% larger than the market share for the simple design.

GENERAL SOCIAL SURVEY: GENDER AND THE DECISION TO WORK FOR ONE'S SELF: SOLUTION

IDENTIFY

The problem objective is to compare two populations (men and women). The data are nominal. The parameter is $p_1 - p_2$ where p_1 = proportion of men who are self-employed and p_2 = proportion of women who are self-employed. The hypotheses are

$$H_0: (p_1 - p_2) = 0$$
$$H_1: (p_1 - p_2) \neq 0$$

The null hypothesis tells us that this is an application of Case 1. Thus, the test statistic is

$$z = \frac{(\hat{p}_1 - \hat{p}_2)}{\sqrt{\hat{p}(1 - \hat{p})\left(\frac{1}{n_1} + \frac{1}{n_2}\right)}}$$

COMPUTE

INTERPRET

There is sufficient evidence to infer that the proportion of men working for themselves differs from the proportion of women working for themselves.

The factors that identify the inference about the difference between two proportions are listed below.

Factors That Identify the z-Test and Estimator of $p_1 - p_2$

1. **Problem objective:** Compare two populations
2. **Data type:** Nominal

EXERCISES

Use a 5% significance level in all tests unless specified otherwise.

13.1 [Xr13-01] The manager of a dairy is in the process of deciding which of two new carton-filling machines to use. The most important attribute is the consistency of the fills. In a preliminary study, she measured the fills in the 1-liter carton and listed them here. Can the manager infer that the two machines differ in their consistency of fills?

Machine 1	Machine 2
.998	1.003
.997	1.004
1.003	.997
1.000	.996
.999	.999
1.000	1.003
.998	1.000
1.003	1.005
1.004	1.002
1.000	1.004
	.996

13.2 [Xr13-02] An operations manager who supervises an assembly line has been experiencing problems with the sequencing of jobs. The problem is that bottlenecks are occurring because of the inconsistency of sequential operations. He decides to conduct an experiment in which two different methods are used to complete the same task. He measures the times (in seconds). The data are listed here. Can he infer that the first method is more consistent than the second method?

Method 1	Method 2
8.8	9.2
9.6	9.4
8.4	8.9
9.0	9.6
8.3	9.7
9.2	8.4
9.0	8.8
8.7	8.9
8.5	9.0
9.4	9.7

13.3 [Xr13-03] A statistics professor hypothesized that not only the means but also the variances would vary if the business statistics course was taught in two different ways but had the same final exam. He organized an experiment in which one section of the course was taught using detailed PowerPoint slides, and the other required students to read the book and answer questions in class discussions. A sample of the marks was recorded and listed next. Can we infer that the variances of the marks differ between the two sections?

Class 1	Class 2
64	73
85	78
80	66
64	69
48	79
62	81
75	74
77	59
50	83
81	79
90	84

The following exercises require the use of a computer and software. The answers may be calculated manually. See Appendix A for the sample statistics.

13.4 [Xr13-04] A new highway has just been completed, and the government must decide on speed limits. There are several possible choices. However, on advice from police who monitor traffic, the objective was to reduce the variation in speeds, which is thought to contribute to the number of collisions. It has been acknowledged that speed contributes to the severity of collisions. It is decided to conduct an experiment to acquire more information. Signs are posted for 1 week indicating that the speed limit is 70 mph. A random sample of cars' speeds is measured. During the second week, signs are posted indicating that the maximum speed is 70 mph and that the minimum speed is 60 mph. Once again a random sample of speeds is measured. Can we infer that limiting the minimum and maximum speeds reduces the variation in speeds?

13.5 [Xr13-05] In Exercise 11.18, we described the problem of whether to change all the lightbulbs at Yankee Stadium or change them one by one as they burn out. Two brands of bulbs can be used. Because both the mean and the variance of the lengths of life are important, it was decided to test the two brands. A random sample of both brands was drawn and left on until they burned out. The times were recorded. Can the Yankee Stadium management conclude that the variances differ?

13.6 [Xr13-06] In deciding where to invest her retirement fund, an investor recorded the weekly returns of two portfolios for 1 year. Can we conclude that portfolio 2 is riskier than portfolio 1?

13.7 [Xr13-07] An important statistical measurement in service facilities (such as restaurants and banks) is the variability in service times. As an experiment, two bank tellers were observed, and the service times for each of 100 customers were recorded. Do these data allow us to infer at the 10% significance level that the variance in service times differs between the two tellers?

13.8 [Xr13-08] Automobile magazines often compare models and rate them in various ways. One question that is often asked of car owners, Would you buy the same model again? Suppose that a researcher for one magazine asked a random sample of Lexus owners and a random sample of Acura owners whether they plan to buy another Lexus or Acura the next time they shop for a new car. The responses (1 = no, 2 = yes) were recorded. Do these data allow the researcher to infer that the two populations of car owners differ in their satisfaction levels?

13.9 [Xr13-09] An insurance company is thinking about offering discounts on its life insurance policies to nonsmokers. As part of its analysis, the company randomly selects 200 men who are 60 years old and asks them whether they smoke at least one pack of cigarettes per day and if they have ever suffered from heart disease (2 = suffer from heart disease, and 1 = do not suffer from heart disease).

a. Can the company conclude at the 10% significance level that smokers have a higher incidence of heart disease than nonsmokers?
b. Estimate with 90% confidence the difference in the proportions of men suffering from heart disease between smokers and nonsmokers.

13.10 [Xr13-10] It has been estimated that the oil sands in Alberta, Canada, contain 2 trillion barrels of oil. However, recovering the oil damages the environment. A survey of Canadians and Americans was asked, What is more important to you with regards to the oil sands: environmental concerns (1) or the potential as a secure nonforeign supply of oil to North America (2)? Do these data allow you to conclude that Canadians and Americans differ in their responses to this question? (*Source:* Flieshman-Hillard Oil Sands Survey.)

13.11 [Xr13-11] Parents often urge their children to get more education, not only for the increased income but also perhaps to work less hard. A survey asked a random sample of Canadians whether they work 11 or more hours a day (1 = no, 2 = yes) and whether they completed high school only or a postsecondary education. Can we infer that those with more education are less likely to work 11 hours or more per day? (*Source:* Harris/Decima Survey.)

13.12 [Xr13-12] Are Americans becoming more unhappy at work? A survey of Americans in 2008 and again this year asked whether they were satisfied with their jobs (1 = no, 2 = yes). Can we infer that more Americans are unhappy compared to 2008?

13.13 [Xr13-13] Clinical depression is linked to several other diseases. Scientists at Johns Hopkins University undertook a study to determine whether heart disease is one of these. A group of 1,190 male medical students was tracked over a 40-year period. Of these, 132 had suffered clinically diagnosed depression. For each student the scientists recorded whether the student died of a heart attack (code = 2) or did not (code = 1). Can we infer at the 1% significance level that men who are clinically depressed are more likely to die from heart diseases?

13.14 [Xr13-14] Many small retailers advertise in their neighborhoods by sending out flyers. People deliver these to homes and are paid according to the number of flyers delivered. Each deliverer is given several streets whose homes become their responsibility. One of the ways retailers check the performance of deliverers is to randomly sample some of the homes and ask home owners whether they received the flyer. Recently, university students started a new delivery service. They have promised better service at a competitive price. A retailer wanted to know whether the new company's delivery rate is better than that of the existing firm. She had both companies deliver her flyers. Random samples of homes were drawn, and home owners were asked whether they received the flyer (2 = yes, and 1 = no). Can the retailer conclude that the new company is better? (Test with α = .10.)

13.15 [Xr13-15] An inspector for the Atlantic City Gaming Commission suspects that a particular blackjack dealer may be cheating (in favor of the casino) when he deals at expensive tables. To test her belief, she observed 500 hands each at the $100-limit table and the $3,000-limit table. For each hand, she recorded whether the dealer won (code = 2) or lost (code = 1). When a tie occurs, there is no winner or loser. Can the inspector conclude at the 10% significance level that the dealer is cheating at the more expensive table?

13.16 [Xr13-16] Obesity among children has become epidemic across North America. Television and video games are part of the problem. To gauge to what extent nonparticipation in organized sports contributes to the crisis, surveys of children 5 to 14 years old were conducted 10 years ago and this year. The gender of the child and whether he or she participated in organized sports (1 = no, 2 = yes) were recorded.

a. Can we conclude that there has been a decrease in participation among boys over the past 10 years?
b. Repeat part (a) for girls.
c. Can we infer that girls are less likely to participate than boys this year?

13.17 [Xr13-17] Cardizem CD is a prescription drug that is used to treat high blood pressure and angina. One common side effect of such drugs is the occurrence of headaches and dizziness. To determine whether its drug has the same side effects, the drug's manufacturer, Marion Merrell Dow, Inc., undertook a study. A random sample of 908 high blood pressure sufferers was recruited; 607 took Cardizem CD, and 301 took a placebo. The subjects reported whether they suffered from headaches or dizziness (2 = yes, 1 = no). Can the pharmaceutical company scientist infer that Cardizem CD users are more likely to suffer headache and dizziness side effects than nonusers?

13.18 [Xr13-18] Have North Americans grown to distrust television and newspaper journalists? A study was conducted this year to compare what Americans currently think of members of the news media versus what they said 3 years ago. The survey asked respondents whether they agreed that the media tends to favor one side when reporting on political and social issues. A random sample of people was asked to participate in this year's survey. The results of a survey of another random sample taken 3 years ago are also available. The responses are 2 = agree and 1 = disagree. Can we conclude at the 10% significance level that Americans have become more distrustful of television and newspaper reporting this year than they were 3 years ago?

General Social Survey Exercises

13.19 [GSS2012*] A generation ago, men were more likely to attend university and acquire a graduate degree than women. However, women now appear to be attending university in greater numbers than men. To gauge the extent of the difference test to determine whether men and women (SEX: 1 = Male, and 2 = Female) differ in completing a graduate degree (DEGREE: 4 = Graduate).

For each of the following four exercises, determine whether men and women are likely to differ in answering each question correctly.

13.20 [GSS2012*] A doctor tells a couple that there is one chance in four that its child will have an inherited disease. Does this mean that if the first child has the illness, the next three will not (ODDS1: 1 = Yes, 2 = No)? Correct answer: No.

13.21 [GSS2012*] A doctor tells a couple that there is one chance in four that its child will have an inherited disease. Does this mean that each of the couple's children will have the same risk of suffering the illness (ODDS2: 1 = Yes, 2 = No)? Correct answer: Yes.

13.22 [GSS2012*] True or false? The center of Earth is very hot. (HOTCORE: 1 = True, 2 = False). Correct answer: True.

13.23 [GSS2012*] Does Earth go around the Sun or does the Sun go around Earth (EARTHSUN: 1 = Earth around Sun, 2 = Sun around Earth)? Correct answer: Earth around Sun.

For each of the following variables, conduct a test to determine whether there is a difference between 2012 and 2010.

13.24 [GSS2010*] [GSS2012*] WRKGOVT: Are (were) you employed by the federal, state, or local government or by a private employer (including not-for-profit organizations)? 1 = Government; 2 = Private.

13.25 [GSS2010*] [GSS2012*] CAPPUN: Do you favor capital punishment for murder? 1 = Favor, 2 = Oppose.

13.26 [GSS2012*] [GSS2010*] GUNLAW: Do you favor requiring a police permit to buy a gun? 1 = Favor, 2 = Oppose.

13.27 [GSS2012*] Test to determine whether Democrats and Republicans (PARTYID: 0 and 1 = Democrat, 5 and 6 = Republicans) differ in terms of completed graduate degree (DEGREE: 4 = Graduate).

American National Election Survey Exercises

For each of the following variables, conduct a test to determine whether Democrats and Republicans differ (PARTY: 1 = Democrats, and 2 = Republicans).

13.28 [ANES2008*] Likely to be employed (EMPLOY: 1 = Working now, 2–8 = Other categories).

13.29 [ANES2008*] Have health insurance (HEALTH 1 = Yes, 5 = No).

13.30 [ANES2008*] Always vote (OFTEN: 1 = Always; 2, 3, 4 = Other categories).

CHAPTER 14

Analysis of Variance

objectives

14-1 One-Way Analysis of Variance

14-2 Multiple Comparisons

14-3 Randomized Block (Two-Way) Analysis of Variance

GENERAL SOCIAL SURVEY: LIBERAL-CONSERVATIVE SPECTRUM AND INCOME

[GSS2012*] Are Americans' political views affected by their incomes or vice versa? If so, we would expect that incomes would differ between groups who define themselves somewhere on the following scale (POLVIEWS):

1 = Extremely liberal

2 = Liberal

3 = Slightly Liberal

4 = Moderate

5 = Slightly conservative

6 = Conservative

7 = Extremely conservative.

This is the question to be answered (on page 227): Are there differences in income between the seven groups of political views?

The technique presented in this chapter allows statistics practitioners to compare two or more populations of interval data. The technique is called the **analysis of variance**, and it is an extremely powerful and commonly used procedure. The analysis of variance technique determines whether differences exist between population means. Ironically, the procedure works by analyzing the sample variance, hence the name. We will examine two different forms of the technique.

One of the first applications of the analysis of variance was conducted in the 1920s to determine whether different treatments of fertilizer produced different crop yields. The terminology of that original experiment is still used. No matter what the experiment, the procedure is designed to determine whether there are significant differences between the **treatment means**.

14-1 One-Way Analysis of Variance

The analysis of variance is a procedure that tests to determine whether differences exist between two or more population means. The name of the technique derives from the way in which the calculations are performed. In other words, the technique analyzes the variance of the data to determine whether we can infer that the population means differ. As in

Chapter 12, the experimental design is a determinant in identifying the proper method to use. In this section, we describe the procedure to apply when the samples are independently drawn. The technique is called the **one-way analysis of variance**. Figure 14.1 depicts the sampling process for drawing independent samples. The mean and variance of population j ($j = 1, 2, \ldots, k$) are labeled μ_j and σ_j^2, respectively. Both parameters are unknown. For each population, we draw independent random samples. For each sample, we can compute the mean $\bar{x}_j$ and the variance s_j^2.

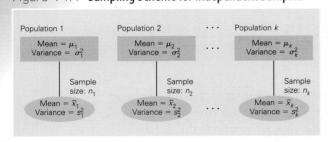

Figure 14.1 **Sampling Scheme for Independent Samples**

© Cengage Learning

NetPhotos/Alamy

EXAMPLE 14.1
Proportion of Total Assets Invested in Stocks[1]

[Xm14-01] In the last decade, stockbrokers have drastically changed the way they do business. Internet trading has become quite common, and

---

[1] Adapted from U.S. Census Bureau, "Asset Ownership of Households, May 2003," *Statistical Abstract of the United States*, 2006, Table 700.

online trades can cost as little $7. It is now easier and cheaper to invest in the stock market than ever before. What are the effects of these changes? To help answer this question, a financial analyst randomly sampled 366 American households and asked each to report the age of the head of the household and the proportion of their financial assets that are invested in the stock market. The age categories are

Young (less than 35)

Early middle age (35 to 49)

Late middle age (50 to 65)

Senior (more than 65)

The analyst was particularly interested in determining whether the ownership of stocks varied by age. Some of the data are listed next. Do these data allow the analyst to determine that there are differences in stock ownership between the four age groups?

Young	Early Middle Age	Late Middle Age	Senior
24.8	28.9	81.5	66.8
35.5	7.3	0.0	77.4
68.7	61.8	61.3	32.9
42.2	53.6	0.0	74.0
⋮	⋮	⋮	⋮

© Cengage Learning

SOLUTION

You should confirm that the data are interval (percentage of total assets invested in the stock market) and that the problem objective is to compare four populations (age categories). The parameters are the four population means μ_1, μ_2, μ_3, and μ_4. The null hypothesis will state that there are no differences between the population means. Hence,

$$H_0: \mu_1 = \mu_2 = \mu_3 = \mu_4$$

The analysis of variance determines whether there is enough statistical evidence to show that the null hypothesis is false. Consequently, the alternative hypothesis will always specify the following:

$$H_1: \text{at least two means differ}$$

The next step is to determine the test statistic, which is somewhat more involved than the test statistics we have introduced thus far. The process of performing the analysis of variance is facilitated by the notation in Table 14.1.

The variable X is called the **response variable**, and its values are called **responses**. The unit that we measure is called an **experimental unit**. In this example, the response variable is the percentage of assets invested in stocks, and the experimental units are the heads of households sampled. The criterion by which we classify the populations is called a **factor**. Each population is called a factor **level**. The factor in Example 14.1 is the age category of the head of the household, and there are four levels.

Table 14.1 Notation for the One-Way Analysis of Variance

	Treatment			
	1	**2**	**j**	**k**
	x_{11}	x_{12}	$\cdots$ x_{1j} $\cdots$	x_{1k}
	x_{21}	x_{22}	$\cdots$ x_{2j} $\cdots$	x_{2k}
	$\vdots$	$\vdots$	$\vdots$	$\vdots$
	x_{n_11}	x_{n_22}	x_{n_jj}	x_{n_kk}
Sample size	n_1	n_2	n_j	n_k
Sample mean	$\bar{x}_1$	$\bar{x}_2$	$\bar{x}_j$	$\bar{x}_k$

x_{ij} = ith observation of the jth sample

n_j = number of observations in the sample taken from the jth population

$\bar{x}_j$ = mean of the jth sample = $\dfrac{\sum\limits_{i=1}^{n_j} x_{ij}}{n_j}$

$\bar{\bar{x}}$ = grand mean of all the observations = $\dfrac{\sum\limits_{j=1}^{k}\sum\limits_{i=1}^{n_j} x_{ij}}{n}$ where $n = n_1 + n_2 + \cdots + n_k$ and k is the number of populations.

© Cengage Learning

14-1a Test Statistic

The test statistic is computed in accordance with the following rationale. If the null hypothesis is true, the population means would all be equal. We would then expect that the sample means would be close to one another. If the alternative hypothesis is true, however, there would be large differences between some of the sample means. The statistic that measures the proximity of the sample means to each other is called the **between-treatments variation** denoted **SST**, which stands for **sum of squares for treatments**.

Sum of Squares for Treatments

$$\text{SST} = \sum_{j=1}^{k} n_j(\bar{x}_j - \bar{\bar{x}})^2$$

As you can deduce from this formula, if the sample means are close to each other, then all of the sample means would be close to the grand mean and SST would be small as a result. In fact, SST achieves its smallest value (zero) when all the sample means are equal; that is, if

$$\bar{x}_1 = \bar{x}_2 = \cdots = \bar{x}_k$$

then

$$\text{SST} = 0$$

It follows that a small value of SST supports the null hypothesis. In this example, we compute the sample means and the grand mean as

$$\bar{x}_1 = 44.40, \quad \bar{x}_2 = 52.47, \quad \bar{x}_3 = 51.14,$$

$$\bar{x}_4 = 51.84, \quad \bar{\bar{x}} = 50.18$$

The sample sizes are

$$n_1 = 84, \quad n_2 = 131, \quad n_3 = 93, \quad n_4 = 58,$$
$$n = n_1 + n_2 + n_3 + n_4 = 84 + 131 + 93 + 58$$
$$= 366$$

Then

$$\text{SST} = \sum_{j=1}^{k} n_j(\bar{x}_j - \bar{\bar{x}})^2$$

$$= 84(44.40 - 50.18)^2 + 131(52.47 - 50.18)^2$$
$$+ 93(51.14 - 50.18)^2 + 58(51.84 - 50.18)^2$$
$$= 3{,}738.8$$

If large differences exist between the sample means, at least some sample means differ considerably from the grand mean, producing a large value of SST. It is then reasonable to reject the null hypothesis in favor of the alternative hypothesis. The key question to be answered in this test (as in all other statistical tests) is, how large does the statistic have to be for us to justify rejecting the null hypothesis? In our example, SST = 3,738.8. Is this value large enough to indicate that the population means differ? To answer this question, we need to know how much variation exists in the percentage of assets, which is measured by the **within-treatments variation**, which is denoted by **SSE** (**sum of squares for error**). The within-treatments variation provides a measure of the amount of variation in the response variable that is not caused by the treatments. In this example, we are trying to determine whether the percentages of total assets invested in stocks vary by the age of the head of the household. However, there are other variables that affect the response variable other than age. We would expect that variables such as household income, occupation, and the size of the family would play a role in determining how much money families invest in stocks. All of these (as well as others we may not even be able to identify) are sources of variation, which we would group together and call it the error. This source of variation is measured by the sum of squares for error.

Sum of Squares for Error

$$\text{SSE} = \sum_{j=1}^{k} \sum_{i=1}^{n_j} (x_{ij} - \overline{x}_j)^2$$

When SSE is partially expanded, we get

$$\text{SSE} = \sum_{i=1}^{n_1} (x_{i1} - \overline{x}_1)^2 + \sum_{i=1}^{n_2} (x_{i2} - \overline{x}_2)^2 + \cdots$$
$$+ \sum_{i=1}^{n_k} (x_{ik} - \overline{x}_k)^2$$

If you examine each of the k components of SSE, you'll see that each is a measure of the variability of that sample. If we divide each component by $n_j - 1$, we obtain the sample variances. We can express this by rewriting SSE as

$$\text{SSE} = (n_1 - 1)s_1^2 + (n_2 - 1)s_2^2 + \cdots + (n_k - 1)s_k^2$$

where s_j^2 is the sample variance of sample j. SSE is thus the combined or pooled variation of the k samples. This is an extension of a calculation we made in Section 12-1, where we tested and estimated the difference between two means using the pooled estimate of the common population variance (denoted s_p^2). One of the required conditions for that statistical technique is that the population variances are equal. That same condition is now necessary for us to use SSE; that is, we require that

$$\sigma_1^2 = \sigma_2^2 = \cdots = \sigma_k^2$$

Returning to our example, we calculate the sample variances as follows:

$$s_1^2 = 386.55, \quad s_2^2 = 469.44, \quad s_3^2 = 471.82,$$
$$s_4^2 = 444.79$$

Thus,

$$\begin{aligned}
\text{SSE} &= (n_1 - 1)s_1^2 + (n_2 - 1)s_2^2 + (n_3 - 1)s_3^2 \\
&\quad + (n_4 - 1)s_4^2 \\
&= (84 - 1)(386.55) + (131 - 1)(469.44) \\
&\quad + (93 - 1)(471.82) + (58 - 1)(444.79) \\
&= 161,871.3
\end{aligned}$$

The next step is to compute quantities called the **mean squares**. The **mean square for treatments** is computed by dividing SST by the number of treatments minus 1.

Mean Square for Treatments

$$\text{MST} = \frac{\text{SST}}{k - 1}$$

The **mean square for error** is determined by dividing SSE by the total sample size (labeled n) minus the number of treatments.

Mean Square for Error

$$\text{MSE} = \frac{\text{SSE}}{n - k}$$

Finally, the test statistic is defined as the ratio of the two mean squares.

Test Statistic

$$F = \frac{\text{MST}}{\text{MSE}}$$

14-1b Sampling Distribution of the Test Statistic

The test statistic is F distributed with $k - 1$ and $n - k$ degrees of freedom provided that the response variable is normally distributed. For Example 14.1, the degrees of freedom are

$$\nu_1 = k - 1 = 4 - 1 = 3$$
$$\nu_2 = n - k = 366 - 4 = 362$$

In our example, we found

$$\text{MST} = \frac{\text{SST}}{k - 1} = \frac{3,738.8}{3} = 1,246.27$$
$$\text{MSE} = \frac{\text{SSE}}{n - k} = \frac{161,871.3}{362} = 447.16$$
$$F = \frac{\text{MST}}{\text{MSE}} = \frac{1,246.27}{447.16} = 2.79$$

14-1c Rejection Region and *p*-Value

The purpose of calculating the *F*-statistic is to determine whether the value of SST is large enough to reject the null hypothesis. As you can see, if SST is large, *F* will be large. Hence, we reject the null hypothesis only if

$$F > F_{\alpha, k-1, n-k}$$

If we let $\alpha = .05$, the rejection region for Example 14.1 is

$$F > F_{\alpha, k-1, n-k} = F_{.05, 3, 362} \approx F_{.05, 3, \infty} = 2.61$$

We found the value of the test statistic to be $F = 2.79$. Thus, there is enough evidence to infer that the mean percentage of total assets invested in the stock market differs between the four age groups.

The p-value of this test is

$$P(F > 2.79)$$

A computer is required to calculate this value, which is .0405.

The results of the analysis of variance are usually reported in an **analysis of variance (ANOVA) table**. Table 14.2 shows the general organization of the ANOVA table, whereas Table 14.3 shows the ANOVA table for Example 14.1.

Table 14.2 ANOVA Table for the One-Way Analysis of Variance

Source of Variation	Degrees of Freedom	Sums of Squares	Mean Squares	F-Statistic
Treatments	$k - 1$	SST	MST = SST/(k − 1)	F = MST/MSE
Error	$n - k$	SSE	MSE = SSE/(n − k)	
Total	$n - 1$	SS (Total)		

© Cengage Learning

Table 14.3 ANOVA Table for Example 14.1

Source of Variation	Degrees of Freedom	Sums of Squares	Mean Squares	F-Statistic
Treatments	3	3,738.8	1,246.27	2.79
Error	362	161,871.3	447.16	
Total	365	165,610.1		

© Cengage Learning

The terminology used in the ANOVA table (and for that matter, in the test itself) is based on the partitioning of the sum of squares. Such partitioning is derived from the following equation (whose validity can be demonstrated by using the rules of summation):

$$\sum_{j=1}^{k} \sum_{i=1}^{n_i} (x_{ij} - \bar{\bar{x}})^2 = \sum_{j=1}^{k} n_j (\bar{x}_j - \bar{\bar{x}})^2$$

$$+ \sum_{j=1}^{k} \sum_{i=1}^{n_i} (x_{ij} - \bar{x}_j)^2$$

The term on the left represents the total variation of all the data. This expression is denoted SS(Total). If we divide SS(Total) by the total sample size minus 1 (that is, by $n - 1$), we would obtain the sample variance (assuming that the null hypothesis is true). The first term on the right of the equal sign is SST, and the second term is SSE. As you can see, the total variation SS(Total) is partitioned into two sources of variation. The sum of squares for treatments (SST) is the variation attributed to the differences between the treatment means, whereas the sum of squares for error (SSE) measures the variation within the samples. The preceding equation can be restated as

$$\text{SS(Total)} = \text{SST} + \text{SSE}$$

The test is then based on the comparison of the mean squares of SST and SSE.

If you've appreciated that the computer and statistical software have spared you the need to manually perform the statistical techniques in earlier chapters, then your appreciation should further grow, because the computer will allow you to avoid the incredibly time-consuming and boring task of performing the analysis of variance by hand. As usual, we've solved Example 14.1 using Excel and Minitab, whose outputs are shown here.

COMPUTE
Excel

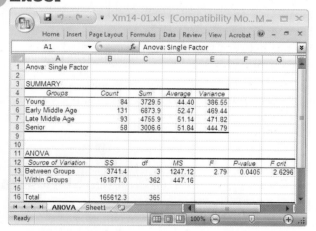

INSTRUCTIONS

1. Type or import the data into adjacent columns. (Open Xm14-01.)

2. Click **Data, Data Analysis,** and **Anova: Single Factor.**

3. Specify the **Input Range** (A1:D132) and a value for $\alpha(.05)$.

One-way ANOVA: Young, Early Middle Age, Late Middle Age, Senior

```
Source   DF      SS       MS     F      P
Factor    3    3741     1247   2.79  0.041
Error   362  161871      447
Total   365  165612

S = 21.15    R-Sq = 2.26%    R-Sq(adj) = 1.45%

Level               N    Mean     StDev
Young              84   44.40     19.66
Early Middle Age  131   52.47     21.67
Late Middle Age    93   51.14     21.72
Senior             58   51.84     21.09

Individual 95% CIs For Mean Based on Pooled StDev
Level           +-------+-------+-------+-------
Young           (-------*-------)
Early Middle Age                (-------*-------)
Late Middle Age                 (-------*-------)
Senior                         (----------*----------)
                +-------+-------+-------+-------
                40.0    45.0    50.0    55.0

Pooled StDev = 21.15
```

INSTRUCTIONS

If the data are unstacked:

1. Type or import the data. (Open Xm14-01.)

2. Click **Stat, ANOVA,** and **Oneway (Unstacked)**. . . .

3. In the **Responses (in separate columns)** box, type or select the variable names of the treatments (Young, Early Middle Age, Late Middle Age, Senior).

If the data are stacked:

1. Type or import the data in two columns.

2. Click **Stat, ANOVA,** and **Oneway**. . . .

3. Type the variable name of the response variable and the name of the factor variable.

INTERPRET

The value of the test statistic is $F = 2.79$ and its p-value is .0405, which means there is evidence to infer that the percentage of total assets invested in stocks are different in at least two of the age categories.

14-1d Checking the Required Conditions

The F-test of the analysis of variance requires that the random variable be normally distributed with equal variances. The normality requirement is easily checked graphically by producing the histograms for each sample. From the Excel histograms in Figure 14.2, we can see that there is no reason to believe that the requirement is not satisfied.

14-1e Violation of the Required Conditions

If the data are not normally distributed we can replace the one-way analysis of variance with its nonparametric counterpart, which is the Kruskal–Wallis test (available

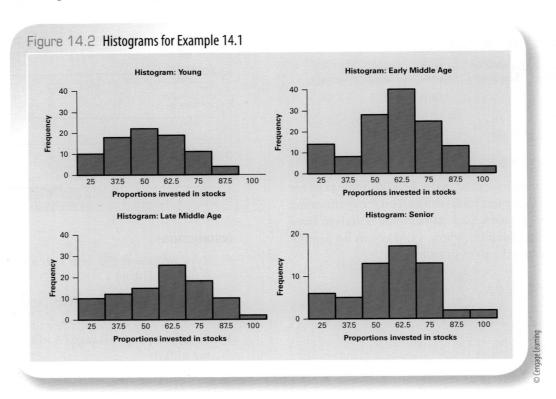

Figure 14.2 **Histograms for Example 14.1**

© Cengage Learning

GENERAL SOCIAL SURVEY: LIBERAL–CONSERVATIVE SPECTRUM AND INCOME: SOLUTION

IDENTIFY

The variable is income of American adults, which is interval. The problem objective is to compare seven populations (the political views), and the experimental design is independent samples. Thus, we apply the one-way analysis of variance.

COMPUTE

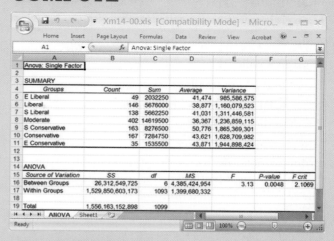

Anova: Single Factor						
SUMMARY						
Groups	*Count*	*Sum*	*Average*	*Variance*		
E Liberal	49	2032250	41,474	985,586,575		
Liberal	146	5676000	38,877	1,160,079,523		
S Liberal	138	5662250	41,031	1,311,446,581		
Moderate	402	14619500	36,367	1,236,859,115		
S Conservative	163	8276500	50,776	1,865,369,301		
Conservative	167	7284750	43,621	1,628,709,982		
E Conservative	35	1535500	43,871	1,944,898,424		
ANOVA						
Source of Variation	*SS*	*df*	*MS*	*F*	*P-value*	*F crit*
Between Groups	26,312,549,725	6	4,385,424,954	3.13	0.0048	2.1069
Within Groups	1,529,850,603,173	1093	1,399,680,332			
Total	1,556,163,152,898	1099				

INTERPRET

The *p*-value is .0048. At the 5% significance level there is sufficient evidence to infer that the incomes differ between the seven political views.

as a Web-site appendix). If the population variances are unequal, we can use several methods to correct the problem. However, these corrective measures are beyond the level of this book.

Let's review how we recognize the need to use the techniques introduced in this section.

Factors that Identify the One-Way Analysis of Variance

1. **Problem objective:** Compare two or more populations
2. **Data type:** Interval
3. **Experimental design:** Independent samples

14-2 Multiple Comparisons

When we conclude from the one-way analysis of variance that at least two treatment means differ, we often need to know which treatment means are responsible for these differences. For example, if an experiment is undertaken to determine whether different locations within a store produce different mean sales, the manager would be keenly interested in determining which locations result in significantly higher sales and which locations result in lower sales. Similarly, a stockbroker would like to know which one of several mutual funds outperforms the others, and a television executive would like to know which television commercials hold the viewers' attention and which are ignored.

Although it may appear that all we need to do is examine the sample means and identify the largest or the smallest to determine which population means are largest or smallest, this is not the case. To illustrate, suppose that in a five-treatment analysis of variance, we discover that differences exist and that the sample means are as follows:

$$\bar{x}_1 = 20 \quad \bar{x}_2 = 19 \quad \bar{x}_3 = 25 \quad \bar{x}_4 = 22 \quad \bar{x}_5 = 17$$

The statistics practitioner wants to know which of the following conclusions are valid:

1. μ_3 is larger than the other means.

2. μ_3 and μ_4 are larger than the other means.

3. μ_5 is smaller than the other means.

4. μ_5 and μ_2 are smaller than the other means.

5. μ_3 is larger than the other means, and μ_5 is smaller than the other means.

From the information we have, it is impossible to determine which, if any, of the statements are true. We need a statistical method to make this determination. The technique is called *multiple comparisons*.

EXAMPLE 14.2

Comparing the Costs of Repairing Car Bumpers

[Xm14-02] North American automobile manufacturers have become more concerned with quality because of foreign competition. One aspect of quality is the cost of repairing damage caused by accidents. A manufacturer is considering several new types of bumpers. To test how well they react to low-speed collisions, the manufacturer installs 10 bumpers of each of four different types on mid-sized cars, which were then driven into a wall at 5 miles per hour. The cost of repairing the damage in each case was assessed. The data are shown below.

a. Is there sufficient evidence at the 5% significance level to infer that the bumpers differ in their reactions to low-speed collisions?

b. If differences exist, which bumpers differ?

Bumper 1	Bumper 2	Bumper 3	Bumper 4
610	404	599	272
354	663	426	405
234	521	429	197
399	518	621	363
278	499	426	297
358	374	414	538
379	562	332	181
548	505	460	318
196	375	494	412
444	438	637	499

© Cengage Learning

SOLUTION
IDENTIFY

The problem objective is to compare four populations, the data are interval, and the samples are independent. The correct statistical method is the one-way analysis of variance, which we perform using Excel and Minitab.

COMPUTE
Excel

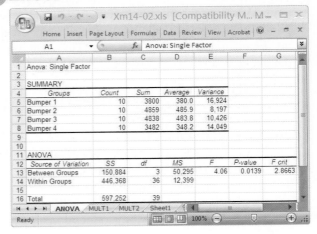

Minitab

One-way ANOVA: Bumper 1, Bumper 2, Bumper 3, Bumper 4

```
Source   DF      SS       MS       F        P
Factor    3    150884    50295    4.06    0.014
Error    36    446368    12399
Total    39    597252

S = 111.4      R-Sq = 25.26%     R-Sq(adj) = 19.03%

Individual 95% CIs For Mean Based on Pooled StDev
Level       N    Mean   StDev   ----+----+----+----+----
Bumper 1   10   380.0   130.1        (------*------)
Bumper 2   10   485.9    90.5               (------*------)
Bumper 3   10   483.8   102.1               (------*------)
Bumper 4   10   348.2   118.5   (------*------)
                                ----+----+----+----+----
                                 320   400   480   560
```

INTERPRET

The test statistic is $F = 4.06$ and the p-value $= .0139$. There is enough statistical evidence to infer that there are differences between some of the bumpers. The question is now, Which bumpers differ?

There are several statistical inference procedures that deal with this problem. We will present three methods that allow us to determine which population means differ. All three methods apply to the one-way experiment only.

14-2a Fisher's Least Significant Difference (LSD) Method

In Chapter 12, we introduced the equal-variances confidence interval estimator of the difference between two means,

$$(\bar{x}_1 - \bar{x}_2) \pm t_{\alpha/2}\sqrt{s_p^2\left(\frac{1}{n_1} + \frac{1}{n_2}\right)}$$

with degrees of freedom $\nu = n_1 + n_2 - 2$.

Recall that s_p^2 is the pooled variance estimate, which is an unbiased estimator of the variance of the two populations.

Statisticians have shown that MSE is an unbiased estimator of the common variance of the populations we're testing. Because MSE is based on all the observations in the k samples, it will be a better estimator than s_p^2 (which is based on only two samples). Thus, we could draw inferences about every pair of means by substituting MSE for s_p^2 in the preceding formula. The number of degrees of freedom would also change to $\nu = n - k$ (where n is the total sample size).

The confidence interval estimator is

$$(\bar{x}_i - \bar{x}_j) \pm t_{\alpha/2}\sqrt{MSE\left(\frac{1}{n_i} + \frac{1}{n_j}\right)}$$

with degrees of freedom $\nu = n - k$. If the interval excludes the value of 0, then we would conclude that μ_i and μ_j differ. For example, if the lower limit is 100 and the upper limit is 200, then the estimate of the difference tells us that there is enough evidence to conclude that the population means differ (by between 100 and 200).

We define the least significant difference LSD as

$$LSD = t_{\alpha/2}\sqrt{MSE\left(\frac{1}{n_i} + \frac{1}{n_j}\right)}$$

If

$$|\bar{x}_i - \bar{x}_j| > LSD$$

then the interval estimator will not include 0. Thus, a simple way of determining whether differences exist between each pair of population means is to compare the absolute value of the difference between their two sample means and LSD. In other words, we will conclude that μ_i and μ_j differ if the absolute difference between sample means is greater than LSD. LSD will be the same for all pairs of means if all k sample sizes are equal. If some sample sizes differ, LSD must be calculated for each combination.

Unfortunately, conducting multiple tests increases the probability of making Type I errors. To understand why, consider a problem where we want to compare six populations, all of which are identical. There are

15 pairs of means to compare [this number is derived from the number of combinations of pairs of means to test, which is $C_2^6 = (6 \times 5)/2 = 15$]. Each test would have a 5% probability of erroneously rejecting the null hypothesis. The probability of committing one or more Type I errors is about 54%.[2] Thus, using a 5% significance level there is a 54% probability of erroneously concluding that at least two population means differ. The 5% figure is now referred to as the *comparisonwise Type I error rate*. The true probability of making at least one Type I error is called the *experimentwise Type I error rate*, denoted α_E. The experimentwise Type I error rate can be calculated as

$$\alpha_E = 1 - (1 - \alpha)^C$$

Here C is the number of pairwise comparisons, which can be calculated by $C = k(k-1)/2$. Statisticians have proven that

$$\alpha_E \le C\alpha$$

which means that if we want the probability of making at least one Type I error to be no more than α_E, we simply specify $\alpha = \alpha_E/C$. The resulting procedure is called the **Bonferroni adjustment**.

14-2b Bonferroni Adjustment to LSD Method

The adjustment is made by dividing the specified experimentwise Type I error rate by the number of combinations of pairs of population means. For example, if $k = 6$, then

$$C = \frac{k(k-1)}{2} = \frac{6(5)}{2} = 15$$

If we want the true probability of a Type I error to be no more than 5%, we divide this probability by C. Thus, for each test we would use a value of α equal to

$$\alpha = \frac{\alpha_E}{C} = \frac{.05}{15} = .0033$$

We use Example 14.2 to illustrate Fisher's LSD method and the Bonferroni adjustment. The four sample means are

$$\bar{x}_1 = 380.0, \quad \bar{x}_2 = 485.9, \quad \bar{x}_3 = 483.8,$$
$$\bar{x}_4 = 348.2$$

---

[2] The probability of committing at least one Type I error is computed from a binomial distribution with $n = 15$ and $p = .05$. Thus,

$$P(X \ge 1) = 1 - P(X = 0) = 1 - .463 = .537$$

The pairwise absolute differences are

$$|\bar{x}_1 - \bar{x}_2| = |380.0 - 485.9| = |-105.9| = 105.9$$
$$|\bar{x}_1 - \bar{x}_3| = |380.0 - 483.8| = |-103.8| = 103.8$$
$$|\bar{x}_1 - \bar{x}_4| = |380.0 - 348.2| = |31.8| = 31.8$$
$$|\bar{x}_2 - \bar{x}_3| = |485.9 - 483.8| = |2.1| = 2.1$$
$$|\bar{x}_2 - \bar{x}_4| = |485.9 - 348.2| = |137.7| = 137.7$$
$$|\bar{x}_3 - \bar{x}_4| = |483.8 - 348.2| = |135.6| = 135.6$$

From the computer output, we learn that MSE = 12,399 and $\nu = n - k = 40 - 4 = 36$. If we conduct the LSD procedure with $\alpha = .05$, we find $t_{\alpha/2,n-k} = t_{.025,36} \approx t_{.025,35} = 2.030$. Thus,

$$t_{\alpha/2}\sqrt{\text{MSE}\left(\frac{1}{n_i} + \frac{1}{n_j}\right)} = 2.030\sqrt{12,399\left(\frac{1}{10} + \frac{1}{10}\right)}$$
$$= 101.09$$

We can see that four pairs of sample means differ by more than 101.09; that is, $|\bar{x}_1 - \bar{x}_2| = 105.9, |\bar{x}_1 - \bar{x}_3| = 103.8, |\bar{x}_2 - \bar{x}_4| = 137.7$, and $|\bar{x}_3 - \bar{x}_4| = 135.6$. Hence, μ_1 and μ_2, μ_1 and μ_3, μ_2 and μ_4, and μ_3 and μ_4 differ. The other two pairs μ_1 and μ_4, and μ_2 and μ_3 do not differ.

If we perform the LSD procedure with the Bonferroni adjustment, the number of pairwise comparisons is 6 [calculated as $C = k(k-1)/2 = 4(3)/2$]. We set $\alpha = .05/6 = .0083$. Thus, $t_{\alpha/2,36} = t_{.0042,36} = 2.794$ (available from Excel and difficult to approximate manually) and

$$\text{LSD} = t_{\alpha/2}\sqrt{\text{MSE}\left(\frac{1}{n_i} + \frac{1}{n_j}\right)}$$
$$= 2.794\sqrt{12,399\left(\frac{1}{10} + \frac{1}{10}\right)} = 139.13$$

Now no pair of means differ because all the absolute values of the differences between sample means are less than 139.19.

The drawback to the LSD procedure is that we increase the probability of at least one Type I error. The Bonferroni adjustment corrects this problem. However, recall that the probabilities of Type I and Type II errors are inversely related. The Bonferroni adjustment uses a smaller value of α, which results in an increased probability of a Type II error. A Type II error occurs when a difference between population means exists, yet we cannot detect it. This may be the case in this example. The next multiple comparison method addresses this problem.

14-2c Tukey's Multiple Comparison Method

A more powerful test is Tukey's multiple comparison method. This technique determines a critical number similar to LSD for Fisher's test, denoted by ω (Greek letter *omega*) such that, if any pair of sample means has a difference greater than ω, we conclude that the pair's two corresponding population means are different.

The test is based on the Studentized range, which is defined as the variable

$$q = \frac{\bar{x}_{\max} - \bar{x}_{\min}}{s/\sqrt{n}}$$

where $\bar{x}_{\max}$ and $\bar{x}_{\min}$ are the largest and smallest sample means, respectively, assuming that there are no differences between the population means. We define ω as follows.

Critical Number ω

$$\omega = q_\alpha(k,\nu)\sqrt{\frac{\text{MSE}}{n_g}}$$

where

k = number of treatments

n = number of observations ($n = n_1 + n_2 + \cdots + n_k$)

ν = number of degrees of freedom associated with MSE ($\nu = n - k$)

n_g = number of observations in each of k samples

α = significance level

$q_\alpha(k, \nu)$ = critical value of the Studentized range

Theoretically, this procedure requires that all sample sizes be equal. However, if the sample sizes are different, we can still use this technique provided that the sample sizes are at least similar. The value of n_g used previously is the *harmonic mean* of the sample sizes; that is,

$$n_g = \frac{k}{\dfrac{1}{n_1} + \dfrac{1}{n_2} + \cdots + \dfrac{1}{n_k}}$$

Table 7 in Appendix B provides values of $q_\alpha(k, \nu)$ for a variety of values of k and ν, and for $\alpha = .01$ and .05. Applying Tukey's method to Example 14.2, we find

$k = 4$

$n_1 = n_2 = n_3 = n_4 = n_g = 10$

$\nu = n - k = 40 - 4 = 36$

MSE = 12,399

$q_{.05}(4,37) \approx q_{.05}(4,40) = 3.79$

Thus,

$$\omega = q_\alpha(k, \nu)\sqrt{\frac{MSE}{n_g}} = (3.79)\sqrt{\frac{12{,}399}{10}} = 133.45$$

There are two absolute values larger than 133.45. Hence, we conclude that μ_2 and μ_4, and μ_3 and μ_4 differ. The other four pairs do not differ.

Excel

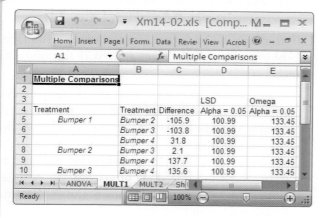

Tukey and Fisher's LSD with the Bonferroni Adjustment ($\alpha = .05/6 = .0083$)

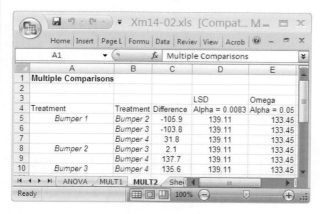

The printout includes ω (Tukey's method), the differences between sample means for each combination of populations, and Fisher's LSD. (The Bonferroni adjustment is made by specifying another value for α.)

INSTRUCTIONS

1. Type or import the data into adjacent columns. (Open Xm14-02.)

2. Click **Add-Ins, Data Analysis Plus,** and **Multiple Comparisons.**

3. Specify the **Input Range** (A1:D11). Type the value of α. To use the Bonferroni adjustment divide, α by $C = k(k - 1)/2$. For Tukey, Excel computes ϖ only for $\alpha = .05$.

Minitab

```
Tukey 95% Simultaneous Confidence Intervals
All Pairwise Comparisons
Individual confidence level = 98.93%

Bumper 1 subtracted from:
          Lower   Center  Upper  ---+----+---+----+---
Bumper 2  -28.3   105.9   240.1        (---*---)
Bumper 3  -30.4   103.8   238.0        (---*---)
Bumper 4  -166.0  -31.8   102.4  (---*---)
                                 ---+----+---+----+---
                                 -150   0  150  300

Bumper 2 subtracted from:
          Lower   Center  Upper  ---+----+---+----+---
Bumper 3  -136.3   -2.1   132.1       (---*---)
Bumper 4  -271.9  -137.7   -3.5 (---*---)
                                 ---+----+---+----+---
                                 -150   0  150  300

Bumper 3 subtracted from:
          Lower   Center  Upper  ---+----+---+----+---
Bumper 4  -269.8  -135.6   -1.4 (---*---)
                                 ---+----+---+----+---
                                 -150   0  150  300


Fisher 99.17% Individual Confidence Intervals
All Pairwise Comparisons
Simultaneous confidence level = 96.04%

Bumper 1 subtracted from:
          Lower   Center  Upper  ---+----+---+----+---
Bumper 2  -33.2   105.9   245.0        (---*---)
Bumper 3  -35.3   103.8   242.9        (---*---)
Bumper 4  -170.9  -31.8   107.3   (---*---)
                                 ---+----+---+----+---
                                 -150   0  150  300

Bumper 2 subtracted from:
          Lower   Center  Upper  ---+----+---+----+---
Bumper 3  -141.2   -2.1   137.0      (---*---)
Bumper 4  -276.8  -137.7   1.4  (---*---)
                                 ---+----+---+----+---
                                 -150   0  150  300

Bumper 3 subtracted from:
          Lower   Center  Upper  ---+----+---+----+---
Bumper 4  -274.7  -135.6   3.5  (---*---)
                                 ---+----+---+----+---
                                 -150   0  150  300
```

Minitab reports the results of Tukey's multiple comparisons by printing interval estimates of the differences between each pair of means. The estimates are computed by calculating the pairwise difference between sample means minus ϖ for the lower limit and plus ϖ for the upper limit. The calculations are described in the following table.

Tukey's Method

Pair of Population Means Compared	Difference	Lower Limit	Upper Limit
Bumper 2 — bumper 1	105.9	−28.3	240.1
Bumper 3 — bumper 1	103.8	−30.4	238.0
Bumper 4 — bumper 1	−31.8	−166.0	102.4
Bumper 3 — bumper 2	−2.1	−136.3	132.1
Bumper 4 — bumper 2	−137.7	−271.9	−3.5
Bumper 4 — bumper 3	−135.6	−269.8	−1.4

© Cengage Learning

A similar calculation is performed for Fisher's method replacing ϖ by LSD.

Fisher's Method

Pair of Population Means Compared	Difference	Lower Limit	Upper Limit
Bumper 2 — bumper 1	105.9	−33.2	245.0
Bumper 3 — bumper 1	103.8	−35.3	242.9
Bumper 4 — bumper 1	−31.8	−170.9	107.3
Bumper 3 — bumper 2	−2.1	−141.2	137.0
Bumper 4 — bumper 2	−137.7	−276.8	1.4
Bumper 4 — bumper 3	−135.6	−274.7	3.5

© Cengage Learning

We interpret the test results in the following way. If the interval includes 0, there is not enough evidence to infer that the pair of means differ. If the entire interval is above or the entire interval is below 0, we conclude that the pair of means differ.

INSTRUCTIONS

1. Type or import the data either in stacked or unstacked format. (Open Xm14-02.)

2. Click **Stat, ANOVA,** and **Oneway (Unstacked).** . . .

3. Type or **Select** the variables in the **Responses (in separate columns)** box (bumper 1, bumper 2, bumper 3, bumper 4).

4. Click **Comparisons.** . . . Select Tukey's method and specify α. Select Fisher's method and specify α. For the Bonferroni adjustment, divide α by $C = k(k - 1)/2$.

INTERPRET

Using the Bonferroni adjustment of Fisher's LSD method, we discover that none of the bumpers

differ. Tukey's method tells us that bumper 4 differs from both bumpers 2 and 3. Based on this sample, bumper 4 appears to have the lowest cost of repair. Because there was not enough evidence to conclude that bumpers 1 and 4 differ, we would consider using bumper 1 if there are advantages that it has over bumper 4.

14-2d Which Multiple Comparison Method to Use

Unfortunately, no one procedure works best in all types of problems. Most statisticians agree with the following guidelines:

If you have identified two or three pairwise comparisons that you wish to make before conducting the analysis of variance, use the Bonferroni method. This means that if in a problem there are 10 populations but you're particularly interested in comparing, say, populations 3 and 7 and populations 5 and 9, then use Bonferroni with $C = 2$.

If you plan to compare all possible combinations, use Tukey.

When do we use Fisher's LSD? If the purpose of the analysis is to point to areas that should be investigated further, then Fisher's LSD method is indicated.

Incidentally, to employ Fisher's LSD or the Bonferroni adjustment, you must perform the analysis of variance first. Tukey's method can be employed instead of the analysis of variance.

14-3 Randomized Block (Two-Way) Analysis of Variance

© Glowimages

The purpose of designing a randomized block experiment is to reduce the within-treatments variation to more easily detect differences between the treatment means. In the one-way analysis of variance, we partitioned the total variation into the between-treatments and the within-treatments variation; that is,

$$SS(Total) = SST + SSE$$

In the randomized block design of the analysis of variance, we partition the total variation into three sources of variation,

$$SS(Total) = SST + SSB + SSE$$

where SSB, the sum of squares for blocks, measures the variation between the blocks. When the variation associated with the blocks is removed, SSE is reduced, making it easier to determine whether differences exist between the treatment means.

At this point in our presentation of statistical inference, we will deviate from our usual procedure of solving examples in three ways: manually, using Excel, and using Minitab. The calculations for this experimental design are so time consuming that solving them by hand adds little to your understanding of the technique. Consequently, although we will continue to present the concepts by discussing how the statistics are calculated, we will solve the problems only by computer.

To help you understand the formulas, we will use the following notation:

$\bar{x}[T]_j$ = mean of the observations in the jth treatment $(j = 1, 2, \ldots, k)$

$\bar{x}[B]_i$ = mean of the observations in the ith block $(i = 1, 2, \ldots, b)$

b = number of blocks

Table 14.4 summarizes the notation we use in this experimental design.

Table 14.4 **Notation for the Randomized Block Analysis of Variance**

Block	Treatments 1	2		k	Block Mean
1	x_{11}	x_{12}	...	x_{1k}	$\bar{x}[B]_1$
2	x_{21}	x_{22}	...	x_{2k}	$\bar{x}[B]_2$
⋮	⋮	⋮		⋮	⋮
b	x_{b1}	x_{b2}	...	x_{bk}	$\bar{x}[B]_b$
Treatment mean	$\bar{x}[T]_1$	$\bar{x}[T]_2$	...	$\bar{x}[T]_k$	

© Cengage Learning

The definitions of SS(Total) and SST in the randomized block design are identical to those in the independent samples design. SSE in the independent samples design is equal to the sum of SSB and SSE in the randomized block design.

Sums of Squares in the Randomized Block Experiment

$$SS(Total) = \sum_{j=1}^{k} \sum_{i=1}^{b} (x_{ij} - \bar{\bar{x}})^2$$

$$SST = \sum_{j=1}^{k} b(\bar{x}[T]_j - \bar{\bar{x}})^2$$

$$SSB = \sum_{i=1}^{b} k(\bar{x}[B]_i - \bar{\bar{x}})^2$$

$$SSE = \sum_{j=1}^{k} \sum_{i=1}^{b} (x_{ij} - \bar{x}[T]_j - \bar{x}[B]_i + \bar{\bar{x}})^2$$

The test is conducted by determining the mean squares, which are computed by dividing the sums of squares by their respective degrees of freedom.

Mean Squares for the Randomized Block Experiment

$$MST = \frac{SST}{k - 1}$$

$$MSB = \frac{SSB}{b - 1}$$

$$MSE = \frac{SSE}{n - k - b + 1}$$

Finally, the test statistic is the ratio of mean squares, as described in the next box.

Test Statistic for the Randomized Block Experiment

$$F = \frac{MST}{MSE}$$

which is F distributed with $\nu_1 = k - 1$ and $\nu_2 = n - k - b + 1$ degrees of freedom.

An interesting, and sometimes useful, by-product of the test of the treatment means is that we can also test to determine whether the block means differ. This will allow us to determine whether the experiment should have been conducted as a randomized block design. (If there are no differences between the blocks, then the randomized block design is less likely to detect real differences between the treatment means.) Such a discovery could be useful in future similar experiments. The test of the block means is almost identical to that of the treatment means except the test statistic is

$$F = \frac{MSB}{MSE}$$

which is F distributed with $\nu_1 = b - 1$ and $\nu_2 = n - k - b + 1$ degrees of freedom.

As with the one-way experiment, the statistics generated in the randomized block experiment are summarized in an ANOVA table, whose general form is exhibited in Table 14.5.

Table 14.5 **ANOVA Table for the Randomized Block Analysis of Variance**

Source of Variation	Degrees of Freedom	Sums of Squares	Mean Squares	F-Statistic
Treatments	$k - 1$	SST	$MST = SST/(k - 1)$	$F = MST/MSE$
Blocks	$b - 1$	SSB	$MSB = SSB/(b - 1)$	$F = MSB/MSE$
Error	$n - k - b + 1$	SSE	$MSE = SSE/(n - k - b + 1)$	
Total	$n - 1$	SS (Total)		

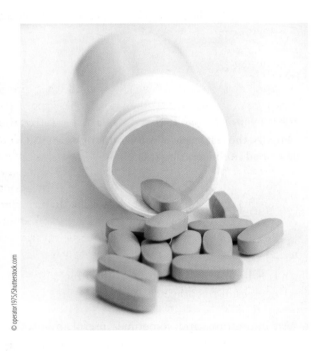

© operator1975/Shutterstock.com

EXAMPLE 14.3

Comparing Cholesterol-Lowering Drugs

[Xm14-03] Many North Americans suffer from high levels of cholesterol, which can lead to heart attacks. For those with very high levels (280 and above),

doctors prescribe drugs to reduce cholesterol levels. A pharmaceutical company has recently developed four such drugs. To determine whether any differences exist in their benefits, an experiment was organized. The company selected 25 groups of four men, each of whom had cholesterol levels in excess of 280. In each group, the men were matched according to age and weight. The drugs were administered over a 2-month period, and the reductions in cholesterol were recorded. Do these results allow the company to conclude that differences exist between the four new drugs?

Group	Drug 1	Drug 2	Drug 3	Drug 4
1	6.6	12.6	2.7	8.7
2	7.1	3.5	2.4	9.3
3	7.5	4.4	6.5	10
4	9.9	7.5	16.2	12.6
5	13.8	6.4	8.3	10.6
6	13.9	13.5	5.4	15.4
7	15.9	16.9	15.4	16.3
8	14.3	11.4	17.1	18.9
9	16	16.9	7.7	13.7
10	16.3	14.8	16.1	19.4
11	14.6	18.6	9	18.5
12	18.7	21.2	24.3	21.1
13	17.3	10	9.3	19.3
14	19.6	17	19.2	21.9
15	20.7	21	18.7	22.1
16	18.4	27.2	18.9	19.4
17	21.5	26.8	7.9	25.4
18	20.4	28	23.8	26.5
19	21.9	31.7	8.8	22.2
20	22.5	11.9	26.7	23.5
21	21.5	28.7	25.2	19.6
22	25.2	29.5	27.3	30.1
23	23	22.2	17.6	26.6
24	23.7	19.5	25.6	24.5
25	28.4	31.2	26.1	27.4

© Cengage Learning

SOLUTION

IDENTIFY

The problem objective is to compare four populations, and the data are interval. Because the researchers recorded the cholesterol reduction for each drug for each member of the similar groups of men, we identify the experimental design as randomized block. The response variable is the cholesterol reduction, the treatments are the drugs, and the blocks are the 25 similar groups of men. The hypotheses to be tested are as follows:

H_0: $\mu_1 = \mu_2 = \mu_3 = \mu_4$

H_1: at least two means differ

COMPUTE
Excel

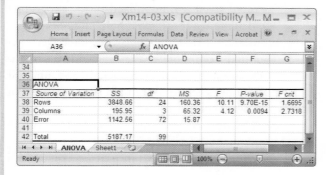

Note the use of scientific notation for one of the p-values. The number 9.70E-15 (E stands for *exponent*) is 9.70 multiplied by 10 raised to the power -15—that is, 9.70×10^{-15}. You can increase or decrease the number of decimal places, and you can convert the number into a regular number, but you would need many decimal places, which is why Excel uses scientific notation when the number is very small. (Excel also uses scientific notation for very large numbers as well.)

The output includes block and treatment statistics (sums, averages, and variances, which are not shown here), and the ANOVA table. The F-statistic to determine whether differences exist between the four drugs (**Columns**) is 4.12. Its p-value is .0094. The other F-statistic, 10.11 (p-value = 9.70×10^{-15} = virtually 0), indicates that there are differences between the groups of men (**Rows**).

INSTRUCTIONS

1. Type or import the data into adjacent columns. (Open Xm14-03.)

2. Click **Data, Data Analysis . . .**, and **Anova: Two-Factor Without Replication**.

3. Specify the **Input Range** (A1:E26). Click **Labels** if applicable. If you do, both the treatments and blocks must be labeled (as in Xm14-03). Specify the value of α(.05).

Minitab

Two-way ANOVA: Reduction versus Group, Drug

Analysis of Variance for Reduction

Source	DF	SS	MS	F	P
Group	24	3848.7	160.4	10.11	0.000
Drug	3	196.0	65.3	4.12	0.009
Error	72	1142.6	15.9		
Total	99	5187.2			

The F-statistic for **Drug** is 4.12 with a p-value of .009. The F-statistic for the blocks (**Group**) is 10.11, with a p-value of 0.

INSTRUCTIONS

The data must be in stacked format in three columns. One column contains the responses, another contains codes for the levels of the blocks, and a third column contains codes for the levels of the treatments.

1. Click **Stat, ANOVA**, and **Twoway. . . .**

2. Specify the **Responses, Row factor**, and **Column factor**.

INTERPRET

A Type I error occurs when you conclude that differences exist when, in fact, they do not. A Type II error is committed when the test reveals no difference when at least two means differ. It would appear that both errors are equally costly. Accordingly, we judge the p-value against a standard of 5%. Because the p-value = .0094, we conclude that there is sufficient evidence to infer that at least two of the drugs differ. An examination reveals that cholesterol reduction is greatest using drugs 2 and 4. Further testing is recommended to determine which is better.

14-3a Checking the Required Conditions

The F-test of the randomized block design of the analysis of variance has the same requirements as the independent samples design. In other words, the random variable must be normally distributed and the population variances must be equal. The histograms (not shown) appear to support the validity of our results; the reductions appear to be normal. The equality of variances requirement also appears to be met.

14-3b Violation of the Required Conditions

When the response is not normally distributed, we can replace the randomized block analysis of variance with the Friedman test, which is available in a appendix.

We now complete this section by listing the factors that we need to recognize to use this experiment of the analysis of variance.

Factors That Identify the Randomized Block of the Analysis of Variance

1. **Problem objective:** Compare two or more populations
2. **Data type:** Interval
3. **Experimental design:** Blocked samples

EXERCISES

14.1 [Xr14-01] How does an MBA major affect the number of job offers received? An MBA student randomly sampled four recent graduates in finance, marketing, and management and asked them to report the number of job offers each received. Can we conclude at the 5% significance level that there are differences in the number of job offers between the three MBA majors?

Finance	Marketing	Management
3	1	8
1	5	5
4	3	4
1	4	6

14.2 [Xr14-02] Spam is the price we pay to easily communicate using e-mail. Does spam affect everyone equally? In a preliminary study, university professors, administrators, and students were randomly sampled. Each person was asked to count the number of spam messages received that day. The results follow. Can we infer at the 2.5% significance level that the differing university communities differ in the amount of spam they receive in their e-mails?

Professors	Administrators	Students
7	5	12
4	9	4
0	12	5
3	16	18
18	10	15

14.3 Refer to Exercise 14.1.

a. Employ Fisher's LSD method to determine which degrees differ (use $\alpha = .10$).
b. Repeat part (a) using the Bonferroni adjustment.

14.4 a. Assuming that the data shown here were generated from a randomized block experiment, calculate SS(Total), SST, SSB, and SSE.
b. Assuming that the following data were generated from a one-way (independent samples) experiment, calculate SS(Total), SST, and SSE.
c. Why does SS(Total) remain the same for both experimental designs?
d. Why does SST remain the same for both experimental designs?
e. Why does SSB + SSE in part (a) equal SSE in part (b)?

Treatment		
1	**2**	**3**
7	12	8
10	8	9
12	16	13
9	13	6
12	10	11

14.5 [Xr14-05] As an experiment to understand measurement error, a statistics professor asks four students to measure the height of the professor, a male student, and a female student. The differences (in centimeters) between the correct dimension and the ones produced by the students are listed here. Can we infer that there are differences in the errors between the subjects being measured? (Use $\alpha = .05$.)

	Errors in Measuring Heights of		
Student	**Professor**	**Male Student**	**Female Student**
1	1.4	1.5	1.3
2	3.1	2.6	2.4
3	2.8	2.1	1.5
4	3.4	3.6	2.9

14.6 [Xr14-06] How well do diets work? In a preliminary study, 20 people who were more than 50 pounds overweight were recruited to compare four diets. The people were matched by age. The oldest four became block 1, the next oldest four became block 2, and so on. The number of pounds that each person lost is listed in the following table. Can we infer at the 1% significance level that there are differences between the four diets?

Block	Diet 1	2	3	4
1	5	2	6	8
2	4	7	8	10
3	6	12	9	2
4	7	11	16	7
5	9	8	15	14

The following exercises require the use of a computer and software. Some answers may be calculated manually. See Appendix A for the sample statistics. Use a 5% significance level unless specified otherwise.

14.7 [Xr14-07] Because there are no national or regional standards, it is difficult for university admission committees to compare graduates of different high schools. University administrators have noted that an 80% average at a high school with low standards may be equivalent to a 70% average at another school with higher standards of grading. In an effort to more equitably compare applications, a pilot study was initiated. Random samples of students who were admitted the previous year from four local high schools were drawn. All the students entered the business program with averages between 70% and 80%. Their average grades in the first year at the university were computed.

a. Can the university admissions officer conclude that there are differences in grading standards between the four high schools?
b. What are the required conditions for the test conducted in part (a)?
c. Does it appear that the required conditions of the test in part (a) are satisfied?

14.8 [Xr14-08] The friendly folks at the Internal Revenue Service (IRS) in the United States and Canada Revenue Agency (CRA) are always looking for ways to improve the wording and format of their tax return forms. Three new forms have been developed recently. To determine which, if any, are superior to the current form, 120 individuals were asked to participate in an experiment. Each of the three new forms and the currently used form were filled out by 30 different people. The amount of time (in minutes) taken by each person to complete the task was recorded.

a. What conclusions can be drawn from these data?
b. What are the required conditions for the test conducted in part (a)?
c. Does it appear that the required conditions of the test in part (a) are satisfied?

14.9 [Xr14-09] Are proficiency test scores affected by the education of the child's parents? (Proficiency tests are administered to a sample of students in private and public schools. Test scores can range from 0 to 500.) To answer this question, a random sample of 9-year-old children was drawn. Each child's test score and the educational level of the parent with the higher level were recorded. The education categories are less than high school, high school graduate, some college, and college graduate. Can we infer that there are differences in test scores between children whose parents have different educational levels? (Adapted from the *Statistical Abstract of the United States*, 2000, Table 286.)

14.10 [Xr14-10] A manufacturer of outdoor brass lamps and mailboxes has received numerous complaints about premature corrosion. The manufacturer has identified the cause of the problem as the low-quality lacquer used to coat the brass. He decides to replace his current lacquer supplier with one of five possible alternatives. To judge which is best, he uses each of the five lacquers to coat 25 brass mailboxes and puts all 125 mailboxes outside. He records, for each, the number of days until the first sign of corrosion is observed.

a. Is there sufficient evidence at the 1% significance level to allow the manufacturer to conclude that differences exist between the five lacquers?
b. What are the required conditions for the test conducted in part (a)?
c. Does it appear that the required conditions of the test in part (a) are satisfied?

14.11 [Xr14-11] In the introduction to this chapter, we mentioned that the first use of the analysis of variance was in the 1920s. It was employed to determine whether different amounts of fertilizer yielded different amounts of crop. Suppose that a scientist at an agricultural college wanted to redo the original experiment using three different types of fertilizer.

Accordingly, he applied fertilizer A to 20 1-acre plots of land, fertilizer B to another 20 plots, and fertilizer C to yet another 20 plots of land. At the end of the growing season, the crop yields were recorded. Can the scientist infer that differences exist between the crop yields?

14.12 [Xr14-12] Does the level of success of publicly traded companies affect the way their board members are paid? Publicly traded companies were divided into four quarters using the rate of return in their stocks to differentiate among the companies. The annual payment (in $1,000s) to their board members was recorded. Can we infer that the amount of payment differs between the four groups of companies?

14.13 [Xr14-07] a. Apply Fisher's LSD method with the Bonferroni adjustment to determine which schools differ in Exercise 14.7.
b. Repeat part (a) applying Tukey's method instead.

14.14 [Xr14-08] a. Apply Tukey's multiple comparison method to determine which forms differ in Exercise 14.8.
b. Repeat part (a) applying the Bonferroni adjustment.

14.15 [Xr14-15] Police cars, ambulances, and other emergency vehicles are required to carry road flares. One of the most important features of flares is their burning times. To help decide which of four brands on the market to use, a police laboratory technician measured the burning time for a random sample of 10 flares of each brand. The results were recorded to the nearest minute.

a. Can we conclude that differences exist between the burning times of the four brands of flares?
b. Apply Fisher's LSD method with the Bonferroni adjustment to determine which flares are better.
c. Repeat part (b) using Tukey's method.

14.16 [Xr14-10] Refer to Exercise 14.10.

a. Apply Fisher's LSD method with the Bonferroni adjustment to determine which lacquers differ.
b. Repeat part (a) applying Tukey's method instead.

14.17 [Xr14-17] An engineering student who is about to graduate decided to survey various firms in Silicon Valley to see which offered the best chance for early promotion and career advancement. He surveyed 30 small firms (size level is based on gross revenues), 30 medium-size firms, and 30 large firms and determined how much time must elapse before an average engineer can receive a promotion.

a. Can the engineering student conclude that speed of promotion varies between the three sizes of engineering firms?
b. If differences exist, which of the following is true? Use Tukey's method.
 i. Small firms differ from the other two.
 ii. Medium-size firms differ from the other two.
 iii. Large firms differ from the other two.
 iv. All three firms differ from one another.
 v. Small firms differ from large firms.

14.18 [Xr14-11] a. Apply Tukey's multiple comparison method to determine which fertilizers differ in Exercise 14.11.
b. Repeat part (a) applying the Bonferroni adjustment.

14.19 [Xr14-19] In recent years, lack of confidence in the U.S. Postal Service has led many companies to send all of their correspondence by private courier. A large company is in the process of selecting one of three possible couriers to act as its sole delivery method. To help in making the decision, an experiment was performed in which letters were sent using each of the three couriers at 12 different times of the day to a delivery point across town. The number of minutes required for delivery was recorded.

a. Can we conclude that there are differences in delivery times between the three couriers?
b. Did the statistics practitioner choose the correct design? Explain.

14.20 [Xr14-20] Refer to Exercise 14.11. Despite failing to show that differences in the three types of fertilizer exist, the scientist continued to believe that there were differences and that the differences were masked by the variation between the plots of land. Accordingly, he conducted another experiment. In the second experiment, he found 20 3-acre plots of land scattered across the county. He divided each into three plots and applied the three types of fertilizer on each of the 1-acre plots. The crop yields were recorded.

a. Can the scientist infer that there are differences between the three types of fertilizer?
b. What do these test results reveal about the variation between the plots?

14.21 [Xr14-21] A recruiter for a computer company would like to determine whether there are differences in sales ability between business, arts, and science graduates. She takes a random sample of 20 business graduates who have been working for the company for the past 2 years. Each is then matched with an arts graduate and a science graduate with similar educational and working experience. The commission earned by each (in $1,000s) in the last year was recorded.

a. Is there sufficient evidence to allow the recruiter to conclude that there are differences in sales ability between the holders of the three types of degrees?
b. Conduct a test to determine whether an independent samples design would have been a better choice.
c. What are the required conditions for the test in part (a)?
d. Are the required conditions satisfied?

14.22 [Xr14-22] Exercise 14.8 described an experiment that involved comparing the completion times associated with four different income tax forms. Suppose the experiment is redone in the following way. Thirty people are asked to fill out all four forms. The completion times (in minutes) are recorded.

a. Is there sufficient evidence at the 1% significance level to infer that differences in the completion times exist between the four forms?
b. Comment on the suitability of this experimental design in this problem.

14.23 [Xr14-23] Do medical specialists differ in the amount of time they devote to patient care? To answer this question, a statistics practitioner organized a study. The numbers of hours of patient care per week were recorded for five specialists. The experimental design was randomized blocks. The physicians were blocked by age. (Adapted from the *Statistical Abstract of the United States*, 2000, Table 190.)

a. Can we infer that there are differences in the amount of patient care between medical specialties?
b. Can we infer that blocking by age was appropriate?

14.24 [Xr14-24] The editor of the student newspaper was in the process of making major changes in the newspaper's layout. He was also contemplating changing the typeface of the print used. To help himself make a decision, he set up an experiment in which 20 individuals were asked to read four newspaper pages, with each page printed in a different typeface. If the reading speed differed, then the typeface that was read fastest would be used. However, if there was not enough evidence to allow the editor to conclude that such differences existed, then the current typeface would continue to be used. The times (in seconds) to completely read one page were recorded. What should the editor do?

General Social Survey Exercises

14.25 [GSS2012*] Is it a myth that Democratic party supporters are more educated than Independents and Republicans (PARTYID: 0, 1 = Democrat, 2,3,4 = Independent, 5,6 = Republican)? Conduct a test to determine whether differences in education (EDUC) actually exist.

14.26 [GSS2012*] Television networks and their advertisers are constantly measuring viewers to determine their likes and dislikes and how much time adults spend watching television per day. Do the data from the General Social Survey in 2012 allow us to infer that the amount of television (TVHOURS) differs by race (RACE: 1 = White, 2 = Black, 3 = Other)?

14.27 [GSS2012*] How are income and degree related? The General Social Survey asked respondents to identify the highest degree completed (DEGREE: 0 = left high school, 1 = high school, 2 = junior college, 3 = bachelor's degree, 4 = graduate degree). Is there enough statistical evidence to conclude that there are differences in income (INCOME) between people with different completed degrees?

CHAPTER 15

Chi-Squared Tests

objectives

15-1 Chi-Squared Goodness-of-Fit Test

15-2 Chi-Squared Test of a Contingency Table

GENERAL SOCIAL SURVEY: HAS SUPPORT FOR CAPITAL PUNISHMENT FOR MURDERERS REMAINED CONSTANT SINCE 2002?

[GSS2006*][GSS2008*][GSS2010*][GSS2012*]

The issue of capital punishment for murderers in the United States has been argued for many years. A number of states have abolished the penalty, and some have kept it on the books but have rarely used

it. Where does the public stand on the issue? Has public support been constant or has it changed from year to year? One of the questions asked in the General Social Survey was:

Do you favor capital punishment for murder? CAPPUN: 1 = Favor, 2 = Oppose

Conduct a test to determine whether public support varies from year to year.

This chapter develops two statistical techniques that involve nominal data. The first is a *goodness-of-fit test* applied to data produced by a *multinomial experiment*, a generalization of a binomial experiment. The second uses data arranged in a table (called a *contingency table*) to determine whether two classifications of a population of nominal data are statistically independent; this test can also be interpreted as a comparison of two or more populations. The sampling distribution of the test statistics in both tests is the chi-squared distribution introduced in Chapter 7.

15-1 Chi-Squared Goodness-of-Fit Test

This section presents another test designed to describe a population of nominal data. The first such test was introduced in Section 10-2, where we discussed the statistical procedure employed to test hypotheses about a population proportion. In that case, the nominal variable could assume one of only two possible values: success or failure. Our tests dealt with hypotheses about the proportion of successes in the entire population. Recall that the experiment that produces the data is called a *binomial experiment*. In this section,

we introduce the **multinomial experiment**, which is an extension of the binomial experiment, in which there are two or more possible outcomes per trial.

Multinomial Experiment

A multinomial experiment is one possessing the following properties:

1. The experiment consists of a fixed number n of trials.
2. The outcome of each trial can be classified into one of k categories called *cells*.
3. The probability p_i that the outcome will fall into cell i remains constant for each trial. Moreover, $p_1 + p_2 + \cdots + p_k = 1$.
4. Each trial of the experiment is independent of the other trials.

When $k = 2$, the multinomial experiment is identical to the binomial experiment. Just as we count the number of successes (recall that we label the number of successes x) and failures in a binomial experiment, we count the number of outcomes falling into each of the k cells in a multinomial experiment. In this way, we obtain a set of observed frequencies $f_1, f_2, \ldots, f_k$ where f_i is the observed frequency of outcomes falling into cell i, for $i = 1, 2, \ldots, k$. Just as we used the number of successes x (by calculating the sample proportion $\hat{p}$, which is equal to x/n) to draw inferences about p, so we use the observed frequencies to draw inferences about the cell probabilities. We'll proceed in what by now has become a standard procedure. We will set up the hypotheses and develop the test statistic and its sampling distribution. We'll demonstrate the process with the following example.

Helen Sessions/Alamy

EXAMPLE 15.1

Testing Market Shares

Company A has recently conducted aggressive advertising campaigns to maintain and possibly increase its share of the market for fabric softener. Its main competitor, company B, has 40% of the market, and a number of other competitors account for the remaining 15%. To determine whether the market shares changed after the advertising campaign, the marketing manager for company A solicited the preferences of a random sample of 200 customers of fabric softener. Of the 200 customers, 102 indicated a preference for company A's product, 82 preferred company B's fabric softener, and the remaining 16 preferred the products of one of the competitors. Can the analyst infer at the 5% significance level that customer preferences have changed from their levels before the advertising campaigns were launched?

SOLUTION

The population in question is composed of the brand preferences of the fabric softener customers. The data are nominal because each respondent will choose one of three possible answers: product A, product B, or other. If there were only two categories, or if we were interested only in the proportion of one company's customers (which we would label as successes and label the others as failures), then we would identify the technique as the z-test of p. However, in this problem, we're interested in the proportions of all three categories. We recognize this experiment as a multinomial experiment, and we identify the technique as the **chi-squared goodness-of-fit test**.

Because we want to know whether the market shares have changed, we specify those precampaign market shares in the null hypothesis.

$$H_0: p_1 = .45, \quad p_2 = .40, \quad p_3 = .15$$

The alternative hypothesis attempts to answer our question, Have the proportions changed? Thus,

H_1: At least one p_i is not equal to its specified value.

15-1a Test Statistic

If the null hypothesis is true, then we would expect the number of customers selecting brand A, brand B, and other to be 200 times the proportions specified under the null hypothesis; that is,

$$e_1 = 200(.45) = 90$$
$$e_2 = 200(.40) = 80$$
$$e_3 = 200(.15) = 30$$

In general, the **expected frequency** for each cell is given by

$$e_i = np_i$$

This expression is derived from the formula for the expected value of a binomial random variable, which was introduced in Section 6-2.

If the expected frequencies e_i and the **observed frequencies** f_i are quite different, then we would conclude that the null hypothesis is false and reject it. However, if the expected and observed frequencies are similar, then we would not reject the null hypothesis. The test statistic defined in the box measures the similarity of the expected and observed frequencies.

Chi-Squared Goodness-of-Fit Test Statistic

$$\chi^2 = \sum_{i=1}^{k} \frac{(f_i - e_i)^2}{e_i}$$

The sampling distribution of the test statistic is approximately chi-squared distributed with $\nu = k - 1$ degrees of freedom, provided that the sample size is large. We will discuss this required condition later. (The chi-squared distribution was introduced in Section 7-3.)

The following table demonstrates the calculation of the test statistic. Thus, the value $\chi^2 = 8.18$. As usual, we judge the size of this test statistic by specifying the rejection region or by determining the p-value.

Company	Observed Frequency f_i	Expected Frequency e_i	$(f_i - e_i)$	$\frac{(f_i - e_i)^2}{e_i}$
A	102	90	12	1.60
B	82	80	2	0.05
Other	16	30	−14	6.53
Total	200	200		$\chi^2 = 8.18$

© Cengage Learning

When the null hypothesis is true, the observed and expected frequencies should be similar, in which case the test statistic will be small. Thus, a small test statistic

supports the null hypothesis. If the null hypothesis is untrue, some of the observed and expected frequencies will differ, and the test statistic will be large. Consequently, we want to reject the null hypothesis when χ^2 is greater than $\chi^2_{\alpha, k-1}$; that is, the rejection region is

$$\chi^2 > \chi^2_{\alpha, k-1}$$

In Example 15.1, $k = 3$; the rejection region is

$$\chi^2 > \chi^2_{\alpha, k-1} = \chi^2_{.05, 2} = 5.99$$

Because the test statistic is $\chi^2 = 8.18$, we reject the null hypothesis. The p-value of the test is

$$p\text{-value} = P(\chi^2 > 8.18)$$

Unfortunately, Table 5 in Appendix B does not allow us to perform this calculation (except for approximation by interpolation). The p-value must be produced by computer.

Excel

INSTRUCTIONS

1. Type the observed values into one column and the expected values into another column. (If you wish, you can type the cell probabilities specified in the null hypothesis and let Excel convert these into expected values by multiplying by the sample size.)

2. Activate an empty cell and type

   = **CHITEST** ([Actual_range], [Expected_range])

   where the ranges are the cells containing the actual observations and the expected values.

   You can also perform what-if analyses to determine for yourself the effect of changing some of the observed values and the sample size.

   If we have the raw data representing the nominal responses, we must first determine the frequency of each category (the observed values) using the **COUNTIF** function described on page 15.

Minitab

Chi-Square Goodness-of-Fit Test for Observed Counts in Variable: C1

Category	Observed	Test Proportion	Expected	Contribution to Chi-Sq
1	102	0.45	90	1.60000
2	82	0.40	80	0.05000
3	16	0.15	30	6.53333

N	DF	Chi-Sq	P-Value
200	2	8.18333	0.017

1. Click **Stat, Tables,** and **Chi-square Goodness-of-Fit Test (One Variable).** . . .

2. Type the observed values into the **Observed counts:** box (102 82 16). If you have a column of data, click **Categorical data:** and specify the column or variable name.

3. Click **Proportions specified by historical counts** and **Input constants.** Type the values of the proportions under the null hypothesis (.45 .40 .15).

INTERPRET

There is sufficient evidence at the 5% significance level to infer that the proportions have changed since the advertising campaigns were implemented. If the sampling was conducted properly, we can be quite confident in our conclusion. This technique has only one required condition, which is satisfied. (See the next subsection.) It is probably a worthwhile exercise to determine the nature and causes of the changes. The results of this analysis will determine the design and timing of other advertising campaigns.

15-1b **Required Condition**

The actual sampling distribution of the test statistic defined previously is discrete, but it can be approximated by the chi-squared distribution provided that the sample size is large. This requirement is similar to the one we imposed when we used the normal approximation to the binomial in the sampling distribution of a proportion. In that approximation, we needed np and $n(1 - p)$ to be 5 or more. A similar rule is imposed for the chi-squared test statistic. It is called the *rule of five*, which states that the sample size must be large enough so that the expected value for each cell must be 5 or more. Where necessary, cells should be combined to satisfy this condition.

Factors that Identify the Chi-Squared Goodness-of-Fit Test

1. **Problem objective:** Describe a single population

2. **Data type:** Nominal

3. **Number of categories:** 2 or more

15-2 Chi-Squared Test of a Contingency Table

We introduce another chi-squared test, this one designed to satisfy two different problem objectives. The chi-squared test of a contingency table is used to determine whether there is enough evidence to infer that two nominal variables are related and to infer that differences exist between two or more populations of nominal variables. Completing both objectives entails classifying items according to two different criteria. To see how this is done, consider the following example.

EXAMPLE 15.2
Relationship between Undergraduate Degree and MBA Major

[Xm15-02] The MBA program was experiencing problems scheduling its courses. The demand for the program's optional courses and majors was quite variable from one year to the next. In one year, students seem to want marketing courses, and in other years accounting or finance is the rage. In desperation, the dean of the business school turned to a statistics professor for assistance. The statistics professor believed that the problem may be the variability in the academic background of the students and that the undergraduate degree affects the choice of major. As a start, he took a random sample of last year's MBA students and recorded the undergraduate degree and the major selected in the graduate program. The undergraduate degrees were BA, BEng, BBA, and several others. There are three possible majors for the MBA students: accounting, finance, and marketing. The results were summarized in a cross-classification table, which is shown here. Can the statistician conclude that the undergraduate degree and choice of major are related?

Under-graduate Degree	MBA Major			
	Accounting	Finance	Marketing	Total
BA	31	13	16	60
BEng	8	16	7	31
BBA	12	10	17	39
Other	10	5	7	22
Total	61	44	47	152

© Cengage Learning

SOLUTION

One way to solve the problem is to consider that there are two variables: undergraduate degree and MBA major. Both are nominal. The values of the undergraduate degree are BA, BEng, BBA, and other. The values of MBA major are accounting, finance, and marketing. The problem objective is to analyze the relationship between the two variables. Specifically, we want to know whether one variable is related to the other.

Another way of addressing the problem is to determine whether differences exist between BA's, BEng's, BBA's, and others. In other words, we treat the holders of each undergraduate degree as a separate population. Each population has three possible values represented by the MBA major. The problem objective is to compare four populations. (We can also answer the question by treating the MBA majors as populations and the undergraduate degrees as the values of the random variable.)

As you will shortly discover, both objectives lead to the same test. Consequently, we address both objectives at the same time.

The null hypothesis will specify that there is no relationship between the two variables. We state this in the following way:

H_0: The two variables are independent.

The alternative hypothesis specifies one variable affects the other, expressed as

H_1: The two variables are dependent.

15-2a Test Statistic

The test statistic is the same as the one used to test proportions in the goodness-of-fit-test; that is, the test statistic is

$$\chi^2 = \sum_{i=1}^{k} \frac{(f_i - e_i)^2}{e_i}$$

where k is the number of cells in the cross-classification table. If you examine the null hypothesis described in the goodness-of-fit test and the one described above, you will discover a major difference. In the goodness-of-fit test, the null hypothesis lists values for the probabilities p_i. The null hypothesis for the chi-squared test of a contingency table only states that the two variables are independent. However, we need the probabilities to compute the expected values e_i, which in turn are needed to calculate the value of the test statistic. (The entries in the table are the observed values f_i.) The question immediately arises, from where do we get the probabilities? The answer is that they must come from the data after we assume that the null hypothesis is true.

In Chapter 5, we introduced independent events and showed that if two events A and B are independent, then the joint probability $P(A$ and $B)$ is equal to the product of $P(A)$ and $P(B)$; that is,

$$P(A \text{ and } B) = P(A) \times P(B)$$

The events in this example are the values each of the two nominal variables can assume. Unfortunately, we do not have the probabilities of A and B. However, these probabilities can be estimated from the data. Using relative frequencies, we calculate the estimated probabilities for the MBA major:

$$P(\text{accounting}) = \frac{61}{152} = .401$$

$$P(\text{finance}) = \frac{44}{152} = .289$$

$$P(\text{marketing}) = \frac{47}{152} = .309$$

We calculate the estimated probabilities for the undergraduate degree.

$$P(BA) = \frac{60}{152} = .395$$

$$P(BEng) = \frac{31}{152} = .204$$

$$P(BBA) = \frac{39}{152} = .257$$

$$P(Others) = \frac{22}{152} = .145$$

Under-graduate Degree	MBA Major		
	Accounting	Finance	Marketing
BA	31 (24.08)	13 (17.37)	16 (18.55)
BEng	8 (12.44)	16 (8.97)	7 (9.59)
BBA	12 (15.65)	10 (11.29)	17 (12.06)
Other	10 (8.83)	5 (6.37)	7 (6.80)

Undergraduate Degree	MBA Major			Total
	Accounting	Finance	Marketing	
BA	$152 \times \frac{60}{152} \times \frac{61}{152} = 24.08$	$152 \times \frac{60}{152} \times \frac{44}{152} = 17.37$	$152 \times \frac{60}{152} \times \frac{47}{152} = 18.55$	60
BEng	$152 \times \frac{31}{152} \times \frac{61}{152} = 12.44$	$152 \times \frac{31}{152} \times \frac{44}{152} = 8.97$	$152 \times \frac{31}{152} \times \frac{47}{152} = 9.59$	31
BBA	$152 \times \frac{39}{152} \times \frac{61}{152} = 15.65$	$152 \times \frac{39}{152} \times \frac{44}{152} = 11.29$	$152 \times \frac{39}{152} \times \frac{47}{152} = 12.06$	39
Others	$152 \times \frac{22}{152} \times \frac{61}{152} = 8.83$	$152 \times \frac{22}{152} \times \frac{44}{152} = 6.37$	$152 \times \frac{22}{152} \times \frac{47}{152} = 6.80$	22
Total	61	44	47	152

Assuming that the null hypothesis is true, we can compute the estimated joint probabilities. To produce the expected values, we multiply the estimated joint probabilities by the sample size, $n = 152$. The results are listed in a **contingency table,** the word *contingency* derived by calculating the expected values contingent on the assumption that the null hypothesis is true (the two variables are independent).

As you can see, the expected value for each cell is computed by multiplying the row total by the column total and dividing by the sample size. For example, the BA and accounting cell expected value is

$$152 \times \frac{60}{152} \times \frac{61}{152} = \frac{60 \times 61}{152} = 24.08$$

All the other expected values would be determined similarly.

Expected Frequencies for a Contingency Table

The expected frequency of the cell in row i and column j is

$$e_{ij} = \frac{\text{Row } i \text{ total} \times \text{Column } j \text{ total}}{\text{Sample size}}$$

The expected cell frequencies are shown in parentheses in the following table. As in the case of the goodness-of-fit test, the expected cell frequencies should satisfy the rule of five.

We can now calculate the value of the test statistic:

$$\chi^2 = \sum_{i=1}^{k} \frac{(f_i - e_i)^2}{e_i} = \frac{(31 - 24.08)^2}{24.08} + \frac{(13 - 17.37)^2}{17.37}$$

$$+ \frac{(16 - 18.55)^2}{18.55} + \frac{(8 - 12.44)^2}{12.44} + \frac{(16 - 8.97)^2}{8.97}$$

$$+ \frac{(7 - 9.59)^2}{9.59} + \frac{(12 - 15.65)^2}{15.65} + \frac{(10 - 11.29)^2}{11.29}$$

$$+ \frac{(17 - 12.06)^2}{12.06} + \frac{(10 - 8.83)^2}{8.83} + \frac{(5 - 6.37)^2}{6.37}$$

$$+ \frac{(7 - 6.80)^2}{6.80}$$

$$= 14.70$$

Notice that we continue to use a single subscript in the formula of the test statistic when we should use two subscripts, one for the rows and one for the columns. We believe that it is clear that for each cell we must calculate the squared difference between the observed and expected frequencies divided by the expected frequency. We don't believe that the satisfaction of using the mathematically correct notation overcomes the unnecessary complication.

15-2b Rejection Region and *p*-Value

To determine the rejection region, we must know the number of degrees of freedom associated with the chi-squared statistic. The number of degrees of freedom for a contingency table with r rows and c columns is

$$\nu = (r - 1)(c - 1)$$

For this example, the number of degrees of freedom is

$$\nu = (r - 1)(c - 1) = (4 - 1)(3 - 1) = 6$$

If we employ a 5% significance level, the rejection region is

$$\chi^2 > \chi^2_{\alpha,\nu} = \chi^2_{.05,6} = 12.6$$

Because $\chi^2 = 14.70$, we reject the null hypothesis and conclude that there is evidence of a relationship between undergraduate degree and MBA major.

The p-value of the test statistic is

$$P(\chi^2 > 14.70)$$

Unfortunately, we cannot determine the p-value manually.

15-2c Using the Computer

Excel and Minitab can produce the chi-squared statistic either from a cross-classification table whose frequencies have already been calculated or from raw data. The respective printouts are almost identical.

File Xm15-02 contains the raw data using the following codes:

Column1 (Undergraduate Degree)	Column 2 (MBA Major)
1 = BA	1 = Accounting
2 = BEng	2 = Finance
3 = BBA	3 = Marketing
4 = Other	

© Cengage Learning

Excel

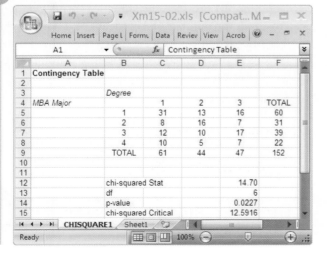

INSTRUCTIONS (RAW DATA)

1. Type or import the data into two adjacent columns. (Open Xm15-02.) The codes must be positive integers greater than 0.

2. Click **Add-Ins, Data Analysis Plus,** and **Contingency Table (Raw Data).**

3. Specify the **Input Range** (A1:B153) and specify the value of $\alpha(.05)$.

INSTRUCTIONS (COMPLETED TABLE)

1. Type the frequencies into adjacent columns.

2. Click **Add-Ins, Data Analysis Plus,** and **Contingency Table.**

3. Specify the **Input Range.** Click **Labels** if the first row and first column of the input range contain the names of the categories. Specify the value for α.

Minitab

Tabulated Statistics: Degree, MBA Major

```
Rows: Degree   Columns: MBA Major

        1    2    3    All

 1     31   13   16    60
 2      8   16    7    31
 3     12   10   17    39
 4     10    5    7    22
All    61   44   47   152

Cell Contents:      Count

Pearson Chi-Square = 14.702, DF = 6, P-Value = 0.023
Likelihood Ratio Chi-Square = 13.781, DF = 6,
P-Value = 0.032
```

INSTRUCTIONS (RAW DATA)

1. Type or import the data into two columns. (Open Xm15-02.)

2. Click **Stat, Tables,** and **Cross Tabulation and Chi-Square. . . .**

3. In the **Categorical variables** box, select or type the variables **For rows** (Degree) and **For columns** (MBA Major). Click **Chi-Square. . . .**

4. Under **Display,** click **Chi-Square analysis.** Specify **Chi-Square analysis.**

INSTRUCTIONS (COMPLETED TABLE)

1. Type the observed frequencies into adjacent columns.

2. Click **Stat, Tables,** and **Chi-Square Test (Table in Worksheet). . . .**

3. Select or type the names of the variables representing the columns.

INTERPRET

There is strong evidence to infer that the undergraduate degree and MBA major are related. This suggests that the dean can predict the number of optional courses by counting the number of MBA students with each type of undergraduate degree. We can see that BA's favor accounting courses, BEng's prefer finance, BBA's drift to marketing, and others show no particular preference.

If the null hypothesis is true, then undergraduate degree and MBA major are independent of one another. This means that whether an MBA student earned a BA, BEng, BBA, or other degree does not affect his or her choice of major program in the MBA. Consequently, there is no difference in major choice among the graduates of the undergraduate programs. If the alternative hypothesis is true, then undergraduate degree does affect the choice of MBA major. Thus, there are differences between the four undergraduate degree categories.

15-2d Rule of Five

In the previous section, we pointed out that the expected values should be at least 5 to ensure that the chi-squared distribution provides an adequate approximation of the sampling distribution. In a contingency table in which one or more cells have expected values of less than 5, we need to combine rows or columns to satisfy the rule of five.

15-2e Data Formats

In Example 15.2, the data were stored in two columns, one column containing the values of one nominal variable and the second column storing the values of the second nominal variable. The data can be stored in another way. In that example, we could have recorded the data in three columns, one column for each MBA major. The columns would contain the codes

GENERAL SOCIAL SURVEY: HAS SUPPORT FOR CAPITAL PUNISHMENT FOR MURDERERS REMAINED CONSTANT SINCE 2006? SOLUTION

IDENTIFY

The problem objective is to compare public opinion in four different years. The variable is nominal because its values are Favor and Oppose, represented by 1 and 2, respectively. The appropriate technique is the chi-squared test of a contingency table. The hypotheses are

H_0: The two variables are independent.

H_1: The two variables are dependent.

In this application the two variables are year (2006, 2008, 2010, and 2012) and the answer to the question posed by the General Social Survey (Favor and Oppose).

Unlike Example 15.2, the data are not stored in two columns. To produce the statistical result, we will need to count the number of Americans in favor and the number opposed in each of the four years. The following table was determined by counting the numbers of 1's and 2's for each year.

	Year			
	2006	**2008**	**2010**	**2012**
Favor	1885	1,263	1,297	1,183
Oppose	930	639	624	641

COMPUTE

INTERPRET

The *p*-value is .3368. There is not enough evidence to infer that the two variables are independent. Thus, there is not enough evidence to conclude that support for capital punishment for murder varies from year to year.

Here is a summary of the factors that tell us when to apply the chi-squared test of a contingency table. Note that there are two problem objectives satisfied by this statistical procedure.

representing the undergraduate degree. Alternatively, we could have stored the data in four columns, one column for each undergraduate degree. The columns would contain the codes for the MBA majors. In either case, we have to count the number of each value and construct the cross-tabulation table using the counts. Both Excel and Minitab can calculate the chi-squared statistic and its *p*-value from the cross-tabulation table. We illustrate this approach with the solution to the chapter-opening example.

Factors that Identify the Chi-Squared Test of a Contingency Table

1. **Problem objectives:** Analyze the relationship between two variables and compare two or more populations

2. **Data type:** Nominal

EXERCISES

15.1 Consider a multinomial experiment involving $n = 300$ trials and $k = 5$ cells. The observed frequencies resulting from the experiment are shown in the accompanying table, and the null hypothesis to be tested is as follows:

$$H_0: p_1 = .1, \quad p_2 = .2, \quad p_3 = .3, \quad p_4 = .2, \quad p_5 = .2$$

Test the hypothesis at the 1% significance level.

Cell	Frequency
1	24
2	64
3	84
4	72
5	56

15.2 The trustee of a company's pension plan has solicited the opinions of a sample of the company's employees about a proposed revision of the plan. A breakdown of the responses is shown in the accompanying table. Is there enough evidence at the 5% significance level to infer that the responses differ between the three groups of employees?

Responses	Blue-Collar Workers	White-Collar Workers	Managers
For	67	32	11
Against	63	18	9

15.3 The operations manager of a company that manufactures shirts wants to determine whether there are differences in the quality of workmanship among the three daily shifts. She randomly selects 600 recently made shirts and carefully inspects them. Each shirt is classified as either perfect or flawed, and the shift that produced it is also recorded. The accompanying table summarizes the number of shirts that fell into each cell. Do these data provide sufficient evidence at the 10% significance level to infer that there are differences in quality between the three shifts?

Shirt Condition	Shift		
	1	2	3
Perfect	240	191	139
Flawed	10	9	11

15.4 One of the issues that came up in a recent national election (and is likely to arise in many future elections) is how to deal with a sluggish economy. Specifically, should governments cut spending, raise taxes, inflate the economy (by printing more money), or do none of the above and let the deficit rise? And, as with most other issues, politicians need to know which parts of the electorate support these options. Suppose that a random sample of 1,000 people was asked which option they support and their political affiliations. The possible responses to the question about political affiliation were Democrat, Republican, and independent (which included a variety of political persuasions). The responses are summarized in the accompanying table. Do these results allow us to conclude at the 1% significance level that political affiliation affects support for the economic options?

Economic Options	Political Affiliation		
	Democrat	Republican	Independent
Cut spending	101	282	61
Raise taxes	38	67	25
Inflate the economy	131	88	31
Let deficit increase	61	90	25

Exercises 15.5 to 15.14 require the use of a computer and software. The answers may be calculated manually. See Appendix A for the sample statistics. Use a 5% significance level unless otherwise directed.

15.5 [Xr15-05] Grades assigned by an economics instructor have historically followed a symmetrical distribution: 5% A's, 25% B's, 40% C's, 25% D's, and 5% F's. This year, a sample of 150 grades was drawn, and the grades were recorded (1 = A, 2 = B, 3 = C, 4 = D, and 5 = F). Can you conclude, at the 10% level of significance, that this year's grades are distributed differently from grades in the past?

15.6 [Xr15-06] Pat Statsdud is about to write a multiple-choice exam but as usual knows absolutely nothing. Pat plans to guess one of the five choices. Pat has been given one of the professor's previous exams with the correct answers marked. The correct choices were recorded where 1 = (a), 2 = (b), 3 = (c), 4 = (d), and 5 = (e). Help Pat determine whether this professor does not randomly distribute the correct answer over the five choices. If this is true, how does it affect Pat's strategy?

15.7 [Xr15-07] Financial managers are interested in the speed with which customers who make purchases on credit pay their bills. In addition to calculating the average number of days that unpaid bills (called *accounts receivable*) remain outstanding, they often prepare an aging schedule. An aging schedule classifies outstanding accounts receivable according to the time that has elapsed since billing and records the proportion of accounts receivable belonging to each classification. A large firm has determined its aging schedule for the past 5 years. These results are shown in the accompanying table. During the past few months, however, the economy has taken a downturn. The company would like to know whether the recession has affected the aging schedule. A random sample of 250 accounts receivable was drawn and each account was classified as follows:

1 = 0–14 days outstanding
2 = 15–29 days outstanding
3 = 30–59 days outstanding
4 = 60 or more days outstanding

Number of Days Outstanding	Proportion of Accounts Receivable Past 5 Years
0–14	.72
15–29	.15
30–59	.10
60 and more	.03

Determine whether the aging schedule has changed.

15.8 [Xr15-08] License records in a county reveal that 15% of cars are subcompacts (1), 25% are compacts (2), 40% are midsize (3), and the rest are an assortment of other styles and models (4). A random sample of accidents involving cars licensed in the county was drawn. The type of car was recorded using the codes in parentheses. Can we infer that certain sizes of cars are involved in a higher than expected percentage of accidents?

15.9 [Xr15-09] In an election held last year that was contested by three parties, party A captured 31% of the vote, party B garnered 51%, and party C received the remaining votes. A survey of 1,200 voters asked each to identify the party that they would vote for in the next election. These results were recorded where 1 = party A, 2 = party B, and 3 = party C. Can we infer at the 10% significance level that voter support has changed since the election?

15.10 [Xr15-10] In a number of pharmaceutical studies, volunteers who take placebos (but are told they have taken a cold remedy) report the following side effects:

Side Effect	Percentage
Headache (1)	5
Drowsiness (2)	7
Stomach upset (3)	4
No side effect (4)	84

A random sample of 250 people who were given a placebo (but who thought they had taken an anti-inflammatory) reported whether they had experienced each of the side effects. These responses were recorded using the codes in parentheses. Do these data provide enough evidence to infer level that the reported side effects of the placebo for an anti-inflammatory differ from that of a cold remedy?

15.11 [Xr09-15*] Refer to Exercise 9.15 where the statistics practitioner estimated the size of market segments based on education among California adults. Suppose that census figures from 10 years ago showed the education levels and the proportions of California adults as follows:

Level	Proportion
1 Did not complete high school	.23
2 Completed high school only	.40
3 Some college or university	.15
4 College or university graduate	.22

Determine whether there has been a change in these proportions.

15.12 [Xr15-12] An investor who can correctly forecast the direction and size of changes in foreign currency exchange rates is able to reap huge profits in the international currency markets. A knowledgeable reader of the *Wall Street Journal* (in particular, of the currency futures market quotations) can determine the direction of change in various exchange rates that is predicted by all investors, viewed collectively. Predictions from 216 investors, together with the subsequent actual directions of change, were recorded in the following way: column 1, predicted change where 1 = positive and 2 = negative; column 2, actual change where 1 = positive and 2 = negative.

a. Can we infer at the 10% significance level that a relationship exists between the predicted and actual directions of change?

b. To what extent would you make use of these predictions in formulating your forecasts of future exchange rate changes?

15.13 [Xr15-13] During the past decade, many cigarette smokers have attempted to quit. Unfortunately, nicotine is highly addictive. Smokers use a large number of different methods to help them quit. These include nicotine patches, hypnosis, and various forms of therapy. A researcher for the Addiction Research Council wanted to determine why some people quit while others attempted to quit successfully but failed. He surveyed 1,000 people who planned to quit smoking. He determined their educational level and whether they continued to smoke 1 year later. Educational level was recorded in the following way:

1 = Did not finish high school
2 = High school graduate
3 = University or college graduate
4 = Completed a postgraduate degree

A continuing smoker was recorded as 1; a quitter was recorded as 2. Can we infer that the amount of education is a factor in determining whether a smoker will quit?

15.14 [Xr15-14] After a thorough analysis of the market, a publisher of business and economics statistics books has divided the market into three general approaches to teach applied statistics. These are (1) use of a computer and statistical software with no manual calculations; (2) traditional teaching of concepts and solution of problems by hand; (3) mathematical approach with emphasis on derivations and proofs. The publisher wanted to know whether this market could be segmented on the basis of the educational background of the instructor. As a result, the statistics editor organized a survey that asked 195 professors of business and economics statistics to report their approach to teaching and which one of the following categories represents their highest degree:

1. Business (MBA or PhD in business)
2. Economics
3. Mathematics or engineering
4. Other

Can the editor infer that there are differences in type of degree among the three teaching approaches? If so, how can the editor use this information?

American National Election Survey Exercise

15.15 [ANES2008*] According to the *Statistical Abstract of the United States*, 2009, Table 55, the proportions for each category of marital status was

never married (including partnered, not married) 25%
married (including separated, but not divorced) 58%
widowed 6%
divorced 11%

Can we infer that the American National Election Survey in 2008 overrepresented at least one category of marital status (MARITAL: 1 = Married, 2 = Widowed,

3 = Divorced, 4 = Separated, 5 = Never married)? (*Hint:* You must combine categories 1 and 4.)

General Social Survey Exercises

According to the *Statistical Abstract of the United States, 2012*, Table 10, the racial mix in the United States was

white 79%
black 13%
other 8%

15.16 [GSS2012*] Test to determine whether there is sufficient evidence that the General Social Survey in 2012 overrepresented at least one race (RACE: 1 = white, 2 = black, 3 = other).

15.17 [GSS2010*] Repeat Exercise 15.16 using the data from 2010.

According to the *Statistical Abstract of the United States, 2012*, Table 56, the proportions for each category of marital status was

never married 26.9%
married (including separated, but not divorced) 56.6%
widowed 6.2%
divorced 10.3%

15.18 [GSS2012*] Can we infer that the General Social Survey in 2008 overrepresented at least one category of marital status (MARITAL: 1 = Married, 2 = Widowed, 3 = Divorced, 4 = Separated, 5 = Never married)? (*Hint:* You must combine categories 1 and 4.)

15.19 [GSS2010*] Repeat Exercise 15.18 using 2010 data.

American National Election Survey Exercises

For each of the following variables, conduct a test to determine whether there are differences between the three political affiliations (PARTY: 1 = Democrat, 2 = Republican, 3 = independent).

15.20 [ANES2008*] Know where to vote (KNOW: 1 = Yes, 2 = No).

15.21 [ANES2008*] Read about campaign in newspaper (READ: 1 = Yes, 5 = No).

15.22 [ANES2008*] Have health insurance (HEALTH: 1 = Yes, 5 = No).

15.23 [ANES2008*] Have access to the Internet (ACCESS: 1 = Yes, 5 = No).

General Social Survey Exercises

15.24 [GSS2006*][GSS2008*][GSS2010*][GSS2012*] The issue of gun control in the United States is often debated, particularly during elections. The question arises, what does the public think about the issue and does support vary from year to year? Test to determine whether there is enough evidence to conclude that support for gun laws (GUNLAW: 1 = Favor, 2 = Oppose) varied from year to year.

15.25 [GSS2006*] [GSS2008*] [GSS2010*][GSS2012*] Can we conclude that the United States' marital status (MARITAL: 1 = Married, 2 = Widowed, 3 = Divorced, 4 = Separated, 5 = Never married) distribution has changed from year to year?

15.26 [GSS2012*] In the last two decades, an increasing proportion of women have entered the workforce. Determine whether there is enough evidence to conclude that men and women (SEX: 1 = Male, 2 = Female) differ in their work status (WRKSTAT: 1 = Working fulltime, 2 = Working part time, 3 = Temporarily not working, 4 = Unemployed, laid off, 5 = Retired, 6 = School, 7 = Keeping house, 8 = Other).

15.27 [GSS2012*] Is there sufficient evidence to infer that support for capital punishment (CAPPUN: 1 = Favor, 2 = Oppose) is related to political affiliation (PARTYID3: 1 = Democrat, 2 = Republican, 3 = independent)?

CHAPTER 16

Simple Linear Regression and Correlation

objectives

16-1 Model

16-2 Estimating the Coefficients

16-3 Error Variable: Required Conditions

16-4 Assessing the Model

16-5 Using the Regression Equation

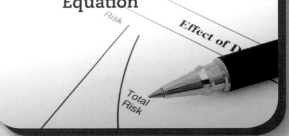

GENERAL SOCIAL SURVEY: EDUCATION AND INCOME—HOW ARE THEY RELATED?

[GSS2012*] If you're taking this course, you're probably a student in an undergraduate or graduate business or economics program. Your plan is to graduate, get a good job, and draw a high salary. You have probably assumed that more education equals better job equals higher income. However, is this true? Fortunately, the General Social Survey recorded two variables that will help determine whether education and income are related and, if so, the value of an additional year of education. On page 268 we will provide our answer.

In Chapter 2, we introduced the scatter diagram, which is a graphical technique to describe the relationship between two interval variables. Recall that in applications in which one variable depends to some degree on the other variable, we label the dependent variable Y and the independent variable X. In this chapter, we expand the technique to develop a mathematical model that more precisely describes the relationship between the two variables.

16-1 Model

Suppose that a real estate agent knows that the cost of building a new house is \$100 per square foot and that most lots sell for about \$100,000. The selling price would be calculated as

$$y = 100,000 + 100x$$

where y = selling price and x = size of the house in square feet. A house of 2,000 square feet would therefore be estimated to sell for

$$y = 100,000 + 100(2,000) = 300,000$$

This type of model is called **deterministic** because we can determine the exact value of y for each value of x. We know, however, that the selling price is not likely to be exactly \$300,000. Prices may actually range from \$200,000 to \$400,000. In other words, the deterministic model is not really suitable. To represent this situation properly, we should use the probabilistic model:

$$y = 100,000 + 100x + \varepsilon$$

where ε (the Greek letter epsilon) represents the **error variable**—the difference between the actual selling price and the estimated price based on the size of the house. The error thus accounts for all the variables that are not part of the model. The value of ε will vary from one sale to the next, even if x remains constant. In other words, houses of exactly the same size will sell for different prices because of differences in location and number of bedrooms and bathrooms, as well as other variables.

This model is called the **first-order linear model**, or sometimes the **simple linear regression model**.[1]

First-Order Linear Model

$$y = \beta_0 + \beta_1 x + \varepsilon$$

where

  y = dependent variable

  x = independent variable

[1] We use the term *linear* in two ways. The "linear" in linear regression refers to the form of the model in which the terms form a linear combination of the coefficients β_0 and β_1. Thus, for example, the model $y = \beta_0 + \beta_1 x^2 + \varepsilon$ is a linear combination, whereas $y = \beta_0 + \beta_1^2 x + \varepsilon$ is not. The simple linear regression model $y = \beta_0 + \beta_1 x + \varepsilon$ describes a straight-line or linear relationship between the dependent variable and one independent variable. In this book, we only use the linear regression technique. Hence, when we use the word *linear*, we are only referring to the straight-line relationship between the variables.

  β_0 = y-intercept

  β_1 = slope of the line (defined as rise/run)

  ε = error variable

The problem objective addressed by the model is to analyze the relationship between two variables, x and y, both of which must be interval. To define the relationship between x and y, we need to know the value of the coefficients β_0 and β_1. However, these coefficients are population parameters, which are almost always unknown. In the next section, we discuss how these parameters are estimated.

16-2 Estimating the Coefficients

We estimate the parameters β_0 and β_1 in a way similar to the methods used to estimate all the other parameters discussed in this book. We draw a random sample from the population of interest and calculate the sample statistics we need. However, because β_0 and β_1 represent the coefficients of a straight line, their estimators are based on drawing a straight line through the sample data. The straight line that we wish to use to estimate β_0 and β_1 is the "best" straight line—best in the sense that it comes closest to the sample data points. This best straight line, called the *least squares line*, is derived from calculus and is represented by the following equation:

$$\hat{y} = b_0 + b_1 x$$

Here b_0 is the y-intercept, b_1 is the slope, and $\hat{y}$ is the predicted or fitted value of y. The formulas are derived using calculus and the least squares method, which produces a straight line that minimizes the sum of the squared differences between the points and the line. The coefficients b_0 and b_1 are calculated so that the sum of squared deviations

$$\sum_{i=1}^{n} (y_i - \hat{y}_i)^2$$

is minimized. In other words, the values of $\hat{y}$ on average come closest to the observed values of y.

Least Squares Line Coefficients

$$b_1 = \frac{s_{xy}}{s_x^2}$$

$$b_0 = \bar{y} - b_1 \bar{x}$$

where

$$s_{xy} = \frac{\sum_{i=1}^{n}(x_i - \bar{x})(y_i - \bar{y})}{n - 1}$$

$$s_x^2 = \frac{\sum_{i=1}^{n}(x_i - \bar{x})^2}{n - 1}$$

$$\bar{x} = \frac{\sum_{i=1}^{n}x_i}{n}$$

$$\bar{y} = \frac{\sum_{i=1}^{n}y_i}{n}$$

The quantity s_{xy} is called the *sample covariance*, which was introduced in Chapter 3, and we remind you that s_x^2 is the sample variance of x.

In Chapter 3, we provided a shortcut formula for the sample variance (page 41) and the sample covariance (page 47). Combining them provides a shortcut method to manually calculate the slope coefficient.

Shortcut Formula for b_1

$$b_1 = \frac{s_{xy}}{s_x^2}$$

$$s_{xy} = \frac{1}{n - 1}\left[\sum_{i=1}^{n}x_i y_i - \frac{\sum_{i=1}^{n}x_i \sum_{i=1}^{n}y_i}{n}\right]$$

$$s_x^2 = \frac{1}{n - 1}\left[\sum_{i=1}^{n}x_i^2 - \frac{\left(\sum_{i=1}^{n}x_i\right)^2}{n}\right]$$

Statisticians have shown that b_0 and b_1 are unbiased estimators of β_0 and β_1, respectively.

Although the calculations are straightforward, we would rarely compute the regression line manually because the work is time consuming. However, we illustrate the manual calculations for a very small sample.

EXAMPLE 16.1
Annual Bonus and Years of Experience

[Xm16-01] The annual bonuses ($1,000s) of six employees with different years of experience were recorded as follows. We wish to determine the straight-line relationship between annual bonus and years of experience.

Years of experience x	Annual bonus y
1	6
2	1
3	9
4	5
5	17
6	12

SOLUTION

To apply the shortcut formula, we need to compute four summations. Using a calculator, we find

$$\sum_{i=1}^{n}x_i = 21, \quad \sum_{i=1}^{n}y_i = 50, \quad \sum_{i=1}^{n}x_i y_i = 212,$$

$$\sum_{i=1}^{n}x_i^2 = 91$$

The covariance and the variance of x can now be computed:

$$s_{xy} = \frac{1}{n - 1}\left[\sum_{i=1}^{n}x_i y_i - \frac{\sum_{i=1}^{n}x_i \sum_{i=1}^{n}y_i}{n}\right]$$

$$= \frac{1}{6 - 1}\left[212 - \frac{(21)(50)}{6}\right] = 7.4$$

$$s_x^2 = \frac{1}{n - 1}\left[\sum_{i=1}^{n}x_i^2 - \frac{\left(\sum_{i=1}^{n}x_i\right)^2}{n}\right]$$

$$= \frac{1}{6 - 1}\left[91 - \frac{(21)^2}{6}\right] = 3.5$$

The sample slope coefficient is calculated next:

$$b_1 = \frac{s_{xy}}{s_x^2} = \frac{7.4}{3.5} = 2.114$$

The y-intercept is computed as follows:

$$\bar{x} = \frac{\sum x_i}{n} = \frac{21}{6} = 3.5$$

$$\bar{y} = \frac{\sum y_i}{n} = \frac{50}{6} = 8.333$$

$$b_0 = \bar{y} - b_1\bar{x} = 8.333 - (2.114)(3.5) = .934$$

Thus, the least squares line is

$$\hat{y} = .934 + 2.114x$$

Figure 16.1 depicts the least squares (or regression) line. As you can see, the line fits the data reasonably well. We can measure how well by computing the value of the minimized sum of squared deviations. The deviations between the actual data points and the line are called **residuals**, denoted e_i; that is,

$$e_i = y_i - \hat{y}_i$$

Figure 16.1 Scatter Diagram with Regression Line for Example 16.1

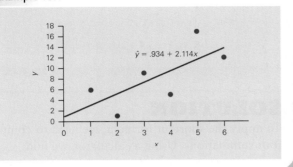

$\hat{y} = .934 + 2.114x$

The residuals are observations of the error variable. Consequently, the minimized sum of squared deviations is called the **sum of squares for error**, denoted SSE.

The calculation of the residuals in this example is shown in Figure 16.2. Notice that we compute $\hat{y}_i$ by substituting x_i into the formula of the regression line. The residuals are the differences between the observed values of y_i and the fitted or predicted values of $\hat{y}_i$. Table 16.1 describes these calculations.

Figure 16.2 Calculation of Residuals in Example 16.1

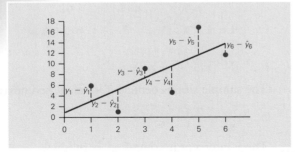

Table 16.1 Calculation of Residuals in Example 16.1

x_i	y_i	$\hat{y}_i = .934 + 2.114x_i$	$y_i - \hat{y}_i$	$(y_i - \hat{y}_i)^2$
1	6	3.048	2.952	8.714
2	1	5.162	−4.162	17.322
3	9	7.276	1.724	2.972
4	5	9.390	−4.390	19.272
5	17	11.504	5.496	30.206
6	12	13.618	−1.618	2.618
			$\Sigma(y_i - \hat{y}_i)^2 =$	81.104

Thus, SSE = 81.104. No other straight line will produce a sum of squared deviations as small as 81.104. In that sense, the regression line fits the data best. The sum of squares for error is an important statistic because it is the basis for other statistics that assess how well the linear model fits the data. We will introduce these statistics in Section 16-4.

EXAMPLE 16.2

Odometer Reading and Prices of Used Honda Accords, Part 1

[Xm16-02*] Car dealers across North America use the Kelley Blue Book to help them determine the value of used cars that their customers trade in when purchasing new cars. The book, which is published monthly, lists the trade-in values for all basic models of cars. It provides alternative values for each car model according to its condition and optional features. The values are determined on the basis of the average paid at recent used-car auctions, the source of supply for many used-car dealers. However, the Blue Book does not indicate the value determined by the odometer reading, despite the fact that a critical factor for used-car buyers is how far the car has been driven. To examine this issue, a used-car dealer randomly selected 100 3-year-old Honda Accords that were sold at auction during the past month. Each car was in top condition and equipped with all the features that come standard with this car. The dealer recorded the price (in $1,000s) and the number of miles (thousands) on the odometer. Some of these data are listed here. The dealer wants to find the regression line.

Car	Price ($1,000)	Odometer (1,000 Mi)
1	14.6	37.4
2	14.1	44.8
3	14.0	45.8
⋮	⋮	⋮
98	14.5	33.2
99	14.7	39.2
100	14.3	36.4

© Cengage Learning

SOLUTION
IDENTIFY

Notice that the problem objective is to analyze the relationship between two interval variables. Because we believe that the odometer reading affects the selling price, we identify the former as the independent variable, which we label x, and the latter as the dependent variable, which we label y.

COMPUTE
Manually

From the data set, we find

$$\sum_{i=1}^{n} x_i = 3{,}601.1, \quad \sum_{i=1}^{n} y_i = 1{,}484.1,$$

$$\sum_{i=1}^{n} x_i y_i = 53{,}155.93, \quad \sum_{i=1}^{n} x_i^2 = 133{,}986.59$$

Next we calculate the covariance and the variance of the independent variable x:

$$s_{xy} = \frac{1}{n-1} \left[\sum_{i=1}^{n} x_i y_i - \frac{\sum_{i=1}^{n} x_i \sum_{i=1}^{n} y_i}{n} \right]$$

$$= \frac{1}{100-1} \left[53{,}155.93 - \frac{(3{,}601.1)(1{,}484.1)}{100} \right]$$

$$= -2.909$$

$$s_x^2 = \frac{1}{n-1} \left[\sum_{i=1}^{n} x_i^2 - \frac{\left(\sum_{i=1}^{n} x_i\right)^2}{n} \right]$$

$$= \frac{1}{100-1} \left[133{,}986.59 - \frac{(3{,}601.1)^2}{100} \right]$$

$$= 43.509$$

The sample slope coefficient is calculated next:

$$b_1 = \frac{s_{xy}}{s_x^2} = \frac{-2.909}{43.509} = -.0669$$

The y-intercept is computed as follows:

$$\bar{x} = \frac{\sum x_i}{n} = \frac{3{,}601.1}{100} = 36.011$$

$$\bar{y} = \frac{\sum y_i}{n} = \frac{1{,}484.1}{100} = 14.841$$

$$b_0 = \bar{y} - b_1 \bar{x} = 14.841 - (-.0669)(36.011)$$

$$= 17.25$$

The sample regression line is

$$\hat{y} = 17.25 - 0.0669x$$

Excel

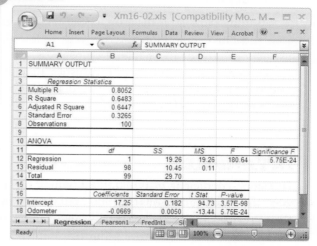

The printout includes more statistics than we need right now. However, we will be discussing the rest of the printouts later.

INSTRUCTIONS

1. Type or import data into two columns, one storing the dependent variable and the other the independent variable. (Open Xm16-02.)

2. Click **Data**, **Data Analysis**, and **Regression**.

3. Specify the **Input Y Range** (A1:A101) and the **Input X Range** (B1:B101).

To draw the scatter diagram, follow the instructions provided in Chapter 2 on page 28.

Minitab
Regression Analysis: Price versus Odometer

```
The regression equation is
Price = 17.2 - 0.0669 Odometer

Predictor     Coef      SE Coef       T        P
Constant    17.2487      0.1821     94.73    0.000
Odometer   -0.066861    0.004975   -13.44    0.000

S = 0.326489  R-Sq = 64.8%  R-Sq(adj) = 64.5%

Analysis of Variance

Source          DF      SS       MS       F       P
Regression       1    19.256   19.256  180.64  0.000
Residual Error  98    10.446    0.107
Total           99    29.702
```

INSTRUCTIONS

1. Type or import the data into two columns. (Open Xm16-02.)

2. Click **Stat**, **Regression**, and **Regression....**

3. Type the name of the dependent variable in the **Response** box (Price) and the name of the independent variable in the **Predictors** box (Odometer).

   To draw the scatter diagram, click **Stat**, **Regression**, and **Fitted Line Plot**. Alternatively, follow the instructions provide in Chapter 2 on page 28.

   The printout includes more statistics than we need right now. However, we will be discussing the rest of the printouts later.

INTERPRET

The slope coefficient b_1 is -0.0669, which means that for each additional 1,000 miles on the odometer, the price decreases by an average of $\$.0669$ thousand. Expressed more simply, the slope tells us that for each additional mile on the odometer, the price decreases on average by $\$.0669$ or 6.69 cents.

   The intercept is $b_0 = 17.250$. Technically, the intercept is the point at which the regression line and the y-axis intersect. This means that when $x = 0$ (i.e., the car was not driven at all) the selling price is $\$17.250$ thousand or $\$17,250$. We might be tempted to interpret this number as the price of cars that have not been driven. However, in this case, the intercept is probably meaningless. Because our sample did not include any cars with zero miles on the odometer, we have no basis for interpreting b_0. As a general rule, we cannot determine the value of $\hat{y}$ for a value of x that is far outside the range of the sample values of x. In this example, the smallest and largest values of x are 19.1 and 49.2, respectively. Because $x = 0$ is not in this interval, we cannot safely interpret the value of $\hat{y}$ when $x = 0$.

It is important to bear in mind that the interpretation of the coefficients pertains only to the sample, which consists of 100 observations. To infer information about the population, we need statistical inference techniques, which are described subsequently.

   In the sections that follow, we will return to this problem and the computer output to introduce other statistics associated with regression analysis.

16-3 Error Variable: Required Conditions

In the previous section, we used the least squares method to estimate the coefficients of the linear regression model. A critical part of this model is the error variable ε. In the next section, we will present an inferential method that determines whether there is a relationship between the dependent and independent variables. Later we will show how we use the regression equation to estimate and predict. For these methods to be valid, however, four requirements involving the probability distribution of the error variable must be satisfied.

Required Conditions for the Error Variable

1. The probability distribution of ε is normal.
2. The mean of the distribution is 0; that is, $E(\varepsilon) = 0$.
3. The standard deviation of ε is σ_ε, which is a constant regardless of the value of x.
4. The value of ε associated with any particular value of y is independent of ε associated with any other value of y.

   Requirements 1, 2, and 3 can be interpreted in another way: For each value of x, y is a normally distributed random variable whose mean is

$$E(y) = \beta_0 + \beta_1 x$$

and whose standard deviation is σ_ε. Notice that the mean depends on x. The standard deviation, however, is not influenced by x, because it is a constant over all values of x. Figure 16.3 depicts this interpretation. Notice that for

Figure 16.3 Distribution of y Given x

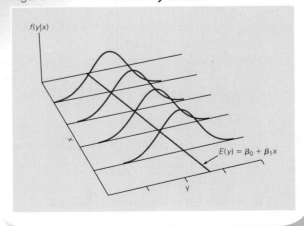

each value of x, $E(y)$ changes, but the shape of the distribution of y remains the same. In other words, for each x, y is normally distributed with the same standard deviation.

16-4 Assessing the Model

The least squares method produces the best straight line. However, there may, in fact, be no relationship or perhaps a nonlinear relationship between the two variables. If so, a straight-line model is likely to be impractical. Consequently, it is important for us to assess how well the linear model fits the data. If the fit is poor, we should discard the linear model and seek another one.

Several methods are used to evaluate the model. In this section, we present two statistics and one test procedure to determine whether a linear model should be employed. They are the standard error of estimate, the t-test of the slope, and the coefficient of determination. All these methods are based on the sum of squares for error.

16-4a Sum of Squares for Error

The least squares method determines the coefficients that minimize the sum of squared deviations between the points and the line defined by the coefficients. Recall from Section 16-2 that the minimized sum of squared deviations is called the *sum of squares for error*, denoted SSE. In that section, we demonstrated the direct method of calculating SSE. For each value of x, we compute the value of $\hat{y}$; that is, for $i = 1$ to n, we compute

$$\hat{y}_i = b_0 + b_1 x_i$$

For each point, we then compute the residual, which is the difference between the actual value of y and the value calculated at the line, which is the residual. We square each residual and sum the squared values. Table 16.1 on page 258 shows these calculations for Example 16.1. To calculate SSE manually requires a great deal of arithmetic. Fortunately, there is a shortcut method available that uses the sample variances and the covariance.

Shortcut Calculation of SSE

$$\text{SSE} = \sum_{i=1}^{n}(y_i - \hat{y}_i)^2 = (n-1)\left(s_y^2 - \frac{s_{xy}^2}{s_x^2}\right)$$

where s_y^2 is the sample variance of the dependent variable.

16-4b Standard Error of Estimate

In Section 16-3, we pointed out that the error variable ε is normally distributed with mean 0 and standard deviation σ_ε. If σ_ε is large, some of the errors will be large, which implies that the model's fit is poor. If σ_ε is small, the errors tend to be close to the mean (which is 0); as a result, the model fits well. Hence, we could use σ_ε to measure the suitability of using a linear model. Unfortunately, σ_ε is a population parameter and, like most other parameters, is unknown. We can, however, estimate σ_ε from the data. The estimate is based on SSE. The unbiased estimator of the variance of the error variable σ_ε^2 is

$$s_\varepsilon^2 = \frac{\text{SSE}}{n-2}$$

The square root of s_ε^2 is called the *standard error of estimate*.

Standard Error of Estimate

$$s_\varepsilon = \sqrt{\frac{\text{SSE}}{n-2}}$$

EXAMPLE 16.3

Odometer Reading and Prices of Used Honda Accords, Part 2

Find the standard error of estimate for Example 16.2 and describe what it tells you about the model's fit.

SOLUTION
COMPUTE
Manually

To compute the standard error of estimate, we must compute SSE, which is calculated from the sample variances and the covariance. We have already determined the covariance and the variance of x. They are -2.909 and 43.509, respectively. The sample variance of y (applying the shortcut method) is

$$s_y^2 = \frac{1}{n-1}\left[\sum_{i=1}^{n}y_i^2 - \frac{\left(\sum_{i=1}^{n}y_i\right)^2}{n}\right]$$

$$= \frac{1}{100-1}\left[22{,}055.23 - \frac{(1{,}484.1)^2}{100}\right] = .300$$

$$\text{SSE} = (n-1)\left(s_y^2 - \frac{s_{xy}^2}{s_x^2}\right)$$

$$= (100-1)\left(.300 - \frac{[-2.909]^2}{43.509}\right) = 10.445$$

The standard error of estimate follows:

$$s_\varepsilon = \sqrt{\frac{\text{SSE}}{n-2}} = \sqrt{\frac{10.445}{98}} = .3265$$

Excel

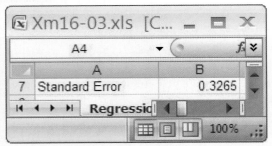

This part of the Excel printout was copied from the complete printout on page 259.

Minitab

`S = .326489`

This part of the Minitab printout was copied from the complete printout on page 259.

INTERPRET

The smallest value that s_ε can assume is 0, which occurs when SSE = 0—that is, when all the points fall on the regression line. Thus, when s_ε is small, the fit is excellent, and the linear model is likely to be an effective analytical and forecasting tool. If s_ε is large, the model is a poor one, and the statistics practitioner should improve it or discard it.

We judge the value of s_ε by comparing it to the values of the dependent variable y or more specifically to the sample mean $\bar{y}$. In this example, because $s_\varepsilon = .3265$ and $\bar{y} = 14.841$, it does appear that the standard error of estimate is small. However, because there is no predefined upper limit on s_ε, it is often difficult to assess the model in this way. In general, the standard error of estimate cannot be used as an absolute measure of the model's utility.

Nonetheless, s_ε is useful in comparing models. If the statistics practitioner has several models from which to choose, the one with the smallest value of s_ε should generally be the one used. As you'll see, s_ε is also an important statistic in other procedures associated with regression analysis.

16-4c Testing the Slope

To understand this method of assessing the linear model, consider the consequences of applying the regression technique to two variables that are not at all linearly related. If we could observe the entire population and draw the regression line, we would observe the scatter diagram shown in Figure 16.4. The line is horizontal, which means that no matter what value of x is used, we would estimate the same value for $\hat{y}$, thus y is not linearly related to x. Recall that a horizontal straight line has a slope of 0—that is, $\beta_1 = 0$.

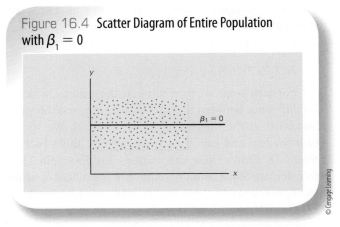

Figure 16.4 Scatter Diagram of Entire Population with $\beta_1 = 0$

© Cengage Learning

Because we rarely examine complete populations, the parameters are unknown. However, we can draw inferences about the population slope β_1 from the sample slope b_1.

The process of testing hypotheses about β_1 is identical to the process of testing any other parameter. We begin with the hypotheses. The null hypothesis specifies that there is no linear relationship, which means that the slope is 0. Thus, we specify

$$H_0: \beta_1 = 0$$

It must be noted that if the null hypothesis is true, it does not necessarily mean that no relationship exists. For example, there may be a quadratic relationship described in Figure 16.5 where $\beta_1 = 0$.

Figure 16.5 **Quadratic Relationship**

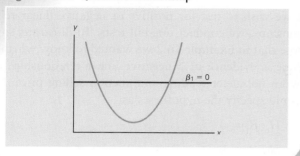

© Cengage Learning

We can conduct one- or two-tail tests of β_1. Most often we perform a two-tail test to determine whether there is sufficient evidence to infer that a linear relationship exists.[2] We test the alternative hypothesis

$$H_1: \beta_1 \neq 0$$

16-4d Estimator and Sampling Distribution

In Section 16-2 we pointed out that b_1 is an unbiased estimator of β_1; that is,

$$E(b_1) = \beta_1$$

The estimated standard error of b_1 is

$$s_{b_1} = \frac{s_\varepsilon}{\sqrt{(n-1)s_x^2}}$$

where s_ε is the standard error of estimate and s_x^2 is the sample variance of the independent variable. If the required conditions outlined in Section 16-3 are satisfied, the sampling distribution of the t-statistic

$$t = \frac{b_1 - \beta_1}{s_{b_1}}$$

is Student t with degrees of freedom $\nu = n - 2$. Notice that the standard error of b_1 decreases when the sample

[2] If the alternative hypothesis is true, it may be that a linear relationship exists or that a nonlinear relationship exists, but that the relationship can be approximated by a straight line.

size increases (which makes b_1 a consistent estimator of β_1) or the variance of the independent variable increases.

Thus, the test statistic and confidence interval estimator are as follows.

Test Statistic for β_1

$$t = \frac{b_1 - \beta_1}{s_{b_1}} \qquad \nu = n - 2$$

Confidence Interval Estimator of β_1

$$b_1 \pm t_{\alpha/2} s_{b_1} \qquad \nu = n - 2$$

EXAMPLE 16.4
Are Odometer Reading and Price of Used Honda Accords Related?

Test to determine whether there is enough evidence in Example 16.2 to infer that there is a linear relationship between the auction price and the odometer reading for all 3-year-old Honda Accords. Use a 5% significance level.

SOLUTION
We test the hypotheses

$$H_0: \beta_1 = 0$$
$$H_1: \beta_1 \neq 0$$

If the null hypothesis is true, no linear relationship exists. If the alternative hypothesis is true, some linear relationship exists.

COMPUTE
Manually
To compute the value of the test statistic, we need b_1 and s_{b_1}. In Example 16.2, we found

$$b_1 = -.0669$$

and

$$s_x^2 = 43.509$$

Thus,

$$s_{b_1} = \frac{s_\varepsilon}{\sqrt{(n-1)s_x^2}} = \frac{.3265}{\sqrt{(99)(43.509)}} = .00497$$

The value of the test statistic is

$$t = \frac{b_1 - \beta_1}{s_{b_1}} = \frac{-.0669 - 0}{.00497} = -13.46$$

The rejection region is

$$t < -t_{\alpha/2,\nu} = -t_{.025,98} \approx -1.984 \quad \text{or}$$

$$t > t_{\alpha/2,\nu} = t_{.025,98} \approx 1.984$$

Excel

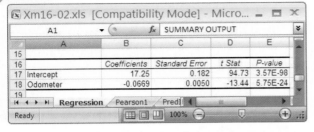

Minitab

Predictor	Coef	SE Coef	T	P
Constant	17.2487	0.1821	94.73	0.000
Odometer	-0.066861	0.004975	-13.44	0.000

INTERPRET

The value of the test statistic is $t = -13.44$, with a p-value of 0. (Excel uses scientific notation, which in this case is 5.75×10^{-24}, or approximately 0.) There is overwhelming evidence to infer that a linear relationship exists. What this means is that the odometer reading may affect the auction selling price of the cars. (See the subsection on the cause-and-effect relationship on page 29.)

As was the case when we interpreted the y-intercept, the conclusion we draw here is valid only over the range of the values of the independent variable. In other words, we can infer that there is a relationship between odometer reading and auction price for the 3-year-old Honda Accords whose odometer readings lie between 19.1 (thousand) and 49.2 (thousand) miles (the minimum and maximum values of x in the sample). Because we have no observations outside this range, we do not know how or even whether the two variables are related.

Notice that the printout includes a test for β_0. However, as we pointed out before, interpreting the value of the y-intercept can lead to erroneous, if not ridiculous, conclusions. Consequently, we generally ignore the test of β_0.

We can also acquire information about the relationship by estimating the slope coefficient. In this example, the 95% confidence interval estimate

(approximating $t_{.025}$ with 98 degrees of freedom with $t_{.025}$ with 100 degrees of freedom) is

$$b_1 \pm t_{\alpha/2}s_{b_1} = -.0669 \pm 1.984(.00497)$$

$$= -.0669 \pm .0099$$

We estimate that the slope coefficient lies between $-.0768$ and $-.0570$.

16-4e One-Tail Tests

If we wish to test for positive or negative linear relationships, we conduct one-tail tests. To illustrate, suppose that in Example 16.2 we wanted to know whether there is evidence of a negative linear relationship between odometer reading and auction selling price. We would specify the hypotheses as

$$H_0: \beta_1 = 0$$

$$H_1: \beta_1 < 0$$

The value of the test statistic would be exactly as computed previously (Example 16.4). However, in this case, the p-value would be the two-tail p-value divided by 2, which using Excel's p-value would be $(5.75 \times 10^{-24})/2 = 2.875 \times 10^{-24}$, which is still approximately 0.

16-4f Coefficient of Determination

The test of β_1 addresses only the question of whether there is enough evidence to infer that a linear relationship exists. In many cases, however, it is also useful to measure the strength of that linear relationship, particularly when we want to compare several different models. The statistic that performs this function is the *coefficient of determination*, which is denoted R^2. Statistics practitioners often refer to this statistic as the "R-square." The coefficient of determination is a measure of the amount of variation in the dependent variable that is explained by the variation in the independent variable.

Coefficient of Determination

$$R^2 = \frac{s_{xy}^2}{s_x^2 s_y^2}$$

With a little algebra, statisticians can show that

$$R^2 = 1 - \frac{SSE}{\Sigma(y_i - \bar{y})^2}$$

We'll return to Example 16.1 to learn more about how to interpret the coefficient of determination. In

Chapter 14, we partitioned the total sum of squares into two sources of variation. We do so here as well. We begin by adding and subtracting $\hat{y}_i$ from the deviation between y_i from the mean $\bar{y}$; that is,

$$(y_i - \bar{y}) = (y_i - \bar{y}) + \hat{y}_i - \hat{y}_i$$

We observe that by rearranging the terms the deviation between y_i and $\bar{y}$ can be decomposed into two parts; that is,

$$(y_i - \bar{y}) = (y_i - \hat{y}_i) + (\hat{y}_i - \bar{y})$$

This equation is represented graphically (for $i = 5$) in Figure 16.6.

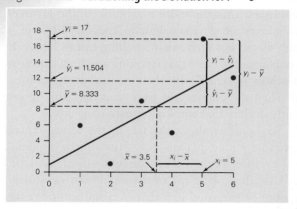

Figure 16.6 **Partitioning the Deviation for $i = 5$**

Now we ask why the values of y are different from one another. From Figure 16.6, we see that part of the difference between y_i and $\bar{y}$ is the difference between $\hat{y}_i$ and $\bar{y}$, which is accounted for by the difference between x_i and $\bar{x}$. In other words, some of the variation in y is explained by the changes to x. The other part of the difference between y_i and $\bar{y}$, however, is accounted for by the difference between y_i and $\hat{y}_i$. This difference is the residual, which represents variables not otherwise represented by the model. As a result, we say that this part of the difference is *unexplained* by the variation in x.

If we now square both sides of the equation, sum over all sample points, and perform some algebra, we produce

$$\Sigma(y_i - \bar{y})^2 = \Sigma(y_i - \hat{y}_i)^2 + \Sigma(\hat{y}_i - \bar{y})^2$$

The quantity on the left side of this equation is a measure of the variation in the dependent variable y. The first quantity on the right side of the equation is SSE, and the second term is denoted SSR, for sum of squares for regression. We can rewrite the equation as

Variation in y = SSE + SSR

As we did in the analysis of variance, we partition the variation of y into two parts: SSE, which measures the amount of variation in y that remains unexplained; and SSR, which measures the amount of variation in y that is explained by the variation in the independent variable x. We can incorporate this analysis into the definition of R^2.

Coefficient of Determination

$$R^2 = 1 - \frac{\text{SSE}}{\Sigma(y_i - \bar{y})^2} = \frac{\Sigma(y_i - \bar{y})^2 - \text{SSE}}{\Sigma(y_i - \bar{y})^2}$$

$$= \frac{\text{Explained variation}}{\text{Variation in } y}$$

It follows that R^2 measures the proportion of the variation in y that can be explained by the variation in x.

EXAMPLE 16.5

Measuring the Strength of the Linear Relationship between Odometer Reading and Price of Used Honda Accords

Find the coefficient of determination for Example 16.2 and describe what this statistic tells you about the regression model.

SOLUTION
COMPUTE
Manually

We have already calculated all the necessary components of this statistic. In Example 16.2, we found

$$s_{xy} = -2.909$$

$$s_x^2 = 43.509$$

and from Example 16.3

$$s_y^2 = .300$$

Thus,

$$R^2 = \frac{s_{xy}^2}{s_x^2 s_y^2} = \frac{(-2.909)^2}{(43.509)(.300)} = .6483$$

Excel

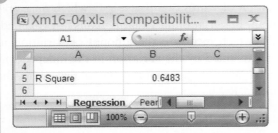

	A	B	C
4			
5	R Square	0.6483	
6			

Regression / Pear

Minitab

`R-Sq = 64.8%`

INTERPRET

We found that R^2 is equal to .6483. This statistic tells us that 64.83% of the variation in the auction selling prices is explained by the variation in the odometer readings. The remaining 35.17% is unexplained. Unlike the value of a test statistic, the coefficient of determination does not have a critical value that enables us to draw conclusions. In general, the higher the value of R^2, the better the model fits the data. From the t-test of β_1 we already know that there is evidence of a linear relationship. The coefficient of determination merely supplies us with a measure of the strength of that relationship. The coefficient of determination is also referred to as the *explanatory power of the model*. As you will discover in the next chapter, when we improve the model, the value of R^2 increases.

16-4g Other Parts of the Computer Printout

The last part of the printout shown on page 259 relates to our discussion of the interpretation of the value of R^2, when its meaning is derived from the partitioning of the variation in y. The values of SSR and SSE are shown in an analysis of variance table similar to the tables introduced in Chapter 14. The general form of the table is shown in Table 16.2. The F-test performed in the ANOVA table will be explained in Chapter 17.

Table 16.2 General Form of the ANOVA Table in the Simple Linear Regression Model

Source	d.f.	Sums of Squares	Mean Squares	*F*-Statistic
Regression	1	SSR	MSR = SSR/1	F = MSR/MSE
Error	n − 2	SSE	MSE = SSE/(n − 2)	
Total	n − 1	Variation in y		

Note: Excel uses the word *residual* to refer to the second source of variation, which we called *error*.

16-4h Cause-and-Effect Relationship

A common mistake is made by many students when they attempt to interpret the results of a regression analysis when there is evidence of a linear relationship. They imply that changes in the independent variable cause changes in the dependent variable. It must be emphasized that we cannot infer a causal relationship from statistics alone. Any inference about the cause of the changes in the dependent variable must be justified by a reasonable theoretical relationship. For example, statistical tests established that the more one smoked, the greater the probability of developing lung cancer. However, this analysis did not prove that smoking causes lung cancer. It only demonstrated that smoking and lung cancer were somehow related. Only when medical investigations established the connection were scientists able to confidently declare that smoking causes lung cancer.

Be cautious about the use of the terms *explained variation* and *explanatory power of the model*. Do not interpret the word *explained* to mean *caused*. We say that the coefficient of determination measures the amount of variation in y that is explained (not caused) by the variation in x. Thus, regression analysis can only show that a statistical relationship exists. We cannot infer that one variable causes another.

Collecting Data

In Chapter 4 we discussed two ways to gather data, by direct observations and by experiments. Example 16.2 is an illustration of observational data. In that example we merely observed the odometer reading and auction selling price of 100 randomly selected Honda Accords.

If you examine Exercise 16.4 you will see experimental data gathered through a controlled experiment. To determine the effect of the length of a television commercial on its viewers' memories of the product advertised, the statistics practitioner arranged for 60 television viewers to watch a commercial of differing lengths and then tested their memories of that commercial. Each viewer was randomly assigned a commercial length. The values of x ranged from 20 to 60 and were set by the statistics practitioner as part of the experiment. For each value of x, the distribution of the memory test scores is assumed to be normally distributed with a constant variance.

We can summarize the difference between the experiment described in Example 16.2 and the one described in Exercise 16.4. In Example 16.2 both the odometer reading and the auction selling price are random variables. We hypothesize that for each possible odometer reading, there is a theoretical population of auction selling prices that are normally distributed with a mean that is a linear function of the odometer reading and a variance that is constant. In Exercise 16.4, the length of the commercial is not a random variable but a series of values selected by the statistics practitioner. For each commercial length, the memory test scores are required to be normally distributed with a constant variance.

Regression analysis can be applied to data generated from either observational or controlled experiments. In both cases our objective is to determine how the independent variable is related to the dependent variable. However, observational data can be analyzed in another way. When the data are observational, both variables are random variables. We need not specify that one variable is independent and the other is dependent. We can simply determine *whether* the two variables are related.

16-4i Coefficient of Correlation

When we introduced the coefficient of correlation (also called the *Pearson coefficient of correlation*) in Chapter 3, we observed that it is used to measure the strength of association between two variables. However, the coefficient of correlation can be useful in another way. We can use it to test for a linear relationship between two variables.

When we are interested in determining *how* the independent variable is related to the dependent variable, we estimate and test the linear regression model. The *t*-test of the slope presented previously allows us to determine whether a linear relationship actually exists. As we pointed out in Section 16-3, the statistical test requires that for each value of *x*, there exists a population of values of *y* that are normally distributed with a constant variance. This condition is required whether the data are experimental or observational.

In many circumstances we're interested in determining only *whether* a linear relationship exists and not the form of the relationship. When the data are observational and the two variables are normally distributed, we can calculate the coefficient of correlation and use it to test for linear association.

As we noted in Chapter 3, the population coefficient of correlation is denoted ρ (the Greek letter *rho*). Because ρ is a population parameter (which is almost always unknown), we must estimate its value from the sample data. Recall that the sample coefficient of correlation is defined as follows.

Sample Coefficient of Correlation

$$r = \frac{s_{xy}}{s_x s_y}$$

Testing the Coefficient of Correlation

When there is no linear relationship between the two variables, $\rho = 0$. To determine whether we can infer that ρ is 0, we test the hypotheses

$$H_0: \rho = 0$$
$$H_1: \rho \neq 0$$

The test statistic is defined in the following way.

Test Statistic for Testing $\rho = 0$

$$t = r\sqrt{\frac{n-2}{1-r^2}}$$

which is Student *t* distributed with $\nu = n - 2$ degrees of freedom provided that the variables are normally distributed.

EXAMPLE 16.6

Are Odometer Reading and Price of Used Honda Accords Linearly Related? Testing the Coefficient of Correlation

Conduct the *t*-test of the coefficient of correlation to determine whether odometer reading and auction selling price are linearly related in Example 16.2. Assume that the two variables are normally distributed.

SOLUTION
COMPUTE
Manually

The hypotheses to be tested are

$$H_0: \rho = 0$$
$$H_1: \rho \neq 0$$

In Example 16.2, we found $s_{xy} = -2.909$ and $s_x^2 = 43.509$. In Example 16.5, we determined that $s_y^2 = .300$. Thus,

$$s_x = \sqrt{43.509} = 6.596$$

$$s_y = \sqrt{.300} = .5477$$

The coefficient of correlation is

$$r = \frac{s_{xy}}{s_x s_y} = \frac{-2.909}{(6.596)(.5477)} = -.8052$$

The value of the test statistic is

$$t = r\sqrt{\frac{n-2}{1-r^2}} = -.8052\sqrt{\frac{100-2}{1-(-.8052)^2}}$$

$$= -13.44$$

Notice that this is the same value we produced in the *t*-test of the slope in Example 16.4. Because both sampling distributions are Student *t* with 98 degrees of freedom, the *p*-value and conclusion are also identical. This should not be surprising because both tests are conducted to determine whether there is evidence of a linear relationship.

Excel

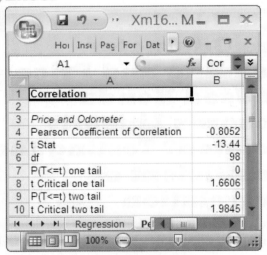

INSTRUCTIONS

1. Type or import the data into two adjacent columns. (Open Xm16-02.)

2. Click **Add-ins, Data Analysis Plus,** and **Correlation (Pearson).**

3. Specify the **Variable 1 Input Range** (A1:A101), **Variable 2 Input Range** (B1:B101), and α(.05).

GENERAL SOCIAL SURVEY: EDUCATION AND INCOME—HOW ARE THEY RELATED? SOLUTION

IDENTIFY

The problem objective is to analyze the relationship between two interval variables. Because we want to know how education affects income, the independent variable is education (EDUC) and the dependent variable is income (INCOME).

COMPUTE

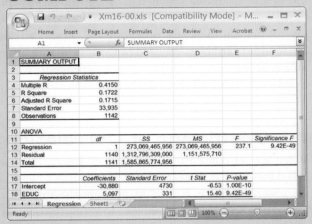

INTERPRET

The regression equation is $\hat{y} = -30,880 + 5097x$. The slope coefficient tells us that on average for each additional year of education income increases by $5,097. The intercept is clearly meaningless. We test to determine whether there is evidence of a linear relationship.

$$H_0: \beta_1 = 0$$
$$H_1: \beta_1 \neq 0$$

The test statistic is $t = 15.40$ and the *p*-value is 9.42×10^{-49}, which is virtually 0. The coefficient of determination is $R^2 = .1722$, which means that 17.22% of the variation in income is explained by the variation in education and the remaining 82.78% is not explained.

Minitab
Correlations: Odometer, Price

```
Pearson correlation of Price and Odometer = -0.805
P-Value = 0.000
```

INSTRUCTIONS

1. Type or import the data into two adjacent columns. (Open Xm16-02.)

2. Click **Stat**, **Basic Statistics**, and **Correlation**.

3. Type the names of the variables in the **Variables** box (Odometer Price).

As is the case with the *t*-test of the slope we can also conduct one-tail tests. We can test for a positive or a negative linear relationship.

16-4j Violation of the Required Condition

When the normality requirement is unsatisfied, we can use a nonparametric technique—the Spearman rank correlation coefficient (Web-site appendix)—to replace the *t*-test of ρ.

16-5 Using the Regression Equation

Using the techniques in Section 16-4, we can assess how well the linear model fits the data. If the model fits satisfactorily, we can use it to forecast and estimate values of the dependent variable. To illustrate, suppose that in Example 16.2, the used-car dealer wanted to predict the selling price of a 3-year-old Honda Accord with 40 (thousand) miles on the odometer. Using the regression equation, with $x = 40$, we get

$$\hat{y} = 17.25 - .0669x = 17.25 - 0.0669(40)$$
$$= 14.574$$

We call this value the **point prediction**, and $\hat{y}$ is the point estimate or predicted value for y when $x = 40$. Thus, the dealer would predict that the car would sell for $14,574.

By itself, however, the point prediction does not provide any information about how closely the value will match the true selling price. To discover that information, we must use an interval. In fact, we can use one of two intervals: the prediction interval of a particular value of y or the confidence interval estimator of the expected value of y.

16-5a Predicting the Particular Value of y for a Given x

The first confidence interval we present is used whenever we want to predict a one-time occurrence for a particular value of the dependent variable when the independent variable is a given value x_g. This interval, often called the **prediction interval**, is calculated in the usual way (point estimator $\pm$ bound on the error of estimation).

Prediction Interval

$$\hat{y} \pm t_{\alpha/2, n-2} s_\varepsilon \sqrt{1 + \frac{1}{n} + \frac{(x_g - \bar{x})^2}{(n-1)s_x^2}}$$

where x_g is the given value of x and $\hat{y} = b_0 + b_1 x_g$.

16-5b Estimating the Expected Value of y for a Given x

The conditions described in Section 16-3 imply that, for a given value of x, there is a population of values of y whose mean is

$$E(y) = \beta_0 + \beta_1 x$$

To estimate the mean of y or long-run average value of y, we would use the following interval referred to simply as the *confidence interval*. Again, the point estimator is $\hat{y}$, but the bound on the error of estimation is different from the prediction interval as follows.

Confidence Interval Estimator of the Expected Value of y

$$\hat{y} \pm t_{\alpha/2, n-2} s_\varepsilon \sqrt{\frac{1}{n} + \frac{(x_g - \bar{x})^2}{(n-1)s_x^2}}$$

Unlike the formula for the prediction interval, this formula does not include the 1 under the square-root sign. As a result, the confidence interval estimate of the expected value of y will be narrower than the prediction interval for the same given value of x and confidence level. This is because there is less error in estimating a mean value as opposed to predicting an individual value.

EXAMPLE 16.7

Predicting the Price and Estimating the Mean Price of Used Honda Accords

a. A used-car dealer is about to bid on a 3-year-old Honda Accord equipped with all the standard features and with 40,000 ($x_g = 40$) miles on the odometer. To help him decide how much to bid, he needs to predict the selling price.

b. The used-car dealer mentioned in part (a) has an opportunity to bid on a lot of cars offered by a rental company. The rental company has 250 Honda Accords all equipped with standard features. All the cars in this lot have about 40,000 ($x_g = 40$) miles on the odometer. The dealer would like an estimate of the selling price of all the cars in the lot.

SOLUTION
IDENTIFY

a. The dealer would like to predict the selling price of a single car. Thus, he must employ the prediction interval

$$\hat{y} \pm t_{\alpha/2, n-2} s_\varepsilon \sqrt{1 + \frac{1}{n} + \frac{(x_g - \bar{x})^2}{(n-1)s_x^2}}$$

b. The dealer wants to determine the mean price of a large lot of cars, so he needs to calculate the confidence interval estimator of the expected value:

$$\hat{y} \pm t_{\alpha/2, n-2} s_\varepsilon \sqrt{\frac{1}{n} + \frac{(x_g - \bar{x})^2}{(n-1)s_x^2}}$$

Technically, this formula is used for infinitely large populations. However, we can interpret our problem as attempting to determine the average selling price of all Honda Accords equipped as described, all with 40,000 miles on the odometer. The crucial factor in part (b) is the need to estimate the mean price of a number of cars. We arbitrarily select a 95% confidence level.

COMPUTE
Manually

From previous calculations, we have the following:

$$\hat{y} = 17.25 - .0669(40) = 14.574,$$
$$s_\varepsilon = .3265, \quad s_x^2 = 43.509, \quad \bar{x} = 36.011$$

From Table 4 in Appendix B, we find

$$t_{\alpha/2} = t_{.025,98} \approx t_{.025,100} = 1.984$$

a. The 95% prediction interval is

$$\hat{y} \pm t_{\alpha/2, n-2} s_\varepsilon \sqrt{1 + \frac{1}{n} + \frac{(x_g - \bar{x})^2}{(n-1)s_x^2}}$$

$$= 14.574 \pm 1.984$$

$$\times .3265 \sqrt{1 + \frac{1}{100} + \frac{(40 - 36.011)^2}{(100 - 1)(43.509)}}$$

$$= 14.574 \pm .652$$

The lower and upper limits of the prediction interval are \$13,922 and \$15,226, respectively.

b. The 95% confidence interval estimator of the mean price is

$$\hat{y} \pm t_{\alpha/2, n-2} s_\varepsilon \sqrt{\frac{1}{n} + \frac{(x_g - \bar{x})^2}{(n-1)s_x^2}}$$

$$= 14.574 \pm 1.984$$

$$\times .3265 \sqrt{\frac{1}{100} + \frac{(40 - 36.011)^2}{(100 - 1)(43.509)}}$$

$$= 14.574 \pm .076$$

The lower and upper limits of the confidence interval estimate of the expected value are \$14,498 and 14,650, respectively.

Excel

	A	B
1	Prediction Interval	
2		
3		Price
4		
5	Predicted value	14.574
6		
7	Prediction Interval	
8	Lower limit	13.922
9	Upper limit	15.227
10		
11	Interval Estimate of Expected Value	
12	Lower limit	14.498
13	Upper limit	14.650

INSTRUCTIONS

1. Type or import the data into two columns. (Open Xm16-02.)

2. Type the given value of x into any cell. We suggest the next available row in the column containing the independent variable.

3. Click **Add-Ins, Data Analysis Plus**, and **Prediction Interval**.

4. Specify the **Input Y Range** (A1:A101), the **Input X Range** (B1:B101), the **Given X Range** (B102), and the **Confidence Level** (.95).

Minitab

```
Predicted Values for New Observations

New
Obs     Fit     SE Fit      95% CI           95% PI
  1   14.5743   0.0382  (14.4985, 14.6501)  (13.9220,
                                             15.2266)

Values of Predictors for New Observations

New
Obs    Odometer
  1     40.0
```

The output includes the predicted value $\hat{y}$ (**Fit**), the standard deviation of $\hat{y}$ (**SE Fit**), the 95% confidence interval estimate of the expected value of y (**CI**), and the 95% prediction interval (**PI**).

INSTRUCTIONS

1. Proceed through the three steps of regression analysis described on page 259. Do not click **OK**. Click **Options....**

2. Specify the given value of x in the **Prediction intervals for new observations** box (40).

3. Specify the confidence level (.95).

INTERPRET

We predict that one car will sell for between $13,925 and $15,226. The average selling price of the population of 3-year-old Honda Accords is estimated to lie between $14,498 and $14,650. Because predicting the selling price of one car is more difficult than estimating the mean selling price of all similar cars, the prediction interval is wider than the interval estimate of the expected value.

EXERCISES

16.1 [Xr16-01] Attempting to analyze the relationship between advertising and sales, the owner of a furniture store recorded the monthly advertising budget ($thousands) and the sales ($millions) for a sample of 12 months. The data are listed here.

Advertising	Sales
23	9.6
46	11.3
60	12.8
54	9.8
28	8.9
33	12.5
25	12.0
31	11.4
36	12.6
88	13.7
90	14.4
99	15.9

a. Draw a scatter diagram. Does it appear that advertising and sales are linearly related?

b. Calculate the least squares line and interpret the coefficients.

c. Determine the standard error of estimate.

d. Is there evidence of a linear relationship between advertising and sales?

e. Estimate β_1 with 95% confidence.

f. Predict with 90% confidence the sales when the advertising budget is $90,000.

16.2 [Xr16-02] Critics of television often refer to the detrimental effects that all the violence shown on television has on children. However, there may be another problem. It may be that watching television also reduces the amount of physical exercise causing weight gains. A sample of 15 10-year-old children was taken. The number of pounds each child was overweight was recorded (a negative number indicates the child is underweight). In addition, the number of hours of television viewing per week was also recorded. These data are listed here.

Television	Overweight
42	18
34	6
25	0
35	−1
37	13
38	14
31	7
33	7
19	−9
29	8
38	8
28	5
29	3
36	14
18	−7

a. Draw the scatter diagram.
b. Calculate the sample regression line and describe what the coefficients tell you about the relationship between the two variables.
c. Is there evidence of a linear relationship between the number of hours of television viewing and how overweight the child is?
d. Predict with 90% confidence the number of pounds overweight for a child who watches 30 hours of television per week.
e. Estimate with 90% confidence the mean number of pounds overweight for children who watch 30 hours of television per week.

16.3 [Xr16-03] To help determine how many beers to stock, the concession manager at Yankee Stadium wanted to know how air temperature affected beer sales. Accordingly, she took a sample of 10 games and recorded the number of beers sold and the temperature in the middle of the game.

Temperature	Number of beers
80	20,533
68	1,439
78	13,829
79	21,286
87	30,985
74	17,187
86	30,240
92	37,596
77	9,610
84	28,742

a. Compute the coefficients of the regression line.
b. Interpret the coefficients.
c. Determine whether there is evidence of a negative linear relationship between temperature and the number of beers sold.
d. Predict with 90% confidence the number of beers to be sold when the temperature is 80 degrees.

The exercises that follow were created to allow you to see how regression analysis is used to solve realistic problems. As a result, most feature a large number of observations. We anticipate that most students will solve these problems using a computer and statistical software. However, for students without these resources, we have computed the means, variances, and covariances for Exercises 16.4 to 16.11 that will permit them to complete the calculations manually. (See Appendix A.)

16.4 [Xr16-04*] In television's early years, most commercials were 60 seconds long. Now, however, commercials can be any length. The objective of commercials remains the same—to have as many viewers as possible remember the product in a favorable way and eventually buy it. In an experiment to determine how the length of a commercial is related to people's memory of it, 60 randomly selected people were asked to watch a 1-hour television program. In the middle of the show, a commercial advertising a brand of toothpaste appeared. Some viewers watched a commercial that lasted for 20 seconds, others watched one that lasted for 24 seconds, 28 seconds,..., 60 seconds. The essential content of the commercials was the same. After the show, each person was given a test to measure how much he or she remembered about the product. The commercial times and test scores (on a 30-point test) were recorded.

a. Draw a scatter diagram of the data to determine whether a linear model appears to be appropriate.
b. Determine the least squares line.
c. Interpret the coefficients.
d. What is the standard error of estimate? Interpret its value.
e. Describe how well the memory test scores and length of television commercial are linearly related.
f. Are the memory test scores and length of commercial linearly related? Test using a 5% significance level.
g. Estimate the slope coefficient with 90% confidence.
h. Predict with 95% confidence the memory test score of a viewer who watches a 36-second commercial.
i. Estimate with 95% confidence the mean memory test score of people who watch 36-second commercials.

16.5 [Xr16-05] Florida condominiums are popular winter retreats for many North Americans. In recent years, the price has steadily increased. A real estate agent wanted to know why prices of similar-size apartments in the same building vary. A possible answer lies in the floor. It may be that the higher the floor, the greater the sale price of the apartment. He recorded the price (in $1,000s) of 1,200-square-foot condominiums in several buildings in the same location that have sold recently and the floor number of the condominium.

a. Determine the regression line.
b. What do the coefficients tell you about the relationship between the two variables?
c. Apply the three methods of assessing the model to determine how well the linear model fits.
d. Predict with 95% confidence the selling price of a 1,200-sq.-ft. condominium on the 25th floor.
e. Estimate with 99% confidence the average selling price of a 1,200-sq.-ft. condominium on the 12th floor.

16.6 [Xr16-06] In 2010, the United States conducted a census of the entire country. The census is completed by mail. To help ensure that the questions are understood, a random sample of Americans took the questionnaire before it was sent out to the entire country. As part of the analysis, the Census Bureau workers recorded the amount of time to complete the questionnaire and ages of the individuals in the sample. Use the least squares method to analyze the relationship between the amount of time taken to complete the questionnaire and the age of the individual answering the questions.

a. What do the coefficients tell you about the relationship between the two variables?
b. Is there enough evidence to infer that age and the amount of time needed to complete the questionnaire are linearly related?

16.7 [Xr16-07] The human resource manager of a telemarketing firm is concerned about the rapid turnover of the firm's telemarketers. It appears that many telemarketers do not work very long before quitting. There may be a number of reasons, including relatively low pay, personal unsuitability for the work, and the low probability of advancement. Because of the high cost of hiring and training new workers, the manager decided to examine the factors that influence workers to quit. He reviewed the work history of a random sample of workers who have quit in the last year and recorded the number of weeks on the job before quitting and the age of each worker when originally hired.

a. Use regression analysis to describe how the work period and age are related.
b. Briefly discuss what the coefficients tell you.
c. Use two statistics to measure the strength of the linear association. What do these statistics tell you?
d. The company has just hired a 25-year-old telemarketer. Predict with 95% confidence how long he will stay with the company.

16.8 [Xr16-08] Besides the known long-term effects of smoking, do cigarettes also cause short-term illnesses such as colds? To help answer this question, a sample of smokers was drawn. Each person was asked to report the average number of cigarettes smoked per day and the number of days absent from work due to colds last year.

a. Determine the regression line.
b. What do the coefficients tell you about the relationship between smoking cigarettes and sick days due to colds?
c. Is there evidence of a linear relationship between number of cigarettes smoked and number of sick days?
d. Predict with 95% confidence the number of sick days for individuals who smoke on average 30 cigarettes per day.

16.9 [Xr16-09] Fire damage in the United States amounts to billions of dollars, much of it insured. The time taken to arrive at the fire is critical. This raises the question, Should insurance companies lower premiums if the home to be insured is close to a fire station? To help make a decision, a study was undertaken in which a number of fires were investigated. The distance to the nearest fire station (in kilometers) and the percentage of fire damage were recorded.

a. Determine the least squares line and interpret the coefficients.
b. Test to determine whether there is evidence of a linear relationship between distance to the nearest fire station and percentage of damage.
c. Estimate the slope coefficient with 95% confidence.
d. Determine the coefficient of determination. What does this statistic tell you about the relationship?
e. Predict with 95% confidence the percentage loss due to fire for a house that is 5 miles away from the nearest fire station.
f. Estimate with 95% confidence the average percentage loss due to fire for houses that are 2 miles away from the nearest fire station.

16.10 [Xr16-10] The manager of Colonial Furniture has been reviewing weekly advertising expenditures. During the past 6 months, all advertisements for the store have appeared in the local newspaper. The number of ads per week has varied from one to seven. The store's sales staff has been tracking the number of customers who enter the store each week. The number of ads and the number of customers per week for the past 26 weeks were recorded.

a. Determine the sample regression line.
b. Interpret the coefficients.
c. Can the manager infer that the larger the number of ads, the larger the number of customers?
d. Find and interpret the coefficient of determination.
e. In your opinion, is it a worthwhile exercise to use the regression equation to predict the number of customers who will enter the store given that Colonial intends to advertise five times in the newspaper? If so, find a 95% prediction interval. If not, explain why not.

16.11 [Xr16-11] The president of a company that manufactures car seats has been concerned about the number and cost of machine breakdowns. The problem is that the machines are old and becoming quite unreliable. However, the cost of replacing them is quite high, and the president is not certain that the cost can be made up in today's slow economy. To help make a decision about replacement, he gathered data about last month's costs for repairs and the ages (in months) of the plant's 20 welding machines.

a. Find the sample regression line.
b. Interpret the coefficients.
c. Determine the coefficient of determination, and discuss what this statistic tells you.
d. Conduct a test to determine whether the age of a machine and its monthly cost of repair are linearly related.
e. Is the fit of the simple linear model good enough to allow the president to predict the monthly repair cost of a welding machine that is 120 months old? If so, find a 95% prediction interval. If not, explain why not.

16.12 [Xr16-12] Every year the United States Federal Trade Commission rates cigarette brands according to their levels of tar and nicotine, substances that are hazardous to smokers' health. In addition, the commission includes the amount of carbon monoxide, which is a by-product of burning tobacco that seriously affects the heart. A random sample of 25 brands was taken.

a. Are the levels of tar and nicotine linearly related?
b. Are the levels of nicotine and carbon monoxide linearly related?

16.13 [Xr16-13] Some critics of television complain that the amount of violence shown on television contributes to violence in our society. Others point out that television also contributes to the high level of obesity among children. We may have to add financial problems to the list. A sociologist theorized that people who watch television frequently are exposed to many commercials, which in turn leads them to buy more, finally resulting in increasing debt. To test this belief, a sample of 430 families was drawn. For each, the total debt and the number of hours the television is turned on per week were recorded. Perform a statistical procedure to help test the theory.

16.14 [Xr16-14] Mutual funds minimize risks by diversifying the investments they make. There are mutual funds that specialize in particular types of investments. For example, the TD Precious Metal Mutual Fund buys shares in gold-mining companies. The value of this mutual fund depends on a number of factors related to the companies in which the fund invests as well as on the price of gold. To investigate the relationship between the value of the fund and the price of gold, an MBA student gathered the daily fund price and the daily price of gold for a 28-day period. Can we infer from these data that there is a positive linear relationship between the value of the fund and the price of gold? (The authors are grateful to Jim Wheat for writing this exercise.)

16.15 [Xr16-15] A computer dating service typically asks for various pieces of information such as height, weight, and income. One such service requested the length of index fingers. The only plausible reason for this request is to act as a proxy on height. Women have often complained that men lie about their heights. If there is a strong relationship between heights and index fingers, the information can be used to "correct" false claims about heights. To test the relationship between the two variables, researchers gathered the heights and lengths of index fingers (in centimeters) of 121 students.

a. Is there sufficient evidence to infer that height and length of index fingers are linearly related?
b. Predict with 95% confidence the height of someone whose index finger is 6.5 cm long. Is this prediction likely to be useful? Explain. (The authors would like to thank Howard Waner for supplying the problem and data.)

American National Election Survey Exercises

16.16 [ANES2008*] Do more educated people spend less time watching or reading news on the Internet? Conduct a regression analysis to determine whether there is enough statistical evidence to conclude that the more education (EDUC) one has the more one watches or reads news on the Internet (TIME1).

16.17 [ANES2008*] In the chapter-opening example, we analyzed the relationship between income and education using the 2012 General Social Survey. Conduct a similar analysis using the 2008 American National Election Survey.

16.18 [ANES2008*] National news on television runs commercials that describe pharmaceutical drugs that treat ailments that plague older people. Apparently, the major networks believe that older people tend to watch national newscasts. Is there sufficient evidence to conclude age (AGE) and number of days watching national news on television (DAYS1) are positively related?

16.19 [ANES2008*] In most presidential elections in the United States, the voter turnout is quite low, often in the neighborhood of 50%. Political workers would like to be able to predict who is likely to vote. Thus, it is important to know which variables are related to intention to vote. One candidate is age. Is there sufficient evidence to infer that age (AGE) and intention to vote (DEFINITE) are linearly related?

16.20 [ANES2008*] Do more affluent people get their news from radio? Answer the question by conducting an analysis of the relationship between income (INCOME) and time listening to news on the radio (TIME4).

General Social Survey Exercises

16.21 [GSS2012*] Does one's income affect his or her position on the question, Should the government reduce income differences between rich and poor? Answer the question by testing the relationship between income (INCOME) and (EQWLTH).

16.22 [GSS2010*] Conduct an analysis of the relationship between income (INCOME) and age (AGE). Estimate with 95% confidence the average increase in income for each additional year of age.

16.23 [GSS2012*] Is there sufficient evidence to conclude that more educated people (EDUC) watch less television (TVHOURS)?

16.24 [GSS2010*] Use the 2010 survey data to determine whether more education (EDUC) leads to higher incomes (INCOME).

CHAPTER 17

Multiple Regression

objectives

17-1 Model and Required Conditions

17-2 Estimating the Coefficients and Assessing the Model

17-3 Regression Diagnostics

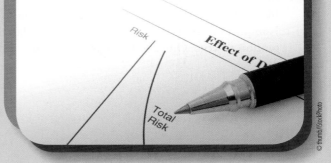

GENERAL SOCIAL SURVEY: VARIABLES THAT AFFECT INCOME

[GSS202012*] In the opening example in Chapter 16, we used the General Social Survey to show that income and education are linearly related. This raises the question, what other variables affect one's income? To answer this question, we need to expand the simple linear regression technique used in the previous chapter to allow for more than one independent variable.

Here is a list of all the interval variables the General Social Survey created in 2012:

Age (AGE)

Years of education of respondent, spouse, father, and mother (EDUC, SPEDUC, PAEDUC, MAEDUC)

Hours of work per week of respondent and of spouse (HRS1 and SPHRS1)

Number of family members earning money (EARNRS)

Number of children (CHILDS)

Age when first child was born (AGEKDBRN)

Number of hours of television viewing per day (TVHOURS)

Score on question, Should government reduce income differences between rich and poor? (EQWLTH)

Score on question, Should government improve standard of living of poor people? (HELPPOOR)

Score on question, Should government do more or less to solve country's problems? (HELPNOT)

Score on question, Is it government's responsibility to help pay for doctor and hospital bills? (HELPSICK)

The goal is to create a regression analysis that includes all variables that you believe affect the amount of time spent watching television. Our answer appears on page 279.

In the previous chapter, we employed the simple linear regression model to analyze how one variable (the dependent variable y) is related to another interval variable (the independent variable x). The restriction of using only one independent variable was motivated by the need to simplify the introduction to regression analysis. Although there are a number of applications where we purposely develop a model with only one independent variable, in general we prefer to include as many independent variables as are believed to affect the dependent variable. Arbitrarily limiting the number of independent variables also limits the usefulness of the model.

In this chapter, we allow for any number of independent variables. In so doing, we expect to develop models that fit the data better than would a simple linear regression model.

17-1) Model and Required Conditions

We now assume that k independent variables are potentially related to the dependent variable. Thus, the model is represented by the following equation:

$$y = \beta_0 + \beta_1 x_1 + \beta_2 x_2 + \cdots + \beta_k x_k + \varepsilon$$

where y is the dependent variable, $x_1, x_2, \ldots, x_k$ are the independent variables, $\beta_0, \beta_1, \ldots, \beta_k$ are the coefficients, and ε is the error variable. The error variable is retained because, even though we have included additional independent variables, deviations between predicted values of y and

actual values of y will still occur. Incidentally, when there is more than one independent variable in the regression model, we refer to the graphical depiction of the equation as a **response surface** rather than as a straight line. Figure 17.1 depicts a scatter diagram of a response surface with $k = 2$. (When $k = 2$, the regression equation creates a plane.) Of course, whenever k is greater than 2, we can only imagine the response surface; we cannot draw it.

Figure 17.1 Scatter Diagram and Response Surface with $k = 2$

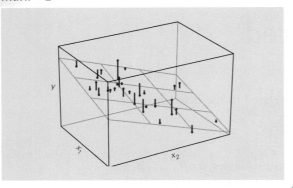

An important part of the regression analysis comprises several statistical techniques that evaluate how well the model fits the data. These techniques require the following conditions, which we introduced in the previous chapter.

Required Conditions for Error Variable

1. The probability distribution of the error variable ε is normal.

2. The mean of the error variable is 0.

3. The standard deviation of ε is σ_ε, which is a constant.

4. The errors are independent.

17-2 Estimating the Coefficients and Assessing the Model

The multiple regression equation is expressed similarly to the simple regression equation. The general form is

$$\hat{y} = b_0 + b_1 x_1 + b_2 x_2 + \cdots + b_k x_k$$

where k is the number of independent variables.

The procedures introduced in Chapter 16 are extended to the multiple regression model. However, in Chapter 16, we first discussed how to interpret the coefficients and then discussed how to assess the model's fit. In practice, we reverse the process—that is, the first step is to determine how well the model fits. If the model's fit is poor, there is no point in a further analysis of the coefficients of that model. Improving the model is of much higher priority. Here is how a regression analysis is performed. The steps we use are as follows:

1. Select variables that you believe are linearly related to the dependent variable.

2. Use a computer and software to generate the coefficients and the statistics used to assess the model.

3. Diagnose violations of required conditions. If there are problems, attempt to remedy them.

4. Assess the model's fit. Three statistics that perform this function are the standard error of estimate, the coefficient of determination, and the *F*-test of the analysis of variance. The first two were introduced in Chapter 16; the third will be introduced here.

5. If we are satisfied with the model's fit and that the required conditions are met, we can interpret the coefficients and test them as we did in Chapter 16. We use the model to predict a value of the dependent variable or estimate the expected value of the dependent variable.

We'll illustrate the procedure with the chapter-opening example.

17-2a Step 1: Select the Independent Variables

Here are the variables we believe may be linearly related to income.

Age (AGE): For most people, income increases with age.

Years of education (EDUC): We've already shown that education is linearly related to income.

Hours of work per week (HRS1): Obviously, more hours of work should equal more income.

Spouse's hours of work (SPHRS1): It is possible that if one's spouse works more and earns more, the other spouse may choose to work less and thus earn less.

Number of family members earning money (EARNRS): As is the case with SPHRS1, if more family members earn income, there may be less pressure on the respondent to work harder.

Number of children (CHILDS): Children are expensive, which may encourage their parents to work harder and thus earn more.

You may be wondering why we don't simply include all the interval variables that are available to us. There are three reasons. First, the objective is to determine whether our hypothesized model is valid and whether the independent variables in the model are linearly related to the dependent variable. In other words, we should screen the independent variables and include only those that, in theory, affect the dependent variable.

Second, by including large numbers of independent variables, we increase the probability of Type I errors. For example, if we include 100 independent variables, none of which are related to the dependent variable, we're likely to conclude that 5 of them are linearly related to the dependent variable. This is a problem we discussed in Chapter 14.

Third, because of a problem called *multicollinearity* (described in Section 17-3) we may conclude that none of the independent variables are linearly related to the dependent variable when, in fact, one or more are.

17-2b Step 2: Use a Computer to Compute All the Coefficients and Other Statistics

Excel

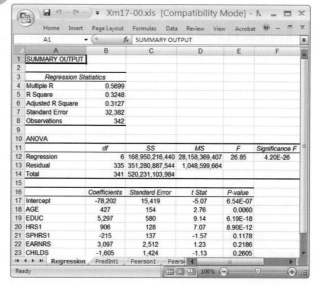

INSTRUCTIONS

1. Type or import the data so that the independent variables are in adjacent columns. Note that all rows with blanks (missing data) must be deleted.

2. Click **Data**, **Data Analysis**, and **Regression**.

3. Specify the **Input Y Range**, the **Input X Range**, and a value for $\alpha(.05)$.

Minitab

Regression Analysis: Income versus AGE, EDUC, . . .

```
The regression equation is
Income = −78202 + 427 AGE + 5297 EDUC + 906 HRS1
          − 215 SPHRS1 + 3097 EARNRS − 1605 CHILDS
```

Predictor	Coef	SE Coef	T	P
Constant	−78202	15419	−5.07	0.000
AGE	426.6	154.3	2.76	0.006
EDUC	5296.9	579.6	9.14	0.000
HRS1	906.0	128.1	7.07	0.000
SPHRS1	−215.1	137.2	−1.57	0.118
EARNRS	3097	2512	1.23	0.219
CHILDS	−1605	1424	−1.13	0.261

S = 32382.1   R-Sq = 32.5%   R-Sq(adj) = 31.3%

Analysis of Variance

Source	DF	SS	MS	F	P
Regression	6	1.68950E+11	28158369407	26.85	0.000
Residual					
Error	335	3.51281E+11	1048599664		
Total	341	5.20231E+11			

1. Click **Stat**, **Regression**, and **Regression.** . . . .

2. Specify the dependent variable in the **Response** box and the independent variables in the **Predictors** box.

INTERPRET

The regression model is estimated by

$$\hat{y}(\text{INCOME}) = -78{,}202 + 427 \text{ AGE}$$
$$+ 5297 \text{ EDUC} + 906 \text{ HRS}$$
$$- 215 \text{ SPHRS1} + 3097 \text{ EARNRS}$$
$$- 1605 \text{ CHILDS}$$

We assess the model in three ways: the standard error of estimate, the coefficient of determination (both introduced in Chapter 16), and the *F*-test of the analysis of variance (presented subsequently).

17-2c Standard Error of Estimate

Recall that σ_ε is the standard deviation of the error variable ε and that, because σ_ε is a population parameter, it is necessary to estimate its value by using s_ε. In multiple regression, the standard error of estimate is defined as follows. (Note that when $k = 1$ the formula is the one defined in Chapter 16.)

Standard Error of Estimate

$$s_\varepsilon = \sqrt{\frac{\text{SSE}}{n - k - 1}}$$

where *n* is the sample size and *k* is the number of independent variables in the model.

As we noted in Chapter 16, each of our software packages reports the standard error of estimate in a different way.

Excel

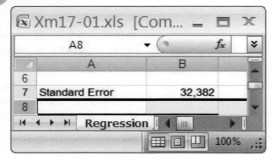

Minitab

`S = 32382.1`

INTERPRET

Recall that we judge the magnitude of the standard error of estimate relative to the values of the dependent variable, and particularly to the mean of *y*. In this example, $\bar{y} = 49{,}417$ (not shown in printouts). It appears that the standard error of estimate is quite large.

17-2d Coefficient of Determination

Recall from Chapter 16 that the coefficient of determination is defined as

$$R^2 = 1 - \frac{\text{SSE}}{\Sigma(y_i - \bar{y})^2}$$

Excel

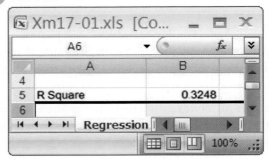

Minitab

`R-Sq = 32.5%`

INTERPRET

This means that 32.48% of the total variation in income is explained by the variation in the six independent variables, whereas 67.52% remains unexplained.

17-2e Testing the Validity of the Model

In the simple linear regression model, we tested the slope coefficient to determine whether sufficient evidence existed to allow us to conclude that there was a linear relationship between the independent variable and the dependent variable. However, because there is only one independent variable in that model, that same *t*-test was used to determine whether that model is valid. When there is more than one independent variable, we need another method to test the overall validity of the model. The technique is a version of the analysis of variance, which we introduced in Chapter 14.

To test the validity of the regression model, we specify the following hypotheses:

$H_0: \beta_1 = \beta_2 = \cdots = \beta_k = 0$

$H_1:$ At least one β_i is not equal to 0.

Table 17.1 Analysis of Variance Table for Regression Analysis

Source of Variation	Degrees of Freedom	Sums of Squares	Mean Squares	F-Statistic
Regression	k	SSR	$MSR = SSR/k$	$F = MSR/MSE$
Residual	$n - k - 1$	SSE	$MSE = SSE/(n - k - 1)$	
Total	$n - 1$	$\Sigma(y_i - \bar{y})^2$		

If the null hypothesis is true, then none of the independent variables $x_1, x_2, \ldots, x_k$ is linearly related to y, and therefore the model is invalid. If at least one β_i is not equal to 0, the model does have some validity.

When we discussed the coefficient of determination in Chapter 16, we noted that the total variation in the dependent variable [measured by $\Sigma(y_i - \bar{y})^2$] can be decomposed into two parts: the explained variation (measured by SSR) and the unexplained variation (measured by SSE); that is,

Total Variation in y = SSR + SSE

Furthermore, we established that, if SSR is large relative to SSE, the coefficient of determination will be high, signifying a good model. On the other hand, if SSE is large, most of the variation will be unexplained, which indicates that the model provides a poor fit and consequently has little validity.

The test statistic is the same one we encountered in Section 14-1, where we tested for the equivalence of two or more population means. To judge whether SSR is large enough relative to SSE to allow us to infer that at least one coefficient is not equal to 0, we compute the ratio of the two mean squares. (Recall that the mean square is the sum of squares divided by its degrees of freedom; recall, too, that the ratio of two mean squares is F distributed as long as the underlying population is normal, a required condition for this application.) The calculation of the test statistic is summarized in an analysis of variance (ANOVA) table, whose general form appears in Table 17.1. The Excel and Minitab ANOVA tables are shown next.

Excel

Minitab

Analysis of Variance

Source	DF	SS	MS	F	P
Regression	6	1.68950E+11	28158369407	26.85	0.000
Residual					
Error	335	3.51281E+11	1048599664		
Total	341	5.20231E+11			

A large value of F indicates that most of the variation in y is explained by the regression equation and that the model is valid. A small value of F indicates that most of the variation in y is unexplained. The rejection region allows us to determine whether F is large enough to justify rejecting the null hypothesis. For this test, the rejection region is

$$F > F_{\alpha, k, n-k-1}$$

In Example 17.1, the rejection region (assuming $\alpha = .05$) is

$$F > F_{\alpha, k, n-k-1} = F_{.05, 6, 335} \approx 2.21$$

As you can see from the printout, $F = 26.85$. The printout also includes the p-value of the test, which is 0. Obviously, there is a great deal of evidence to infer that the model is valid.

17-2f Interpreting the Coefficients

The coefficients $b_0, b_1, \ldots, b_k$ describe the relationship between each of the independent variables and the dependent variable in the sample. We need to use inferential methods (described below) to draw conclusions about the population. In our example, the sample consists of the 341 observations. The population is composed of all American adults.

Intercept

The intercept is $b_0 = -78,202$. This is the average income when all the independent variables are zero.

As we observed in Chapter 16, it is often misleading to try to interpret this value, particularly if 0 is outside the range of the values of the independent variables (as is the case here).

Age

The relationship between income and age is described by $b_1 = 427$. From this number, we learn that, in this model, for each additional year of age, income increases on average by $427, assuming that the other independent variables in this model are held constant.

Education

The coefficient $b_2 = 5,297$ specifies that, in this sample, for each additional year of education, the income increases on average by $5,297, assuming the constancy of the other independent variables.

Hours of Work

The relationship between hours of work per week is expressed by $b_3 = 906$. We interpret this number as the average increase in annual income for each additional hour of work per week, keeping the other independent variables fixed in this sample.

Spouse's Hours of Work

The relationship between annual income and a spouse's hours of work per week is described in this sample: $b_4 = -215$, which we interpret to mean that for each additional hour a spouse works per week income decreases on average by $215 when the other variables are constant.

Number of Family Members Earning Income

In this data set, the relationship between annual income and the number of family members who earn money is expressed by $b_5 = 3,097$, which tells us that for each additional family member earner, annual income increases on average by $3,097, assuming that the other independent variables are constant.

Number of Children

The relationship between annual income and number of children is expressed by $b_6 = -1,605$, which tells us that in this sample for each additional child annual income decreases on average by $1,605 keeping the other variables constant.

© Gladskikh Tatiana/Shutterstock

17-2g Testing the Coefficients

In Chapter 16, we described how to test to determine whether there is sufficient evidence to infer that in the simple linear regression model x and y are linearly related. The null and alternative hypotheses were

$$H_0: \beta_1 = 0$$
$$H_1: \beta_1 \neq 0$$

The test statistic was

$$t = \frac{b_1 - \beta_1}{s_{b_1}}$$

which is Student t distributed with $\nu = n - 2$ degrees of freedom.

In the multiple regression model, we have more than one independent variable. For each such variable, we can test to determine whether there is enough evidence of a linear relationship between it and the dependent variable for the entire population when the other independent variables are included in the model.

Testing the Coefficients

$$H_0: \beta_i = 0$$
$$H_1: \beta_i \neq 0$$

(for $i = 1, 2, \ldots, k$); the test statistic is

$$t = \frac{b_i - \beta_i}{s_{b_i}}$$

which is Student t distributed with $\nu = n - k - 1$ degrees of freedom.

To illustrate, we test each of the coefficients in the multiple regression model in the chapter-opening example. The tests that follow are performed just as all other tests in this book have been performed. We set up the null and alternative hypotheses, identify the test statistic, and use the computer to calculate the value of the test statistic and its p-value. For each independent variable, we test ($i = 1, 2, 3, 4, 5, 6$)

$$H_0: \beta_i = 0$$
$$H_1: \beta_i \neq 0$$

Refer to page 279 and examine the computer output. The output includes the t-tests of β_i. The results of these tests pertain to the entire population of the United States in 2012. Note that these test results were determined when the other independent variables were included in the model. We add this statement because a simple linear regression will very likely result in different values of the test statistics and possibly the conclusion.

Test of β_1 (coefficient of age)

Value of the test statistic: $t = 2.76$; p-value $= .0060$

Test of β_2 (coefficient of education)

Value of the test statistic: $t = 9.14$; p-value $= 0$

Test of β_3 (coefficient of number of hours of work per week)

Value of the test statistic: $t = 7.07$; p-value $= 0$

Test of β_4 (coefficient of spouse's number of hours of work per week)

Value of the test statistic: $t = -1.57$; p-value $= .1178$

Test of β_5 (coefficient of number of earners in family)

Value of the test statistic: $t = 1.23$; p-value $= .2186$

Test of β_6 (coefficient of number of children)

Value of the test statistic: $t = -1.13$; p-value $= .2605$

There is sufficient evidence at the 5% significance level to infer that each of the following variables is linearly related to income:

Age

Education

Number of hours of work per week

In this model, there is not enough evidence to conclude that each of the following variables is linearly related to income:

Spouse's number of hours of work per week

Number of earners in the family

Number of children

Note that this may mean that there is no evidence of a linear relationship between these three independent variables and income. However, it may also mean that there is a linear relationship, but because of a condition called *multicollinearity*, the t-tests revealed no linear relationship. We will discuss multicollinearity in Section 17-3.

17-2h A Cautionary Note about Interpreting the Results

Care should be taken when interpreting the results of this and other regression analyses. We might find that in one model there is enough evidence to conclude that a particular independent variable is linearly related to the dependent variable, but that in another model no such evidence exists. Consequently, whenever a particular t-test is *not* significant, we state that there is not enough evidence to infer that the independent and dependent variable are linearly related *in this model*. The implication is that another model may yield different conclusions.

Furthermore, if one or more of the required conditions are violated, the results may be invalid. In Section 17-3, we will introduce the procedures that allow the statistics practitioner to examine the model's requirements. We also remind you that it is dangerous to extrapolate far outside the range of the observed values of the independent variables.

17-2i Using the Regression Equation

As was the case with simple linear regression, we can use the multiple regression equation in two ways: we can produce the prediction interval for a particular value of y, and we can produce the confidence interval estimate of the expected value of y. Like the other calculations associated with multiple regression, we call on the computer to do the work.

To illustrate, we'll predict the income of a 50-year old, with 12 years of education, who works 40 hours per week, whose spouse also works 40 hours per week, who has 2 earners in the family, and who has 2 children.

Excel

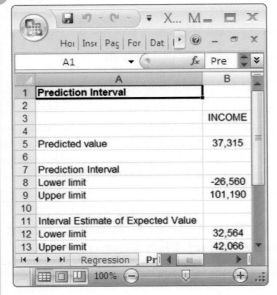

	A	B
1	Prediction Interval	
2		
3		INCOME
4		
5	Predicted value	37,315
6		
7	Prediction Interval	
8	Lower limit	-26,560
9	Upper limit	101,190
10		
11	Interval Estimate of Expected Value	
12	Lower limit	32,564
13	Upper limit	42,066

INSTRUCTIONS
See the instructions on page 271. In cells B343 to G343, we input the values 50 12 40 40 2 2, respectively. We specified 95% confidence.

Minitab
```
Predicted Values for New Observations
New
Obs   Fit    SE Fit     95% CI           95% PI
 1   37315   2415   (32564, 42066)   (-26560, 101190)

Values of Predictors for New Observations

New
Obs  AGE  EDUC  HRS  SPHRS  PRESTG80  CHILDS  EARNRS  CUREMPYR
 1  50.0  12.0  40.0  40.0    50.0     2.00    2.00     5.00
```

INSTRUCTIONS
See the instructions on page 271. We input the values 50 12 40 40 2 2. We specified 95% confidence.

INTERPRET
The prediction interval is $-25,560$, $101,190$. It is so wide as to be completely useless. To be useful in predicting values, the model must be considerably better. The confidence interval estimate of the expected income of the population we're addressing is 32,564, 42,066.

17-3 Regression Diagnostics

In Section 17-1, we described the required conditions for the validity of regression analysis. Simply put, the error variable must be normally distributed with a constant variance, and the errors must be independent of each other. In this section, we show how to diagnose violations.

17-3a Residual Analysis
Most departures from required conditions can be diagnosed by examining the residuals. Most computer packages allow you to output the values of the residuals and apply various graphical and statistical techniques to this variable.

We can also compute the standardized residuals. We standardize residuals in the same way we standardize all variables: by subtracting the mean and dividing by the standard deviation. The mean of the residuals is 0; because the standard deviation σ_ε is unknown, we must estimate its value. The simplest estimate is the standard error of estimate s_ε. Thus,

$$\text{Standardized residuals for point } i = \frac{e_i}{s_\varepsilon}$$

Excel
Excel calculates the standardized residuals by dividing the residuals by the standard deviation of the residuals. (The difference between the standard error of estimate and the standard deviation of the residuals is that in the formula of the former the denominator is $n - 2$, whereas in the formula for the latter, the denominator is $n - 1$.)

Part of the printout (we show only the first five and last five values) for the chapter-opening example follows.

	A	B	C	D
29	Observation	Predicted INCOME	Residuals	Standard Residuals
30	1	53141.84	14358.16	0.45
31	2	56369.07	43630.93	1.36
32	3	45555.81	-555.81	-0.02
33	4	63347.63	36652.37	1.14
34	5	51034.90	48965.10	1.53
35				
36				
369	338	46111.25	-1111.25	-0.03
370	339	72111.47	27888.53	0.87
371	340	97215.95	-52215.95	-1.63
372	341	85093.19	-17593.19	-0.55
373	342	47951.89	7048.11	0.22

Proceed with the three steps of regression analysis described on page 279. Before clicking **OK**, select **Residuals** and **Standardized Residuals**. The predicted values, residuals, and standardized residuals will be printed.

We can also standardize by computing the standard deviation of each residual. Statisticians have determined that the standard deviation of the residual for observation i is defined as follows.

Standard Deviation of the ith Residual

$$s_{r_i} = s_\varepsilon \sqrt{1 - h_i}$$

where

$$h_i = \frac{1}{n} + \frac{(x_i - \bar{x})^2}{(n-1)s_x^2}$$

The quantity h_i should look familiar; it was used in the formula for the prediction interval and confidence interval estimate of the expected value of y in Section 16-5. Minitab computes this version of the standardized residuals. Part of the printout (we show only the first five and last five values) for the chapter-opening example is shown below.

Minitab

Obs	AGE	INCOME	Fit	SE Fit	Residual	St Resid
1	54.0	67500	53142	3044	14358	0.45
2	45.0	100000	56369	2075	43631	1.35
3	42.0	45000	45556	3517	-556	-0.02
4	29.0	100000	63348	4136	36652	1.14
5	42.0	100000	51035	2275	48965	1.52
338	60.0	45000	46111	3258	-1111	-0.03
339	36.0	100000	72111	4578	27889	0.87
340	50.0	45000	97216	4794	-52216	-1.63
341	65.0	67500	85093	5123	-17593	-0.55
342	48.0	55000	47952	4866	7048	0.22

Proceed with the three steps of regression analysis as described on page 280. After specifying the **Response** and **Predictors**, click **Results . . .** , and **In addition, the full table of fits and residuals**.

The predicted values, residuals, and standardized residuals will be printed.

An analysis of the residuals will allow us to determine whether the error variable is nonnormal and whether the error variance is constant. We begin with nonnormality.

17-3b Nonnormality

As we've done throughout this book, we check for normality by drawing the histogram of the residuals. Figure 17.2 is Excel's version (Minitab's is similar). As you can see, the histogram is bell shaped, leading us to believe that the error is normally distributed.

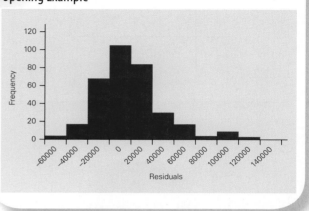

Figure 17.2 **Histogram of Residuals for Chapter-Opening Example**

17-3c Heteroscedasticity

The variance of the error variable σ_ε^2 is required to be constant. When this requirement is violated, the condition is called **heteroscedasticity**. (You can impress friends and relatives by using this term. If you can't pronounce it, try **homoscedasticity**, which refers to the condition where the requirement is satisfied.) One method of diagnosing heteroscedasticity is to plot the residuals against the predicted values of y. We then look for a change in the spread of the plotted points. Figure 17.3 describes such a situation. Notice that in this illustration, σ_ε^2 appears to be small when $\hat{y}$ is small and large when $\hat{y}$ is large. Of course, many other patterns could be used to depict this problem.

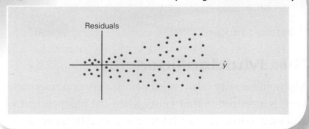

Figure 17.3 **Plot of Residuals Depicting Heteroscedasticity**

Figure 17.4 illustrates a case in which σ_ε^2 is constant. As a result, there is no apparent change in the variation of the residuals. Excel's plot of the residuals versus the predicted values of y for the chapter opening example is shown in Figure 17.5. There may be a problem in this example. It appears that the variance of the residuals increases for larger values of the predicted value. The methods used to fix the problem are beyond the level of this book.

Figure 17.4 Plot of Residuals Depicting Homoscedasticity

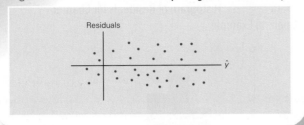

© Cengage Learning

Figure 17.5 Plot of Predicted Values versus Residuals for Chapter-Opening Example

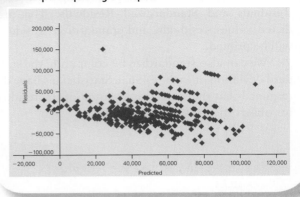

© Cengage Learning

© Layland Masuda/Shutterstock.com

17-3d Multicollinearity

Multicollinearity (also called *collinearity* and *intercorrelation*) is a condition that exists when the independent variables are correlated with one another. The adverse effect of multicollinearity is that the estimated regression coefficients of the independent variables that are correlated tend to have large sampling errors. There are two consequences of multicollinearity. First, because the variability of the coefficients is large, the sample coefficient may be far from

the actual population parameter, including the possibility that the statistic and parameter may have opposite signs. Second, when the coefficients are tested, the *t*-statistics will be small, which leads to the inference that there is no linear relationship between the affected independent variables and the dependent variable. In some cases, this inference will be wrong. Fortunately, multicollinearity does not affect the *F*-test of the analysis of variance.

Consider the chapter-opening example where we found that the number of children in the family not statistically significant at the 5% significance level. However, when we tested the coefficient of correlation between income and number of children, we found it to be statistically significant. The Excel printout follows. How do we explain the appare nt contradiction between the multiple regression *t*-test of the coefficient of the number of children and the result of the *t*-test of the correlation coefficients? The answer is multicollinearity.

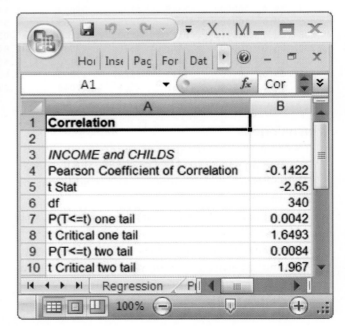

	A	B
1	**Correlation**	
2		
3	*INCOME and CHILDS*	
4	Pearson Coefficient of Correlation	-0.1422
5	t Stat	-2.65
6	df	340
7	P(T<=t) one tail	0.0042
8	t Critical one tail	1.6493
9	P(T<=t) two tail	0.0084
10	t Critical two tail	1.967

There is a relatively high degree of correlation between number of family members who earn income and number of children. The result of the *t*-test of the correlation between number of earners and number of children is shown next. The result should not be surprising since more earners in a family are very likely children.

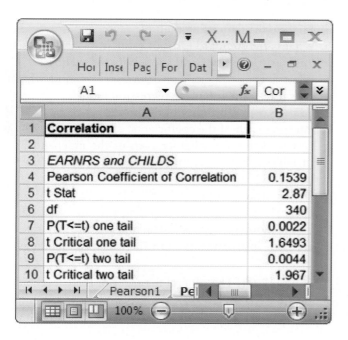

Multicollinearity affected the result of the multiple regression *t*-test so that it appeared that number of children is not significantly related to income, when in fact it is.

Another problem caused by multicollinearity is the interpretation of the coefficients. We interpret the coefficients as measuring the change in the dependent variable when the corresponding independent variable increases by one unit while all the other independent variables are held constant. This interpretation may be impossible when the independent variables are highly correlated, because when the independent variable increases by one unit, some or all of the other independent variables will change.

This raises two important questions for the statistics practitioner. First, how do we recognize the problem of multicollinearity when it occurs? Second, how do we avoid or correct it?

Multicollinearity exists in virtually all multiple regression models. In fact, finding two completely uncorrelated variables is rare. The problem becomes serious, however, only when two or more independent variables are highly correlated. Unfortunately, we do not have a critical value that indicates when the correlation between two independent variables is large enough to cause problems. To complicate the issue, multicollinearity also occurs when a combination of several independent variables is correlated with another independent variable or with a combination of other independent variables. Consequently, even with access to all the correlation coefficients, determining when the multicollinearity problem has reached the serious stage may be extremely difficult. A good indicator of the problem is a large *F*-statistic but small *t*-statistics.

Minimizing the effect of multicollinearity is often easier than correcting it. The statistics practitioner must try to include independent variables that are independent of each other.

EXERCISES

The following exercises require the use of a computer and statistical software. Exercises 17.1–17.4 can be solved manually (except for the prediction intervals). See Appendix A for the sample statistics. Use a 5% significance level.

17.1 [Xr17-01] A developer who specializes in summer cottage properties is considering purchasing a large tract of land adjoining a lake. The current owner of the tract has already subdivided the land into separate building lots and has prepared the lots by removing some of the trees. The developer wants to forecast the value of each lot. From previous experience, she knows that the most important factors affecting the price of the lot are size, number of mature trees, and distance to the lake. From a nearby area, she gathers the relevant data for 60 recently sold lots.

a. Find the regression equation.
b. What is the standard error of estimate? Interpret its value.
c. What is the coefficient of determination? What does this statistic tell you?
d. Test the validity of the model. What does the *p*-value of the test statistic tell you?
e. Interpret each of the coefficients.
f. Test to determine whether each of the independent variables is linearly related to the price of the lot in this model.

g. Predict with 90% confidence the selling price of a 40,000-square-foot lot that has 50 mature trees and is 25 feet from the lake.

h. Estimate with 90% confidence the average selling price of 50,000-square-foot lots that have 10 mature trees and are 75 feet from the lake.

17.2 [Xr17-02] Pat Statsdud, a student who ranks near the bottom of the statistics class, decided that a certain amount of studying could actually improve final grades. However, too much studying would not be warranted, because Pat's ambition (if that's what one could call it) was to ultimately graduate with the absolute minimum level of work. Pat was registered in a statistics course, which had only 3 weeks to go before the final exam and in which the final grade was determined in the following way:

Total mark = 20% (assignment)
+ 30% (midterm test) + 50% (final exam)

To determine how much work to do in the remaining 3 weeks, Pat needed to be able to predict the final exam mark on the basis of the assignment mark (worth 20 points) and the midterm mark (worth 30 points). Pat's marks on these were 12/20 and 14/30, respectively. Accordingly, Pat undertook the following analysis. The final exam mark, assignment mark, and midterm test mark for 30 students who took the statistics course last year were collected.

a. Determine the regression equation.

b. What is the standard error of estimate? Briefly describe how you interpret this statistic.

c. What is the coefficient of determination? What does this statistic tell you?

d. Test the validity of the model.

e. Interpret each of the coefficients.

f. Can Pat infer that the assignment mark is linearly related to the final grade in this model?

g. Can Pat infer that the midterm mark is linearly related to the final grade in this model?

h. Predict Pat's final exam mark with 95% confidence.

i. Predict Pat's final grade with 95% confidence.

17.3 [Xr17-03] The president of a company that manufactures drywall wants to analyze the variables that affect demand for his product. Drywall is used to construct walls in houses and offices. Consequently, the president decides to develop a regression model in which the dependent variable is monthly sales of drywall (in hundreds of 4 × 8 sheets) and the independent variables are:

number of building permits issued in the county, 5-year mortgage rates (in percentage points), vacancy rate in apartments (in percentage points), and vacancy rate in office buildings (in percentage points).

To estimate a multiple regression model, he took monthly observations from the past 2 years.

a. Analyze the data using multiple regression.

b. What is the standard error of estimate? Can you use this statistic to assess the model's fit? If so, how?

c. What is the coefficient of determination, and what does it tell you about the regression model?

d. Test the overall validity of the model.

e. Interpret each of the coefficients.

f. Test to determine whether each of the independent variables is linearly related to drywall demand in this model.

g. Predict next month's drywall sales with 95% confidence if the number of building permits is 50, the 5-year mortgage rate is 9.0%, and the vacancy rates are 3.6% in apartments and 14.3% in office buildings.

17.4 [Xr17-04] The general manager of the Cleveland Indians baseball team is in the process of determining which minor-league players to draft. He is aware that his team needs home-run hitters and would like to find a way to predict the number of home runs a player will hit. Being an astute statistician, he gathers a random sample of players and records the number of home runs each player hit in his first two full years as a major-league player, the number of home runs he hit in his last full year in the minor leagues, his age, and the number of years of professional baseball.

a. Develop a regression model and use a software package to produce the statistics.

b. Interpret each of the coefficients.

c. How well does the model fit?

d. Test the model's validity.

e. Do each of the independent variables belong in the model?

f. Calculate the 95% interval of the number of home runs in the first two years of a player who is 25 years old, has played professional baseball for 7 years, and hit 22 home runs in his last year in the minor leagues.

g. Calculate the 95% interval of the expected number of home runs in the first two years of players who are 27 years old, have played professional baseball for 5 years, and hit 18 home runs in their last year in the minors.

17.5 [Xr17-05] When one company buys another company, it is not unusual that some workers are terminated. The severance benefits offered to the laid-off workers are often the subject of dispute. Suppose that the Laurier Company recently bought the Western Company and subsequently terminated 20 of Western's employees. As part of the buyout agreement, it was promised that the severance packages offered to the former Western employees would be equivalent to those offered to Laurier employees who had been terminated in the past year. Thirty-six-year-old Bill Smith, a Western employee for the past 10 years, earning $32,000 per year, was one of those let go. His severance package included an offer of 5 weeks' severance pay. Bill complained that this offer was less than that offered to Laurier's employees when they were laid off, in contravention of the buyout agreement. A statistician was called in to settle the dispute. The statistician was told that severance is determined by three factors: age, length of service with the company, and pay. To determine how generous the severance package had been, a random sample of 50 Laurier ex-employees was taken. For each, the following variables were recorded:

> Number of weeks of severance pay
> Age of employee
> Number of years with the company
> Annual pay (in thousands of dollars)

a. Determine the regression equation.

b. Comment on how well the model fits the data.

c. Do all the independent variables belong in the equation? Explain.

d. Perform an analysis to determine whether Bill is correct in his assessment of the severance package.

17.6 [Xr17-06] The admissions officer of a university is trying to develop a formal system of deciding which students to admit to the university. She believes that determinants of success include the standard variables: high school grades and SAT scores. However, she also believes that students who have participated in extracurricular activities are more likely to succeed than those who have not. To investigate the issue, she randomly sampled 100 fourth-year students and recorded the following variables:

> GPA for the first 3 years at the university (range: 0 to 12)
> GPA from high school (range: 0 to 12)
> SAT score (range: 400 to 1600)
> Number of hours on average spent per week in organized extracurricular activities in the last year of high school

a. Develop a model that helps the admissions officer decide which students to admit, and use the computer to generate the usual statistics.

b. What is the coefficient of determination? Interpret its value.

c. Test the overall validity of the model.

d. Test to determine whether each of the independent variables is linearly related to the dependent variable in this model.

e. Determine the 95% interval of the GPA for the first 3 years of university for a student whose high school GPA is 10, whose SAT score is 1200, and who worked an average of 2 hours per week on organized extracurricular activities in the last year of high school.

f. Find the 90% interval of the mean GPA for the first 3 years of university for all students whose high school GPA is 8, whose SAT score is 1100, and who worked an average of 10 hours per week on organized extracurricular activities in the last year of high school.

17.7 [Xr17-07] The marketing manager for a chain of hardware stores needed more information about the effectiveness of the three types of advertising that the chain used. These are localized direct mailing (in which flyers describing sales and featured products are distributed to homes in the area surrounding a store), newspaper advertising, and local television advertisements. To determine which type is most effective, the manager collected 1 week's data from 100 randomly selected stores. For each store, the following variables were recorded:

> Weekly gross sales
> Weekly expenditures on direct mailing
> Weekly expenditures on newspaper advertising
> Weekly expenditures on television commercials

All variables were recorded in thousands of dollars.

a. Find the regression equation.

b. What is the coefficient of determination? What does this statistic tell you about the regression equation?

c. What does the standard error of estimate tell you about the regression model?

d. Test the validity of the model.

e. Which independent variables are linearly related to weekly gross sales in this model? Explain.

f. Compute the 95% interval of the week's gross sales if a local store spent $800 on direct mailing, $1,200 on newspaper advertisements, and $2,000 on television commercials.

g. Calculate the 95% interval of the mean weekly gross sales for all stores that spend $800 on direct mailing, $1,200 on newspaper advertising, and $2,000 on television commercials.

h. Discuss the difference between the two intervals found in parts (f) and (g).

17.8 [Xr17-08] For many cities around the world, garbage is an increasing problem. Many North American cities have virtually run out of space to dump their garbage. A consultant for a large American city decided to gather data about the problem. She took a random sample of houses and determined the following:

> Y = the amount of garbage per average week (pounds)
> X_1 = size of the house (square feet)
> X_2 = number of children
> X_3 = number of adults who are usually home during the day

a. Conduct a regression analysis.
b. Is the model valid?
c. Interpret each of the coefficients.
d. Test to determine whether each of the independent variables is linearly related to the dependent variable.

17.9 [Xr17-09] The administrator of a school board in a large county was analyzing the average mathematics test scores in the schools under her control. She noticed that there were dramatic differences in scores among the schools. In an attempt to improve the scores of all the schools, she attempted to determine the factors that account for the differences. Accordingly, she took a random sample of 40 schools across the county and, for each, determined the mean test score last year, the percentage of teachers in each school who have at least one university degree in mathematics, the mean age, and the mean annual income (in $thousands) of the mathematics teachers.

a. Conduct a regression analysis to develop the equation.
b. Is the model valid?
c. Interpret and test the coefficients.
d. Predict with 95% confidence the test score at a school where 50% of the mathematics teachers have mathematics degrees, the mean age is 43, and the mean annual income is $48,300.

17.10 [Xr17-10] Life insurance companies are keenly interested in predicting how long their customers will live, because their premiums and profitability depend on such numbers. An actuary for one insurance company gathered data from 100 recently deceased male customers. He recorded the age at death of the customer plus the ages at death of his mother and father, the mean ages at death of his grandmothers, and the mean ages at death of his grandfathers.

a. Perform a multiple regression analysis on these data.
b. Is the model valid?
c. Interpret and test the coefficients.
d. Determine the 95% interval of the longevity of a man whose parents lived to the age of 70, whose grandmothers averaged 80 years, and whose grandfathers averaged 75 years.
e. Find the 95% interval of the mean longevity of men whose mothers lived to 75 years, whose fathers lived to 65 years, whose grandmothers averaged 85 years, and whose grandfathers averaged 75 years.

17.11 [Xr17-11] University students often complain that universities reward professors for research but not for teaching, and they argue that professors react to this situation by devoting more time and energy to the publication of their findings and less time and energy to classroom activities. Professors counter that research and teaching go hand in hand: more research makes better teachers. A student organization at one university decided to investigate the issue. It randomly selected 50 economics professors who are employed by a multicampus university. The students recorded the salaries (in $thousands) of the professors, their average teaching evaluations (on a 10-point scale), and the total number of journal articles published in their careers. Perform a complete analysis (produce the regression equation, assess it, and report your findings).

17.12 [Xr17-12] One critical factor that determines the success of a catalog store chain is the availability of products that consumers want to buy. If a store is sold out, then future sales to that customer are less likely. Accordingly, delivery trucks operating from a central warehouse regularly resupply stores. In an analysis of a chain's operations, the general manager wanted to determine the factors that are related to how long it takes to unload delivery trucks. A random sample of 50 deliveries to one store was observed. The times (in minutes) to unload the truck, the total number of boxes, and the total weight (in hundreds of pounds) of the boxes were recorded.

a. Determine the multiple regression equation.
b. How well does the model fit the data? Explain.
c. Interpret and test the coefficients.
d. Produce a 95% interval of the amount of time needed to unload a truck with 100 boxes weighing 5,000 pounds.

e. Produce a 95% interval of the average amount of time needed to unload trucks with 100 boxes weighing 5,000 pounds.

17.13 [Xr17-13] Lotteries have become important sources of revenue for governments. Many people have criticized lotteries, however, referring to them as a tax on the poor and uneducated. In an examination of the issue, a random sample of 100 adults was asked how much they spend on lottery tickets and about various socioeconomic variables. The purpose of this study is to test the following beliefs:

1. Relatively uneducated people spend more on lotteries than do relatively educated people.
2. Older people buy more lottery tickets than younger people.
3. People with more children spend more on lotteries than people with fewer children.
4. Relatively poor people spend a greater proportion of their income on lotteries than relatively rich people.

The following data were recorded:

> Amount spent on lottery tickets as a percentage of total household income
> Number of years of education
> Age
> Number of children
> Personal income (in thousands of dollars)

a. Develop the multiple regression equation.
b. Is the model valid?
c. Test each of the beliefs. What conclusions can you draw?

17.14 [Xr17-14] The MBA program at a large university is facing a pleasant problem: too many applicants. The current admissions policy requires students to have completed at least 3 years of work experience and an undergraduate degree with a B– average or better. Until 3 years ago, the school admitted any applicant who met these requirements. However, because the program recently converted from a 2-year program (four semesters) to a 1-year program (three semesters), the number of applicants has increased substantially. The dean, who teaches statistics courses, wants to raise the admissions standards by developing a method that more accurately predicts how well an applicant will perform in the MBA program. She believes that the primary determinants of success are the following:

> Undergraduate grade point average (GPA)
> Graduate Management Admissions Test (GMAT) score
> Number of years of work experience

She randomly sampled students who completed the MBA and recorded their MBA program GPA, as well as the three variables listed here.

a. Develop a multiple regression model.
b. Test the model's validity.
c. Test to determine which of the independent variables is linearly related to MBA GPA.

General Social Survey Exercises

17.15 [GSS2012*] How does the amount of education of one's parents (PAEDUC, MAEDUC) affect your education (EDUC)?

a. Develop a regression model.
b. Test the validity of the model.
c. Test the two slope coefficients.
d. Interpret the coefficients.

17.16 [GSS2012*] What determines people's opinion on the following question? Should the government reduce income differences between rich and poor (EQWLTH: 1 = government should reduce differences; 2, 3, 4, 5, 6, 7 = No government action.)

a. Develop a regression analysis using demographic variables education (EDUC), age (AGE), and number of children (CHILDS).
b. Test the model's validity.
c. Test each of the slope coefficients.
d. Interpret the coefficient of determination.

17.17 [GSS2012*] The Nielsen ratings estimate the numbers of televisions tuned to various channels. However, television executives need more information. The General Social Survey may be the source of this information. Respondents were asked to report the number of hours per average day of television viewing (TVHOURS). Conduct a regression analysis using the following independent variables:

> Education (EDUC)
> Age (AGE)
> Hours of work (HRS)
> Number of children (CHILDS)
> Number of family members earning money (EARNRS)

a. Test the model's validity.
b. Test each slope coefficient.
c. Determine the coefficient of determination and describe what it tells you.

17.18 [GSS2012*] What determines people's opinion on the following question? Should the government improve the standard of living of poor people (HELPPOOR: 1 = Government act; 2, 3, 4, 5 = People should help themselves)?

a. Develop a regression analysis using demographic variables education (EDUC), age (AGE), and number of children (CHILDS).
b. Test the model's validity.
c. Test each of the slope coefficients.
d. Interpret the coefficient of determination.

17.19 [GSS2008*] Use the General Social Survey of 2008 to undertake a regression analysis of income (INCOME) using the following independent variables:

Age (AGE)
Education (EDUC)
Hours of work per week (HRS)
Spouse's hours of work (SPHRS)
Occupation prestige score (PRESTG80)
Number of children (CHILDS)
Years with current job (YEARSJOB)

a. Test the model's validity.
b. Test each of the slope coefficients.

American National Election Survey Exercises

17.20 [ANES2008*] With voter turnout during presidential elections around 50%, a vital task for politicians is predicting who will actually vote. Develop a regression model to predict intention to vote (DEFINITE) using the following demographic independent variables:

Age (AGE)
Education (EDUC)
Income (INCOME)

a. Determine the regression equation.
b. Test the model's validity.
c. Test to determine whether there is sufficient evidence to infer a linear relationship between the dependent variable and each independent variable.

17.21 [ANES2008*] Does watching news on television or reading newspapers provide indicators of who will vote? Conduct a regression analysis with intention to vote (DEFINITE) as the dependent variable and the following independent variables:

Number of days in previous week watching national news on television (DAYS1)

Number of days in previous week watching local television news in afternoon or early evening (DAYS2)
Number of days in previous week watching local television news in late evening (DAYS3)
Number of days in previous week reading a daily newspaper (DAYS4)
Number of days in previous week reading a daily newspaper on the Internet (DAYS5)
Number of days in previous week listening to news on the radio (DAYS6)

a. Compute the regression equation.
b. Is there enough evidence to conclude that the model is valid?
c. Test each slope coefficient.

17.22 Compute the residuals and the predicted values for the regression analysis in Exercise 17.1.

a. Is the normality requirement violated? Explain.
b. Is the variance of the error variable constant? Explain.

17.23 Calculate the coefficients of correlation for each pair of independent variables in Exercise 17.1. What do these statistics tell you about the independent variables and the t-tests of the coefficients?

17.24 Refer to Exercise 17.2.

a. Determine the residuals and predicted values.
b. Does it appear that the normality requirement is violated? Explain.
c. Is the variance of the error variable constant? Explain.
d. Determine the coefficient of correlation between the assignment mark and the midterm mark. What does this statistic tell you about the t-tests of the coefficients?

17.25 Compute the residuals and predicted values for the regression analysis in Exercise 17.3.

a. Does it appear that the error variable is not normally distributed?
b. Is the variance of the error variable constant?
c. Is multicollinearity a problem?

17.26 Refer to Exercise 17.4. Find the coefficients of correlation of the independent variables.

a. What do these correlations tell you about the independent variables?
b. What do they say about the t-tests of the coefficients?

17.27 Calculate the residuals and predicted values for the regression analysis in Exercise 17.5.

a. Does the error variable appear to be normally distributed?
b. Is the variance of the error variable constant?
c. Is multicollinearity a problem?

17.28 Are the required conditions satisfied in Exercise 17.6?

17.29 Refer to Exercise 17.7.

a. Conduct an analysis of the residuals to determine whether any of the required conditions are violated.
b. Does it appear that multicollinearity is a problem?
c. Identify any observations that should be checked for accuracy.

CHAPTER 18

Review of Statistical Inference

We have completed our presentation of statistical inference. The list of statistical techniques in Table 18.1 and the flowchart in Figure 18.1 now contain all the statistical inference methods presented in this book. Our Web site contains review exercises. Use the flowchart to determine the appropriate technique to use to solve these exercises. Because they were drawn from a wide variety of applications and collectively require the use of all the techniques introduced in this book, they provide the same kind of challenge faced by real statistics practitioners. By attempting to solve these problems, you will be getting realistic exposure to statistical applications. Incidentally, this also provides practice in the approach required to succeed in a statistics course examination. Note: Figure 18.1 includes nonparametric techniques (introduced on our Web site) that are used when the data are ordinal and when the data are interval and the normality requirement is not satisfied. If you have not covered these tests, ignore the entries in the flowchart.

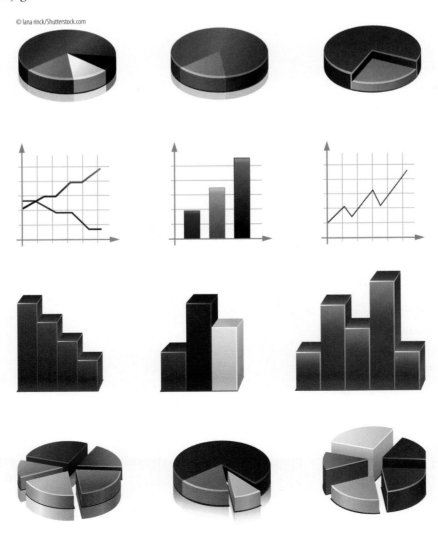

Table 18.1 Summary of Statistical Techniques

Problem objective: Describe a population

  Data type: Interval

    Descriptive measurement: Central location

      Parameter: μ

      Test statistic: $t = \dfrac{\bar{x} - \mu}{s/\sqrt{n}}$

      Interval estimator: $\bar{x} \pm t_{\alpha/2}\dfrac{s}{\sqrt{n}}$

      Required condition: Population is normal.

    Descriptive measurement: Variability

      Parameter: σ^2

      Test statistic: $\chi^2 = \dfrac{(n-1)s^2}{\sigma^2}$

      Interval estimator: $LCL = \dfrac{(n-1)s^2}{\chi^2_{\alpha/2}}$ $UCL = \dfrac{(n-1)s^2}{\chi^2_{1-\alpha/2}}$

      Required condition: Population is normal.

  Data type: Nominal

    Number of categories: Two

      Parameter: p

      Test statistic: $z = \dfrac{\hat{p} - p}{\sqrt{p(1-p)/n}}$

      Interval estimator: $\hat{p} \pm z_{\alpha/2}\sqrt{\hat{p}(1-\hat{p})/n}$

      Required condition: $np \geq 5$ and $n(1-p) \geq 5$ (for test)

                    $n\hat{p} \geq 5$ and $n(1-\hat{p}) \geq 5$ for estimate

    Number of categories: Two or more

      Parameters: $p_1, p_2, \ldots, p_k$

      Statistical technique: Chi-squared goodness-of-fit

      Test statistic: $\chi^2 = \Sigma \dfrac{(f_i - e_i)^2}{e_i}$

      Required condition: $e_i \geq 5$

Problem objective: Compare two populations

  Data type: Interval

    Descriptive measurement: Central location

    Experimental design: Independent samples

    Population variances: $\sigma_1^2 = \sigma_2^2$

      Parameter: $\mu_1 - \mu_2$

      Test statistic: $t = \dfrac{(\bar{x}_1 - \bar{x}_2) - (\mu_1 - \mu_2)}{\sqrt{s_p^2\left(\dfrac{1}{n_1} + \dfrac{1}{n_2}\right)}}$

      Interval estimator: $(\bar{x}_1 - \bar{x}_2) \pm t_{\alpha/2}\sqrt{s_p^2\left(\dfrac{1}{n_1} + \dfrac{1}{n_2}\right)}$

      Required condition: Populations are normal.

    Population variances: $\sigma_1^2 \neq \sigma_2^2$

      Parameter: $\mu_1 - \mu_2$

      Test statistic: $t = \dfrac{(\bar{x}_1 - \bar{x}_2) - (\mu_1 - \mu_2)}{\sqrt{\left(\dfrac{s_1^2}{n_1} + \dfrac{s_2^2}{n_2}\right)}}$

(continued)

Table 18.1 **Summary of Statistical Techniques** (*continued*)

Interval estimator: $(\bar{x}_1 - \bar{x}_2) \pm t_{\alpha/2} \sqrt{\dfrac{s_1^2}{n_1} + \dfrac{s_2^2}{n_2}}$

Required condition: Populations are normal.

Experimental design: Matched pairs

Parameter: μ_D

Test statistic: $t = \dfrac{\bar{x}_D - \mu_D}{s_D/\sqrt{n_D}}$

Interval estimator: $\bar{x}_D \pm t_{\alpha/2} \dfrac{s_D}{\sqrt{n_D}}$

Required condition: Differences are normal.

Descriptive measurement: Variability

Parameter: σ_1^2/σ_2^2

Test statistic: $F = \dfrac{s_1^2}{s_2^2}$

Interval estimator: $\text{LCL} = \left(\dfrac{s_1^2}{s_2^2}\right) \dfrac{1}{F_{\alpha/2,\nu_1,\nu_2}}$ $\text{UCL} = \left(\dfrac{s_1^2}{s_2^2}\right) F_{\alpha/2,\nu_2,\nu_1}$

Required condition: Populations are normal.

Data type: Nominal

Number of categories: Two

Parameter: $p_1 - p_2$

Test statistic: Case 1: $H_0: p_1 - p_2 = 0$ $z = \dfrac{(\hat{p}_1 - \hat{p}_2)}{\sqrt{\hat{p}(1 - \hat{p})\left(\dfrac{1}{n_1} + \dfrac{1}{n_2}\right)}}$

Case 2: $H_0: p_1 - p_2 = D\ (D \neq 0)$ $z = \dfrac{(\hat{p}_1 - \hat{p}_2) - (p_1 - p_2)}{\sqrt{\dfrac{\hat{p}_1(1 - \hat{p}_1)}{n_1} + \dfrac{\hat{p}_2(1 - \hat{p}_2)}{n_2}}}$

Interval estimator: $(\hat{p}_1 - \hat{p}_2) \pm z_{\alpha/2} \sqrt{\dfrac{\hat{p}_1(1 - \hat{p}_1)}{n_1} + \dfrac{\hat{p}_2(1 - \hat{p}_2)}{n_2}}$

Required condition: $n_1\hat{p}_1$, $n_1(1 - \hat{p}_1)$, $n_2\hat{p}_2$, and $n_2(1 - \hat{p}_2) \geq 5$

Number of categories: Two or more

Statistical technique: Chi-squared test of a contingency table

Test statistic: $\chi^2 = \Sigma \dfrac{(f_i - e_i)^2}{e_i}$

Required condition: $e_i \geq 5$

Problem objective: Compare two or more populations

Data type: Interval

Experimental design: Independent samples

Parameters: $\mu_1, \mu_2, \ldots, \mu_k$

Statistical technique: One-way analysis of variance

Test statistic: $F = \dfrac{\text{MST}}{\text{MSE}}$

Statistical technique: Multiple comparisons:

Fisher and Bonferroni adjustment: $\text{LSD} = t_{\alpha/2} \sqrt{\text{MSE}\left(\dfrac{1}{n_i} + \dfrac{1}{n_j}\right)}$

(*continued*)

Table 18.1 **Summary of Statistical Techniques (*continued*)**

Tukey: $\omega = q_\alpha(k, v)\sqrt{\dfrac{MSE}{n_g}}$

Required conditions: Populations are normal with equal variances.

Experimental design: Randomized blocks

Parameters: $\mu_1, \mu_2, \ldots, \mu_k$

Statistical technique: Two-way analysis of variance

Test statistics: $F = \dfrac{MST}{MSE}$ $F = \dfrac{MSB}{MSE}$

Required conditions: Populations are normal with equal variances.

Data type: Nominal

Number of categories: Two or more

Statistical technique: Chi-squared test of a contingency table

Test statistic: $\chi^2 = \sum \dfrac{(f_i - e_i)^2}{e_i}$

Required condition: $e_i \geq 5$

Problem objective: Analyze the relationship between two variables

Data type: Interval

Parameters: β_0, β_1, ρ

Statistical technique: Simple linear regression and correlation

Test statistic: $t = \dfrac{b_1 - \beta_1}{s_{b_1}}$

Prediction interval: $\hat{y} \pm t_{\alpha/2, n-2} s_\varepsilon \sqrt{1 + \dfrac{1}{n} + \dfrac{(x_g - \bar{x})^2}{(n-1)s_x^2}}$

Interval estimator of expected value:

$$\hat{y} \pm t_{\alpha/2, n-2} s_\varepsilon \sqrt{\dfrac{1}{n} + \dfrac{(x_g - \bar{x})^2}{(n-1)s_x^2}}$$

Required conditions: ε is normally distributed with mean 0 and standard deviation σ_ε; ε values are independent.
To test whether two normally distributed variables are linearly related:

Parameter: ρ

Test statistic: $t = r\sqrt{\dfrac{n-2}{1-r^2}}$

Data type: Nominal

Statistical technique: Chi-squared test of a contingency table

Test statistic: $\chi^2 = \sum \dfrac{(f_i - e_i)^2}{e_i}$

Required condition: $e_i \geq 5$

Problem objective: Analyze the relationship among two or more variables

Data type: Interval

Parameters: $\beta_0, \beta_1, \beta_2, \ldots, \beta_k$

Statistical technique: multiple regression

Test statistics: $t = \dfrac{b_i - \beta_i}{s_{b_i}} (i = 1, 2, \ldots, k); F = \dfrac{MSR}{MSE}$

Required conditions: ε is normally distributed with mean 0 and standard deviation σ_ε; ε values are independent.

Figure 18.1 Flowchart of All Statistical Inference Techniques

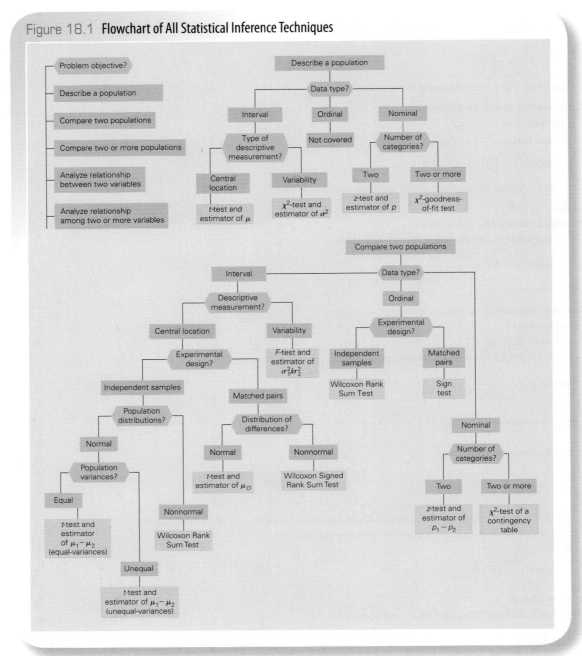

(continued)

Figure 18.1   **Flowchart of All Statistical Inference Techniques** (*continued*)

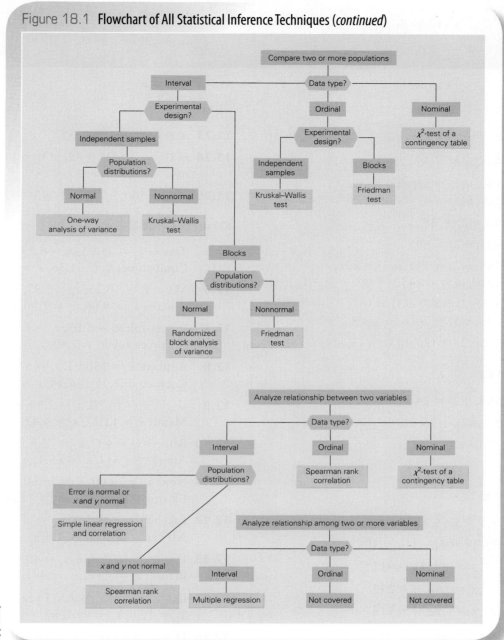

APPENDIX A
Data File Sample Statistics

Chapter 9

9.8 $n(1) = 466, n(2) = 55$

9.10 $n(1) = 140, n(2) = 59, n(3) = 39,$
$n(4) = 106, n(5) = 47$

9.11 $n(1) = 92, n(2) = 28$

9.12 $n(1) = 603, n(2) = 905$

9.13 $n(1) = 245, n(2) = 745, n(3) = 238,$
$n(4) = 1319, n(5) = 2453$

9.14 $n(1) = 81, n(2) = 47, n(3) = 167,$
$n(4) = 146, n(5) = 34$

9.15 $n(1) = 63, n(2) = 125, n(3) = 45, n(4) = 87$

Chapter 10

10.10 $n(1) = 153, n(2) = 24$

10.11 $n(1) = 57, n(2) = 35, n(3) = 4, n(4) = 4$

10.13 $n(1) = 786, n(2) = 254$

10.14 $n(1) = 287, n(2) = 113$

Chapter 11

11.8 $\bar{x} = 7.15, s = 1.65, n = 200$

11.9 $\bar{x} = 15{,}137, s = 5{,}263, n = 306$

11.10 $\bar{x} = 59.04, s = 20.62, n = 122$

11.11 $\bar{x} = 13.94, s = 2.16, n = 212$

11.12 $\bar{x} = 15.27, s = 5.72, n = 116$

11.13 $\bar{x} = 3.79, s = 4.25, n = 564$

11.14 $\bar{x} = 89.27, s = 17.30, n = 85$

11.15 $s^2 = 270.58, n = 25$

11.16 $s^2 = 22.56, n = 245$

11.17 $s^2 = 4.72, n = 90$

11.18 $s^2 = 174.47, n = 100$

11.19 $s^2 = 19.68, n = 25$

11.20 $n(1) = 418, n(2) = 536, n(3) = 882$

11.21 $n(1) = 290, n(2) = 35$

11.22 $n(1) = 72, n(2) = 77, n(3) = 37,$
$n(4) = 50, n(5) = 176$

11.23 $n(1) = 289, n(2) = 51$

11.24 $n(1) = 77, n(2) = 42, n(3) = 11,$
$n(4) = 58, n(5) = 27$

11.25 $n(1) = 860, n(2) = 74, n(3) = 210$

Chapter 12

12.5 Tastee: $\bar{x}_1 = 36.93, s_1 = 4.23, n_1 = 15;$
Competitor: $\bar{x}_2 = 31.36, s_2 = 3.35, n_2 = 25$

12.6 Male: $\bar{x}_1 = 10.23, s_1 = 2.87, n_1 = 100;$
Female: $\bar{x}_2 = 9.66, s_2 = 2.90, n_2 = 100$

12.7 Successful: $\bar{x}_1 = 5.02, s_1 = 1.39, n_1 = 200;$
Unsuccessful: $\bar{x}_2 = 7.80, s_2 = 3.09, n_2 = 200$

12.8 Applied: $\bar{x}_1 = 130.93, s_1 = 31.99, n_1 = 100;$
Contacted: $\bar{x}_2 = 126.14, s_2 = 26.00, n_2 = 100$

12.9 Cork: $\bar{x}_1 = 14.20, s_1 = 2.84, n_1 = 130;$
Metal: $\bar{x}_2 = 11.27, s_2 = 4.42, n_2 = 130$

12.10 Before: $\bar{x}_1 = 497, s_1 = 73.8, n_1 = 355;$
After: $\bar{x}_2 = 511, s_2 = 69.1, n_2 = 288$

12.11 New: $\bar{x}_1 = 73.60, s_1 = 15.60, n_1 = 20;$
Existing: $\bar{x}_2 = 69.20, s_2 = 15.06, n_2 = 20$

12.12 Facebook: $\bar{x}_1 = 3.24, s_1 = .447, n_1 = 148;$
No Facebook: $\bar{x}_2 = 3.48, s_2 = .336, n_2 = 71$

12.13 During: $\bar{x}_1 = 5{,}746, s_1 = 409, n_1 = 15;$
Before: $\bar{x}_2 = 5{,}372, s_2 = 441, n_2 = 24$

12.14 D = X[This year] − X[5 years ago]:
$\bar{x}_D = 12.4, s_D = 99.1, n_D = 150$

12.15 D = X[Waiter] − X[Waitress]:
$\bar{x}_D = -1.16, s_D = 2.22, n_D = 50$

12.16 D = X[This year] − X[Last year]:
$\bar{x}_D = 19.75, s_D = 30.63, n_D = 40$

12.17 D = X[Uninsulated] − X[Insulated]:
$\bar{x}_D = 57.40, s_D = 13.14, n_D = 15$

12.18 D = X[Men] − X[Women]:
$\bar{x}_D = -42.94, s_D = 317.16, n_D = 45$

12.19 D = X[Last year] − X[Previous year]:
$\bar{x}_D = -183.35, s_D = 1568.94, n_D = 170$

12.20 D = X[This year] − X[Last year]:
$\bar{x}_D = .0422, s_D = .1634, n_D = 38$

12.21 Dry Cleaner: X[Before] − X[After]:
$\bar{x}_D = 2.50$, $s_D = 9.77$, $n_D = 14$
Donut Shop: X[Before] − X[After]:
$\bar{x}_D = 12.86$, $s_D = 14.85$, $n_D = 14$
Convenience Store: X[Before] − X[After]:
$\bar{x}_D = 26.50$, $s_D = 13.51$, $n_D = 14$

12.22 D = X[New] − X[Existing]:
$\bar{x}_D = 4.55$, $s_D = 7.22$, $n_D = 20$

12.24 D = X[Company 1] − X[Company 2]:
$\bar{x}_D = 520.85$, $s_D = 1854.92$, $n_D = 55$

12.25 D = X(Drug − Placebo):
$\bar{x}_D = -3.60$, $s_D = 5.91$, $n_D = 100$

Chapter 13

13.4 Week 1: $s_1^2 = 19.38$, $n_1 = 100$;
Week 2: $s_2^2 = 12.70$, $n_2 = 100$

13.5 A: $s_1^2 = 41,309$, $n_1 = 100$;
B: $s_2^2 = 19,850$, $n_2 = 100$

13.6 Portfolio 1: $s_1^2 = .0261$, $n_1 = 52$;
Portfolio 2: $s_2^2 = .0875$, $n_2 = 52$

13.7 Teller 1: $s_1^2 = 3.35$, $n_1 = 100$;
Teller 2: $s_2^2 = 10.95$, $n_2 = 100$

13.8 Lexus: $n_1(1) = 33$, $n_1(2) = 317$;
Acura: $n_2(1) = 33$, $n_2(2) = 261$

13.9 Smokers: $n_1(1) = 28$, $n_1(2) = 10$;
Non-smokers: $n_2(1) = 150$, $n_2(2) = 12$

13.10 Canada: $n_1(1) = 230$, $n_1(2) = 215$;
U.S.: $n_2(1) = 165$, $n_2(2) = 275$

13.11 High school: $n_1(1) = 27$, $n_1(2) = 167$;
Post-secondary: $n_2(1) = 17$, $n_2(2) = 63$

13.12 Year 2008: $n_1(1) = 63$, $n_1(2) = 41$;
Year 2011: $n_2(1) = 81$, $n_2(2) = 44$

13.13 Depressed: $n_1(1) = 94$, $n_1(2) = 38$;
Not depressed: $n_2(1) = 846$, $n_2(2) = 212$

13.14 New: $n_1(1) = 13$, $n_1(2) = 237$;
Older: $n_2(1) = 20$, $n_2(2) = 230$

13.15 \$100 limit: $n_1(1) = 234$, $n_1(2) = 257$;
\$3000 limit: $n_2(1) = 218$, $n_2(2) = 272$

13.16 Year 2001 boys: $n_1(1) = 93$, $n_1(2) = 178$;
Year 2011 boys: $n_2(1) = 139$, $n_2(2) = 174$
Year 2001 girls: $n_3(1) = 144$, $n_3(2) = 137$;
Year 2011 girls: $n_4(1) = 167$, $n_4(2) = 137$

13.17 Cardizem: $n_1(1) = 556$, $n_1(2) = 51$;
Placebo: $n_2(1) = 277$, $n_2(2) = 24$

13.18 This year: $n_1(1) = 222$, $n_1(2) = 171$;
Three years ago: $n_2(1) = 248$, $n_2(2) = 137$

Chapter 14

14.7

Sample	$\bar{x}_i$	s_i^2	n_i
1	68.83	52.28	20
2	65.08	37.38	26
3	62.01	63.46	16
4	64.64	56.88	19

14.8

Sample	$\bar{x}_i$	s_i^2	n_i
1	90.17	991.5	30
2	95.77	900.9	30
3	106.8	928.7	30
4	111.2	1023	30

14.9

Sample	$\bar{x}_i$	s_i^2	n_i
1	196.8	914.1	41
2	207.8	861.1	73
3	223.4	1195	86
4	232.7	1080	79

14.10

Sample	$\bar{x}_i$	s_i^2	n_i
1	164.6	1164	25
2	185.6	1720	25
3	154.8	1114	25
4	182.6	1658	25
5	178.9	841.8	25

14.11

Sample	$\bar{x}_i$	s_i^2	n_i
1	551.5	2742	20
2	576.8	2641	20
3	559.5	3129	20

14.12

Sample	$\bar{x}_i$	s_i^2	n_i
1	74.10	250.0	30
2	75.67	184.2	30
3	78.50	233.4	30
4	81.30	242.9	30

14.15

Sample	$\bar{x}_i$	s_i^2	n_i
1	61.60	80.49	10
2	57.30	70.46	10
3	61.80	22.18	10
4	51.80	75.29	10

14.17

Sample	$\bar{x}_i$	s_i^2	n_i
1	53.17	194.6	30
2	49.37	152.6	30
3	44.33	129.9	30

14.19 $k = 3$, $b = 12$, SST = 204.2,
SSB = 1150.2, SSE = 495.1

14.20 $k = 3$, $b = 20$, SST = 7131,
SSB = 177,465, SSE = 1098

14.21 $k = 3$, $b = 20$, SST = 10.26,
SSB = 3020.30, SSE = 226.7

14.22 $k = 4, b = 30, \text{SST} = 4206,$
$\text{SSB} = 126{,}843, \text{SSE} = 5764$

14.23 $k = 5, b = 36, \text{SST} = 1406.4,$
$\text{SSB} = 7309.7, \text{SSE} = 4593.9$

14.24 $k = 4, b = 20, \text{SST} = 4437.6,$
$\text{SSB} = 43{,}979.6, \text{SSE} = 6113.1$

Chapter 15

15.5 $n(1) = 11, n(2) = 32, n(3) = 62,$
$n(4) = 29, n(5) = 16$

15.6 $n(1) = 8, n(2) = 4, n(3) = 3,$
$n(4) = 8, n(5) = 2$

15.7 $n(1) = 159, n(2) = 28, n(3) = 47, n(4) = 16$

15.8 $n(1) = 36, n(2) = 58, n(3) = 74, n(4) = 29$

15.9 $n(1) = 408, n(2) = 571, n(3) = 221$

15.10 $n(1) = 19, n(2) = 23, n(3) = 14, n(4) = 194$

15.11 $n(1) = 63, n(2) = 125, n(3) = 45, n(4) = 87$

15.12

	Actual	
Predicted	Positive	Negative
Positive	65	64
Negative	39	48

15.13

	Smoking	
Education	Continuing	Quitter
1	34	23
2	251	212
3	159	248
4	16	57

15.14

	Degree			
Approach	1	2	3	4
1	51	8	5	11
2	24	14	12	8
3	26	9	19	8

Chapter 16

16.4 Lengths: $\bar{x} = 38.00, s_x^2 = 193.90,$
Test: $\bar{y} = 13.80, s_y^2 = 47.96; n = 60,$
$s_{xy} = 51.86$

16.5 Floors: $\bar{x} = 13.68, s_x^2 = 59.32,$
Price: $\bar{y} = 210.42, s_y^2 = 496.41; n = 50,$
$s_{xy} = 86.93$

16.6 Age: $\bar{x} = 45.49, s_x^2 = 107.51,$
Time: $\bar{y} = 11.55, s_y^2 = 42.54; n = 229,$
$s_{xy} = 9.67$

16.7 Age: $\bar{x} = 37.28, s_x^2 = 55.11,$ Employment:
$\bar{y} = 26.28, s_y^2 = 4.00; n = 80, s_{xy} = -6.44$

16.8 Cigarettes: $\bar{x} = 37.64, s_x^2 = 108.3,$
Days: $\bar{y} = 14.43, s_y^2 = 19.80; n = 231,$
$s_{xy} = 20.55$

16.9 Distance: $\bar{x} = 4.88, s_x^2 = 4.27,$ Percent:
$\bar{y} = 49.22, s_y^2 = 243.94; n = 85, s_{xy} = 22.83$

16.10 Ads: $\bar{x} = 4.12, s_x^2 = 3.47,$ Customers:
$\bar{y} = 384.81, s_y^2 = 18{,}552; n = 26, s_{xy} = 74.02$

16.11 Age: $\bar{x} = 113.35, s_x^2 = 378.77,$ Repairs: $\bar{y} =$
$395.21, s_y^2 = 4{,}094.79; n = 20, s_{xy} = 936.82$

Chapter 17

17.1 $R^2 = .2425, s_\varepsilon = 40.24, F = 5.97,$
$p\text{-value} = .0013$

	Coefficients	Standard error	t statistic	p-value
Intercept	51.39	23.52	2.19	.0331
Lot size	.700	.559	1.25	.2156
Trees	.679	.229	2.96	.0045
Distance	−.378	.195	−1.94	.0577

17.2 $R^2 = .7629, s_\varepsilon = 3.75, F = 43.43, p\text{-value} = 0$

	Coefficients	Standard error	t statistic	p-value
Intercept	13.01	3.53	3.69	.0010
Assignment	.194	.200	.97	.3417
Midterm	1.11	.122	9.12	0

17.3 $R^2 = .8935, s_\varepsilon = 40.13, F = 39.86, p\text{-value} = 0$

	Coefficients	Standard error	t statistic	p-value
Intercept	−111.83	134.34	−.83	.4155
Permits	4.76	.395	12.06	0
Mortgage	16.99	15.16	1.12	.2764
Apartment vacancy	−10.53	6.39	−1.65	.1161
Office vacancy	1.31	2.79	.47	.6446

17.4 $R^2 = .3511, s_\varepsilon = 6.99, F = 22.01, p\text{-value} = 0$

	Coefficients	Standard error	t statistic	p-value
Intercept	−1.97	9.55	−.21	.8369
Minor HR	.666	.087	7.64	0
Age	.136	.524	.26	.7961
Years Pro	1.18	.671	1.75	.0819

APPENDIX B
Tables

Table 1 Binomial Probabilities

Tabulated values are $P(X \le k) = \sum_{x=0}^{k} p(x)$. (Values are rounded to four decimal places.)

$p: X \le k$

n = 5

k	\multicolumn{15}{c}{p}
	0.01	0.05	0.10	0.20	0.25	0.30	0.40	0.50	0.60	0.70	0.75	0.80	0.90	0.95	0.99
0	0.9510	0.7738	0.5905	0.3277	0.2373	0.1681	0.0778	0.0313	0.0102	0.0024	0.0010	0.0003	0.0000	0.0000	0.0000
1	0.9990	0.9774	0.9185	0.7373	0.6328	0.5282	0.3370	0.1875	0.0870	0.0308	0.0156	0.0067	0.0005	0.0000	0.0000
2	1.0000	0.9988	0.9914	0.9421	0.8965	0.8369	0.6826	0.5000	0.3174	0.1631	0.1035	0.0579	0.0086	0.0012	0.0000
3	1.0000	1.0000	0.9995	0.9933	0.9844	0.9692	0.9130	0.8125	0.6630	0.4718	0.3672	0.2627	0.0815	0.0226	0.0010
4	1.0000	1.0000	1.0000	0.9997	0.9990	0.9976	0.9898	0.9688	0.9222	0.8319	0.7627	0.6723	0.4095	0.2262	0.0490

n = 6

k	\multicolumn{15}{c}{p}
	0.01	0.05	0.10	0.20	0.25	0.30	0.40	0.50	0.60	0.70	0.75	0.80	0.90	0.95	0.99
0	0.9415	0.7351	0.5314	0.2621	0.1780	0.1176	0.0467	0.0156	0.0041	0.0007	0.0002	0.0001	0.0000	0.0000	0.0000
1	0.9985	0.9672	0.8857	0.6554	0.5339	0.4202	0.2333	0.1094	0.0410	0.0109	0.0046	0.0016	0.0001	0.0000	0.0000
2	1.0000	0.9978	0.9842	0.9011	0.8306	0.7443	0.5443	0.3438	0.1792	0.0705	0.0376	0.0170	0.0013	0.0001	0.0000
3	1.0000	0.9999	0.9987	0.9830	0.9624	0.9295	0.8208	0.6563	0.4557	0.2557	0.1694	0.0989	0.0159	0.0022	0.0000
4	1.0000	1.0000	0.9999	0.9984	0.9954	0.9891	0.9590	0.8906	0.7667	0.5798	0.4661	0.3446	0.1143	0.0328	0.0015
5	1.0000	1.0000	1.0000	0.9999	0.9998	0.9993	0.9959	0.9844	0.9533	0.8824	0.8220	0.7379	0.4686	0.2649	0.0585

n = 7

k	\multicolumn{15}{c}{p}
	0.01	0.05	0.10	0.20	0.25	0.30	0.40	0.50	0.60	0.70	0.75	0.80	0.90	0.95	0.99
0	0.9321	0.6983	0.4783	0.2097	0.1335	0.0824	0.0280	0.0078	0.0016	0.0002	0.0001	0.0000	0.0000	0.0000	0.0000
1	0.9980	0.9556	0.8503	0.5767	0.4449	0.3294	0.1586	0.0625	0.0188	0.0038	0.0013	0.0004	0.0000	0.0000	0.0000
2	1.0000	0.9962	0.9743	0.8520	0.7564	0.6471	0.4199	0.2266	0.0963	0.0288	0.0129	0.0047	0.0002	0.0000	0.0000
3	1.0000	0.9998	0.9973	0.9667	0.9294	0.8740	0.7102	0.5000	0.2898	0.1260	0.0706	0.0333	0.0027	0.0002	0.0000
4	1.0000	1.0000	0.9998	0.9953	0.9871	0.9712	0.9037	0.7734	0.5801	0.3529	0.2436	0.1480	0.0257	0.0038	0.0000
5	1.0000	1.0000	1.0000	0.9996	0.9987	0.9962	0.9812	0.9375	0.8414	0.6706	0.5551	0.4233	0.1497	0.0444	0.0020
6	1.0000	1.0000	1.0000	1.0000	0.9999	0.9998	0.9984	0.9922	0.9720	0.9176	0.8665	0.7903	0.5217	0.3017	0.0679

Table 1 (*Continued*)

n = 8								p							
k	**0.01**	**0.05**	**0.10**	**0.20**	**0.25**	**0.30**	**0.40**	**0.50**	**0.60**	**0.70**	**0.75**	**0.80**	**0.90**	**0.95**	**0.99**
0	0.9227	0.6634	0.4305	0.1678	0.1001	0.0576	0.0168	0.0039	0.0007	0.0001	0.0000	0.0000	0.0000	0.0000	0.0000
1	0.9973	0.9428	0.8131	0.5033	0.3671	0.2553	0.1064	0.0352	0.0085	0.0013	0.0004	0.0001	0.0000	0.0000	0.0000
2	0.9999	0.9942	0.9619	0.7969	0.6785	0.5518	0.3154	0.1445	0.0498	0.0113	0.0042	0.0012	0.0000	0.0000	0.0000
3	1.0000	0.9996	0.9950	0.9437	0.8862	0.8059	0.5941	0.3633	0.1737	0.0580	0.0273	0.0104	0.0004	0.0000	0.0000
4	1.0000	1.0000	0.9996	0.9896	0.9727	0.9420	0.8263	0.6367	0.4059	0.1941	0.1138	0.0563	0.0050	0.0004	0.0000
5	1.0000	1.0000	1.0000	0.9988	0.9958	0.9887	0.9502	0.8555	0.6846	0.4482	0.3215	0.2031	0.0381	0.0058	0.0001
6	1.0000	1.0000	1.0000	0.9999	0.9996	0.9987	0.9915	0.9648	0.8936	0.7447	0.6329	0.4967	0.1869	0.0572	0.0027
7	1.0000	1.0000	1.0000	1.0000	1.0000	0.9999	0.9993	0.9961	0.9832	0.9424	0.8999	0.8322	0.5695	0.3366	0.0773

n = 9								p							
k	**0.01**	**0.05**	**0.10**	**0.20**	**0.25**	**0.30**	**0.40**	**0.50**	**0.60**	**0.70**	**0.75**	**0.80**	**0.90**	**0.95**	**0.99**
0	0.9135	0.6302	0.3874	0.1342	0.0751	0.0404	0.0101	0.0020	0.0003	0.0000	0.0000	0.0000	0.0000	0.0000	0.0000
1	0.9966	0.9288	0.7748	0.4362	0.3003	0.1960	0.0705	0.0195	0.0038	0.0004	0.0001	0.0000	0.0000	0.0000	0.0000
2	0.9999	0.9916	0.9470	0.7382	0.6007	0.4628	0.2318	0.0898	0.0250	0.0043	0.0013	0.0003	0.0000	0.0000	0.0000
3	1.0000	0.9994	0.9917	0.9144	0.8343	0.7297	0.4826	0.2539	0.0994	0.0253	0.0100	0.0031	0.0001	0.0000	0.0000
4	1.0000	1.0000	0.9991	0.9804	0.9511	0.9012	0.7334	0.5000	0.2666	0.0988	0.0489	0.0196	0.0009	0.0000	0.0000
5	1.0000	1.0000	0.9999	0.9969	0.9900	0.9747	0.9006	0.7461	0.5174	0.2703	0.1657	0.0856	0.0083	0.0006	0.0000
6	1.0000	1.0000	1.0000	0.9997	0.9987	0.9957	0.9750	0.9102	0.7682	0.5372	0.3993	0.2618	0.0530	0.0084	0.0001
7	1.0000	1.0000	1.0000	1.0000	0.9999	0.9996	0.9962	0.9805	0.9295	0.8040	0.6997	0.5638	0.2252	0.0712	0.0034
8	1.0000	1.0000	1.0000	1.0000	1.0000	1.0000	0.9997	0.9980	0.9899	0.9596	0.9249	0.8658	0.6126	0.3698	0.0865

Table 1 (*Continued*)

n = 10

k	0.01	0.05	0.10	0.20	0.25	0.30	0.40	0.50	0.60	0.70	0.75	0.80	0.90	0.95	0.99
								p							
0	0.9044	0.5987	0.3487	0.1074	0.0563	0.0282	0.0060	0.0010	0.0001	0.0000	0.0000	0.0000	0.0000	0.0000	0.0000
1	0.9957	0.9139	0.7361	0.3758	0.2440	0.1493	0.0464	0.0107	0.0017	0.0001	0.0000	0.0000	0.0000	0.0000	0.0000
2	0.9999	0.9885	0.9298	0.6778	0.5256	0.3828	0.1673	0.0547	0.0123	0.0016	0.0004	0.0001	0.0000	0.0000	0.0000
3	1.0000	0.9990	0.9872	0.8791	0.7759	0.6496	0.3823	0.1719	0.0548	0.0106	0.0035	0.0009	0.0000	0.0000	0.0000
4	1.0000	0.9999	0.9984	0.9672	0.9219	0.8497	0.6331	0.3770	0.1662	0.0473	0.0197	0.0064	0.0001	0.0000	0.0000
5	1.0000	1.0000	0.9999	0.9936	0.9803	0.9527	0.8338	0.6230	0.3669	0.1503	0.0781	0.0328	0.0016	0.0001	0.0000
6	1.0000	1.0000	1.0000	0.9991	0.9965	0.9894	0.9452	0.8281	0.6177	0.3504	0.2241	0.1209	0.0128	0.0010	0.0000
7	1.0000	1.0000	1.0000	0.9999	0.9996	0.9984	0.9877	0.9453	0.8327	0.6172	0.4744	0.3222	0.0702	0.0115	0.0001
8	1.0000	1.0000	1.0000	1.0000	1.0000	0.9999	0.9983	0.9893	0.9536	0.8507	0.7560	0.6242	0.2639	0.0861	0.0043
9	1.0000	1.0000	1.0000	1.0000	1.0000	1.0000	0.9999	0.9990	0.9940	0.9718	0.9437	0.8926	0.6513	0.4013	0.0956

n = 15

k	0.01	0.05	0.10	0.20	0.25	0.30	0.40	0.50	0.60	0.70	0.75	0.80	0.90	0.95	0.99
								p							
0	0.8601	0.4633	0.2059	0.0352	0.0134	0.0047	0.0005	0.0000	0.0000	0.0000	0.0000	0.0000	0.0000	0.0000	0.0000
1	0.9904	0.8290	0.5490	0.1671	0.0802	0.0353	0.0052	0.0005	0.0000	0.0000	0.0000	0.0000	0.0000	0.0000	0.0000
2	0.9996	0.9638	0.8159	0.3980	0.2361	0.1268	0.0271	0.0037	0.0003	0.0000	0.0000	0.0000	0.0000	0.0000	0.0000
3	1.0000	0.9945	0.9444	0.6482	0.4613	0.2969	0.0905	0.0176	0.0019	0.0001	0.0000	0.0000	0.0000	0.0000	0.0000
4	1.0000	0.9994	0.9873	0.8358	0.6865	0.5155	0.2173	0.0592	0.0093	0.0007	0.0001	0.0000	0.0000	0.0000	0.0000
5	1.0000	0.9999	0.9978	0.9389	0.8516	0.7216	0.4032	0.1509	0.0338	0.0037	0.0008	0.0001	0.0000	0.0000	0.0000
6	1.0000	1.0000	0.9997	0.9819	0.9434	0.8689	0.6098	0.3036	0.0950	0.0152	0.0042	0.0008	0.0000	0.0000	0.0000
7	1.0000	1.0000	1.0000	0.9958	0.9827	0.9500	0.7869	0.5000	0.2131	0.0500	0.0173	0.0042	0.0000	0.0000	0.0000
8	1.0000	1.0000	1.0000	0.9992	0.9958	0.9848	0.9050	0.6964	0.3902	0.1311	0.0566	0.0181	0.0003	0.0000	0.0000
9	1.0000	1.0000	1.0000	0.9999	0.9992	0.9963	0.9662	0.8491	0.5968	0.2784	0.1484	0.0611	0.0022	0.0001	0.0000
10	1.0000	1.0000	1.0000	1.0000	0.9999	0.9993	0.9907	0.9408	0.7827	0.4845	0.3135	0.1642	0.0127	0.0006	0.0000
11	1.0000	1.0000	1.0000	1.0000	1.0000	0.9999	0.9981	0.9824	0.9095	0.7031	0.5387	0.3518	0.0556	0.0055	0.0000
12	1.0000	1.0000	1.0000	1.0000	1.0000	1.0000	0.9997	0.9963	0.9729	0.8732	0.7639	0.6020	0.1841	0.0362	0.0004
13	1.0000	1.0000	1.0000	1.0000	1.0000	1.0000	1.0000	0.9995	0.9948	0.9647	0.9198	0.8329	0.4510	0.1710	0.0096
14	1.0000	1.0000	1.0000	1.0000	1.0000	1.0000	1.0000	1.0000	0.9995	0.9953	0.9866	0.9648	0.7941	0.5367	0.1399

Table 1 (*Continued*)

	p														
k	0.01	0.05	0.10	0.20	0.25	0.30	0.40	0.50	0.60	0.70	0.75	0.80	0.90	0.95	0.99
0	0.8179	0.3585	0.1216	0.0115	0.0032	0.0008	0.0000	0.0000	0.0000	0.0000	0.0000	0.0000	0.0000	0.0000	0.0000
1	0.9831	0.7358	0.3917	0.0692	0.0243	0.0076	0.0005	0.0000	0.0000	0.0000	0.0000	0.0000	0.0000	0.0000	0.0000
2	0.9990	0.9245	0.6769	0.2061	0.0913	0.0355	0.0036	0.0002	0.0000	0.0000	0.0000	0.0000	0.0000	0.0000	0.0000
3	1.0000	0.9841	0.8670	0.4114	0.2252	0.1071	0.0160	0.0013	0.0000	0.0000	0.0000	0.0000	0.0000	0.0000	0.0000
4	1.0000	0.9974	0.9568	0.6296	0.4148	0.2375	0.0510	0.0059	0.0003	0.0000	0.0000	0.0000	0.0000	0.0000	0.0000
5	1.0000	0.9997	0.9887	0.8042	0.6172	0.4164	0.1256	0.0207	0.0016	0.0000	0.0000	0.0000	0.0000	0.0000	0.0000
6	1.0000	1.0000	0.9976	0.9133	0.7858	0.6080	0.2500	0.0577	0.0065	0.0003	0.0000	0.0000	0.0000	0.0000	0.0000
7	1.0000	1.0000	0.9996	0.9679	0.8982	0.7723	0.4159	0.1316	0.0210	0.0013	0.0002	0.0000	0.0000	0.0000	0.0000
8	1.0000	1.0000	0.9999	0.9900	0.9591	0.8867	0.5956	0.2517	0.0565	0.0051	0.0009	0.0001	0.0000	0.0000	0.0000
9	1.0000	1.0000	1.0000	0.9974	0.9861	0.9520	0.7553	0.4119	0.1275	0.0171	0.0039	0.0006	0.0000	0.0000	0.0000
10	1.0000	1.0000	1.0000	0.9994	0.9961	0.9829	0.8725	0.5881	0.2447	0.0480	0.0139	0.0026	0.0000	0.0000	0.0000
11	1.0000	1.0000	1.0000	0.9999	0.9991	0.9949	0.9435	0.7483	0.4044	0.1133	0.0409	0.0100	0.0001	0.0000	0.0000
12	1.0000	1.0000	1.0000	1.0000	0.9998	0.9987	0.9790	0.8684	0.5841	0.2277	0.1018	0.0321	0.0004	0.0000	0.0000
13	1.0000	1.0000	1.0000	1.0000	1.0000	0.9997	0.9935	0.9423	0.7500	0.3920	0.2142	0.0867	0.0024	0.0000	0.0000
14	1.0000	1.0000	1.0000	1.0000	1.0000	1.0000	0.9984	0.9793	0.8744	0.5836	0.3828	0.1958	0.0113	0.0003	0.0000
15	1.0000	1.0000	1.0000	1.0000	1.0000	1.0000	0.9997	0.9941	0.9490	0.7625	0.5852	0.3704	0.0432	0.0026	0.0000
16	1.0000	1.0000	1.0000	1.0000	1.0000	1.0000	1.0000	0.9987	0.9840	0.8929	0.7748	0.5886	0.1330	0.0159	0.0000
17	1.0000	1.0000	1.0000	1.0000	1.0000	1.0000	1.0000	0.9998	0.9964	0.9645	0.9087	0.7939	0.3231	0.0755	0.0010
18	1.0000	1.0000	1.0000	1.0000	1.0000	1.0000	1.0000	1.0000	0.9995	0.9924	0.9757	0.9308	0.6083	0.2642	0.0169
19	1.0000	1.0000	1.0000	1.0000	1.0000	1.0000	1.0000	1.0000	1.0000	0.9992	0.9968	0.9885	0.8784	0.6415	0.1821

n = 25	*p*														
k	0.01	0.05	0.10	0.20	0.25	0.30	0.40	0.50	0.60	0.70	0.75	0.80	0.90	0.95	0.99
0	0.7778	0.2774	0.0718	0.0038	0.0008	0.0001	0.0000	0.0000	0.0000	0.0000	0.0000	0.0000	0.0000	0.0000	0.0000
1	0.9742	0.6424	0.2712	0.0274	0.0070	0.0016	0.0001	0.0000	0.0000	0.0000	0.0000	0.0000	0.0000	0.0000	0.0000
2	0.9980	0.8729	0.5371	0.0982	0.0321	0.0090	0.0004	0.0000	0.0000	0.0000	0.0000	0.0000	0.0000	0.0000	0.0000
3	0.9999	0.9659	0.7636	0.2340	0.0962	0.0332	0.0024	0.0001	0.0000	0.0000	0.0000	0.0000	0.0000	0.0000	0.0000
4	1.0000	0.9928	0.9020	0.4207	0.2137	0.0905	0.0095	0.0005	0.0000	0.0000	0.0000	0.0000	0.0000	0.0000	0.0000
5	1.0000	0.9988	0.9666	0.6167	0.3783	0.1935	0.0294	0.0020	0.0001	0.0000	0.0000	0.0000	0.0000	0.0000	0.0000
6	1.0000	0.9998	0.9905	0.7800	0.5611	0.3407	0.0736	0.0073	0.0003	0.0000	0.0000	0.0000	0.0000	0.0000	0.0000
7	1.0000	1.0000	0.9977	0.8909	0.7265	0.5118	0.1536	0.0216	0.0012	0.0000	0.0000	0.0000	0.0000	0.0000	0.0000
8	1.0000	1.0000	0.9995	0.9532	0.8506	0.6769	0.2735	0.0539	0.0043	0.0001	0.0000	0.0000	0.0000	0.0000	0.0000
9	1.0000	1.0000	0.9999	0.9827	0.9287	0.8106	0.4246	0.1148	0.0132	0.0005	0.0000	0.0000	0.0000	0.0000	0.0000
10	1.0000	1.0000	1.0000	0.9944	0.9703	0.9022	0.5858	0.2122	0.0344	0.0018	0.0002	0.0000	0.0000	0.0000	0.0000
11	1.0000	1.0000	1.0000	0.9985	0.9893	0.9558	0.7323	0.3450	0.0778	0.0060	0.0009	0.0001	0.0000	0.0000	0.0000
12	1.0000	1.0000	1.0000	0.9996	0.9966	0.9825	0.8462	0.5000	0.1538	0.0175	0.0034	0.0004	0.0000	0.0000	0.0000
13	1.0000	1.0000	1.0000	0.9999	0.9991	0.9940	0.9222	0.6550	0.2677	0.0442	0.0107	0.0015	0.0000	0.0000	0.0000
14	1.0000	1.0000	1.0000	1.0000	0.9998	0.9982	0.9656	0.7878	0.4142	0.0978	0.0297	0.0056	0.0000	0.0000	0.0000
15	1.0000	1.0000	1.0000	1.0000	1.0000	0.9995	0.9868	0.8852	0.5754	0.1894	0.0713	0.0173	0.0001	0.0000	0.0000
16	1.0000	1.0000	1.0000	1.0000	1.0000	0.9999	0.9957	0.9461	0.7265	0.3231	0.1494	0.0468	0.0005	0.0000	0.0000
17	1.0000	1.0000	1.0000	1.0000	1.0000	1.0000	0.9988	0.9784	0.8464	0.4882	0.2735	0.1091	0.0023	0.0000	0.0000
18	1.0000	1.0000	1.0000	1.0000	1.0000	1.0000	0.9997	0.9927	0.9264	0.6593	0.4389	0.2200	0.0095	0.0002	0.0000
19	1.0000	1.0000	1.0000	1.0000	1.0000	1.0000	0.9999	0.9980	0.9706	0.8065	0.6217	0.3833	0.0334	0.0012	0.0000
20	1.0000	1.0000	1.0000	1.0000	1.0000	1.0000	1.0000	0.9995	0.9905	0.9095	0.7863	0.5793	0.0980	0.0072	0.0000
21	1.0000	1.0000	1.0000	1.0000	1.0000	1.0000	1.0000	0.9999	0.9976	0.9668	0.9038	0.7660	0.2364	0.0341	0.0001
22	1.0000	1.0000	1.0000	1.0000	1.0000	1.0000	1.0000	1.0000	0.9996	0.9910	0.9679	0.9018	0.4629	0.1271	0.0020
23	1.0000	1.0000	1.0000	1.0000	1.0000	1.0000	1.0000	1.0000	0.9999	0.9984	0.9930	0.9726	0.7288	0.3576	0.0258
24	1.0000	1.0000	1.0000	1.0000	1.0000	1.0000	1.0000	1.0000	1.0000	0.9999	0.9992	0.9962	0.9282	0.7226	0.2222

Table 2 Poisson Probabilities

Tabulated values are $P(X \leq k) = \sum_{x=0}^{k} p(x)$. (Values are rounded to four decimal places.)

k	0.10	0.20	0.30	0.40	0.50	1.0	1.5	2.0	2.5	3.0	3.5	4.0	4.5	5.0	5.5	6.0
								μ								
0	0.9048	0.8187	0.7408	0.6703	0.6065	0.3679	0.2231	0.1353	0.0821	0.0498	0.0302	0.0183	0.0111	0.0067	0.0041	0.0025
1	0.9953	0.9825	0.9631	0.9384	0.9098	0.7358	0.5578	0.4060	0.2873	0.1991	0.1359	0.0916	0.0611	0.0404	0.0266	0.0174
2	0.9998	0.9989	0.9964	0.9921	0.9856	0.9197	0.8088	0.6767	0.5438	0.4232	0.3208	0.2381	0.1736	0.1247	0.0884	0.0620
3	1.0000	0.9999	0.9997	0.9992	0.9982	0.9810	0.9344	0.8571	0.7576	0.6472	0.5366	0.4335	0.3423	0.2650	0.2017	0.1512
4		1.0000	1.0000	0.9999	0.9998	0.9963	0.9814	0.9473	0.8912	0.8153	0.7254	0.6288	0.5321	0.4405	0.3575	0.2851
5				1.0000	1.0000	0.9994	0.9955	0.9834	0.9580	0.9161	0.8576	0.7851	0.7029	0.6160	0.5289	0.4457
6						0.9999	0.9991	0.9955	0.9858	0.9665	0.9347	0.8893	0.8311	0.7622	0.6860	0.6063
7						1.0000	0.9998	0.9989	0.9958	0.9881	0.9733	0.9489	0.9134	0.8666	0.8095	0.7440
8							1.0000	0.9998	0.9989	0.9962	0.9901	0.9786	0.9597	0.9319	0.8944	0.8472
9								1.0000	0.9997	0.9989	0.9967	0.9919	0.9829	0.9682	0.9462	0.9161
10									0.9999	0.9997	0.9990	0.9972	0.9933	0.9863	0.9747	0.9574
11									1.0000	0.9999	0.9997	0.9991	0.9976	0.9945	0.9890	0.9799
12										1.0000	0.9999	0.9997	0.9992	0.9980	0.9955	0.9912
13											1.0000	0.9999	0.9997	0.9993	0.9983	0.9964
14												1.0000	0.9999	0.9998	0.9994	0.9986
15													1.0000	0.9999	0.9998	0.9995
16														1.0000	0.9999	0.9998
17															1.0000	0.9999
18																1.0000
19																
20																

Table 2 (*Continued*)

							μ						
k	**6.50**	**7.00**	**7.50**	**8.00**	**8.50**	**9.00**	**9.50**	**10**	**11**	**12**	**13**	**14**	**15**
0	0.0015	0.0009	0.0006	0.0003	0.0002	0.0001	0.0001	0.0000	0.0000	0.0000	0.0000	0.0000	0.0000
1	0.0113	0.0073	0.0047	0.0030	0.0019	0.0012	0.0008	0.0005	0.0002	0.0001	0.0000	0.0000	0.0000
2	0.0430	0.0296	0.0203	0.0138	0.0093	0.0062	0.0042	0.0028	0.0012	0.0005	0.0002	0.0001	0.0000
3	0.1118	0.0818	0.0591	0.0424	0.0301	0.0212	0.0149	0.0103	0.0049	0.0023	0.0011	0.0005	0.0002
4	0.2237	0.1730	0.1321	0.0996	0.0744	0.0550	0.0403	0.0293	0.0151	0.0076	0.0037	0.0018	0.0009
5	0.3690	0.3007	0.2414	0.1912	0.1496	0.1157	0.0885	0.0671	0.0375	0.0203	0.0107	0.0055	0.0028
6	0.5265	0.4497	0.3782	0.3134	0.2562	0.2068	0.1649	0.1301	0.0786	0.0458	0.0259	0.0142	0.0076
7	0.6728	0.5987	0.5246	0.4530	0.3856	0.3239	0.2687	0.2202	0.1432	0.0895	0.0540	0.0316	0.0180
8	0.7916	0.7291	0.6620	0.5925	0.5231	0.4557	0.3918	0.3328	0.2320	0.1550	0.0998	0.0621	0.0374
9	0.8774	0.8305	0.7764	0.7166	0.6530	0.5874	0.5218	0.4579	0.3405	0.2424	0.1658	0.1094	0.0699
10	0.9332	0.9015	0.8622	0.8159	0.7634	0.7060	0.6453	0.5830	0.4599	0.3472	0.2517	0.1757	0.1185
11	0.9661	0.9467	0.9208	0.8881	0.8487	0.8030	0.7520	0.6968	0.5793	0.4616	0.3532	0.2600	0.1848
12	0.9840	0.9730	0.9573	0.9362	0.9091	0.8758	0.8364	0.7916	0.6887	0.5760	0.4631	0.3585	0.2676
13	0.9929	0.9872	0.9784	0.9658	0.9486	0.9261	0.8981	0.8645	0.7813	0.6815	0.5730	0.4644	0.3632
14	0.9970	0.9943	0.9897	0.9827	0.9726	0.9585	0.9400	0.9165	0.8540	0.7720	0.6751	0.5704	0.4657
15	0.9988	0.9976	0.9954	0.9918	0.9862	0.9780	0.9665	0.9513	0.9074	0.8444	0.7636	0.6694	0.5681
16	0.9996	0.9990	0.9980	0.9963	0.9934	0.9889	0.9823	0.9730	0.9441	0.8987	0.8355	0.7559	0.6641
17	0.9998	0.9996	0.9992	0.9984	0.9970	0.9947	0.9911	0.9857	0.9678	0.9370	0.8905	0.8272	0.7489
18	0.9999	0.9999	0.9997	0.9993	0.9987	0.9976	0.9957	0.9928	0.9823	0.9626	0.9302	0.8826	0.8195
19	1.0000	1.0000	0.9999	0.9997	0.9995	0.9989	0.9980	0.9965	0.9907	0.9787	0.9573	0.9235	0.8752
20			1.0000	0.9999	0.9998	0.9996	0.9991	0.9984	0.9953	0.9884	0.9750	0.9521	0.9170
21				1.0000	0.9999	0.9998	0.9996	0.9993	0.9977	0.9939	0.9859	0.9712	0.9469
22					1.0000	0.9999	0.9999	0.9997	0.9990	0.9970	0.9924	0.9833	0.9673
23						1.0000	0.9999	0.9999	0.9995	0.9985	0.9960	0.9907	0.9805
24							1.0000	1.0000	0.9998	0.9993	0.9980	0.9950	0.9888
25									0.9999	0.9997	0.9990	0.9974	0.9938
26									1.0000	0.9999	0.9995	0.9987	0.9967
27										0.9999	0.9998	0.9994	0.9983
28										1.0000	0.9999	0.9997	0.9991
29											1.0000	0.9999	0.9996
30												0.9999	0.9998
31												1.0000	0.9999
32													1.0000

Table 3   Cumulative Standardized Normal Probabilities

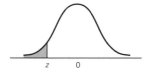

P(Z < z)

Z	0.00	0.01	0.02	0.03	0.04	0.05	0.06	0.07	0.08	0.09
−3.0	0.0013	0.0013	0.0013	0.0012	0.0012	0.0011	0.0011	0.0011	0.0010	0.0010
−2.9	0.0019	0.0018	0.0018	0.0017	0.0016	0.0016	0.0015	0.0015	0.0014	0.0014
−2.8	0.0026	0.0025	0.0024	0.0023	0.0023	0.0022	0.0021	0.0021	0.0020	0.0019
−2.7	0.0035	0.0034	0.0033	0.0032	0.0031	0.0030	0.0029	0.0028	0.0027	0.0026
−2.6	0.0047	0.0045	0.0044	0.0043	0.0041	0.0040	0.0039	0.0038	0.0037	0.0036
−2.5	0.0062	0.0060	0.0059	0.0057	0.0055	0.0054	0.0052	0.0051	0.0049	0.0048
−2.4	0.0082	0.0080	0.0078	0.0075	0.0073	0.0071	0.0069	0.0068	0.0066	0.0064
−2.3	0.0107	0.0104	0.0102	0.0099	0.0096	0.0094	0.0091	0.0089	0.0087	0.0084
−2.2	0.0139	0.0136	0.0132	0.0129	0.0125	0.0122	0.0119	0.0116	0.0113	0.0110
−2.1	0.0179	0.0174	0.0170	0.0166	0.0162	0.0158	0.0154	0.0150	0.0146	0.0143
−2.0	0.0228	0.0222	0.0217	0.0212	0.0207	0.0202	0.0197	0.0192	0.0188	0.0183
−1.9	0.0287	0.0281	0.0274	0.0268	0.0262	0.0256	0.0250	0.0244	0.0239	0.0233
−1.8	0.0359	0.0351	0.0344	0.0336	0.0329	0.0322	0.0314	0.0307	0.0301	0.0294
−1.7	0.0446	0.0436	0.0427	0.0418	0.0409	0.0401	0.0392	0.0384	0.0375	0.0367
−1.6	0.0548	0.0537	0.0526	0.0516	0.0505	0.0495	0.0485	0.0475	0.0465	0.0455
−1.5	0.0668	0.0655	0.0643	0.0630	0.0618	0.0606	0.0594	0.0582	0.0571	0.0559
−1.4	0.0808	0.0793	0.0778	0.0764	0.0749	0.0735	0.0721	0.0708	0.0694	0.0681
−1.3	0.0968	0.0951	0.0934	0.0918	0.0901	0.0885	0.0869	0.0853	0.0838	0.0823
−1.2	0.1151	0.1131	0.1112	0.1093	0.1075	0.1056	0.1038	0.1020	0.1003	0.0985
−1.1	0.1357	0.1335	0.1314	0.1292	0.1271	0.1251	0.1230	0.1210	0.1190	0.1170
−1.0	0.1587	0.1562	0.1539	0.1515	0.1492	0.1469	0.1446	0.1423	0.1401	0.1379
−0.9	0.1841	0.1814	0.1788	0.1762	0.1736	0.1711	0.1685	0.1660	0.1635	0.1611
−0.8	0.2119	0.2090	0.2061	0.2033	0.2005	0.1977	0.1949	0.1922	0.1894	0.1867
−0.7	0.2420	0.2389	0.2358	0.2327	0.2296	0.2266	0.2236	0.2206	0.2177	0.2148
−0.6	0.2743	0.2709	0.2676	0.2643	0.2611	0.2578	0.2546	0.2514	0.2483	0.2451
−0.5	0.3085	0.3050	0.3015	0.2981	0.2946	0.2912	0.2877	0.2843	0.2810	0.2776
−0.4	0.3446	0.3409	0.3372	0.3336	0.3300	0.3264	0.3228	0.3192	0.3156	0.3121
−0.3	0.3821	0.3783	0.3745	0.3707	0.3669	0.3632	0.3594	0.3557	0.3520	0.3483
−0.2	0.4207	0.4168	0.4129	0.4090	0.4052	0.4013	0.3974	0.3936	0.3897	0.3859
−0.1	0.4602	0.4562	0.4522	0.4483	0.4443	0.4404	0.4364	0.4325	0.4286	0.4247
−0.0	0.5000	0.4960	0.4920	0.4880	0.4840	0.4801	0.4761	0.4721	0.4681	0.4641

Table 3 (*Continued*)

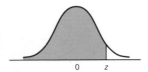

P(Z < z)

Z	0.00	0.01	0.02	0.03	0.04	0.05	0.06	0.07	0.08	0.09
0.0	0.5000	0.5040	0.5080	0.5120	0.5160	0.5199	0.5239	0.5279	0.5319	0.5359
0.1	0.5398	0.5438	0.5478	0.5517	0.5557	0.5596	0.5636	0.5675	0.5714	0.5753
0.2	0.5793	0.5832	0.5871	0.5910	0.5948	0.5987	0.6026	0.6064	0.6103	0.6141
0.3	0.6179	0.6217	0.6255	0.6293	0.6331	0.6368	0.6406	0.6443	0.6480	0.6517
0.4	0.6554	0.6591	0.6628	0.6664	0.6700	0.6736	0.6772	0.6808	0.6844	0.6879
0.5	0.6915	0.6950	0.6985	0.7019	0.7054	0.7088	0.7123	0.7157	0.7190	0.7224
0.6	0.7257	0.7291	0.7324	0.7357	0.7389	0.7422	0.7454	0.7486	0.7517	0.7549
0.7	0.7580	0.7611	0.7642	0.7673	0.7704	0.7734	0.7764	0.7794	0.7823	0.7852
0.8	0.7881	0.7910	0.7939	0.7967	0.7995	0.8023	0.8051	0.8078	0.8106	0.8133
0.9	0.8159	0.8186	0.8212	0.8238	0.8264	0.8289	0.8315	0.8340	0.8365	0.8389
1.0	0.8413	0.8438	0.8461	0.8485	0.8508	0.8531	0.8554	0.8577	0.8599	0.8621
1.1	0.8643	0.8665	0.8686	0.8708	0.8729	0.8749	0.8770	0.8790	0.8810	0.8830
1.2	0.8849	0.8869	0.8888	0.8907	0.8925	0.8944	0.8962	0.8980	0.8997	0.9015
1.3	0.9032	0.9049	0.9066	0.9082	0.9099	0.9115	0.9131	0.9147	0.9162	0.9177
1.4	0.9192	0.9207	0.9222	0.9236	0.9251	0.9265	0.9279	0.9292	0.9306	0.9319
1.5	0.9332	0.9345	0.9357	0.9370	0.9382	0.9394	0.9406	0.9418	0.9429	0.9441
1.6	0.9452	0.9463	0.9474	0.9484	0.9495	0.9505	0.9515	0.9525	0.9535	0.9545
1.7	0.9554	0.9564	0.9573	0.9582	0.9591	0.9599	0.9608	0.9616	0.9625	0.9633
1.8	0.9641	0.9649	0.9656	0.9664	0.9671	0.9678	0.9686	0.9693	0.9699	0.9706
1.9	0.9713	0.9719	0.9726	0.9732	0.9738	0.9744	0.9750	0.9756	0.9761	0.9767
2.0	0.9772	0.9778	0.9783	0.9788	0.9793	0.9798	0.9803	0.9808	0.9812	0.9817
2.1	0.9821	0.9826	0.9830	0.9834	0.9838	0.9842	0.9846	0.9850	0.9854	0.9857
2.2	0.9861	0.9864	0.9868	0.9871	0.9875	0.9878	0.9881	0.9884	0.9887	0.9890
2.3	0.9893	0.9896	0.9898	0.9901	0.9904	0.9906	0.9909	0.9911	0.9913	0.9916
2.4	0.9918	0.9920	0.9922	0.9925	0.9927	0.9929	0.9931	0.9932	0.9934	0.9936
2.5	0.9938	0.9940	0.9941	0.9943	0.9945	0.9946	0.9948	0.9949	0.9951	0.9952
2.6	0.9953	0.9955	0.9956	0.9957	0.9959	0.9960	0.9961	0.9962	0.9963	0.9964
2.7	0.9965	0.9966	0.9967	0.9968	0.9969	0.9970	0.9971	0.9972	0.9973	0.9974
2.8	0.9974	0.9975	0.9976	0.9977	0.9977	0.9978	0.9979	0.9979	0.9980	0.9981
2.9	0.9981	0.9982	0.9982	0.9983	0.9984	0.9984	0.9985	0.9985	0.9986	0.9986
3.0	0.9987	0.9987	0.9987	0.9988	0.9988	0.9989	0.9989	0.9989	0.9990	0.9990

Table 4 Critical Values of the Student t Distribution

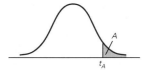

Degrees of Freedom	$t_{.100}$	$t_{.050}$	$t_{.025}$	$t_{.010}$	$t_{.005}$	Degrees of Freedom	$t_{.100}$	$t_{.050}$	$t_{.025}$	$t_{.010}$	$t_{.005}$
1	3.078	6.314	12.706	31.821	63.657	29	1.311	1.699	2.045	2.462	2.756
2	1.886	2.920	4.303	6.965	9.925	30	1.310	1.697	2.042	2.457	2.750
3	1.638	2.353	3.182	4.541	5.841	35	1.306	1.690	2.030	2.438	2.724
4	1.533	2.132	2.776	3.747	4.604	40	1.303	1.684	2.021	2.423	2.704
5	1.476	2.015	2.571	3.365	4.032	45	1.301	1.679	2.014	2.412	2.690
6	1.440	1.943	2.447	3.143	3.707	50	1.299	1.676	2.009	2.403	2.678
7	1.415	1.895	2.365	2.998	3.499	55	1.297	1.673	2.004	2.396	2.668
8	1.397	1.860	2.306	2.896	3.355	60	1.296	1.671	2.000	2.390	2.660
9	1.383	1.833	2.262	2.821	3.250	65	1.295	1.669	1.997	2.385	2.654
10	1.372	1.812	2.228	2.764	3.169	70	1.294	1.667	1.994	2.381	2.648
11	1.363	1.796	2.201	2.718	3.106	75	1.293	1.665	1.992	2.377	2.643
12	1.356	1.782	2.179	2.681	3.055	80	1.292	1.664	1.990	2.374	2.639
13	1.350	1.771	2.160	2.650	3.012	85	1.292	1.663	1.988	2.371	2.635
14	1.345	1.761	2.145	2.624	2.977	90	1.291	1.662	1.987	2.368	2.632
15	1.341	1.753	2.131	2.602	2.947	95	1.291	1.661	1.985	2.366	2.629
16	1.337	1.746	2.120	2.583	2.921	100	1.290	1.660	1.984	2.364	2.626
17	1.333	1.740	2.110	2.567	2.898	110	1.289	1.659	1.982	2.361	2.621
18	1.330	1.734	2.101	2.552	2.878	120	1.289	1.658	1.980	2.358	2.617
19	1.328	1.729	2.093	2.539	2.861	130	1.288	1.657	1.978	2.355	2.614
20	1.325	1.725	2.086	2.528	2.845	140	1.288	1.656	1.977	2.353	2.611
21	1.323	1.721	2.080	2.518	2.831	150	1.287	1.655	1.976	2.351	2.609
22	1.321	1.717	2.074	2.508	2.819	160	1.287	1.654	1.975	2.350	2.607
23	1.319	1.714	2.069	2.500	2.807	170	1.287	1.654	1.974	2.348	2.605
24	1.318	1.711	2.064	2.492	2.797	180	1.286	1.653	1.973	2.347	2.603
25	1.316	1.708	2.060	2.485	2.787	190	1.286	1.653	1.973	2.346	2.602
26	1.315	1.706	2.056	2.479	2.779	200	1.286	1.653	1.972	2.345	2.601
27	1.314	1.703	2.052	2.473	2.771	∞	1.282	1.645	1.960	2.326	2.576
28	1.313	1.701	2.048	2.467	2.763						

Table 5 Critical Values of the χ^2 Distribution

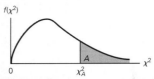

Degrees of Freedom	$\chi^2_{.995}$	$\chi^2_{.990}$	$\chi^2_{.975}$	$\chi^2_{.950}$	$\chi^2_{.900}$	$\chi^2_{.100}$	$\chi^2_{.050}$	$\chi^2_{.025}$	$\chi^2_{.010}$	$\chi^2_{.005}$
1	0.000039	0.000157	0.000982	0.00393	0.0158	2.71	3.84	5.02	6.63	7.88
2	0.0100	0.0201	0.0506	0.103	0.211	4.61	5.99	7.38	9.21	10.6
3	0.072	0.115	0.216	0.352	0.584	6.25	7.81	9.35	11.3	12.8
4	0.207	0.297	0.484	0.711	1.06	7.78	9.49	11.1	13.3	14.9
5	0.412	0.554	0.831	1.15	1.61	9.24	11.1	12.8	15.1	16.7
6	0.676	0.872	1.24	1.64	2.20	10.6	12.6	14.4	16.8	18.5
7	0.989	1.24	1.69	2.17	2.83	12.0	14.1	16.0	18.5	20.3
8	1.34	1.65	2.18	2.73	3.49	13.4	15.5	17.5	20.1	22.0
9	1.73	2.09	2.70	3.33	4.17	14.7	16.9	19.0	21.7	23.6
10	2.16	2.56	3.25	3.94	4.87	16.0	18.3	20.5	23.2	25.2
11	2.60	3.05	3.82	4.57	5.58	17.3	19.7	21.9	24.7	26.8
12	3.07	3.57	4.40	5.23	6.30	18.5	21.0	23.3	26.2	28.3
13	3.57	4.11	5.01	5.89	7.04	19.8	22.4	24.7	27.7	29.8
14	4.07	4.66	5.63	6.57	7.79	21.1	23.7	26.1	29.1	31.3
15	4.60	5.23	6.26	7.26	8.55	22.3	25.0	27.5	30.6	32.8
16	5.14	5.81	6.91	7.96	9.31	23.5	26.3	28.8	32.0	34.3
17	5.70	6.41	7.56	8.67	10.1	24.8	27.6	30.2	33.4	35.7
18	6.26	7.01	8.23	9.39	10.9	26.0	28.9	31.5	34.8	37.2
19	6.84	7.63	8.91	10.1	11.7	27.2	30.1	32.9	36.2	38.6
20	7.43	8.26	9.59	10.9	12.4	28.4	31.4	34.2	37.6	40.0
21	8.03	8.90	10.3	11.6	13.2	29.6	32.7	35.5	38.9	41.4
22	8.64	9.54	11.0	12.3	14.0	30.8	33.9	36.8	40.3	42.8
23	9.26	10.2	11.7	13.1	14.8	32.0	35.2	38.1	41.6	44.2
24	9.89	10.9	12.4	13.8	15.7	33.2	36.4	39.4	43.0	45.6
25	10.5	11.5	13.1	14.6	16.5	34.4	37.7	40.6	44.3	46.9
26	11.2	12.2	13.8	15.4	17.3	35.6	38.9	41.9	45.6	48.3
27	11.8	12.9	14.6	16.2	18.1	36.7	40.1	43.2	47.0	49.6
28	12.5	13.6	15.3	16.9	18.9	37.9	41.3	44.5	48.3	51.0
29	13.1	14.3	16.0	17.7	19.8	39.1	42.6	45.7	49.6	52.3
30	13.8	15.0	16.8	18.5	20.6	40.3	43.8	47.0	50.9	53.7
40	20.7	22.2	24.4	26.5	29.1	51.8	55.8	59.3	63.7	66.8
50	28.0	29.7	32.4	34.8	37.7	63.2	67.5	71.4	76.2	79.5
60	35.5	37.5	40.5	43.2	46.5	74.4	79.1	83.3	88.4	92.0
70	43.3	45.4	48.8	51.7	55.3	85.5	90.5	95.0	100	104
80	51.2	53.5	57.2	60.4	64.3	96.6	102	107	112	116
90	59.2	61.8	65.6	69.1	73.3	108	113	118	124	128
100	67.3	70.1	74.2	77.9	82.4	118	124	130	136	140

Table 6(a) Critical Values of the F-Distribution: $A = .05$

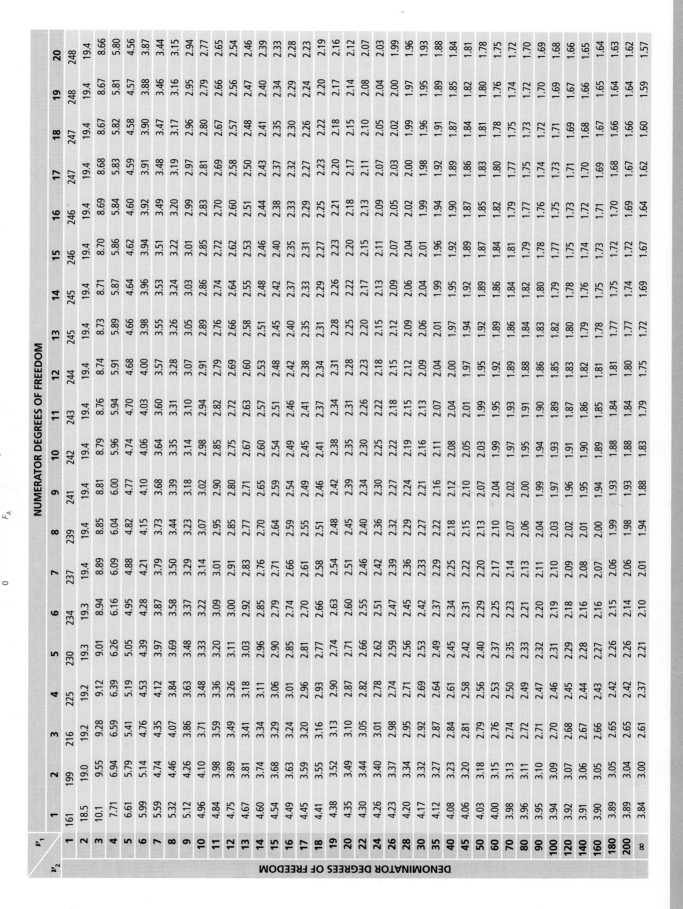

NUMERATOR DEGREES OF FREEDOM

ν_2 \ ν_1	1	2	3	4	5	6	7	8	9	10	11	12	13	14	15	16	17	18	19	20
1	161	199	216	225	230	234	237	239	241	242	243	244	245	245	246	246	247	247	248	248
2	18.5	19.0	19.2	19.2	19.3	19.3	19.4	19.4	19.4	19.4	19.4	19.4	19.4	19.4	19.4	19.4	19.4	19.4	19.4	19.4
3	10.1	9.55	9.28	9.12	9.01	8.94	8.89	8.85	8.81	8.79	8.76	8.74	8.73	8.71	8.70	8.69	8.68	8.67	8.67	8.66
4	7.71	6.94	6.59	6.39	6.26	6.16	6.09	6.04	6.00	5.96	5.94	5.91	5.89	5.87	5.86	5.84	5.83	5.82	5.81	5.80
5	6.61	5.79	5.41	5.19	5.05	4.95	4.88	4.82	4.77	4.74	4.70	4.68	4.66	4.64	4.62	4.60	4.59	4.58	4.57	4.56
6	5.99	5.14	4.76	4.53	4.39	4.28	4.21	4.15	4.10	4.06	4.03	4.00	3.98	3.96	3.94	3.92	3.91	3.90	3.88	3.87
7	5.59	4.74	4.35	4.12	3.97	3.87	3.79	3.73	3.68	3.64	3.60	3.57	3.55	3.53	3.51	3.49	3.48	3.47	3.46	3.44
8	5.32	4.46	4.07	3.84	3.69	3.58	3.50	3.44	3.39	3.35	3.31	3.28	3.26	3.24	3.22	3.20	3.19	3.17	3.16	3.15
9	5.12	4.26	3.86	3.63	3.48	3.37	3.29	3.23	3.18	3.14	3.10	3.07	3.05	3.03	3.01	2.99	2.97	2.96	2.95	2.94
10	4.96	4.10	3.71	3.48	3.33	3.22	3.14	3.07	3.02	2.98	2.94	2.91	2.89	2.86	2.85	2.83	2.81	2.80	2.79	2.77
11	4.84	3.98	3.59	3.36	3.20	3.09	3.01	2.95	2.90	2.85	2.82	2.79	2.76	2.74	2.72	2.70	2.69	2.67	2.66	2.65
12	4.75	3.89	3.49	3.26	3.11	3.00	2.91	2.85	2.80	2.75	2.72	2.69	2.66	2.64	2.62	2.60	2.58	2.57	2.56	2.54
13	4.67	3.81	3.41	3.18	3.03	2.92	2.83	2.77	2.71	2.67	2.63	2.60	2.58	2.55	2.53	2.51	2.50	2.48	2.47	2.46
14	4.60	3.74	3.34	3.11	2.96	2.85	2.76	2.70	2.65	2.60	2.57	2.53	2.51	2.48	2.46	2.44	2.43	2.41	2.40	2.39
15	4.54	3.68	3.29	3.06	2.90	2.79	2.71	2.64	2.59	2.54	2.51	2.48	2.45	2.42	2.40	2.38	2.37	2.35	2.34	2.33
16	4.49	3.63	3.24	3.01	2.85	2.74	2.66	2.59	2.54	2.49	2.46	2.42	2.40	2.37	2.35	2.33	2.32	2.30	2.29	2.28
17	4.45	3.59	3.20	2.96	2.81	2.70	2.61	2.55	2.49	2.45	2.41	2.38	2.35	2.33	2.31	2.29	2.27	2.26	2.24	2.23
18	4.41	3.55	3.16	2.93	2.77	2.66	2.58	2.51	2.46	2.41	2.37	2.34	2.31	2.29	2.27	2.25	2.23	2.22	2.20	2.19
19	4.38	3.52	3.13	2.90	2.74	2.63	2.54	2.48	2.42	2.38	2.34	2.31	2.28	2.26	2.23	2.21	2.20	2.18	2.17	2.16
20	4.35	3.49	3.10	2.87	2.71	2.60	2.51	2.45	2.39	2.35	2.31	2.28	2.25	2.22	2.20	2.18	2.17	2.15	2.14	2.12
22	4.30	3.44	3.05	2.82	2.66	2.55	2.46	2.40	2.34	2.30	2.26	2.23	2.20	2.17	2.15	2.13	2.11	2.10	2.08	2.07
24	4.26	3.40	3.01	2.78	2.62	2.51	2.42	2.36	2.30	2.25	2.22	2.18	2.15	2.13	2.11	2.09	2.07	2.05	2.04	2.03
26	4.23	3.37	2.98	2.74	2.59	2.47	2.39	2.32	2.27	2.22	2.18	2.15	2.12	2.09	2.07	2.05	2.03	2.02	2.00	1.99
28	4.20	3.34	2.95	2.71	2.56	2.45	2.36	2.29	2.24	2.19	2.15	2.12	2.09	2.06	2.04	2.02	2.00	1.99	1.97	1.96
30	4.17	3.32	2.92	2.69	2.53	2.42	2.33	2.27	2.21	2.16	2.13	2.09	2.06	2.04	2.01	1.99	1.98	1.96	1.95	1.93
35	4.12	3.27	2.87	2.64	2.49	2.37	2.29	2.22	2.16	2.11	2.07	2.04	2.01	1.99	1.96	1.94	1.92	1.91	1.89	1.88
40	4.08	3.23	2.84	2.61	2.45	2.34	2.25	2.18	2.12	2.08	2.04	2.00	1.97	1.95	1.92	1.90	1.89	1.87	1.85	1.84
45	4.06	3.20	2.81	2.58	2.42	2.31	2.22	2.15	2.10	2.05	2.01	1.97	1.94	1.92	1.89	1.87	1.86	1.84	1.82	1.81
50	4.03	3.18	2.79	2.56	2.40	2.29	2.20	2.13	2.07	2.03	1.99	1.95	1.92	1.89	1.87	1.85	1.83	1.81	1.80	1.78
60	4.00	3.15	2.76	2.53	2.37	2.25	2.17	2.10	2.04	1.99	1.95	1.92	1.89	1.86	1.84	1.82	1.80	1.78	1.76	1.75
70	3.98	3.13	2.74	2.50	2.35	2.23	2.14	2.07	2.02	1.97	1.93	1.89	1.86	1.84	1.81	1.79	1.77	1.75	1.74	1.72
80	3.96	3.11	2.72	2.49	2.33	2.21	2.13	2.06	2.00	1.95	1.91	1.88	1.84	1.82	1.79	1.77	1.75	1.73	1.72	1.70
90	3.95	3.10	2.71	2.47	2.32	2.20	2.11	2.04	1.99	1.94	1.90	1.86	1.83	1.80	1.78	1.76	1.74	1.72	1.70	1.69
100	3.94	3.09	2.70	2.46	2.31	2.19	2.10	2.03	1.97	1.93	1.89	1.85	1.82	1.79	1.77	1.75	1.73	1.71	1.69	1.68
120	3.92	3.07	2.68	2.45	2.29	2.18	2.09	2.02	1.96	1.91	1.87	1.83	1.80	1.78	1.75	1.73	1.71	1.69	1.67	1.66
140	3.91	3.06	2.67	2.44	2.28	2.16	2.08	2.01	1.95	1.90	1.86	1.82	1.79	1.76	1.74	1.72	1.70	1.68	1.66	1.65
160	3.90	3.05	2.66	2.43	2.27	2.16	2.07	2.00	1.94	1.89	1.85	1.81	1.78	1.75	1.73	1.71	1.69	1.67	1.66	1.64
180	3.89	3.05	2.65	2.42	2.26	2.15	2.06	1.99	1.93	1.88	1.84	1.81	1.77	1.75	1.72	1.70	1.68	1.66	1.65	1.63
200	3.89	3.04	2.65	2.42	2.26	2.14	2.06	1.98	1.93	1.88	1.84	1.80	1.77	1.74	1.72	1.69	1.67	1.66	1.64	1.62
∞	3.84	3.00	2.61	2.37	2.21	2.10	2.01	1.94	1.88	1.83	1.79	1.75	1.72	1.69	1.67	1.64	1.62	1.60	1.59	1.57

DENOMINATOR DEGREES OF FREEDOM

Table 6(a) (Continued)

NUMERATOR DEGREES OF FREEDOM

ν_1 \ ν_2	22	24	26	28	30	35	40	45	50	60	70	80	90	100	120	140	160	180	200	∞
1	249	249	249	250	250	251	251	251	252	252	252	253	253	253	253	253	254	254	254	254
2	19.5	19.5	19.5	19.5	19.5	19.5	19.5	19.5	19.5	19.5	19.5	19.5	19.5	19.5	19.5	19.5	19.5	19.5	19.5	19.5
3	8.65	8.64	8.63	8.62	8.62	8.60	8.59	8.59	8.58	8.57	8.57	8.56	8.56	8.55	8.55	8.55	8.54	8.54	8.54	8.53
4	5.79	5.77	5.76	5.75	5.75	5.73	5.72	5.71	5.70	5.69	5.68	5.67	5.67	5.66	5.66	5.65	5.65	5.65	5.65	5.63
5	4.54	4.53	4.52	4.50	4.50	4.48	4.46	4.45	4.44	4.43	4.42	4.41	4.41	4.41	4.40	4.39	4.39	4.39	4.39	4.37
6	3.86	3.84	3.83	3.82	3.81	3.79	3.77	3.76	3.75	3.74	3.73	3.72	3.72	3.71	3.70	3.70	3.70	3.69	3.69	3.67
7	3.43	3.41	3.40	3.39	3.38	3.36	3.34	3.33	3.32	3.30	3.29	3.29	3.28	3.27	3.27	3.26	3.26	3.25	3.25	3.23
8	3.13	3.12	3.10	3.09	3.08	3.06	3.04	3.03	3.02	3.01	2.99	2.99	2.98	2.97	2.97	2.96	2.96	2.95	2.95	2.93
9	2.92	2.90	2.89	2.87	2.86	2.84	2.83	2.81	2.80	2.79	2.78	2.77	2.76	2.76	2.75	2.74	2.74	2.73	2.73	2.71
10	2.75	2.74	2.72	2.71	2.70	2.68	2.66	2.65	2.64	2.62	2.61	2.60	2.59	2.59	2.58	2.57	2.57	2.57	2.56	2.54
11	2.63	2.61	2.59	2.58	2.57	2.55	2.53	2.52	2.51	2.49	2.48	2.47	2.46	2.46	2.45	2.44	2.44	2.43	2.43	2.41
12	2.52	2.51	2.49	2.48	2.47	2.44	2.43	2.41	2.40	2.38	2.37	2.36	2.36	2.35	2.34	2.33	2.33	2.33	2.32	2.30
13	2.44	2.42	2.41	2.39	2.38	2.36	2.34	2.33	2.31	2.30	2.28	2.27	2.27	2.26	2.25	2.25	2.24	2.24	2.23	2.21
14	2.37	2.35	2.33	2.32	2.31	2.28	2.27	2.25	2.24	2.22	2.21	2.20	2.19	2.19	2.18	2.17	2.17	2.16	2.16	2.13
15	2.31	2.29	2.27	2.26	2.25	2.22	2.20	2.19	2.18	2.16	2.15	2.14	2.13	2.12	2.11	2.11	2.10	2.10	2.10	2.07
16	2.25	2.24	2.22	2.21	2.19	2.17	2.15	2.14	2.12	2.11	2.09	2.08	2.07	2.07	2.06	2.05	2.05	2.04	2.04	2.01
17	2.21	2.19	2.17	2.16	2.15	2.12	2.10	2.09	2.08	2.06	2.05	2.03	2.03	2.02	2.01	2.00	2.00	1.99	1.99	1.96
18	2.17	2.15	2.13	2.12	2.11	2.08	2.06	2.05	2.04	2.02	2.00	1.99	1.98	1.98	1.97	1.96	1.96	1.95	1.95	1.92
19	2.13	2.11	2.10	2.08	2.07	2.05	2.03	2.01	2.00	1.98	1.97	1.96	1.95	1.94	1.93	1.92	1.92	1.91	1.91	1.88
20	2.10	2.08	2.07	2.05	2.04	2.01	1.99	1.98	1.97	1.95	1.93	1.92	1.91	1.91	1.90	1.89	1.88	1.88	1.88	1.84
22	2.05	2.03	2.01	2.00	1.98	1.96	1.94	1.92	1.91	1.89	1.88	1.86	1.86	1.85	1.84	1.83	1.82	1.82	1.82	1.78
24	2.00	1.98	1.97	1.95	1.94	1.91	1.89	1.88	1.86	1.84	1.83	1.82	1.81	1.80	1.79	1.78	1.78	1.77	1.77	1.73
26	1.97	1.95	1.93	1.91	1.90	1.87	1.85	1.84	1.82	1.80	1.79	1.78	1.77	1.76	1.75	1.74	1.73	1.73	1.73	1.69
28	1.93	1.91	1.90	1.88	1.87	1.84	1.82	1.80	1.79	1.77	1.75	1.74	1.73	1.73	1.71	1.71	1.70	1.69	1.69	1.65
30	1.91	1.89	1.87	1.85	1.84	1.81	1.79	1.77	1.76	1.74	1.72	1.71	1.70	1.70	1.68	1.68	1.67	1.66	1.66	1.62
35	1.85	1.83	1.82	1.80	1.79	1.76	1.74	1.72	1.70	1.68	1.66	1.65	1.64	1.63	1.62	1.61	1.61	1.60	1.60	1.56
40	1.81	1.79	1.77	1.76	1.74	1.72	1.69	1.67	1.66	1.64	1.62	1.61	1.60	1.59	1.58	1.57	1.56	1.55	1.55	1.51
45	1.78	1.76	1.74	1.73	1.71	1.68	1.66	1.64	1.63	1.60	1.59	1.57	1.56	1.55	1.54	1.53	1.52	1.52	1.51	1.47
50	1.76	1.74	1.72	1.70	1.69	1.66	1.63	1.61	1.60	1.58	1.56	1.54	1.53	1.52	1.51	1.50	1.49	1.49	1.48	1.44
60	1.72	1.70	1.68	1.66	1.65	1.62	1.59	1.57	1.56	1.53	1.52	1.50	1.49	1.48	1.47	1.46	1.45	1.44	1.44	1.39
70	1.70	1.67	1.65	1.64	1.62	1.59	1.57	1.55	1.53	1.50	1.49	1.47	1.46	1.45	1.44	1.42	1.42	1.41	1.40	1.35
80	1.68	1.65	1.63	1.62	1.60	1.57	1.54	1.52	1.51	1.48	1.46	1.45	1.44	1.43	1.41	1.40	1.39	1.38	1.38	1.33
90	1.66	1.64	1.62	1.60	1.59	1.55	1.53	1.51	1.49	1.46	1.44	1.43	1.42	1.41	1.39	1.38	1.37	1.36	1.36	1.30
100	1.65	1.63	1.61	1.59	1.57	1.54	1.52	1.49	1.48	1.45	1.43	1.41	1.40	1.39	1.38	1.36	1.35	1.35	1.34	1.28
120	1.63	1.61	1.59	1.57	1.55	1.52	1.50	1.47	1.46	1.43	1.41	1.39	1.38	1.37	1.35	1.34	1.33	1.32	1.32	1.26
140	1.62	1.60	1.57	1.56	1.54	1.51	1.48	1.46	1.44	1.41	1.39	1.38	1.36	1.35	1.33	1.32	1.31	1.30	1.30	1.23
160	1.61	1.59	1.57	1.55	1.53	1.50	1.47	1.45	1.43	1.40	1.38	1.36	1.35	1.34	1.32	1.31	1.30	1.29	1.28	1.22
180	1.60	1.58	1.56	1.54	1.52	1.49	1.46	1.44	1.42	1.39	1.37	1.35	1.34	1.33	1.31	1.30	1.29	1.28	1.27	1.20
200	1.60	1.57	1.55	1.53	1.52	1.48	1.46	1.43	1.41	1.39	1.36	1.35	1.33	1.32	1.30	1.29	1.28	1.27	1.26	1.19
∞	1.54	1.52	1.50	1.48	1.46	1.42	1.40	1.37	1.35	1.32	1.29	1.28	1.26	1.25	1.22	1.21	1.19	1.18	1.17	1.00

DENOMINATOR DEGREES OF FREEDOM

Table 6(b) Values of the F-Distribution: $A = .025$

NUMERATOR DEGREES OF FREEDOM

ν_2 \ ν_1	1	2	3	4	5	6	7	8	9	10	11	12	13	14	15	16	17	18	19	20
1	648	799	864	900	922	937	948	957	963	969	973	977	980	983	985	987	989	990	992	993
2	38.5	39.0	39.2	39.2	39.3	39.3	39.4	39.4	39.4	39.4	39.4	39.4	39.4	39.4	39.4	39.4	39.4	39.4	39.4	39.4
3	17.4	16.0	15.4	15.1	14.9	14.7	14.6	14.5	14.5	14.4	14.4	14.3	14.3	14.3	14.3	14.2	14.2	14.2	14.2	14.2
4	12.2	10.6	10.0	9.60	9.36	9.20	9.07	8.98	8.90	8.84	8.79	8.75	8.71	8.68	8.66	8.63	8.61	8.59	8.58	8.56
5	10.0	8.43	7.76	7.39	7.15	6.98	6.85	6.76	6.68	6.62	6.57	6.52	6.49	6.46	6.43	6.40	6.38	6.36	6.34	6.33
6	8.81	7.26	6.60	6.23	5.99	5.82	5.70	5.60	5.52	5.46	5.41	5.37	5.33	5.30	5.27	5.24	5.22	5.20	5.18	5.17
7	8.07	6.54	5.89	5.52	5.29	5.12	4.99	4.90	4.82	4.76	4.71	4.67	4.63	4.60	4.57	4.54	4.52	4.50	4.48	4.47
8	7.57	6.06	5.42	5.05	4.82	4.65	4.53	4.43	4.36	4.30	4.24	4.20	4.16	4.13	4.10	4.08	4.05	4.03	4.02	4.00
9	7.21	5.71	5.08	4.72	4.48	4.32	4.20	4.10	4.03	3.96	3.91	3.87	3.83	3.80	3.77	3.74	3.72	3.70	3.68	3.67
10	6.94	5.46	4.83	4.47	4.24	4.07	3.95	3.85	3.78	3.72	3.66	3.62	3.58	3.55	3.52	3.50	3.47	3.45	3.44	3.42
11	6.72	5.26	4.63	4.28	4.04	3.88	3.76	3.66	3.59	3.53	3.47	3.43	3.39	3.36	3.33	3.30	3.28	3.26	3.24	3.23
12	6.55	5.10	4.47	4.12	3.89	3.73	3.61	3.51	3.44	3.37	3.32	3.28	3.24	3.21	3.18	3.15	3.13	3.11	3.09	3.07
13	6.41	4.97	4.35	4.00	3.77	3.60	3.48	3.39	3.31	3.25	3.20	3.15	3.12	3.08	3.05	3.03	3.00	2.98	2.96	2.95
14	6.30	4.86	4.24	3.89	3.66	3.50	3.38	3.29	3.21	3.15	3.09	3.05	3.01	2.98	2.95	2.92	2.90	2.88	2.86	2.84
15	6.20	4.77	4.15	3.80	3.58	3.41	3.29	3.20	3.12	3.06	3.01	2.96	2.92	2.89	2.86	2.84	2.81	2.79	2.77	2.76
16	6.12	4.69	4.08	3.73	3.50	3.34	3.22	3.12	3.05	2.99	2.93	2.89	2.85	2.82	2.79	2.76	2.74	2.72	2.70	2.68
17	6.04	4.62	4.01	3.66	3.44	3.28	3.16	3.06	2.98	2.92	2.87	2.82	2.79	2.75	2.72	2.70	2.67	2.65	2.63	2.62
18	5.98	4.56	3.95	3.61	3.38	3.22	3.10	3.01	2.93	2.87	2.81	2.77	2.73	2.70	2.67	2.64	2.62	2.60	2.58	2.56
19	5.92	4.51	3.90	3.56	3.33	3.17	3.05	2.96	2.88	2.82	2.76	2.72	2.68	2.65	2.62	2.59	2.57	2.55	2.53	2.51
20	5.87	4.46	3.86	3.51	3.29	3.13	3.01	2.91	2.84	2.77	2.72	2.68	2.64	2.60	2.57	2.55	2.52	2.50	2.48	2.46
22	5.79	4.38	3.78	3.44	3.22	3.05	2.93	2.84	2.76	2.70	2.65	2.60	2.56	2.53	2.50	2.47	2.45	2.43	2.41	2.39
24	5.72	4.32	3.72	3.38	3.15	2.99	2.87	2.78	2.70	2.64	2.59	2.54	2.50	2.47	2.44	2.41	2.39	2.36	2.35	2.33
26	5.66	4.27	3.67	3.33	3.10	2.94	2.82	2.73	2.65	2.59	2.54	2.49	2.45	2.42	2.39	2.36	2.34	2.31	2.29	2.28
28	5.61	4.22	3.63	3.29	3.06	2.90	2.78	2.69	2.61	2.55	2.49	2.45	2.41	2.37	2.34	2.32	2.29	2.27	2.25	2.23
30	5.57	4.18	3.59	3.25	3.03	2.87	2.75	2.65	2.57	2.51	2.46	2.41	2.37	2.34	2.31	2.28	2.26	2.23	2.21	2.20
35	5.48	4.11	3.52	3.18	2.96	2.80	2.68	2.58	2.50	2.44	2.39	2.34	2.30	2.27	2.23	2.21	2.18	2.16	2.14	2.12
40	5.42	4.05	3.46	3.13	2.90	2.74	2.62	2.53	2.45	2.39	2.33	2.29	2.25	2.21	2.18	2.15	2.13	2.11	2.09	2.07
45	5.38	4.01	3.42	3.09	2.86	2.70	2.58	2.49	2.41	2.35	2.29	2.25	2.21	2.17	2.14	2.11	2.09	2.07	2.04	2.03
50	5.34	3.97	3.39	3.05	2.83	2.67	2.55	2.46	2.38	2.32	2.26	2.22	2.18	2.14	2.11	2.08	2.06	2.03	2.01	1.99
60	5.29	3.93	3.34	3.01	2.79	2.63	2.51	2.41	2.33	2.27	2.22	2.17	2.13	2.09	2.06	2.03	2.01	1.98	1.96	1.94
70	5.25	3.89	3.31	2.97	2.75	2.59	2.47	2.38	2.30	2.24	2.18	2.14	2.10	2.06	2.03	2.00	1.97	1.95	1.93	1.91
80	5.22	3.86	3.28	2.95	2.73	2.57	2.45	2.35	2.28	2.21	2.16	2.11	2.07	2.03	2.00	1.97	1.95	1.92	1.90	1.88
90	5.20	3.84	3.26	2.93	2.71	2.55	2.43	2.34	2.26	2.19	2.14	2.09	2.05	2.02	1.98	1.95	1.93	1.91	1.88	1.86
100	5.18	3.83	3.25	2.92	2.70	2.54	2.42	2.32	2.24	2.18	2.12	2.08	2.04	2.00	1.97	1.94	1.91	1.89	1.87	1.85
120	5.15	3.80	3.23	2.89	2.67	2.52	2.39	2.30	2.22	2.16	2.10	2.05	2.01	1.98	1.94	1.92	1.89	1.87	1.84	1.82
140	5.13	3.79	3.21	2.88	2.66	2.50	2.38	2.28	2.21	2.14	2.09	2.04	2.00	1.96	1.93	1.90	1.87	1.85	1.83	1.81
160	5.12	3.78	3.20	2.87	2.65	2.49	2.37	2.27	2.19	2.13	2.07	2.03	1.99	1.95	1.92	1.89	1.86	1.84	1.82	1.80
180	5.11	3.77	3.19	2.86	2.64	2.48	2.36	2.26	2.19	2.12	2.07	2.02	1.98	1.94	1.91	1.88	1.85	1.83	1.81	1.79
200	5.10	3.76	3.18	2.85	2.63	2.47	2.35	2.26	2.18	2.11	2.06	2.01	1.97	1.93	1.90	1.87	1.84	1.82	1.80	1.78
∞	5.03	3.69	3.12	2.79	2.57	2.41	2.29	2.19	2.11	2.05	1.99	1.95	1.90	1.87	1.83	1.80	1.78	1.75	1.73	1.71

DENOMINATOR DEGREES OF FREEDOM

Table 6(b) (Continued)

NUMERATOR DEGREES OF FREEDOM

ν_2 \ ν_1	22	24	26	28	30	35	40	45	50	60	70	80	90	100	120	140	160	180	200	∞
1	995	997	999	1000	1001	1004	1006	1007	1008	1010	1011	1012	1013	1013	1014	1015	1015	1015	1016	1018
2	39.5	39.5	39.5	39.5	39.5	39.5	39.5	39.5	39.5	39.5	39.5	39.5	39.5	39.5	39.5	39.5	39.5	39.5	39.5	39.5
3	14.1	14.1	14.1	14.1	14.1	14.1	14.0	14.0	14.0	14.0	14.0	14.0	14.0	14.0	13.9	13.9	13.9	13.9	13.9	13.9
4	8.53	8.51	8.49	8.48	8.46	8.43	8.41	8.39	8.38	8.36	8.35	8.33	8.33	8.32	8.31	8.30	8.30	8.29	8.29	8.26
5	6.30	6.28	6.26	6.24	6.23	6.20	6.18	6.16	6.14	6.12	6.11	6.10	6.09	6.08	6.07	6.06	6.06	6.05	6.05	6.02
6	5.14	5.12	5.10	5.08	5.07	5.04	5.01	4.99	4.98	4.96	4.94	4.93	4.92	4.92	4.90	4.90	4.89	4.89	4.88	4.85
7	4.44	4.41	4.39	4.38	4.36	4.33	4.31	4.29	4.28	4.25	4.24	4.23	4.22	4.21	4.20	4.19	4.18	4.18	4.18	4.14
8	3.97	3.95	3.93	3.91	3.89	3.86	3.84	3.82	3.81	3.78	3.77	3.76	3.75	3.74	3.73	3.72	3.71	3.71	3.70	3.67
9	3.64	3.61	3.59	3.58	3.56	3.53	3.51	3.49	3.47	3.45	3.43	3.42	3.41	3.40	3.39	3.38	3.38	3.37	3.37	3.33
10	3.39	3.37	3.34	3.33	3.31	3.28	3.26	3.24	3.22	3.20	3.18	3.17	3.16	3.15	3.14	3.13	3.13	3.12	3.12	3.08
11	3.20	3.17	3.15	3.13	3.12	3.09	3.06	3.04	3.03	3.00	2.99	2.97	2.96	2.96	2.94	2.94	2.93	2.92	2.92	2.88
12	3.04	3.02	3.00	2.98	2.96	2.93	2.91	2.89	2.87	2.85	2.83	2.82	2.81	2.80	2.79	2.78	2.77	2.77	2.76	2.73
13	2.92	2.89	2.87	2.85	2.84	2.80	2.78	2.76	2.74	2.72	2.70	2.69	2.68	2.67	2.66	2.65	2.64	2.64	2.63	2.60
14	2.81	2.79	2.77	2.75	2.73	2.70	2.67	2.65	2.64	2.61	2.60	2.58	2.57	2.56	2.55	2.54	2.54	2.53	2.53	2.49
15	2.73	2.70	2.68	2.66	2.64	2.61	2.59	2.56	2.55	2.52	2.51	2.49	2.48	2.47	2.46	2.45	2.44	2.44	2.44	2.40
16	2.65	2.63	2.60	2.58	2.57	2.53	2.51	2.49	2.47	2.45	2.43	2.42	2.40	2.40	2.38	2.37	2.37	2.36	2.36	2.32
17	2.59	2.56	2.54	2.52	2.50	2.47	2.44	2.42	2.41	2.38	2.36	2.35	2.34	2.33	2.32	2.31	2.30	2.29	2.29	2.25
18	2.53	2.50	2.48	2.46	2.44	2.41	2.38	2.36	2.35	2.32	2.30	2.29	2.28	2.27	2.26	2.25	2.24	2.23	2.23	2.19
19	2.48	2.45	2.43	2.41	2.39	2.36	2.33	2.31	2.30	2.27	2.25	2.24	2.23	2.22	2.20	2.19	2.19	2.18	2.18	2.13
20	2.43	2.41	2.39	2.37	2.35	2.31	2.29	2.27	2.25	2.22	2.20	2.19	2.18	2.17	2.16	2.15	2.14	2.13	2.13	2.09
22	2.36	2.33	2.31	2.29	2.27	2.24	2.21	2.19	2.17	2.14	2.13	2.11	2.10	2.09	2.08	2.07	2.06	2.05	2.05	2.00
24	2.30	2.27	2.25	2.23	2.21	2.17	2.15	2.12	2.11	2.08	2.06	2.05	2.03	2.02	2.01	2.00	1.99	1.99	1.98	1.94
26	2.24	2.22	2.19	2.17	2.16	2.12	2.09	2.07	2.05	2.03	2.01	1.99	1.98	1.97	1.95	1.94	1.94	1.93	1.92	1.88
28	2.20	2.17	2.15	2.13	2.11	2.08	2.05	2.03	2.01	1.98	1.96	1.94	1.93	1.92	1.91	1.90	1.89	1.88	1.88	1.83
30	2.16	2.14	2.11	2.09	2.07	2.04	2.01	1.99	1.97	1.94	1.92	1.90	1.89	1.88	1.87	1.86	1.85	1.84	1.84	1.79
35	2.09	2.06	2.04	2.02	2.00	1.96	1.93	1.91	1.89	1.86	1.84	1.82	1.81	1.80	1.79	1.77	1.77	1.76	1.75	1.70
40	2.03	2.01	1.98	1.96	1.94	1.90	1.88	1.85	1.83	1.80	1.78	1.76	1.75	1.74	1.72	1.71	1.70	1.70	1.69	1.64
45	1.99	1.96	1.94	1.92	1.90	1.86	1.83	1.81	1.79	1.76	1.74	1.72	1.70	1.69	1.68	1.66	1.66	1.65	1.64	1.59
50	1.96	1.93	1.91	1.89	1.87	1.83	1.80	1.77	1.75	1.72	1.70	1.68	1.67	1.66	1.64	1.63	1.62	1.61	1.60	1.55
60	1.91	1.88	1.86	1.83	1.82	1.78	1.74	1.72	1.70	1.67	1.64	1.63	1.61	1.60	1.58	1.57	1.56	1.55	1.54	1.48
70	1.88	1.85	1.82	1.80	1.78	1.74	1.71	1.68	1.66	1.63	1.60	1.59	1.57	1.56	1.54	1.53	1.52	1.51	1.50	1.44
80	1.85	1.82	1.79	1.77	1.75	1.71	1.68	1.65	1.63	1.60	1.57	1.55	1.54	1.53	1.51	1.49	1.48	1.47	1.47	1.40
90	1.83	1.80	1.77	1.75	1.73	1.69	1.66	1.63	1.61	1.58	1.55	1.53	1.52	1.50	1.48	1.47	1.46	1.45	1.44	1.37
100	1.81	1.78	1.76	1.74	1.71	1.67	1.64	1.61	1.59	1.56	1.53	1.51	1.50	1.48	1.46	1.45	1.44	1.43	1.42	1.35
120	1.79	1.76	1.73	1.71	1.69	1.65	1.61	1.59	1.56	1.53	1.50	1.48	1.47	1.45	1.43	1.42	1.41	1.40	1.39	1.31
140	1.77	1.74	1.72	1.69	1.67	1.63	1.60	1.57	1.55	1.51	1.48	1.46	1.45	1.43	1.41	1.39	1.38	1.37	1.36	1.28
160	1.76	1.73	1.70	1.68	1.66	1.62	1.58	1.55	1.53	1.50	1.47	1.45	1.43	1.42	1.39	1.38	1.36	1.35	1.35	1.26
180	1.75	1.72	1.69	1.67	1.65	1.61	1.57	1.54	1.52	1.48	1.46	1.43	1.42	1.40	1.38	1.36	1.35	1.34	1.33	1.25
200	1.74	1.71	1.68	1.66	1.64	1.60	1.56	1.53	1.51	1.47	1.45	1.42	1.41	1.39	1.37	1.35	1.34	1.33	1.32	1.23
∞	1.67	1.64	1.61	1.59	1.57	1.52	1.49	1.46	1.43	1.39	1.36	1.33	1.31	1.30	1.27	1.25	1.23	1.22	1.21	1.00

DENOMINATOR DEGREES OF FREEDOM

Table 6(c) Values of the F-Distribution: $A = .01$

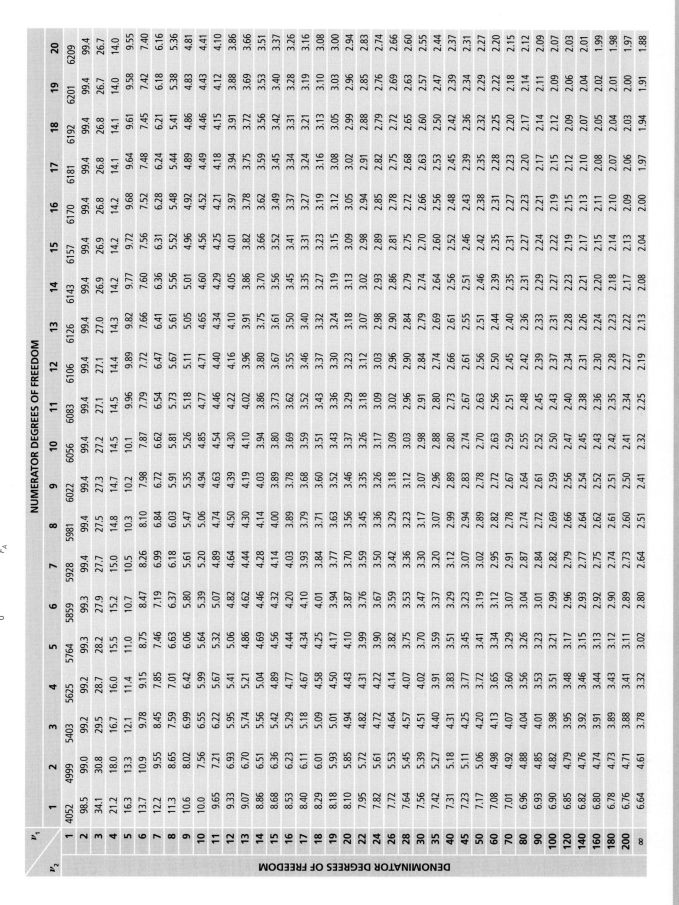

NUMERATOR DEGREES OF FREEDOM

ν_2 \ ν_1	1	2	3	4	5	6	7	8	9	10	11	12	13	14	15	16	17	18	19	20
1	4052	4999	5403	5625	5764	5859	5928	5981	6022	6056	6083	6106	6126	6143	6157	6170	6181	6192	6201	6209
2	98.5	99.0	99.2	99.2	99.3	99.3	99.4	99.4	99.4	99.4	99.4	99.4	99.4	99.4	99.4	99.4	99.4	99.4	99.4	99.4
3	34.1	30.8	29.5	28.7	28.2	27.9	27.7	27.5	27.3	27.2	27.1	27.1	27.0	26.9	26.9	26.8	26.8	26.8	26.7	26.7
4	21.2	18.0	16.7	16.0	15.5	15.2	15.0	14.8	14.7	14.5	14.5	14.4	14.3	14.2	14.2	14.2	14.1	14.1	14.0	14.0
5	16.3	13.3	12.1	11.4	11.0	10.7	10.5	10.3	10.2	10.1	9.96	9.89	9.82	9.77	9.72	9.68	9.64	9.61	9.58	9.55
6	13.7	10.9	9.78	9.15	8.75	8.47	8.26	8.10	7.98	7.87	7.79	7.72	7.66	7.60	7.56	7.52	7.48	7.45	7.42	7.40
7	12.2	9.55	8.45	7.85	7.46	7.19	6.99	6.84	6.72	6.62	6.54	6.47	6.41	6.36	6.31	6.28	6.24	6.21	6.18	6.16
8	11.3	8.65	7.59	7.01	6.63	6.37	6.18	6.03	5.91	5.81	5.73	5.67	5.61	5.56	5.52	5.48	5.44	5.41	5.38	5.36
9	10.6	8.02	6.99	6.42	6.06	5.80	5.61	5.47	5.35	5.26	5.18	5.11	5.05	5.01	4.96	4.92	4.89	4.86	4.83	4.81
10	10.0	7.56	6.55	5.99	5.64	5.39	5.20	5.06	4.94	4.85	4.77	4.71	4.65	4.60	4.56	4.52	4.49	4.46	4.43	4.41
11	9.65	7.21	6.22	5.67	5.32	5.07	4.89	4.74	4.63	4.54	4.46	4.40	4.34	4.29	4.25	4.21	4.18	4.15	4.12	4.10
12	9.33	6.93	5.95	5.41	5.06	4.82	4.64	4.50	4.39	4.30	4.22	4.16	4.10	4.05	4.01	3.97	3.94	3.91	3.88	3.86
13	9.07	6.70	5.74	5.21	4.86	4.62	4.44	4.30	4.19	4.10	4.02	3.96	3.91	3.86	3.82	3.78	3.75	3.72	3.69	3.66
14	8.86	6.51	5.56	5.04	4.69	4.46	4.28	4.14	4.03	3.94	3.86	3.80	3.75	3.70	3.66	3.62	3.59	3.56	3.53	3.51
15	8.68	6.36	5.42	4.89	4.56	4.32	4.14	4.00	3.89	3.80	3.73	3.67	3.61	3.56	3.52	3.49	3.45	3.42	3.40	3.37
16	8.53	6.23	5.29	4.77	4.44	4.20	4.03	3.89	3.78	3.69	3.62	3.55	3.50	3.45	3.41	3.37	3.34	3.31	3.28	3.26
17	8.40	6.11	5.18	4.67	4.34	4.10	3.93	3.79	3.68	3.59	3.52	3.46	3.40	3.35	3.31	3.27	3.24	3.21	3.19	3.16
18	8.29	6.01	5.09	4.58	4.25	4.01	3.84	3.71	3.60	3.51	3.43	3.37	3.32	3.27	3.23	3.19	3.16	3.13	3.10	3.08
19	8.18	5.93	5.01	4.50	4.17	3.94	3.77	3.63	3.52	3.43	3.36	3.30	3.24	3.19	3.15	3.12	3.08	3.05	3.03	3.00
20	8.10	5.85	4.94	4.43	4.10	3.87	3.70	3.56	3.46	3.37	3.29	3.23	3.18	3.13	3.09	3.05	3.02	2.99	2.96	2.94
22	7.95	5.72	4.82	4.31	3.99	3.76	3.59	3.45	3.35	3.26	3.18	3.12	3.07	3.02	2.98	2.94	2.91	2.88	2.85	2.83
24	7.82	5.61	4.72	4.22	3.90	3.67	3.50	3.36	3.26	3.17	3.09	3.03	2.98	2.93	2.89	2.85	2.82	2.79	2.76	2.74
26	7.72	5.53	4.64	4.14	3.82	3.59	3.42	3.29	3.18	3.09	3.02	2.96	2.90	2.86	2.81	2.78	2.75	2.72	2.69	2.66
28	7.64	5.45	4.57	4.07	3.75	3.53	3.36	3.23	3.12	3.03	2.96	2.90	2.84	2.79	2.75	2.72	2.68	2.65	2.63	2.60
30	7.56	5.39	4.51	4.02	3.70	3.47	3.30	3.17	3.07	2.98	2.91	2.84	2.79	2.74	2.70	2.66	2.63	2.60	2.57	2.55
35	7.42	5.27	4.40	3.91	3.59	3.37	3.20	3.07	2.96	2.88	2.80	2.74	2.69	2.64	2.60	2.56	2.53	2.50	2.47	2.44
40	7.31	5.18	4.31	3.83	3.51	3.29	3.12	2.99	2.89	2.80	2.73	2.66	2.61	2.56	2.52	2.48	2.45	2.42	2.39	2.37
45	7.23	5.11	4.25	3.77	3.45	3.23	3.07	2.94	2.83	2.74	2.67	2.61	2.55	2.51	2.46	2.43	2.39	2.36	2.34	2.31
50	7.17	5.06	4.20	3.72	3.41	3.19	3.02	2.89	2.78	2.70	2.63	2.56	2.51	2.46	2.42	2.38	2.35	2.32	2.29	2.27
60	7.08	4.98	4.13	3.65	3.34	3.12	2.95	2.82	2.72	2.63	2.56	2.50	2.44	2.39	2.35	2.31	2.28	2.25	2.22	2.20
70	7.01	4.92	4.07	3.60	3.29	3.07	2.91	2.78	2.67	2.59	2.51	2.45	2.40	2.35	2.31	2.27	2.23	2.20	2.18	2.15
80	6.96	4.88	4.04	3.56	3.26	3.04	2.87	2.74	2.64	2.55	2.48	2.42	2.36	2.31	2.27	2.23	2.20	2.17	2.14	2.12
90	6.93	4.85	4.01	3.53	3.23	3.01	2.84	2.72	2.61	2.52	2.45	2.39	2.33	2.29	2.24	2.21	2.17	2.14	2.11	2.09
100	6.90	4.82	3.98	3.51	3.21	2.99	2.82	2.69	2.59	2.50	2.43	2.37	2.31	2.27	2.22	2.19	2.15	2.12	2.09	2.07
120	6.85	4.79	3.95	3.48	3.17	2.96	2.79	2.66	2.56	2.47	2.40	2.34	2.28	2.23	2.19	2.15	2.12	2.09	2.06	2.03
140	6.82	4.76	3.92	3.46	3.15	2.93	2.77	2.64	2.54	2.45	2.38	2.31	2.26	2.21	2.17	2.13	2.10	2.07	2.04	2.01
160	6.80	4.74	3.91	3.44	3.13	2.92	2.75	2.62	2.52	2.43	2.36	2.30	2.24	2.20	2.15	2.11	2.08	2.05	2.02	1.99
180	6.78	4.73	3.89	3.43	3.12	2.90	2.74	2.61	2.51	2.42	2.35	2.28	2.23	2.18	2.14	2.10	2.07	2.04	2.01	1.98
200	6.76	4.71	3.88	3.41	3.11	2.89	2.73	2.60	2.50	2.41	2.34	2.27	2.22	2.17	2.13	2.09	2.06	2.03	2.00	1.97
∞	6.64	4.61	3.78	3.32	3.02	2.80	2.64	2.51	2.41	2.32	2.25	2.19	2.13	2.08	2.04	2.00	1.97	1.94	1.91	1.88

DENOMINATOR DEGREES OF FREEDOM

Table 6(c) (*Continued*)

NUMERATOR DEGREES OF FREEDOM

ν_2 \ ν_1	22	24	26	28	30	35	40	45	50	60	70	80	90	100	120	140	160	180	200	∞
1	6223	6235	6245	6253	6261	6276	6287	6296	6303	6313	6321	6326	6331	6334	6339	6343	6346	6348	6350	6366
2	99.5	99.5	99.5	99.5	99.5	99.5	99.5	99.5	99.5	99.5	99.5	99.5	99.5	99.5	99.5	99.5	99.5	99.5	99.5	99.5
3	26.6	26.6	26.6	26.5	26.5	26.5	26.4	26.4	26.4	26.3	26.3	26.3	26.3	26.2	26.2	26.2	26.2	26.2	26.2	26.1
4	14.0	13.9	13.9	13.9	13.8	13.8	13.7	13.7	13.7	13.7	13.6	13.6	13.6	13.6	13.6	13.5	13.5	13.5	13.5	13.5
5	9.51	9.47	9.43	9.40	9.38	9.33	9.29	9.26	9.24	9.20	9.18	9.16	9.14	9.13	9.11	9.10	9.09	9.08	9.08	9.02
6	7.35	7.31	7.28	7.25	7.23	7.18	7.14	7.11	7.09	7.06	7.03	7.01	7.00	6.99	6.97	6.96	6.95	6.94	6.93	6.88
7	6.11	6.07	6.04	6.02	5.99	5.94	5.91	5.88	5.86	5.82	5.80	5.78	5.77	5.75	5.74	5.72	5.72	5.71	5.70	5.65
8	5.32	5.28	5.25	5.22	5.20	5.15	5.12	5.09	5.07	5.03	5.01	4.99	4.97	4.96	4.95	4.93	4.92	4.92	4.91	4.86
9	4.77	4.73	4.70	4.67	4.65	4.60	4.57	4.54	4.52	4.48	4.46	4.44	4.43	4.41	4.40	4.39	4.38	4.37	4.36	4.31
10	4.36	4.33	4.30	4.27	4.25	4.20	4.17	4.14	4.12	4.08	4.06	4.04	4.03	4.01	4.00	3.98	3.97	3.97	3.96	3.91
11	4.06	4.02	3.99	3.96	3.94	3.89	3.86	3.83	3.81	3.78	3.75	3.73	3.72	3.71	3.69	3.68	3.67	3.66	3.66	3.60
12	3.82	3.78	3.75	3.72	3.70	3.65	3.62	3.59	3.57	3.54	3.51	3.49	3.48	3.47	3.45	3.44	3.43	3.42	3.41	3.36
13	3.62	3.59	3.56	3.53	3.51	3.46	3.43	3.40	3.38	3.34	3.32	3.30	3.28	3.27	3.25	3.24	3.23	3.23	3.22	3.17
14	3.46	3.43	3.40	3.37	3.35	3.30	3.27	3.24	3.22	3.18	3.16	3.14	3.12	3.11	3.09	3.08	3.07	3.06	3.06	3.01
15	3.33	3.29	3.26	3.24	3.21	3.17	3.13	3.10	3.08	3.05	3.02	3.00	2.99	2.98	2.96	2.95	2.94	2.93	2.92	2.87
16	3.22	3.18	3.15	3.12	3.10	3.05	3.02	2.99	2.97	2.93	2.91	2.89	2.87	2.86	2.84	2.83	2.82	2.81	2.81	2.75
17	3.12	3.08	3.05	3.03	3.00	2.96	2.92	2.89	2.87	2.83	2.81	2.79	2.78	2.76	2.75	2.73	2.72	2.72	2.71	2.65
18	3.03	3.00	2.97	2.94	2.92	2.87	2.84	2.81	2.78	2.75	2.72	2.70	2.69	2.68	2.66	2.65	2.64	2.63	2.62	2.57
19	2.96	2.92	2.89	2.87	2.84	2.80	2.76	2.73	2.71	2.67	2.65	2.63	2.61	2.60	2.58	2.57	2.56	2.55	2.55	2.49
20	2.90	2.86	2.83	2.80	2.78	2.73	2.69	2.67	2.64	2.61	2.58	2.56	2.55	2.54	2.52	2.50	2.49	2.49	2.48	2.42
22	2.78	2.75	2.72	2.69	2.67	2.62	2.58	2.55	2.53	2.50	2.47	2.45	2.43	2.42	2.40	2.39	2.38	2.37	2.36	2.31
24	2.70	2.66	2.63	2.60	2.58	2.53	2.49	2.46	2.44	2.40	2.38	2.36	2.34	2.33	2.31	2.30	2.29	2.28	2.27	2.21
26	2.62	2.58	2.55	2.53	2.50	2.45	2.42	2.39	2.36	2.33	2.30	2.28	2.26	2.25	2.23	2.22	2.21	2.20	2.19	2.13
28	2.56	2.52	2.49	2.46	2.44	2.39	2.35	2.32	2.30	2.26	2.24	2.22	2.20	2.19	2.17	2.15	2.14	2.13	2.13	2.07
30	2.51	2.47	2.44	2.41	2.39	2.34	2.30	2.27	2.25	2.21	2.18	2.16	2.14	2.13	2.11	2.10	2.09	2.08	2.07	2.01
35	2.40	2.36	2.33	2.30	2.28	2.23	2.19	2.16	2.14	2.10	2.07	2.05	2.03	2.02	2.00	1.98	1.97	1.96	1.96	1.89
40	2.33	2.29	2.26	2.23	2.20	2.15	2.11	2.08	2.06	2.02	1.99	1.97	1.95	1.94	1.92	1.90	1.89	1.88	1.87	1.81
45	2.27	2.23	2.20	2.17	2.14	2.09	2.05	2.02	2.00	1.96	1.93	1.91	1.89	1.88	1.85	1.84	1.83	1.82	1.81	1.74
50	2.22	2.18	2.15	2.12	2.10	2.05	2.01	1.97	1.95	1.91	1.88	1.86	1.84	1.82	1.80	1.79	1.77	1.76	1.76	1.68
60	2.15	2.12	2.08	2.05	2.03	1.98	1.94	1.90	1.88	1.84	1.81	1.78	1.76	1.75	1.73	1.71	1.70	1.69	1.68	1.60
70	2.11	2.07	2.03	2.01	1.98	1.93	1.89	1.85	1.83	1.78	1.75	1.73	1.71	1.70	1.67	1.65	1.64	1.63	1.62	1.54
80	2.07	2.03	2.00	1.97	1.94	1.89	1.85	1.82	1.79	1.75	1.71	1.69	1.67	1.65	1.63	1.61	1.60	1.59	1.58	1.50
90	2.04	2.00	1.97	1.94	1.92	1.86	1.82	1.79	1.76	1.72	1.68	1.66	1.64	1.62	1.60	1.58	1.57	1.55	1.55	1.46
100	2.02	1.98	1.95	1.92	1.89	1.84	1.80	1.76	1.74	1.69	1.66	1.63	1.61	1.60	1.57	1.55	1.54	1.53	1.52	1.43
120	1.99	1.95	1.92	1.89	1.86	1.81	1.76	1.73	1.70	1.66	1.62	1.60	1.58	1.56	1.53	1.51	1.50	1.49	1.48	1.38
140	1.97	1.93	1.89	1.86	1.84	1.78	1.74	1.70	1.67	1.63	1.60	1.57	1.55	1.53	1.50	1.48	1.47	1.46	1.45	1.35
160	1.95	1.91	1.88	1.85	1.82	1.76	1.72	1.68	1.66	1.61	1.58	1.55	1.53	1.51	1.48	1.46	1.45	1.43	1.42	1.32
180	1.94	1.90	1.86	1.83	1.81	1.75	1.71	1.67	1.64	1.60	1.56	1.53	1.51	1.49	1.47	1.45	1.43	1.42	1.41	1.30
200	1.93	1.89	1.85	1.82	1.79	1.74	1.69	1.66	1.63	1.58	1.55	1.52	1.50	1.48	1.45	1.43	1.42	1.40	1.39	1.28
∞	1.83	1.79	1.76	1.73	1.70	1.64	1.59	1.56	1.53	1.48	1.44	1.41	1.38	1.36	1.33	1.30	1.28	1.26	1.25	1.00

DENOMINATOR DEGREES OF FREEDOM

Table 6(d) Values of the F-Distribution: $A = .005$

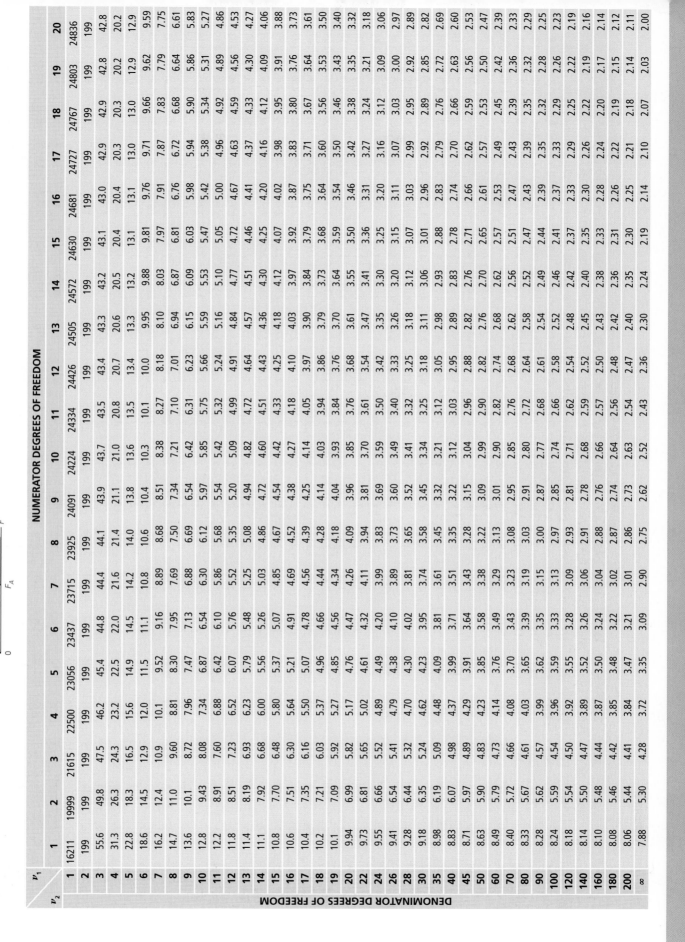

NUMERATOR DEGREES OF FREEDOM

ν_2 \ ν_1	1	2	3	4	5	6	7	8	9	10	11	12	13	14	15	16	17	18	19	20
1	16211	19999	21615	22500	23056	23437	23715	23925	24091	24224	24334	24426	24505	24572	24630	24681	24727	24767	24803	24836
2	199	199	199	199	199	199	199	199	199	199	199	199	199	199	199	199	199	199	199	199
3	55.6	49.8	47.5	46.2	45.4	44.8	44.4	44.1	43.9	43.7	43.5	43.4	43.3	43.2	43.1	43.0	42.9	42.9	42.8	42.8
4	31.3	26.3	24.3	23.2	22.5	22.0	21.6	21.4	21.1	21.0	20.8	20.7	20.6	20.5	20.4	20.4	20.3	20.3	20.2	20.2
5	22.8	18.3	16.5	15.6	14.9	14.5	14.2	14.0	13.8	13.6	13.5	13.4	13.3	13.2	13.1	13.1	13.0	13.0	12.9	12.9
6	18.6	14.5	12.9	12.0	11.5	11.1	10.8	10.6	10.4	10.3	10.1	10.0	9.95	9.88	9.81	9.76	9.71	9.66	9.62	9.59
7	16.2	12.4	10.9	10.1	9.52	9.16	8.89	8.68	8.51	8.38	8.27	8.18	8.10	8.03	7.97	7.91	7.87	7.83	7.79	7.75
8	14.7	11.0	9.60	8.81	8.30	7.95	7.69	7.50	7.34	7.21	7.10	7.01	6.94	6.87	6.81	6.76	6.72	6.68	6.64	6.61
9	13.6	10.1	8.72	7.96	7.47	7.13	6.88	6.69	6.54	6.42	6.31	6.23	6.15	6.09	6.03	5.98	5.94	5.90	5.86	5.83
10	12.8	9.43	8.08	7.34	6.87	6.54	6.30	6.12	5.97	5.85	5.75	5.66	5.59	5.53	5.47	5.42	5.38	5.34	5.31	5.27
11	12.2	8.91	7.60	6.88	6.42	6.10	5.86	5.68	5.54	5.42	5.32	5.24	5.16	5.10	5.05	5.00	4.96	4.92	4.89	4.86
12	11.8	8.51	7.23	6.52	6.07	5.76	5.52	5.35	5.20	5.09	4.99	4.91	4.84	4.77	4.72	4.67	4.63	4.59	4.56	4.53
13	11.4	8.19	6.93	6.23	5.79	5.48	5.25	5.08	4.94	4.82	4.72	4.64	4.57	4.51	4.46	4.41	4.37	4.33	4.30	4.27
14	11.1	7.92	6.68	6.00	5.56	5.26	5.03	4.86	4.72	4.60	4.51	4.43	4.36	4.30	4.25	4.20	4.16	4.12	4.09	4.06
15	10.8	7.70	6.48	5.80	5.37	5.07	4.85	4.67	4.54	4.42	4.33	4.25	4.18	4.12	4.07	4.02	3.98	3.95	3.91	3.88
16	10.6	7.51	6.30	5.64	5.21	4.91	4.69	4.52	4.38	4.27	4.18	4.10	4.03	3.97	3.92	3.87	3.83	3.80	3.76	3.73
17	10.4	7.35	6.16	5.50	5.07	4.78	4.56	4.39	4.25	4.14	4.05	3.97	3.90	3.84	3.79	3.75	3.71	3.67	3.64	3.61
18	10.2	7.21	6.03	5.37	4.96	4.66	4.44	4.28	4.14	4.03	3.94	3.86	3.79	3.73	3.68	3.64	3.60	3.56	3.53	3.50
19	10.1	7.09	5.92	5.27	4.85	4.56	4.34	4.18	4.04	3.93	3.84	3.76	3.70	3.64	3.59	3.54	3.50	3.46	3.43	3.40
20	9.94	6.99	5.82	5.17	4.76	4.47	4.26	4.09	3.96	3.85	3.76	3.68	3.61	3.55	3.50	3.46	3.42	3.38	3.35	3.32
22	9.73	6.81	5.65	5.02	4.61	4.32	4.11	3.94	3.81	3.70	3.61	3.54	3.47	3.41	3.36	3.31	3.27	3.24	3.21	3.18
24	9.55	6.66	5.52	4.89	4.49	4.20	3.99	3.83	3.69	3.59	3.50	3.42	3.35	3.30	3.25	3.20	3.16	3.12	3.09	3.06
26	9.41	6.54	5.41	4.79	4.38	4.10	3.89	3.73	3.60	3.49	3.40	3.33	3.26	3.20	3.15	3.11	3.07	3.03	3.00	2.97
28	9.28	6.44	5.32	4.70	4.30	4.02	3.81	3.65	3.52	3.41	3.32	3.25	3.18	3.12	3.07	3.03	2.99	2.95	2.92	2.89
30	9.18	6.35	5.24	4.62	4.23	3.95	3.74	3.58	3.45	3.34	3.25	3.18	3.11	3.06	3.01	2.96	2.92	2.89	2.85	2.82
35	8.98	6.19	5.09	4.48	4.09	3.81	3.61	3.45	3.32	3.21	3.12	3.05	2.98	2.93	2.88	2.83	2.79	2.76	2.72	2.69
40	8.83	6.07	4.98	4.37	3.99	3.71	3.51	3.35	3.22	3.12	3.03	2.95	2.89	2.83	2.78	2.74	2.70	2.66	2.63	2.60
45	8.71	5.97	4.89	4.29	3.91	3.64	3.43	3.28	3.15	3.04	2.96	2.88	2.82	2.76	2.71	2.66	2.62	2.59	2.56	2.53
50	8.63	5.90	4.83	4.23	3.85	3.58	3.38	3.22	3.09	2.99	2.90	2.82	2.76	2.70	2.65	2.61	2.57	2.53	2.50	2.47
60	8.49	5.79	4.73	4.14	3.76	3.49	3.29	3.13	3.01	2.90	2.82	2.74	2.68	2.62	2.57	2.53	2.49	2.45	2.42	2.39
70	8.40	5.72	4.66	4.08	3.70	3.43	3.23	3.08	2.95	2.85	2.76	2.68	2.62	2.56	2.51	2.47	2.43	2.39	2.36	2.33
80	8.33	5.67	4.61	4.03	3.65	3.39	3.19	3.03	2.91	2.80	2.72	2.64	2.58	2.52	2.47	2.43	2.39	2.35	2.32	2.29
90	8.28	5.62	4.57	3.99	3.62	3.35	3.15	3.00	2.87	2.77	2.68	2.61	2.54	2.49	2.44	2.39	2.35	2.32	2.28	2.25
100	8.24	5.59	4.54	3.96	3.59	3.33	3.13	2.97	2.85	2.74	2.66	2.58	2.52	2.46	2.41	2.37	2.33	2.29	2.26	2.23
120	8.18	5.54	4.50	3.92	3.55	3.28	3.09	2.93	2.81	2.71	2.62	2.54	2.48	2.42	2.37	2.33	2.29	2.25	2.22	2.19
140	8.14	5.50	4.47	3.89	3.52	3.26	3.06	2.91	2.78	2.68	2.59	2.52	2.45	2.40	2.35	2.30	2.26	2.22	2.19	2.16
160	8.10	5.48	4.44	3.87	3.50	3.24	3.04	2.88	2.76	2.66	2.57	2.50	2.43	2.38	2.33	2.28	2.24	2.20	2.17	2.14
180	8.08	5.46	4.42	3.85	3.48	3.22	3.02	2.87	2.74	2.64	2.56	2.48	2.42	2.36	2.31	2.26	2.22	2.19	2.15	2.12
200	8.06	5.44	4.41	3.84	3.47	3.21	3.01	2.86	2.73	2.63	2.54	2.47	2.40	2.35	2.30	2.25	2.21	2.18	2.14	2.11
∞	7.88	5.30	4.28	3.72	3.35	3.09	2.90	2.75	2.62	2.52	2.43	2.36	2.30	2.24	2.19	2.14	2.10	2.07	2.03	2.00

DENOMINATOR DEGREES OF FREEDOM

Table 6(d) (*Continued*)

NUMERATOR DEGREES OF FREEDOM

ν_2 \ ν_1	22	24	26	28	30	35	40	45	50	60	70	80	90	100	120	140	160	180	200	∞
1	24892	24940	24980	25014	25044	25103	25148	25183	25211	25253	25283	25306	25323	25337	25359	25374	25385	25394	25401	25464
2	199	199	199	199	199	199	199	199	199	199	199	199	199	199	199	199	199	199	199	199
3	42.7	42.6	42.6	42.5	42.5	42.4	42.3	42.3	42.2	42.1	42.1	42.1	42.0	42.0	42.0	42.0	41.9	41.9	41.9	41.8
4	20.1	20.0	20.0	19.9	19.9	19.8	19.8	19.7	19.7	19.6	19.6	19.5	19.5	19.5	19.5	19.4	19.4	19.4	19.4	19.3
5	12.8	12.8	12.7	12.7	12.7	12.6	12.5	12.5	12.5	12.4	12.4	12.3	12.3	12.3	12.3	12.3	12.2	12.2	12.2	12.1
6	9.53	9.47	9.43	9.39	9.36	9.29	9.24	9.20	9.17	9.12	9.09	9.06	9.04	9.03	9.00	8.98	8.97	8.96	8.95	8.88
7	7.69	7.64	7.60	7.57	7.53	7.47	7.42	7.38	7.35	7.31	7.28	7.25	7.23	7.22	7.19	7.18	7.16	7.15	7.15	7.08
8	6.55	6.50	6.46	6.43	6.40	6.33	6.29	6.25	6.22	6.18	6.15	6.12	6.10	6.09	6.06	6.05	6.04	6.03	6.02	5.95
9	5.78	5.73	5.69	5.65	5.62	5.56	5.52	5.48	5.45	5.41	5.38	5.36	5.34	5.32	5.30	5.28	5.27	5.26	5.26	5.19
10	5.22	5.17	5.13	5.10	5.07	5.01	4.97	4.93	4.90	4.86	4.83	4.80	4.79	4.77	4.75	4.73	4.72	4.71	4.71	4.64
11	4.80	4.76	4.72	4.68	4.65	4.60	4.55	4.52	4.49	4.45	4.41	4.39	4.37	4.36	4.34	4.32	4.31	4.30	4.29	4.23
12	4.48	4.43	4.39	4.36	4.33	4.27	4.23	4.19	4.17	4.12	4.09	4.07	4.05	4.04	4.01	4.00	3.99	3.98	3.97	3.91
13	4.22	4.17	4.13	4.10	4.07	4.01	3.97	3.94	3.91	3.87	3.84	3.81	3.79	3.78	3.76	3.74	3.73	3.72	3.71	3.65
14	4.01	3.96	3.92	3.89	3.86	3.80	3.76	3.73	3.70	3.66	3.62	3.60	3.58	3.57	3.55	3.53	3.52	3.51	3.50	3.44
15	3.83	3.79	3.75	3.72	3.69	3.63	3.58	3.55	3.52	3.48	3.45	3.43	3.41	3.39	3.37	3.36	3.34	3.34	3.33	3.26
16	3.68	3.64	3.60	3.57	3.54	3.48	3.44	3.40	3.37	3.33	3.30	3.28	3.26	3.25	3.22	3.21	3.20	3.19	3.18	3.11
17	3.56	3.51	3.47	3.44	3.41	3.35	3.31	3.28	3.25	3.21	3.18	3.15	3.13	3.12	3.10	3.08	3.07	3.06	3.05	2.99
18	3.45	3.40	3.36	3.33	3.30	3.25	3.20	3.17	3.14	3.10	3.07	3.04	3.02	3.01	2.99	2.97	2.96	2.95	2.94	2.87
19	3.35	3.31	3.27	3.24	3.21	3.15	3.11	3.07	3.04	3.00	2.97	2.95	2.93	2.91	2.89	2.87	2.86	2.85	2.85	2.78
20	3.27	3.22	3.18	3.15	3.12	3.07	3.02	2.99	2.96	2.92	2.88	2.86	2.84	2.83	2.81	2.79	2.78	2.77	2.76	2.69
22	3.12	3.08	3.04	3.01	2.98	2.92	2.88	2.84	2.82	2.77	2.74	2.72	2.70	2.69	2.66	2.65	2.63	2.62	2.62	2.55
24	3.01	2.97	2.93	2.90	2.87	2.81	2.77	2.73	2.70	2.66	2.63	2.60	2.58	2.57	2.55	2.53	2.52	2.51	2.50	2.43
26	2.92	2.87	2.84	2.80	2.77	2.72	2.67	2.64	2.61	2.56	2.53	2.51	2.49	2.47	2.45	2.43	2.42	2.41	2.40	2.33
28	2.84	2.79	2.76	2.72	2.69	2.64	2.59	2.56	2.53	2.48	2.45	2.43	2.41	2.39	2.37	2.35	2.34	2.33	2.32	2.25
30	2.77	2.73	2.69	2.66	2.63	2.57	2.52	2.49	2.46	2.42	2.38	2.36	2.34	2.32	2.30	2.28	2.27	2.26	2.25	2.18
35	2.64	2.60	2.56	2.53	2.50	2.44	2.39	2.36	2.33	2.28	2.25	2.22	2.20	2.19	2.16	2.15	2.13	2.12	2.11	2.04
40	2.55	2.50	2.46	2.43	2.40	2.34	2.30	2.26	2.23	2.18	2.15	2.12	2.10	2.09	2.06	2.05	2.03	2.02	2.01	1.93
45	2.47	2.43	2.39	2.36	2.33	2.27	2.22	2.19	2.16	2.11	2.08	2.05	2.03	2.01	1.99	1.97	1.95	1.94	1.93	1.85
50	2.42	2.37	2.33	2.30	2.27	2.21	2.16	2.13	2.10	2.05	2.02	1.99	1.97	1.95	1.93	1.91	1.89	1.88	1.87	1.79
60	2.33	2.29	2.25	2.22	2.19	2.13	2.08	2.04	2.01	1.96	1.93	1.90	1.88	1.86	1.83	1.81	1.80	1.79	1.78	1.69
70	2.28	2.23	2.19	2.16	2.13	2.07	2.02	1.98	1.95	1.90	1.86	1.84	1.81	1.80	1.77	1.75	1.73	1.72	1.71	1.62
80	2.23	2.19	2.15	2.11	2.08	2.02	1.97	1.94	1.90	1.85	1.82	1.79	1.77	1.75	1.72	1.70	1.68	1.67	1.66	1.57
90	2.20	2.15	2.12	2.08	2.05	1.99	1.94	1.90	1.87	1.82	1.78	1.75	1.73	1.71	1.68	1.66	1.64	1.63	1.62	1.52
100	2.17	2.13	2.09	2.05	2.02	1.96	1.91	1.87	1.84	1.79	1.75	1.72	1.70	1.68	1.65	1.63	1.61	1.60	1.59	1.49
120	2.13	2.09	2.05	2.01	1.98	1.92	1.87	1.83	1.80	1.75	1.71	1.68	1.66	1.64	1.61	1.58	1.57	1.55	1.54	1.43
140	2.11	2.06	2.02	1.99	1.96	1.89	1.84	1.80	1.77	1.72	1.68	1.65	1.62	1.60	1.57	1.55	1.53	1.52	1.51	1.39
160	2.09	2.04	2.00	1.97	1.93	1.87	1.82	1.78	1.75	1.69	1.65	1.62	1.60	1.58	1.55	1.52	1.51	1.49	1.48	1.36
180	2.07	2.02	1.98	1.95	1.92	1.85	1.80	1.76	1.73	1.68	1.64	1.61	1.58	1.56	1.53	1.50	1.49	1.47	1.46	1.34
200	2.06	2.01	1.97	1.94	1.91	1.84	1.79	1.75	1.71	1.66	1.62	1.59	1.56	1.54	1.51	1.49	1.47	1.45	1.44	1.32
∞	1.95	1.90	1.86	1.82	1.79	1.72	1.67	1.63	1.59	1.54	1.49	1.46	1.43	1.40	1.37	1.34	1.31	1.30	1.28	1.00

DENOMINATOR DEGREES OF FREEDOM

Table 7(a) Critical Values of the Studentized Range, $\alpha = .05$

ν	k																		
	2	3	4	5	6	7	8	9	10	11	12	13	14	15	16	17	18	19	20
1	18.0	27.0	32.8	37.1	40.4	43.1	45.4	47.4	49.1	50.6	52.0	53.2	54.3	55.4	56.3	57.2	58.0	58.8	59.6
2	6.08	8.33	9.80	10.9	11.7	12.4	13.0	13.5	14.0	14.4	14.7	15.1	15.4	15.7	15.9	16.1	16.4	16.6	16.8
3	4.50	5.91	6.82	7.50	8.04	8.48	8.85	9.18	9.46	9.72	9.95	10.2	10.3	10.5	10.7	10.8	11.0	11.1	11.2
4	3.93	5.04	5.76	6.29	6.71	7.05	7.35	7.60	7.83	8.03	8.21	8.37	8.52	8.66	8.79	8.91	9.03	9.13	9.23
5	3.64	4.60	5.22	5.67	6.03	6.33	6.58	6.80	6.99	7.17	7.32	7.47	7.60	7.72	7.83	7.93	8.03	8.12	8.21
6	3.46	4.34	4.90	5.30	5.63	5.90	6.12	6.32	6.49	6.65	6.79	6.92	7.03	7.14	7.24	7.34	7.43	7.51	7.59
7	3.34	4.16	4.68	5.06	5.36	5.61	5.82	6.00	6.16	6.30	6.43	6.55	6.66	6.76	6.85	6.94	7.02	7.10	7.17
8	3.26	4.04	4.53	4.89	5.17	5.40	5.60	5.77	5.92	6.05	6.18	6.29	6.39	6.48	6.57	6.65	6.73	6.80	6.87
9	3.20	3.95	4.41	4.76	5.02	5.24	5.43	5.59	5.74	5.87	5.98	6.09	6.19	6.28	6.36	6.44	6.51	6.58	6.64
10	3.15	3.88	4.33	4.65	4.91	5.12	5.30	5.46	5.60	5.72	5.83	5.93	6.03	6.11	6.19	6.27	6.34	6.40	6.47
11	3.11	3.82	4.26	4.57	4.82	5.03	5.20	5.35	5.49	5.61	5.71	5.81	5.90	5.98	6.06	6.13	6.20	6.27	6.33
12	3.08	3.77	4.20	4.51	4.75	4.95	5.12	5.27	5.39	5.51	5.61	5.71	5.80	5.88	5.95	6.02	6.09	6.15	6.21
13	3.06	3.73	4.15	4.45	4.69	4.88	5.05	5.19	5.32	5.43	5.53	5.63	5.71	5.79	5.86	5.93	5.99	6.05	6.11
14	3.03	3.70	4.11	4.41	4.64	4.83	4.99	5.13	5.25	5.36	5.46	5.55	5.64	5.71	5.79	5.85	5.91	5.97	6.03
15	3.01	3.67	4.08	4.37	4.59	4.78	4.94	5.08	5.20	5.31	5.40	5.49	5.57	5.65	5.72	5.78	5.85	5.90	5.96
16	3.00	3.65	4.05	4.33	4.56	4.74	4.90	5.03	5.15	5.26	5.35	5.44	5.52	5.59	5.66	5.73	5.79	5.84	5.90
17	2.98	3.63	4.02	4.30	4.52	4.70	4.86	4.99	5.11	5.21	5.31	5.39	5.47	5.54	5.61	5.67	5.73	5.79	5.84
18	2.97	3.61	4.00	4.28	4.49	4.67	4.82	4.96	5.07	5.17	5.27	5.35	5.43	5.50	5.57	5.63	5.69	5.74	5.79
19	2.96	3.59	3.98	4.25	4.47	4.65	4.79	4.92	5.04	5.14	5.23	5.31	5.39	5.46	5.53	5.59	5.65	5.70	5.75
20	2.95	3.58	3.96	4.23	4.45	4.62	4.77	4.90	5.01	5.11	5.20	5.28	5.36	5.43	5.49	5.55	5.61	5.66	5.71
24	2.92	3.53	3.90	4.17	4.37	4.54	4.68	4.81	4.92	5.01	5.10	5.18	5.25	5.32	5.38	5.44	5.49	5.55	5.59
30	2.89	3.49	3.85	4.10	4.30	4.46	4.60	4.72	4.82	4.92	5.00	5.08	5.15	5.21	5.27	5.33	5.38	5.43	5.47
40	2.86	3.44	3.79	4.04	4.23	4.39	4.52	4.63	4.73	4.82	4.90	4.98	5.04	5.11	5.16	5.22	5.27	5.31	5.36
60	2.83	3.40	3.74	3.98	4.16	4.31	4.44	4.55	4.65	4.73	4.81	4.88	4.94	5.00	5.06	5.11	5.15	5.20	5.24
120	2.80	3.36	3.68	3.92	4.10	4.24	4.36	4.47	4.56	4.64	4.71	4.78	4.84	4.90	4.95	5.00	5.04	5.09	5.13
∞	2.77	3.31	3.63	3.86	4.03	4.17	4.29	4.39	4.47	4.55	4.62	4.68	4.74	4.80	4.85	4.89	4.93	4.97	5.01

Table 7(b) Critical Values of the Studentized Range, $\alpha = .01$

								k											
ν	2	3	4	5	6	7	8	9	10	11	12	13	14	15	16	17	18	19	20
1	90.0	135	164	186	202	216	227	237	246	253	260	266	272	277	282	286	290	294	298
2	14.0	19.0	22.3	24.7	26.6	28.2	29.5	30.7	31.7	32.6	33.4	34.1	34.8	35.4	36.0	36.5	37.0	37.5	37.9
3	8.26	10.6	12.2	13.3	14.2	15.0	15.6	16.2	16.7	17.1	17.5	17.9	18.2	18.5	18.8	19.1	19.3	19.5	19.8
4	6.51	8.12	9.17	9.96	10.6	11.1	11.5	11.9	12.3	12.6	12.8	13.1	13.3	13.5	13.7	13.9	14.1	14.2	14.4
5	5.70	6.97	7.80	8.42	8.91	9.32	9.67	9.97	10.2	10.5	10.7	10.9	11.1	11.2	11.4	11.6	11.7	11.8	11.9
6	5.24	6.33	7.03	7.56	7.97	8.32	8.61	8.87	9.10	9.30	9.49	9.65	9.81	9.95	10.1	10.2	10.3	10.4	10.5
7	4.95	5.92	6.54	7.01	7.37	7.68	7.94	8.17	8.37	8.55	8.71	8.86	9.00	9.12	9.24	9.35	9.46	9.55	9.65
8	4.74	5.63	6.20	6.63	6.96	7.24	7.47	7.68	7.87	8.03	8.18	8.31	8.44	8.55	8.66	8.76	8.85	8.94	9.03
9	4.60	5.43	5.96	6.35	6.66	6.91	7.13	7.32	7.49	7.65	7.78	7.91	8.03	8.13	8.23	8.32	8.41	8.49	8.57
10	4.48	5.27	5.77	6.14	6.43	6.67	6.87	7.05	7.21	7.36	7.48	7.60	7.71	7.81	7.91	7.99	8.07	8.15	8.22
11	4.39	5.14	5.62	5.97	6.25	6.48	6.67	6.84	6.99	7.13	7.25	7.36	7.46	7.56	7.65	7.73	7.81	7.88	7.95
12	4.32	5.04	5.50	5.84	6.10	6.32	6.51	6.67	6.81	6.94	7.06	7.17	7.26	7.36	7.44	7.52	7.59	7.66	7.73
13	4.26	4.96	5.40	5.73	5.98	6.19	6.37	6.53	6.67	6.79	6.90	7.01	7.10	7.19	7.27	7.34	7.42	7.48	7.55
14	4.21	4.89	5.32	5.63	5.88	6.08	6.26	6.41	6.54	6.66	6.77	6.87	6.96	7.05	7.12	7.20	7.27	7.33	7.39
15	4.17	4.83	5.25	5.56	5.80	5.99	6.16	6.31	6.44	6.55	6.66	6.76	6.84	6.93	7.00	7.07	7.14	7.20	7.26
16	4.13	4.78	5.19	5.49	5.72	5.92	6.08	6.22	6.35	6.46	6.56	6.66	6.74	6.82	6.90	6.97	7.03	7.09	7.15
17	4.10	4.74	5.14	5.43	5.66	5.85	6.01	6.15	6.27	6.38	6.48	6.57	6.66	6.73	6.80	6.87	6.94	7.00	7.05
18	4.07	4.70	5.09	5.38	5.60	5.79	5.94	6.08	6.20	6.31	6.41	6.50	6.58	6.65	6.72	6.79	6.85	6.91	6.96
19	4.05	4.67	5.05	5.33	5.55	5.73	5.89	6.02	6.14	6.25	6.34	6.43	6.51	6.58	6.65	6.72	6.78	6.84	6.89
20	4.02	4.64	5.02	5.29	5.51	5.69	5.84	5.97	6.09	6.19	6.29	6.37	6.45	6.52	6.59	6.65	6.71	6.76	6.82
24	3.96	4.54	4.91	5.17	5.37	5.54	5.69	5.81	5.92	6.02	6.11	6.19	6.26	6.33	6.39	6.45	6.51	6.56	6.61
30	3.89	4.45	4.80	5.05	5.24	5.40	5.54	5.65	5.76	5.85	5.93	6.01	6.08	6.14	6.20	6.26	6.31	6.36	6.41
40	3.82	4.37	4.70	4.93	5.11	5.27	5.39	5.50	5.60	5.69	5.77	5.84	5.90	5.96	6.02	6.07	6.12	6.17	6.21
60	3.76	4.28	4.60	4.82	4.99	5.13	5.25	5.36	5.45	5.53	5.60	5.67	5.73	5.79	5.84	5.89	5.93	5.98	6.02
120	3.70	4.20	4.50	4.71	4.87	5.01	5.12	5.21	5.30	5.38	5.44	5.51	5.56	5.61	5.66	5.71	5.75	5.79	5.83
∞	3.64	4.12	4.40	4.60	4.76	4.88	4.99	5.08	5.16	5.23	5.29	5.35	5.40	5.45	5.49	5.54	5.57	5.61	5.65

Source: From E. S. Pearson and H. O. Hartley, *Biometrika Tables for Statisticians*, 1 : 176–77. Reproduced by permission of the Biometrika Trustees.

Chapter 1

1.2 Descriptive statistics summarizes a set of data. Inferential statistics makes inferences about populations from samples.

1.4 **a.** The complete production run
b. 1,000 chips
c. Proportion of the production run that is defective
d. Proportion of sample chips that are defective (7.5%)
e. Parameter
f. Statistic
g. Because the sample proportion is less than 10%, we can conclude that the claim is true.

1.6 **a.** Flip the coin 100 times and count the number of heads and tails.
b. Outcomes of flips
c. Outcomes of the 100 flips
d. Proportion of heads
e. Proportion of heads in the 100 flips

1.8 **a.** The population consists of the fuel mileage of all the taxis in the fleet.
b. The owner would like to know the mean mileage.
c. The sample consists of the 50 observations.
d. The statistic the owner would use is the mean of the 50 observations.
e. The statistic would be used to estimate the parameter from which the owner can calculate total costs.

We computed the sample mean to be 19.8 mpg.

Chapter 2

2.2 **a.** Interval **b.** Interval
c. Nominal **d.** Ordinal
e. Interval

2.4 **c.** Excel is the choice of about half the sample, one-quarter have opted for Minitab, and a small fraction chose SAS and SPSS.

2.6 **c.** The histogram is positively skewed.

2.8 Total health care expenditures are rising faster than inflation.

2.10 Before the last four years, consumption was increasing and production was falling. In the last four years, consumption decreased while production slightly increased.

2.12 **b.** There is a positive linear relationship between calculus and statistics marks.

2.16 The histogram is symmetric, unimodal, and bell shaped.

2.18 **a.** The histogram should contain 9 or 10 bins. We chose 10.
c. The histogram is positively skewed.
d. The histogram is not bell shaped.

2.20 Imports from Canada have greatly exceeded exports to Canada.

2.22 The inflation-adjusted index displays far less volatility.

2.24 **b.** There is a very weak positive linear relationship.

2.26 There is a weak positive linear relationship.

Chapter 3

3.2 $\bar{x} = 6.0$; Median = 5; Mode = 5

3.4 **a.** $\bar{x} = 11.19$; median = 11

3.6 $\bar{x} = 5.0$, $s^2 = 6.57$

3.8 The data in (b) appear to be most similar to one another.

3.10 Variance cannot be negative because it is the sum of *squared* differences.

3.12 **a.** about 68% **b.** about 95%
c. About 99.7%

3.14 Range = 25.85, $s^2 = 29.46$, and $s = 5.43$; there is considerable variation between prices; approximately 95% of the prices lie within 10.86 of the mean; approximately 99.7% of the prices lie within 16.29 of the mean.

3.16 $s^2 = .0858$ cm^2, and $s = .2929$ cm; approximately 95% of the lengths lie within .5858 of the mean; approximately 99.7% of the rods will lie within .8787 cm of the mean.

3.18 30th percentile = 22.3; 80th percentile = 30.8

3.20 The quartiles are 13.05, 14.7, 15.6

3.22 **a.** The quartiles are 2, 4, 8
b. Most executives spend little time reading resumes. Keep it short.

3.24 **a.** The quartiles are 26, 28.5, and 32
b. The times are positively skewed.

3.26 $r = -.7813$; There is a moderately strong negative linear relationship.

3.28 $r = .0744$ (Excel); There is a weak positive linear relationship.

Chapter 5

5.2 {Adams wins. Brown wins, Collins wins, Dalton wins}

5.4 **a.** {0, 1, 2, 3, 4, 5} **b.** {4, 5}
c. $P(5) = .10$
d. $P(2, 3, \text{ or } 4) = .65$
e. $P(6) = 0$

5.6 **a.** .36 **b.** .49 **c.** .83

5.8 **a.** .35 **b.** .538 **c.** .714
d. (a) is the joint probability and (b) and (c) are conditional probabilities

5.10 **a.** .103 **b.** .316
c. Yes, because $P(\text{new}) = .19$ $P(\text{new} \mid \text{overdue})$

5.12 .038

5.14 .698

5.16 .6125

5.18 .825

5.20 **a.** .49 **b.** .44
c. .449 **d.** No

5.22 $^2/_3$

Chapter 6

6.2 **a.** 0, 1, 2, ..., 100 **b.** Yes
c. Yes, there are 101 values.
d. The variable is discrete.

6.4 **a.** .48 **b.** .52

6.6 2.25, 1.26

6.8 E(Value of coin) = 460. Take the $500.

6.10 **a.** .4219 **b.** .3114 **c.** .25810

6.12 .0081

6.14 .08748

6.16 **a.** .38174 **b.** .25880
c. .14355 **d.** .29680

6.18 .30440

6.20 **a.** .0302 **b.** .2746
c. .3033

6.22 **a.** .20269 **b.** .26761

6.24 **a.** .4911 **b.** .4457
c. .4040

Chapter 7

7.2 **a.** .1667 **b.** .3333
c. 0

7.4 **a.** .5762 **b.** .2119
c. .2119

7.6 **a.** .6759 **b.** .3745
c. .1469

7.8 **a.** .1056 **b.** .1056
c. .8882

7.10 **a.** .3336 **b.** .0314
c. .0436 **d.** 32.88

7.12 .6915

7.14 **a.** .2643 **b.** .0301

7.16 A: 82.8; B: 72.5; C: 61.6; D: 53.55

7.18 **a.** 1.341 **b.** 1.319
c. 1.988 **d.** 1.653

7.20 **a.** 1.3406 **b.** 1.3195
c. 1.9890 **d.** 1.6527

7.22 **a.** .0189 **b.** .0341
c. .0927 **d.** .0324

7.24 **a.** 9.24 **b.** 136
c. 9.39 **d.** 37.5

7.26 **a.** 73.3441 **b.** 102.946
c. 16.3382 **d.** 24.7690

7.28 **a.** .2688 **b.** 1.0
c. .9903 **d.** 1.0

7.30 **a.** 4.35 **b.** 8.89
c. 3.29 **d.** 2.50

7.32 **a.** 1.4857 **b.** 1.7633
c. 1.8200 **d.** 1.1587

7.34 **a.** .0510 **b.** .1634
c. .0222 **d.** .2133

Chapter 8

8.2   **a.** 1/36   **b.** 1/36

8.4   The variance of $\overline{X}$ is smaller than the variance of X.

8.6   No, because the sample mean is approximately normally distributed.

8.8   We can answer part (c) and possibly part (b), depending on how nonnormal the population is.

8.10   **a.** .2514   **b.** .0475

8.12   .3085

8.14   .9332

8.16   No because the central limit theorem says that the sample mean is approximately normally distributed.

8.18   0; the defective rate appears to be larger than 2%.

8.20   .8749

8.22   .0838

8.24   .0096

Chapter 9

9.2   **a.** .50 ± .0490
       b. .33 ± .0461
       c. .10 ± .0294
       d. The interval narrows.

9.4   LCL = .6057, UCL = .6943

9.6   LCL = .1332, UCL = .2068

9.8   **a.** LCL = .0792, UCL = .1320

9.10   LCL = .0880, UCL = .1524

9.12   LCL = .575, UCL = .625; Total number of Canadians who prefer artificial Christmas trees: LCL = 3.45 million, UCL = 3.75 million

9.14   Codes 3 and 4 were changed to 5.
       LCL = .6906, UCL = .7704; Market segment size: LCL = 21,870,611, UCL = 24,397,798

9.16   752

9.18   **a.** .75 ± .0260
       b. The interval is narrower.
       c. Yes, because the interval estimate is better than specified.

9.20   **a.** .75 ± .03
       b. Yes, because the sample size was chosen to produce this interval.

9.22   **a.** .5 ± .0346
       b. The interval is wider.
       c. No, because the interval estimate is wider (worse) than specified.

Chapter 10

10.2 H_0: Risky investment is more successful

       H_1: Risky investment is not more successful

10.4   The defendant in both cases was O. J. Simpson. The verdicts were logical because in the criminal trial the amount of evidence to convict is greater than the amount of evidence required in a civil trial. The two juries concluded that there was enough (preponderance of) evidence in the civil trial, but not enough evidence (beyond a reasonable doubt) in the criminal trial.

10.6   **a.** .2578   **b.** .3300
       c. .4129
       d. The z-statistic decreases and the p-value increases.

10.8 $z = .33$, p-value = .3707, no

10.10 $z = -1.58$, p-value = .0571, no

10.12   Codes 1, 2, and 3 have been recoded to 5. $z = 2.00$, p-value = .0228, yes

10.14   **a.** $z = 1.74$, p-value = .0409, yes
       b. $z = 1.07$, p-value = .1423, no

10.16   .2233

10.18   **a.** .6480

       b. .7764
       c. When α decreases, β increases.

10.20   **a.** .6217

       b. .2327
       c. When n increases, β decreases.

10.22   .6141

10.24   .3156

Chapter 11

11.2   LCL = 12.73, UCL = 23.53

11.4   LCL = .00046, UCL = .00300

11.6 $\chi^2 = 5.02$, p-value = .6854, no

11.8   LCL = 6.92, UCL = 7.38

11.10   **a.** LCL = 55.34, UCL = 62.74
       Total spent on other products:
       LCL = \$154,952, UCL = \$175,672

11.12 $t = .51$, p-value = .3061, no

11.14 $t = 2.28$, p-value $= .0127$, yes

11.16 $\chi^2 = 305.81$, p-value $= .0044$, yes

11.18 $\chi^2 = 86.36$, p-value $= .1863$, no. Replace the bulbs as they burn out.

11.20 **a.** LCL $= .2711$, UCL $= .3127$
b. LCL $= 32{,}729{,}361$
UCL $= 37{,}751{,}646$

11.22 LCL $= .1440$, UCL $= .2056$; Number: LCL $= 29{,}360{,}448$, UCL $= 41{,}920{,}195$

11.24 LCL $= .3043$, UCL $= .4119$

Chapter 12

12.2 $t = 1.12$, p-value $= .2761$, no

12.4 $t = 1.98$, p-value $= .0473$, yes

12.6 **a.** $t = 1.40$, p-value $= .1640$, no
b. LCL $= -.23$, UCL $= 1.37$
c. The histograms are bell shaped.

12.8 **a.** $t = 1.16$, p-value $= .2467$, no

12.10 $t = -2.54$, p-value $= .0057$, yes

12.12 $z = -4.53$, p-value $= 0$, yes

12.14 $t = 1.53$, p-value $= .0638$, no

12.16 **a.** LCL $= 11.59$, UCL $= 27.91$
b. $t = 4.08$, p-value $= .0001$, yes
c. The histogram of the differences is bell shaped.
d. No, because we expect a great deal of variation between stores.

12.18 $t = -.91$, p-value $= .3687$, no

12.20 $t = 1.59$, p-value $= .0599$, no

12.22 $t = 2.82$, p-value $= .0055$, yes

12.24 $t = 2.08$, p-value $= .0210$, yes

Chapter 13

13.2 $F = .98$, p-value $= .4879$, no

13.4 $F = 1.53$, p-value $= .0183$, yes

13.6 $F = .298$, p-value $= 0$, yes

13.8 **a.** $z = .75$, p-value $= .4532$, no

13.10 (1 = Success) $z = 4.24$, p-value $= 0$, yes

13.12 $z = -0.66$, p-value $= .2551$, no

13.14 $z = 1.26$, p-value $= .1037$, no

13.16 **a.** $z = 2.49$, p-value $= .0065$, yes
b. $z = .893$, p-value $= .1859$, no
c. $z = 2.61$, p-value $= .0045$, yes

13.18 $z = 2.26$, p-value $= .0119$, yes

13.20 $z = 0.864$, p-value $= .3876$, no

13.22 $z = 1.30$, p-value $= .1952$, no

13.24 $z = 0.485$, p-value $= .6276$, no

13.26 $z = -0.536$, p-value $= .5916$, no

13.28 $z = 2.23$, p-value $= .0258$, yes

13.30 $z = -0.626$, p-value $= .5316$, no

Chapter 14

14.2 $F = .87$, p-value $= .4445$, no

14.4 **a.** SS(Total) $= 99.6$, SST $= 15.6$, SSB $= 48.3$, SSE $= 35.7$
b. SS(Total) $= 99.6$, SST $= 15.6$, SSE $= 84.0$
c. The variation between all the data is the same for both designs.
d. The variation between treatments is the same for both designs.
e. Because the randomized block design divides the sum of squares for error in the one-way analysis of variance into two parts.

14.6 $F = 1.65$, p-value $= .2296$, no

14.8 **a.** $F = 2.94$, p-value $= .0363$, yes
b. The times for each form must be normally distributed with the same variance.
c. The histograms are approximately bell shaped, and the sample variances are similar.

14.10 **a.** $F = 3.32$, p-value $= .0129$, no
b. The times until first sign of corrosion for each lacquer must be normally distributed with a common variance.
c. The histograms are approximately bell shaped with similar sample variances.

14.12 $F = 1.33$, p-value $= .2675$, no

14.14 **a.** The means for Forms 1 and 4 differ.
b. No means differ.

14.16 **a.** The means of lacquers 2 and 3 differ.
b. The means of lacquers 2 and 3 differ.

14.18 **a.** There are no differences.
b. There are no differences.

14.20 **a.** $F = 123.36$, p-value $= 0$, yes
b. $F = 323.16$, p-value $= 0$, yes

14.22 **a.** $F = 21.16$, p-value $= 0$, yes
b. $F = 66.02$, p-value $= 0$, yes

14.24 $F = 13.79$, p-value $= 0$, yes

14.26 $F = 25.35$, p-value $= 0$, yes

Chapter 15

15.2 $\chi^2 = 2.27$, p-value $= .3221$, no

15.4 $\chi^2 = 70.675$, p-value $= 0$, yes

15.6 $\chi^2 = 6.40$, p-value $= .1712$, no

15.8 $\chi^2 = 6.00$, p-value $= .1116$, no

15.10 $\chi^2 = 7.93$, p-value $= .0475$, yes

15.12 a. $\chi^2 = .64$, p-value $= .4225$, no
b. Ignore what the other investors are doing.

15.14 $\chi^2 = 20.89$, p-value $= .0019$, yes

15.16 $\chi^2 = 21.22$, p-value $= 0$, yes

15.18 $\chi^2 = 97.03$, p-value $= 0$, yes

15.20 $\chi^2 = 31.40$, p-value $= 0$, yes

15.22 $\chi^2 = 29.81$, p-value $= 0$, yes

15.24 $\chi^2 = 24.52$, p-value $= 0$, yes

15.26 $\chi^2 = 148.1$, p-value $= 0$, yes

Chapter 16

16.2 b. $\hat{y} = -24.72 + .9675x$

The slope coefficient indicates that for each additional hour of television weight increases on average by .9675 pounds. The y-intercept is has no practical meaning.
c. $t = 6.55$, p-value $= 0$, yes
d. Lower prediction limit $= -2.702$, Upper prediction limit $= 11.31$
e. LCL $= 2.514$, UCL $= 6.096$

16.4 $\hat{y} = 3.635 + .2675x$
c. For each additional second of commercial, the memory test score increases on average by .2675.
d. 5.888. The standard error of estimate appears to be large indicating a weak linear relationship.
e. $R^2 = .2892$
f. $t = 4.86$, p-value $= 0$, yes
g. LCL $= .1756$, UCL $= .3594$
h. Lower prediction limit $= 1.39$, Upper prediction limit $= 25.15$
i. LCL $= 11.73$, UCL $= 14.81$

16.6 a. $\hat{y} = 7.460 + .0899x$. The slope coefficient tells us that for each additional year of age time increases on average by .0899 minutes.
b. $t = 2.17$, p-value $= .0305$, yes

16.8 a. $\hat{y} = 7.286 + .1898x$

b. For each additional cigarette, the number of days absent from work increases on average by .1898. The y-intercept has no meaning.
c. $t = 7.50$, p-value $= 0$, yes
Lower prediction limit $= 5.12$, Upper prediction limit $= 20.84$

16.10 a. $\hat{y} = 296.93 + 21.33x$
b. On average each additional ad generates 21.33 customers.
c. $t = 1.49$, p-value $= .0740$, no
d. $R^2 = .0852$
e. The linear relationship is too weak for the model to produce predictions.

16.12 a. $r = .9766$, $t = 21.78$, p-value $= 0$, yes
b. $r = .9259$, $t = 11.76$, p-value $= 0$, yes

16.14 $t = 6.63$, p-value $= 0$, yes

16.16 $t = -1.45$, p-value $= .0741$, no

16.18 $t = 10.68$, p-value $= 0$, yes

16.20 $t = .69$, p-value $= .4915$, no

16.22 \$367.90, \$672.50

16.24 $t = 15.17$, p-value $= 0$, yes

Chapter 17

17.2 a. $\hat{y} = 13.01 + .194x_1 + 1.11x_2$
b. 3.75   **c.** .7629
d. $F = 43.43$, p-value $= 0$, evidence that the model is valid
f. $t = .97$, p-value $= .3417$, no
g. $t = 9.12$, p-value $= 0$, yes
h. 23, 39   **i.** 49, 65

17.4 c. $s_\varepsilon = 6.99$ and $R^2 = .3511$; the model's fit is not very good.
d. $F = 22.01$, p-value $= 0$, evidence that the model is valid
e. Minor-league home runs: $t = 7.64$, p-value $= 0$
Age: $t = .26$, p-value $= .7961$
Years professional: $t = 1.75$, p-value $= .0819$
Only the number of minor-league home runs is linearly related to the number of major-league home runs.
f. 9.86 (rounded to 10), 38.76 (rounded to 39)
g. 14.66, 24.47

17.6 **b.** .2882
  c. $F = 12.96$, p-value $= 0$, evidence that the model is valid
  d. High school GPA: $t = 6.06$, p-value $= 0$
    SAT: $t = .94$, p-value $= .3485$
    Activities: $t = .72$, p-value $= .4720$
    Only the high school GPA is linearly related to the university GPA.
  e. 4.45, 12.00 (12 is the maximum)
  f. 6.90, 8.22

17.8 **b.** $F = 29.80$, p-value $= 0$, evidence that the model is valid
  d. House size: $t = 3.21$, p-value $= .0014$
    Number of children: $t = 7.84$, p-value $= 0$
    Number of adults at home: $t = 4.48$, p-value $= 0$
    All three independent variables are linearly related to the amount of garbage.

17.10 **b.** $F = 67.97$, p-value $= 0$, evidence that the model is valid
  c. Mothers: $t = 8.27$, p-value $= 0$
    Fathers: $t = 8.26$, p-value $= 0$
    Grandmothers: $t = .25$, p-value $= .8028$
    Grandfathers: $t = 1.32$, p-value $= .1890$
    Only the ages of mothers and fathers are linearly related to the ages of their children.
  d. 65.54, 77.31
  e. 68.75, 74.66

17.12 **a.** $\hat{y} = -28.43 + .604x_1 + .374x_2$
  b. $s_\varepsilon = 7.07$ and $R^2 = .8072$; the model fits well.
  c. Boxes: $t = 10.85$, p-value $= 0$
    Weight: $t = 4.42$, p-value $= .0001$
    Both variables are linearly related to time to unload.
  d. 35.16, 66.24
  e. 44.43, 56.96

17.14 **b.** $F = 24.48$, p-value $= 0$, evidence that the model is valid
  c. Undergraduate GPA: $t = .524$, p-value $= .6017$
    GMAT: $t = 8.16$, p-value $= 0$

Work experience: $t = 3.00$, p-value $= .0036$
Both the GMAT and work experience are linearly related to MBA GPA.

17.16 **b.** $F = 12.06$, p-value $= 0$, evidence that the model is valid
  c. AGE: $t = 4.12$, p-value $= 0$
    EDUC: $t = 4.12$, p-value $= 0$
    CHILDS: $t = -0.85$, p-value $= .3967$
    Only CHILDS is not linearly related to EQWLTH.
  d. .0268

17.18 **a.** $F = 11.16$, p-value $= 0$, evidence that the model is valid
  b. AGE: $t = 3.75$, p-value $= 0.0002$
    EDUC: $t = 4.13$, p-value $= 0$
    CHILDS: $t = -0.81$, p-value $= .4209$
    Only AGE and EDUC are linearly related to HELPPOOR.
  c. .0254

17.20 **b.** $F = 41.92$, p-value $= 0$, evidence that the model is valid
    AGE: $t = 6.93$, p-value $= 0$
    EDUC: $t = 8.07$, p-value $= 0$
    INCOME: $t = 1.72$, p-value $= .0858$
    AGE and EDUC are linearly related to DEFINITE.

17.22 **a.** The normality requirement is satisfied.
  b. The variance of the error variable appears to be constant.

17.24 **b.** The normality requirement has not been violated.
  c. The variance of the error variable appears to be constant.
  d. The absence of multicollinearity means that the t–tests were valid.

17.26 **a.** Age and years as a professional are highly correlated. The correlations of the other combinations are small.
  b. The t–tests may not be valid.

17.28 The error variable is approximately normally distributed, and the variance is constant.

"And whatever your labors and aspirations, in the noisy confusion of life, keep peace in your soul. With all its sham, drudgery and broken dreams, it is still a beautiful world. Be cheerful. Strive to be happy"	...
arithmicmean	The arithmetic mean, a.k.a. average, shortened to mean, is the most popular & useful measure of central location. It is computed by simply adding up all the observations and dividing by the total number of observations:
bar charts show	frequency
The best type of chart for comparing two sets of nominal (categorical) data is: a. a line chart b. a scatter diagram c. a histogram d. a bar chart	D
Charts used for categorical data	pic chart and bar chart
Confidence level measures: a. The proportion of times that an estimating procedure will be correct b. The variability of a sample around the mean c. The proportion of times that an estimating procedure will be wrong in the long run d. The Central Location in a set of observations	A
Histograms and stem & leaf displays are used to graphically describe	interval data
If I say I flip a coin 10 times and 8 times came up tails. Interested in every time I flip that coin. Population or sample	sample
In a given bell-shaped distribution, the mean is 100 and the standard deviation is 10. What percentage of observations would be between 70 and 130? a. 0% b. 65% c. 95% d. 99.7%	D
Interval DATA	Real numbers, i.e. heights, weights, prices, etc • Also referred to as quantitative or numerical

		PROBLEM OBJECTIVES			
	Describe a Population	**Compare Two Populations**	**Compare Two or More Populations**	**Analyze Relationship between Two Variables**	**Analyze Relationship among Two or More Variables**
Interval	Histogram **Section 2.3** Stem-and-leaf **Section 2.3** Box plot **Section 3.3** Mean, median, and mode **Section 3.1** Range, variance, and standard deviation **Section 3.2** Percentiles and quartiles **Section 3.3** *t*-test and estimator of a mean **Section 11.1** Chi-squared test and estimator of a variance **Section 11. 2**	Equal-variances *t*-test and estimator of the difference between two means: independent samples **Section 12.1** Unequal-variances *t*-test and estimator of the difference between two means: independent samples **Section 12.1** *t*-test and estimator of mean difference **Section 12.2** *F*-test and estimator of ratio of two variances **Section 13.1** Wilcoxon rank sum test **Web site appendix** Wilcoxon signed rank sum test **Web site appendix**	One-way analysis of variance **Section 14.1** LSD multiple comparison method **Section 14.2** Tukey's multiple comparison method **Section 14.2** Two-way analysis of variance **Section 14.3** Kruskal–Wallis test **Web site appendix** Friedman test **Web site appendix**	Scatter diagram **Section 2.5** Simple linear regression and correlation **Chapter 16** Spearman rank correlation **Web site appendix**	Multiple regression **Chapter 17**
Nominal	Frequency distribution **Section 2.2** Bar chart **Section 2.2** Pie chart **Section 2.2** Line chart **Section 2.4** *z*-test and estimator of a proportion **Sections 10.2 & 9.2** Chi-squared goodness-of-fit test **Section 15.1**	*z*-test and estimator of the difference between two proportions **Section 13.2** Chi-squared test of a contingency table **Section 15.2**	Chi-squared test of a contingency table **Section 15.2**	Chi-squared test of a contingency table **Section 15.2**	Not covered

DATA TYPES

		Describe a Population	Compare Two Populations	Compare Two or More Populations	Analyze Relationship between Two Variables	Analyze Relationship among Two or More Variables
DATA TYPES	Ordinal	Box plot **Section 3.3** Median **Section 3.1** Percentiles and quartiles **Section 3.3**	Wilcoxon rank sum test **Web site appendix** Sign test **Web site appendix**	Kruskal–Wallis test **Web site appendix** Friedman test **Web site appendix**	Spearman rank correlation **Web site appendix**	Not covered

APPENDIX E
Index of Computer Output and Instructions

Techniques	Excel	Minitab
Graphical		
Frequency distribution	15	15
Bar chart	16	17
Pie chart	16	17
Histogram	20	21
Stem-and-leaf display	24	24
Line chart	25	25
Scatter diagram	27	27
Box plot	45	45
Numerical descriptive techniques		
Mean	37	37
Median	37	37
Mode	38	–
Variance	41	41
Probability/random variables		
Binomial	89	89
Poisson	92	92
Normal	108	108
Student t	110	111
Chi-squared	113	113
F	114	114
Inference about p		
Test statistic	157	158
Interval estimator	140	140
Probability of Type II error	163	163
Inference about μ (σ unknown)		
Test statistic	171	172
Interval estimator	174	174
Inference about σ^2		
Test statistic	177	177
Interval estimator	178	178

Techniques	Excel	Minitab
Inference about $\mu_1 - \mu_2$		
Equal-variances test statistic	189	189
Equal-variances interval estimator	190	190
Unequal-variances test statistic	192	192
Unequal-variances interval estimator	193	193
Inference about μ_D		
Test statistic	199	200
Interval estimator	200	200
Inference about σ_1^2/σ_2^2		
Test statistic	188 & 209	189 & 209
Interval estimator	210	210
Inference about $p_1 - p_2$		
Test statistic	212	212
Interval estimator	215	215
Analysis of variance		
One-way	225	226
Multiple comparison methods	230	230
Two-way	235	235
Chi-squared tests		
Goodness-of-fit test	243	243
Contingency table	247	247
Linear regression		
Coefficients and tests	259	259
Correlation (Pearson)	268	268
Prediction interval	264	264
Multiple regression		
Coefficients and tests	279	279
Prediction interval	284	284
Regression diagnostics	285	285

Index

A

Accuracy and Coverage Evaluation, 54
Addition rule, 73–74
Alternative hypothesis, 150, 152, 158–159
American National Election Survey, 8
  Republican vs. Democrat levels of education, 184, 193–194
  survey results vs. election results, 148, 160
Analysis of variance, 220–236
  Bonferroni adjustment to LSD method, 229–230
  comparing cholesterol-lowering drugs example, 234–236
  comparing costs of repairing car bumpers example, 228
  Fisher's least significant difference (LSD) method, 229
  multiple comparisons, 227–232
  one-way analysis of variance, 221–227
  proportion of assets invested in stocks example, 222–223
  randomized block (two-way) analysis of variance, 232–236
  test statistic, 223
  Tukey's multiple comparison method, 230–232
Analysis of variance (ANOVA) table, 225
  for one-way analysis of variance, 225
  for randomized block analysis of variance, 234
  for stock asset example, 225
Arithmetic mean, 36

B

Bar charts, 14–18
  displaying frequencies with, 15–17
Bell shaped histogram, 23
  Empirical Rule and, 42
Bernoulli process, 86
Between-treatments variation, 223
Bias, 62
Bimodal histogram, 22
Binomial distribution, 86–90, 97
  approximating with normal distribution, 127–130
  binomial random variable, 86, 87–88
  binomial table, 88–89
  cumulative probability, 88
  mean and variance of, 89–90
  student taking the statistics quiz (example), 87–88
Binomial experiment, 86, 127, 241
  probability tree for, 87
Binomial probabilities, 101
  table, 88–89, 303–306
Binomial table, 88–89, 303–306
Bonferroni adjustment to LSD method, 229–230
Box plots, 44–47
  long-distance telephone bill analysis and, 45
  outliers, 45
  service times of fast-food drive-throughs analysis, 36

C

Categorical data, 12
Census Bureau, 54, 60–61
Central limit theorem, 125

(continued)

Chi-squared distribution, 111–113
Chi-squared statistic, 176
Chi-squared tests, 240–249
  of contingency table, 244–253
  goodness-of-fit test, 241–244
  testing market shares example, 242–244
Classes, 19–20
  class interval widths, 21–22
  determining number of class intervals, 21
  modal class, 22
Classical approach, 66–67
Cluster sample, 60
Coefficient of correlation, 47–48, 267
  and scatter diagram/covariance compared, 48
Coefficient of determination, 264–265
Coefficients, estimating, 256–260
Coin toss probability, 82
Collinearity, 286
Complement rule, 72
Confidence interval, 269
Confidence interval estimates, 155, 164
Confidence level, 7
  interpreting estimate of, 141–143
  producing estimator of, 140–141
Consumer Price Index, 26
Contingency table, chi-squared test of, 244–253
  data formats, 248
  expected frequencies for, 246
  interpreting, 248
  rejection region and p-value, 246–247
  relationship between undergraduate degree/MBA major, 244–245

rule of five, 248
test statistic, 245–246
Continuity correction factor,
128–129
Continuous probability
distributions, 96–118
approximating a discrete
distribution with, 100
chi-squared distribution, 111–113
F distribution, 113–115
finding minus $Z_{.05}$, 107
normal distribution, 100–108
probability density functions,
98–100
Student t distribution, 108–111
uniform distribution, 99
Continuous random variable, 82
Covariance
and coefficiency of correlation
compared, 48
measures of linear relationship
and, 47
sample covariance, 257
Criminal trial, as hypothesis
testing, 149–150
Critical value, determining, 114
Cross-sectional data, 24
Cumulative probability, 88
Cumulative standardized normal
probabilities (table), 309–310

D

Data
acquisition errors, 61
calculations for types of, 12–13
cross-sectional, 24
defined, 12, 55
formats, 195
graphical methods of presenting,
4, 14–18, 44
hierarchy of, 13
histograms, 18–23
interval (quantitative/numerical)
data, 12–13, 35
nominal (qualitative/categorical)
data, 12, 14

numerical techniques for
summarizing, 4
ordinal data, 13
problem objectives and
information, 13
time-series, 24
types of, 12–13
Data Analysis Plus, 8
Data collection
direct observation, 55–56
experiments, 56
personal interviews, 56
self-administered survey, 57
surveys, 56
telephone interviews, 57
Data file sample statistics, 300–302
Data sampling, 57–58
cluster sampling, 60
nonsampling error, 61–62
sample size, 60
sampling error, 61
simple random sampling, 58–61
stratified random sampling, 59–60
U.S. census and, 54, 60–61
Deciles, 43
Deming, W. Edwards, 162
Denominator degrees of freedom,
113, 208
Dependent variables, 27, 165
Derivations, 165
Descriptive statistics, 3–5, 11
business statistic course marks
example, 3
graphical techniques in, 4, 11
numerical techniques in, 4, 11
Pepsi example, 4–5
Deterministic model, 256
Dice throws, 82
probability and, 68
sampling distribution of the
mean, 122
Direct observation, 55–56
Discrete probability distributions, 97
using continuous distribution to
approximate, 100
Discrete random variable, 82
Diversity index, 64, 75

E

Empirical Rule, 42
Equal-variances interval estimator,
186
Equal-variances test statistic, 186
Errors in data acquisition, 61
Error variable, 256
required conditions, 260–261
Estimate, 135
Estimation, 134–145
concepts of, 135–137
consistency and, 137
error of, 144
interval estimator, 136
number of American government
workers, 134, 141
point estimator, 136
political polling and population
proportion, 138
prescription drug effectiveness
example, 139
relative efficiency and, 137
sample size selection, 143–145
unbiased estimator, 136–137
Estimator, 135
Events, probability of
addition rule, 73–74
complement rule, 72
defined, 67
independent, 70–71
intersection of, 68
multiplication rule, 72
union of, 71–72
Excel (Microsoft), 8
Exercise answers, 323–328
Expected frequency, 243
Experimental data, 56, 266
Experimental unit, 223
Explained variation, 266
Explanatory power of the model,
266

F

Factor, 223
Fast-food drive through service
times analysis, 36

F distribution, 113–115, 314–320
    table of critical values, 313–314
    tables of values of, 315–320
First-order linear model, 256
Fisher's least significant difference
    (LSD) method, 229
    Bonferroni adjustment to,
        229–230
Frequencies, 20
Frequency distribution, 14–15
F-test of randomized block design,
    235

G

Gallup Poll, 56
Gasoline prices, 24–26
Gasoline sales, uniformly
    distributed (example), 99–100
General Social Survey, 7–8
    education of American adults,
        10, 17–18
    gender and decision to work for
        self, 206, 215–216
    liberal-conservative spectrum
        and income, 220, 227
    number of American government
        workers, 134, 141
    relation between education and
        income, 254, 268
    support for capital punishment,
        240, 248
    television watching and level of
        education, 34, 50
    time American adults spend
        watching television, 168, 175
    variables that affect income, 276,
        279
GMAT (Graduate Management
    Admission Test), 43
Goodness-of-fit test, 241–244
Gosset, William S., 108, 170

H

Harris Survey, 56
Heteroscedasticity, 285–286

Histograms, 18–23, 35
    bell shaped, 23
    bimodal, 22
    for probability of ranges, 98
    shapes of, 22
    skewed, 22
    symmetry, 22
    telephone bill analysis example,
        18–19
    unimodal, 22, 23
Homoscedasticity, 285
Honda Accord, 258–268, 270
House price/house size analysis,
    27–28, 48–49
Hypothesis testing, 148–165
    calculating probability of Type II
        error, 160–164
    concepts, 149–152
    election day exit poll example,
        152
    left-tail test, 163
    one-tail tests, 159
    of population proportion,
        152–160
    power of a test, 162–163
    p-value approach, 153, 154
    rejection region method,
        153–154
    right-tail test, 163
    standardized test statistic, 154
    terminology of, 150
    two-tail tests, 159
    value of larger sample size and,
        162

I

Independent variable, 27, 165
Inferential statistics, 5
    exit polls example, 5–6
Inflation, measuring, 26
Intercorrelation, 286
Internet, time spent on (study)
    measures of central location,
        36–37
    measures of relative standing, 43

Interquartile range
    factors that identify when to
        compute, 47
    of long-distance telephone bills,
        44–46
Interval data, 12, 13, 35
Interval estimator, 136
    information and width of
        interval, 143

J

Joint probability, 68

K

Kruskal-Wallis test, 226–227

L

Landon, Alfred, 57
Large real data sets, 7–8
Least squares line, 256–257
Least squares method, 29
Left-tail test, 163
Linear relationship, 28–29
    interpreting, 29
    scatter diagrams depicting, 29
Line charts, 24–27
Literary Digest, 57, 62
Long-distance telephone bill
    analysis
    box plots and, 44–45
    interquartile range of, 44
    quartiles of, 44
    using histograms, 18–19
Lottery tickets, 80, 86

M

Marginal probability, 69
Matched pairs experiment, 196–202
Mean (average), 36
Mean of the population of
    differences, 199

Mean square for error, 224
Mean square for treatment, 224
Mean squares, 224
Measures of central location, 4,
  36–39
  Excel and Minitab for, 38–39
  Internet time example, 36–37
  long-distance telephone bills
    example, 37
  mean, median, and mode, 36–38
  for ordinal and nominal data, 39
Measures of linear relationship,
  47–50
  coefficient of correlation, 47–48
  covariance, 47
Measures of relative standing,
  42–44
Measures of variability, 4, 39–42
  standard deviation, 39–42
  summer jobs data example, 41
  variance, 39–40
Median, 4, 36
Medium, 13
Microsoft Excel, 8
Minitab, 8
Missing data, 8
Mitofsky, Warren, 152n
Modal class, 22
Mode, 36
Multicollinearity, 279, 286
Multinomial experiment, 241, 242
Multiple regression, 276–287
  coefficient of determination, 280
  computing coefficients and other
    statistics, 279
  estimating coefficients/assessing
    the model, 278–284
  heteroscedasticity, 285
  interpreting coefficients, 281–282
  interpreting results, cautionary
    note, 283
  model and required conditions,
    277–278
  regression diagnostics, 284–293
  regression equation use, 283–284
  required conditions for error
    variable, 278

selecting independent variables,
  279
standard error of estimate, 280
testing coefficients, 282–283
testing model validity, 280–281

N

Negatively skewed histogram, 22
Nielsen ratings, 57
Nominal data, 12, 14
  calculations for, 13
  measures of central location
    for, 39
  measures of variability for, 42
Nonresponse error, 62
Nonsampling errors, 61–62
Normal distribution, 100–108
  calculating, 101
  finding values of Z, 105–106
  gasoline sales example, 101
  minimum GMAT score to enter
    MBA program example, 94,
    107
Null hypothesis, 150–152
  use of equal sign in, 151
Numerator degrees of freedom,
  113, 115, 208
Numerical data, 12
Numerical descriptive techniques,
  34–50
  arithmetic mean, 36
  box plots, 44–47
  measures of central location,
    36–39
  measures of linear relationship,
    47–50
  measures of relative standing,
    42–44
  measures of variability, 39–42

O

Observational data, 55, 266
Observed frequencies, 243
Odometer reading, and price of
  used cars, 258–268, 270

One-tail tests, 159, 264
Ordinal data, 13
  measures of central location
    for, 39
  measures of variability for, 42
Outliers, 45

P

Parameter, 6, 35
Pearson coefficient of correlation,
  267
Percentiles, 42–43
  factors to consider when
    computing, 77
Pie charts, 14–18
  displaying relative frequencies
    with, 15–17
Point estimator, 136
Point prediction, 269
Poisson distribution, 90–92
Poisson experiment, 90
Poisson probabilities, 90, 101
  table, 91–92, 307–308
Poisson random variable, 90
Poisson table, 91–92, 307–308
Pooled proportion estimate, 211
Pooled variance estimator, 186
Population, 6
  sampled population, 57
  sample size selection to estimate
    proportion of, 143–145
  target population, 57
  testing proportion of, 152–160
Population inferences, 168–169,
  184–202, 206–291
  checking required conditions,
    174, 178, 202
  consistency of container-filling
    machine, 176–179
  data formats, 195
  deciding if variances differ, 187
  difference between two means
    (independent samples),
    185–196
  difference between two means
    (matched pairs experiment),
    196–202

Population inferences, *(Continued)*
　on difference between two
　　population proportions,
　　210–219
　direct and broker-purchased
　　mutual funds (example),
　　187–190
　effect of new CEO in family-run
　　businesses (example), 191
　estimating equal variances, 190
　estimating totals of finite
　　populations, 174–175
　estimating unequal variances, 193
　independent samples or matched
　　pairs result comparisons, 201
　newspaper recycling plant
　　example, 170–171
　on population means, 170–175
　population variance and, 175–176
　on ratio of two population
　　variances, 207–210
　review, 179
　salary offer comparisons
　　(example), 196–200
　statistic and sampling
　　distribution, 176
　tax collected from audited
　　returns (example), 172–174
　testing quality of bottle-filling
　　machines example, 208–210
　test marketing of package
　　designs, 212–215
　violation of required condition,
　　195, 202
Population means, analysis of
　variance and. *See* Analysis of
　variance
Population proportion, estimating,
　138
Population standard deviation,
　85–86
Population variance, 85
Positively skewed histogram, 22
Prediction interval, 269
Probability, 64–79
　addition rule, 73–74

assigning to events, 65–68
classical approach, 66–67
complement rule, 72
conditional probability, 69–70
defining events, 67
diversity index, 64, 75
of events, 67
identifying correct method for
　calculating, 75–79
independence, 70–71
interpreting, 67
joint probability, 68, 75
marginal probability, 69
multiplication rule, 72
mutual fund applications, 68–72
random experiment, 65–66
relative frequency approach, 67
rules and trees, 72–75
selecting two students example,
　72–75
subjective approach, 67
Probability density functions,
　98–100
Probability distribution, 83
　describing number of persons per
　　household (example), 85–86
　of number of sales (example), 84
　of persons per household
　　(example), 83–84
　populations and, 84–85
Probability trees, 74
p-value approach, 153, 154–159
　describing *p*-value, 157
　interpreting, 155–157
　rejection region methods and,
　　157
　solving with Excel and Minitab,
　　157–158

Q

Qualitative data, 12
Quantitative data, 12
Quartiles, 43
　factors that identify when to
　　compute, 47, 77

of long-distance telephone
　bills, 44
Questionnaires, 57
Quintiles, 43

R

Random experiment, 65–66
Randomized block (two-way)
　analysis of variance, 232–236
Random variable, 82
Range, 4
Ratio data, 12n
Rectangular probability
　distribution, 99
Regression diagnostics, 284–293
　multicollinearity, 279, 286
　nonnormality, 285
　residual analysis, 284–285
Regression equation, 269–275
Rejection region method,
　153–154
　p-value and, 157
Relative efficiency, 137
Relative frequency approach, 67
Relative frequency distribution,
　14, 15
Research hypothesis, 150
Response rate, 56
Responses, 223
Response variable, 223
Right-tail test, 163
Roosevelt, Franklin D., 57
R-square, 264

S

Sample, 6–7
Sample covariance, 257
Sampled population, 57
Sample mean, 61
Sample variance, 40n
Sampling distributions, 120–130
　central limit theorem, 125

determining sales of business school grads (example), 120, 126

of the mean, 121–127

of a proportion, 127–130

32-oz. bottle contents (example), 125–126

using for inference, 126–127

Sampling error, 61

SAT (Scholastic Achievement Test), 43

Scatter diagrams, 27–29, 35

and covariance/coefficient of correlation compared, 48

patterns of, 28–29

Selection bias, 62

Self-selected samples, 57

Significance level, 7, 150

Simple event, 67

Simple linear regression and correlation

annual bonus and years of experience (example), 257–258

cause-and-effect relationship, 266

coefficient of correlation, 267

coefficient of determination, 264–265

data collection, 266

estimating the coefficients, 256–260

estimator and sampling distribution, 263

model, 256

model assessment, 261–269

odometer reading and price of used cars, 258–268, 270

one-tail tests, 264

regression equation and, 269–275

standard error of estimate, 261

sum of squares for error (SSE), 258, 261

testing the slope, 262–263

violation of required condition, 269

Simple linear regression model, 256

Simple random sample, 58

of income tax returns (example), 58–59

Skewed histograms, 22

Spearman rank correlation coefficient, 269

SSE (sum of squares for error), 223, 258, 261

SST (sum of squares for treatments), 223

Stacked data format, 195

Standard deviation, 39, 41–42

using empirical rule to interpret, 42

Standard error of estimate, 261

Standard error of the mean, 170

Standard error of the proportion, 129

Standardized test statistic, 154

Standard normal random variable, 101

Statistical Abstract of the United States, 83

Statistical inference, 7

guide to techniques, 165

Statistical inference review, 294–299

flowchart of statistical inference techniques, 298–299

statistical techniques summary, 295–297

Statistical techniques guide, 329–330

Statistician, defined, 2n

Statistics

computers and, 8

defined, 2

descriptive, 3–5

inferential, 5

key concepts, 6–7

objective of, 12

Statistics practitioner, defined, 2n

Stem-and-leaf display, 23–24

Stratified random sample, 59–60

Studentized range, tables of critical values of, 321, 322

Student *t* distribution, 170

table of critical values, 311

Subjective approach, 67

Sum of squares for error (SSE), 223, 258, 261

Sum of squares for treatments (SST), 223

Surveys, 56

American National Election Survey, 8

General Social Survey, 7–8

light beer preference, 14–17

political survey (sampling distribution), 130

self-administered, 57

Symmetric histograms, 22

T

Target population, 57

Telephone bill analysis, 18–20

Test statistic (standardized test statistic), 152, 154, 223–226

checking required conditions, 226

rejection region and *p*-value, 224–225

sampling distribution of, 224

violation of required conditions, 226–227

Time-series data, 24

t-statistic, 170

Tukey, John, 23

Two-tail tests, 159, 163

Type I error, 150–151

Type II error, 150–151

calculating probability of, 160–164

judging the test, 161–162

U

Unbiased estimator, 136–137

Undercounting, 54

Undergraduate degree/MBA major, 244–245

Unequal-variances confidence interval, 187
Unequal-variances test statistic, 187
Uniform distribution, 99
Unimodal histogram, 22, 23
Union, 71–72
Unstacked data format, 195

V

Values of the variable, 12
Variable, 12
Variance, 39–41
  interpreting, 41
  shortcut (optional) method for, 41

W

Within-treatments variation, 223

X

x^2 distribution, table of critical values, 312

Learning Objectives and Outcomes

1-1 Key Statistical Concepts

Know the difference between population and sample. Know the difference between a parameter and a statistic. Understand statistical inference. Understand the purpose of exit polls and how statistical inference works to predict the winner.

1-2 Large Real Data Sets

Know about the General Social Survey and the American National Election Survey.

1-3 Statistics and the Computer

Understand the need for computers and software in real applications of statistics. Know where to find the data sets and (for Excel users) Data Analysis Plus.

Key Concepts

Vocabulary

Descriptive statistics deals with methods of organizing, summarizing, and presenting data in a convenient and informative way.

Inferential statistics is a body of methods used to draw conclusions or inferences about characteristics of populations based on sample data.

A **population** is the group of all items of interest to a statistics practitioner. It is frequently very large and may, in fact, be infinitely large.

A descriptive measure of a population is called a **parameter**.

A **sample** is a set of data drawn from the population.

A descriptive measure of a sample is called a **statistic**.

Statistical inference is the process of making an estimate, prediction, or decision about a population based on sample data.

The **confidence level** is the proportion of times that an estimating procedure will be correct.

The **significance level** measures how frequently the conclusion of a testing procedure will be wrong in the long run.

Practice Test

Part I: Knowing the Definitions

1.1 What does GSS stand for?

1.2 What does ANES stand for?

Part II: Applying the Techniques

1.3 List the type of information needed in Example 1.1.

1.4 Why isn't the mean enough information in Example 1.1?

1.5 Why is the mean an important statistic in Example 1.2?

1.6 What is the difference between the information needed in Examples 1.1 and 1.2?

1.7 What are the parameters needed in Examples 1.2 and 10.1?

1.8 Why is there missing data in the General Social Surveys and the American National Election Surveys?

1.9 In a survey of 350 students each was asked whether they planned to go to graduate school. The number who responded affirmatively was 35. If we want to acquire information about the graduate school plans of all students what is the parameter?

1.10 Refer to Exercise 1.9. What is the statistic?

1.11 Refer to Exercise 1.9. Is 350 the population or sample size?

1.12 Refer to Exercise 1.7. Do we know the population parameter?

Part III: Understanding the Concepts

1.13 Discuss why it is often necessary to use inferential statistical techniques.

1.14 As you will discover there are two forms of inference, estimation and hypothesis testing. In Example 1.2 which form of inference should you use?

1.15 Which form of inference should you use in Example 10.1?

1.16 There are three steps that statistics practitioners use when applying inferential methods. They are identifying the technique, calculating the statistics, and interpreting the results. Put the steps in order of importance.

Additional exercises and cases may be found on the CourseMate BSTAT Web site, www.cengagebrain.com.

Learning Objectives and Outcomes

2-1 Types of Data and Information

Know how to identify interval, ordinal, and nominal data. Understand what calculations are permitted for each type of data. Understand that we can treat interval data as ordinal or nominal and ordinal as nominal, but in doing so we lose information. Know that we cannot treat nominal data as ordinal or interval, and we cannot treat ordinal data as interval.

2-2 Bar and Pie Charts

Manually create bar and pie charts for small samples and use computer software to create these charts for small and large samples. Understand that bar charts depict frequencies, and pie charts depict relative frequencies.

2-3 Histograms and Stem-and-Leaf Displays

Manually draw histograms and stem-and-leaf displays for small samples and use computer software to create these charts for small and large samples. Know how to describe a histogram in terms of symmetry or skewness, unimodal or bimodal, and bell shape. Know the difference between positive and negative skewness.

2-4 Line Charts

Manually draw line charts for small samples and use computer software to create these charts for small and large samples. Understand the Consumer Price Index and how it is used to remove the effect of inflation.

2-5 Scatter Diagrams

Manually draw scatter diagrams for small samples and use computer software to create these charts for small and large samples. Know how to interpret the chart in terms of linearity and strength of the linear relationship.

Key Concepts

Vocabulary

A variable is some characteristic of a population or sample.

The va**lues** of the variable are the possible observations of the variable.

Data are the observed values of a variable.

Interval data are real numbers, such as heights, weights, incomes, and distances.

The values of **nominal** data are categories.

Ordinal data appear to be nominal, but their values are in order.

A **frequency distribution** summarizes the data in a table that presents the categories and their counts.

Relative frequency distribution lists the categories and the proportion with which each occurs.

A **bar chart** graphically depicts the frequencies in a set of ordinal data.

A **pie chart** graphically depicts the relative frequencies of a set of ordinal data.

A **histogram** is similar to a bar chart. The key difference is that it is used to graphically describe interval data.

A histogram is said to be **symmetric** if, when we draw a vertical line down the center of the histogram, the two sides are identical in shape and size.

A **skewed** histogram is one with a long tail extending to either the right or the left. The former is called **positively skewed**, and the latter is called **negatively skewed**.

A **modal class** is the class with the largest number of observations. A **unimodal histogram** is one with a single peak. A **bimodal histogram** is one with two peaks that are not necessarily equal in height. Bimodal histograms often indicate that two different distributions are present.

A special type of symmetric unimodal histogram is one that is **bell shaped**.

Excel Commands

Bar and Pie Charts: Click **Insert, Column,** and **2-D Column**
Histogram: Click **Data, Data Analysis,** and **Histogram**
Stem-and Leaf Display: Click **Add-Ins, Data Analysis Plus,** and **Stem-and-Leaf Display**
Line Chart: Click **Insert, Line,** and **2-D Line**
Scatter Diagram: Click **Insert** and **Scatter**

Minitab Commands

Bar Chart: Click **Graph** and **Bar Chart**
Pie Chart: Click **Graph** and **Pie Chart**
Histogram: Click **Graph** and **Histogram**
Stem-and Leaf Display: Click **Graph** and **Stem-and-Leaf**
Line Chart: Click **Graph** and **Time Series Plot**
Scatter Diagram: Click **Graph** and **Scatterplot**

Practice Test

Part I: Knowing the Definitions

2.1 What calculations are permitted on interval data?

2.2 What calculations are permitted on ordinal data?

2.3 What calculations are permitted on nominal data?

2.4 What is the difference between an interval variable and an ordinal variable?

2.5 What is the difference between an ordinal variable and a nominal variable?

2.6 Residents of condominiums were recently surveyed and asked a series of questions. Identify the type of data for each question.

    a. What is your age?
    b. On what floor is your condominium?
    c. Do you own or rent?
    d. How large is your condominium (in square feet)?
    e. Does your condominium have a pool?

2.7 Information about a magazine's readers is of interest to both the publisher and the magazine's advertisers. A survey of readers asked respondents to complete the following:

    a. Age
    b. Gender
    c. Marital status
    d. Number of magazine subscriptions
    e. Annual income
    f. Rate the quality of our magazine: excellent, good, fair, or poor

For each item identify the resulting data type.

A **stem-and-leaf display** is similar to a histogram. The key difference is that digits make up the heights of the classes.

A **scatter diagram** is a graph that depicts the relationship between two interval variables.

Time-series data are often graphically depicted on a **line chart**, which is a plot of the variable over time.

Part II: Applying the Techniques

2.8 A large investment firm on Wall Street wants to review the distribution of ages of its stockbrokers. The firm believes that this information can be useful in developing plans to recruit new brokers. The ages of a sample of 200 brokers were recorded. Which graphical technique should be used to summarize the data?

2.9 Are younger workers less likely to stay with their jobs? To help answer this question a random sample of workers was selected. All were asked to report their ages and how many months they had been employed with their current employers. Which graphical technique should be used to summarize these data?

2.10 Subway train riders frequently pass the time by reading a newspaper. New York City has a subway and four newspapers. A sample of 360 subway riders who regularly read a newspaper was asked to identify that newspaper. The responses are

    1. *New York Daily News*
    2. *New York Post*
    3. *New York Times*
    4. *Wall Street Journal*

Identify the graphical method that best summarizes these data.

2.11 The number of property crimes (burglary, larceny, theft, car theft) (in thousands) for the years 1981 to 2011 was recorded. Which graphical method should be used to summarize these data?

Part III: Understanding the Concepts

2.12 Why do you lose information when you treat an interval variable as ordinal or nominal?

2.13 Why do you lose information when you treat ordinal data as nominal?

Additional exercises and cases may be found on the CourseMate BSTAT Web site, www.cengagebrain.com.

Learning Objectives and Outcomes

3-1 Measures of Central Location

Manually calculate the mean, median, and mode of a small sample and use computer software for small and large samples. Know when to use each statistic. Know when the median should be used instead of the mean. Know why the mode is seldom used as a measure of central location. Know that the mean is calculated from interval data only and the median can be used for interval or ordinal data.

3-2 Measures of Variability

Manually calculate the range, variance, and standard deviation in small samples and use computer software for small and large samples. Understand why we square the deviations (differences between the observations and the mean) when calculating the variance. Understand why we divide the sum of squared deviations by $n - 1$ instead of n in the formula for sample variance. Understand why we cannot interpret the variance but we can interpret the standard deviation. Understand how the Empirical Rule works. Know that the variance and standard deviation can be calculated from interval data only.

3-3 Measures of Relative Standing and Box Plots

Know what percentiles and quartiles are. Manually calculate the location of any percentile. Know how to create a box plot and how to interpret box plots. Know that the interquartile range is another measure of variation that can be used for both interval and ordinal data.

Key Concepts

Vocabulary

The **mean, median**, and the **mode** are measures of central location.

The **range,** the **variance,** and the **standard deviation** are measures of variability.

The **P**th **percentile** is the value for which P percent are less than that value and $(100 - P)\%$ are greater than that value.

Quartiles divide the data into quarters.

The **first** or **lower quartile** is labeled Q_1.

The **second quartile**, $Q2$, is equal to the 50th percentile, which is also the median.

The **third** or **upper quartile**, Q_3, is equal to the 75th percentile.

Quintiles divide the data into fifths, and **deciles** divide the data into tenths.

A **box plot** graphs five statistics, the minimum and maximum observations, and the first, second, and third quartiles. It also depicts other features of a set of data.

The **covariance** and the **coefficient of correlation** are measures of linear relationship.

Symbols

Symbol	Pronounced	Represents
μ	Mu	Population mean
$\bar{x}$	X-bar	Sample mean
σ^2	Sigma–squared	Population variance
σ	Sigma	Population standard deviation
σ_{xy}	Sigma-sub-xy	Population covariance
ρ	Rho	Population coefficient of correlation

Key Formulae

Population mean: $\mu = \dfrac{\sum\limits_{i=1}^{N} x_i}{N}$

Sample mean: $\bar{x} = \dfrac{\sum\limits_{i=1}^{n} x_i}{n}$

Population variance: $\sigma^2 = \dfrac{\sum\limits_{i=1}^{N}(x_i - \mu)^2}{N}$

Sample variance: $s^2 = \dfrac{\sum\limits_{i=1}^{n}(x_i - \bar{x})^2}{n - 1}$

Shortcut for Sample Variance

$s^2 = \dfrac{1}{n-1}\left[\sum\limits_{i=1}^{n} x_i^2 - \dfrac{\left(\sum\limits_{i=1}^{n} x_i\right)^2}{n}\right]$

Standard Deviation

Population standard deviation: $\sigma = \sqrt{\sigma^2}$
Sample standard deviation: $s = \sqrt{s^2}$

Location of a Percentile

$L_P = (n + 1)\dfrac{P}{100}$

where L_p is the location of the Pth percentile.

Interquartile Range

Interquartile range $= Q_3 - Q_1$

Covariance

Population covariance:

$\sigma_{xy} = \dfrac{\sum\limits_{i=1}^{N}(x_i - \mu_x)(y_i - \mu_y)}{N}$

Sample covariance:

$s_{xy} = \dfrac{\sum\limits_{i=1}^{n}(x_i - \bar{x})(y_i - \bar{y})}{n - 1}$

Shortcut for Sample Covariance

$s_{xy} = \dfrac{1}{n-1}\left[\sum\limits_{i=1}^{n} x_i y_i - \dfrac{\sum\limits_{i=1}^{n} x_i \sum\limits_{i=1}^{n} y_i}{n}\right]$

Coefficient of Correlation

Population coefficient of correlation:

$\rho = \dfrac{\sigma_{xy}}{\sigma_x \sigma_y}$

Sample coefficient of correlation:

$r = \dfrac{s_{xy}}{s_x s_y}$

3-3 Measures of Linear Relationship

Manually calculate the covariance and the coefficient of correlation for small samples and use computer software for small and large samples. Understand the relationship between scatter diagrams and the coefficient of correlation. Understand why the covariance does not provide as much information as the coefficient of correlation.

Excel Commands

Measures of Central Location and Variation: Use functions AVERAGE, MEDIAN, VAR, and STDEV

Box Plot: Click **Add-Ins, Data Analysis Plus,** and **Box Plot**

Measures of Linear Relationship: Use functions CORREL and COVAR

Minitab Commands

Measures of Central Location, Variation, Percentiles, and Linear Relationship: Click **Stat, Basic Statistics,** and **Descriptive Statistics**

Box Plot: Click **Graph** and **Box Plot**

Practice Test

Part I: Knowing the Definitions

3.1 What is the Empirical Rule?

3.2 What are the statistics depicted in a box plot?

Part II: Applying the Techniques

3.3 Compute the three statistics that measure central location for the following data.

   5 3 2 7 4 9 1 3 7 9

3.4 Calculate the mean, median, and mode for the following data.

   16 12 9 15 13 8 5 19 12 14

3.5 Refer to Exercise 3.3. Calculate the variance and standard deviation.

3.6 Refer to Exercise 3.4. Calculate the variance and standard deviation.

3.7 Find the variance and standard deviation of the following sample.

   0 −5 −3 6 4 −4 1 −5 0 3

3.8 Refer to Exercise 3.3. Calculate the quartiles.

3.9 Refer to Exercise 3.4. Calculate the quartiles.

3.10 Calculate the covariance for the following data.

X	5	7	8	11	17
Y	20	14	23	27	19

3.11 Refer to Exercise 3.10. Compute the coefficient of correlation.

Part III: Understanding the Concepts

3.12 If a histogram is positively skewed, which is larger—the mean or the median?

3.13 If a histogram is negatively skewed, which is larger—the mean or the median?

3.14 Why is it impossible for a variance to be negative?

3.15 What useful information about the relationship between two interval variables can one derive from the covariance?

3.16 What useful information about the relationship between two interval variables is not possible from the covariance?

Additional exercises and cases may be found on the CourseMate BSTAT Web site, www.cengagebrain.com.

Learning Objectives and Outcomes

4-1 Methods of Collecting Data

Know the three methods of collecting data discussed in this section. Know the three types of surveys. Understand the differences between the three surveys in terms of costs and response rates. Understand the difference between observational data and experimental data.

4-2 Sampling

Understand why it is necessary to sample. Understand what went wrong with *The Literary Digest* in 1936.

4-3 Sampling Plans

Know that there are three sampling plans and how they are conducted. Understand under what circumstances each should be used.

4-4 Sampling and Nonsampling Errors

Know the difference between the two types of errors and how each can occur.

Key Concepts

Vocabulary

The simplest method of obtaining data is by **direct observation**. When data are gathered in this way, they are said to be **observational**.

A more expensive but better way to produce data is through **experiments**. Data produced in this manner are called **experimental**.

One of the most familiar methods of collecting data is the **survey**, which solicits information from people concerning such things as their income, family size, and opinions on various issues.

Many researchers feel that the best way to survey people is by means of a **personal interview**, which involves an interviewer soliciting information from a respondent by asking prepared questions.

A **telephone interview** is usually less expensive, but it is also less personal and has a lower expected response rate.

A third popular method of data collection is the **self-administered questionnaire**, which is usually mailed to a sample of people.

A **simple random sample** is a sample selected in such a way that every possible sample with the same number of observations is equally likely to be chosen.

A **stratified random sample** is obtained by separating the population into mutually exclusive sets, or strata, and then drawing simple random samples from each stratum.

A **cluster sample** is a simple random sample of groups or clusters of elements.

Sampling error refers to differences between the sample and the population that exists only because of the observations that happened to be selected for the sample.

Nonsampling error is more serious than sampling error, because taking a larger sample won't diminish the size, or the possibility of occurrence, of this error.

Practice Test

Part I: Knowing the Definitions

4.1 What is observational data?

4.2 What is experimental data?

4.3 What is a simple random sample?

4.4 What is a stratified random sample?

4.5 What is a cluster sample

Part II: Applying the Techniques

4.6 Describe how to conduct a simple random survey.

4.7 Describe how to conduct a stratified random survey.

4.8 Describe how to conduct a cluster survey.

Part III: Understanding the Concepts

4.9 Why did *The Literary Digest* survey in 1936 go so wrong?

4.10 What is a sampling error?

4.11 How do sampling errors occur?

4.12 What is a nonsampling error?

4.13 How do nonsampling errors occur?

Additional exercises and cases may be found on the CourseMate BSTAT Web site, www.cengagebrain.com.

Learning Objectives and Outcomes

Key Concepts

5-1 Assigning Probability to Events

Know what a random experiment, a sample space, and simple events are. Know what is meant by exhaustive and mutually exclusive. Know the three methods of assigning probabilities and understand when each is used. Know the requirements of probability.

5-2 Joint, Marginal, and Conditional Probability

Know what joint, marginal, and conditional probabilities are. Understand that the joint probability represents the probability of the intersection of two events. Know how to compute marginal probabilities from joint probabilities. Know how to calculate conditional probabilities. Understand the concept of independence and how to determine if two events are independent. Know what the probability of the union of two events means and how it is calculated.

5-3 Probability Rules and Trees

Know the complement, multiplication, and addition rules. Know the special cases of the multiplication rule and the addition rule. Know how to apply each rule to compute the probability of the events of interest. Know how to set up probability trees to describe events and how to calculate joint probabilities at the ends of branches. Know how to add the joint probabilities to determine the probability of the event of interest.

5-4 Identifying the Correct Method

Understand that for many problems one needs to determine whether joint probabilities are given or must be calculated from the information provided.

Vocabulary

A **random experiment** is an action or process that leads to one of several possible outcomes.

The listed outcomes must be **exhaustive**, which means that all possible outcomes must be included. In addition, the outcomes must be **mutually exclusive**, which means that no two outcomes can occur at the same time.

A **sample space** of a random experiment is a list of all possible outcomes of the experiment. The outcomes must be exhaustive and mutually exclusive.

An **event** is a collection or set of one or more simple events in a sample space.

The **probability of an event** is the sum of the probabilities of the simple events that constitute the event.

The **intersection** of events A and B is the event that occurs when both A and B occur.

The probability of the intersection is called the **joint probability**.

The probability of event A given event B is called **conditional probability**.

Two events are **independent** if the occurrence of one of the events does not affect the probability of the other event.

The **union** of events A and B is the event that occurs when either A or B or both occur.

The **complement rule** calculates the probability that an event will occur from the probability that the event won't occur.

The **multiplication rule** calculates the **joint probability**.

The **addition rule** computes the probability that at least one of two events will occur.

Key Formulae

Conditional Probability

The probability of event A given event B is

$$P(A|B) = \frac{P(A \text{ and } B)}{P(B)}$$

The probability of event B given event A is

$$P(B|A) = \frac{P(A \text{ and } B)}{P(A)}$$

Independent Events

Two events A and B are said to be **independent** if

$$P(A|B) = P(A)$$

or

$$P(B|A) = P(B)$$

Union of Events A and B

The **union** of events A and B is the event that occurs when either A or B or both occur. It is denoted as

$$A \text{ or } B$$

Complement Rule

$$P(A^C) = 1 - P(A)$$

for any event A.

Multiplication Rule

The joint probability of any two events A and B is

$$P(A \text{ and } B) = P(B)P(A|B)$$

or altering the notation

$$P(A \text{ and } B) = P(A)P(B|A)$$

Multiplication Rule for Independent Events

The joint probability of any two independent events A and B is

$$P(A \text{ and } B) = P(A)P(B)$$

Addition Rule

The probability that event A, or event B, or both occur is

$$P(A \text{ or } B) = P(A) + P(B) - P(A \text{ and } B)$$

Practice Test

Part I: Knowing the Definitions

5.1 What is a random experiment?

5.2 Define mutually exclusive events.

5.3 What are the three methods of assigning probabilities to events?

5.4 What are the requirements for probability?

Part II: Applying the Techniques

5.5 The following table lists the joint probabilities associated with smoking and lung disease among 60- to 65-year-old men.

	He is a smoker	He is a nonsmoker
He has lung disease	.12	.03
He does not have lung disease	.19	.66

One 60- to 65-year-old man is selected at random. What is the probability of the following events?

a. He is a smoker.
b. He does not have lung disease.
c. He has lung disease given that he is a smoker.
d. He has lung disease given that he does not smoke.

5.6 Refer to Exercise 5.5. Are smoking and lung disease among 60- to 65-year-old men related? Explain.

5.7 A retail outlet wanted to know whether its weekly advertisement in the daily newspaper works. To acquire this critical information the store manager surveyed the people who entered the store and determined whether each individual saw the ad and whether a purchase was made. From the information developed the manager produced the following table of joint probabilities. Are the ads effective? Explain.

	Purchase	No purchase
Saw ad	.18	.42
Did not see ad	.12	.28

5.8 To gauge the relationship between education and unemployment an economist turned to the U.S. Census from which the following table of joint probabilities was produced.

Education	Employed	Unemployed
Not a high school graduate	.091	.008
High school graduate	.282	.014
Some college, no degree	.166	.007
Associate's degree	.095	.003
Bachelor's degree	.213	.004
Advanced degree	.115	.002

Source: Statistical Abstract of the United States, 2009, Table 223

a. What is the probability that a high school graduate is unemployed?
b. Determine the probability that a randomly selected individual is employed.
c. Find the probability that an unemployed person possesses an advanced degree.
d. What is the probability that a randomly selected person did not finish high school?

5.9 A survey of middle-age men reveals that 28% of them are balding at the crown of their heads. Moreover, it is known that such men have an 18% probability of suffering a heart attack in the next 10 years. Men who are not balding in this way have an 11% probability of a heart attack. Find the probability that a middle-age man will suffer a heart attack sometime in the next 10 years.

5.10 Researchers at the University of Pennsylvania School of Medicine have determined that children under 2 years old who sleep with the lights on have a 36% chance of becoming myopic before they are 16. Children who sleep in darkness have a 21% probability of becoming myopic. A survey indicates that 28% of children under 2 sleep with some light on. Find the probability that a child under 16 is myopic.

5.11 All printed circuit boards (PCBs) that are manufactured at a certain plant are inspected. An analysis of the company's records indicates that 22% of all PCBs are flawed in some way. Of those that are flawed, 84% are reparable and the rest must be discarded. If a newly produced PCB is randomly selected, what is the probability that it does not have to be discarded?

Additional exercises and cases may be found on the CourseMate BSTAT Web site, www.cengagebrain.com.

Learning Objectives and Outcomes

Key Concepts

6-1 Random Variables and Probability Distributions

Know what a random variable is. Understand the difference between discrete and continuous random variables. Know how discrete probability distributions are created. Understand that probability distributions can be used to represent populations. Know how to calculate the mean, variance, and standard deviation of these populations.

6-2 Binomial Distribution

Know how to recognize a binomial experiment. Know how to manually calculate binomial probabilities. Know how to use Table 1 to compute cumulative probabilities as well as probabilities of individual values. Know the mean, variance, and standard deviation of a binomial random variable.

6-3 Poisson Distribution

Know how to recognize a Poisson experiment. Know how to manually calculate Poisson probabilities. Know how to use Table 2 to compute cumulative probabilities as well as probabilities of individual values. Know the mean and variance of a Poisson random variable.

Vocabulary

A **random variable** is a function or rule that assigns a number to each outcome of an experiment.

There are two types of random variables, discrete and continuous. A **discrete random variable** is one that can take on a countable number of values. A **continuous random variable** is one whose values are uncountable.

A **probability distribution** is a table, formula, or graph that describes the values of a random variable and the probability associated with these values.

A **binomial experiment** consists of a fixed number of trials. We represent the number of trials by n. On each trial there are two possible outcomes. We label one outcome a *success,* and the other a *failure*. The probability of success is p. The probability of failure is $1 - p$. The trials are independent, which means that the outcome of one trial does not affect the outcomes of any other trials.

Binomial probability distribution computes the probability of x successes in n trials

A **Poisson experiment** is characterized by the following properties: The number of successes that occur in any interval is independent of the number of successes that occur in any other interval. The probability of a success in an interval is the same for all equal-size intervals. The probability of a success in an interval is proportional to the size of the interval. The probability of more than one success in an interval approaches 0 as the interval becomes smaller.

Poisson probability distribution calculates the probability of the number of successes in a specific interval.

Symbols

Symbol	Pronounced	Represents
C_x^n	n-choose x	Number of combinations
$n!$	n-factorial	$n(n - 1)(n - 2) \cdots (3)(2)(1)$
e		$2.71828\ldots$

Key Formulae

Population Mean

$$E(X) = \mu = \sum_{\text{all } x} xP(x)$$

Population Variance

$$V(X) = \sigma^2 = \sum_{\text{all } x} (x - \mu)^2 P(x)$$

Shortcut Calculation for Population Variance

$$V(X) = \sigma^2 = \sum_{\text{all } x} x^2 P(x) - \mu^2$$

Population Standard Deviation

$$\sigma = \sqrt{\sigma^2}$$

Binomial Probability Distribution
The probability of x successes in a binomial experiment with n trials and probability of success $= p$ is

$$P(x) = \frac{n!}{x!(n - x)!} p^x (1 - p)^{n-x}$$

$$\text{for } x = 0, 1, 2, \ldots, n$$

Poisson Probability Distribution
The probability that a Poisson random variable assumes a value of x in a specific interval is

$$P(x) = \frac{e^{-\mu}\mu^x}{x!} \qquad \text{for } x = 0, 1, 2, \ldots$$

where μ is the mean number of successes in the interval or region and e is the base of the natural logarithm (approximately 2.71828).

Excel Commands

Binomial probability: Use function BINOMDIST

Poisson probability: Use function POISSON

Minitab Commands

Click **Calc, Probability Distributions**, and **Binomial**.

Click **Calc, Probability Distributions**, and **Poisson**.

Practice Test

Part I: Knowing the Definitions

6.1   What is a random variable?

6.2   How do discrete and continuous random variables differ?

6.3   List the four conditions that define a binomial experiment.

6.4   What is a cumulative probability?

Part II: Applying the Techniques

6.5   After watching a number of children playing games at a video arcade, a statistics practitioner estimated the following probability distribution of X, the number of games per visit.

x	1	2	3	4	5	6	7
P(x)	.05	.15	.15	.25	.20	.10	.10

a. What is the probability that a child will play more than four games?

b. What is the probability that a child will play at least two games?

6.6   Refer to Exercise 6.5. Determine the mean and variance of the number of games played.

6.7   According to the American Academy of Cosmetic Dentistry, 75% of adults believe that an unattractive smile hurts career success. Suppose that 25 adults are randomly selected. What is the probability that 15 or more of them would agree with the claim?

6.8   Most Internet service providers (ISPs) attempt to provide a large enough service so that customers seldom encounter a busy signal. Suppose that the customers of one ISP encounter busy signals 8% of the time. During the week a customer of this ISP called 25 times. What is the probability that she did not encounter any busy signals?

6.9   The number of arrivals at a car wash is Poisson distributed with a mean of eight per hour.

a. What is the probability that 10 cars will arrive in the next hour?

b. What is the probability that more than 5 cars will arrive in the next hour?

c. What is the probability that fewer than 12 cars will arrive in the next hour?

6.10   The percentage of customers who enter a restaurant and ask to be seated in a smoking section is 15%. Suppose that 100 people enter the restaurant.

a. What is the expected number of people who request a smoking table?

b. What is the standard deviation of the number of requests for a smoking table?

c. What is the probability that 20 or more people request a smoking table?

6.11   Lotteries are an important income source for various governments around the world. However, the availability of lotteries and other forms of gambling have created a social problem—addicts. A critic of government-controlled gambling contends that 30% of people who regularly buy lottery tickets are gambling addicts. If we randomly select 10 people among those who report that they regularly buy lottery tickets, what is the probability that more than five of them are addicts?

Part III: Understanding the Concepts

6.12   Describe the difference between a binomial and Poisson experiment.

Additional exercises and cases may be found on the CourseMate BSTAT Web site, www.cengagebrain.com.

Learning Objectives and Outcomes

7-1 Probability Density Functions

Know how density functions can be created. Know the requirements for a probability density function. Know how to calculate probability from a uniform distribution.

7-2 Normal Distribution

Know that a normal distribution is described by its mean and standard deviation. Know how to standardize a random variable. Be capable of using Table 3 to calculate cumulative probabilities. Be able to determine values of Z_A for any value of A. Be capable of using computer software to compute both probabilities and values of Z_A.

7-3 Other Continuous Distributions

Know the shape of the Student t distribution, chi-squared distribution, and F distribution. Understand that the shape of the Student and the chi-squared distribution depend on the number of degrees of freedom. Know that the F distribution's shape is determined by two sets of degrees of freedom. Know how to use Tables 4, 5, and 6 to determine critical values of t, χ^2, and F. Be able to use computer software to find Student t, chi-squared, and F probabilities and critical values.

Key Concepts

Vocabulary

Uniform probability density function is a function that looks like a rectangle.

Normal density function is a function that is bell shaped.

Z_A is the value of Z such that the area to its right under the standard normal curve is A.

Student t distribution, chi-squared distribution, and F distribution are continuous distributions that will be used extensively throughout the book.

Symbols

Symbol	Pronounced	Represents
π	pi	3.14159...
Z_A	z-sub-A or z-A	Value of Z such that area to its right is A
ν	nu	Degrees of freedom
t_A	t-sub-A or t-A	Value of t such that area to its right is A
χ_A^2	chi-squared-sub-A or chi-squared-A	Value of chi-squared such that area to its right is A
F_A	F-sub-A or F-A	Value of F such that area to its right is A
ν_1	nu-sub-one or nu-one	Numerator degrees of freedom
ν_2	nu-sub-two or nu-two	Denominator degrees of freedom

Key Formulae

Uniform Probability Density Function
The uniform distribution is described by the function

$$f(x) = \frac{1}{b-a} \quad \text{where } a \le x \le b$$

The probability that a uniformly distributed variable falls between x_1 and x_2 is

$$\frac{x_2 - x_1}{b - a}$$

Normal Density Function

The **normal distribution** is the most important of all probability distributions because of its crucial role in statistical inference. The probability density function of a **normal random variable** is

$$f(x) = \frac{1}{\sigma\sqrt{2\pi}} e^{-\frac{1}{2}\left(\frac{x-\mu}{\sigma}\right)^2} \quad -\infty < x < \infty$$

where $e = 2.71828...$ and $\pi = 3.14159...$

Standardizing a Normal Random Variable

$$Z = \frac{X - \mu}{\sigma}$$

Excel Commands

Normal distribution: Use function NORMDIST or NORMSDIST (for probability) and NORMINV or NORMSINV (for critical values)

Student *t* distribution: Use function TDIST (for probability) and TINV (for critical values)

Chi-squared distribution: Use function CHIDIST (for probability) and CHIINV (for critical values)

F distribution: Use function FDIST (for probability) and FINV (for critical values)

Minitab Commands

Normal distribution and critical values: Click **Calc, Probability Distributions**, and **Normal**.

Student *t* distribution and critical values: Click **Calc, Probability Distributions**, and ***t***

Chi-squared distribution and critical values: Click **Calc, Probability Distributions**, and **Chi-square**

F distribution and critical values: Click **Calc, Probability Distributions**, and ***F***

Practice Test

Part I: Knowing the Definitions

7.1 What is the theoretical range of a normal random variable?

7.2 Who created the Student *t* distribution?

7.3 Why don't we need a list of left-tail values for the *F* distribution?

Part II: Applying the Techniques

7.4 A random variable is uniformly distributed between 5 and 25.
  a. Find $P(X > 25)$.
  b. Find $P(10 < X < 15)$.
  c. Find $P(5.0 < X < 5.1)$.

7.5 *X* is normally distributed with mean 1,000 and standard deviation 250. What is the probability that *X* lies between 800 and 1,100?

7.6 *X* is normally distributed with mean 50 and standard deviation 8. What value of *X* is such that only 8% of values are below it?

7.7 The heights of children 2 years old are normally distributed with a mean of 32 inches and a standard deviation of 1.5 inches. Pediatricians regularly measure the heights of toddlers to determine whether there is a problem. There may be a problem when a child is in the top or bottom 5% of heights. Determine the heights of 2-year-old children that could be a problem.

7.8 Refer to Exercise 7.7. Find the probability of these events.
  a. A 2-year-old child is taller than 36 inches.
  b. A 2-year-old child is shorter than 34 inches.
  c. A 2-year-old child is between 30 and 33 inches tall.

7.9 University and college students average 7.2 hours of sleep per night with a standard deviation of 40 minutes. If the amount of sleep is normally distributed, what proportion of university and college students sleep for more than 8 hours?

7.10 Refer to Exercise 7.9. Find the amount of sleep that is exceeded by only 25% of students.

7.11 The lifetimes of televisions produced by the Hishobi Company are normally distributed with a mean of 75 months and a standard deviation of 8 months. If the manufacturer wants to have to replace only 1% of its televisions, what should its warranty be?

7.12 According to the *Statistical Abstract of the United States* (2000, Table 764) the mean family net worth of families whose head is between 35 and 44 years old is approximately $99,700. If family net worth is normally distributed with a standard deviation of $30,000, find the probability that a randomly selected family whose head is between 35 and 44 years old has a net worth greater than $150,000.

7.13 Find the following critical values of *t*.
  a. $t_{.05,14}$ b. $t_{.01,5}$ c. $t_{.10,17}$

7.14 Find the following critical values of χ^2.
  a. $\chi^2_{.05,22}$ b. $\chi^2_{.95,6}$ c. $\chi^2_{.01,14}$

7.15 Find the critical values of *F*.
  a. $F_{.05,5,10}$ b. $F_{.99,8,5}$ c. $F_{.025,3,12}$

Part III: Understanding the Concepts

7.16 Why is the probability that a continuous random variable takes on one single value always equal to 0?

Additional exercises and cases may be found on the CourseMate BSTAT Web site, www.cengagebrain.com.

Learning Objectives and Outcomes

8-1 Sampling Distribution of the Mean

Know how a sampling distribution can be created. Know how the sample mean is distributed and its parameters. Be capable of identifying this type of problem and using the normal table to calculate probabilities.

8-2 Sampling Distribution of a Proportion

Know that a binomial random variable can be approximated by a normal distribution. Know the distribution of a sample proportion and its parameters. Know how to recognize this type of problem and use the normal table to calculate probabilities.

Key Concepts

Vocabulary

Sampling distribution is the distribution created by repeated sampling from a population.

Sampling distribution of the sample mean is the distribution of the sample means.

The **central limit theorem** states that the sampling distribution of the mean of a random sample drawn from any population is approximately normal for a sufficiently large sample size. The larger the sample size, the more closely the sampling distribution of $\bar{X}$ will resemble a normal distribution.

Sampling distribution of a sample proportion is the distribution of the sample proportions.

Symbols

Symbol	Pronounced	Represents
$\mu_{\bar{x}}$	mu-x-bar	Mean of the sampling distribution of the sample mean
$\sigma^2_{\bar{x}}$	sigma-squared-x-bar	Variance of the sampling distribution of the sample mean
$\sigma_{\bar{x}}$	sigma-x-bar	Standard deviation (standard error) of the sampling distribution of the sample mean
α	alpha	Probability
$\hat{P}$	p-hat	Sample proportion
$\sigma^2_{\hat{p}}$	sigma-squared-p-hat	Variance of the sampling distribution of the sample proportion
$\sigma_{\hat{p}}$	sigma-p-hat	Standard deviation (standard error) of the sampling

Key Formulae

Sampling Distribution of the Sample Mean

1. $\mu_{\bar{x}} = \mu$
2. $\sigma^2_{\bar{x}} = \sigma^2/n$ and $\sigma_{\bar{x}} = \sigma/\sqrt{n}$

Sampling Distribution of a Sample Proportion

1. $\hat{P}$ is approximately normally distributed provided that np and $n(1 - p)$ are greater than or equal to 5.

2. The expected value: $E(\hat{P}) = p$
3. The variance: $V(\hat{P}) = \sigma^2_{\hat{p}} = \dfrac{p(1 - p)}{n}$
4. The standard deviation:

$$\sigma_{\hat{p}} = \sqrt{p(1 - p)/n}$$

(The standard deviation of $\hat{P}$ is called the **standard error of the proportion**.)

Practice Test

Part I: Knowing the Definitions

8.1 What is the central limit theorem?

8.2 What is the standard error of the mean?

8.3 What is the standard error of the proportion?

Part II: Applying the Techniques

8.4 Given a normal population whose mean is 50 and whose standard deviation is 5,

    a. find the probability that a random sample of 4 has a mean between 49 and 52.

    b. find the probability that a random sample of 16 has a mean between 49 and 52.

    c. find the probability that a random sample of 25 has a mean between 49 and 52.

8.5 An automatic machine in a manufacturing process is operating properly if the lengths of an important subcomponent are normally distributed with mean = 117 cm and standard deviation = 5.2 cm.

    a. Find the probability that one selected subcomponent is longer than 120 cm.

    b. Find the probability that if four subcomponents are randomly selected, their mean length exceeds 120 cm.

8.6 The marks on a statistics midterm test are normally distributed with a mean of 78 and a standard deviation of 6.

    a. What proportion of the class has a midterm mark of less than 75?

    b. What is the probability that a class of 50 has an average midterm mark that is less than 75?

8.7 The amount of time spent by North American adults watching television per day is normally distributed with a mean of 6 hours and a standard deviation of 1.5 hours.

    a. What is the probability that a randomly selected North American adult watches television for more than 7 hours per day?

    b. What is the probability that the average time watching television by a random sample of five North American adults is more than 7 hours?

8.8 The restaurant in a large commercial building provides coffee for the building's occupants. The restaurateur has determined that the mean number of cups of coffee consumed in a day by all the occupants is 2.0 with a standard deviation of .6. A new tenant of the building intends to have a total of 125 new employees. What is the probability that the new employees will consume more than 240 cups per day?

8.9 The number of pages produced by a fax machine in a busy office is normally distributed with a mean of 275 and a standard deviation of 75. Determine the probability that in 1 week (5 days) more than 1,500 faxes will be received?

8.10 In a binomial experiment with $n = 300$ and $p = .55$, find the probability that $\hat{P}$ is greater than 60%.

8.11 The probability of success on any trial of a binomial experiment is 25%. Find the probability that the proportion of successes in a sample of 500 is less than 22%.

8.12 An accounting professor claims that no more than one-quarter of undergraduate business students will major in accounting. What is the probability that in a random sample of 1,200 undergraduate business students, 336 or more will major in accounting?

8.13 Refer to Exercise 8.12. A survey of a random sample of 1,200 undergraduate business students indicates that there are 336 students who plan to major in accounting. What does this tell you about the professor's claim?

Part III: Understanding the Concepts

8.14 Does the actual distribution of X affect the central limit theorem?

Learning Objectives and Outcomes

9-1 Concepts of Estimating

Know why we need to estimate parameters. Know the difference between a point estimator and an interval estimator and why the latter is better. Know the three qualities of estimators.

9-2 Estimating the Population Proportion

Understand that the confidence interval estimator of p is derived from the sampling distribution of $\hat{p}$ and thus is another form of probability statement. Be capable of manually calculating the confidence interval estimator of p. Be capable of using computer software to produce the interval estimator of p. Understand how to properly interpret the confidence interval estimate.

9-3 Selecting the Sample Size to Estimate the Proportion

Understand the effect of the sample size on the width of the confidence interval estimator. Know what is meant by the error of estimation and bound on the error of estimation. Be capable of determining the sample size using both methods.

Key Concepts

Vocabulary

A **point estimator** draws inferences about a population by estimating the value of an unknown parameter using a single value or point.

An **interval estimator** draws inferences about a population by estimating the value of an unknown parameter using an interval.

An **unbiased estimator** of a population parameter is an estimator whose expected value is equal to that parameter.

An unbiased estimator is said to be **consistent** if the difference between the estimator and the parameter grows smaller as the sample size grows larger.

If there are two unbiased estimators of a parameter, the one whose variance is smaller is said to be **relatively more efficient**.

Confidence interval estimator of p estimates the unknown population proportion.

The **lower confidence limit (LCL)** is the lower limit of the interval estimator.

The **upper confidence limit (UCL)** is the upper limit of the interval estimator.

The **confidence level** is the probability that in the long run the interval estimator will be correct.

Symbols

Symbol	Pronounced	Represents
$1 - \alpha$	*One-minus-alpha*	Confidence level
B		Bound on the error of estimation
$z_{\alpha/2}$	*z-alpha-by-2*	Value of Z such that the area to its right is equal to $\alpha/2$

Key Formulae

Confidence Interval Estimator of p

$$\hat{p} - Z_{\alpha/2}\sqrt{\frac{\hat{p}(1 - \hat{p})}{n}},$$

$$\hat{p} + Z_{\alpha/2}\sqrt{\frac{\hat{p}(1 - \hat{p})}{n}}$$

The probability $1 - \alpha$ is called the **confidence level**.

$\hat{p} - Z_{\alpha/2}\sqrt{\frac{\hat{p}(1 - \hat{p})}{n}}$ is called the **lower confidence limit (LCL)**.

$\hat{p} + Z_{\alpha/2}\sqrt{\frac{\hat{p}(1 - \hat{p})}{n}}$ is called the **upper confidence limit (UCL)**.

We often represent the confidence interval estimator as

$$\hat{p} \pm Z_{\alpha/2}\sqrt{\frac{\hat{p}(1 - \hat{p})}{n}}$$

where the minus sign defines the lower confidence limit and the plus sign defines the upper confidence limit.

Estimating the Total Number of Successes in a Large Finite Population

$$N\left(\hat{p} \pm z_{\alpha/2}\sqrt{\frac{\hat{p}(1 - \hat{p})}{n}}\right)$$

Sample Size to Estimate a Proportion

$$n = \left(\frac{z_{\alpha/2}\sqrt{p(1 - p)}}{B}\right)^2$$

Excel Commands

Click **Add-Ins, Data Analysis Plus**, and **z-Estimate: Proportion**

Minitab Commands

Click **Stat, Basic Statistics**, and **1 Proportion**

Practice Test

Part I: Knowing the Definitions

9.1 How do point estimators and interval estimators differ?

9.2 Define unbiasedness.

9.3 Define consistency.

9.4 Define relative efficiency.

Part II: Applying the Techniques

9.5 Compute the 95% confidence interval estimate of a population proportion when the sample proportion is .6 and the sample size is 400.

9.6 Determine the 90% confidence interval estimate of a population proportion when the number of successes is 650 and the sample size is 900.

9.7 A survey asked 250 adults whether they had visited a museum in the last year. A total of 40 said that they had. Estimate with 90% confidence the proportion of all adults who had visited a museum.

9.8 A marketing manager wanted to know whether his new product design was going to be popular. He asked a random sample of 500 potential customers whether they liked the new design better than the current design. A total of 320 people said that they did. Estimate with 95% confidence the proportion of all potential customers who would prefer the new design.

9.9 Determine the sample size to estimate a population proportion to within .02 with 99% confidence when you have no prior knowledge about the value of p.

9.10 Find the sample size required to estimate a population proportion to within .01 with 90% confidence assuming no prior knowledge of p.

Part III: Understanding the Concepts

9.11 Why is it logical to believe that increasing the sample size produces narrower intervals?

Additional exercises and cases may be found on the CourseMate BSTAT Web site, www.cengagebrain.com.

Learning Objectives and Outcomes

10-1 Concepts of Hypothesis Testing

Understand the purpose of hypothesis testing. Know what the null hypothesis and alternative hypothesis are. Know the two types of error and their probabilities. Understand how the two probabilities are related. Know the two possible decisions.

10-2 Testing the Population Proportion

Know how to identify the parameter to be tested and know how to set up the null and alternative hypothesis. Be capable of conducting the test using the rejection approach and by using the unstandardized test statistic and the standardized test statistic. Know how to calculate the *p*-value of the test and understand what it tells us about the hypotheses. Be capable of using computer software to conduct the test.

10-3 Calculating the Probability of a Type II Error

Understand that to calculate β you must use the two-stage approach where in stage 1 you set up the rejection region in terms of the unstandardized test statistic. In stage 2 you find the probability that the unstandardized test statistic does not fall into the rejection region given a specific value of the parameter. Understand what happens to β when α increases or decreases. Understand what happens to β when n increases.

10-4 The Road Ahead

Understand that most of the remainder of the book addresses the problem of estimating and hypothesis testing for other parameters. The most important skill to develop is the ability to identify the parameter and the correct statistical technique to use. The two most important factors in identifying the appropriate technique is the objective of the statistical analysis and the type of data.

Key Concepts

Vocabulary

Hypothesis testing is the process used to determine whether sufficient evidence exists to draw a conclusion about a parameter.

The **null hypothesis** states the value of a parameter to be tested.

The **alternative** or **alternate hypothesis** represents whatever you're trying to show statistically.

A **Type I error** occurs when we reject a true null hypothesis.

A **Type II error** occurs when we don't reject a false null hypothesis.

The **test statistic** is the statistic we use to decide whether to reject the null hypothesis.

The **rejection region** is a range of values such that if the test statistic falls into that range, we decide to reject the null hypothesis in favor of the alternative hypothesis.

The **significance level** determines the rejection region.

When a null hypothesis is rejected, the test is said to be **statistically significant** at whatever significance level the test was conducted.

The **p-value** of a test is the probability of observing a test statistic at least as extreme as the one computed given that the null hypothesis is true.

If the *p*-value is less than .01, we say that the test is **highly significant**.

If the *p*-value lies between .01 and .05, the result is deemed to be **significant**.

If the *p*-value is between .05 and .10, we say that the result is **not statistically significant**.

Symbols

Symbol	Pronounced	Represents
H_0	H-nought	Null hypothesis
H_1	H-one	Alternative (research) hypothesis
α	alpha	Probability of a Type I error
β	beta	Probability of a Type II error
$\hat{p}_L$	P-bar-sub L or P-bar-L	Value of $\hat{p}$ large enough to reject H_0
$\|z\|$	Absolute z	Absolute value of z

Key Formulae

Test statistic for *p*

$$z = \frac{\hat{p} - p}{\sqrt{p(1-p)/n}}$$

Excel Commands

Click **Add-Ins**, **Data Analysis Plus**, and **Z-Test: Mean**

Minitab Commands

Click **Stat**, **Basic Statistics**, and **1-Sample Z**

Practice Test

Part I: Knowing the Definitions

10.1 Define Type I error.

10.2 Define Type II error.

10.3 What is the probability of a Type I error?

10.4 What is the probability of a Type II error?

10.5 What is the significance level?

10.6 Define p-value.

10.7 What is a rejection region?

Part II: Applying the Techniques

10.8 Calculate the p-value of the test of the following hypotheses given that $\hat{p} = .66$ and $n = 400$:

$$H_0: p = .60$$
$$H_1: p > .60$$

10.9 A statistics practitioner wants to test the following hypotheses:

$$H_0: p = .70$$
$$H_1: p < .70$$

A random sample of 900 produced $\hat{p} = .68$. Calculate the p-value of the test.

10.10 In some states the law requires drivers to turn on their headlights when driving in the rain. A highway patrol officer believes that less than one-quarter of all drivers follow this rule. As a test, he randomly samples 200 cars driving in the rain and counts the number whose headlights are turned on. He finds this number to be 36. Does the officer have enough evidence at the 10% significance level to support his belief?

10.11 Before the recent downturn one airline bragged that 92% of its flights were on time. A random sample of 165 flights completed this year reveals that 153 were on time. Can we conclude at the 5% significance level that the airline's on-time performance has improved?

10.12 A professor of business statistics recently adopted a new textbook. At the completion of the course, 100 randomly selected students were asked to assess the book. The responses and frequencies are as follows.

Excellent (57), Good (35), Adequate (4), Poor (4)

Do the data allow us to conclude at the 10% significance level that more than 50% of all business students would rate the book as excellent?

10.13 Refer to Exercise 10.12. Find the probability of a Type II error when the actual proportion is 60%.

Part III: Understanding the Concepts

10.14 What does a large p-value tell you about the alternative hypothesis?

10.15 What does a small p-value tell you about the alternative hypothesis?

10.16 Why does the probability of a Type II error increase when the value of p under the alternative hypothesis and the value of p under the null hypothesis grow closer?

10.17 Why does the probability of a Type II error increase when the probability of a Type I error decreases?

10.18 Why does the probability of a Type II error decrease when the sample size increases?

Additional exercises and cases may be found on the CourseMate BSTAT Web site, www.cengagebrain.com.

Learning Objectives and Outcomes

11–1 Inference about a Population Mean

Know the sampling distribution to use to test and estimate a population mean. Know the required condition and how to check if it has been violated. Be capable of setting up the hypotheses and manually calculating the test statistic. Know the method to use to estimate the population mean. Be capable of using computer software to produce the results. Know how to convert the confidence interval estimate of μ into the total for a finite population.

> **Factors That Identify the t-Test and Estimator of μ**
> 1. Problem objective: Describe a population
> 2. Data type: Interval
> 3. Type of descriptive measurement: Central location

11–2 Inference about a Population Variance

Know the sampling distribution to use to test and estimate a population variance. Know the required condition and how to check if it has been violated. Be capable of setting up the hypotheses and manually calculating the test statistic. Know the method to use to estimate the population variance. Be capable of using computer software to produce the results.

> **Factors That Identify the Chi-Squared Test and Estimator of σ^2**
> 1. Problem objective: Describe a population
> 2. Data type: Interval
> 3. Type of descriptive measurement: Variability

11–3 Review of Inference about a Population Proportion

Be capable of testing and estimating p (introduced in Chapters 10 and 9, respectively).

> **Factors That Identify the z-Test and Interval Estimator of p**
> 1. Problem objective: Describe a population
> 2. Data type: Nominal

Key Concepts

Vocabulary

The **t-statistic** is used to test hypotheses about a population mean.

A statistical procedure is called **robust** if violations of the required conditions do not invalidate the results.

The **chi-squared statistic** is used to test hypotheses about the population variance.

Symbols

Symbol	Pronounced	Represents
ν	nu	Degrees of freedom
χ^2	chi-squared	Chi-squared statistic
$\hat{p}$	p-hat	Sample proportion

Key Formulae

Test Statistic for μ

The test statistic for testing hypotheses about μ is

$$t = \frac{\bar{x} - \mu}{s/\sqrt{n}}$$

Confidence Interval Estimator of μ

$$\bar{x} \pm t_{\alpha/2}\frac{s}{\sqrt{n}} \quad \nu = n - 1$$

Test Statistic for σ^2

$$\chi^2 = \frac{(n - 1)s^2}{\sigma^2}$$

Confidence Interval Estimator of σ^2

Lower confidence limit

$$(LCL) = \frac{(n - 1)s^2}{\chi^2_{\alpha/2}}$$

Upper confidence limit

$$(UCL) = \frac{(n - 1)s^2}{\chi^2_{1-\alpha/2}}$$

Test Statistic for p

$$z = \frac{\hat{p} - p}{\sqrt{p(1 - p)/n}}$$

Confidence Interval Estimator of p

$$\hat{p} \pm z_{\alpha/2}\sqrt{\hat{p}(1 - \hat{p})/n}$$

Excel Commands

t-test of μ: Click **Add-Ins**, **Data Analysis Plus**, and **t-Test: Mean**

t-estimate of μ: Click **Add-Ins**, **Data Analysis Plus**, and **t-Estimate: Mean**

χ^2—test of σ^2: Click **Add-Ins**, **Data Analysis Plus**, and **Chi-squared Test: Variance**

χ^2—estimate of σ^2: Click **Add-Ins**, **Data Analysis Plus**, and **Chi-squared Estimate: Variance**

t-test of μ: Click **Stat**, **Basic Statistics**, and **1-Sample t**

t-estimate of μ: Click **Stat**, **Basic Statistics**, and **1-Sample t**

χ^2—test of σ^2: Click **Stat**, **Basic Statistics**, and **1 Variance**

χ^2—estimate of σ^2: Click **Stat**, **Basic Statistics**, and **1 Variance**

Practice Test

Part I: Knowing the Definitions

11.1 What is the number of degrees of freedom of the t-test of μ?

11.2 What is the number of degrees of freedom of the chi-squared test of σ^2?

Part II: Applying the Techniques

11.3 How much money do winners take home from the television quiz show *Jeopardy*? To determine an answer, a random sample of winners was drawn and the amount of money each won was recorded and is listed here. Estimate with 95% confidence the mean winnings for all the show's players.

26,650	6,060	52,820	8,490	13,660	25,840
49,840	23,790	51,480	18,960	990	11,450
41,810	21,060	7,860			

11.4 The routes of postal deliverers are carefully planned so that each deliverer works between 7 and 7.5 hours per shift. The planned routes assume an average walking speed of 2 miles per hour and no shortcuts across lawns. In an experiment to examine the amount of time deliverers actually spend completing their shifts, a random sample of 75 postal deliverers was secretly timed. The mean and standard deviation are 6.91 and .226, respectively.

   a. Estimate with 99% confidence the mean shift time for all postal deliverers.

   b. Is there enough evidence at the 10% significance level to conclude that postal workers are on average spending less than 7 hours per day doing their jobs?

11.5 An oil company sends out monthly statements to its customers who purchased gasoline and other items using the company's credit card. Until now, the company has not included a preaddressed envelope for returning payments. The average and the standard deviation of the number of days before payment is received are 9.8 and 3.2, respectively. As an experiment to determine whether enclosing preaddressed envelopes speeds up payment, 150 customers selected at random were sent preaddressed envelopes with their bills. The numbers of days to payment were recorded. The mean and standard deviation are 9.16 and 2.64, respectively.

   a. Do the data provide sufficient evidence at the 10% level of significance to establish that enclosure of preaddressed envelopes improves the average speed of payments?

   b. Can we conclude at the 10% significance level that the variability in payment speeds decreases when a preaddressed envelope is sent?

11.6 An increasing number of people are giving gift certificates as Christmas presents. To measure the extent of this practice, a random sample of people was asked (survey conducted December 26–29) whether they had received a gift certificate for Christmas. The frequencies of the responses are No (92) and Yes (28). Estimate with 95% confidence the proportion of people who received a gift certificate for Christmas.

11.7 The results of an annual Claimant Satisfaction Survey of policyholders who have had a claim with State Farm Insurance Company revealed a 90% satisfaction rate for claim service. To check the accuracy of this claim, a random sample of State Farm claimants was asked to rate whether they were satisfied with the quality of the service. The number who were satisfied was 153, unsatisfied 24. Can we infer at the 5% significance level that the satisfaction rate is less than 90%?

11.8 A company that produces universal remote controls wanted to determine the number of remote control devices American homes contain. The company hired a statistician to survey 240 randomly selected homes and determine the number of remote controls. If there are 100 million households, estimate with 99% confidence the total number of remote controls in the United States. The mean and standard deviation are 4.66 and 2.37, respectively.

11.9 An important decision faces Christmas holiday celebrators: buy a real or an artificial tree? A sample of 1,508 male and female respondents 18 years of age and over was interviewed. Respondents were asked whether they preferred a real or an artificial tree. The frequencies are real (603) and artificial (905). If there are 6 million Canadian households that buy Christmas trees, estimate with 95% confidence the total number of Canadian households that would prefer artificial Christmas trees.

Additional exercises and cases may be found on the CourseMate BSTAT Web site, www.cengagebrain.com.

Learning Objectives and Outcomes

12-1 Inference about the Difference between Two Means: Independent Samples

Know that there are two experimental designs, independent samples and matched pairs. For independent samples, know that there are two sets of formulas for drawing inferences about the difference between two means and know how to decide which set to use. Be capable of manually testing and estimating the difference between two means. Be capable of using computer software to produce the results. Know how to set up hypotheses and interpret results. Know the required condition and how to check them.

Factors That Identify the Equal-Variances t-Test and Estimator of $\mu_1 - \mu_2$:

1. Problem objective: Compare two populations.
2. Data type: Interval.
3. Descriptive measurement: Central location.
4. Experimental design: Independent samples.
5. Population variances: Equal

Factors That Identify the Unequal-Variances t-Test and Estimator of $\mu_1 - \mu_2$:

1. Problem objective: Compare two populations.
2. Data type: Interval.
3. Descriptive measurement: Central location.
4. Experimental design: Independent samples.
5. Population variances: Unequal

12-2 Inference about the Difference between Two Means: Matched Pairs Experiment

Know how to distinguish between independent samples and matched pairs. Know how to conduct the test and estimator of the mean of the matched pairs. Understand how the matched pairs experiment can often reduce variation. Know the required condition and how to check if it has been violated.

Key Concepts

Vocabulary

Independent samples are samples taken independently of each other.

Pooled variance estimator is the estimator of the common population variances.

F-test is conducted to determine whether the population variances are equal or unequal.

Matched pairs are samples that are matched by some criterion.

Symbols

Symbol	Pronounced	Represents
s_p^2	s-sub-p-squared	Pooled variance estimator
μ_D	mu-sub-D or mu-D	Mean of the paired differences
$\bar{x}_D$	x-bar-sub-D or x-bar-D	Sample mean of the paired differences
s_D	s-sub-D or s-D	Sample standard deviation of the paired differences
n_D	n-sub-D or n-D	Sample size of the paired differences

Key Formulae

Test Statistic for $\mu_1 - \mu_2$ when $\sigma_1^2 = \sigma_2^2$

$$t = \frac{(\bar{x}_1 - \bar{x}_2) - (\mu_1 - \mu_2)}{\sqrt{s_p^2\left(\frac{1}{n_1} + \frac{1}{n_2}\right)}}$$

$$\nu = n_1 + n_2 - 2$$

$$s_p^2 = \frac{(n_1 - 1)s_1^2 + (n_2 - 1)s_2^2}{n_1 + n_2 - 2}$$

Confidence Interval Estimator of $\mu_1 - \mu_2$ when $\sigma_1^2 = \sigma_2^2$

$$(\bar{x}_1 - \bar{x}_2) \pm t_{\alpha/2}\sqrt{s_p^2\left(\frac{1}{n_1} + \frac{1}{n_2}\right)}$$

$$\nu = n_1 + n_2 - 2$$

Test Statistic for $\mu_1 - \mu_2$ When $\sigma_1^2 \neq \sigma_2^2$

$$t = \frac{(\bar{x}_1 - \bar{x}_2) - (\mu_1 - \mu_2)}{\sqrt{\frac{s_1^2}{n_1} + \frac{s_2^2}{n_2}}}$$

$$\nu = \frac{(s_1^2/n_1 + s_2^2/n_2)^2}{\frac{(s_1^2/n_1)^2}{n_1 - 1} + \frac{(s_2^2/n_2)^2}{n_2 - 1}}$$

Confidence Interval Estimator of $\mu_1 - \mu_2$ When $\sigma_1^2 \neq \sigma_2^2$

$$(\bar{x}_1 - \bar{x}_2) \pm t_{\alpha/2}\sqrt{\frac{s_1^2}{n_1} + \frac{s_2^2}{n_2}}$$

$$\nu = \frac{(s_1^2/n_1 + s_2^2/n_2)^2}{\frac{(s_1^2/n_1)^2}{n_1 - 1} + \frac{(s_2^2/n_2)^2}{n_2 - 1}}$$

Test for σ_1^2/σ_2^2

$$F = s_1^2/s_2^2$$

Test Statistic for μ_D

$$t = \frac{\bar{x}_D - \mu_D}{s_D/\sqrt{n_D}}$$

Confidence Interval Estimator of μ_D

$$\bar{x}_D \pm t_{\alpha/2}\frac{s_D}{\sqrt{n_D}}$$

Factors That Identify the t-Test and Estimator of μ_D

1. Problem objective: Compare two populations
2. Data type: Interval
3. Descriptive measurement: Central location
4. Experimental design: Matched pairs

Excel Commands

F-test of two variances: Click **Data, Data Analysis**, and **F-test Two-Sample for Variances**

Equal-variances t-test of $\mu_1 - \mu_2$: Click **Data, Data Analysis**, and **t-Test: Two-Sample Assuming Equal Variances**

Equal-variances t-estimator of $\mu_1 - \mu_2$: Click **Add-Ins, Data Analysis Plus**, and **t-Estimate: Two Means**

Unequal-variances t-test of $\mu_1 - \mu_2$: Click **Data, Data Analysis**, and **t-Test: Two-Sample Assuming Unequal Variances**

Unequal-variances t-estimator of $\mu_1 - \mu_2$: Click **Add-Ins, Data Analysis Plus**, and **t-Estimate: Two Means**

t Test of μ_D: Click **Data, Data Analysis**, and **t-Test: Paired Two-Sample for Means**

t Estimate of μ_D: Click **Data, Data Analysis Plus**, and **t-Estimate: Two Means**

Minitab Commands

F-test of two variances: Click **Stat, Basic Statistics**, and **2 Variances**

Equal-variances t-test of $\mu_1 - \mu_2$: Click **Stat, Basic Statistics**, and **2-Sample t**

Equal-variances t-estimator of $\mu_1 - \mu_2$: Click **Stat, Basic Statistics**, and **2-Sample t**

Unequal-variances t-test of $\mu_1 - \mu_2$: Click **Stat, Basic Statistics**, and **2-Sample t**

Unequal-variances t-estimator of $\mu_1 - \mu_2$: Click **Stat, Basic Statistics**, and **2-Sample t**

t Test of μ_D: Click **Stat, Basic Statistics**, and **Paired t**

t Estimate of μ_D: Click **Stat, Basic Statistics**, and **Paired t**

Practice Test

Part I: Knowing the Definitions

12.1 What is meant by independent samples?

12.2 What is a matched pairs experiment?

Part II: Applying the Techniques

12.3 In an effort to determine whether a new type of fertilizer is more effective than the type currently in use, researchers took six 2-acre plots of land scattered throughout the county. Each plot was divided into two equal-size subplots, one of which was treated with the current fertilizer and the other with the new fertilizer. Wheat was planted, and the crop yields were measured.

Plot	1	2	3	4	5	6
Current fertilizer	56	45	68	72	61	69
New fertilizer	60	56	66	73	59	77

a. Can we conclude at the 10% significance level that the new fertilizer is more effective than the current one?
b. Estimate with 95% confidence the difference in mean crop yields between the two fertilizers.

12.4 Many people use scanners to read documents and store them in a Word (or some other software) file. To help determine which brand of scanner to buy, a student conducts an experiment wherein eight documents are scanned by each of the two scanners that he is interested in. He records the number of errors made by each. These data are listed here. Can he infer that brand A is better than brand B?

Document	1	2	3	4	5	6	7	8
Brand A	17	29	18	14	21	25	22	29
Brand B	21	38	15	19	22	30	31	37

12.5 An important component of the cost of living is the amount of money spent on housing. An economist undertook a 5-year study to determine how housing costs have changed. Five years ago, he took a random sample of 200 households and recorded the percentage of total income spent on housing. This year, he took another sample of 200 households. Conduct a test (with $\alpha = .10$) to determine whether the economist can infer that housing cost as a percentage of total income has increased over the last 5 years. (Statistics: 5 years ago $\bar{x} = 32.42$, $s = 6.08$. This year $\bar{x} = 33.72$, $s = 6.75$.)

12.6 The cruise ship business is rapidly increasing. Although cruises have long been associated with seniors, it now appears that younger people are choosing a cruise as their vacations. To determine whether this is true, an executive for a cruise line sampled passengers 2 years ago and this year and determined their ages. (Statistics: Two years ago $\bar{x} = 59.81$, $s = 7.02$, $n_1 = 125$. This year $\bar{x} = 57.40$, $s = 6.99$, $n_2 = 159$.)

a. Do these data allow the executive to infer with $\alpha = .01$ that cruise ships are attracting younger customers?
b. Estimate with 99% confidence the difference in ages between this year and 2 years ago.

Learning Objectives and Outcomes

13-1 Inference about the Ratio of Two Population Variances

Be capable of manually testing and estimating the ratio of two population variances. Be capable of using computer software to produce the results. Know how to set up hypotheses. Know the required condition and how to check them.

> Factors That Identify the *F*-Test and Estimator of σ_1^2/σ_2^2
>
> 1. Problem objective: Compare two populations
> 2. Data type: Interval
> 3. Descriptive measurement: Variability

13-2 Inference about the Difference between Two Population Proportions

Be capable of manually testing and estimating the difference between two population proportions. Understand the difference between Case 1 and Case 2. Be capable of using computer software to produce the results. Know how to set up hypotheses and interpret results. Know the required condition.

> Factors That Identify the *z*-Test and Estimator of $p_1 - p_2$
>
> 1. Problem objective: Compare two populations
> 2. Data type: Nominal

Key Concepts

Vocabulary

The **mean of the population of differences** is the unknown mean of the population created by taking the difference in each matched pair.

The **F distribution** is used to test the ratio of two population variances.

The **numerator degrees of freedom** and the **denominator**

degrees of freedom are the degrees of freedom of the *F* distribution.

The **pooled proportion estimator** is the estimator of the two population proportions, which are assumed to be equal. The two samples are combined or pooled to create this estimator.

Symbols

Symbol	Pronounced	Represents
ν_1	Nu-sub-1	Numerator degrees of freedom
ν_2	Nu-sub-2	Numerator degrees of freedom
$\hat{p}$	p-hat	Pooled proportion

Key Formulae

Test Statistic for σ_1^2/σ_2^2

$$F = \frac{s_1^2}{s_2^2}$$

Confidence Interval Estimator of σ_1^2/σ_2^2

$$LCL = \left(\frac{s_1^2}{s_2^2}\right)\frac{1}{F_{\alpha/2, \nu_1, \nu_2}}$$

$$UCL = \left(\frac{s_1^2}{s_2^2}\right)F_{\alpha/2, \nu_2, \nu_1}$$

Test Statistic for $p_1 - p_2$: Case 1

If the null hypothesis specifies

$$H_0: (p_1 - p_2) = 0$$

the test statistic is

$$z = \frac{(\hat{p}_1 - \hat{p}_2)}{\sqrt{\hat{p}(1-\hat{p})\left(\frac{1}{n_1} + \frac{1}{n_2}\right)}}$$

Test Statistic for $p_1 - p_2$: Case 2

If the null hypothesis specifies

$$H_0: (p_1 - p_2) = D \qquad (D \neq 0)$$

the test statistic is

$$z = \frac{(\hat{p}_1 - \hat{p}_2) - (p_1 - p_2)}{\sqrt{\frac{\hat{p}_1(1-\hat{p}_1)}{n_1} + \frac{\hat{p}_2(1-\hat{p}_2)}{n_2}}}$$

which can also be expressed as

$$z = \frac{(\hat{p}_1 - \hat{p}_2) - D}{\sqrt{\frac{\hat{p}_1(1-\hat{p}_1)}{n_1} + \frac{\hat{p}_2(1-\hat{p}_2)}{n_2}}}$$

Confidence Interval Estimator of $p_1 - p_2$

$$(\hat{p}_1 - \hat{p}_2)$$

$$\pm z_{\alpha/2}\sqrt{\frac{\hat{p}_1(1-\hat{p}_1)}{n_1} + \frac{\hat{p}_2(1-\hat{p}_2)}{n_2}}$$

Excel Commands

F-test of two variances: Click **Data**, **Data Analysis**, and **F-test Two-Sample for Variances**

F-Estimate of two variances: Click **Add-ins**, **Data Analysis Plus**, and **F Estimate 2 Variances**

z-Test of $p_1 - p_2$: Click **Add-ins**, **Data Analysis Plus**, and **Z-Test: 2 Proportions**

z-Estimate of $p_1 - p_2$: Click **Add-ins**, **Data Analysis Plus**, and **Z-Estimate: 2 Proportions**

Minitab Commands

F-test of two variances: Click **Stat**, **Basic Statistics**, and **2 Variances**

F-Estimate of two variances: Minitab does not perform this calculation.

z-Test of $p_1 - p_2$: Click **Stat**, **Basic Statistics**, and **2 Proportions**

z-Estimate of $p_1 - p_2$: Click **Stat**, **Basic Statistics**, and **2 Proportions**

Practice Test

Part I: Knowing the Definitions

13.1 What is the pooled proportion estimate?

13.2 What is Case 1 of the z-test of $p_1 - p_2$?

13.3 What is Case 2 of the z-test of $p_1 - p_2$?

Part II: Applying the Techniques

13.4 Random samples from two normal populations produced the following statistics:

$s_1^2 = 350$ $n_1 = 30$ $s_2^2 = 700$ $n_2 = 30$

Can we infer at the 10% significance level that the two population variances differ?

13.5 Random samples from two normal populations produced the following statistics:

$s_1^2 = 28$ $n_1 = 10$ $s_2^2 = 19$ $n_2 = 10$

Estimate with 95% confidence the ratio of the two population variances.

13.6 Random samples from two binomial populations yielded the following statistics:

$\hat{p}_1 = .45$ $n_1 = 100$ $\hat{p}_2 = .40$ $n_2 = 100$

Calculate the p-value of a test to determine whether we can infer that the population proportions differ.

13.7 Cold and allergy medicines have been available for a number of years. One serious side effect of these medications is that they cause drowsiness, which makes them dangerous for industrial workers. In recent years, a nondrowsy cold and allergy medicine has been developed. One such product, Hismanal, is claimed by its manufacturer to be the first once-a-day nondrowsy allergy medicine. The nondrowsy part of the claim is based on a clinical experiment in which 1,604 patients were given Hismanal and 1,109 patients were given a placebo. Of the first group 7.1% reported drowsiness; of the second group, 6.4% reported drowsiness. Do these results allow us to infer at the 5% significance level that Hismanal's claim is false?

13.8 Many stores sell extended warranties for products they sell. These are very lucrative for store owners. To learn more about who buys these warranties, a random sample of a store's customers who recently purchased a product for which an extended warranty was available was drawn. Among other variables respondents reported whether they paid the regular price or a sale price and whether they purchased an extended warranty.

	Regular price	Sale price
Sample size	229	178
Number who bought extended warranty	47	25

Can we conclude at the 10% significance level that those who paid the regular price are more likely to buy an extended warranty?

13.9 Plavix is a drug that is given to angioplasty patients to help prevent blood clots. A researcher at McMaster University organized a study that involved 12,562 patients in 482 hospitals in 28 countries. All the patients had acute coronary syndrome, which produces mild heart attacks or unstable angina, chest pain that may precede a heart attack. The patients were divided into two equal groups. Group 1 received daily Plavix pills, while group 2 received a placebo. After 1 year 9.3% of patients on Plavix suffered a stroke or new heart attack, or had died of cardiovascular disease, compared with 11.5% of those who took the placebo. Can we infer at the 10% significance level that Plavix is effective?

13.10 A firm has classified its customers in two ways: (1) according to whether the account is overdue and (2) whether the account is new (less than 12 months) or old. To acquire information about which customers are paying on time and which are overdue, a random sample of 292 customer accounts was drawn. Each was categorized as a new account (less than 12 months) and old, and whether the customer has paid or is overdue. The results are summarized next.

	New account	Old account
Sample size	83	209
Overdue account	12	49

Is there enough evidence at the 5% significance level to infer that new and old accounts are different with respect to overdue accounts?

Additional exercises and cases may be found on the CourseMate BSTAT Web site, www.cengagebrain.com.

Learning Objectives and Outcomes

14-1 One-Way Analysis of Variance

Understand what SST and SSE represent. Be capable of manually producing the ANOVA table for small samples and using computer software for small and large samples. Know the required conditions and how to check to see if they are violated.

> Factors That Identify the One-Way Analysis of Variance
> 1. Problem objective: Compare two or more populations
> 2. Data type: Interval
> 3. Experimental design: Independent samples

14-2 Multiple Comparisons

Understand why multiple comparisons are necessary. Know how to conduct the three forms of multiple comparisons manually and using computer software. Understand the need for the Bonferroni adjustment. Know how to decide which method to use.

14-3 Randomized Block (Two-Way) Analysis of Variance

Understand that this experimental design is an extension of the matched pairs experiment described in Chapter 12. Understand that SSE in the one-way analysis of variance is now being divided into two sources of variation in this design, SSB and SSE. Be capable of manually producing the ANOVA table for small samples and using computer software for small and large samples. Know the required conditions and how to check to see if they are violated.

Key Concepts

Vocabulary

Populations are called **treatments**.

One-way analysis of variance is a statistical procedure that determines whether there is evidence of a difference between population (treatment) means when the samples are drawn independently.

Sum of squares for treatments measures the amount of variation between treatments.

Sum of squares for error measures the amount of variation within treatments.

Mean square for treatments is the sum of squares for treatment divided by the number of treatments minus 1.

Mean square for error is the sum of squares for error divided by the total sample size minus the number of treatments.

ANOVA table for the one-way analysis of variance is a summary of the calculations in the one-way analysis of variance.

Multiple comparisons are methods that allow us to determine which pairs of means differ.

Fisher's least significant difference (LSD) method is a multiple comparison method based on the mean square for error.

Bonferroni adjustment to LSD method is a variation of the LSD method.

Tukey's method is another multiple comparison method.

Randomized block (two-way) analysis of variance is a statistical procedure that determines whether there is evidence of a difference between population (treatment) means when the samples are drawn from a blocked experiment.

Symbols

Symbol	Pronounced	Represents
$\bar{\bar{x}}$	x-double-bar	Overall or grand mean
q		Studentized range
ω	Omega	Critical value of Tukey's multiple comparison method
$q_\alpha(k, \nu)$	q-sub-alpha-k-ν	Critical value of the Studentized range
n_g		Number of observations in each of k samples
$\bar{x}[T]_j$	x-bar-T-sub-j	Mean of the jth treatment
$\bar{x}[B]_i$	x-bar-B-sub-i	Mean of the ith block

Key Formulae

Sum of Squares for Treatments

$$SST = \sum_{j=1}^{k} n_j(\bar{x}_j - \bar{\bar{x}})^2$$

Sum of Squares for Error

$$SSE = \sum_{j=1}^{k} \sum_{i=1}^{n_j} (x_{ij} - \bar{x}_j)^2$$

Mean Square for Treatments

$$MST = \frac{SST}{k-1}$$

Mean Square for Error

$$MSE = \frac{SSE}{n-k}$$

Test Statistic

$$F = \frac{MST}{MSE}$$

Fisher's Least Significant Difference (LSD) Method

$$LSD = t_{\alpha/2}\sqrt{MSE\left(\frac{1}{n_i} + \frac{1}{n_j}\right)}$$

Bonferroni Adjustment to LSD Method

$$\alpha = \frac{\alpha_E}{C} \quad \text{where } C = \frac{k(k-1)}{2}$$

Tukey's Method: Critical Number ω

$$\omega = q_\alpha(k, \nu)\sqrt{\frac{MSE}{n_g}}$$

Sums of Squares in the Randomized Block Experiment

$$SS(Total) = \sum_{j=1}^{k}\sum_{i=1}^{b}(x_{ij} - \bar{\bar{x}})^2$$

$$SST = \sum_{j=1}^{k} b(\bar{x}[T]_j - \bar{\bar{x}})^2$$

$$SSB = \sum_{i=1}^{b} k(\bar{x}[B]_i - \bar{\bar{x}})^2$$

$$SSE = \sum_{j=1}^{k}\sum_{i=1}^{b}(x_{ij} - \bar{x}[T]_j - \bar{x}[B]_i + \bar{\bar{x}})^2$$

Mean Squares for the Randomized Block Experiment

$$MST = \frac{SST}{k-1}$$

$$MSB = \frac{SSB}{b-1}$$

$$MSE = \frac{SSE}{n - k - b + 1}$$

Test Statistic for the Randomized Block Experiment

$$F = \frac{MST}{MSE}$$

Factors That Identify the Randomized Block of the Analysis of Variance
1. Problem objective: Compare two or more populations
2. Data type: Interval
3. Experimental design: Blocked samples

Excel Commands

One-way analysis of variance: Click Data, Data Analysis, and Anova: Single factor

Multiple comparisons: Click Add-ins, Data Analysis Plus, and Multiple Comparisons

Randomized block analysis of variance: Click Data, Data Analysis, and Anova: Two-Factor Without Replication

Minitab Commands

One-way analysis of variance: Click Stat, ANOVA, and Oneway (Unstacked)

Multiple comparisons: Click Stat, ANOVA, and Oneway (Unstacked) and then Comparisons

Randomized block analysis of variance: Click Stat, ANOVA, and Twoway

Practice Test

Part I: Knowing the Definitions

14.1 Why are populations referred to as "treatments" in the analysis of variance?

14.2 How many pairwise comparisons are there when there are 8 treatments?

Part II: Applying the Techniques

14.3 A consumer organization was concerned about the differences between the advertised sizes of containers and the actual amount of product. In a preliminary study, six packages of three different brands of margarine that are supposed to contain 500 ml were measured. The differences from 500 ml are listed here. Do these data provide sufficient evidence to conclude that differences exist between the three brands? Use $\alpha = .10$.

Brand 1	Brand 2	Brand 3
1	2	1
3	2	2
3	4	4
0	3	2
1	0	3
0	4	4

14.4 Many college and university students obtain summer jobs. A statistics professor wanted to determine whether students in different degree programs earn different amounts. A random sample of five students in the BA, BSc, and BBA programs were asked to report what they earned the previous summer. The results (in $1,000s) are listed here. Can the professor infer at the 10% significance level that students in different degree programs differ in their summer earnings?

BA	BSc	BBA
3.3	3.9	4.0
2.5	5.1	6.2
4.6	3.9	6.3
5.4	6.2	5.9
3.9	4.8	6.4

14.5 Refer to Exercise 14.3. Use the Bonferroni adjustment to the LSD method (with $\alpha = .05$) to determine which pairs of means differ.

Additional exercises and cases may be found on the CourseMate BSTAT Web site, www.cengagebrain.com.

Learning Objectives and Outcomes

15–1 Chi-Squared Goodness-of-Fit Test

Know what a multinomial experiment is. Be capable of calculating the test statistic in the goodness-of-fit test.

> Factors That Identify the Chi-Squared Goodness-of-Fit Test
>
> 1. Problem objective: Describe a single population
> 2. Data type: Nominal
> 3. Number of categories: 2 or more

15–2 Chi-Squared Test of a Contingency Table

Be capable of manually calculating and using computer software to find the value of the test statistic. Understand that there are two problem objectives addressed by this technique.

> Factors That Identify the Chi-Squared Test of a Contingency Table
>
> 1. Problem objectives: Analyze the relationship between two variables and compare two or more populations
> 2. Data type: Nominal

Key Concepts

Vocabulary

A **multinomial experiment** is one possessing the following properties. The experiment consists of a fixed number n of trials. The outcome of each trial can be classified into one of k categories, called cells. The probability p_i that the outcome will fall into cell i remains constant for each trial. Each trial of the experiment is independent of the other trials.

The **chi-squared goodness-of-fit test** determines whether there is enough evidence to infer that at least one hypothesized proportion differs

The **expected frequency** is the frequency we expect to see if the null hypothesis is true.

The **chi-squared test of a contingency table** determines whether there is enough evidence to conclude that two nominal variables are dependent.

Symbols

Symbol	Pronounced	Represents
f_i	f-sub-i	Frequency of the ith category
e_i	e-sub-i	Expected value of the ith category
χ^2	Chi-squared	Test statistic

Key Formulae
Chi-Squared Test Statistic

$$\chi^2 = \sum_{i=1}^{k} \frac{(f_i - e_i)^2}{e_i}$$

Expected Frequencies for a Contingency Table

The expected frequency of the cell in row i and column j is

$$e_{ij} = \frac{\text{Row } i \text{ total} \times \text{Column } j \text{ total}}{\text{Sample size}}$$

Excel Commands

Excel Commands

Chi-squared goodness-of-fit test: Use function CHITEST

Chi-squared test of a contingency table from raw data: Click **Add-ins**, **Data Analysis Plus**, and **Contingency Table (Raw Data)**

Chi-squared test of a completed contingency table: Click **Add-ins**, **Data Analysis Plus**, and **Contingency Table**

Minitab Commands

Chi-squared goodness-of-fit test: Click **Stat**, **Tables**, and **Chi-square Goodness-of-Fit Test (One Variable)**

Chi-squared test of a contingency table from raw data: Click **Stat**, **Tables**, and **Cross Tabulation and Chi-Square**. . . .

Chi-squared test of a completed contingency table: Click **Stat**, **Tables**, and **Chi-Square Test (Table in Worksheet)**. . . .

Practice Test

Part I: Knowing the Definitions

15.1 What is a multinomial experiment?

Part II: Applying the Techniques

15.2 To determine whether a single die is balanced, or fair, the die was rolled 600 times. The frequencies are:

1	2	3	4	5	6
114	92	84	101	107	102

Is there sufficient evidence at the 5% significance level to allow you to conclude that the die is not fair?

15.3 It has been estimated that employee absenteeism costs North American companies more than $100 billion per year. As a first step in addressing the rising cost of absenteeism, the personnel department of a large corporation recorded the weekdays during which individuals in a sample of 362 absentees were away over the past several months. Do these data suggest that absenteeism is higher on some days of the week than on others? (Use $\alpha = .05$.)

Day of the week	Monday	Tuesday	Wednesday	Thursday	Friday
Number absent	87	62	71	68	74

15.4 Suppose that the personnel department in Exercise 15.3 continued its investigation by categorizing absentees according to the shift on which they worked, as shown in the accompanying table. Is there sufficient evidence at the 10% significance level of a relationship between the days on which employees are absent and the shift on which the employees work?

Shift	Monday	Tuesday	Wednesday	Thursday	Friday
Day	52	28	37	31	33
Evening	35	34	34	37	41

15.5 A management behavior analyst has been studying the relationship between male–female supervisory structures in the workplace and the level of employees' job satisfaction. The results of a recent survey are shown in the accompanying table. Is there sufficient evidence at the 1% significance level to infer that the level of job satisfaction depends on the boss–employee gender relationship?

Level of satisfaction	Boss–employee			
	Female–male	Female–female	Male–male	Male–female
Satisfied	21	25	54	71
Neutral	39	49	50	38
Dissatisfied	31	48	10	11

15.6 Stress is a serious medical problem that costs businesses and government billions of dollars annually. In a survey, American and Canadian adults were asked to report their primary source of stress in their lives. The responses are

1. Job   2. Finances   3. Health   4. Family life   5. Other

The table below summarizes the data. Do these data provide sufficient evidence at the 5% significance level to conclude that Americans and Canadians differ in their sources of stress?

Stress type	U.S.	Canada
1	266	315
2	347	276
3	153	187
4	164	128
5	92	79

15.7 Trying to pinpoint his market's characteristics, a newspaper publisher wondered whether the way people read a newspaper is related to the reader's educational level. A survey asked adult readers which section of the paper they read first and asked to report their highest educational level. These data were recorded (column 1 = first section read where 1 = front page, 2 = sports, 3 = editorial, and 4 = other; and column 2 = educational level where 1= did not complete high school, 2 = high school graduate, 3 = university or college graduate, and 4 = postgraduate degree). What do these data tell the publisher about how educational level affects the way adults read the newspaper? (Use $\alpha = .01$)

Section	Education			
	1	2	3	4
1	4	21	31	14
2	27	32	18	2
3	1	20	42	22
4	10	44	22	3

Additional exercises and cases may be found on the CourseMate BSTAT web site, www.cengagebrain.com.

Learning Objectives and Outcomes

16–1 Model

Know the difference between deterministic and probabilistic models. Know what is meant by the simple linear regression model. Understand what the slope and what the *y*-intercept represent. Understand the need for the error term.

16–2 Estimating the Coefficients

Understand the least squares method and how it produces the coefficients b_0 and b_1. Know how to interpret the values of the coefficients. Be capable of manually calculating the coefficients for small samples and use computer software for small and large samples.

16–3 Error Variable: Required Conditions

Know the required conditions.

16–4 Assessing the Model

Know the different methods used to assess the model. Be capable of manually calculating the sum of squares, the standard error of estimate, the *t*-test of the slope, the coefficient of correlation, and the coefficient of determination for small samples. Be capable of using computer software to produce the regression statistics, for all sizes of samples. Know how the *t*-test of the slope and the *t*-test of the correlation are related. Understand what the coefficient of determination measures.

16–5 Using the Regression Equation

Know the difference between predicting the particular value of *y* and estimating the expected value of *y*. Be capable of calculating both intervals manually and with computer software.

> Factors That Identify Simple Linear regression
> 1. Problem objective: Analyze the relationship between two variables
> 2. Data type: Interval

Key Concepts

Vocabulary

Regression analysis is a procedure to analyze the relationship among interval variables.

First-Order Linear Model: $y = \beta_0 + \beta_1 x + \varepsilon$

The **error variable** is represented by ε

The **least squares method** produces a straight line through the data that minimizes the sum of squared differences.

Residuals are the observed values of the error variable.

The **sum of squares for error** is the minimized sum of squared differences.

The **standard error of estimate** is the estimate of the standard deviation of the error variable.

The **coefficient of determination** is the proportion of the total variation in *y* that is explained by the variation in *x*.

The **prediction interval** is the interval that predicts the value of the dependent variable given a value of *x*.

The **confidence interval estimator of the expected value of *y*** is the confidence interval estimator of the mean value of *y* given a value of *x*.

Symbols

Symbol	Pronounced	Represents
β_0	Beta-sub-zero or beta-zero	*y*-intercept coefficient
β_1	Beta-sub-one or beta-one	Slope coefficient
ε	Epsilon	Error variable
$\hat{y}$	y-hat	Fitted or calculated value of *y*
b_0	b-sub-zero or b-zero	Sample *y*-intercept coefficient
b_1	b-sub-one or b-one	Sample slope coefficient
σ_ε	Sigma-sub-epsilon or sigma-epsilon	Standard deviation of error variable
s_ε	s-sub-epsilon or s-epsilon	Standard error of estimate
s_{b_1}	s-sub-b-sub-one or s-b-one	Standard error of b_1
R^2	R-squared	Coefficient of determination
x_g	x-sub-g or x-g	Given value of *x*
ρ	Rho	Pearson coefficient of correlation
r		Sample coefficient of correlation

Key Formulae

Covariance

$$s_{xy} = \frac{\sum_{i=1}^{n}(x_i - \bar{x})(y_i - \bar{y})}{n - 1}$$

$$= \frac{1}{n-1}\left[\sum_{i=1}^{n} x_i y_i - \frac{\sum_{i=1}^{n} x_i \sum_{i=1}^{n} y_i}{n}\right]$$

Sample Slope

$$b_1 = \frac{s_{xy}}{s_x^2}$$

Sample y-intercept

$$b_0 = \bar{y} - b_1 \bar{x}$$

Sum of Squares for Error

$$SSE = \sum_{i=1}^{n}(y_i - \hat{y}_i)^2$$

Short-cut Calculation of SSE

$$SSE = \sum_{i=1}^{n}(y_i - \hat{y}_i)^2 = (n-1)\left(s_y^2 - \frac{s_{xy}^2}{s_x^2}\right)$$

Standard Error of Estimate

$$s_\varepsilon = \sqrt{\frac{SSE}{n-2}}$$

Test Statistic for the Slope

$$t = \frac{b_1 - \beta_1}{s_{b_1}}$$

Standard Error of b_1

$$s_{b_1} = \frac{s_\varepsilon}{\sqrt{(n-1)s_x^2}}$$

Prediction Interval

$$\hat{y} \pm t_{\alpha/2,n-2}\, s_\varepsilon \sqrt{1 + \frac{1}{n} + \frac{(x_g - \bar{x})^2}{(n-1)s_x^2}}$$

Confidence Interval Estimator of the Expected Value of y

$$\hat{y} \pm t_{\alpha/2,n-2}\, s_\varepsilon \sqrt{\frac{1}{n} + \frac{(x_g - \bar{x})^2}{(n-1)s_x^2}}$$

Sample Coefficient of Correlation

$$r = \frac{s_{xy}}{s_x s_y}$$

Test Statistic for Testing $\rho = 0$

$$t = r\sqrt{\frac{n-2}{1-r^2}}$$

Confidence Interval Estimator of β_1

$$b_1 \pm t_{\alpha/2} s_{b_1} \quad \nu = n - 2$$

Coefficient of Determination

$$R^2 = \frac{s_{xy}^2}{s_x^2 s_y^2} = 1 - \frac{SSE}{\Sigma(y_i - \bar{y})^2}$$

$$= \frac{\text{Explained variation}}{\text{Variation in } y}$$

Excel Commands

Regression: Click **Data**, **Data Analysis**, and **Regression**

Prediction interval and confidence interval estimator of the expected value of y: Click **Add-Ins**, **Data Analysis Plus**, and **Prediction Interval**

Test of coefficient of correlation: Click **Add-Ins**, **Data Analysis Plus**, and **Correlation (Pearson)**

Minitab Commands

Regression and prediction interval and confidence interval estimator of the expected value of y: Click **Stat**, **Regression**, and **Regression . . .**

Test of coefficient of correlation: Click **Stat**, **Basic Statistics**, and **Correlation**

Practice Test

Part I: Knowing the Definitions

16.1 Define slope.

16.2 Define y-intercept.

16.3 What is the sum of squares for error?

Part II: Applying the Techniques

16.4 To determine how the number of housing starts is affected by mortgage rates an economist recorded the average mortgage rate and the number of housing starts in a large county for the past 10 years. These data are listed here.

Rate	8.5	7.8	7.6	7.5	8.0	8.4	8.8	8.9	8.5	8.0
Starts	115	111	185	201	206	167	155	117	133	150

a. Determine the regression line.
b. What do the coefficients of the regression line tell you about the relationship between mortgage rates and housing starts?
c. Calculate the coefficient of determination and describe the information it provides.
d. Estimate with 90% confidence the mean monthly number of housing starts when the mortgage interest rate is 8%.

Part III: Understanding the Concepts

16.5 If there is evidence of a linear relationship can we say that x causes y

THREE METHODS TO DETERMINE PROBABILITY	...
Three types of DATA	INTERVAL ORDINAL NOMINAL
Topical DATA	...
We used pivot tables in excel to count the number of observations across two nominal categories, this is called a a. Tally Table b. Cross-tabulation table c. Assemble Table d. Reference Table	B
What is another name for the 2nd quartile? a. The 25th percentile b. The 4th decile c. The median d. The 75th percentile	C
what is put on x and what is put on y	y is dependent and x is independent
What is Sample Statistics	A sample is a set of data drawn from the population. — Potentially very large, but less than the population. E.g. a sample of 765 voters exit polled on election day.
What is the function key to make a cell reference absolute in Excel. a. F1 b. F2 c. F3 d. F4	...
What is the name given to extreme observations that are 1.5 times the IQR beyond the 1st or 3rd Quartiles. a. Extremists b. Sentinels c. Extraneous Observations d. Outliers	D
When comparing two sets of data what chart would you use	Scatter Diagram

Learning Objectives and Outcomes

17-1 Model and Required Conditions

Know the required conditions.

17-2 Estimating the Coefficients and Assessing the Model

Be capable of using computer software to produce all the statistics. Understand what each part of the printout represents.

17-3 Regression Diagnostics

Be capable of producing the residuals. Know how to check the normality requirement. Know how to check for homoscedasticity. Understand multicollinearity and how to recognize it and how to avoid it.

Factors That Identify Multiple Regression

1. Problem objective: Analyze the relationship among two or more variables
2. Data type: Interval

Key Concepts

Vocabulary

The **response surface** is the multiple regression counterpart to the straight line in simple linear regression.

Heteroscedasticity refers to the situation where the error variable is not constant.

Homoscedasticity refers to the situation where the error variable is constant.

Multicollinearity occurs when some of the independent variables are correlated with other independent variables.

Symbols

Symbol	Pronounced	Represents
β_i	Beta-sub-i or beta-i	Coefficient of ith independent variable
b_i	b-sub-i or b-i	Sample coefficient

Key Formulae

Standard Error of Estimate

$$s_\varepsilon = \sqrt{\frac{SSE}{n - k - 1}}$$

Test Statistic for β_i

$$t = \frac{b_i - \beta_i}{s_{b_i}}$$

Coefficient of Determination

$$R^2 = \frac{s_{xy}^2}{s_x^2 s_y^2} = 1 - \frac{SSE}{\Sigma(y_i - \overline{y})^2}$$

Mean Square for Error

$$MSE = SSE/k$$

Mean Square for Regression

$$MSR = SSR/(n - k - 1)$$

F-statistic

$$F = MSR/MSE$$

Excel Commands

Regression: Click **Data**, **Data Analysis**, and **Regression**

Prediction interval and confidence interval estimator of the expected value of y: Click **Add-Ins**, **Data Analysis Plus**, and **Prediction Interval**

Minitab Commands

Regression and prediction interval and confidence interval estimator of the expected value of y: Click **Stat**, **Regression**, and **Regression...**

Practice Test

Part I: Knowing the Definitions

17.1 Define residual.

17.2 What is multicollinearity?

17.3 What is heteroscedasticity?

17.4 What is homoscedasticity?

17.5 How do you test for the validity of a model?

Part II: Applying the Techniques

17.6 An agronomist wanted to investigate the factors that determine crop yield. She conducted an experiment in the following way. Thirty greenhouses were rented. In each, the amount of fertilizer and the amount of water were varied. At the end of the growing season, the amount of corn was recorded.

Here are the statistics generated by a regression analysis.

$R^2 = .4752, S_\varepsilon = 63.08, F = 12.23, p\text{-value} = .0002$

Variable	Coefficient	Standard error	t	p-value
Fertilizer	.140	.081	1.72	.0974
Water	.0313	.0067	4.64	.0001

a. Test the validity of the model with $\alpha = .05$.

b. Do these data allow us to infer at the 5% significance level that there is a linear relationship between the amount of fertilizer and the crop yield?

c. Do these data allow us to infer at the 5% significance level that there is a linear relationship between the amount of water and the crop yield?

d. What can you say about the fit of the multiple regression model?

17.7 A real estate agent specializing in commercial real estate wanted a more precise method of judging the likely selling price (in $1,000s) of apartment buildings. As a first effort, she recorded the price of a number of apartment buildings sold recently, the number of square feet (in 1,000s) in the building, the number of apartments, the age, and the number of floors. Here are the statistics generated by a regression analysis.

$R^2 = .4736, S_\varepsilon = 2644, F = 7.87, p\text{-value} = .0001$

Variable	Coefficient	Standard error	t	p-value
Size	−14.55	20.70	−.70	.4866
Apartments	113.0	24.01	4.70	0
Age	−50.10	98.81	−.51	.6153
Floors	−223.8	171.1	−1.31	.1994

a. Test the validity of the model with $\alpha = .05$.

b. Which independent variables(s) is linearly related to the price? Test with $\alpha = .05$.

17.8 An economist wanted to investigate the relationship between office rents (the dependent variable) and vacancy rates. Accordingly, he took a random sample of monthly office rents and the percentage of vacant office space in 30 different cities. It was decided to add another variable that measures the state of the economy. The city's unemployment rate was chosen for this purpose. Here are the statistics generated by a regression analysis.

$R^2 = .6123, S_\varepsilon = 2.16, F = 21.32, p\text{-value} = 0$

Variable	Coefficient	Standard error	t	p-value
Vacancy	−.309	.067	−4.58	.0001
Unemployment	−1.11	.24	−4.73	.0001

a. Is there sufficient evidence at the 1% significance level to conclude that the model is valid?

b. Determine the coefficient of determination and describe what this value means.

c. Determine which of the two independent variables is linearly related to rents. Test at the 5% significance level.

Additional exercises and cases may be found on the CourseMate BSTAT Web site, www.cengagebrain.com.

Figure 18.1 **Flowchart of All Statistical Inference Techniques**

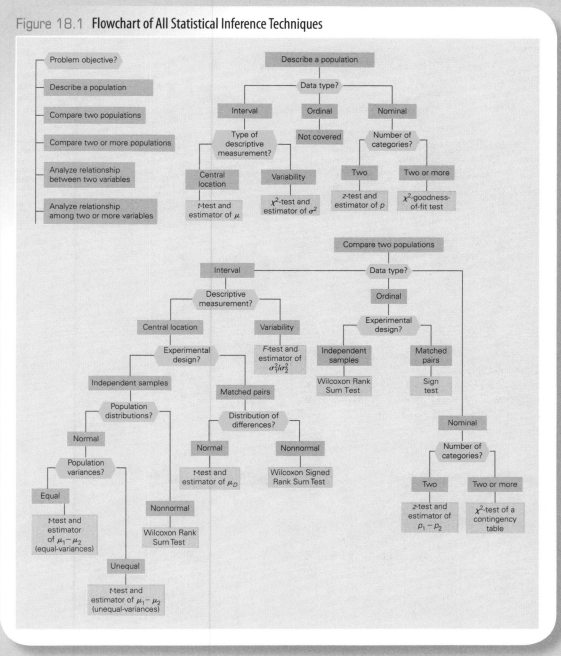

(continued)

Figure 18.1 Flowchart of All Statistical Inference Techniques (*continued*)

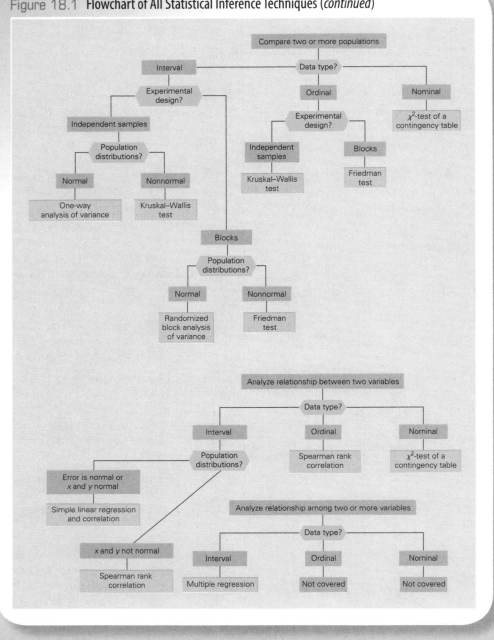

Additional exercises and cases may be found on the CourseMate BSTAT Web site, www.cengagebrain.com.

The purpose of this appendix is to introduce you to Microsoft Excel and provide enough instruction to allow you to use Excel to produce statistical results. The information and instructions below pertain to Office 2007 and 2010, Microsoft's latest version.

Installing Excel

Installing Excel on your computer is easy. Simply follow the instructions in the booklet that accompanies your edition of Microsoft Excel. In most cases you will install some edition of Office, which includes Excel, Word, and PowerPoint, as well as several other programs.

Excel Screen

At this point the screen is blank except for the top where as many as five rows or bars appear. These are the locations of most of the commands that you will issue to Excel. Move the mouse, which in turn will move the pointer to different positions on the screen. To select a command, position the pointer over the command, and click once.

The first row is called the **Title bar**. In the center you see the name of the program, Microsoft Excel. At the right side there are three small boxes, which (moving left to right) minimize, restore, or close the Excel program. You can see what the box does before you execute it by placing the mouse pointer over it and waiting a second before moving or clicking. On the left side of this row you can see the Office icon. Clicking that will open a list of choices including New, Open, Save, Print, and others.

The second row contains the following choices.

Home	**Data**
Insert	**Review**
Page Layout	**View**
Formulas	**Add-Ins** (or **Developer**)

Clicking any one of these provides you with a number of other selections. Try clicking each of the options to see the additional list. The third row contains the commands that save, open a new worksheet, open an existing file, or several other choices. The fourth row displays the contents of the active cell.

Excel Workbook and Worksheet

Excel files are called *workbooks;* these contain worksheets. A worksheet consists of rows and columns. The rows are numbered, and letters identify the columns. The intersection of a row and column is called a **cell**, which is a box that can store a number, word, or formula.

Inputting Data

To input data, open a new workbook. Activate the cell in the first row of the column in which you plan to type the data. If you wish, you may type the name of the variable. For example, if you plan to type your assignment marks in row A, you may type "Assignment Marks" in cell A1. Hit the **Enter** key, and cell A2 becomes active. Begin typing the marks following each one by **Enter**. Use the arrow key or mouse pointer to move to a new column if you wish to enter another set of numbers. Note that data are usually stored in columns.

Importing Data Files

A data file stored on the our Web site accompanies most of the examples, exercises, and cases in this book. For example, the data set accompanying Example 2.1 contains 285 numbers. These data are stored in a file called **Xm02-01**, which is stored in a directory (or folder) called **CH02**. (The **Xm** refers to files attached to e**Xam**ples, **Xr** is used for e**Xer**cises, and **C** is used for **C**ases.)

Performing Statistical Procedures

There are several ways to conduct a statistical analysis. The two most frequently used are **Data Analysis** and **Data Analysis Plus**.

Data Analysis/Analysis ToolPak

The Analysis ToolPak is a Microsoft Office Excel add-in (add-in: a supplemental program that adds custom commands or custom features to Microsoft Office.) program that is available when you install Microsoft Office or Excel. To use it in Excel, however, you need to load it first.

1. Click the **Microsoft Office Button**, and then click **Excel Options**.
2. Click **Add-Ins**, and then in the **Manage** box, select **Excel Add-ins**.
3. Click **Go**.
4. In the **Add-Ins available** box, select the **Analysis ToolPak** check box, and then click **OK**. If **Analysis ToolPak** is not listed in the **Add-Ins available** box, click **Browse** to locate it.
5. If you get prompted that the **Analysis ToolPak** is not currently installed on your computer, click **Yes** to install it.

After you load the **Analysis ToolPak**, the **Data Analysis** command is available in the **Analysis** group on the **Data** tab.

Data Analysis Plus

Data Analysis Plus is the collection of macros we created to augment Excel's list of statistical procedures. **Data Analysis Plus (STATS.xls)** is supplied on our Web site. The installation program that saves the data files on your computer will also save a copy of **STATS.xls** in a file called **XlSTART**. When this file is correctly saved on your computer, **Data Analysis Plus** will become a menu item in the **Add-ins** heading in the **Menu bar**. The instructions for **Data Analysis Plus** are also described in this book. The Web site also contains a help file that is associated with **Data Analysis Plus**.

Below is an example of how to use Excel to tally for discrete variables:

Excel

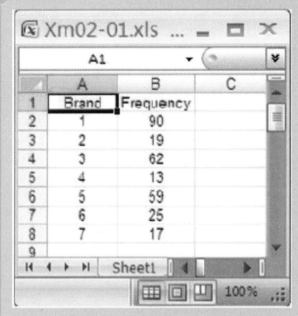

INSTRUCTIONS

1. Type or import the data into one or more columns. (Open Xm02-01.)

2. Activate any empty cell and type

   `=COUNTIF ([Input range], [Criteria])`

Input range are the cells that contain the data. In this example, the range is B1:B286. The criteria are the codes you want to count: (1) (2) (3) (4) (5) (6) (7). To count the number of 1s (Bud Light), type

   `=COUNTIF (B1:B286, 1)`

and the frequency will appear in the dialog box. Change the criteria to produce the frequency of the other categories.

Below is an example of how to use Excel to create a box plot.

Box Plot of Long-Distance Telephone Bills

[Xm02-02] Draw the box plot for Example 2.2.

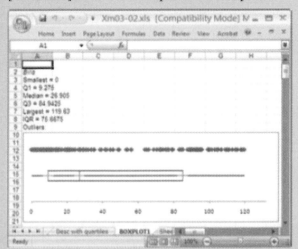

Excel

INSTRUCTIONS

1. Type or import the data into one column or two or more adjacent columns. (Open Xm02-02.)

2. Click **Add-Ins, Data Analysis Plus,** and **Box Plot.**

3. Specify the **Input Range** (A1:A201).

A box plot will be created for each column of data that you have specified or highlighted.

Notice that the quartiles produced in the **Box Plot** are not exactly the same as those produced by **Descriptive Statistics.** The **Box Plot** command uses a slightly different method than the **Descriptive Methods** command.

Additional exercises and cases may be found on the CourseMate BSTAT Web site, www.cengagebrain.com.

minitabcard Introduction to Minitab

Minitab Release 16 for Windows is a statistical software package that is extremely easy to use and understand. This software features a wide variety of statistical methods. However, we will use only a fraction of its capabilities. Our goal in this appendix is to introduce you to the basics of Minitab. When we use this software to solve an example in this book, we will provide both the output and the specific instructions.

Within Minitab you will find a number of different windows and tools. Here is brief description of each.

Minitab Environment

The **Session window** displays the statistical output requested. Most of what you command Minitab to do will appear here.

The **Data window** shows the data in the worksheet you are conducting your analysis on. Each column represents a variable.

The **History window** keeps track of all the commands you have issued.

Graph windows exhibit the graphs you requested.

The **Info window** summarizes each open worksheet.

Menus and Tools

The **menu bar** is the starting point for selecting commands.

The **Toolbar** displays buttons for functions that are used most frequently.

The **status bar** shows an explanation when you point at a menu item.

Commands

There are three ways to issue commands. These are

    Clicking menu items
    Toolbar selections
    Session commands

In this book we describe the menu items only. For example, to produce a histogram (see page 21) from the menu bar click **Graph**. From the list that appears click **Histogram. . . .** A dialog box will appear requesting you to identify the variable or variables you wish to describe as well as other information.

Dialog Boxes

Among other things, you will have to identify the variable that you wish to compute statistics or graphs from. Minitab displays the **variable list**, which contains all the variables, constants, or matrices in the current worksheet. (The current worksheet is the one associated with the active Data window. You activate a Data window by clicking on it.) If the variables have been named, the names will appear in the list. If the variables are unnamed, the column in which the variable is stored appears. To select a variable, type its name or column in the **Variables** box. Alternatively, click in the text box you wish to fill, highlight the variable in the variable list, and click **Select**.

Data Input

Activate the data window and start typing the data into a column starting in row 1. You can type the name of the variable in the cell immediately under the column number (e.g., C1). When finished, you may issue commands.

Importing Data

Most of the examples, exercises, and cases in this book have data sets associated with them. To import the data, you will have to download the Minitab files from our Web site.

To open a file, click **File** and **Open Worksheet . . .** (Do not click the file symbol. The reasons are explained below.) Select the folder containing the data files. All the data files are saved in chapter subdirectories. To open a file in Chapter 2 click **CH02**. A complete list of files will appear. The files beginning with Xm refer to files for examples. The data files associated with exercises begin with Xr, and files connected to cases begin with C. For example, to get the data for Example 2.2 click **Xm02-02**.

Minitab Projects and Worksheets

A Minitab project contains all the data, the output from any commands issued on the data set, and graphs. When you save the project all of this will be saved. You may have as many worksheets as you like in any project. For example, one worksheet can contain the data; a second, a graph; a third, descriptive statistics; and so on. All the data files on the disk are worksheets. If you click the file symbol on the toolbar, Minitab will attempt to open a project. The only projects you will have are the ones you yourself previously created.

Below is an example of how to use Minitab to tally for discrete variables:

Minitab

Tally for Discrete Variables: Brand

Brand	Count	Percent
1	90	31.58
2	19	6.67
3	62	21.75
4	13	4.56
5	59	20.70
6	25	8.77
7	17	5.96

$N = 285$

INSTRUCTIONS

(Specific commands for this example are highlighted.)

1. Type or import the data into one column. (Open Xm02-01.)

2. Click **Stat, Tables,** and **Tally Individual Variables.**

3. Type or use the **Select** button to specify the name of the variable or the column where the data are stored in the **Variables** box (Brand). Under **Display,** click **Counts** and **Percents.**

Below is an example of how to use Minitab to create a box plot.

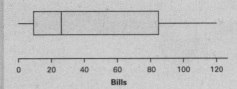

INSTRUCTIONS

1. Type or import the data into one column or more columns. (Open Xm02-02.)

2. Click **Graph** and **Box Plot . . . .**

3. Click **Simple** if there is only one column of data or **Multiple Y's** if there are two or more columns.

4. Type or **Select** the variable or variables in the **Graph variables** box. (Bills).

5. The box plot will be drawn so that the values (Bills) will appear on the vertical axis. To turn the box plot on its side click **Scale . . . , Axes and Ticks,** and **Transpose value and category scales.**